Lillian Gish

Lillian Gish

A Life on Stage and Screen

by

STUART ODERMAN

McFarland & Company, Inc., Publishers
Jefferson, North Carolina, and London

ALSO BY STUART ODERMAN

Roscoe "Fatty" Arbuckle:
A Biography of the Silent Film Comedian, 1887–1933
(McFarland, 1994)

Cover: Publicity shot for the play *Life with Father* (1939).

Library of Congress Cataloguing-in-Publication Data

Oderman, Stuart, 1940–
　　Lillian Gish : a life on stage and screen / by Stuart Oderman.
　　　　p.　　cm.
　　Includes bibliographical references and index.
　　ISBN 0-7864-0644-5 (illustrated case binding : 50# alkaline paper) ∞
　　1. Gish, Lillian, 1893–1993.　 2. Motion picture actors and
　　actresses — United States — Biography.　 I. Title.
　　PN2287.G55O34　 2000
　　791.43'028'092 — dc21
　　[B]　　　　　　　　　　　　　　　　　　　　　　　99-28402 CIP

British Library Cataloguing-in-Publication data are available

Manufactured in the United States of America

McFarland & Company, Inc., Publishers
　Box 611, Jefferson, North Carolina 28640
　　www.mcfarlandpub.com

To my first wife with love

Table of Contents

Acknowledgments

I am more than grateful to the many people who, over the years, shared their recollections, memories, and anecdotes: George Abbott, Alan Alda, Minta Durfee Arbuckle, Joan Bennett, Joan Blondell, Guy Bolton, John Britton, Alan Brock, Louise Brooks, Gene Brown, Frank Capra, Frank Carrington, Sir Noel Coward, Donald Crisp, Agnes DeMille, Jerry Devine, Colleen Dewhurst, Allan Dwan, William K. Everson, Neil Fitzgerald, James L. Frasher, Roy Frumkes, Sir John Gielgud, Margalo Gillmore, Peter Glenville, Paulette Goddard, Sheila Graham, Dorothy Kirstein Greenwald, Mary Hara, Carl Harms, Helen Hayes, Lou Jacobi, George Jessel, Leatrice Joy, Henri Langlois, Linda Lee, Viveca Lindfors, Anita Loos, Myrna Loy, Alfred Lunt, Donald Mackenzie, Enid Markey, Colleen Moore, Nita Naldi, Dame Anna Neagle, Edmund O'Brien, Ann Pennington, Lester Polakov, Michael Powell, Harold Prince, Aileen Pringle, Dorothy Davenport Reid, Joanna Roos, Adela Rogers St. Johns, Albert Salmi, Herman Shumlin, Leonard Sillman, Anthony Slide, Janet Sovey, Milan Stitt, Clifford Stonely, Jessica Stonely, Blanche Sweet, Constance Talmadge, Frances Tannehill, Howard Teichmann, Herman G. Weinberg, Glenway Wescott, Cornel Wilde, Tennessee Williams, Lois Wilson, Ralph Haven Wolfe, and John Wolfson.

For their research assistance and the supplying of out-of-print books and magazines from their personal libraries, I am grateful to Sam Affoumado, Patrick Baskwell, Charles and Linda D'Addario, Salvatore Di Gerlando, Frank Evans, Beatrice Herring, Victoria Michaels, Paul R. Miller, Lawrence Natanson, Cynthia Salzano, Ron Sproat, and Inge Vandormael.

Thanks to Yiannis Kardoulakis and the Elounda Residence on Crete.

Special thanks to Lena Tymczyna for her expert help with the photographs.

I am grateful to the New Jersey public libraries in East Orange, Maplewood, and Millburn in addition to the Jerome Library at Bowling Green State University in Bowling Green, Ohio, and the Library of the Performing Arts at Lincoln Center, New York City.

I am especially grateful to Lillian Gish, not only for the beauty and professionalism of her life, but for the 39 years of correspondence and friendship she extended to me, beginning in my days as a 14-year-old pianist who cut high school classes in Newark, New Jersey to watch silent films at the Museum of Modern Art in New York and had the good fortune to be sitting near her on one of those stolen Wednesdays in 1954.

I am lucky to have a wife who not only read all of the drafts of this biography, but also has been a constant source of support and love.

Preface

It isn't easy being a Lillian Gish.
— Lillian Gish
Conversation with author (1954)

New York City: March 12, 1993.

There were 700 mourners in attendance at St. Bartholomew's. The pews were already filled before the start of the eleven o'clock memorial service.[1] Even before it was announced in the newspapers and on radio and television, many knew that Lillian Gish had passed away in her sleep at her East 57th Street apartment, where she had lived alone for many years.

"It was what she had wanted," James Frasher, her longtime personal manager, told the press.[2] "She died at 7:03 p.m. on February 27 in her own bed. She was film. Film started in 1893, and so did she."[3]

Film, in the days of its infancy, meant a quickly cranked black-and-white one-reeler exhibited in nickelodeons for an audience of poor people, immigrants eager to plunk down their nickels for a new minutes of escapism from the factories, tenements, and drudgeries of the day.

"I don't remember everything, Stuart," Lillian Gish said to me during our first meeting. It was 1954. I was fourteen years old and cutting school in Newark, New Jersey, to attend a Wednesday matinee of a Broadway show. When the cheapest balcony seats weren't available, I walked uptown to the Museum of Modern Art to watch a silent film.

The film that day was *Broken Blossoms*, a film she made for D.W. Griffith in 1920. "Nostalgia" had not become part of the American language. The term used by the general public was the all-encompassing phrase, "old movies." *Old* people during the day watched *old* movies. Fourteen-year-olds belonged in school, not on the streets of New York, and certainly not at the Museum of Modern Art.

But I was precocious. People were throwing away their 78 rpm recordings and buying 45 rpm "singles" and 33 and ⅓ "long-playing albums" called "LP's." I had read about Bix Beiderbecke, and Bessie Smith, and Moran and Mack, and I could explain what "10-20-30" melodrama was.

I also knew about silent films and the music that was often played. Music stores still stocked *Hearts and Flowers* and *The Perfect Song*, which was written for Lillian Gish in *The Birth of a Nation* in 1914.

In 1954, I was sitting next to Lillian Gish. We were both by ourselves. Unlike Greta Garbo, who would have a continuing career by *not* working and always remained visible enough to tell people she

1

wanted to be *alone*, Miss Gish *was* alone. She also looked very approachable.

It was the beginning of a thirty-nine year friendship — postcards and letters from all over the world, and meetings backstage and at parties — that ended with her passing. She was a constant source of encouragement, and gave me a life that I would never have had otherwise.

"I don't remember everything," she said that first time, before she began to research her life in preparation for her autobiography. "I was just another Griffith player, and those films were just jobs to us. We finished one film, and then we went to another film. Sometimes we made two films side by side, depending on the weather and the location."[4]

In her silent film years, Lillian had risen from a $5-a-day player hired off the street for the Biograph Company in 1912 by D.W. Griffith[5] to co-star with her sister Dorothy in a one-reel melodrama, *An Unseen Enemy*, to a Metro-Goldwyn-Mayer leading lady who, in 1927, could command a salary of $400,000,[6] along with her choice of director, script and cast approval, and the added luxury of extra rehearsal time.[7]

She had lived long enough to see the "flickers" become "talkies," which became multi-million dollar color extravaganzas that commanded high ticket prices, sometimes required reserved seats, and caused traffic jams.

On March 31, 1982, the Warner Bros. screening room was filled to capacity. Several people gladly stood behind the last row. It was the final night of a film series that featured the introduction by the leading man or lady.

Lillian Gish was going to introduce *The Wind* (1923), and I would be accompanying it on the piano. My fantasy had come true — my hope that one evening, I would be playing, and Miss Gish would be in the audience.

As the lights dimmed after Miss Gish's introduction, she walked over to the piano and gave me a soft kiss and whisper of encouragement. "Play well. I have always been proud of you."

She returned to her seat next to James Frasher. By now my eyes were misty. I could hardly see the MGM lion on the screen.

I quickly wiped away my tears with my tuxedoed right arm as I *tremoloed* with my left hand. The main title flashed across the screen and there was a burst of applause as Miss Gish's name appeared.

There was no time for sentiment, except in the music. This was another job in the series of jobs I had been playing for thirty-five years. All that was required was to sustain a dramatic mood for a nonstop two hours.

The lights came up, and Miss Gish rose to the applause. Now the audience rose, as she walked to the piano. She took my hand and whispered, "Follow me to the stage."

Now the two of us were in front of an enthusiastic audience. Miss Gish took a step away from me, leaving me alone at center stage.

She returned and, taking another bow, asked the audience, "May I share your applause with Stuart Oderman?"

She lifted my arm and whispered, "Bow your head with me... Count to five... Raise your head slowly... Turn to your left. Follow me... Exit."

Four days later, the following letter arrived. It is still on my desk.

> Dear Stuart:
> This note is of double purpose: first to wish you a Happy Easter and joy. Thank you for *The Wind*. You played beautifully and AT LAST we got to work together. It was exciting for me and, as always, I am terribly proud of you.
> May your life be filled with your

every wish which you so richly deserve.

Your co-star in happiness,
Lillian Gish

It was to be expected that among the attendees at the memorial service would be fellow professionals whose lives were touched by her art and blessed by her presence: Anne Jackson, Douglas Fairbanks, Jr., Jane Powell and husband Dick Moore, William Roehrick, James MacArthur, Irene Worth, Lauren Hutton, Jack Warden, Tammy Grimes, Mary Steenburgen, Teresa Wright, Malcolm MacDowell. Most had come in by themselves, sometimes pausing in front of the altar rail where bouquets of flowers, discreetly placed cards, and long-stemmed roses sent from all over the world were in full view.

Their conversations were whispered as they acknowledged one another. William Roehrick had appeared on stage with her in a 1936 production of *Hamlet* that starred John Gielgud. Teresa Wright was featured in the 1968 production of *I Never Sang for my Father*. Jack Warden had a sup-

porting role in PBS's *Hobson's Choice*. With Laurence Hutton, Lillian had appeared in Robert Altman's film *A Wedding* (Lillian's 100th movie). Mary Steenburgen was in Lillian's last film, *The Whales of August*.

Lillian Gish never married, although she was never at a loss for beaus and proposals. She had inherited the Protestant work ethic from her controlling mother: What you make is a living; what you give is a life. From her absentee alcoholic father, she received a lifelong insecurity which would never allow her to be totally satisfied with her achievements. She, more than her sister Dorothy, would always want employment. Observing at an early age the toll that marriage had taken on her mother, she knew she could never share her life with any husband.

This is a biography of someone who devoted her life to her work and her mother's happiness. It was a life that kept her constantly busy for almost 100 years. Her formula was talent, time, and tenacity.

Stuart Oderman
Silent film pianist

CHAPTER 1

Father, Dear Father

The Springfield, Ohio, where Lillian Diana Gish was born to James Leigh and Mary (McConnell) Robinson Gish on October 14, 1893,[1] wasn't very far removed from the wilderness of an earlier time. True, there was a post office, town newspaper, and Covenant Presbyterian church,[2] but Springfield was still regarded as a rural area where many of its citizens eked out a living using the barter system: eggs for butter, calico, and lace.[3] Corn, which would grow "as long as a man's forearm,"[4] could always be marketed in areas beyond the hills and mountains with a horse and wagon, so long as the seller was willing to travel.

If one wanted to learn of the latest births or deaths or new arrivals settling down, or attempt an honorable courtship, the church was of central importance as a proper meeting place. In Springfield and the surrounding areas, there were small churches of different denominations. To attract and maintain new and established congregants, "dinner on the ground" (a link to a time when churches were hard to find — and preachers harder) became very popular.[5] It was a common sight to see pioneer wives with food baskets coming to worship in the morning and then staying for the afternoon service.

Everything was conducted honorably and in full view. Occasionally there were ice-cream suppers, song nights, and amateur theatricals to tempt the young and unmarried from the outside mysteries and dangers of the woods.

Always an active theatre state, Ohio was home to touring companies featuring the likes of Jane Cowl, Maude Adams,[6] and playwright Eugene O'Neill's father, James, who left the security of a tailor's job in Cincinnati to join a touring company.[7]

Nomadic acting troupes travelled the dangerous rivers performing on showboats (such as the Cotton Blossom and Golden Rod) while their on-land counterparts, the tent show people, were always sure to find an audience for their minstrel shows and "purple melodrama." Tent shows and showboat actors performed the same program generation after generation.[8] Despite their loose reputation, most of the performers were married. It was the only way they could survive and have some degree of respectability within the community.

To this nomadic life, with its frustration and heartbreak, Mary Robinson Gish would have to surrender herself and her daughters if they wished to survive.

The origins of James Leigh Gish were not known or easily traceable. Everyone knew that Lillian's mother, once known as "pretty May McConnell,"[9] could trace her solid American ancestry back to President Zachary Taylor, a poetess named Emily

5

Ward, and an Ohio state Senator, who was their Grandfather McConnell.[10]

Even in an era when townspeople discussed their kith and kin with unabashed alacrity, nobody could speak a complete paragraph about Mary Gish's husband. James often described himself as a travelling salesman, a "drummer."

Although the most skilled drummers (which James wasn't) could charm their way through town after town, changing their stories and lines of patter as the occasion required, the only James Gish story about which there was complete agreement was his courtship of young, pretty May McConnell. They had met in May's hometown, Urbana,[11] and were married very quickly. Thanks to Mary McConnell's father, James was able to get a job in a grocery store with the hope that one day he and his wife would have saved enough money to open a confectionery business of their own.[12]

Despite the long hours at the store, the money they had hoped to save never really materialized. There were always expenses that the former Mary McConnell would question without receiving satisfactory answers. Often James would be away from the store in search of business opportunities elsewhere, and he could only remain at home with his wife for a short time.

To a suspicious but knowing father, Mary would offer no explanation. Daughter Lillian was always shielded from James' drinking problems and inability to manage his financial responsibilities and moral obligations. Mary often improvised a flimsy excuse about James' wanderings, adding that everyone would have a nice surprise when he returned.

During James' days away from Springfield, Lillian and her mother would exist on a "diet of oatmeal and milk. One portion for breakfast, and two for dinner."[13]

Of course, when James would return there was some money provided to use for groceries and rent, but the bulk of what he was expected to bring home from these business opportunities was just never there. James provided no explanation, and the silences between James and his wife told Lillian more than if there had been an honest argument or quarrel. Holding on to money was just beyond him. Often Mary would take in a neighbor's sewing, never telling Lillian just how close to eviction they really were.[14] Mary would remind her quiet, serious young daughter that she was born with a caul,[15] and that was a sign that good things were straight ahead.

Lillian sensed the tension that arose when her father's name was mentioned. It was never said with a smile or any expression of joy or love. She only knew her mother was upset, and it made her want to do everything perfectly — the right way with no mistakes. It was the way she thought her mother would like things to be done. If mother was happy, she could be happy too. It would be the beginning of a lifelong calling: to somehow divert her mother's attention away from problems.[16]

The problem was her father.

On March 11, 1898, sister Dorothy was born in Dayton, Ohio, the family's new address.

James again attempted to make a success of his confectionery business, often setting up a stand at fairs and celebrations, hoping that this new venture would help him pay the rent.[17] The rent was paid, but it came from secret stipends given to Mary from her father's harness business. James, Mary grew to realize, was a dreamer whose best plans and dreams were discussed at a local tavern with anyone who would lend a sympathetic ear.

Lillian was a frequent listener, happy to hear James' plans for the future as she contented herself with a plate of beans,[18] one of her favorite meals. It was one of the ways James could lure her out of the house and away from a wife he knew was constantly undermining everything he said. So long as she had a plate of beans to eat in a friendly atmosphere, she was very happy and relaxed. What James said seemed to be very logical. James just wasn't meant to be in business, where people did the same things every day, the same boring things. America was a big, wide country. Why not see it all?

Mary never criticized her husband or his ideas in front of Lillian or her younger sister, Dorothy. Lillian's retelling of what had been said to her was greeted with a stony silence. It was bad enough to subject other townspeople to drunken reveries in the subdued light of a local tavern, but to put these wandering notions into the mind of an innocent little girl? Where did he get his upbringing? When would he assume the responsibilities of a Christian, God-fearing father and stop playing the role of a feckless ne'er-do-well?

Without James' knowledge, she and her daughter joined the Episcopal church and were regular worshippers, maintaining the tradition that had begun in Springfield. Perhaps if Mary's thoughts were spoken in proper prayer and constant Sunday devotion, there might be salvation for James. Indeed, for everyone. We must *bear and forbear*. Amen.[19]

The Episcopal church was a step up socially and an opportunity to be with what Mary believed to be a better class of people. The parishioners did not appear to be Saturday night drinkers like James, but thoughtful, pious citizens on the road to righteousness. Lillian would remain an active member of the Episcopal church all of her life.

In the summer they journeyed to Aunt Emily's farm in Massillon. They continued to be active churchgoers. Lillian and Dorothy were baptized by Bishop Leonard of Cleveland. The Massillon church also provided suppers for a quarter. It was another chance for the Gishes to stuff themselves with real homecooked food.[20]

Before the summer ended, James left his family in search of business opportunities in other cities, tightening the bond between Mary and her daughters. Lillian, somehow becoming aware of James' erratic behavior patterns, knew not to upset her mother with painful questions. Everything Lillian wanted she had found on her Aunt Emily's farm: chickens, a cat who was always asleep, and a friendly dog. There was no need to think about an absentee alcoholic father who made her mother cry and wasted money on drink.

On one occasion, Mary had told her daughters that their father was sending his love from the city of Baltimore, where he had entered the confectionery business with a Mr. Meixner.[21]

In December, Lillian learned from her mother that James was no longer working with Mr. Meixner in Baltimore, but had gone to New York in search of another business opportunity. If all went well, everyone would be together.

There was no reaction from either Dorothy, who was beginning to realize something was wrong, or from Lillian, who already knew.

> It was a shock, hearing my father's name mentioned by mother. We had become so accustomed to *not* seeing him every night at the table. So we stopped thinking about him, and we knew we shouldn't talk about him because it would upset mother, and she would walk into the bedroom or the hallway and cry.
>
> We were living a very orderly life. Dorothy was always playing outside with some of the local children. I liked to play alone with the animals, who were always friendly. Sometimes, I would stay indoors and be with

mother and try to make things easier for her.

Children are much more resilient to sad times. I learned how to make quick outward adjustments. Nothing ever seemed to bother Dorothy, but I wanted to think that deep down she knew something wasn't the way it should be.

Some children are afraid to grow up. They still cling to their innocence… But what can a child do? Sometimes, it's better not to ask.

We, at least *I*, didn't want to further upset mother. Outwardly she had been very stoic, but I knew she must have been hurt. She hardly knew my father before they were married.

She was taken in the way thousands of naive, overprotected women were taken in. If the man *looked* presentable and spoke nicely, that was all that was necessary. You judged someone by manners and appearance.

Today we would say my father was an alcoholic, and we would try to send him someplace where he could be helped. In those days, people simply whispered *he drinks*, and nothing more was said.

Mother never argued with my father in front of us, and she would never admit to us that the marriage was a failure.

In those days, and in many families today, the failure would be the woman's. The ladies at the church would probably blame my mother, and *not* my father. It was a *man's* world, and a man who drank was considered by some people better than no man at all.

What man would want a single women with two very young, dependent children? A woman, like my mother, who was unable to earn a living? Where could she go? Who would want her?[22]

As promised, James Gish sent some money from New York to Massillon. Then he sent less, and less, and then nothing.

The prolonged absence of James Gish put Dorothy and Lillian completely under the influence of their mother. It established beliefs and patterns of behavior that would stay with Lillian for her entire life.

Men were not to be trusted.

Be thrifty.

Be self-reliant.

And men were not to be trusted.

In desperation, Mary contacted James' former business partner, Edward Meixner. After hearing how they had been abandoned, Meixner, sympathetic and compassionate, sent some money to cover their travel expenses to Baltimore, where Mary could get employment as a packager in her husband's former business.

Not wishing to take any further advantage of sister Emily's hospitality, Mary packed her bags and her two daughters and left for Baltimore. They had hoped that James' "problem" was only temporary, and that he would return and assume his responsibilities.

For a short time, Mary's plan worked. James did send some money from New York, but it was hardly enough to sustain the three of them. Still, Mary believed, any money from James was better than no money. He was acknowledging their circumstances, even if he wasn't contributing very much to help matters.

And then the money stopped. Without any explanation.

Meixner again gave some money to the three Gishes and told them to go to New York.

There they *might* find him.

They arrived in New York in September 1899 and secured a third-floor apartment on West 39th Street in the vicinity of Pennsylvania Station. To help offset the rent, Mary took in two boarders. They were actresses who had theatrical engagements in the city and didn't want to pay the prices even second class hotels charged.[23] Mary's apartment was presentable. With two young daughters, there was a semblance of a family, even though there seemed to be no husband or *any* man present.

Having no man on the premises was a blessing. Actresses were always alluring to men. They wore exotic makeup and clothing and, if one read the stories in *The Police Gazette*, were women of easy virtue.

In an effort to fix up her new quarters for herself and the boarders, May purchased some used furniture, payable on the three-dollars-a-week installment plan. All payments were to be made in cash to the collector who would visit them on Fridays.[24]

At the age of twenty-five, Mary Gish had assumed an awesome responsibility: the maintaining of a family without a husband in a large, impersonal city. Mary's day would begin at five in the morning with the preparation of the breakfasts. Then she would make sure her daughters, who would be alone for the day while she worked as a product demonstrator in a Brooklyn department store, were going to be properly supervised by a neighbor. The subway fare, each direction, was a nickel, and the journey was almost forty minutes.

When she returned at night, there was the preparation of the suppers for the actress-boarders before they left for the theatre, as well as supper for Lillian and Dorothy. Lillian always requested *beans*, perhaps stemming from a frugality she was acquiring from a penny-pinching mother, or trying to recapture, by scents, the memories of earlier times when she and her father would go to one of the local bars where he spun his dreams. Lillian knew not to mention the *real* reason she liked baked beans. The thought of Mary's absentee, alcoholic husband, who had not tried to find them, would upset everyone's day. Lillian wanted to make *everyone's* day wonderful.

After the actresses had gone, Mary would sew for the neighborhood residents.

Sewing a torn piece of clothing was always a good source of extra money. It enabled her to stay at home and be with her daughters.

Lillian's clothes were rarely in need of repair, and that made her mother happy.

But Dorothy's...

> Dorothy (recalled Lillian) was always lively and active. She got the happy side that God left out of me. Dorothy could always play anywhere.
>
> During the day, when mother was working in Brooklyn, Dorothy would race through the rooms and laugh, and do tumbling tricks on the floor, and tear her clothes mother had just mended.
>
> I liked to be quiet and thoughtful, and sit at the living room window and look out at the city, and wonder when mother was coming home to be with us.[25]

One day in the early part of October 1899, there was a surprise which Mary Gish must have received with mixed feelings. After she had made the breakfasts for Lillian and Dorothy, there was a knocking on the door.

The three Gishes looked at each other. It wasn't Friday. There were no furniture payments to be made.

Mary opened the door.

Standing in the hallway was James Gish.

He entered their apartment quite naturally, as if he'd done nothing worse than return a few minutes later than usual with the morning rolls and newspaper.

There were no exclamations of surprise or delight from Mary Gish or her daughters. If Lillian had said anything to her younger sister, it might have been, "It's father."[26]

Not wanting to be late for work in Brooklyn, and not able to ask James too many questions in front of her curious daughters, Mary poured a second cup of coffee. She informed her neighbor that her *husband* James would be staying with them, watching the children, and taking responsibility for paying the three-dollars-a-week installment on the furniture to the collector on Friday.[27]

The furniture was second-hand and typical of the period: "maple and rather shoddy."[28] Still, it was all Mary Gish could afford, as she was living on a tight budget. Lillian remembered that they were so poor they walked to save the nickel fare the streetcars charged.[29]

James' presence was a mixed blessing. Apparently unemployed, he was another mouth to feed; but Mary could save on the small monies she had been paying the neighbor for watching Lillian and Dorothy while she was at work. The words *very tight budget* were well implanted in Lillian's young mind, when she and mother and Dorothy walked to church on Sundays to save the fifteen cent fare.[30] Whether he stayed home while they were out is a matter of conjecture.

A father, even though James Gish wasn't the best example, was still a father. He was the man of the house, and Mary would treat and respect him as such, even though he was contributing nothing financially in the way of support. That total burden still fell on Mary. Until he secured employment, he would have two specific responsibilities: to watch his daughters during the day and, most important, to remember to give the collector, who would appear on Fridays, the three dollars for the furniture.

Things went smoothly for a while. The young daughters were supervised, and on Fridays the three dollar payments were collected.

Four or five weeks after James' arrival, Mary had another surprise when she returned home to the apartment at the end of her day's work in Brooklyn.

Lillian and Dorothy were on hand to greet her, but husband and father James was gone.

So was most of the second-hand furniture: the sofa in the living room, Dorothy's and Lillian's beds, the two beds on which the actress-boarders slept, and Mary's bedroom set. All gone.

It was Friday, Mary realized, and James hadn't been making those payments to the collector for the last two weeks. While Lillian and Dorothy cut out paper dollies from the newspapers Mary kept in the dining room, James packed his cardboard suitcase and left minutes before two men came to repossess the furniture. Dorothy and Lillian had been alone in the apartment all day.[31]

For Mary, it was the final hurt. James' drinking, taking his daughter Lillian to those taverns, the days into weeks of wandering away in search for business opportunities, could somehow be tolerated. Abandoning his children, walking out on his daughters, was an unforgivable sin.[32] May had lived for her children. To leave them alone in a big city without any means of protection was the lowest crime anyone could commit.

The marriage of James Leigh and Mary McConnell Gish was now over. Mary would now obtain legal separation.[33]

The two actresses boarding at the apartment were more than willing to sleep on the floor, as they were behind in their rent. If Mary could wait a few weeks until some of the current plays were seeking replacements or new plays were casting, she would be more than compensated. One or both of them would be on hand to supervise the young daughters.

Mary agreed, but there were still debts to pay. The three ladies pawned whatever jewelry they had, and Mary pawned her wedding ring.[34] She no longer had any use for it. It hadn't brought her any happiness, except two daughters: Dorothy, who was too young and playful to understand, and Lillian, who was always serious and thoughtful, and whose eyes saw and understood perhaps too much.

She had seen her mother's love and trust betrayed. Betrayed by her father. Betrayed by a man.

What Mary had been telling her finally made sense. Be self-reliant. Watch your money, and don't trust men.

Oatmeal, which had been a staple diet before, was now frequently served. If Lillian had any thoughts of taking a streetcar to different parts of the city, they were put aside.

Thrift and self-reliance were the order of the day. Mary had instilled in Lillian and Dorothy that *they* were all they had, and that nobody in the world would care for them better than themselves.

The actress-boarders kept their promise to see that Mary was compensated, but it was an offer that wasn't totally to Mary's liking. Actress-boarder Dolores Lorne was hired by a theatrical company, and suggested that Mary visit the offices of producer E.J. Proctor to see if she could get work on the stage, too.[35]

At first Mary was reluctant, having been raised by a proper churchgoing family. To have actresses as boarders would be quite unheard of in Springfield, Ohio. In New York, one had to accept anyone, no matter what they did for a living. Actresses needed places to stay, and if they could pay their bills and not cause any disturbances, they were as good as anybody else.

Mary Gish, the former "pretty May McConnell," on the *stage*? Dolores persisted, telling Mary that the money she would easily make in the theatre could be used for Lillian's and Dorothy's education.

Proctor had entered the theatrical profession in the 1870s, as Fred Levantine. After thirty years, he owned six prestigious theatres all over the city. So successful was he that a new theatre would soon open in Montreal.[36]

The Proctor's Theatre circuit was primarily vaudeville: "first class acts willing to play three times daily."[37] Usually within the vaudeville presentation, there was a stock company that showcased a famous artist who utilized them as a supporting cast. It was quite common and acceptable for Broadway stars who were "at liberty" to "take a flier" and appear on vaudeville stages for good money.[38]

Mary Gish visited the Proctor offices and was hired as the ingenue for fifteen dollars a week. It was more money than she had ever made as a product demonstrator at the Brooklyn department store. Proctor's work was less demanding, as far as hours and travel time were concerned, and on matinee days Lillian and Dorothy could join her at the theatre on West 28th Street.

West 28th Street was only a few streets from their apartment. An easy walk! Even at night!

One evening, returning home after the theatre, Mary was approached again by Dolores. Dolores' New York show was going to close. She had been visiting the agencies, hoping to be cast immediately in another New York production. No luck. The only work available was a touring company of a popular 1862 melodrama called *East Lynne*. Dolores' being hired was dependent on one factor: a little boy was needed to play the minor but important part of Little Willie.[39]

Young Dorothy, whom she called Doatsie, was the right size. Dorothy loved going to the theatre with Lillian. Both girls loved watching their mother on the stage when seats were available.

Would Mary...?

Mary's reaction was quick. No! Dorothy and Mary had never been apart from each other, except for the time James was staying with them and Dorothy had to go to Brooklyn. She would never be separated from Dorothy or Lillian. What would people think if they knew Mary had a daughter, a little girl, on the stage? Few people in her family knew that Mary was earning her living as an actress. An actress stood for every value they shunned.

How would Dorothy survive in strange, faraway places without the right supervision? Dorothy and Lillian were lucky they weren't kidnapped by a passing stranger after the furniture had been removed. Children in big cities disappeared quite often. Did Dolores actually believe Mary would surrender her baby to a company of vagabonds who lived out of suitcases and could be stranded someplace they never heard of?

The salary offer quickly changed Mary's mind: fifteen dollars a week plus a week's salary in advance. Dorothy would be touring in the same company as Dolores, who would look after her. There would be no problems. Dorothy had to pretend that Dolores was her Aunt Dolores. Dorothy would be her niece, "Doatsie," the favorite nickname she had been called when they were together in the apartment after James had abandoned them. Fifteen dollars a week for Dorothy!

What would Mary tell Lillian, who would be left behind? Dolores had anticipated the problem, and she had provided a logical solution. Her friend, Alice Niles, was looking for a little girl to be in a touring company of *In Convict's Stripes*, which would be playing in a barn in the village of Risingsun, Ohio.[40]

Lillian's salary was ten dollars a week, and Alice Niles was just as honorable as Mary. There would be no cause for worry. Alice and Lillian would be together all of the time. They would stay in the same room, and she would never let Lillian out of her sight.

The total of the combined salaries was overwhelming. Ten dollars a week for Lillian. Fifteen dollars a week for Dorothy.

Mary knew that Lillian wouldn't be able to save the total amount. It would cost at least three dollars a week to live.[41]

Where would Lillian be rooming?

Alice promised "a mother's care," inferring that being on the road was the equivalent of "a long pleasure trip."[42] Wisely, she had omitted the hazards: long nights on terrible trains, the sometimes barely edible food, and the general drudgery of it all.

Ten dollars a week for Lillian. Fifteen dollars a week for Dorothy.

Again, Mary wondered. Was the combined salary of her daughters worth the emotional toll it would take on her life, being without them? How would she explain this to her sister, Emily, in Massillon?

A glance at the wall calendar brought Mary's problem to a quick solution. One needed money to exist. With James, there was never any steady money, and since he had left them, there had been no money from him. With the Proctor's Theatre closing for the summer, there would be no employment. Now both Lillian and Dorothy had been offered legitimate jobs with acceptable chaperons. Two jobs, with two salaries.

Just like a "long pleasure trip…"

The Gish sisters, Lillian and Dorothy, would be on the road. It was an actor's life!

Lillian made her debut as "Little Florence Niles" (the supposed niece of her chaperon, Aunt Alice Niles) in 1902 in a touring production of *In Convict's Stripes* in Risingsun, Ohio. The theatre was actually a barn with an upstairs hall, reserved for touring theatricals playing limited engagements of two or three performances, with one day to travel to the next town. When travelling by train, there was rarely the luxury of booking a sleeper. One slept in the same clothes one wore out of the theatre.

Lillian's company arrived in time for one rehearsal before the performance. The stage manager would make sure the cast knew their blocking and where the scenery would be placed. Not all theatres were the same size, and sometimes the scenery they used was too small or too large. Audiences were not upset by the lack of total perfection.

In the third act, Lillian knew to hide behind one of the papier mâché rocks that were supposed to represent a stone quarry, where her character had been placed by the villain. When someone said "Boom!" there was going to be an explosion and a dummy would be tossed into the air, which would be grabbed by the hero of the play in his attempt to "rescue" her.

When the great moment occurred in the performance, however, something unexpected happened. Nobody backstage said "Boom!" There was a *real* "Boom!" that shook the Risingsun barn-theatre, surprising the capacity audience and so upsetting Lillian that, without thinking of her dummy-double, she jumped from her hiding place, shrieked, and ran across the stage.

The audience yelled and hooted its approval at "Little Florence Niles" and a star was born. For the next performances in the next towns in the next theatres, Lillian would remember to put cotton inside her ears.

Lillian knew her numbers and sums, and she soon realized that, because of her mother's tutoring before the departure, she could quickly calculate the price of the hotel and her meals from her weekly ten dollar salary. Hotel clerks were constantly amazed at her mathematical wizardry. She did it all in her head, while they used pencil and paper![43]

Lillian knew that being thrifty, as her mother had taught, did not always mean that one had to hold tightly onto one's money, but to spend it *wisely*, on things that would help one. As the child of an alcoholic who was now operating in adult situations, she couldn't help thinking about how James Gish had spent his money at local taverns on the afternoons when she

went for her favorite plate of beans. It was money that could have been put to better use supporting the family, specifically her mother who sometimes had spent the better part of the night mending Dorothy's clothes and those of the neighbors.

Lillian sent home the promised seven dollars each week. It was a promise she would keep for the duration of the tour, and the tour lasted forty weeks. Forty times seven...[44]

Dorothy, Lillian realized, was making *fifteen* dollars a week, five more than herself. How much did Dorothy send home? And why was Dorothy making *more* money?

Mary Gish had the answer: the producer told her Dorothy's tour was playing bigger theatres in bigger cities. Lillian was more fortunate. The producer of her show paid the expensive train fare, leaving the troupers to pay only for their hotel and food.

After a few weeks of touring, Lillian learned to overlook the quick naps on the "stone floors" in the waiting rooms and sleeping on conveniently placed newspapers.[45]

Most of the time, the travelling was done on day coaches or milk trains that arrived at small towns late in the evening. The troupe had to be met by someone who would escort them to a theatrical boarding house or a cheaper hotel.

Some boarding houses had rooms that were infested with bugs and cockroaches. There were theatres that often had chilly dressing rooms, hot dressing rooms, sinks with only cold water, sinks with barely enough hot water. Often there were all kinds of insects on the mirrors.

Sometimes there were cynical signs backstage:

WE KNOW THE THEATRE IS ROTTEN. HOW'S YOUR SHOW?[46]

Still, it was work, and the actors hoped the next theatre in the next town would be better. Touring actors had spent their careers in "Don't look under the bed" rooms.[47]

Nobody ever trusted "show people." Show people were little better than "strollers, vagabonds, vagrants, harlots and trollops."[48] The prejudice had originated centuries ago in England, but the assassination of President Lincoln by an actor did little to raise the prestige of actors a few decades later.

The child actor was always learning lines, or rehearsing lines, or packing, or unpacking. They had little time to make friends with any of the ordinary kids in the neighborhood. Child actors would often lament, in later years, that they never had a childhood.[49]

Lillian would never express such sentiments. Like Eve Harrington, the memorable heroine of Joseph Mankiewicz's *All About Eve*, Lillian found that acting became the reason for her existence. While Mary Gish constantly admonished Lillian to speak up or the producers would "hire another little girl," Lillian knew from the moment she stepped onstage that she, more than Dorothy, had the power and ability to control the financial future of her family. Mary Gish was a very controlling mother offstage, but in the course of a performance, the situation was reversed. Lillian had firm control, and Mary was the subordinate player. Lillian could temporarily forget the furniture men who removed sections of her house in front of her eyes. She could briefly banish thoughts of an alcoholic father who had escaped responsibility and stolen their mother's money while she and her younger sister had had to sit on a bare floor and wonder when their mother was returning and what they would say to her.

On a theatre stage, she could put aside her private agonies and enter the world of her character. The child had become the adult and would be rewarded with waves of approval, love, and applause from a receptive audience.

The stage was the only reality Lillian could control, a reality she would covet for nine decades. That she made her mother happy was also a source of satisfaction, but in an era when the rights of women were subordinate to those of men, and they weren't even allowed to vote, Lillian would begin to realize how much power she would derive from her art. Unlike her mother, who paid the price for being subservient to her father, *no* man would ever put Lillian in a position to depend on men for help.

The melodramas in which Lillian and Dorothy would appear in the next ten years (1902–12) were a combination of "black villainy, sticky sweetness, and a good dose of hokum."[50] There were no compromises or shadings of character delineation. What was good was totally good. What was evil was beyond redemption. Of course, there were times when the villain saw the evil of his ways, but this didn't occur until the final minutes of the last act.

Often the melodrama became a vehicle for the star — as long as the star was willing to play to the paying audiences who were willing to watch the same play season after season. James O'Neill, for instance, spent a lifetime touring as Edmond Dantes in *The Count of Monte Cristo*.[51]

The plight of little children always moved audiences to tears. How they must have wept in *East Lynne* when Dorothy Gish, appearing as Little Willie, in her death scene spoke:

> It is nothing to die when our Savior loves us…. It will be pleasant to go up there, and never be tired or ill anymore. Do you think my Mama will be there?[52]

Or when Lillian, dressed as a newsboy in a 1903 touring production of *Her First False Step*, knelt beside her sick mother (who was played by her *real* mother for a short time) and asked:

> Oh, mother, what are you doing out here in the snow?[53]

One can't help but notice the mixture of "humble worthiness amidst the quarts of tears."[54]

On the few occasions when Mary Gish joined one of her daughters, or when all three were fortunate to be touring together, the ritual was the same whenever they arrived in a new hotel or rooming house: Mary would cleanse the walls and shake the sheets to be rid of the bugs, roaches, and accumulations of dirt. Only then would it be safe for the night or the duration of the run![55]

When Lillian was appearing in Fort Wayne, Indiana in a tour of *In Convict's Stripes*, the actor playing the guard dropped his rifle and Lillian's leg was powder-burned. In great pain (after a doctor in the audience removed most of the poisonous grains), Lillian went on with the play.

Although Alice Niles, acting in the same company and also as Lillian's chaperon, did not notify family members, a news item in one of the Fort Wayne papers somehow reached Lillian's grandfather in Dayton, Ohio. The injury was regarded as "retribution" for working in the theatre![56]

The lack of a formal education for touring stage children was always a problem. Touring actors rarely spent time in a public school for an entire academic year. Lillian and Dorothy learned their lines by rote, the constant repetition of the same words to whomever was coaching them. The teacher was anyone who spent time with children and thought it more important to be able to know how to pay a hotel bill or order a meal in a restaurant than to be constantly drilling young actors in line rehearsals hour after hour.[57]

When Mary Gish was on the road with Lillian or Dorothy, she would often read to them from their favorite book, *Black Beauty*.[58] The cities they played on tour often served as a natural background for a geography or history lesson.

Despite the hardships of travel, what struck instant terror in the minds of juveniles and their families was the Gerry Society.

The Gerry Society was an organization formed by New York attorney Elbridge T. Gerry to protect the rights of children being forced to work for long hours and little compensation in dangerous and unsanitary sweatshops and factories. While Gerry might have had sincere intentions in policing the children appearing in the legitimate theatre and the enforcement of child labor laws, he was not appreciated by the families for whom these children were earning their living. Child actress Gladys Smith, before she made her film debut as Mary Pickford, was the sole support of her family.

Once in Chicago, where Lillian played at the age of ten, she had an encounter with the Gerry Society. To conceal her age, she appeared before a judge, dressing up in "long skirts, padding, and veils" as if she were sixteen, the age which didn't require a license to perform. In most small towns, where the Gerry Society was not active or rarely had time to visit the theatres, the disguises and lies about her age worked. The problems occurred when she and Dorothy went eastward.[59]

Lillian remembered:

> There were some parents who would whisper to their children that the Society would take you away from your family, and that you would never see them again. Mother would never say things like that to either Dorothy or me. She always told us, "If they can't hear you in the back of the theatre or upstairs in the balcony, the managements would hire another

little girl." And then what would we do? This is our only livelihood.[60]

What Lillian neglected to tell her mother or chaperon Alice Niles was

that I sometimes dreamed about my father, that he was in the audiences where we played.

After he left us in New York, there was never any mention of him. Neither Dorothy nor I ever asked about him. Mother never mentioned his name. But that doesn't mean that I ever forgot about him and some of the nice times we had together when I was having a dish of beans at one of the taverns.

Once I asked Mother if she would ever marry again, and she answered something like "Your father destroyed me. Another man would destroy us."

I'm speaking as an adult now, but I think Mother made the adjustment to *not* having anyone around but Dorothy and me. She never said a bad word about my father. She just erased him from her mind. Maybe she hoped we would do the same. But I knew she was hurting inside. When she hurt, *I* hurt for her.

I never told her that there were some nights I would look out into the darkness of the theatre during the performance, and I would see him, and I would wish he would come back and see us, and talk to us. I wouldn't be angry with him. I would just want to talk to him, so he could see that *I* was okay.

I just knew he was there sometimes. Standing in the back, just smiling. I knew he was proud of me. I just *knew* it.[61]

With more than four hundred stock and touring companies crisscrossing the country and constantly changing from state to state and sometimes city to city in the course of a season, nothing on the road was totally constant.[62] For a short time Lillian played Dorothy's "Little Willie" role in a company of *East Lynne*.[63] Dorothy played the role of the "sister" in *The Child Wife*.[64]

When Dolores Lorne, now Lillian's chaperon, became ill in Buffalo, New York, touring with *The Little Red Schoolhouse*, Mrs. Gish requested that Lillian return to her in New York rather than remain with strangers.

To replace Lillian, a young Canadian actress named Gladys Smith, later to emerge in motion pictures as Mary Pickford, was hired.[65] Like Lillian, Gladys was a seasoned juvenile trouper, playing with her brother Jack, sister Lottie, and their mother, the over-watchful Charlotte. Gladys longed to be on Broadway. Broadway meant respectability, prestige, and money. With the exception of Charlie Chaplin, no other performer was ever so money-driven. At this period in her life, young Gladys had to tolerate whatever salary she could get, even if it meant playing fourteen performances a week.[66]

To support their mother, the Pickford children had sacrificed their childhood. While the loss of childhood experiences was a lifelong source of regret to Judy Garland, Jackie Coogan, Jerry Devine, and Mickey Rooney, no such statement was ever spoken by Lillian Gish. Lillian knew that the money she earned would support her mother, who she felt had sacrificed so much for her. She had kept her daughters out of orphanages and foster homes, and had seen that there was always something to eat, in the wake of her husband's — their father's — desertion.

Opposite: A program of "10-20-30" melodramas performed in the early years of the twentieth century. In such theatrical fare a young Dorothy and Lillian Gish learned to perfect their craft before varying audiences. *Moths and the Flame* seems to be the crowdpleaser here, having matinee and evening performances.

Plans for Lillian, Dorothy, and Gladys to play together on Broadway in *The Truth Teller* in 1905 were cancelled, and Lillian quickly landed a small dancing role in Sarah Bernhardt's company in New York, which opened at the Lyric Theatre on December 15, 1905. With another little girl, she would dance across the stage, which was covered with canvas. Until she appeared in the musical *Anya*, sixty years later in 1965, her work with the Divine Sarah was the only time she ever appeared onstage in a play that required some dancing.

When Lillian had become famous years after the short New York engagement, she would receive wonderful letters from the Divine Sarah. Lillian would always remember her as the "tall lady" who waited with her in the wings and who, just before she made her entrance, would place an encouraging hand on her head and whisper in French: "Le petit ange aux cheveux d'or" (The little angel with the hair of gold).

At the end of the engagement, Lillian and Dorothy were on the road together in *At Duty's Call*, a melodrama which closed unexpectedly and left them without funds.[67]

Being stranded on the road was every actor's nightmare. There were no unions to protect the artist, who had to pay his own fare back.

A dressing room interview for a role in Maude Adams' *Peter Pan* yielded nothing. The short Maude Adams wanted an even shorter child to play opposite her. Lillian was too tall. Ironically, when *Peter Pan* was filmed, Lillian claimed she was author James M. Barrie's choice for *Peter Pan*.[68]

It was a story Lillian loved to tell. Maude Adams, for all of the praise she gathered from her stage success, never appeared in the film. Nor did she ever make a film.[69]

To make ends meet and have some money to tide them over until the next job,

Mary Gish opened a candy and popcorn stand at Fort George amusement park in northern Manhattan. Lillian and Dorothy took jobs posing for artists and photographers at a fee of five dollars a day.[70]

Although there had been little mention of James Gish, Lillian still harbored the dream that he would surface backstage at one of the theatres and a grand family reunion would take place. Everything would be forgiven, and the family would live happily ever after. Mary, on the other hand, dreaded that James would suddenly appear and kidnap Lillian or Dorothy or both.[71] Sometimes Mary wondered if James was still living, and where, and how.

An October 1910 letter sent to Mary from Shawnee, Oklahoma put everyone's mind at ease. The sender wasn't James, but his brother, Grant. James, he wrote, had been in ill health and was confined to a sanitarium. There were no further details.

To a tearful Lillian's constant pleas that everyone go to Shawnee, Oklahoma, Mary turned a deaf ear. No matter what his condition was, she had no desire to see the man who had ruined her life, the man who failed to make the furniture payments, the man who knowingly abandoned his own children in a strange city.

No. Mary would never go to see James Gish. Let him die.

The train pulled into a forsaken train station at two a.m. Lillian had made the cross-country trip alone, in defiance of her mother's wishes. She was barely a teenager, but she knew from her ten years of performing that this trip was nothing more than a tour without a chaperon. Hadn't everyone said she was very *aware* for her age? All of her life she had been in adult situations. She sensed that she was a survivor, although she was too young to articulate her reasons for exerting this first attempt at independence.

A surviving letter sent to Nell Dorr,

an Ohio childhood friend and confidant, explained Lillian's feelings:

> I didn't want to come, dear, but I thought it was my duty. It's awfully hard to do your duty sometimes, and you know that I met with opposition on all sides, but I have done what I think is right, and I am glad that I did it.[72]

Nobody, neither her aunt nor uncle, was there to greet her.

In the immediate vicinity of the train station was a hotel, whose only sign of life was the light emitted from a single bulb on the ground floor. The room itself was depressing, with the sounds of rats running and squeaking within the walls. One light at the end of the string dangling from a cracked ceiling was the only source of luminescence.

Taking every precaution she had been taught by her mother and her chaperons, Dolores and Alice, Lillian pushed her chair against the locked door. She undressed away from the window and went to sleep on top of the faded blanket. She didn't turn off the light.

Whether Lillian actually saw or spoke with her father has always been a matter of conjecture. There are conflicting versions of what actually occurred during her stay at Shawnee, Oklahoma. Certainly James' bouts with the bottle must have taken their toll, and in that condition he might not have wanted to see Lillian, although she might have insisted that she be allowed to spend some time with him.

She could not have gone to any sanitarium in Shawnee, because the population at that time couldn't have supported one. The nearest facility was a hospital in Oklahoma City, some thirty-five miles away.[73]

Lillian claimed she never saw her father, preferring to yield to the wishes of her uncle and keep alive a memory of a much younger looking James Gish,[74] who always made sure she was given a fine dish of beans whenever they went on their excursions.

Blanche Sweet believed that James Gish might have seen his daughter once or twice (at most), but she never pressed for details. Blanche was also the daughter of an alcoholic father. Like Lillian, she viewed her father with a mixture of love and frustration.

Lillian's survival instincts may have had their first testing at Shawnee. When the situation was too much to bear, she would shrug her shoulders and look for an alternative solution. Living with herself, and within herself, was more important. Her father had done all he could do. It remained for Lillian to continue.

It was a pattern she learned from her mother: to solve problems as they occurred, not to look for them. There was slowly developing a hardness beneath the seemingly fragile innocence. So long as she was a butterfly, albeit an iron butterfly, she wasn't a threat to anyone. She would tell people what she wished them to know with the calculated restraint of a child and the maturity of a woman. It was this quality that in later years would endear her to millions.

James Gish was a topic she rarely discussed with anyone.[75] He was never visited by his wife, nor did Lillian ever say if her sister Dorothy ever saw him.

Deciding to remain in Shawnee was an easy decision for Lillian to make. Her aunt and uncle were more than willing to have her. Dorothy was staying at Aunt Emily's farm in Massillon. Mother Gish was trying to earn a living working at her other sister's confectionery store in East St. Louis.

Lillian had no problem adjusting to the comparative quiet of a Western small town. There were no prospects of touring, and it was wiser to wait out the season until something happened.

After Lillian returned to Ohio at the end of the year, James Gish passed away.[76] She had heard that prior to his passing that he had "gone mental," but it was not a topic on which she wished to elaborate or discuss. She had seen, on several occasions, the hardships her mother had to endure and keep within herself. She would do the same. James had never been there for them.

He had taken a toll on Lillian's mother, the most wonderful, most important person in her life.[77]

The business of living and working were what mattered most; that, and making life as easy and tolerable for Mother as possible.

Mother was everything.

CHAPTER 2

The Road to Biograph and Mr. Griffith

With the arrival of summer 1911, Lillian returned to Aunt Emily's farm in Massillon, Ohio, while her mother remained in Fort George to manage her taffy and popcorn stand.[1] In September, Dorothy went on tour with Fiske O'Hara, the Irish singing comedian, who made sure that Mrs. Gish joined the tour in the second year and had a role in each of his plays.

At the end of the engagement, Mrs. Gish took her daughters to East St. Louis, where she managed an ice cream parlor, assisting the wife of her recently deceased brother. The workday was long, sometimes twelve to fourteen hours. It left her little time to spend with Dorothy or Lillian.[2] Lillian, never an outgoing person, especially needed to be helped. She had been maturing into a young lady and hadn't received the benefits of an education or childhood experiences. When not acting on stage, she preferred to be alone, spending those quiet hours looking out of the window or curled in a chair, reading books. Sometimes she helped her mother.

Dorothy was always the more outgoing. She could make friends quickly with young girls and boys. She was always, and would always be, the more spirited and popular of the sisters.

To provide a place for Lillian to play and receive a much *wanted* education, the Ursuline Academy would supply properly cooked meals, a room, and schooling for twenty dollars a month.[3]

It would be a financial burden, but Mary Gish acquiesced to Lillian's pleas. With an education, she could play "serious, grown-up parts," and perhaps read better for a director. Without the right education, she would always sound like a little girl.

After the initial weeks of adjustment to convent life, Lillian welcomed the opportunity to be removed from the pressures of touring, the lack of constancy, and the nomadic existence of a stage player. The Ursuline Academy provided her with the first stability she had ever received.

> The Ursuline Academy was peaceful. It was serene. I had time to sit and think about myself, and what I wanted to do with my life.
>
> I think if circumstances hadn't forced my mother to put us on the stage, I would have liked to be a children's librarian in Massillon, or a nun.
>
> When *The White Sister* was filmed in Rome (1923), I often thought of the days at the Ursuline Academy.[4]

21

What Lillian probably didn't realize while she was living at the Ursuline Academy was that her entrance into her teenage years meant fewer opportunities for performing. She was too old and too tall to continue in the children's parts, and she wasn't quite adult enough to make a smooth transition to more suitable roles.[5] What's more, the number of road companies was dwindling.

Something called "flickers" was beginning to affect the attendance at theatres. While some stage veterans might have viewed these primitive entertainments as the latest novelty for the lower classes and recent non–English speaking immigrants, it did not take producers long to realize that the nickel price for a program of short films and newsreels, accompanied by a pianist whose melodies could soften the noise of the hand-cranked projector and underscore the action on the screen, was less than the dime needed for a seat in the upper gallery.

Suddenly, "live" players didn't mean that much. "Flickers" could be shown over and over, from the early morning until the very late evening. There would always be a steady stream of customers.

In 1903, a twelve minute one-reeler in fourteen scenes called *The Great Train Robbery*, filmed by the Thomas Edison Studios in West Orange, New Jersey,[6] was causing a sensation — whether exhibited in formerly empty storerooms with hastily assembled screen and chairs or in specially built nickelodeon parlors.[7] By 1908, the year of the release of D. W. Griffith's first film, *The Adventures of Dollie*,[8] there were more than 10,000 nickelodeons across the United States.[9]

Neither Gladys Smith nor Lillian Gish saw any real artistic merit in those early one- and two-minute films whose subject matter centered on putting out fires "somebody getting in or out of a car."[10] Gladys, always the business woman, claimed after seeing *Hale's Tours*, a one-reeler which gave

viewers the illusion of being on a train, that the experience made her carsick. Still, the "economic potential" of the movies might be popular enough to attract a lot of paying customers.[11] Surveys of the day estimated that between two and three million people were going to the movies each week.[12]

If an actor or actress were successful enough to demand a percentage of the gross, even if only one or two percent...

Gladys' mother Charlotte, blessed with an even greater business acumen than Mother Gish, urged her theatrically-minded daughter to shelve her theatrical pride and get over to Biograph at 11 East 14th Street, New York City, and speak to Mr. D. W. Griffith about getting a job as a "day-player" for five dollars a day. Five dollars a day could keep the family together.[13]

D. W. Griffith's American Mutoscope and Biograph Company was a typical New York brownstone of the 1850s: four stories with a commercial basement that opened onto the street. Originally, the brownstone had been a private home prior to being tenanted by the Steck Piano Company. When Steck vacated the premises, the basement stores were rented, and the building was leased to Biograph for five thousand dollars.[14]

Because some stage actors had scruples about being recognized entering a place that manufactured such low entertainment, they reported to work through a basement store that served as a rented tailor's shop. Their fear was not of being seen by the public, but by fellow stage professionals who might spread the scandalous news that they knew someone who had to resort to the "flickers" to pay their room rent or feed their (obviously destitute) families.

Nobody with any self-respect would appear in "flickers." They might as well sing in waterfront taverns, where drunken customers rewarded the performer's efforts with tossed pennies!

Both Lillian and Dorothy had seen the "flicker" *Lena and the Geese* by chance during the summer of 1912 while they were playing in Baltimore.[15] Like all seasoned stage actors, they were appalled at seeing their friend and fellow trouper Gladys Smith on a movie screen, making gestures and not speaking.

Lillian, in particular, was quite shocked.

> There she was! Our friend, Gladys! She was in one of those "flickers" we would sneak away to see! But now she was Mary Pickford! Imagine changing her name, the name she was born with!
> We were afraid to tell our Mother that our friend Gladys had fallen on hard times. Her family must be *destitute*![16]

When Lillian and Dorothy learned that their destitute fellow trouper was earning a salary of one hundred–and–seventy-five dollars a week, and was being driven to work from an uptown Riverside Drive apartment in a studio-supplied automobile (complete with a chauffeur),[17] Mrs. Gish and her high-minded, artistic daughters thought it best to leave their confectionery business to their Baltimore aunt and head for New York.[18] Perhaps the Gish troupers could lower their artistic standards and find some employment in this entertainment novelty.

They quickly found a place to sleep in a rooming house on 424 Central Park West.[19] It was a fairly quiet area, but too far from the Biograph Studio. Both the trolley and the subway would require transfers. At six fares each day, and the waste of time in travel, living so far away from the city's activities would be too costly.

They found barely suitable accommodations near the top floor of the Hotel Marlton, a Greenwich Village structure on 5 West Eighth Street. Built in the 1880s, the Hotel Marlton was a natural haven for transients, writers, singers, and artists who didn't mind climbing step after step to rooms whose windows were covered by dirty shades that covered a steady stream of traffic. The Marlton lodgers viewed their residence as a temporary one, until they were secure enough to move to a better address. The occasional drunk who might have slept in the lobby until daybreak rarely returned.[20] (In the 1940s, writer Jack Kerouac and jazz trumpeter Miles Davis would be among the Marlton residents.)

Once the Gishes were settled, Mary Gish and her daughters walked to the Biograph studios on East 14th Street, hoping to find their friend, Gladys. Of course, Mrs. Gish had chosen and coached both Dorothy and Lillian in prepared monologues which, if Mr. Griffith so desired, they would be happy to deliver in voices that would show their stage experience and their ability to project to the last rows of the balcony.

After some initial confusion at the Biograph front desk regarding this "Gladys" actress they had seen in *Lena and the Geese*, the receptionist summoned Mary Pickford.[21]

Mary, always loyal to the Gish family, introduced a hopeful Dorothy and a very eager Lillian to Mr. Griffith, who disregarded their monologue as being of little value. Spoken words were immaterial to the motion picture camera that only photographed images. Instead, Mr. Griffith thrust Lillian and Dorothy into the center of an improvised action sequence, where words weren't needed.

Recalling the initial Griffith meeting years later, Lillian remembered that in order for Mr. Griffith to differentiate between the two sisters, each was given a hair ribbon: blue for Lillian and red for Dorothy. Both Lillian and Dorothy would be addressed by their ribbon colors. "Blue, raise your left hand! Red, smile at Blue…"[22]

And then Mr. Griffith instructed Blue and Red not to look at the camera lens and not to look at him while taking direction.

> "*Blue* and *Red*, hold each other! Cower in the corner!"
>
> Mr. Griffith pulled a real gun from his pocket and began chasing the two of us around the room.
>
> *He's gone mad!* I thought, and we scurried around the room, looking for an exit.
>
> Mr. Griffith began to fire several shots, and we screamed….
>
> And then he yelled, "Cut!" and we stopped running, and he put away his gun.
>
> He was smiling, evidently pleased with the results.
>
> "That will make a wonderful scene," he said. "You have expressive bodies. I can use you. Do you want to work for me?"[23]

Neither Dorothy nor Lillian required any prompting from their mother. A combined salary of ten dollars a day, and living within *walking* distance of their place of employment was more than adequate.

With the possibility of day work for Mrs. Gish in the wardrobe department, it had been a perfect day. Lillian and Dorothy had come through, and the family could stay together.

In their first Griffith venture, *An Unseen Enemy* (1912), Lillian and Dorothy played sisters, whose on-screen persona was not far removed from their off-screen identities: a younger, livelier Dorothy and a more serene and thoughtful Lillian. What Mr. Griffith had put the sisters through as an audition piece would effectively serve as part of the finished product's story line. Two sisters, alone in their house, would be terrorized by men, who would try to rob them!

The camera would register their horrified expressions as the robbers would try to pry open the windows, knock down a door, and attempt to kill them by shooting through a hole in the stovepipe. At the film's conclusion, both sisters would be rescued by their brother, but not before the audience has had a good dose of scares!

From his first film, *The Adventures of Dollie* (1908), Griffith proved he was the master showman. *The Adventures of Dollie* contained all of the elements of melodrama that would appeal to an audience: a child is kidnapped by villains, imprisoned in a barrel, and sent down the river, over the waterfalls, and rescued in the final minutes by a group of boys fishing in a stream.

An Unseen Enemy continued the pattern set by *The Adventures of Dollie*. By constantly changing the point of view, the audience could not avoid being drawn into the plight of the Gish heroines. Like good storytelling worthy of his favorite author, Edgar Allan Poe, Griffith successfully utilized Poe's short story techniques of presenting the main character and a particular problem, then adding further complications that leads to the climax and denouement. "Scare 'em," and then "save 'em."

David Wark Griffith, often described by Lillian Gish as "the father of film" and "the man who gave motion pictures its grammar,"[24] was a failed stage actor and playwright. Born on January 22, 1875, in the farm country of Crestwood, Kentucky, he had grown up in a world of literature and escapism. His father, Jacob, would constantly remind him that he was a wounded Confederate soldier in the recently lost Civil War, and the only joys with which to conquer the bitterness of frustration and defeat was to seek solace in the classics. Young Griffith's childhood was filled with his father's readings of works by Shakespeare, Dickens, Longfellow, and Sir Walter Scott.[25]

Seeing the infant motion picture business as a possible market for his stories, thirty-three-year-old Griffith tried to peddle his material to the Edison studio in the Bronx in 1908, only to have his work rejected for having too many scenes. Mr. Edison's 1903 one-reeler, *The Great Train Robbery*, had established the acceptable length requirement: twelve minutes. A longer film would lose the audience's concentration.

Acting on a suggestion from actor Max Davidson,[26] Griffith went to American Biograph on East 14th Street in New York City. He had heard that a *director* was needed. Although Griffith had not done any directing and had never actively been employed in films (except for a short time as an actor in Edison's *Rescued From an Eagle's Nest*), he agreed to try his hand — with the proviso that should this directing venture fail, he could still continue as an actor and writer. He still harbored hopes that he would sell his words to the screen, there to be translated into pictures.[27]

In the beginning, Griffith was not very proud of his association with motion pictures. Films were not the legitimate stage, which he viewed as the purest of the arts. Theatre catered to educated people who understood the beauty of the spoken word, not the vulgar pantomime that drew on cultural stereotypes.

The sight of a tall man entering a motion picture studio with his hat over his face and his collar turned up in an effort not to be recognized by fellow stage actors was a commonplace sight in the early hours of the morning. Most shooting began an hour or two after the sun rose. To prepare for the day's work, Lillian, her mother, and Dorothy would walk from their hotel room at the Marlton to the Biograph studio in darkness. Having stood by themselves or with fellow actors at quiet train stations during the last hours of the night when they were on tour, it was eas-ier to keep moving than to remain still. On cold days, when the streets were covered with snow, walking kept you warmer.[28]

Inside the Biograph studio were other stage actors, who often resorted to similar tricks of disguise or camouflage. Blanche Sweet, Lionel Barrymore, James Kirkwood, Henry B. Walthall — their opinion of this renegade art form did not differ from Griffith's. At best it was a means of support until the next tour, which would take them away from East 14th Street and be so successful that they wouldn't have to return to the "flickers."

Film work, Mr. Griffith informed Lillian and Dorothy and their fellow players, was not the same as stage work. There were no speeches to memorize, although there were mouthed sentences which would be used as titles later inserted into the finished product. Mr. Griffith, standing behind the camera, would instruct and "walk" his players through constantly running commentary regarding their actions. Most important was the presence of the camera lens. Avoid looking at it!

Lillian remembered:

> Griffith shot his scenes separately and then edited everything in the cutting room when everything was done: all of those cross-cuts and sudden jumps.
>
> He could communicate with the simple lifting of a finger. He didn't use big gestures, because he wanted us to think of *him* as camera lens.
>
> The camera lens would *magnify* everything. What would look permissible on the stage would look ridiculous, given the intimacy of the camera.
>
> We soon realized that anything we did in front of a camera would tell all about us, if we stayed there long enough.
>
> John Barrymore said the camera would tell people what you had for breakfast, and who your ancestors were.[29]

Despite the successes of earlier Biograph arrivals Mary Pickford and Blanche Sweet, Lillian in her first film, *An Unseen Enemy*, would prove to be Griffith's romantic notion of the perfect heroine.[30] Through film after film, she would maintain, no matter how great the danger, a vision of spiritual purity[31] worthy of the respect one would show to one's mother or sister. It was an innocence that did not yield to desire. You wanted nothing to happen to her. You wanted to save her, to cherish her, to protect her from corruption and the evils of the world she might encounter if she left the house. She would rise above any negative environment like an angel heaven-bound. Beneath her outer fragility was the undying strength of iron.

Offscreen, Lillian had the same aura, recalled Hearst journalist Adela Rogers St. Johns, who began her long newspaper career in 1913, one year after the arrival of the Gish sisters.

Lillian knew how to present herself. She always created her own atmosphere. She had none of the features you would associate with the "vamps" or the bad girls. She had blonde hair and big blue eyes, which we would associate with the fairy tale princess illustrations or the little dolls girls would play with.

Lillian was always radiant, like the children you see in holy pictures: not of this earth, and very ethereal. Because she moved with such elegance and grace, like a trained ballet dancer, I think she intimidated men. She would look them directly in the eye and then turn away very demurely.

Men loved it. They *respected* her. Respect for any lady in Hollywood was very rare. Yet Lillian *inspired* respect. Even in her Griffith days, in an era before women had the right to vote, men would stand up when she approached their table.

Mary Pickford, who was "America's Sweetheart" and queen of the industry, also was respected, but it was a respect one gives to someone with power, the power to see that you wouldn't work again.

Mrs. Gish was always with Lillian. Lillian took her everywhere. Miriam Cooper, Mae Marsh, Blanche Sweet: they didn't go to parties with their mothers.

With Lillian, a function, no matter who was present, was a business function. It was to her advantage to be seen there. She was never a nightlife person.

Dorothy would stop by for a few minutes, make sure she was seen, and then head for the beach and the cafes. She was always a little more playful, if you know what I mean. Dorothy came to life in an easier atmosphere, away from her mother and her sister. She was always a lot of fun, and all of the men loved Dorothy. Men respected Lillian, and they loved Dorothy.

And men, then and now, will always be men. And what man would ever make a pass at any woman if her mother is in the same room?[32]

Being an actress, Lillian would say in later years, was an around-the-clock job. At Biograph, you arrived at five in the morning, put on your own makeup and costume, and waited for Mr. Griffith's directions. His players would receive five dollars a day, and would remain at the studio until the dismissal at the end of the shooting day, whenever that occurred.

No stars worked at Biograph, he would say in response to an increasing awareness that his players were developing followings. All players were unbilled.

Working for Griffith, Lillian soon learned, meant turning out a reel (ten to twelve minutes) of finished film a week. It was a full-time job, seven days a week, "year in and year out."

Being an actress meant being an observer. Griffith would tell his players to watch the behavior of people in all kinds of situations: weddings, funerals, an arrival of a new baby.

Lillian recalled: "We were made to visit hospitals, insane asylums, death prisons, houses of prisoners, all to catch, as he put it, humanity off guard."[33]

It was one of the basic tenets of good storytelling.

Lillian, in addition to sharing the same physical attributes of being "small, slim, and young," with Mary Pickford, Miriam Cooper, and Blanche Sweet, discovered that most of the Griffith actresses also had similar family backgrounds: "poverty, and the need to support a mother who was without a husband."[34]

Griffith's attitude toward women was a popular saying of the day: "Catch 'em young, treat 'em rough, tell 'em nothing."[35]

Wisely, Griffith showed no favoritism to any of his teenage players, although it was rumored that the young lady to whom he had been devoting the most shooting time during the day would serve as company that same evening at a restaurant or hotel.

Anita Loos always believed that Dorothy Gish, the more humorous of the two sisters, first attracted Mr. Griffith's admiring glance, only to be pushed aside by a quiet but more aggressive Lillian. Pensive, thoughtful Lillian's interest in motion pictures went beyond the work of acting in front of a camera.

From the outset, Lillian was interested in the creative process of moviemaking: the blocking of scenes, the shooting schedule, and the editing which took place at the end of the day and often went far into the night.

She was a familiar face at Biograph, even on days when she wasn't working, watching Griffith instructing the other players and learning from cameramen Karl Brown and Billy Bitzer about the intricacies of the camera and the moods proper lighting could effect.[36]

Karl Brown, in his autobiography *Adventures with D. W. Griffith*, recalled that, "Lillian's eyes were alive with beaming life. Her dimpled smile was so real. She could be as lucid as a mirror lake in repose, but who could become heartbreakingly tragic."[37]

From the endless hours after work Lillian spent with cameramen Brown and Bitzer, trying to attain the best lighting possible, she mastered techniques she would be able to use in the future. Photography, in those early days, was often terrible. An attractive young actress of eighteen, improperly lit, sometimes resembled "an old hag."[38]

Lillian, now in her teenage years, must have wondered about her future. Who would want her, and how could she take care of Mother?

Miriam Cooper, who had joined Biograph in 1910, always felt that the extra hours Lillian spent on the set after the end of the day's shoot weren't without an ulterior motive. Lillian and Mr. Griffith were going beyond the traditional employer-employee relationship. The puritanical Mr. Griffith had specific rules regarding his young female players: no boyfriends, no smoking, and no drinking.[39]

Dorothy Gish had dates, however secret, but it was never discussed. Had Mr. Griffith even broached the subject to her, she would have laughed and walked away. Dorothy was always independent and fun-loving. She knew that her quiet, serious sister, the older, more mature Lillian, was the more important of the two, but paid it little mind. She and Lillian were never the same character type, so there was never a sense of jealousy or competition when Mr. Griffith was casting his players. Had Dorothy been Lillian's age or older, she might easily have walked out on her mother, which James Gish had done. It was something she would occasionally suggest to Lillian when she was told to be more cooperative and less belligerent.[40]

For the purpose of defying the on-slaught of rules, and ignoring Mother Gish's often-voiced admonition that "men might leave you,"[41] Dorothy and Miriam Cooper formed a "Hen's Club" for the se-cret purpose of sharing a few beers and cig-arettes in someone's apartment on Thurs-day nights.

Miriam thought it would be fun to pay a surprise visit to the always proper Lillian, who was never part of any group and whose apartment had never been seen. On the set, Lillian rarely spoke with fellow players, preferring to stay close to Mr. Griffith as he instructed the cameramen concerning the next set-ups and the mood he wished to achieve. Lillian never invited anyone to visit her in the evening, claim-ing she was tired and had to rise and do her makeup early.

Miriam, fortified with courage ob-tained from a few extra beers at Dorothy's apartment, decided to go across the hall to Lillian's. She

> opened her door, yelling something inane like surprise! and then stopped in our tracks. There was Lillian, lying on her bed, wearing something filmy, with her long golden hair spread over the pillow. She was reading Shake-speare. It was the only time I ever saw her look annoyed.[42]

Blanche Sweet tried to explain the al-leged Trilby-Svengali relationship between Lillian and Mr. Griffith:

> The three of us — Lillian, Dorothy, and I — came from broken homes. We were the daughters of alcoholic fathers who were unable to keep any sort of job very long. When things got too tough, they walked out. They aban-doned us. Sometimes they came back. Sometimes they didn't.
>
> What could our mothers do, be-sides cook and sew? We, the daugh-ters, were our mothers' salvation.

They were helpless, like orphaned children. So we went on the stage in some touring show, or we did some kind of kid act that would take us on the road, or we went into the movies. If we were any good in any of those fields, we lasted, and families had a source of income.

I don't know what Lillian or Dorothy would have become if they hadn't been good actresses. Maybe they would have packed off from one relative to another.

Dorothy and Lillian were sur-vivors. They already had the talent. The family problem only brought it out sooner.

Mr. Griffith was separated from his wife [Linda Arvidson] when the three of us eventually wound up at Bio-graph. He was kind to us. We would have picnics together when we weren't working. He would tell us his plans and what types of parts he thought we could play in the future. I suppose people in those days made all kinds of jokes about Mr. Griffith and his harem, but we didn't pay at-tention to them. Mr. Griffith was the father we never had.[43]

The Musketeers of Pig Alley, which cast Lillian in the sympathetic role of "Little Lady," utilized the gritty realism of the streets in New York's Jewish Lower East Side, chronicling their lives as if they were struggling in Emile Zola's Paris of the nineteenth century. Famine and death were common everyday occur-rences long before they were pho-tographed and noted by Jacob Riis in *The Shame of the Cities*. Nobody was sur-prised to see an undertaker's wagon at all hours of the day and night. Those who survived, noted a socially conscious Griffith in his daily walks to the area, lived a hand-to-mouth, day-to-day exis-tence in filthy, rat-infested tenements. Easy money only came with a life of crime. Everyone lived on dreams.

Against the film's conflicting backgrounds (the *spiritual*, as exemplified by the innocence of "Little Lady," and the *sordid*, demonstrated by a very brutal, realistic picture of the slums), the gunfight for territorial control provided an exciting climax.

Throughout the picture, Lillian's character remained faithful to her musician-boyfriend, while being pursued by a gangster named Snapper Kid.

Of her work in *The Musketeers of Pig Alley*, one of many Griffith films which would pit her innocence against an evil, corrupt world, Lillian would say:

> I created a heroine who was the essence of virginity, purity, and goodness, with nobility of heart. But I'm not those ladies. I never was… That's why it's called *acting*![44]

In response to an increasing awareness that the unbilled actresses and actors at Biograph were developing followings and admirers, Mr. Griffith would remind his players there were no stars working at Biograph. "Not until your name becomes a household word in every family, not only in America, but in the world, if the world feels it knows you, and loves you, will you be a star in motion pictures."[45]

To support his "no stars" belief, Griffith continued to treat his players like actors in a repertory theatre. Bit players and leads were interchangeable. Only Mary Pickford, who appeared in more films than anyone, would challenge Griffith's autocratic rules.

At the time of *The New York Hat* (1912), which was a story written by Anita Loos and purchased for $25, Mary was earning $300 a week, a salary Mary's mother felt was $200 short of her worth.[46] In contrast, Mr. Griffith felt Mary was pricing herself out of the Biograph budget.

Lillian and Dorothy Gish were used as extras in *The New York Hat*, appearing with the parishioners outside the church at the conclusion of the service. While Lillian might have wondered why she had been cast as an extra, having had an important role in *The Musketeers of Pig Alley*, Mrs. Gish understood Mr. Griffith's reasoning: he was trying to prevent Lillian from becoming "big-headed." Didn't Dorothy have a very small role in Lillian's film? Now it was Lillian's turn…[47]

At the conclusion of the filming of *The New York Hat*, Mary Pickford and D. W. Griffith parted company.

For Lillian and Dorothy, the timing had been perfect. With Mary setting her sights on returning to the legitimate theatre and respectability, Lillian, more than Dorothy, could think of becoming the next queen of the studio. "We didn't know we were the beginnings of an industry. We were too young. Movies were just something we were just working in to make a living until we were old enough to be accepted in the theatre as an ingenue."[48]

Mrs. Gish, in anticipating Lillian's future success in motion pictures, offered advice to her. "Mother said, 'You may feel secure to be making so much money now, but break your leg and then see how much you have left. If you want to save enough money to live on when you get older and are no longer starring in pictures, live simply.'"[49]

Reminding Lillian that she no longer had a father, she, too,

> had a feeling she was going to die and leave us alone with the result that when we got our salaries, Mother would go to a bank and ask about what was good and what wasn't.
>
> She tried to make us save and invest; sometimes we did, and sometimes we didn't know what to do about it. She was trying to train us to take care of what we had worked so hard for.[50]

In an era when a woman's horizon was limited to the kitchen and childbearing, Lillian had been exposed to the creativity of driven men whose genius redirected the course of human thinking. The twentieth century would record its history on moving pictures, and would not be confined to paintings, photographs, and written eyewitness accounts. Lillian had been allowed to participate in the birth of film, and given a life which would free her from being a girl.

CHAPTER 3

Events Leading to The Birth: *I*

Before the close of 1912, movies, despite their successes in nickelodeons and converted storefronts, were still regarded as little more than cheap entertainment for immigrants and the lower classes. A standard program consisted of compilations of simple stories or primitive newsreel footage of local events of the day (changing horses in Linden, New Jersey, or John Philip Sousa's Band marching down the muddy streets of Scranton, Pennsylvania).[1]

One-reelers were twelve minute entertainments produced for a few hundred dollars. A D. W. Griffith one-reeler starring Lillian Gish, however, was an extravaganza that went way over budget, showing little concern for production costs. The product was all that mattered, but Mr. Griffith completed his work on time. At Biograph, he worked to the schedule.

Unlike other directors, who photographed their players with an immobile camera (as if the motion picture were little more than a stage play viewed from an advantageous seat in the audience), Mr. Griffith kept his camera moving. The audiences saw Lillian's emotions. There were close-ups of her face, something rarely seen even in the best seat in a legitimate theatre. Griffith's camera brought the viewer into the action. An audience didn't observe, an audience participated.

Griffith constructed his photoplays in

sections, and increased the tension by switching from one character to another, from one scene to another, even from one angle to another. It was quite common to move the camera from a living room fireplace point-of-view to a large picture window that overlooked a rural landscape, then return to the same fireplace before the start of the action.[2]

Lillian remembered that the idea of seeing only "the face and shoulders" of the actor on the screen wasn't received with total acceptance by the Biograph production office.

Mr. Griffith was always being told that the audience would think the actor had no body, only a head and shoulders, and we're paying for the entire actor. We want to see an entire actor on the screen the same way we see an entire actor on the stage.

Mr. Griffith would step closer to the person who was talking.

"Look at me," he would say to the speaker, "Look at me right in the eye! Does it make any difference that you can't see my feet? How did you react when I stepped closer? Didn't you think I was going to say something very important?!"

For Mr. Griffith, movies were pictures in motion, and the camera told the story. The camera was our eyes. The camera couldn't speak words. It was the job of the actors to convey the emotions. We did this with gestures and facial expressions, which were recorded with Mr. Griffith's camera.[3]

With Mary Pickford's departure, Griffith needed someone to fill the gap and take her place. Fast. Mary, in her four years at Biograph (1909–1912), had made over seventy films.

Looking at his roster of female players for a possible successor, Griffith chose Lillian Gish, whose output her first year (1912) was a mere eleven films — not all of them successful. Was she worth the risk?

Across the ocean, Louis Mercanton of France convinced Sarah Bernhardt, the leading French tragedienne of her day, to immortalize her Queen Elizabeth on four reels.

Madam Sarah, knowing that "every stage actor's tragedy is that his art dies with him," saw this venture, even without sound, as her "one chance of immortality."[4]

Using the slogan, "Famous Players in Famous Plays," Adolph Zukor convinced Broadway producer Daniel Frohman to import the film and present it at his Lyceum Theatre. It would be mutually advantageous: an international stage star gaining exposure for both herself *and* the new medium of the motion picture. Yes, the French titles would be translated into English.

At an "invitation only" matinee on July 12, 1912, an appreciative crowd of "political, artistic, and financial celebrities" watched the four-reel import and applauded wildly at its conclusion.[5]

Griffith was envious and enraged! A French import had upstaged what he had considered an American product!

What Griffith had feared would come true *had* come true: an outside organization, not an American studio like Biograph, had made the "flickers" into an ac-

ceptable art form that could be exhibited to sophisticated, well-dressed, wealthy patrons in a legitimate theatre. Madam Sarah, unlike her American counterparts, did not believe that going from the theatre to the motion picture studio was a step down or a sign of hard times. Her regret that her voice would not be united with her screen image was cast aside when she heard that recordings of speeches from the play were easily available in the theatre lobby and at record stores. Discerning patrons could hear Madam Sarah's "smoky" voice in their homes at all hours of the day and night![6]

Griffith turned to Lillian, who had acted in less than a dozen films, and whose popularity was nowhere near that of Mary Pickford's. Would the Biograph production office take a chance on her? Was she worth the risk?

Before he could spend any significant time to ponder this question, Lillian had provided the answer. It was yet another blow.

Prior to appearing before the Biograph camera in their first film, *An Unknown Enemy* (1912), she and Dorothy, along with hundreds of other hopefuls, had visited the Belasco office and auditioned for a role in the play *A Good Little Devil*. Not hearing anything, both sisters turned to the "flickers" for temporary employment until the opportunity to return to their first love, the theatre, would present itself.[7]

The opportunity presented itself.

Not only did Mr. Belasco hire Lillian, but, to her surprise, he had released a statement about her, which she recalled many years later:

> David Belasco told the press that I was the most beautiful blonde in the world. I didn't care about being a beauty. I wanted to be an actress!
>
> I thought it was a terrible thing for him to say, because I felt I was too

gauche and awkward. I also knew that next month there would be another "most beautiful blonde."[8]

In addition to the Belasco statement to the press, there was another surprise: her friend, Mary Pickford, with whom she had been working at Biograph, was playing the lead role of blind Juliet in the same play. They would be together again!

Anita Loos, a close friend of both Mary Pickford and Lillian, always had doubts about the casting of Mr. Belasco's play.

> I wouldn't put it past Mary Pickford's mother to tell Mr. Belasco to hire Lillian. Mary's mother believed that with a little pressure Griffith would have kept her (Mary). Mary had helped Lillian with Mr. Griffith. Now that Mary was with Mr. Belasco, having Lillian around would make things easier. The theatre was new territory for them both, although they had done stage work. This wasn't barnstorming somewhere on the road. This was New York!
>
> Lillian and Mary were always friends. They were never a threat to each other, nor were they competition.
>
> I can't prove it, and I never asked Lillian, but I wouldn't put it past Mary's mother to keep the girls together at any cost."[9]

Now that Lillian was hired as one of the three "angels," her problem for the future was not to jeopardize any chances of employment at Biograph once *A Good Little Devil* had concluded its New York run. Would Mr. Griffith believe that the exodus of his two favorite players was not a planned conspiracy? Mary, always supported by her mother, had no qualms about telling anybody how she felt. Lillian, always providing support to her mother, would forever be reluctant to alienate anyone who could possibly employ her.[10]

The Belasco salary Lillian would re-

ceive was only twenty-five dollars a week. Not a very large sum. But this was the theatre, and, in the theatre, one worked at one's art.

Griffith, if Lillian chose to remain with him, would pay twice as much — a salary of fifty dollars! Fifty dollars a week was more than she had ever earned!

What career decision would she make?

Before she could answer, Griffith counseled her, reminding her that he had once wanted to be an actor in the theatre and write plays. And he had failed at both...

> "Mr. Griffith," said Lillian, "told me to go with Mr. Belasco, even though it was for less money. The name Belasco was worth ten times anything he (Griffith) could offer."[11]

To spare any concern regarding Dorothy, Mr. Griffith offered to take Dorothy with him to his studio in California. Her salary would be fifteen dollars a week, plus five dollars a day each day she worked. Mr. Gish, who had returned to Springfield, Ohio to work for the caterer who had previously employed her, was also guaranteed train fare to Los Angeles.

It would be like before: a temporary separation. It was the life they had chosen. Somehow, unlike many others, they had been strong and tough enough to survive: Lillian in New York, Dorothy in California, and mother on her way from Ohio.[12]

A Good Little Devil, written by the mother and son playwriting team of Rosemunde and Maurice Rostand, was a "fairy tale for grownups," a "memory of the joys and sorrows of Childhood." Set in a garden where a blind Juliet, played by nineteen-year-old Mary Pickford acting as a twelve year old, waits for her sweetheart in a world of birds, beasts, fairies, and gnomes, it was the perfect showcase for the popular film star. Lillian played Morganie, one of the three flying angels.[13]

If Griffith harbored any animosity over Mary's return to the theatre — or of Lillian's departure, however temporary — he never indicated how he felt. He was present at the out-of-town tryouts in Philadelphia and Baltimore. At the end of each performance, he was enthusiastic and encouraging.[14]

An incident in Baltimore remained in Lillian's memory for many years.

Before the start of every matinee and evening performance, a company of eighteen men would check all of the wires used by the flying angels as a safety precaution. Lillian would also take a few flying solos to practice her flights which would occur in the play.

As rehearsed, there were only two flights: the first, from the ceiling to the stage and up to a seven foot ledge, all in one continuous motion, and the second, down from the ledge, where she had been sitting, to the stage. Both flights were done in full view of the audience while the spotlight shone on her radiant face. The flights would begin in darkness, allowing the spotlight to catch and follow her.

During the evening performance (the matinee had gone without a hitch), the wire which had flown her from the ceiling to the ledge must have become disengaged, unbeknownst to her, seconds after she landed on the ledge. When she heard the cue to begin her second descent, she calmly leapt from the wall into space, and with the spotlight on her, she fell to the stage in full view of the stunned audience — who laughed.

As much as the unexpected shock of the unexpected fall had unnerved her, the laughter and humiliation in front of the audience were too much to bear. She ran off the stage, hid in her dressing room, and did not finish the performance.[15] An understudy, Clare Booth, later to marry publisher Henry Luce and become a playwright (*The Women*) and diplomat, went on and played her part.[16]

Lillian never forgot

> seeing Mr. Belasco in my dressing room seconds after I ran off the stage. I didn't know he was in the audience! And here he was — looking at me and laughing!
>
> I burst into tears, not because of the pain, which I still felt, but because of what I had done. I had ruined his play, and the audience was laughing at me, and he would fire me! A fired actress was the worst thing you could be! People in the profession would talk secretly about you, the way they did about certain actors who went on stage drunk until it was reported. And then the only work left, *if* you got any work, would be in places far from New York.
>
> What was I going to tell Mother?
>
> Mr. Belasco kept repeating the audience wasn't laughing at me, but at what had happened. They would have laughed at anybody. But *anybody* didn't fall down seven feet in full view. *I* did! And I knew I had ruined his play … and in front of everybody![17]

When the troupe returned to New York, Lillian moved back to her first room at the Marlton Hotel on West 8th Street in an effort to save money.

Once again she was cooking "tinned things with a Sterno lamp"[18] and sending ten dollars a week to her mother in Ohio.[19]

Nothing had changed, except that Lillian was living alone and on her own. She had come full circle, maintaining her lifestyle in the manner she and Dorothy had been taught by their mother. If she could be thrifty and wise, she would always be independent and not need anyone to help her. Especially men.

With rehearsals sometimes lasting until the early hours of the following morning, Lillian's thriftiness and Spartan way of living had begun to take a toll on her health. At first, she had blamed her gaunt, tired look on the extra hours she devoted to the wires and the two flights she had insisted on taking. She ignored the concern shown by Mary and her mother.[20]

When she mentioned being tired in a letter to childhood friend Nell Dorr, Nell invited her to join her at the family home in Ohio.

Lillian also responded by letter:

> You ... can't know how wonderful it is to have someone offer me a home, and how I would love to follow the desire of my heart and come to you. But I can't. I can't because I have to make my way in this world from now on. Mother has worked all her life; surely it's my turn now.[21]

The dangerous winter weather continued to assault the streets with ice, snow, and rain. Lillian continued to attend the rehearsals, never realizing how demoralizing to the rest of the company the sight of her must have been.

Finally, both Mrs. Pickford and her daughter Mary confronted Lillian and insisted she do something. Her weight loss could no longer be concealed. A tired actress was a liability to herself. A sick actress was a liability to the company.

When Mary threatened to send a telegram to Lillian's mother, a telegram that would bring Mrs. Gish immediately to New York, Lillian relented. She visited a physician, who told her that unless she took quick steps, her pernicious anemia would be fatal.[22]

Trouper Mary Pickford's outlook was more practical: nobody fools around with personal health so close to Opening Night in New York!

With both Dorothy and Mrs. Gish out of the city, to what family member could Lillian turn for help? Nobody. The show must go on.

A Good Little Devil opened at the Re-public Theatre on January 8, 1913. As anticipated, Mary Pickford earned the praise of the critics, with *The New York Times* reviewer suggesting that the new medium of the motion picture was a desirable place for actors to improve their diction. How a silent film could improve one's voice was never explained.

Lillian's performance as Morganie was described in only one word: "alluring."[23] Fortunately the out-of-town accident with the wires was never reported to the press. She was safe.

She stayed with the play, somehow managing to gather enough strength and willpower to do the required eight performances a week, despite the doctor's diagnosis of pernicious anemia.

At the end of January her health hadn't improved. With Dorothy and her mother and Mr. Griffith at the Biograph Studio in Los Angeles, there was no reason to remain in New York. She took Mr. Belasco's offer of railroad fare to Los Angeles and left *A Good Little Devil*, although business was strong enough to continue the run until May.[24]

Mary Pickford remained in New York for the run of the play, never missing a performance. When Adolph Zukor of Famous Players-Paramount offered Mary the chance to repeat her stage role in the film version for the salary of $5,000 a week, she accepted.[25]

Mary remembered Lillian's reaction to her good fortune in an article she wrote for *Movie Weekly*, eleven years later, in 1925: Lillian said, "How happy you must be, Mary, to have attained the position where you can give your mother so much. My sole aim is to reach that place, too, some day."[26]

Lillian's Biograph salary in Los Angeles would be fifty dollars a week — considerably less than friend Mary's. While she never challenged Mr. Griffith's claim that the theatre was "true art," it must have rankled when she compared the salaries.

Of her first venture into the world of "true art," she would say *A Good Little Devil* was a "good little failure!"[27]

The Hollywood of 1913, to which Lillian had journeyed cross-country by train for five days, hadn't yet become a major industry with motion picture, television, and recording studios within close proximity. Lillian Gish's Hollywood was an area most known for its orange groves and good weather. Hollywood was a safe place for Eastern émigrés looking for a prime location to produce their product far away from the roving eye of Thomas Edison's goon squads, who tried to destroy film stock that didn't bear the Edison trademark.

Formerly vacant land had become sprinkled with quickly assembled shacks and tents. The names Griffith, Horsley, Selig, Lasky, Zukor, and DeMille were becoming familiar to people living in the area.

Griffith had returned to supervise the construction of a larger studio in Los Angeles on Georgia and Girard Streets, which afforded its actors more modern facilities, including a smooth — instead of rough — wooden stage, lockers for the players, and running water.[28]

Griffith's Hollywood company had included many of the former New York people with whom Lillian and Dorothy worked: Lionel Barrymore, Henry B. Walthall, Blanche Sweet, Robert Harron, Harry Carey, Mae Marsh.

The seed of ambition had been well planted in Lillian's childhood by her mother. The unfortunate Belasco experience was behind her.

With an earnestness, zeal, and determination that would attempt to remove any memories of previous actresses who acted in front of the Biograph cameras, Lillian vowed to pursue her career under Griffith that would summon comparisons of Trilby under the domination of Svengali. She would be more than a Griffith actress. There were plenty of those. Weren't Griffith girls called his "harem" by insiders?

Lillian wanted to be the Griffith heroine, and she knew the way to impress audiences was to be photographed in as many close-ups as possible, close-ups which would project desirability as well as vulnerability.

While Lillian, the blossoming adult, was more than willing to be molded in the Griffith manner and quite capable of assuming her professional responsibilities, the child in Lillian desperately wanted her mother's approval and forever would crave her mother's affection. Perhaps love would come with achievement.

As Lillian's star continued to ascend at Biograph, Mary Gish's words of hope and cheer would be tempered with words of caution. *Can you keep this up? If you're not good enough, they'll hire another little girl…*

The thought of "another little girl," however quietly suggested by Lillian's mother, was enough to send Lillian into a rage. It was a rage Lillian knew not to have her mother see. Young ladies didn't ever rage at their mothers, especially when they were doing their best to keep the family together without a husband.

Invoking the name of James to Lillian often brought unashamed tears. No matter what her mother would say, Lillian still regarded James Gish as basically a good man overwhelmed by responsibilities he couldn't handle.

In the wake of growing male admirers, Mrs. Gish would counsel Lillian at strategic moments when she felt Lillian might be swayed by her less inhibited female co-workers who were keeping late hours and being seen drinking and smoking at impossible places.

Men will leave you. And then what will you do? Who will take care of us?

We are all we have, and all we will ever have.

Griffith's principal photography was done outside, on a raised stage, in broad daylight. Curtains were arranged to determine the degree of necessary sunlight.

On rainy days, when shooting became impossible, the company would rehearse their future scenes in the carpentry shop in order to salvage some hours and avoid the cancellation of work. Knowing that nobody was paid on days when they had no work, the company did not balk at having to rehearse in cramped quarters. The inconvenience was only temporary, and time and money were of the essence. Griffith, as extravagant as he sometimes appeared to be to the production office, constantly attempted to show that he was keeping production costs and salaries within reason. Even in cramped quarters, it was still possible to give actors their blocking.

There were no "lines" to recite. The players could say whatever they thought appropriate, except at "silent rehearsals" when pantomime had to indicate what could be a filmed emotion.[29]

According to Lillian, some of Mr. Griffith's stories were mere suggestions made to him by members of the company. One was developed from Lionel Barrymore's casual remark that Lillian couldn't kill a cockroach. The remark became *The Lady and the Mouse*.[30]

Lillian played the granddaughter of curmudgeonly Lionel Barrymore, who hated mice and would set traps for them.

Then, as now, the short film was an audience-pleaser, a very charming little comedy, a typical programmer of its time, but hardly the career-maker for Barrymore, Gish, or Mr. Griffith that would make the production office sit up and take notice.

It would remain for *The Mothering Heart* to do that.

The Mothering Heart was a two-reeler filmed in two weeks at a cost of $1,800. For Lillian, it was the role she had always wanted. It was the chance to "play old." In *The Mothering Heart*, Lillian would be a thirty-year-old married woman, a most welcome change from the fragile one-reel heroines with one-dimensional problems.[31]

The character was quite a stretch, and Griffith left her alone to develop it. Unlike Dorothy, who was quick at realizing what Mr. Griffith wanted, Lillian was a slow worker who analyzed every step and motion her screen character would use. Griffith would say that Lillian "conceived an ideal and patiently sought to realize it. Genius is like that. The ideal becomes real to it."[32]

When Lillian first approached Griffith about playing the role, she was rejected as being too young. Lillian, ever since her screen debut in *An Unseen Enemy*, was the ideal Griffith heroine: wistful, fragile, delicate as porcelain, with a shining innocence that would raise her above any sordid environment.

At the second meeting, Griffith changed his mind. Lillian, determined to play the part, reported to the studio wearing padded clothes to add maturity and age to her figure.[33]

Her role was "tailored specifically for her talents,"[34] requiring her to play a jealous, pregnant wife whose husband is enamored of a cabaret dancer.

Once again, Griffith's direction and Lillian's strict adherence to his instructions conjured up in the minds of her fellow players the image of Svengali hypnotizing Trilby.[35]

As the filming progressed, Griffith would softly speak to her, telling her how she should react and what she should do for the camera. "You feel that you've been humiliated by your husband. You think that he doesn't love you any longer because you are carrying his child. You are afraid that he wants to get rid of you."[36]

What is obvious in viewing the film is the absence of the grand gestures so often associated with early silent film acting. Griffith-style acting emphasized restraint and small, subtle gestures which when seen close-up, would read as intimate. A close-up meant impact, and it had to be used with discretion.[37]

Unlike James O'Neill, who virtually repeated his stage performance in the filmed version of his touring hit, *The Count of Monte Cristo*, there was no need to address the audience through the camera lens.

Griffith used the "hidden emotion," the "reverse acknowledgment of the lens," to emphasize private feelings. He avoided "camera consciousness."

In *The Mothering Heart*, Lillian, seeing her husband driving away, stands behind a tree to avoid her husband and the other woman. Rather than show a tear-stained face, which Lillian could easily have done, the camera focuses on Lillian's hand slowly moving across the tree.[38]

She has her baby alone, a plot device later repeated in *Way Down East*. When the baby in *The Mothering Heart* is born dead, she goes into the garden and furiously hits the rose bushes until every rose has been torn away.

Lillian remembered:

> The beating of the rose bushes occurred during the actual shooting. Whether Mr. Griffith wanted an unrehearsed one camera-take, natural reaction, I don't know.
>
> He was quietly talking me through the actions, and he, without any warning, suddenly raised his voice and yelled "You've given birth to a dead baby, and your husband has gone away, and you are saddened by one and are enraged at the other...
>
> "Do something!"
>
> The action was continuous, and I was so involved in my character, I just struck the rose bushes in frustration.

I was reacting to Mr. Griffith's directorial command.

I often think of *The Mothering Heart* as a milestone in my career.[39]

While *The New York Dramatic Mirror* called *The Mothering Heart* "a most notable production" and praised Lillian, "despite her extreme youth," as portraying the mother "with pleasing taste and remarkable intelligence,"[40] Griffith's contributions were still unacknowledged. He still was fighting with the production office who didn't want him to make longer films.[41]

The Battle of Elderbridge Gulch, which seems not to have been reviewed upon its original release (1913),[42] was a combination of Griffith's attempt to tell a complex story within the conventional two-reel length and use the camera in a more spectacular manner.

The sets, Mr. Griffith told *The Motion Picture World* (a trade paper), were going to be constructed in San Fernando Valley, and they were going to be three-dimensional with an authentic look.[43]

There would be more threads to the story than in previous efforts. More than one character would have a problem to solve.

Sally (Mae Marsh), staying at the Cameron cabin of her aunt and uncle, has been told to keep her two puppies outside. When an Indian tries to take the puppies, her uncle shoots him. The dead Indian is the chief's son.

A young married couple (Lillian Gish and Robert Haron) and their baby are on their way to Elderbridge Gulch. Their baby, the title announces, will be the town's first.

While the local Indian tribe terrorizes the town as an act of reprisal, Bobby has stepped inside the saloon for a drink. He hands the baby to a lady, who, in turn, gives the baby to a young cowboy.

Hearing the noises outside, Bobby

panics and seeks shelter, forgetting that the baby is no longer in his possession.

Suddenly, Bobby is hit by a stray bullet...

Lillian, who has sought refuge at the Cameron cabin, is doubly grief-stricken: her husband and baby are missing.

The cabin is surrounded by Indians...

Help, desperately needed, will come if somebody can get to the cavalry, which is far away. The route is treacherous and fraught with the dangers of sudden attacks...

Anthony Slide, writing in *Early American Cinema*, has stated why *The Battle of Elderbridge Gulch* has remained a vital work and an indication of the more effective Griffith films to follow.

If the baby is not rescued, Lillian and Bobby are tragic figures.

If Bobby does not survive, the same is true.

If help from the cavalry does not arrive..."[44]

Using constantly changing points of view and close-ups (a crying baby, Lillian's anguish-ridden face, the death throes of a dying cowboy), *The Battle of Elderbridge Gulch* is a prime example of "nervous cutting."[45]

Until the film's conclusion, when a wounded Bobby, who has been picked up by the rescuing army and reunited with his wife at the Cameron cabin — only to have their happiness postponed because they are without their baby, Griffith has engaged his audience's interest and sustained it without a break in the tension.

Of course, the young baby and puppies emerge from hiding, but that is only moments before The End title is flashed on the screen.

The Battle of Elderbridge Gulch is a film rich in cinema language and its use of parallel action and changing points of view.[46]

With the success of Griffith's *The Birth of a Nation* (1915), there was a mad scramble to re-release earlier efforts in an effort to capitalize on his name. *The Battle of Elderbridge Gulch* was brought back to theatres as an "encore" attraction. It was the only Griffith film to receive this honor at this time.[47]

According to Lillian Gish, Griffith used no systemized script. He preferred to keep the ideas in his head, and experimented during the actual shooting. When filming *The Mothering Heart*, he and Lillian, beside him at the end of the day, would help the film editor clip certain sections together to form a smoothly flowing narrative. To the outsider, and even to people within the industry, the D. W. Griffith work method was disorganized and haphazard.

Enid Markey, whose career began in silents at the rival Essanany Studios in Chicago in 1915 (and who played in William S. Hart westerns, the first *Tarzan* film, and later supported Lillian Gish onstage in 1942 in Ketti Frings' play, *Mr. Sycamore*, for the Theatre Guild), always thought Mr. Griffith's methods were "a bit bizarre."

Still active and appearing onstage in New York in the Edward Albee adaptation of Carson McCullers' *The Ballad of the Sad Cafe*, she reminisced about Lillian Gish between Saturday performances in November 1963.

> Once, I asked Lillian, "How did you keep your concentration in those days with all of that jumping around?" And Lillian, who was always Griffith's greatest champion, calmly answered, "Mr. Griffith did all of your thinking for you." He would say, "Stop!" and we would stop, and we would have to remember all of our places, and he would try something else.
>
> I knew I couldn't work for Griffith ... unless he called me! Which he didn't!
>
> When Lillian and Dorothy were going through their ballet movements

at Biograph, and playing those delicate virgins, I was playing Jane and swinging through the trees with barechested Elmo Lincoln in *Tarzan of the Apes*! Thank God the director (Scott Sydney) didn't call Stop! while I was swinging through the air. Elmo would have dropped me on my ass![48]

With the importing of another foreign film, the Italian *Quo Vadis?* and the raised admission price of one dollar, the day of the one- and two-reeler and old nickelodeon prices were a thing of the past.[49] Whatever doubts exhibitors may have had about audience attention span were swept aside on the April 27, 1913 premiere.[50]

The appeal of Italian filmmaking lay in spectacular camera sweeps of large casts and great crowds who filled the screen with a virtual sea of people. Like Italian opera, everything was done on a grand scale, from the bravura style of acting to the visual magnificence of the sets.[51] The one-set society drama, popular on American stages, was photographed from one perspective. Now, there were outdoor panoramic shots of castles, mountains, and ships at sea.

With movie-making on a grand scale, it was quite easy for producers and theatres to ask for a higher admission price. A higher admission price stood for prestige and respectability.

Griffith, who might have seen *Quo Vadis?* in its twenty-two day engagement in New York[52] must have realized immediately that his own film output, no matter how popular and successful in the rented storefronts and nickelodeons, would not hold up to these new imported spectacles that were exhibited in theatres and ran for sixty minutes. Theatre owners knew that if you wanted to attract big audiences who would pay big prices, you had to provide a big picture.

To accomplish that goal, Griffith re-

called the 1904 hit play *Judith of Bethulia* by Thomas Bailey Aldrich, a successful vehicle that starred Nance O'Neil and Lowell Sherman.[53] Sherman, eight years later, in 1920, would co-star with Lillian Gish and Richard Barthelmess in *Way Down East*.

Secretly, Griffith spoke to Lee Dougherty of the Biograph story department[54] and had Dougherty purchase not the play, but a script fashioned from the playwright's original source, the biblical story from the Apocrypha in the Old Testament. The writer was Grace A. Pierce of Santa Monica.[55]

To avoid any plagiarism suit from either Aldrich or Pierce, Griffith assigned Frank Woods to fashion Pierce's *Judith and Holofernes* and the Aldrich play into a vehicle for filming which would not use any dialogue from either version for screen titles. Wisely, he kept a copy of Aldrich's play on the set at all times during the shooting.[56]

Theatre actor and playwright that he once was, Griffith invited Nance O'Neil to visit his set and reminisce about the 1904 production. Whatever details he inserted into the shooting of the film did not come from the printed play text but from the recollections of an old friend from touring days.[57]

The elements of success were inherent in the story: a captured fortress, a beautiful widow who wants to save her people, a powerful adversary, a vision to visit the camp of the adversary, unexpected and forbidden love, a beheading of the enemy, victory, and freedom.

With the shrewd casting of a voluptuous seventeen-year-old Blanche Sweet, clad only in a "snug crepe shirt and a tiny pair of panties,"[58] it was easy to see why audiences, unaccustomed to any visual representation of biblical characters, would flock to behold *Judith of Bethulia* and future films on "religious themes!"

The set for *Judith of Bethulia* would be constructed in Chatsworth Park outside Los Angeles. With the success of *The Battle of Elderbridge Gulch*, spending more money for what would be his greatest effort was easily justifiable.

Judith of Bethulia utilized twelve square miles for an ancient walled city, armies of extras, several babies, trained horses, and expert riders.[59]

Transportation to Chatsworth Park was furnished by streetcar, train, and, at the very end, haywagon. The players had to be on the set for the makeup call at four or five in the morning. Filming began at six, the hour when the sun rose. Since snakes were much in evidence, strategically placed bottles of snakebite antidote were always available, thus eliminating any long work stoppage.[60]

With Griffith still maintaining his troupe as players-in-repertory, Lillian, who had a leading role in the recently completed *The Battle of Elderbridge Gulch*, was cast in a very small role as a mother in Egypt. Dorothy, prominent in Griffith's *Her Old Teacher*, was cast as the crippled beggar.

Lillian remembered that her role in *Judith of Bethulia* required her to

>merely run around, clutching this dying hungry baby, in search of food while this city was being besieged.
>
>Dorothy was luckier. All or most of her scenes were played near a wall. I think she had some shade.
>
>The weather was always hot, and we had long shooting days with desert scenes and charging horses.
>
>Mr. Griffith had sent out a call for babies, and they were easy to get. Dozens and dozens of young Mexican mothers came with babies. Most of the babies, because of the heat, were crying, and I say this looking back, that I wished we had silent babies for silent films!

>Dorothy had a wonderful sense of humor. When we had to break for lunch, she would tell me to put my baby down and join her. We were given box-lunches: a sandwich, a piece of fruit, something on that order. All of those endless box-lunches tasted alike. I don't eat sandwiches anymore!
>
>When the shooting resumed, and I was given back my baby, I saw that it wasn't the same baby I was working with before we broke for lunch. I mentioned this to Dorothy and she calmly put down her sandwich and answered, "Lillian, that baby went on tour and had to be replaced!"[61]

When Blanche Sweet wasn't in a scene, she would ride her horse to the sets where the battle sequences were being shot. Like Lillian, she knew that *Judith of Bethulia* was D. W. Griffith's first long film, a four-reeler, and she (Blanche) was going to make sure that Mr. Griffith was aware of the degree of seriousness and total commitment she was giving this role. Like Lillian, she knew Mr. Griffith was always planning and thinking of future projects.

If *Judith of Bethulia* succeeded, and there was every reason to think it would, perhaps Mr. Griffith would consider her for a leading role in his next film.

At the end of each shooting day, Blanche and Lillian were familiar sights in the cutting room, each watching Mr. Griffith carefully assembling what would be the final product.[62]

Silent films were never meant to be seen in silence. When the early film exhibitors needed something to camouflage the noise made by handcranked projectors, pianists or organists were engaged to provide suitable music to underscore the action and mood being depicted on the screen. Most of the time, the early musicians resorted to popular music of the day. In the larger cities, small orchestras were utilized, and the handbook of selections

Lillian: *Judith of Bethulia* (1914: American Biograph, directed by D. W. Griffith). Lillian was required to "merely run around, clutching this dying hungry baby, in search of food, while this city was being besieged."

bearing descriptive titles was common-place: *Neutral Society Drama, Racing Down the Rapids, First Love, First Loss*, etc.

For *Judith of Bethulia*, Griffith, who had a vast knowledge of opera and symphonic music, wanted classical themes to accompany the on-screen action.

Lillian remembered that some of the music that accompanied the showings of *Judith of Bethulia* was hummed by Mr. Griffith during the actual shooting of the film.

> Mr. Griffith would talk/direct us through our actions and movements, and then sometimes gesture with his arms and start to sing or hum a phrase of music. It was never a distraction, because we had become used to his work habits, and his humming gave an added emotion to the scene.
>
> Nowadays, everyone can hear classical music on the radio or television, or go to concerts, but we were working before phonograph records were so common to find in every home. You couldn't take this sort of luxury for granted in those days. Culture was something only for the very wealthy or educated.[63]

Griffith's specific requests for the accompanying score for *Judith of Bethulia* included portions of Rossini's *William Tell*, Von Suppe's *Poet and Peasant Overture*, and Grieg's *Peer Gynt Suite*.[64] It was common when the titles "Comes the dawn" or "The next day" were seen during the course of any film to hear strains of Grieg's *Morning Mood* to establish the scene.

"A fascinating work of high artistry," wrote Louis Reeves Harrison of *Judith of Bethulia* in *The Moving Picture World* of March 7, 1914, while *Variety*, in their March 27 edition, termed the Griffith four-reeler "a full grown man's job."[65]

Despite high words of praise, the Biograph production office was not impressed. *Judith of Bethulia*, budgeted at the already exorbitant price of $18,000, had cost twice as much to complete. Mr. Griffith had become a company risk, a liability rather than an asset.

While the film was being completed and edited in New York, Griffith was summoned to the Biograph production office and told that if he wished to continue employment at Biograph, it would be in the capacity of supervising the work of other directors.[66] Under no circumstances would he be allowed to direct any picture of his own.

Griffith's increasing restlessness, which had been escalating over the last few months, had reached the boiling point. A film without any message, he told cameraman Billy Bitzer, is just a waste of time. To continue employment at Biograph in the capacity of supervisor would mean "grinding out sausages" which would have little or nothing of his personal vision. There was no reason to stay. It was time to go.[67]

The production office, remembered Lillian Gish, did not look at Mr. Griffith's decision to leave very kindly.

> They [the Biograph production office] were so angry at Mr. Griffith's decision to leave — they had expected him to thank them for maintaining him in the face of the financial loss they expected. [They] were afraid to release the film when it was completed. They wanted to have a profit from other films to offset what they thought they would lose on *Judith of Bethulia*.
>
> Biograph withheld it in the wake of other European imports and productions from rival studios. They wanted to see how much their films made before deciding to take a chance with Griffith's film.
>
> By the time they decided it was safe to release it, hoping to recoup some of the initial loss, it was too late. The public had become accustomed to longer

films, and they naturally thought nothing was special about an American four-reeler.

Griffith practically *forced* them to release *Judith of Bethulia*. Biograph was a one- and two-reeler production house, and they were afraid that this film wouldn't show a profit, and this would make Mr. Griffith a bigger risk, since the film had gone over budget.

Mr. Griffith had no choice but to resign. He couldn't work under those restrictive conditions anymore. He was a serious artist, not a pattern maker. Everything was an uphill battle, a continual fight to survive.

What was ironic about all of this is that the film was reissued a few years later (1917). It was brought back, and the footage that had been cut from the original release was restored — this same film that they didn't want to release because it had gone over the production budget! Biograph even changed the title to *Her Condoned Sin*, but it didn't do the business they had hoped. Everything is in the timing.

In the beginning, he was way ahead of the competitors. Now, they were ahead of him. For the moment....

There was also a problem that Dorothy and I had to face, and tell our mother: if Mr. Griffith goes, what will happen to the two of us? We weren't under contract to Biograph. We were employed by Mr. Griffith, and neither Dorothy nor I had ever signed or had ever been presented with any kind of contract that required our signature. He told us from that very first day when to report, and when not to report. We were working for Mr. Griffith, and now we weren't working for anyone![68]

CHAPTER 4

Events Leading to The Birth: *II*

Dorothy and I had to go to work early. I think that's a good thing, to put children out into the world so they learn what to expect and be ready for — before it hurts.

I never had any hobbies. I never learned how to really cook. I don't know how to sew. I didn't make friends with the other children the way Dorothy could.

I never learned how to play.

— Lillian Gish
Conversation with author
January 1968

October 1, 1913: With Griffith's resignation from Biograph came the end of the one- and two-reel "flickers" and the beginning of an art form. The full length feature was no longer only an excuse for raising the price of admission nor merely an imported foreign novelty exhibited in a legitimate theatre. Full length features on serious themes required attention, thought, and the respect you could give to dramas. Only comedies were one or two reels, because motion picture producers believed audiences couldn't laugh longer than ten or twenty minutes.

Griffith knew that if he didn't secure immediate employment and turn out a successful product that would keep his name before the public, the industry he had helped to create would soon relegate his name to history.

Lillian knew her little output, unless she appeared in front of the cameras,

would soon be forgotten, or she and Dorothy would be dimly recalled as "those two sisters who worked for a man who couldn't make transitions."[1]

In a burgeoning industry whose workers knew everybody and functioned like a small town, names were synonymous with reputations. Lillian was "a queen, very fine, very gentle," and Dorothy was "a clown."[2]

While Griffith would advertise his achievements and innovations in the December 3, 1913 edition of *The New York Mirror* (close-up figures, the switchback, sustained suspense, raising motion picture acting to a higher plane),[3] neither Lillian nor Dorothy knew which road to take. Should they return to the legitimate theatre and subject themselves to the hazards of touring? Of should they risk their lives in something uncertain called motion pictures?

How long either or both of them would remain "at liberty" was a mystery they couldn't solve. As Griffith actresses, they had removed themselves from the minds of other producers.

Griffith, they had heard, had tried to negotiate a new contract with his former employer, Biograph, on terms under which he would be able to work. But, once again, he and the production office had reached an impasse. He would not be held accountable to accountants who had no eye nor regard for artistry. He had also rejected an offer of $50,000-a-year to work for Adolph Zukor at Paramount, because he felt a large salary might place more demands on his work.[4]

Allan Dwan, involved with the film industry as an engineer and director since 1908, believed Griffith thought he was accountable only to his product. He showed little concern for studio politics.

One couldn't help but feel sorry for Lillian and Dorothy Gish, who were dependent on Griffith. Without Griffith, they had no career.[5] Or work.

Although unemployed, there was still a certain amount of professional socializing they were obligated to do if they wished to keep their names on the minds of fellow players and directors. Griffith, always the proper Victorian regarding his relationship with Lillian, tried to maintain an even stricter code of morality regarding her appearances in public places.

Lillian, who would prefer to make "disappearances,"[6] would, when it was absolutely necessary, attend the dance evenings at the Hollywood Hotel, a thirty-two room building on an unpaved Hollywood Boulevard between Orchid and Highland Avenue. Its architecture was a mix of Spanish and Moorish, with a roof garden.[7]

These Thursday night evenings were rather conservative, but it gave the film colony an opportunity to dress up in their finest and provide the adoring public an opportunity to see their favorite players away from the studio. Although there was a certain degree of public scrutiny, such evenings provided publicity and gossip and the opportunity for fans to "see" just "who" was having a "romance."

Lillian and her mother would make a brief appearance, not staying long enough to have dinner or a brief whirl around the dance floor with any of the popular leading men who were eligible bachelors.

A familiar face at the weekly Hollywood Hotel dances was Charlie Chaplin, the popular Sennett comedian who, until he was given a Sennett Keystone contract, had been appearing with the Fred Karno troupe as part of an English music hall revue.[8] Chaplin, who was awestruck by Lillian's beauty, introduced himself at one of these Thursday night evenings and requested the pleasure of dancing with her, only to be politely refused. Chaplin, it was rumored, was having a romance with blonde, voluptuous Peggy Pearce of the Sennett lot — and with any Sennett bathing beauty who would respond to his wit and winning smile.

Chaplin girls, as they were sometimes called, were, in the nomenclature of the day, "loose" girls who sometimes had to suddenly take a Mexican "vacation" (the polite term used for a quick weekend to Tijuana, a well known place for abortions).[9]

Charlie, warned Lillian's mother, was not the type for Lillian, even if only for a brief waltz around the ballroom in view of everyone.

Constance Talmadge, who appeared with Lillian in Griffith's *Intolerance* (1916), would laughingly compare the chaperoning attitudes of their mothers at the Hollywood Hotel dances:

> My mother was always taking me and my sisters (Natalie and Norma) to places where we could meet men.

Lillian's mother was always taking her away from men.

Mrs. Gish never tried to chaperon any of Dorothy's activities. Dorothy, from the time I first met her, was always independent. She always had boyfriends, but nothing serious.

Dorothy wouldn't have listened to anything her mother said, but Lillian always did. Lillian was slavishly devoted to her mother.[10]

While Dorothy partied and danced until the late hours of the evening at the Pier at Santa Monica, Lillian never left her mother's side. Lillian was more than an ordinary Griffith player, she would hear her mother say. Lillian was a personal investment in their family's future.

Mother Gish had warned Lillian of the consequences that could befall her if she befriended Mr. Sennett's girlfriend, actress Mabel Normand. Mabel, rumored to be addicted to drugs, was often seen at the wrong places when Mr. Sennett wasn't with her. Whether Sennett knew of Mabel's secret problems was never openly discussed. Mabel moved with a "fast" crowd, and was someone to be avoided if one wanted to maintain self-respect.[11]

What would Mrs. Gish say to her Ohio relatives if Lillian brought disgrace to her family? Despite Lillian's slowly accumulating fame, none of Mary Gish's relatives ever thought the arts, especially the "flickers," a redeeming profession. Weren't some of those actors and actresses living sinful lives? Weren't some of those movie people "drinkers" like Mary's husband and Lillian's father, James?

Lillian listened to her mother, once again.

Help, in the form of employment, came to Griffith from the least likely source. An insurance man with a love of motion pictures named Harry Aitken had purchased the former Clara Morris estate in Yonkers, New York, and had rented a second studio, a former loft, at 16th Street and Union Square West in New York.[12]

Both Harry and his brother Roy were in their early twenties. Beginning as nickelodeon owners in the early years of the twentieth century, they exercised their daring and within two years were operating film exchanges around the world, purchasing films and renting them to exhibitors.[13]

Neither Harry nor Roy knew of Griffith's penchant for extravagance and spending money beyond his means. In their young eyes, whatever Griffith spent was justified. *The Battle of Elderbridge Gulch* and *Judith of Bethulia* looked quite impressive on the screen. Unlike Griffith's previous employer, the Aitken brothers were willing to allow Griffith a free hand.[14]

A free hand! It was the moment and opportunity for which Griffith had been laboring all of his cinematic career: to be able to film his visions, to tell his stories in moving pictures without consulting an accountant to see if funds were available.

With the signing of the Aitken brothers' Reliance-Majestic studio contract, Griffith had a free hand. Of course, they told him afterwards, this would be the case only when adequate monies were available. The Aitken brothers operated on "very little money," and Griffith was almost broke.[15]

The Aitken brothers had honorable intentions, but nothing had been set aside to cover the salaries of an acting company. Indeed, the studio, at the time of the contract signing, had no acting company! They had secured the services of Mr. Griffith in writing, and only Mr. Griffith! Nobody else!

It was like starting at the very beginning. Griffith was practical enough to know that he couldn't sit at a desk and hire fresh, unknown actors or interested parties off the street the way he did at Biograph. The public was more sophisticated and would not pay higher admission prices to watch unknowns on a theatre screen. The uptown audiences wanted to know the names of the players they were paying good money to see. Even more important than names, which Griffith thought would be forgotten, were their faces. Lillian and Dorothy Gish were very recognizable. It was time to bring them back.

Donald Crisp, wizened at eighty-seven and living at the Actors' Home in Woodland Hills, California in August 1968, recalled that he

> was one of the actors who answered Griffith's call for help. Biograph had no future without him, and we had no future without him. He had molded us into a stock company capable of performing without having to explain very much. Everybody was used to each other.
>
> The only problem was money. His new studio [Reliance-Majestic] couldn't pay a cent. There were other studios like that, fly-by-night operations, but they folded almost as soon as they were up. They weren't worth the risk. D. W. Griffith was.
>
> The only question was: would we be willing to work at Griffith's new place for nothing? Even though it would be for a few days, it still was nothing. No money ... nothing.
>
> None of us had any sign of employment once Biograph was finished. So we said we would. We were both in trouble.
>
> He knew the Gish girls would do anything he wanted. Especially Lillian. Lillian was in love with him.[16]

Griffith's initial production, *The Escape*, was abruptly halted when the leading lady (Blanche Sweet) contracted scarlet fever during the early days of shooting in December 1913.[17] Knowing it would be foolish to totally abandon any project, he temporarily shelved what had been filmed and hustled the remaining cast (Donald Crisp, Owen Moore, and Robert Harron) into his second planned film, *The Battle of the Sexes*. The original title *The Single Standard*, was withdrawn for fear it might be objectionable to more prudent patrons.

To round out the cast, Griffith added Fay Tincher and Lillian Gish.[18] Lillian played the leading role in *The Battle of the Sexes*, "a daughter who suffers and brings her father to remorse." Fay Tincher played the vamp, the destroyer of the family.

In the climactic scene, Lillian, brandishing a gun aimed at the vamp, is about to shoot her when her father arrives. Shocked, he gestures at the vamp's apartment and its high-toned elegance and asks, "You, my daughter, what are you doing here?"

Enraged at such a question, Lillian answers, "You, my father, what are you doing here?"[19]

Budgeted and actually shot for the incredibly low cost of $5,000, *The Battle of the Sexes*, a five-reeler, was filmed in five non-stop days and nights.

To maintain the frantic pace, Lillian remembered that

> Mother was on the set at all times, working in wardrobe and doing a lot of the sewing, while making sure I didn't get sick or collapse with exhaustion. I was so worried for her....
>
> Mr. Griffith had already lost days because of Blanche [Sweet], and it was important that he show something to the Aitken brothers, who were the source of our future. Mr. Griffith had done so much for us, we had to show our loyalty to him, and our confidence. He knew he wasn't going to make a great film. He wanted to turn out a programmer as quickly as he could, so the Aitken brothers could show it right away. That was the only way the company was going to get on its feet.
>
> Billy Bitzer [cameraman] told Mr. Griffith he couldn't shoot too many

close-ups of me because my eyes were bloodshot from lack of sleep. Mother was afraid I would collapse, and she said this to Mr. Griffith against my wishes. I told her Mr. Griffith was working on a tight schedule. Nobody made a five-reeler in less than a week! The shooting schedule when we made our first film [*An Unseen Enemy* 1912] was a reel a week. And here he was: trying to do the impossible!

He looked closely at me, and let us go home for a few hours. I wouldn't have asked for a few hours of sleep if I were there by myself.

Mother didn't argue with Mr. Griffith. And she didn't plead. She charmed.[20]

Opening at Weber's Theatre in New York on April 12, 1914, at an admission price of twenty-five cents, and providing no billing for anyone except D. W. Griffith ("a 5-reel masterpiece staged by D. W. Griffith"), the film was shown four times a day (with an added performance on Saturdays and Sunday).[21]

On the second day of its seven day engagement, Mr. Griffith's name was removed from the advertisement. Only a boxed title remained.

The film critic for *The New York Dramatic Mirror* praised "the lavish sets" that were "true to the highest social sphere," but of Lillian's performance, nothing was written. She and the entire cast were summarily lumped together as "an eventful piece of artistic work."[22]

Everyone was happy. *The Battle of the Sexes* played to receptive audiences, and that was all that mattered. Employment would continue.

In the wake of freezing weather and a very cold winter, Griffith deemed it foolhardy for his company to remain in New York and chance pneumonia or the flu, either of which would cripple the future of Reliance-Majestic.

To acquire quick funds to offset any

unforeseeable problems, he pawned *The Great Leap*, a feature directed by Christy Cabanne, one of his assistants, to cover the players' train fare from New York to Los Angeles.

Though successful, *The Battle of the Sexes* "quickie" didn't gross what the Aitken brothers had anticipated.

Still, they were satisfied. Griffith had, under extreme pressure, turned out a more than passable five-reel feature that could be exhibited without apology.[23] The film had proven that the risk Roy and Harry Aitken had taken was a good one. Everyone believed in the Aitkens' and Griffith's future. Ironically, Griffith's five day and night effort had a longer running time than the much heralded *Judith of Bethulia*.[24]

Traveling cross-country with the three Gishes was nineteen-year-old Robert Harron. Bobby, a former Griffith prop, began working at Biograph in 1907 when he was twelve years old, and his school day was completed. By simply standing and watching the players listening to Griffith's directions during the shooting, the shy youngster, who, at times, was the sole support of his twelve member Irish family, began to master the fundamentals of screen acting. From bit parts he had progressed to playing opposite both Dorothy and Lillian.[25]

To Dorothy, who had never had a boyfriend, Bobby was everything. Lillian had thought Bobby "sensitive and poetic looking," and had given no disapproval at the sight of Dorothy and Bobby holding hands everywhere they were seen together.[26] They were "two young kids, and nothing more." Mrs. Gish, for whom no man was of any value, remained silent, but the moment to voice her disapproval was not far away.[27]

The company was temporarily housed in rooms at the Hotel Alexandria, while preparations for filming were begun at the new studio on Sunset and Gower. The new place of operations was little more than "a few bungalows amid a tract of fig trees" with a large barn serving as an indoor stage and dressing rooms. Outside, a raised platform would satisfy all of the requirements for the outdoor shots.

The move to California was a mixed blessing. What extra hours they had gained because of the availability of the sun would be lost when the film would have to be sent back to New York for processing. The high alkali content in the water, they had immediately discovered, would not provide the clearest prints.[28]

For Griffith, who was very conscious of the time factor, he was grateful for the longer shooting days and the possible extra footage. The product was of prime importance. Since the Aitkens respected his achievements, no longer would he call his products "sausages."[29]

Home Sweet Home was the film biography of lyricist John Howard Payne, best remembered for the time-honored popular song which begins," 'Mid pleasures and palaces, though we may roam, Be it ever so humble, There's no place like home."

The large cast included Lillian and Dorothy, Robert Harron, Blanche Sweet, and Donald Crisp.

Originally opening in Los Angeles at Clune's Auditorium on May 4, 1914,[30] *Home Sweet Home* had its New York premiere at the recently completed 3,500 seat Strand Theatre on May 17. The Strand was the largest picture-house in the city, charging three different prices (ten, fifteen, and twenty-five cents) in the manner of theatres presenting legitimate plays. Not only was seeing Griffith's latest motion picture important, it was important to see it from a good seat![31]

Home Sweet Home was actually three separate stories, a precursor of the narrative technique Griffith would successfully utilize two years later in *Intolerance.*[32]

Blanche Sweet, who appeared as "the

wife" in the third story, told a small group of people at the Museum of Modern Art that

> each section of *Home Sweet Home* could exist on its own. Griffith filmed it that way in case the total product wasn't satisfactory. He would still be able to salvage something and possibly use it as a one-reeler.[33]

Lillian's response to questions about *Home Sweet Home* was less than enthusiastic: "I don't really remember much about it."

It was a sentence she would often say when she did not wish to recall a film that brought back painful memories, either of filming or of a performance she believed was less than satisfactory.

Maybe she was remembering the Epilogue in which she, as Payne's childhood sweetheart, had to descend to Hell (on wires) to usher her first love into heaven. Did the use of wires recall her angel role in Belasco's 1913 stage play *The Good Little Devil* when she was humiliated in front of an audience? Was this embarrassment still painful fifty years later?

Or was she remembering back fifty years to Dorothy's adolescent crush on young Robert Harron, an innocent friendship which had incurred the wrath of their mother?

Neither Mrs. Gish nor Lillian anticipated that Bobby's friendship with Dorothy, which had begun on the set during the final days of *Judith of Bethulia,* would take its natural course from sly stares and blushes (remember this is 1914) to handholding every place they were seen together.[34]

To her mother's stinging rebukes that Dorothy had "no common sense," a usually docile Lillian became surprisingly defensive about Dorothy's "budding independence."[35] Younger Dorothy not only could field wisecracks from the crew and her fellow actors about her friendship with Bobby, she could respond with retorts just as quickly and sometimes just as scathingly. She was a thorough professional, and everyone's delight. Except her mother's...[36]

Lillian, to placate her mother, tried to stop the off-the-set bickering. As the older sister, she was told to counsel the younger and teach her the way to behave like a lady. Dorothy was a teenaged rebel, maturing more quickly than her mother wished to acknowledge. The Gish sisters were a study in contrasts. Dorothy was the hoyden; Lillian, the angel.

Lillian would always lunch with her mother away from everyone. Dorothy and Bobby would eat with the men on the crew. Dorothy preferred their raucous stories to mother's sermons regarding behavior and morality.

Still, Lillian would try to reason with Dorothy, only to hear the same answer. "You're just like she is! There's no difference!"[37]

Angered by the negative comparison, Lillian would remain silent.

Mother Gish was given the ideal opportunity for the final word. Not for Dorothy, but for Lillian. Dorothy's behavior was like her father's.[38]

Mr. Griffith had no time for family squabbles. He had more important things on his mind. He had optioned Thomas Dixon's *The Clansman*, a novel of the Reconstruction following The War Between the States, for ten thousand dollars. Only two-thousand five hundred dollars had been paid. Money was owed—money Mr. Griffith did not have.

Blanche Sweet had been promised one of the leading roles that Lillian coveted. Because Blanche was her close friend (and, as the child of an alcoholic father, subject to the same insecurities as Lillian), she knew better than to openly pressure Mr. Griffith. He had given good roles to both women.[39]

Still, nothing was final until the day of the first shooting, and, even then, unpredictable things could happen. Hadn't Blanche contracted scarlet fever during the early days of *The Escape*?

Lillian knew better than to stand and wait. That kind of behavior was for the newcomers, the "extras" who were strictly background. Biograph player Mae Marsh would jokingly refer to Griffith (when he wasn't around) as "Mr. Heinz," because he liked "fifty-seven varieties of available girls."[40]

To land the role of Elsie Stoneman, the daughter of the Leader of the House, Lillian knew she would have to rely on charm—even more charm than she had seen her mother use.

By mutual consent, Griffith had finally separated from his wife, actress Linda Arvidson, whom he had married in 1906 when he was a touring actor with hopes of becoming a writer like Charles Dickens.[41] The marriage had been a well-kept secret, allowing Griffith mobility amongst his eager young female players when he joined Biograph that same year.

It wasn't until the advent of Lillian Gish that Linda Arvidson Griffith became more than concerned. Lillian Gish, of all the Griffith female players, was never liked by Linda Arvidson Griffith. With her heightened career drive, Lillian Gish was giving Griffith's wife some "anxious moments."[42]

CHAPTER 5

The Birth of a Nation

The only thing I remember about filming *The Birth of a Nation* was that I didn't have enough money to rent a horse.

— Lillian Gish
Conversation with author (1960)

D. W. Griffith's masterpiece, *The Birth of a Nation*, was not a spur-of-the moment idea. Lillian recalled seeing "assorted pieces of paper of all shapes and sizes, with quickly scrawled notes and phrases, descriptions of characters, and suggestions for music," dangling outside Griffith's pants and jacket pockets while she was filming *The Battle of Elderbridge Gulch*.[1] Dorothy, too, had noticed Griffith "catching up on his schoolwork" during the breaks between crowd scenes during the filming of *Judith of Bethulia*.[2] Occasionally, Griffith, at the completion of a day's shooting, would confide to Lillian that he needed to make "a big picture, an epic"[3] on the order of the European spectaculars that were proving so popular with American audiences. Given the opportunity to make a picture with a big theme, American Cinema — specifically the cinema of D. W. Griffith — would be as respected as the European efforts. American motion pictures would no longer languish in the vulgar pie-in-the-face Mack Sennett comedy or Pearl White's last-minute rescues. The time had come to remove the "flickers" image lingering from the 14th Street nickelodeon

parlors. Films warranted exhibitions in legitimate theatres like serious drama. No longer would Griffith be content to "grind out sausages."[4] With the nations in Europe readying for war following the assassination of the Archduke at Sarajevo, Griffith knew that this and all future wars would be remembered not only in print and newspaper photographs but on film.

The Civil War in America had been over for fifty years. Feelings of bitterness, of the loss of personal dignity, self-esteem, and family fortunes, still existed. As a young boy, Griffith constantly heard firsthand accounts of Southern gallantry and courage amidst a field of destruction. The War Between the States, and its aftermath of Union pillaging and Reconstruction, had never been filmed in its fullest intensity. Here was a golden opportunity for the Southern viewpoint to be immortalized on film with a large cast and spectacular effects.

Thomas Dixon's novel, *The Clansman* (also a play in which Griffith had toured as an actor in 1907),[5] was the perfect vehicle to show how the South had risen from the smoldering ashes of defeat. With the addition of Griffith's personal beliefs, and supplementary material from Dixon's 1902 novel, *The Leopard's Spots (A Romance of the White Man's Burden 1868–1900)*, it was only a matter of time and financial backing before filming would begin.

That the material glorified racism and the Ku Klux Klan was unimportant. Nobody had ever considered the Civil War from the viewpoint of the vanquished. While Griffith clearly understood that this would not win the war, in his version attention would be paid to those who had sacrificed their lives and honor on the bloodstained battlefields of Dixie.

The titles he would supply would be history lessons,[6] and also serve as an opportunity to reshape American thinking via the use of the motion picture as a tool for propaganda. *The Birth of a Nation* was Griffith's Civil War revisited in terms of classic storytelling: divided households, deprivation, and destruction.[7]

The Birth of a Nation set new precedents for filmmaking: six weeks of rehearsal, nine weeks to film, and three months to edit. Originally budgeted at an unheard of forty thousand dollars, the costs would spiral to one hundred thousand dollars and a twelve-reel product![8]

Robert Edgar Long, an early Griffith biographer, noted some of the spectacular effects that blazed across the screen at the film's initial viewing on January 1, 1915 at the Loring Opera House in Riverside, California:[9]

> the battle of Petersburg, fought by eighteen thousand men on a field five miles across; the march of Sherman to the sea, culminating in the burning of Atlanta; the assassination of President Lincoln in the crowded Ford's Theatre in Washington; the wild rides of the Ku Klux Klan, and the session of the South Carolina Legislature under the Negro carpetbagger regime.[10]

In the role of one of the "Southern flowers" was Lillian Gish, playing Elsie Stoneman, the daughter of a Southern congressman.

Years later, viewing an original still she inscribed to this biographer ("To dear Stuart Oderman: Be careful of what you wish for, you're apt to get it"), Lillian held up the photograph and laughed:

> Stuart, that's what Mr. Griffith wrote to me on a photograph he had given to me after I had started to work for him [1912].
>
> I wanted the Elsie Stoneman role in *The Birth of a Nation* very much, and I knew I wasn't Mr. Griffith's first choice. He had always given roles to the people who were with him the longest. Dorothy and I were the last to join his Biograph unit.
>
> I don't know how I really wound up with the role. What you forget, history remembers, and I've been told all sorts of things over the years by people who were too young to have been there.
>
> I know that Blanche Sweet was Mr. Griffith's original choice, and she was a good choice, too. I was told she lost the role because she was sick, because she didn't photograph well, and because she was taller than Henry B. Walthall. I never thought about it at the time. I just wanted to work, and I wanted that role.
>
> One day when we were rehearsing the scene when the black man lifts up the girl from the North, Mr. Griffith said I could have the part. I had very blonde hair and it fell to my waist when the actor playing the mulatto [George Siegmann] suddenly grabbed me and says he wants to marry me. The camera picked up on the color contrast.
>
> For those days, and maybe even today, it was a very brutal scene. Probably more so at that time [1915] because you had never depicted that sort of behavior on the screen in any film. In polite company, you never

discussed things like that. And here was Mr. Griffith courageously daring to film it!

Billy Bitzer whispered that even with all of the effects Mr. Griffith was planning to use, *The Birth of a Nation* was another sausage. He saw the basic story as nothing more than a black man chasing after a white woman. Fifty years after the Civil War, lynchings were still a common occurrence, and Bitzer said the picture would incite riots. Of course, Billy knew not to say any of this to Mr. Griffith.

Billy saw this film as a variation on the American western. You were keeping the cowboys, and just changing the Indians....

After I got the part, I didn't like it. It wasn't what I thought it was. The rehearsals were too long, and I didn't have the money to rent a horse, to be able to watch the battle scenes."[11]

As a novel, Thomas Dixon's *The Clansman* was little more than bigotry cloaked in the protective blanket of fiction. Griffith's incendiary film version, retitled *The Birth of a Nation* to give it wider appeal, contained all of the "clichés of the genre: divided friends and families, a mulatto governor trying to rape Lillian Gish, and a grand rescue by the Ku Klux Klan."[12] After viewing the film at a private showing in the East Room of the White House, President Woodrow Wilson (a former history professor at Princeton University and college chum of Dixon) made the often quoted remark that, "It was like writing history with lightning, and it is all so terribly true."[13]

The Birth of a Nation gave Lillian another opportunity to play a frail heroine in a classic battle of good versus evil: her blonde purity combating the lustful intentions of the black man, Silas Lynch.[14] Although Lynch's ambitious character was conscienceless and without fidelity to anybody in his drive for advancement in the

Reconstruction era, his portrayal of the "uppity black" was considered offensive,[15] invoking riots and controversy at the time of the film's release. Griffith had classified blacks in two categories: Uncle Toms or menaces. Clearly, Silas Lynch was a menace.

The origin of the Ku Klux Klan, as depicted in the film, was not the result of clandestine meetings or streetcorner soliciting, but the fears of young black children thinking a bedsheet was a ghost! It was an incident very human and understandable, and it had unknowingly created a stereotype. Why not utilize this fear by combining Rip Van Winkle's Headless Horseman with ghost riders?[16]

While Griffith would remember his mother sitting up nights to sew costumes for the Ku Klux Klan, an organization he felt was necessary "in those days," he was genuinely astonished at the newspaper attacks from the Northern press accusing him of racism.[17] Responding, he would invite his detractors to consult his historical sources: the writings of Woodrow Wilson, John Ford Rhodes, and William Dunning.[18] It was Thomas Dixon who was the racist, claimed Griffith, adding in his own defense that black people, more than any other race, had made the most progress in history. Still, because they were never conditioned to being free, they would have to be "shown their place."[19]

A stunned Griffith would remark to Lillian Gish, "To say I am against blacks is like saying I am against children, as they [the blacks] were our children whom we loved and cared for all our lives."[20]

In a letter to this biographer, after a performance of *The Birth of a Nation* at Kean College in Union, New Jersey on November 14, 1960 (at which he played the original score heard at the March 3, 1915 premiere at the Liberty Theatre in New York), Miss Gish wrote:

I do not understand the objection to the film. Griffith was shocked when told it was anti–Negro, as he had been raised by them, claimed he loved and understood them better than anyone else, and certainly they loved and adored him. He said, "Can't they see in my picture that when the colored people are bad, they are made so by the whites?" And if you study it, you will find this to be true. The white man is the villain, and the colored man his victim.[21]

Griffith filmed *The Birth of a Nation* without a "clearly formulated script," preferring to carry the story ideas around in his head. While this might have been viewed as a costly and wasteful method of working, it was not without precedent. So long as one didn't waste film stock, it was permissible, even advisable, to "rehearse the blocking of the actors"[22] until the moment it was advantageous to begin the shooting.

In the course of filming, Griffith reduced the names of his players to initials and scene numbers in columns reading from left to right. Also included were a brief hint of the action, the number of feet shot, the exit direction and the aperture of the lens. A scene shot six times would carry six different numbers.

A typical Griffith entry for a scene with Lillian and Robert Harron made during *The Birth of a Nation* might read: LG ER MRH PS LG XL 35 4.5.

Cameraman Karl Brown would know how to interpret this. Lillian Gish (LG) enters right (ER), meets Robert Harron (MRH), plays scene (PS) and exits left (XL). The scene would run thirty-five feet (35) and would be shot with a lens aperture of 4.5.[23] Griffith's method of staging a scene was very similar to a composer writing a theme with variations. The variations were as many as Griffith could create.[24]

With constant repetition, the players,

hearing Griffith count as the action progressed, learned "Griffith acting." It was simply performing by the numbers, much as people do on those "connect the dots" puzzles so popular in newspapers and magazines with children. When the call for Action! came, Lillian performed by rote.[25]

The unending grind of learning something over and over again had begun to take a toll on some of the Griffith veterans during the shooting of *The Birth of a Nation*— more so than on any other production. Never a careless worker, Griffith knew he had more at stake. Mae Marsh, who played the ill-fated little sister of Henry B. Walthall, would threaten to resign,[26] but Lillian, who later would remark that the filming and rehearsing were "strenuous," would persevere.

Mae, whose career soared as a barely-clad cavewoman in Griffith's *Man's Genesis* (1912), a role that Mary Pickford refused to do, often said Griffith told her she was a more "intuitive" actress than her co-worker, Lillian, and that Lillian couldn't act at all. Every movement Lillian made was done after much study and practice away from the set. Lillian did achieve perfection, but it was done at the cost of personal fun. Lillian always worked too hard, and she missed out on a lot of good times.

In answer to Mae's stinging criticism, Lillian and Dorothy would tell her that her windswept hair looked at though it were put up with a bellows.[27]

Donald Crisp, playing General U.S. Grant, dismissed any negative remarks about Lillian, calling her "the girl you wanted to protect":

> And Griffith, when he cast her [Lillian] in *The Birth of a Nation* was aware of this. He knew audiences, both men and women, would feel the same way. Lillian was always projecting an air of fragility. Which, of course, she wasn't. But from the moment she came on the set, until she

and her mother left, you wanted to shield her from some of the language the crew and some of us would occasionally use.

When that emancipated slave is going to rape her, audiences shrieked with horror. At every performance! To rape any woman is unthinkable, but to rape Lillian... No! And Griffith knew this.[28]

The shooting schedule for *The Birth of a Nation* was always subject to the whims of the rising sun. Work preparations would start at five in the morning, the hour the players rose to be ready at seven. Close-ups were taken later in the morning (before it was too hot) or just before the sun went down. Many times, the players worked through their lunch hour, eating when it was convenient. Rarely would Lillian have a complete meal without some interruption. Often the battle scenes were played at noontime, when the sun was at its peak.[29]

Lillian's mother's sewing skills were in constant demand, particularly before the shooting of the battle scenes.

Mother and I would look through copies of *Godey's Ladies Book* for costume ideas. Mr. Griffith wanted *The Birth of a Nation* to be virtually a photographic reproduction of the Civil War, almost like a Matthew Brady photograph in motion.

I think he was using *The Birth of a Nation* to pay tribute to his father, who fought on the Confederate side and was wounded.

Throughout the shooting, Mr. Griffith worked like a man possessed. Everything had to be perfect, more perfect than anything he had ever undertaken.

Even though mother and I didn't think a missing button on a uniform would be noticed in a long shot, mother and her assistants checked the uniforms. When you see hundreds of men battling in uniform on a large

battlefield, you don't think of any missing buttons on a uniform. Clothing is torn, and, of course, you would have buttons hanging or missing.

Mr. Griffith was a perfectionist. In the South, where he grew up, the son of a Confederate officer, manners were everything. Good manners meant good breeding. "Even though we lost the Civil War," Mr. Griffith would joke, "in my film we are going to look good doing it!"...

The best part of the picture were the horses. I tried to ride one whenever I could, if they would let me. Most of the time, they were being used in the battle scenes, the time I wanted to have one.

Mr. Griffith had a horse, but he was always with that same horse, watching the filming from high up on a hill. He told me to rent a horse. All of his were taken!

I had no intention of renting a horse, and I wasn't going to climb up a hill for a few minutes of filming and then somehow get down and face a camera. Not in that heat!

I knew better than to ask for insurance. I suppose we had some kind of protection. I saw medical personnel on the set. If I fell, who would replace me? Who *could*?[30]

With the success of the White House showing for President Wilson, and the preview at the Loring Opera House in Riverside, California on January 1, 1915, followed by the February 8 premiere at Los Angeles's Clune's auditorium, it remained for the New York premiere at the Liberty Theatre on March 3 to assure its place in cinema history.[31]

The ticket price was an unprecedented two dollars. Seats were reserved. *The Birth of a Nation* was making a bid for the same kind of deference one would bestow on a long-established classic work of music or literature. While Cyril Chesterton and John Cowper Powys were debating Nietzsche at the Hudson Theatre, and reformer Jane Addams was speaking for "Woman's Obligations for World Peace" at the Cort theatre, patrons who preferred lighter fare could attend a performance of Marie Dressler in *A Mix-Up* at the 39th Street theatre or try to get tickets for *Watch Your Step* (featuring the dancing team of Vernon and Irene Castle) at the New Amsterdam. Upstairs, on the New Amsterdam Roof, Ziegfeld's *Midnight Frolic* ("Tango in the Air") was the perfect way to close the evening.[32]

The advertisement in *The New York Times* wasted no space, nor was it the full-page hoopla later generations would come to expect whenever a new attraction, theatre or film, was coming to town.

Readers of the day learned about

> the dawn of a new art which marks an epoch in the theatres of the world: 18,000 people in the mightiest Spectacle ever produced. Symphony orchestra of 40.[33]

The first part of *The Birth of a Nation*, concluding with the assassination of President Lincoln, was never the source of the problem, for both Thomas Dixon and D. W. Griffith had great respect and admiration for the man who did his best to keep the United States from becoming a house divided.[34]

During the intermission, Thomas Dixon addressed the New York audience, telling them he would allow only the son of a Confederate soldier to direct the film. The New York audience accepted Dixon's remarks in good faith. Then they settled back in their seats to watch part two, which was more Thomas Dixon than D. W. Griffith.

The Birth of a Nation, part two, was "an impressive new illustration of the scope of the motion picture camera." Its Southern, Dixon-dominated treatment of Reconstruction caused some New Yorkers to "carp at old wounds." The Ku Klux Klan resembled a "company of avenging spectral

crusaders sweeping along the moonlit roads."[35]

In the last ten minutes of the film, as the Ku Klux Klan rushed to rescue Dr. Cameron (a white Southerner), director D. W. Griffith skillfully "cut between six simultaneous situations," creating a pitch of tension that left the audience gasping for its breath.

While no single player, not even Lillian Gish, was singled out for an outstanding performance, Griffith and his company must have been ecstatic when they read that *The Birth of a Nation* made *Cabiria* (The Italian import which caused Griffith a lot of worry) seem "insignificant by comparison."[36]

The twelve reels of *The Birth of a Nation*, directed by D. W. Griffith and starring Lillian Gish, had thrust the American motion picture solidly in the center of the world cinema arena.

Still, the controversy continues regarding Griffith's alleged racism. At the Kean College showing in Union, New Jersey, for which this biographer played the original score on November 14, 1960, the entrance of the Klan brought whistles, cheers, and stomps from the same audience who had winced silently earlier in the presentation when the first scene of the slaves on the plantation was scored to "Turkey in the Straw." The film's love theme, meaningless in 1915 when first heard, now drew suppressed laughter when recognized as the radio (and later television) theme for *The Amos n' Andy Show*.

Critic-writer Anthony Slide states that Griffith, at the very outset of the filming of *The Birth of a Nation*, knew that Reconstruction was a topic "too hot to handle." If he wished to tell the truth as he saw it,[37] it would naturally be from a Southern point of view. There could be no other way, stated novelist James Agee (*A Death in the Family*). D. W. Griffith approached the Southern aftermath of the

Civil War with "absolute passion, pity, and honesty."

The Birth of a Nation was a "perfect realization of a collective dream of what the Civil War was like, as veterans might remember it fifty years later, or as children, fifty years later, might imagine it."[38]

Backstage in June 1961 at New York's Belasco Theatre, where Lillian was appearing in Tad Mosel's Pulitzer Prize-winning play, *All the Way Home* (a dramatization of James Agee's *A Death in the Family*), Lillian provided the last words on D. W. Griffith's still-controversial film.

> I don't think you could possibly realize, Stuart, the emotional toll the Civil War took on those whose families participated in it.... The Civil War, not any other war, was fought on American soil between Americans! The Civil War wasn't a war fought in a foreign country because someone was assassinated in the Balkans, or because a bomb was dropped on some unsuspecting ships. The Civil War was an all–American war.
>
> One section of the country disagreed with the policies of another section of the country. It was the North versus the South: machines and technology versus rural agrarianism. The South never had a chance. And I think Mr. Griffith knew this.
>
> I like to think he believed that slavery, from its very outset, was a doomed institution. And the people whose families were slaveowners must have realized that you can't hold a race of people in bondage and servitude forever.
>
> Mr. Griffith said that Negroes, of all the races, made the most progress of anyone after they were freed. He also believed that the South had suffered two defeats: one on the battlefield, and one at home. A freed slave, said Mr. Griffith, was an "economic threat to the social fabric that had shackled him."
>
> Now there was a bigger problem: what do you do to educate these people? Without education and a family structure, how could anyone be equal? How can you suddenly assume a position of responsibility, without learning how to care for yourself and provide for your family?
>
> Mr. Griffith used to tell us, while we were filming *The Birth of a Nation*, that his father used to see freed colored people walking on the roads everywhere. Aimlessly, and without purpose. Without a place to sleep or eat. These people, grownups and children, couldn't read or write.
>
> Mr. Griffith's father, who was wounded as a soldier fighting for the Confederacy, used to ask him, "What favor did Lincoln do for them?" and, "How dare the North tell the South what to do?"
>
> Segregation still exists. All things are not equal for everyone, including women.
>
> *The Birth of a Nation* established box-office records, and at the same time raised a lot of still unanswered questions. Mr. Griffith knew he would have to make another film, if only to answer the critics who called him a racist and a bigot. Mr. Griffith knew film would be used as propaganda, and propaganda could sway an audience in any direction.
>
> The time was ripe for a film about man's intolerance.[39]

CHAPTER 6

Triangle Time

Fortunately for Lillian, the personal attacks on Mr. Griffith's *The Birth of a Nation* were never extended to her. Although she would live to be the film's surviving player and spokesperson, her role in the controversial interpretation of life and labor in the post–Civil War South was never a topic for debate.

Griffith screenwriter Anita Loos recalled

> that the original newspaper advertisements never mentioned any of the actors' names. *The Birth of a Nation* was a Griffith picture. Nobody had billing, which, in this case, was a good thing.
>
> I don't think the public would have held any actor responsible. The public was sophisticated enough to know that the actors were acting and doing what Griffith directed them to do.
>
> Lillian's roles were always sympathetic. She wasn't a Theda Bara homewrecking vamp. The public always liked Lillian.
>
> With Theda, it was fascination. With Lillian, it was adoration. You wanted to shelter her from the moment she made her first entrance.
>
> Still, Mr. Griffith wasn't going to take any chances, which would jeopardize — and maybe end — her career. Lillian was Mr. Griffith's future.
>
> And they both knew it.[1]

The uniting of the three most successful creative minds in the motion picture industry, D. W. Griffith (epics), Thomas Ince (Westerns), and Mack Sennett (slapstick two-reelers) into one company turning out a product under one banner, Triangle, was the brainchild of Harry Aitken. Aitken, with his brother Roy, had gone from the nickelodeon business to founding a film exchange which distributed motion pictures across the country.[2]

The Triangle Film Corporation was an uneasy alliance of egos which fortunately did not invade or challenge the participants' field of expertise. Mr. Griffith, Lillian would tell players on the Ince lot, could film anything, but did not wish to be geographically restricted.[3] Mack Sennett, who was ignored by a "high-toned" Lillian during the days when he and Griffith worked at Biograph, must have been delighted upon learning that his "vulgar, slapstick two-reelers would be on the same bill as the efforts of his "high-toned" coworker![4]

Anybody walking past New York's Knickerbocker Theatre at Broadway and 38th Street during July 1915 would have seen and heard workmen converting the former stage house into a showcase for Harry Aitken's newly formed company. All of the Triangle films would have their first showing at the Knickerbocker and then play at neighborhood movie houses. Should the neighborhood house, which could be uptown on 81st Street, wish to change the program twice a week to meet the demands of the customers, it was possible to provide a wide array of offerings. No longer would they have to wait a week. Programmers (quickly and inexpensively produced films) were always available.

In addition to Lillian and Dorothy Gish, and Norma and Constance Talmadge, the close proximity of the legitimate theatres and vaudeville houses always provided a steady flow of actors who were willing to try their chances in another medium. Occasionally, a stage performer would view possible employment at Triangle with condescension.

Lillian remembered how the Aitkens treated this attitude.

> Either Roy or Harry [Aitken] would tell these people they were a risk, no matter how successful their act was on the stage.
> "Why should we hire you? You don't have any camera experience?"
> If these people were willing to work for less money — and remember, some of the greatest people in the theatre, then and now, sometimes do not register on film — they were hired on a film-to-film basis, depending on the audience's response.
> Film has always been an intangible mystery. The camera likes you, or doesn't like you. If you don't register on film, it doesn't mean you are a bad actor.
> In silent films, you had to use your body to convey emotion. It was impossible to use your voice.
> Metropolitan Opera star Geraldine Farrar had a nice career in films [fourteen films made between 1915 and 1921]. Enrico Caruso didn't: one film — and it wasn't a success.[5]

Wisely, Griffith, involved with his most ambitious project — the filming of the four-story epic *Intolerance*, distanced himself from the directorial reins during Lillian's time at Triangle. His trusted assistants, Christy Cabanne and Allan Dwan, were given that responsibility.

Sister Dorothy enjoyed success playing opposite Wallace Reid in *Old Heidelberg*, the original source of Sigmund Romberg's musical, *The Student Prince*.

Old Heidelberg, directed by John Emerson, the husband of Anita Loos, was not totally devoid of problems.

Dorothy refused to kiss her leading man, Wallace Reid, claiming that Mr. Griffith once instructed her that kissing actors wasn't healthy, and that Wally, who was married and much older, could possibly give her a disease she called the "Chinese gongo."[6]

A quick telephone call to Mrs. Wallace Reid (actress Dorothy Davenport) solved the problem, and Dorothy Gish kissed her leading man.

Sixty years later, in 1975, Dorothy Davenport Reid laughingly recalled the incident to this biographer at a film convention, at which their son, Wallace Reid, Jr., was present.

> I don't know if this was a publicity stunt. I know it meant thinking back a lot of years, and also looking at Lillian's coffee table photo album [*Dorothy and Lillian Gish*, published by Charles Scribner's Sons, New York, 1973].
> Wally, at the time he made *Old Heidelberg*, was 22 or 23 but to any teen-age girl, he must have been *older*— certainly a lot of ladies did want to kiss Wally, and I'm sure plenty did. So the Dorothy Gish incident certainly would be the opposite attitude, which would have made a good story.
> Wally worked with both of the Gish girls. He worked with Lillian in *The Birth of a Nation* and *Enoch Arden*, and they didn't have any problems.

Lillian was always chaperoned by her mother. Dorothy, who was younger, was the more outgoing and friendlier. Had Dorothy been Lillian's age, she most definitely would have kissed him. He most definitely would have kissed her!

If Lillian would have kissed Wally on *The Birth of a Nation* set, that would have been a problem. They had no scenes together.

If Lillian would have kissed anyone on the set, it would have been Mr. Griffith! If she could get away from her mother. And Mr. Griffith could get away from his wife![7]

With Lillian's career maintaining its definite ascent since she and Dorothy had begun as five-dollar-a-day players at Biograph in 1912, mother and Dorothy thought it was advisable in the fall of 1915 to stop riding the streetcar everyday from their modest five room apartment on Hope Street in downtown Los Angeles[8] to Griffith's studio on 4500 Sunset Boulevard on the outskirts of Hollywood. It was time to live respectably in a home.

When dancer Ruth St. Denis, with whom Lillian had been taking classes, said she was going on tour, the opportunity to move came at the perfect moment. For the duration of the tour, Lillian, her mother, and her sister, would lease Denishawn, which was also the site of Ruth's husband Ted Shawn's dancing school.

In addition to residing there, Lillian would have round-the-clock access to the horizontal ballet bar.

What Miss St. Denis neglected to tell Lillian was that a small collection of birds also resided on the premises! By December, the menagerie, thanks to gifts from Lillian's friends, had noticeably increased. Very visible were a "one-eyed gray owl, eight Japanese finches, two parakeets, two or three canaries, one little poll-parrot, squirrels, a pair of golden pheasants, and a pair of peacocks![9]

Lillian Gish remembered:

> We were never at a loss for greeters whenever any of us came home from the studio. A secretary once told me she heard somebody practicing operatic scales over and over again in a strange voice... I opened one of the closed doors and introduced her to my parrot, John.[10]

Still wishing to maintain a professional relationship with Lillian and maintain the personal ties away from the studio, Griffith, at the suggestion of Harry Aitken, used the pseudonym Granville Warwick when he wrote the script for Lillian's first Triangle-Fine Arts film, *The Lily and the Rose*. The film was directed by Paul Powell, whose body of work consists of one film.

In this "Warwick-Powell" collaboration, Lillian once again played a sympathetic role which would endear her to audiences: an abandoned mother, whose husband has succumbed to the wiles of an exotic dancer. When the dancer's flirtations are too much to bear, the errant husband commits suicide, thus paving the way for Lillian, after forgiving him at his coffin, to marry the man she should have married — a rejected bookwormish neighbor who has since written a successful book and dedicated it to her.[11]

One cannot help but wonder if the "successful author" is not the frustrated playwright Griffith, who, unable to obtain a divorce from his wife, would have married Lillian had he been given the opportunity.

The Lily and the Rose, which opened at the Knickerbocker Theatre on November 8, 1915, at ticket prices ranging from twenty-five cents for hard balcony seats to two dollars for plush orchestra seats, was the first of the Triangle Fine Arts films exhibited in the New York metropolitan area with a planned marketing strategy designed to attract the widest possible audiences who wished to see the latest features at popular prices.[12]

Unlike *The Birth of a Nation*, still playing as a solo offering and long enough to be seen by itself, Triangle films were to be shown as part of a program of features and short subjects in neighborhoods where family trips to the local moviehouse were a weekly ritual.

The Knickerbocker Theatre premiere, in addition to *The Lily and the Rose*, also included *Aloha Oe!* with Enid Markey and Willard Mack, and two Mack Sennett comedies featuring one of the Keystone Kops playing a leading role.

The policy of the Triangle booking schedule varied from neighborhood theatre to neighborhood. Film programs were changed once or twice a week. The Spooner Theatre in the Bronx ran the latest Triangle offering with three other features (15 reels) in a three hour program designed to attract less affluent patrons who were willing to pay ten to twenty-five cents. The same program would return to New York City and play the 81st Street Theatre on a ten to fifty cent price schedule.[13]

Where the programs would differ was in the musical accompaniment. Instead of the symphony orchestra which had been synonymous with the two dollar ticket price at the Knickerbocker, patrons in the Bronx and Brooklyn had to be satisfied with a local pianist or organist, who *may* have had the chance to practice the musical score — if the studio remembered to supply one.

Very few patrons bothered to inquire about the musical accompaniment. As long as there was "something" to accompany the screen action, everybody was happy (including the manager, the ticket collectors, the ushers, the candy sellers, and the luckily employed musician).

The Gishes left the Dennishawn residence before their lease expired. Why they moved back to the security of an apartment was explained to Lillian's friend, Nell Dorr, in a letter:

> We have moved from that huge house I told you about. We were there eight months, and during the last four, we had four burglars. One was so bold as to come through the dining room window, all the way upstairs into Mother's room, at the improper hour of 2:30 in the morning.
>
> Being an old house with many squeaks, Mother knew all about him before he made his appearance, and greeted him with two bullets, the first of which hit the ceiling (she would have been terrified if she hit him), and the second went through the railing in the hall. However, the man ran away, and the police never did catch him. All this time I was out on the sleeping porch, petrified — could not utter a sound or move an inch. On, I am very brave. Imagine, Nell, being awakened from a sound sleep by your Mother tearing through the house, shooting a gun.[14]

Film scholars have always believed that Lillian and Dorothy were "wasted" at Triangle.[15] Lillian's professional relationship with Griffith-appointed director Christy Cabanne was satisfying. Cabanne, who was told by Griffith to "leave her [Lillian] alone because she'll do it her own way anyway,"[16] did as he was told. He gave Lillian carte blanche and allowed her the opportunity to offer any suggestions and ideas without any fear of rejection. Lillian was also allowed to view the results before the film was edited.[17]

Wisely, Griffith authorized the inclusion of Lillian's name above the title in the newspaper advertisements for her third Triangle release, *Sold for Marriage*.[18] Lillian's prior films had always been publicized with only Griffith's name, as they were Griffith productions rather than star

Did You Select Your Husband—

Or did some one else do it for you?

Suppose ,you had picked out the man you wanted to marry, and then your relatives cold-bloodedly *sold* you to another man. Impossible, you may say! In the newest TRIANGLE PLAY,

"Sold For Marriage"

which we are showing you for the first time this week this very condition is pictured for you vividly, delineated clearly, so that you are *compelled* to recognize the importance of it. And the condition *does* exist, right here in America. In this play

Lillian Gish

in the star role rises to dramatic heights that will make you remember her work as you recall great performances of other players.

If you have ever seen TRIANGLE PLAYS you know they represent the highest motion picture excellence. If you have not, there is no time like the present. "Sold For Marriage" is at the

KNICKERBOCKER THEATRE
Broadway and 38th Street.
"And There's a Triangle Theatre Near You"

1916 advertisement for *Sold for Marriage.*

vehicles for any of his players (no matter how fond he was of them).

Using Lillian's name was a good move. Some patrons had been taking notice of her. Without her name, *Sold for Marriage* would be just another listing, and would not attract an audience.

To see Lillian's name listed above the title had taken four years and forty-four films!

The story was timely and could have been an article in any newspaper of the day. Lillian, playing an innocent Russian peasant girl, had been brought to America by her aunt and uncle to marry a prosperous Russian farmer, a bachelor who had emigrated earlier, a man she had never met.

Lillian had not seen *Sold for Marriage* since its original April 10, 1916 opening at the Knickerbocker Theatre in New York.

When Professor William K. Everson announced in the New School for Social Research Bulletin that *Sold for Marriage* was going to be shown as part of his much-attended Friday film series, Lillian asked to see the film in a private showing at his home.

She shared her 1972 impressions with this biographer:

> When Bill [William K. Everson] told me he had located a print of *Sold for Marriage*, I was more than curious. There are films I would like to forget. This one I don't remember!
>
> I had no idea how to play a Russian peasant, and I didn't have any time to do any character research or look at photographs to check for authenticity the way I was able to do for *The Birth of a Nation*. The Russian girl I played could have been Polish! She could have been German! She could have been Yugoslavian! No matter which nation they came, I always associated peasant women with scarves... So I wore a scarf, and an old dark blouse and skirt, and I reported to work.

I knew prearranged marriages had always existed amongst certain groups in America, and it certainly occurred many times between recent immigrant arrivals and older, wealthier settlers from the same villages in their native countries. Women were needed to work on the farms in the country or the factories in the city. The men wanted women for companionship, and marriage came with it. Sometimes, love. The women had no choice, but to obey. It was written in the marriage vows: love, honor, and obey.

A woman's life was charted like a boat.

Those marriages must have been dreadful, and the women, like my mother, suffered in silence and kept quiet about it. To whom could these women turn for help? Certainly not another woman, and definitely not any man. An unmarried woman, unless she inherited some money or property from her parents, was at the mercy of her relatives. She was helpless. She was a burden, and often the object of family ridicule. Nobody wanted to be responsible for her, especially if she had no property. What was she going to leave them when she died?

Of course, if a relative became ill, the family had no reason to hire a nurse. They had the family Old Maid for that....

Mr. Cabanne was very patient with me. I had so many questions about the Russian side of her character. What were her possibilities and limitations?

Looking at *Sold for Marriage* all of these years later [1972], I can honestly say that at the time I made that film [1916], I didn't really know what I was doing.

But that scarf was a good choice![19]

Lillian's next film, *An Innocent Magdalene*, was directed by Allan Dwan from a story by Granville Warwick, the pen name of D. W. Griffith.

Lillian was cast as the wife of a jailed Southern gambler who is believed to be married to another woman. When Lillian discovers she is pregnant, rumors of the legitimacy of the baby force her father to disown her, and she has her baby alone.[20]

Was Griffith using the audience's reaction to Lillian's illegitimate baby in *An Innocent Magdalene* as justification for the future purchase of the screen rights to *Way Down East* (1920)?

Or was the still-married Griffith with the "wife in the background" trying to work out a way of balancing Lillian and the possibility of a baby entering their off-screen relationship (which was now entering its fifth year with no sign of commitment)?

Allan Dwan who also directed Dorothy that same year (1916) in Triangle's *Jordan Is a Hard Road* and *Betty of Greystone*, pondered the question regarding Griffith and the Gishes almost sixty years later at a Los Angeles film convention:

> Both Gishes, Dorothy and Lillian, were products, with Lillian being the more successful because she was more ambitious. Cabanne [director Christy Cabanne] and I both learned how to survive under Griffith's permission to direct Lillian.
>
> As the writer "Granville Warwick," Mr. Griffith was always on the set in anticipation of unexpected problems. To Griffith's credit, he didn't interfere with anything we did, but we knew he was still exercising tight control and using his blocking. We trained under him, and we tried to approximate what he would do. And he knew what he was doing.
>
> Remember: from the very beginning, audiences always loved Lillian. And Griffith did, too. He was always looking for situations and stories that might serve as future material for the two of them.
>
> The public was becoming aware of the faces they saw on the screen, and Griffith knew that you only had to see the face and you knew the type of role the actor or actress was playing and maybe a hint of the story line from the title. Lillian was always the innocent girl, and audiences loved it.
>
> Dorothy was a great clown, full of fun. She was the more versatile actress. She was a quick study, a real "just-tell-me-what-you-want-me-to-do" type, and she could provide an instant characterization that needed little refining. I never thought of Dorothy *acting*. Dorothy *was* that character.
>
> Lillian was always the queen, but a queen who worked all of the time and never let her guard down. Lillian *worked* at being casual.
>
> She was very professional, but I always felt that every movement she made, even walking to where the lunch table was, was blocked, as if a camera recorded her every movement.
>
> Dorothy, you loved. Lillian, you respected. Both ladies were great audience pleasers.
>
> It was probably the material, but whatever Lillian did always had the audience pulling for her.[21]

In some cities where *The Birth of a Nation* was still doing record business in its second year (1916), there were still protesters who threatened to break through police barricades and disrupt the performance.

The recently formed National Association for the Advancement of Colored People saw the Griffith interpretation of the Civil War and its aftermath as the ideal launching pad from which to present racist ideas and create further divisions between blacks and whites.

Griffith, to his amazement, found himself continually on the defensive.

Had the film been less successful commercially and less innovative in its use of camera techniques, perhaps its only audiences would have been curious historians and scholars.

But that didn't happen.

Lillian, because of her association with the films of D. W. Griffith, many times throughout her career found herself on the defensive regarding Griffith's attitudes shown toward blacks, attitudes which may have overshadowed his artistic achievements and immortalized him as a bigot with a camera.

Milan Stitt, playwright (*The Runner Stumbles*) and executive director of New York's Circle Repertory Theatre, recalled such a discussion in 1965 while he was doing press relations for Miss Gish during her summer engagement as the Nurse in *Romeo and Juliet* at the American Shakespeare Festival in Stratford, Connecticut.

> I was driving Lillian and Blanche Sweet to the theatre on one of the Thursdays when Lillian had had an afternoon tea with either Claudette Colbert — when Miss Colbert was in town — or with Greta Garbo.
>
> Neither Lillian nor Blanche were what we would call wistful ladies who sighed when they recalled their early days with Mr. Griffith. Being wistful was an attitude Lillian knew how to use when the occasion required it. Lillian was a thorough professional at all times.
>
> For some reason, Griffith's name came into their conversation. I don't know who mentioned his name first. The ladies were in the back seat, and I was just driving and not saying anything. I never talked to anybody when Lillian was with them.
>
> It was probably Lillian who said Griffith's name, because she was working on her autobiography [*The Movies, Mr. Griffith, and Me*] and she wanted Blanche to clarify something. Lillian didn't remember specific details about everything she did. She retained a good overall impression, and

easily handled herself during the interviews, which I arranged.

> Something came up about attacks on Griffith and his treatment of blacks in *The Birth of a Nation*, and I could see that even in 1965, with only Blanche around and nobody else, Lillian was getting upset. She knew she would have to deal with the reaction from some people to *The Birth of a Nation*. There was no way it could have been avoided.
>
> Had she avoided the controversy that still exists over *The Birth of a Nation*, the critics would have taken her to task over something that wasn't her fault. She didn't write the film. Griffith did.
>
> Lillian maintained her composure and remembered an incident from *The Greatest Thing in Life* [1918], which was a title she thought of on the set while eating a cheese sandwich and drinking a milkshake with Mr. Griffith.
>
> She said to Blanche, "You know Mr. Griffith made this war film, now lost, that contained one of the most powerful trench warfare scenes ever put on a screen. Bobby [Robert Harron] played a young Southern fighter who rids himself of his prejudice against black people by kissing, actually kissing a black soldier right on the lips as he is calling for his beloved mother to be with him… Right on the lips! And the camera didn't pull away!
>
> "Nobody in any of the audiences in California, where we previewed the film, shouted or laughed, or made any rude remarks. Blanche, how could anyone accuse of Mr. Griffith of racism when he films a scene like that?"[22]

Although Griffith knew that Lillian would always publicly defend him, words of denial, no matter how often they were repeated and sincerely stated, were insufficient. The film was all that mattered.

Griffith knew the way to answer his detractors was to make another film.

Intolerance was more than a film. It was an obligation.

Griffith's plans for *Intolerance: A Sun Play of the Ages*, did not include a role for Lillian. This new epic, designed to run for eight hours (two four-hour presentations with an intermission for dinner), was rejected immediately by the same group of exhibitors who deemed the length of *The Birth of a Nation* too taxing for an audience.

Intolerance comprised four historical events which, when shown together, would stress compassion and a universal call for brotherhood: *Babylon* (the betrayal to the Persians), *Jerusalem* (the cries for the crucifixion of Jesus), *Paris* (the slaughter of the Huguenots), and *New York* (a love story of the slums).[23]

The New York story, titled "The Mother and the Law," had already been filmed, and starred Robert Harron and Mae Marsh.

Though received with enthusiasm by a small group of loyal employees (Lillian Gish, Blanche Sweet, and Anita Loos), the general consensus was that to follow a motion picture possessing the scope of *The Birth of a Nation* with a film that was little more than a Triangle programmer (albeit well-crafted and acted) was asking for a critical panning.

Anita Loos explained her reasoning years later:

> I liked Griffith's *The Mother and the Law*, but I felt that the critics would believe it was turned out too quickly in an effort to supply something for the audience.
>
> A powerful little film like this was deserved more than a week's run. It should be part of a bigger film, which is what Mr. Griffith did.[24]

To tie the four independent films together, Griffith needed a unifying symbol. In his 1914 *Home, Sweet Home*, it was a musical motif of John Howard Payne's song. For *Intolerance* the unifying symbol had to be stronger.

What better symbol than that of a mother rocking a cradle endlessly to lines from Walt Whitman's *Leaves of Grass*?

> ...endlessly rocks the cradle,
> Uniter of Here and Hereafter.[25]

It was another opportunity to film Lillian Gish.

The entire process of filming Lillian rocking a cradle for the four sequences took less than an hour.[26] The film itself took almost two years to complete.[27]

The audiences attending the Liberty Theatre opening on September 5, 1916 saw the Standing Room Only card posted on the box office window.[28]

Having played endangered virginal heroines in perilous situations from the moment she and sister Dorothy stepped in front of a camera in 1912, Lillian wanted to play a vamp.

Her reasons were logical.

> Vamps had an easier time of it because most of the work has been done. The role plays itself. You wear exotic costumes, darken the eyebrows, apply heavy makeup, and let a cigarette dangle from your lips.[29]

Witness Louise Glaum vamping cowboy William S. Hart at the bar in *Hell's Hinges*, or Theda Bara, the perpetual homewrecker, ruining the life of a married man in *A Fool There Was*.

The audiences knew what to anticipate. No surprises.

Lillian, however, had never had an on-screen passionate encounter.

Her private life was also free of involvement and gossip. While Dorothy's romance with leading man Robert Harron still continued away from the studio, Lillian's friendship with Mr. Griffith was little more than that. Mrs. Gish always accompanied Lillian and Mr. Griffith whenever they appeared in public. Lillian was certainly aware that co-workers must have remarked that she never socialized with anyone after hours.

To audiences attending her presentation *Lillian Gish in Person: Lillian Gish and the Movies* at the Westport Country Playhouse, Westport, Connecticut on April 15, 1970, she explained her work ethic, and briefly compared her solitary lifestyle to the more gregarious Dorothy:

> My work has always been my fun. When I'm by myself, I like to read.
>
> Dorothy was always the fun person. When Dorothy went to a party, the party would become a bigger party.
>
> I'm as funny as a barrel of dead babies!

Diane of the Follies, written by D. W. Griffith (as Granville Warwick), was Lillian's attempt at vamping, but this cinematic journey into the private life of a Follies girl was a very guarded excursion.

Even with material dealing with showgirls, Griffith was a moralist.

With Lillian, his fantasies had limits...

Lillian's character was a radical departure from the "Gaga-baby" sweet little girl types.[30]

Follies girl Diane is trapped in a boring marriage to an amateur sociologist who married her to raise her level of intelligence by exposing her to what he thinks is the best of what culture has to offer. When the opportunity presents itself to return to the theatre, she leaves her husband and their daughter, Bijou. Bijou dies, and Diane announces to her husband that they can remain married, but they must never see each other again.[31]

One cannot help but comment upon the daughter's name, Bijou. Had Diane produced twins, would she have named her other daughter Rialto? Was Bijou Griffith's attempt at humor? Or were his frustrations at not succeeding as a playwright so overwhelming that, had he been a playwright, would his plays have been mounted at theatres named Bijou and Rialto?

Was the separation that occurs between Diane and her husband parallel to Griffith's from his wife?

Anita Loos offered her thoughts on Griffith's literary ambitions:

> Mr. Griffith, for all of his film successes, was a frustrated playwright. He regarded himself as a playwright.
>
> The more success he had as a filmmaker, the more reluctant he was to try to return to the theatre. The theatre world was less secure than pictures. A play closes and is hopefully forgotten. Nobody makes anything from a flop. A movie can partially recoup its losses, should it play small towns for a very short time. Some money can be made, but not much.
>
> Mr. Griffith, whether he liked it or not, always thought in cinema terms: big, lots of people to fill the lens.
>
> Lillian's theatre work at that time was very limited, but I think if Mr. Griffith were willing to take the chance, she would have returned to the theatre with him. With Lillian, Griffith or no Griffith, work always came first.[32]

It is highly likely that Griffith had attended a few performances of Florenz Ziegfeld's *Follies of 1916*, which was playing in New York at the time he was working on a film for Lillian that could place her in more worldly — but still acceptable — circumstances.

The *Follies of 1916*, with a cast that included Ina Claire, Fanny Brice, W. C. Fields, Ann Pennington, and Bert Williams,[33] had sketches using a "Shakespearean" theme[34] (Ina Claire as Juliet and Bert Williams as Othello). The beautiful Follies girls in period costumes in front of a Sphinx background must have convinced Griffith that filming in New York and utilizing the Follies name would appeal to a substantial metropolitan audience (as well as audiences across the United States who may never have the opportunity to see any part of a Ziegfeld show).

With the inclusion of Lillian as the lead, this latest Triangle film might be a box-office bonanza.

Dancer Ann Pennington, who headlined in the *Follies of 1916* (and eight other *Follies* editions), easily remembered meeting Lillian Gish in her dressing room a few times after evening performances. Accompanying Lillian on all of the visits were her mother and Mr. Griffith. Fifty-four years later, in 1970, Pennington still remembered meeting Lillian Gish:

> Mr. Ziegfeld told us to try and help her [Lillian] for this film about a Follies girl.
>
> She [Lillian] was as beautiful up close as she photographed on the screen. She had reddish-blonde hair and large blue eyes that the camera loved.
>
> At Fanny's [Brice] suggestion, we took Lillian and her mother and Mr. Griffith on-stage and watched Lillian walk around a few times, then take a few turns on the runway.
>
> She had a very good figure, but she wasn't Follies girl material. I don't think Mr. Ziegfeld would have hired her, had she shown up for an audition.
>
> She had no ... allure, and her balance was a little off. You could tell she never practiced walking to music. Mr. Griffith should have taught her how to walk, but maybe that would be later, when the actual filming started.
>
> I always thought she should have come backstage alone. Then we could have talked about our lives, and she could have picked up some simple dance steps. With Watching Mama there, we were very polite, and the conversation never really went anywhere.
>
> Lillian was very professional in what she asked and how she asked it.
>
> We couldn't talk about men, and men were certainly a big part of our lives. Men were one of the reason pretty young girls came to New York. They wanted to be in the Follies, and they wanted to meet men.
>
> Men who met Follies girls were always wealthy, and they could show you a good time, and, if you played your cards right, you could get one of them to marry you, if you know what I mean...
>
> Lillian never became a Follies girl in that film. There was nothing inside her character. She didn't know what a Follies girl was, or what she had to go through everyday. It isn't just walking down a staircase, or smiling on a runway to beautiful music and wearing pretty clothes. But Lillian Gish did look wonderful, and the clothing fit very well.
>
> It would have been a better picture if Joan Crawford or Clara Bow played that part. Men fantasized about Joan Crawford and Clara Bow. Lillian Gish was only Mr. Griffith's fantasy. He was very Victorian, and she was very prissy.
>
> Why did she always bring her mother? Her mother gave me the impression that being a Follies girl meant you were only slightly better than a chorus girl, and chorus girls were low class....
>
> When I saw the film, I thought Lillian Gish reminded me of an eleven-year-old girl playing dress up![35]

December 1916: In the fourth month of what was hoped to be an engagement as successful as *The Birth of a Nation*, business for *Intolerance* had taken a noticeable dive. Reasons for the box-office slump were numerous — and, of course, logical.

Anita Loos claimed it was the film's length, that audiences who sat for *The Birth of a Nation* were "too cushion-conscious" to sit that extra time.[36]

Some newspaper critics lamented the lack of a "dramatic technique" and the inability of the audience to follow four separately constructed stories.[37]

Griffith assistant and Triangle director Allan Dwan believed the scenery in the Babylonian sequence was so overwhelming that audiences couldn't find the actors.[38]

Constance Talmadge, who appeared in the Babylonian sequence as the Mountain Girl, succinctly summarized all of the prevailing attitudes years later: *Intolerance* did nothing for anyone involved. Especially Mr. Griffith.[39]

Intolerance, one of the greatest financial calamities in the history of the motion picture, was the last time Griffith used a wide narrative canvas and bold strokes to connect any commonality between eras.

In an effort to recoup some of the losses he had incurred, he released *The Fall of Babylon* as a "complete evening," and *The Mother and the Law* as the programmer it perhaps should have been.[40]

The warm and friendly relationship with Roy and Harry Aitken at the beginning of Griffith's association was strained.

On March 11, 1917, Griffith broke his contract, claiming the funding had dwindled and the "creative challenge" was no longer there.[41]

Once again, D. W. Griffith was unemployed.

When Griffith had no work, neither did Dorothy nor Lillian.

CHAPTER 7

Dark Crossings

The insecurity and fear that always accompanied the lives of the three Gishes whenever Mr. Griffith was unemployed was fortunately short-lived. On March 17, six days after Griffith had broken his contract with Triangle, he signed with Adolph Zukor at Paramount to direct their Artcraft pictures.[1] The crafty Zukor, a one-time Hungarian immigrant furrier who successfully imported Sarah Bernhardt's four-reeler, *Queen Elizabeth*, made his entrance into motion pictures via a 14th Street penny arcade he managed. He had twice attempted to entice Griffith away from Biograph.

Although Zukor was aware that Griffith's *Intolerance* was a box-office failure, he was also well aware of what *The Birth of a Nation* had grossed, and that it was continuing to gross more money than anyone in the industry had anticipated. Sizable orchestras were providing musical accompaniment for the film in cities and towns across the United States.[2]

Places like Morristown, New Jersey, who had once banned showings at the time of its original release (1915), now deemed it safe to allow the twelve-reel epic to be shown.[3]

Lillian, whose name was not above the title in the original release of the film, had since achieved solo billing in Triangle's *Sold for Marriage* the following year (1916). She was no longer a mere Griffith player. Just as with her friend Mary Pickford (with whom Lillian once appeared at Biograph, and who was also employed by Zukor at Paramount), Zukor knew the names of Gish and Griffith could lure customers into the theatre.

Zukor presented Griffith with a most attractive salary: ten thousand dollars (an amount neither Harry nor Roy Aitken could meet, and an offer Griffith knew he could not to refuse).[4] With the acquisition of D. W. Griffith, Adolph Zukor had practically decimated the Triangle studio— since Mack Sennett and Thomas Ince had also expressed a desire to work at Paramount. Griffith would call Zukor's triumphant accomplishment a "virtual raid,"[5] but it was a raid for which Griffith was most grateful.

When Griffith had work, so did Lillian and Dorothy.

April 6, 1917: On the morning of the London premiere of Griffith's *Intolerance*, Woodrow Wilson, President of the United States, declared war on Germany. The motion picture industry, in the sudden emergence of songs with the topical titles *I Didn't Raise My Boy to Be a Soldier, Good Bye Broadway, Hello France,* and *When a Yankee Doodle Learns to Parlez Vous Francais*, could no longer remain neutral and hope to keep the paying customers happy with films about vamps and cigarette girls.[6] For instance, Mary Pickford's *The Little American* featured a storyline that bore more than a passing reference to the May 7, 1915 German torpedoing of the Lusitania, on which 1,200 people (114 Americans) lost their lives off the coast of Ireland.[7]

Unlike the wars of the past, this Great War would be preserved on film (in addition to the magazines and newspapers of the day). Griffith was not caught totally off guard with the issuing of former employee Mary Pickford's film. Nor was he unaware of the world events which would shape his first film at Artcraft for Mr. Zukor.

At the invitation of English Prime Minister Lloyd George and Lord Beaverbrook,[8] Griffith pushed aside his pacifist leanings[9] long enough to visit and photograph the actual war front in France while he was in London to arrange for the showing of *Intolerance* at the Drury Lane Theatre. He knew an eventual American entry was unavoidable.

In the fall of 1917, the Germans had retreated one hundred miles — from Arras to Soissons — along the Hindenburg lines. In the abandoned territory were totally demolished villages, castles, churches, vineyards, and orchards.[10]

In one of those abandoned villages, Griffith found the ideal setting for *Hearts of the World*, a film about the suffering of simple French people under German occupation. *Hearts of the World*, strictly constructed as anti–German propaganda, would be Griffith's war effort, designed to make the Americans give up their isolationist policy and help the Allies.[11]

The casting was pure Griffith formula, players who knew each other's timing as well as their own: Lillian Gish (the Girl), Robert Harron (the Boy), Dorothy Gish (the Little Disturber, a role that finally showcased her comic talents), George Siegmann (a German soldier). Mary Gish, who was usually on the set as often as pos-

sible while Lillian was working, was given a small part as the Refugee Mother.

Hearts of the World was a story of pure and ideal young love threatened by the War. Its message could not be overlooked by anyone. The Germans alone were responsible for the War, which was a "deliberate blow aimed at civilization."[12] Audiences reading titles such as, "Month after month piled up with its legend of Hunnish crimes in the book of God,"[13] could not help but be aroused.

For poignancy, it was hard to surpass scenes of Lillian Gish, in her wedding dress, aimlessly wandering through the ruins in search of her beloved. Griffith weighed the scales of propaganda quite heavily when Lillian asks her beloved to shoot her rather than be captured and tortured by the Germans.

To insure the safety of his players, Griffith insisted that they sail from New York to England on separate camouflaged ships. The *St. Louis*, which carried Lillian and her mother, and the *Baltic*, which carried Dorothy, Robert Harron, and cameraman Billy Bitzer (a problem, since his birthname was Johann Wilhelm Gottlob Bitzer),[14] would depart on different days.

Lillian's ship, which carried a group of doctors, nurses, and medical equipment, was without any military protection. The nurses were instructed to sleep on deck and wear their life belts at all times. Lillian and her mother were privileged to sleep in one of the cabins. They were also supplied with rubber suits with "weighted feet" and emergency supplies that would enable them to remain alive for a period of two weeks if they were torpedoed.[15]

On Dorothy's ship were General John Pershing, a few auto trucks, and three-hundred-and-eighty-five officers of the American Expeditionary Forces. The *Baltic*, for all of its military might, ironically was devoid of any means of protection against a sudden German attack. The *Baltic* was a lone ship without a convoy to search the ocean for a periscope, the sign of a German submarine patrolling the waters.[16]

Lillian's ship, the *St. Louis*, was the first to arrive, naturally. Dorothy's crossing, with its constant changes of course, took thirteen days!

Upon her arrival, Dorothy was reunited with a frantic mother and sister in their elegant fourth floor suite at the elegant Savoy Hotel, long a host to visiting celebrities and prominent people from all over the world. Times for the Gishes had certainly changed from when they worked at Biograph five years ago and slept in the same room at the Marlton in New York's Greenwich Village!

Still, even with the change of surroundings, the Gishes had to contend with nightly noises. These new noises weren't from the constant flow of traffic on West Eighth Street. These new sounds were louder and dangerous: German Zeppelins patrolling the London sky, ready to strike at any moment!

At eleven o'clock nightly, the sounds of the British anti-aircraft guns practicing in the event of an air attack was something for which everyone had to be prepared.[17] On some nights there were no Zeppelins, but nothing in a time of war was ever permanent

Except death...

A few evenings later, the Gishes were awakened by the sound of the British anti-aircraft guns. Lillian looked at her clock in the moonlight. It was ten-thirty, one half-hour earlier than the British drill time.

Looking out of her window, she knew the reason from the break in pattern. It was a German bombing raid—this time on London's East End.

A passing waiter in the hallway, who was trying to calm down the panicking guests, let the three Gishes view the "black speck"—the source of the damage as it flew eighteen thousand feet above the hotel.

Lillian, her mother, and sister, took a taxi to Whitechapel. There they saw the devastation of the War at first hand, including

> a schoolhouse where ninety-six children had been killed. Crazed mothers swarmed about, looking for fragments of their dead.
>
> Other bombs had fallen in the neighborhood. People were insane from grief. A schoolmaster carried out his own child. A woman standing near had just discovered that her boy was among the victims. Her face was distorted—it was as if someone had pulled it out of shape.[18]

Sometimes there was only one nightly bombing. Sometimes, two or three. There were nights when the German planes circled over London and dropped nothing.

And then there was an occasional night of silence. No warnings of approaching German Zeppelins.

It was the silence without sirens that could be the most terrifying...

To her friend Nell, Lillian wrote:

> You cannot imagine what terrible things those big things in the sky are, dropping death wherever they go. If this war would only end...[19]

There were few, if any, air-raid shelters.

Griffith saw everything as material for the actor to draw upon when the occasion warranted.

> "All the time," recounted Lillian, "Mr. Griffith kept telling us not to hide in the closet or under the beds, but to pull far enough away from the danger to be able to watch. Watch and remember everything.
>
> Whenever we had a day off from shooting, he'd send us to Waterloo Station and make us stay there until nightfall, watching.

"You want to be in the acting profession," he would say to us, "then you must know life. You'll never have another chance like this!" and he would wave his hand across all of the destruction. You are a witness to history! Watch the women's faces! Watch their farewells! Watch the homecomings! Watch the burying of the dead husbands and children! *Watch* and *learn!*[20]

The raids continued, the sounds of explosions and screaming ripped through the night air, shattering windows and setting houses and streets on fire. Lives, old and young, were suddenly ended.

In the vicinity of Cleopatra's Needle, a bomb fell, hitting a streetcar blowing away the legs of the conductor and killing eleven people. Several others were wounded.

Theatres crumbled: one on Adelphi Terrace, one at Piccadilly Circus, one near Charing Cross Hospital.

It was a world without end.[21]

Still, Griffith continued the filming of *Hearts of the World*. Lillian, Dorothy, and their mother would rise at four in the morning, step onto the hotel balcony, and look down at the latest debris before setting off for work.

In Worcestershire, Sir Noel Coward, then seventeen years old and a five-dollar-a-day extra,[22] reported for work at five o'clock in the morning, his face made up in bright yellow. He had received his first set of professional notices in the June 28, 1911 edition of *The Daily Telegraph* for a minor role in the stage play *The Goldfish*.[23] *Hearts of the World*, with Lillian and Dorothy Gish, was his film debut.

On December 4, 1969, the opening night of the New York revival of Sir Noël's play, *Private Lives*, the renowned playwright-composer-screenwriter-actor could still recall his times with the Gishes on the set in 1917:

I had a little part in that film.

Actually, it was a walk-on, with a wheelbarrow for a prop.

Lillian was in the scene with me. I was supposed to push the wheelbarrow up a hill, away from the camera. But I convinced somebody, maybe it was Mr. Griffith, that I thought our scene would be more effective if I pushed the wheelbarrow toward the camera. They went along with it, dear boy, but if you blink, you'll miss me.

I was living on practically nothing in those days, and Lillian's mother, a dear, dear lady, always made sure there was something for this seventeen-year-old English boy, which is what she called me, to eat: a piece of chicken, some fruit, or a sandwich. She looked after Dorothy and Lillian with equal devotion.

Mother Gish was very ... strong. She always supervised her little girls and made sure they did the right thing.[24]

The Coward-Gish friendship would continue down the years. Whenever Sir Noel chanced to be in New York, either on a visit or to appear in one of his plays, he always called on the Gishes in their apartment. So fond was he of Mrs. Gish that he presented her with one of his original paintings, *Fishing at Dawn*, which they hung in their living room.

When the summer of 1917 arrived, Griffith thought it safe and advisable to take the *Hearts of the World* company to the war front in France. In secrecy, the three Gishes and Robert Harron packed their bags and traveled to Southampton, where they boarded a troop ship to take them across the Channel to Le Havre, from where a train would complete their journey to Paris.[25]

To be present at the front was the goal of every war correspondent and photographer. You had to secure a permit from the American Embassy before you could travel to France.[26] The Channel was the danger zone. Twice they had been forced to return to Southampton because of the presence of floating mines.[27]

Billy Bitzer, to Griffith's frustration, had to remain behind.

Mrs. Gish, still suffering from the aftereffects of the bombing raids, wanted to be with her daughters. Even in the trenches.

"There are only three members left in our family," she said to Lillian, "and if one of us is going to die, all of us are going to die together."[28]

As Griffith, Dorothy, Lillian, and their mother drove across the land outside Paris, everything seemed to be barbed wire and trenches. Griffith knew he was working against time, that shooting actual locations was risky and would not always transfer effectively onto film. There were days, he would tell assistant Allan Dwan after the company had returned to complete sequences at the Sunset Boulevard studio, that one trench looked like "another and another," and the look of the devastated French villages housing the wounded and dying men was sometimes dreary and monotonous.

An artist-created war was often more dramatic than the actual one. In a real war, it was perfectly logical for the doughboys to remain in their foxholes for hours — until the sound of enemy awakened them from their lethargy and mobilized them into action. To try to turn this actual reality into film reality was well-nigh impossible. Film created its own urgency and time.[29]

Griffith's energy seemed to be tireless. He often worked eighteen hours a day. There were seemingly endless rehearsals involving learning new body movements as well as the blocking of the scene.

Years later, Lillian told this biographer she still retained strong memories of what Griffith told the military photographer, sent in place of Billy Bitzer, to shoot. She could also recall the footage Griffith was afraid, or told not to include in the final print of *Hearts of the World*.

> In one of the villages going to the front from Senlis, we saw a house that had been destroyed. Bits and sections of old furniture, an old tea kettle on its side… Everyone in the house had been killed.
>
> On the walls of one empty house, we could see the smears of blood on the wall.
>
> We drove to places where trained nurses weren't sent. Trained nurses had value, but actors? We were a dime a dozen.
>
> We couldn't help but see the astonished look on the faces of all of the soldiers. They couldn't believe that we — and we were sometimes dressed as we would if we were going to an Opening Night party — were actually with them.
>
> We were within the range of the long distance guns. Mother was still shell shocked. Occasionally, when she heard the noise of the bombs, she would involuntarily shake so violently that either Dorothy or I had to hold her until the shaking stopped. Sometimes, she was afraid to feed herself, because she thought she would spill her food, and people would look at her and laugh. She was fighting her own war…[30]

The war-weary company returned to Los Angeles and Griffith's Hollywood and Sunset studio in November to complete the film.[31] The shooting overseas in England and on the war front in France, with the accompanying pressure, tension, and day-to-day anxiety, had taken their toll on the Gishes. Lillian and Dorothy had tried to create art from life under terrible circumstances.

Mrs. Gish had lost thirty-five pounds, and had developed a nervous condition. Daughter Dorothy had lost ten pounds, but with her usual sense of humor, would tell people, "Lillian is brave. She couldn't afford to lose. She gained a whole pound."

To Lillian, the filming overseas was a dream to which she had no desire to return.[32]

Shooting resumed on a twenty-four day schedule after the new sets were built and other roles were cast. Lillian, who had been functioning as an editor at the end of each day's shoot, was given more leeway than she had had in previous films. If a room in her scene needed a different type of furniture than had been supplied to her liking, Griffith would yell, "Then go and find it! It's your room!"

On Christmas Eve, while peace negotiations were continuing between the Bolshevik government and the Central Powers (Germany and Austria), Griffith kept Dorothy and Lillian on the set until midnight, and then all of Christmas Day.[33] His twelve-reel war was coming to an end.

The real war would continue for another eleven months until Germany surrendered and the Armistice was signed on November 11, 1918. By that time, *Hearts of the World* was in general release.

The Los Angeles opening of *Hearts of the World* at Clune's Auditorium on March 12 was a major event that attracted the celebrities of the day. In the audience were (beside Griffith and the three Gishes) Blanche Sweet, Charlie Chaplin, Douglas Fairbanks, Mae Murray, Mary Miles Minter, Mack Sennett, Roscoe Arbuckle, and Dustin Farnum.[34]

The April 4 premiere at New York's Forty-fourth Street Theatre confirmed the West Coast consensus that Lillian had tallied another personal triumph, and the film's war scenes were realistic.

Until the signing of the Armistice, Griffith's film was as topical as the headlines. After the signing, *Hearts of the World*, despite the war footage, had become "trite and sentimental," a history few wished to relive so immediately.[35]

Sir Noël Coward provided an opinion on why *Hearts of the World* failed to maintain its initial momentum:

> *Hearts of the World*, to be an unqualified success, required immediacy. The signing of the armistice dated the material. Had Griffith made this film at the start—instead of near the end—of the war, the suspense of the reality of the situation could have sustained the suspense of the screen story. Once the armistice was signed, the Germans on the screen became laughable. They had started a war they couldn't finish and their on-screen villainy became cheap melodrama. Hiss the villain, hiss the Germans. No matter how well their villainy was presented, audiences knew that they had lost the war. The propaganda had become dated overnight, and the audiences felt superior to the material.
>
> Films like *Wings* (1927), and plays like *What Price Glory* (1924) and *Journey's End* (1929), were successful because they were presented years after the armistice. Audiences could become involved with the characters instead of the propaganda. *Gone with the Wind* was not written to make its readers anti–Union or pro Confederacy. Scarlett O'Hara was a memorably drawn heroine.
>
> *Hearts of the World* was a period piece in its own time, because Griffith was stirring the audiences to be anti–German. Those characters became stick figures—typical propaganda types. When you're seeing that film now, you can see how laughable the propaganda is.
>
> Some of the photographic effects are still quite spectacular, and they can engage an audience.
>
> The appeal of *Hearts of the World* is Dorothy and Lillian Gish. Those wonderful sisters can transcend anything![36]

CHAPTER 8

Little Poems

Mr. Griffith would call *The Birth of a Nation* and *Intolerance* big pictures, and *A Romance of Happy Valley, Broken Blossoms*, and *True Heart Susie* little poems.

—Lillian Gish
Conversation with author (1954)

Never one to abandon unused footage, D. W. Griffith (writing under his reliable pseudonym, Granville Warwick) hastily fashioned *The Hun Within* as a vehicle for Dorothy Gish. Directed by assistant Chester Withey, *The Hun Within* served as an opportunity to utilize the talents of Erich Von Stroheim as a quintessential German,[1] a role he had to surrender in *Hearts of the World* to George Siegmann, who had been with Griffith at Biograph since 1909.[2] Dorothy played Beth, a young orphan torn between two young admirers: one a school chum, and the other a German-American who turns out to be a spy.[3]

First publicly shown in Pasadena in May 1918, the programmer was released in New York the following September, a few weeks before the signing of the armistice. Unlike *Hearts of the World*, its temporarily successful predecessor, *The Hun Within* had even less opportunity to do even minimal business at the box-office.

The 155 tons of ticker tape greeting the victorious soldiers parading down New York's Fifth Avenue was the signaling of a new era. Nothing would be as it once was.

The "older generation"[4] that had wrecked the world before passing it on, had to step aside. The pre-war traditions of restraint and propriety were permanently shattered as the newly emerging modern woman, who called herself a flapper, proceeded to bob her hair and shorten her skirts. Some would even be so bold as to smoke in public, but that would be seen only in a smart café where sophistication sometimes meant indiscretion. No longer would literature and motion pictures be content to concentrate on provincial problems. The Great War, the first to be photographed with a moving picture camera, had made men — disillusioned men — out of boys. The restraining bonds of Victorian morality that had hitherto held sway were now being challenged by a new permissiveness and freedom.

In the face of the post-war "moral laxity,"[5] a stubborn D. W. Griffith pursued, via the films of Lillian Gish, his personal vision: that "spiritual values would always overcome the forces that threatened them."[6] Let flaming youth flame on![7] Both Lillian and Dorothy had their own, Griffith-reinforced, philosophy: "Love could not withstand the waste of the carnal," and that "love could not be bought nor ravaged by it."[8]

Lillian's next films (the sentimental *A Romance of Happy Valley* and *True Heart Susie*, and the "genuinely poetic"[9] *Broken Blossoms*), while smart and clever in the entertainment sense, would link her with the Victorian era[10]—the era in which Griffith felt most comfortable, a time when forgiveness and salvation were granted after "tear-dimmed repentance."[11]

In defense of her characters ("child-women with a strong maternal streak")[12] who were free from moral blemish and any taint of sin, Lillian told an interviewer: "Virgins are the hardest role to play, those dear little girls. To make them interesting takes great vitality."[13]

Both Lillian and D. W. Griffith were savvy enough to know that "eighty percent of all movie audiences were women."[14]

A Romance of Happy Valley, set in the rural Kentucky of Griffith's childhood, was a simple tale of two different worlds: the temptations of the big city versus the security of a small town. Will the heroine (Lillian) faithfully wait for the hero (Robert Harron), an inventor who has spent eight years of his life developing a mechanical frog, to return from a sinful New York where he has gone to make his fortune?

One cannot help but notice certain autobiographical parallels in the story written by Captain Victor Marier, another of Griffith's pseudonyms.[15] Its handling of the relationship between the inventor (Griffith, the struggling artist) and the innocent Jennie (Lillian), who patiently and devotedly waits, must have been a topic of gossip amongst Griffith's players. As another variation on the Svengali-Trilby dynamic, Griffith must have certainly have enjoyed it.[16] But not because of Griffith's still-attached marital status, which showed no signs of changing—he and Lillian hav-

ing been considered an "item" since they met at Biograph in 1912.

Appearing in a New York dancehall sequence in *A Romance of Happy Valley* was seventeen-year-old former Denishawn dancer Carol Dempster, who made her film debut as one of the dancers in the ill-fated *Intolerance* (1916). By virtue of her tenacity and aggression, Dempster had slowly risen to larger roles in film, and—away from the cameras—in Griffith's personal life.

Actress Colleen Moore, who met Lillian in 1917 and remained a close friend, was quite outspoken about the Dempster-Griffith relationship in a conversation fifty years later, in Chicago:

> Carol Dempster was a pushy little bitch who threw herself at old man Griffith, who was more than twice her age and liked the attention—any attention—he could get from a well-developed young girl, who was often the source of her family's income.
>
> The Dempster-Griffith relationship was mutually advantageous. He always played one young girl against another, offering both a part in one of his next films as the prize. He was always discovering and testing young girls for possible roles.
>
> I don't know if he ever told these naive hopefuls that he was married. Lillian certainly knew he was, and so did her mother, who might have tolerated these liaisons because they didn't involve her daughters. So she liked to think....
>
> Sponsoring new talent was nothing new to anyone who's been in the business. A lot of producers would use wealthy backers' girlfriends, who could supply their own wardrobe for background in society-type films.
>
> It must have been hard for Lillian to watch old man Griffith making an ass out of himself over this absolute no-talent airhead Dempster, but she was very stoic about it. For the first time in Lillian's life, something had

happened which she couldn't control. None of us could say anything to her, because she never discussed her social life. I never knew if Lillian had a social life of any kind.

I knew, everybody knew, what Dorothy did. Dorothy always talked about Bobby (Robert Harron) and where they went....

Lillian, on the set, was very professional. Whenever she was with Griffith, her mother was always there, acting as a chaperon.

Mr. Griffith, everybody knew, always had a roving eye. With Carol Dempster, he had found himself another little girl.[17]

True Heart Susie, with its depiction of idyllic love in a rural setting, can almost be considered as a companion piece to Griffith's *A Romance of Happy Valley*. Filmed in the spring of 1919,[18] *True Heart Susie* is the story of country neighbors Susie May Trueheart (Lillian) and ministry student William Jenkins (Robert Harron) who seem destined to be married. In anticipation of a proposal when William returns home from his studies in Chicago, Susie, in order to help finance his education, has secretly sold her cow and a few household possessions. To her surprise and dismay, William returns home with a wife, Bettina, a gaudily dressed milliner who prefers to party instead of assuming her churchly responsibilities. Susie, content to be William's friend, allows this Chicago hussy to stay overnight at her home during a rainstorm because she forgot to take her housekeys while sneaking away to party. Bettina even supplies Susie with a lie to tell the innocent William: she was borrowing a book for William, and she wanted to avoid catching a cold. Bettina still manages to catch a cold, which kills her. William, learning the truth about his erring wife, vows never to marry again — until he hears about the sacrifices his neighbor, Susie, had made for him. At the film's end, Susie and William are reunited.

Although there was genuine screen chemistry between Lillian and Robert Harron in *True Heart Susie*, the film, at the time of its original release, was not well-received. Many voiced complaints regarding its length. It ran approximately one hour. Had this film been a Triangle programmer designed for the neighborhood theatres on a prescribed circuit in the manner of Lillian Gish's *Sold for Marriage*, the reception of *True Heart Susie* may have been more favorable. Griffith's films were prestige films, whose look reflected a high budget: impressive scenery, fancy camera work, and a large cast. Was Griffith purposely placing Lillian in a smaller production to keep his name in front of the public while he was planning another epic?

The June 8, 1919 edition of *Wid's Film Daily* suggested that had *True Heart Susie* been shorter (perhaps a two-reeler like Gish and Harron's *The Battle of Elderbridge Gulch?*) it would have become a "masterpiece of screen character fiction."[19] Had writer Griffith taken Marion Fremont's scenario and expanded its ideal "short story material" to "novel" length with its "too frequent repetition of scenes that in their meaning and expression of emotion were virtually the same"?[20]

Still, the original *Wid's* review was not a total dismissal of the film. The reviewer was aware that Lillian's Susie May Trueheart was not played as a "simple country girl"[21] whose motivations could be handled within the confines of a one or two column analysis. Susie was someone who "loves, and to her, love means sacrifice and an abiding faith in the ultimate goodness of things."

Critic Anthony Slide adds:

> The Gish characterization hints not so much at a selfless sacrifice, but at a sacrifice that eventually will bring her the man she loves. When that sacrifice

does not work out exactly as she had planned, and the man she loves marries another woman, then her spite may not be openly visible, but it is there nevertheless, only just beneath the surface. Watch Lillian's eyes... They are not the eyes of a selfless simple girl. They are the eyes of a devoted creature until Harron (William Jenkins) meets Clarine Seymour (Betting), and then those eyes are filled with spite and hatred. You know Lillian gets her man, no matter how long she may have to wait.[22]

Lillian, journeying around the world fifty years later in 1969 presenting her lecture, *The Art of the Film*, centering on her work with D. W. Griffith, was surprised and gratified to learn that *True Heart Susie* was one of Mr. Griffith's "most respected films." It was part of the Buckingham Palace film library and a favorite of Queen Mother Alexandra.[23]

Depending on the source of information, Thomas Burke's *Limehouse Nights*, a collection of short stories ("admittedly violent stuff, written hastily") set in London's Chinatown district,[24] came to Griffith's attention while he was in London in preparation for shooting *Hearts of the World*.[25] Hearst columnist Adela Rogers St. Johns, a friend of Mary Pickford, believed it was the actress herself who sent a copy of the book to her former Biograph boss as a suggestion for a film to be made under the auspices of United Artists — a company formed by Mary, her husband Douglas Fairbanks, Charlie Chaplin, and Griffith for the purpose of distributing their own films and those made by independent studios. Everyone would have a greater share of the profits.

From the Burke collection, Griffith was most impressed with "The Chink and the Child," an interracial love story of a fifteen-year-old Chinese boy and his love for a twelve-year-old abused white girl

(the daughter of a prizefighter) he encounters in a house of ill-repute. What intrigued Griffith more than the taboo theme of miscegenation was Burke's descriptions of the mist and fog which created a sense of mystery and danger as well as atmosphere. Griffith had spent time on the docks, and the thought of photographing this was an artistic challenge he could not turn away.

The use of three main characters — the young girl, her father, and the young boy — required only a small cast that would be easy to manage given the short amount of time he would need to make the film. A business-smart Mary knew that economics would govern the success of United Artists' first venture. She was quite aware of Griffith's penchant for extravagance. Griffith, if not constantly watched by the production office, was capable of sending any studio into bankruptcy. He was either totally unaware or totally indifferent to the financial matters of moviemaking.

Because Griffith had acquired and maintained a stock company of reliable players who could anticipate each other's reactions, he knew he was confident in the casting of Lillian as the waif-like Lucy, reliable Donald as her father (the prizefighter Battling Burrows), and a newcomer, Trinity College (Hartford, Connecticut) graduate Richard Barthelmess (who made his film debut in the 1916 film *War Brides*, starring Alla Nazimova[26]) as the boy.

The weeks before Lillian began shooting *Broken Blossoms* were not without problems. Both Lillian and Griffith knew each other's work habits. There was no need to renew a past relationship and go through the ritual of becoming reacquainted with the beginning of each new creative venture. Lillian and her mother would simply report to the studio and await further instructions.

Said Griffith: "I gave her an outline of

what I hoped to accomplish, and let her work it out her own way. When she got it, she had something of her own."[27]

Cameraman Billy Bitzer commented: "Griffith conditioned her [Lillian Gish] to the part she was to play and once she had the action in mind, she wouldn't forget or deviate by so much as a flicker of the eye."[28]

The weight loss Lillian had suffered while making *Hearts of the World* had begun to take its toll. Costumes had to be altered.[29] The costumes Griffith had selected for *Broken Blossoms* were "part of his conception of realism, dusted over with fantasy and a sexually-charged Victorianism derived from the ... novels of Charles Dickens and their illustrations."[30]

Even with the briefest of rehearsals, it was impossible for Lillian, at the end of the day, to walk a few feet without feeling dizzy. There were occasions when the walk home took longer than usual, because she had to lie down, away from public view, in protective areas near bushes or trees to gather the strength to continue.

Arriving four hours late one afternoon just before sundown, she collapsed on the bed. Alarmed, her mother hurriedly summoned a doctor who noted Lillian's 106 degree temperature and immediately diagnosed her illness: the Spanish influenza, a pandemic that was bombarding the United States. It was often fatal. Five had already died at Griffith's studio, including Robert Harron's five-year-old sister.[31]

Until a nurse was found, Lillian remained in her mother's care, while sister Dorothy was sent to the Talmadge home. Griffith, not wanting to lose valuable rehearsal time, assigned Lillian's role to Carol Dempster.

Against doctor's orders, Lillian reported to the set a few days later.[32] Her face was covered by a surgical mask. She was assisted by her mother, who remained —

even more than usual — at her side. As sick as she was, Lillian, the trouper, knew the show must go on. She also had no intention of surrendering a role — any role — to Carol Dempster, described by Hearst columnist Adela Rogers St. Johns as a "third rate actress."[33]

Carol, in an effort to convince a beleaguered Griffith to keep her employed, had new and more flattering pictures of herself taken at another studio by portrait photographer Hendrick Sartov. Sartov, who had no experience with a motion picture camera, photographed actresses in soft focus, which diminished any sharp features and concealed any signs of aging.

Griffith, Carol knew, was constantly pouring over submitted photographs of young girls who wanted to be in pictures. Seventeen-year-old Carol, with the addition of Sartov's lighting, looked much younger than twenty-six-year-old Lillian, the oldest female player on the Griffith lot.[34]

Cameraman Billy Bitzer, present during the tense early days of Lillian's recovery, witnessed and recorded the impact of Lillian's determination to resume work, and the affect it had on a scheming Carol Dempster:

> I saw her [Carol] in the back lot ... talking to Griffith. She had called him David! No one ever called him by his first name, and he had responded. I chuckled to myself. I looked around to see if anyone else had witnessed this. Lillian was standing as though transfixed, not far from where I stood. She merely smiled as she passed, and in her usual soft voice said, "There he goes again." She continued walking, with her shoulders straight, and her back stiff, that Mona Lisa smile masking her thoughts.[35]

There were two rehearsals now going on at the Griffith studio for the upcoming

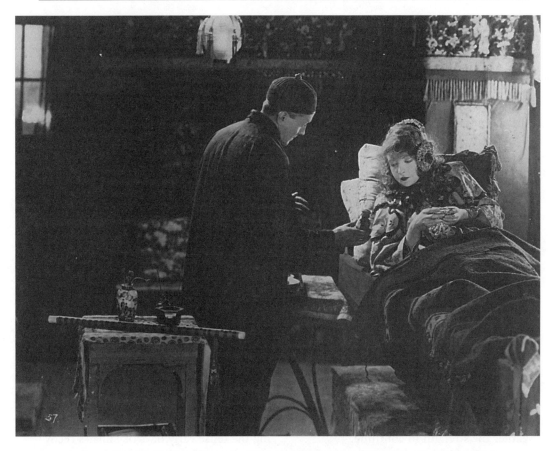

As Lucy, the girl: *Broken Blossoms* (1919, United Artists, directed by D. W. Griffith).

shooting of *Broken Blossoms*. Griffith, now legally separated from his wife Linda Arvidson, was rehearsing with Carol. Lillian was rehearsing with her leading man, Richard Barthelmess, coaching him with the same intensity of purpose Griffith had used with her seven years earlier when she first went to work for him at Biograph in New York.[36]

It was important for Barthelmess to register strongly on screen in this, his first, role as her leading man. *Broken Blossoms* had been announced as a Lillian Gish picture, and it would be a Lillian Gish picture. Lillian Gish would star.

Not Carol Dempster!

An undercurrent of fear and insecurity ran deep through the *Broken Blossoms* company during the early days of re-

hearsal. Established careers were in jeopardy and personal lives were in danger of becoming fodder for the fan magazines. Photographer Hendrick Sartov had been hired as an assistant to Billy Bitzer, who was now shooting Lillian through a silk net to give her a younger and more ethereal look.[37]

Lillian, aware of Carol Dempster's hovering presence, was struggling to stay on her feet and concentrate on her new role.

D. W. Griffith, pressuring his wife to divorce him, was torn between two fierce and powerful women: Lillian — quiet, faithful, and a consummate professional, and Carol — younger, and very manipulative.

The first days of shooting were not

without trepidation. Lillian, more than once, had expressed doubts about her ability to portray Thomas Burke's battered heroine, "a little girl of twelve" with "a starved face and the transfixed air" who had "a lurking beauty about her, a something that cried for kisses and was fed with blows."[38]

Lillian knew she couldn't be photographed as a twelve year old. After much discussion, Griffith raised the age of Lucy to fifteen, which seemed to be more logical.[39]

Lillian's work hours, Griffith assured her, would be short, with provisions arranged to allow her nine hours of sleep a night. She agreed to such an arrangement.

Neither kept their word. Both Lillian and Griffith remained on the set for long stretches, just as they had done in previous collaborations when their involvement and professionalism superseded any awareness of time.

On the set of *Broken Blossoms*, their professional relationship must have shown signs of strain. Lillian wasn't totally recovered from her illness, and Griffith had an "almost neurotic fear of germs."[40] Lillian was ordered to wear a face mask when not appearing in front of the camera, and to stay at least ten feet away from him.[41]

The actual filming, due to the small, well-rehearsed cast and limited sets and action shots, took only eighteen days.[42] There were no retakes or "added scenes."[43]

Broken Blossoms, unlike Griffith's previous films, was a "genuinely poetic film"[44] heightened by the use of "misty photography" for the Chinatown and waterfront sequences. In addition to artificial fog blown onto the sets for realism, Griffith used rough reflecting surfaces that scattered the lighting for the love scenes between Lillian and Richard Barthelmess.[45]

Lillian's acting, wrote cameraman Billy Bitzer, was quiet and unemotional. The often-imitated sad smile she gave her father, before he beat her for the last time, was made by placing her second and third fingers at opposite end of her upper lip and gently pushing upwards.[46] It was a truly inspired "bit" that Griffith insisted be kept in. That tiny gesture remained in the minds of everyone who saw the film. It justified Griffith's rehearsal methods, where every movement and gesture were noted.

Lillian, a firm believer in rehearsals and the Griffith method of rehearsing, would later say:

> In the daily rushes, you could see what you had done, and you could correct your mistakes. Mr. Griffith would let you work on your part and keep finding new things to do with it. He was never stingy about using film to instruct, and he shot a lot of it. It was only during the actual shooting that he didn't want to waste film. There was no wasted footage in *Broken Blossoms*.
>
> By the time we made *Broken Blossoms*, I knew almost as much as he did. I knew about lights, camera angles, and lenses.[47]

For the famous scene which required Lillian to be trapped inside a closet, Lillian knew nobody could tell her how to act it but herself. She rehearsed it "almost without sleep" for three days and nights.[48]

On the day of the shooting, Griffith closed the set. Only cameraman Billy Bitzer, Griffith, and Lillian would be present.[49] Gaping outsiders, Griffith felt, would only make Lillian feel self-conscious as she systematically reduced herself to a quivering mass of hysteria. The noise from the hammers of the stage carpenters were silenced. A "cathedral hush"[50] now blanketed the Hollywood studio.

Bitzer listened for Griffith's instructions:

"Load the camera with plenty of film. I'm going to shoot this scene without stopping, even if it takes all day to shoot it." Then turning to Lillian, he [Griffith] said, "Are you ready?"

Yes, Mr. Griffith was her obedient reply, as she walked into the three-frame closet set.[51]

Outside the perimeter of the *Broken Blossoms* set stood a group of people in total silence: technicians and carpenters, grips, a few actors who somehow had managed to get through the gates. They had seen everything, and now they were waiting for this: Lillian's screams, which would never be recorded. One simply had to be there to hear them.

A journalist witnessing the filming of Lillian's father smashing the door with an ax recorded:

> She [Lillian] pressed her body closer to the wall — hugged it, threw her arms high above her head, dug her fingers into the plaster. A trickle of dust fell beneath her nails. She screamed a high-pitched, terrifying sound, a cry of fear and anguish. Then she turned and faced the camera.[52]

The closet scene became the silent cinema's most famous example of emotional hysteria. Unlike Carol Dempster, who once required six hours of non-stop Griffith direction to induce a few tears, Lillian, the consummate artist, could achieve emotional highs quite easily. Her screams were of such intensity they could be heard on the streets outside the studio.[53]

She told a *Sight and Sound* interviewer:

> I worked that [closet scene] out myself. I never told Griffith what I was going to do. You see, if I had told him, he'd have made me rehearse it over and over again; and that would

have spoilt it. It had to be spontaneous, the hysterical terror of a child. Well, when I came to play the scene in front of the camera, I did it as I planned — spinning and screaming terribly [I was a good screamer; Mr. Griffith used to encourage me to scream at the top of my voice]. When we finished, Mr. Griffith was very pale.[54]

There was silence in the studio.

Mr. Griffith then whispered to Lillian, "My God, why didn't you warn me you were going to do that?"[55]

It remained for Paramount boss Adolph Zukor to see the film.

Donald Crisp, who played Lillian's father, remembered Zukor's reaction to *Broken Blossoms* at a studio screening for the Paramount employees:

> Zukor hated it! He watched the picture with us and said nothing the entire time. Some of us, who had seen the daily rushes and knew what to expect, were still moved to tears, especially in Lillian's closet scene. But Zukor didn't react to anything. He was unmoved, and sat there stone-faced. He hated the whole thing: the story, the innovative photography. He didn't even say a kind word about the *tinting*! Just silence the entire time....
>
> Lillian said Zukor told Griffith the next day in his office, "A little sadness, is okay. But where's the happiness at the end of the picture if this is a love story? This film is a total tragedy! Nobody lives! At the end of this film, everyone is dead! The whole cast! You wasted your time and my money! People won't sit through this! They like to laugh! They like to see a happy picture!"
>
> I think Zukor was afraid of another *Birth of a Nation* problem — the racial thing, but with the Chinese.
>
> When he finished telling Mr. Griffith why he didn't want to release the picture, Mr. Griffith asked if he

could buy the negative. Zukor immediately said yes, and said the price of the negative was $250,000, a price I think had a little profit built into it, if you know what I mean.

Mr. Griffith didn't bat an eyelash, or bother to argue. He quickly got the money — he was able to do that in those days — and paid Mr. Zukor in full right on the spot! He had worked too hard to see his film stay on the shelf.

He handed *Broken Blossoms* over to United Artists, the company he had founded with Mary [Pickford] and Charlie [Chaplin], and it was their first release.

It was a bigger success than anybody could have imagined![56]

Running ninety minutes, *Broken Blossoms* opened at New York's George M. Cohan Theatre on May 13, 1919 as the initial offering of a D. W. Griffith "repertory season"[57] that would include *The Fall of Babylon* and *The Mother and the Law* (which were reassembled sequences from Griffith's less successful *Intolerance*).

The New York premiere, unlike the premieres *Broken Blossoms* would have in other major cities, had an additional staged prologue, a "dance play in one act" titled *The Dance of Life*,[58] which featured the dancing talents of Carol Dempster.

Although *Broken Blossoms* ran shorter than *The Birth of a Nation*, Griffith had no qualms about asking the public to pay three dollars a ticket,[59] one dollar more than the asking price for any of his previous releases.

With the use of pale blue lighting to highlight the Chinese scenes, it was no wonder that the New York newspapers hailed *Broken Blossoms* as a major cinematic achievement. *The Sun* and *The Tribune* called the Griffith and Gish offering, "the most artistic photoplay yet produced" and "the most beautiful motion picture we have ever seen, or expect to see. When it was over, we wanted to rush up to everyone we met and cry, 'Oh don't miss it, don't miss it!'"[60]

Lillian was heralded as "the supreme technician of the screen."[61]

What pleased Griffith, besides the words of praise heaped upon him and Lillian, were the box-office returns. *Broken Blossoms*, which was filmed at a cost of $88,000 and rejected by Adolph Zukor as "not commercial," turned a profit of $700,000![62]

The Master had brought home the bacon!

Broken Blossoms came at the end of the era in which women "protected their ankles with spats or with high-laced walking boots,"[63] milk was priced at fifteen cents a quart,[64] and the New York speed limit was thirty miles an hour.[65] The next decade would change everything, and America would be on the "greatest, gaudiest shopping spree" in recorded time.[66]

Both Lillian and Griffith knew they would have to make an adjustment. Neither had any intention of sitting out the decade until the short skirts were longer and the flappers stopped misbehaving. To continue filming life in rural America was impractical. The "chaste Victorian terrain"[67] no longer had any appeal to the returning soldiers. A quick decision for the sake of both of their careers had to be made.

When Mr. Griffith announced his intentions, Lillian Gish knew she would be out in the cold.

CHAPTER 9

A Reward

Will you see the players well bestowed?
— William Shakespeare
Hamlet (II, ii)

It was time for rewards. At Keystone, studio boss Mack Sennett had been letting players Charlie Chaplin, Mabel Normand, and Roscoe Arbuckle work behind the camera in a directorial capacity, but not for extra money, as they would be receiving their regular salary for acting in front of the camera. Their regular salary, Sennett believed, was large enough. Both Chaplin and Arbuckle soon left Keystone when their directorial efforts weren't met with an increase in salary. Their reason was logical: Sennett could no longer deny them any increase in salary when his "risk-taking" was successful.[1]

Griffith knew Lillian would never leave. After eight years of steady employment, her mother would never allow it, even though she was aware that rival studios would probably offer greater salaries. Where there was Mr. Griffith, there would always be Lillian. Only occasionally did Mrs. Gish warn her daughters to beware of fortune-hunters who might take advantage of them.

Working with Richard Barthelmess was an enjoyable experience. Richard, like Lillian, also had an equally domineering mother next to him on the set almost every day, and Mrs. Barthelmess knew that her son's success would depend on how well he played opposite Mrs. Gish's daughter. And both children knew better than to sacrifice their careers for the sake of an off-camera romance.

Griffith had a problem: how could he and director Elmer Clifton go to Florida without Lillian to film exteriors for his next two pictures, and still keep Lillian busily employed for the months of November and December? In the days when he was an actor on the road, Griffith was never fond of wintertime. Cold, damp weather was always a good reason to film in California as much as possible.

Before he had finished formulating the question, he had the answer: give Lillian a directing job, a job which would not require her to act in front of the camera (unlike Sennett's people). In her eight years of employment, she had voluntarily spent thousands of hours in the editing room, watching how the final product was assembled, learning about the cost of film, how to set up the shots, where to place the camera, and how to give the right blocking to the actors. She would have a budget of $50,000, the choice of material, and of performers.

As predicted, Lillian chose her sister Dorothy. Their film could be made in the unheated Mamaroneck studio.[2]

Lillian, who always felt Dorothy's off-camera antics should be preserved on film, knew not to waste precious time choosing a stage vehicle, which would invite comparisons between Dorothy and the stage actor. Working within a limited budget, and given only two months, she wanted to impress Griffith with her professionalism by minimizing the productions costs and completing the film within the scheduled time.

She Made Him Behave, the working title for Lillian's directing debut, was a cartoon Dorothy found in a humor magazine. A husband, complaining that his wife always wore dowdy clothes, is suddenly amazed when she becomes the center of attention as he follows her down New York's Fifth Avenue.

To help Lillian flesh out this cartoon to five reels,[3] Lillian enlisted the services of Dorothy Parker, then a drama critic for *Vanity Fair* magazine. This film would be Parker's first screen-writing credit.

While Parker formulated a script with witty titles, Lillian visited Griffith's unheated Mamaroneck studio with her mother and sister Dorothy. Without Mr. Griffith there to guide them, Lillian realized that her new assignment was a heavier responsibility than she realized. On Sennett's lot, Sennett was always available for advice. At Mamaroneck, Lillian was working without the security of her mentor's presence.

There was much work to be done before she called "Action!

[I know] nothing at all of practical mechanics, Lillian remembered, "[or the] measurements for a set, and was afraid the company would lose respect for me if they found it out. I went home and paced the floor, measuring the number of feet, to try to get some idea of what I wanted to talk about. As a result, I ordered a room that was too big for the height of it. The camera couldn't get far enough away without shooting over the back wall.

Then the worst developed. Mr. Griffith had bought an engine to transform alternating to direct current, and when we were ready to shoot the picture, we didn't have enough juice for the lights."[4]

When Sunday arrived and forty extras reported at Mamaroneck to shoot the big wedding scene, there were no lights. Lights would not be available until six in the evening...

In the first week of shooting, she would sit by the camera from nine in the morning until eleven at night, directing her actors, ready to meet any sudden emergencies. When the early rushes failed to conceal the breath of the cold actors, the company moved to the smaller Fisher studio in New Rochelle, an easier commute for the Gishes who were rooming at the Hotel Commodore near New York's Grand Central Station.[5]

November was a cold month, with low temperatures and the constant threat of freezing rain and snow. To the Gishes and the other actors making the daily commute to work, the shorter distance of a few miles made little difference. Luckily, there was a working furnace, and the sight of recently arrived actors huddling around the heat, waiting for the shooting day to begin, or trying to warm themselves between takes, was a familiar one. Still, the Fisher studio was damp, and the cellar was always full of water. To generate further additional electricity because of the extra lights, Lillian needed miles of telegraph poles to withstand the strain on the wires.[6]

When the opportunity arose for the company to return to Mamaroneck, Lillian seized it. The moving between New Rochelle and Mamaroneck was made three times. Electricity and heat were a hard combination to get for any sustained amount of time.[7]

Dorothy, to Lillian's surprise, became a problem. She had fallen in love with her leading man, Canadian actor James Rennie, and she wanted to reshoot her love scenes whenever possible. Rennie, a former member of the Royal Flying Corps.,[8] had come to films from the Broadway stage, where he and William Powell had appeared in *Spanish Love* earlier in the season.[9]

Lillian had expected problems on the set, but only technical ones. Loving your leading man had never been a problem. Leading men were only co-workers. Dorothy's relations with Wallace Reid were platonic, and whatever time she had spent away from her sister and mother to be with Robert Harron never interrupted the work schedule. She always reported on time and knew her blocking. Lillian's relationship with Griffith, always a subject of rumors, was on-the-set professional. That Dorothy had fallen in love, in full view of everyone, was quite obvious when she requested that Lillian reshoot their love scenes several times. James Rennie was Dorothy's choice to play opposite her, having selected him from a group of available glossy photographs and accompanying resumes.

Recalled actress Aileen Pringle, a sometimes diner at the Algonquin Hotel, where she would occasionally meet her friend, Dorothy Parker:

> James Rennie liberated Dorothy from a prolonged adolescence both Gish girls had because of their controlling mother. And I say liberated with a long, meaningful wink. Rennie and Dorothy couldn't wait to be with each other, and Mrs. Gish, benevolent ogre that she was, had little she could about it. Dorothy wasn't Lillian, and never would be. What worked on-screen between Rennie

and Dorothy worked off-screen, without director Lillian around to yell "cut."

> It was nothing like the Garbo-Gilbert romance during *Flesh and the Devil* a few years later, [1926] when observers said that director Clarence Brown should hose them down until the next set-up was ready.

> Dotty [Dorothy Parker] used to laugh and say that this was the first time the three Gishes didn't eat together. Dorothy and Rennie used to go for walks. Probably to his dressing room.

> I suppose Lillian might have spoken to her, but I don't think she could have said very much. Dorothy was doing more than handholding, and to deal with this problem you would have to know if this is a problem. Lillian probably found this too confusing.

> She and Griffith were probably handholding too, when they thought nobody was around![10]

Battling terrible weather and moving sets, camera equipment, and a chilly company of actors between New Rochelle and Mamaroneck naturally took its toll on the budget and the shooting schedule. Lillian knew she couldn't possibly bring her film, now retitled *Remodeling Her Husband*, to completion on time. Wisely, she had kept the crew on salary over the Christmas holiday, a welcome remuneration for the extra hours they had worked. Now, during the last day of shooting, she had to take a risk.

One of the final scenes had to be shot in New York, on Fifth Avenue. A double-deckered bus had to pass a taxi cab. The wife sitting on top of the bus would see her husband sitting with another woman in the cab. It was a short scene lasting a brief moment on the screen — but very crucial to the plot.[11]

The scene required a police permit. Without the police permit, no scene. Mr. Griffith never mentioned anything about police permits!

Lillian asked her crew and company if they would take the chance of being carted off to jail for filming on the streets of New York without a police permit.

Everyone nodded in the affirmative. They would take the chance.

Lillian recalled the sequence:

> West 57th Street and Fifth Avenue is the longest section in New York... We had the cameras in the car ahead, and as we turned a policeman saw what was happening, and held up his hand. Then he looked at me, and he looked again, and then he put his fingers to his mouth (the way Lillian did in *Broken Blossoms* to form a V), and forced a smile. I said, "Yes." He waved us on, and we got by.[12]

Remodeling Her Husband was completed during Christmas week for $58,000.[13] While Lillian went over the allotted budget of $50,000, the film was finished before Griffith's arrival from Florida. Everything was "cut and ready."[14] Griffith, viewing the film, told Lillian the first two reels were "as good as anything

he had done." When shown to the public, the Gish-directed production netted a profit of $160,000![15]

When Lillian asked why Griffith neglected to mention all of the technical problems she might encounter, his answer was quite candid:

> Because I needed my studio built quickly, and I knew they'd work faster for a girl than they did for me. I'm no fool.[16]

With the studio Lillian readied for immediate use, Griffith began working on the camera setups for the next two films he was planning to make. His trip to Florida with Elmer Clifton had been successful. Both men seemed healthier, and the exteriors they had photographed were accomplished without any problems. Like Lillian, they had maintained their work schedule.

Aileen Pringle, filming in Florida with newcomer Rudolph Valentine (the change to Valentino would come shortly) in the low-budgeted *Stolen Moments* for the Pioneer Film Corporation, remembered seeing Elmer Clifton and D. W. Griffith dining at a Fort Lauderdale restaurant with a third party — Carol Dempster.[17]

CHAPTER 10

Ice Floes

Griffith couldn't look at an ice floe — unless I were on top of it.
— Lillian Gish
Conversation with author
April 1961

Not every Gish and Griffith collaboration was a happy one. *The Greatest Question* (1919) was a prime example of "the best use of landscape for lyrical and dramatic symbolism" with a "melodramatic and rambling plot" that attempted to cover "too much ground."[1] When questioned about the film in later years, Lillian would simply state it was "hastily made," and "not successful."[2] A quick nod, followed by a short, hard stare at the interviewer was her way of dismissing any further inquiries. The film was privately screened for her in 1964 at the home of Professor William K. Everson, who was not aware that this "lost" Griffith effort would draw such hostility. Lillian's reaction afterwards was, "I don't remember this film at all," a phrase she repeated after a screening of *Sold for Marriage* (1916) at a later occasion. Everson, whose private collection of film was legendary, often ran films for Lillian, who was more interested in preserving Griffith's work for archivists and historians than in agonizing through those early performances she wanted to forget.

The Greatest Question, based on a story by S. E. V. Taylor (another Griffith pseudonym),[3] cast Lillian as a Kentucky maid who, in the employment of a married couple is witness to their murder of a young girl. The film was subtitled, "a story of the strange meandering river of life."[4] Audiences, aware of Griffith's love for Kentucky (which he had utilized effectively in the earlier *A Romance of Happy Valley*), may have been shocked as they viewed Lillian being whipped in the same elegiac setting by employer Josephine Crowell as too much of a resemblance to her whipping by Donald Crisp in another 1919 release, *Broken Blossoms*.[5]

Perhaps Miss Gish's reluctance to discuss *The Greatest Question* was best explained to this author years later by Anita Loos:

> I'll tell you in two words: Carol Dempster. She was always on the set, determined to scratch and claw her way in the employment. Remember: Griffith never signed a contract with anyone. He just kept using the same actors.
>
> At this point in her less than illustrious career Carol Dempster hadn't done that much. Lillian came out of the theatre. Carol had nothing.

Lillian's bout with the flu gave Carol the opportunity to convince Griffith that she, not Lillian, could play the lead in *The Girl Who Stayed at Home*, a film slated for Lillian.

Anyone looking at Carol could have told Griffith to change the title to *The Girl Who Stayed on the Streets*, if you can get my drift. Carol knew how to convince Griffith if he had any doubts. Everywhere he went, she went. Always ready to convince him that she was the right choice. Apparently, she couldn't convince anybody else. It wouldn't have done her any good, because Griffith always made the final decision.

On the first day of shooting, everybody on the set knew Carol Dempster had no talent, certainly not enough to sustain a lead. Nobody spoke to her unless it was absolutely necessary.

That picture, like all of her pictures, was not a success, but Griffith kept employing her. When Lillian and Griffith made *The Greatest Question*, Carol, who had no part in the picture, was right there on the set. Maybe she was trying to convince Griffith to ignore the bad reviews, [that] a Western they made [*Scarlet Days*] got.

We used to say that Lillian never asked The Greatest Question, which should have been, "Who is this Carol Dempster, what is she doing on this set, and where are we going?"

Maybe Lillian was afraid of what Griffith would answer. Lillian had two great fears: being abandoned the way her mother was, and being out of work. Lillian had come to believe that work, ultimately, was more important than love. You could always fall in love. Actresses did that all the time ... and still do![6]

Lillian wasn't particularly enthusiastic when Griffith told her he had spent $175,000 to acquire the motion picture rights from theatrical producer William Brady to film Lottie Blair Parker's stage success, *Way Down East*, a popular touring favorite with America's heartland audiences since its first production in 1897.[7] The story of Anna, a New England country girl tricked into a false marriage to a city playboy (who abandons her right after she tells him she is pregnant), was right out of the pages of the penny dreadfuls. The abandoned country girl delivers her baby alone in a cheap rooming house and baptizes the baby minutes before the baby dies. Thrown out by an unfeeling landlady, she finds employment on a farm next to the home where her seducer lives! A gossiping spinster, hearing of the background of the new employee, causes her to be thrown out a second time.

Lillian, aware that her friend, playwright Eugene O'Neill, had just won a Pulitzer Prize for his first Broadway play, *Beyond the Horizon*, viewed the earlier Parker play as "horse and buggy"[8] melodrama. It would be greeted with guffaws by more sophisticated audiences as an attempt to "make a grand opera out of *The Old Oaken Bucket*.[9]

And yet she knew there was good reasoning behind Griffith's wish to film an old-fashioned melodrama:

> Films were visual, unlike the theatre which depended on words.
>
> Griffith didn't succeed in the theatre as a playwright or an actor because he couldn't take the constant insecurity. In wanting to film a stage play, he would be bringing the kind of theatre he best understood to the screen on his terms. Even though it was a very dated play, he saw something that would make this play work on film. It had to be a visual effect, something that would register strongly on film. And I soon learned what it was, and it all made sense."[10]

After Anna's banishment from the farm, she would wander aimlessly into a blizzard — a blizzard that would blind her and cause her to step onto a large mass of

As Anna Moore attempting to escape disgrace in D. W. Griffith's 1920 *Way Down East*. The ice floe is just ahead!

floating ice on a frozen river, whose current would take her to a waterfall. For that single dramatic effect, he had purchased *Way Down East*!

Now Lillian would be a "frail floating heroine,"[11] a portrait of "idealized femininity"[12] thrust into a situation fraught with danger…

In contrast to heroic Richard Barthlemess' valiant attempts to save Lillian as the slab of ice on which she is barely conscious floats toward the waterfall, Griffith planned to capture his rhapsodic love of nature in the manner he had done with Lillian in *Romance of Happy Valley* and *True Heart Susie*, released the previous year (1919). Barthelmess, who had scored a critical and popular success opposite Lillian in *Broken Blossoms* (1920), once again would be fighting for her love. This time, he would be valiantly leaping from ice floe to ice floe.

For this sustained dramatic sequence, Griffith would risk a considerable amount of money, his reputation, and the lives of Richard Barthelmess and Lillian Gish.

Before rehearsals began, Lillian knew *Way Down East*, more than any earlier film she had made for Griffith, would be an endurance test. Her body would be subjected to freezing and below freezing temperatures. She would have to be in peak physical condition to withstand snow, ice, and frost, in addition to being able to maintain her balance on the ice floes. As the action required, she would even have to give the impression of sleeping on the ice floe as the current carried her to the waterfall. This was going to be an outdoor production with plenty of close-ups. Nothing could be faked. Audiences were too aware of tricks. The blizzard would have to be a real blizzard.[13]

Lillian's mother, always on the scene

when Lillian was working, now had to assist with the grueling preparations.

> Mother would fill the Claridge Hotel bathtub with buckets and buckets of ice everyday, and then run cold water into the tub until it was filled almost to the top. Only my head would be above the water. My entire body had to be immersed. She did this early in the morning when I was barely awake.
>
> Without pausing on my way to the bathroom, I made a direct line to the bathtub and sat down. I couldn't do it gradually, because you don't gradually run away from adverse weather conditions. You do your best to get away quickly. I used the same reasoning when I quickly sat in the tub. The whole entire body had to realize what was happening, not only my feet.
>
> When I did this the first time, the windows were closed. I think I lasted a minute before I had to jump out, wrap myself in a towel, and shakily hold the hot cup of tea mother had waiting for me. I don't remember what shook more — that teacup or my body, or my teeth! I had to put the cup down on the sink and hug myself, only to see if my blood was still flowing.
>
> Mother, who was quite alarmed, suggested that I stop, rest, and wait for the water to warm. I had to explain to her that waiting for the water to warm wouldn't make conditions any easier when we had to work in the blizzard. This film needed a real blizzard, not any passing snowstorm. We had to be able to act in a real blizzard. Audiences want to see a real blizzard, not a sub-title with a two sentence description. If this film was going to work, the audiences wanted to see the real thing. Otherwise, whatever we did would be laughable...
>
> I sat down in the tub again and, by clutching my hands together, managed to remain that way for thirty or so seconds longer than the first time. I was still shaking when I got out, but

> I now knew what to expect. It would only take a few more tries before I would be able to stay in the tub for five minutes.
>
> Mother returned with another bucket of ice to replace what had somehow melted. She opened the bathroom window. Outside, there was snow starting to fall, and I could feel the lower temperature. Now that I had been exposed to the ice, a little snow wouldn't affect me that much. Cold is cold, and would be colder when we would be working outside in the cold.
>
> I braced myself, and sat down in the tub again.[14]

Being able to withstand cold water and ice cubes was only the beginning of what she would be facing when filming began. In order to prepare for the ordeal, she also had to follow a program of specific exercises and maintain a proper diet.

In the days to follow, the sight of Lillian standing outside in the rain or snow — minus a coat — was a familiar one. She would run around the block (without a coat) in the hour before dawn, her mother several paces behind her. By the time the late night party-goers thought they recognized the passing runner, it was too late, and their questions had gone away as quickly as they came.[15]

Ice cubes in cold bathtubs, windows fully opened to the snow and rain, exercises, running around the block at impossible hours — it was part of the life she had chosen. Jokingly, she would remind her mother of the early days when she and Dorothy and Bobby Harron were extras employed for one summer day as congregants standing outside a church at the conclusion of the morning service in *The New York Hat* (1912). For their work, each received five dollars ... and a box-lunch!

Eight years later (in 1920), Lillian would still be working outside. The salary was much higher, and the temperature

As Anna Moore in *Way Down East* (1920, United Artists, directed by D. W. Griffith). No amount of rehearsal time could have prepared her for the reality: a snowstorm and a ninety-mile-an-hour gale.

much lower. Bobby hadn't worked in over a year. His last picture with Lillian was *True Heart Susie* (1919). There being no sign of future employment, he naturally stayed away.

In the beginning, there were constant visits. Everyone was working, and the Griffith lot fostered a family feeling. But things changed, and the camaraderie so evident in the quickly-made one- and two-reelers lessened with the increase of features. Lillian's work demands were more strenuous. She was spending more time with Mr. Griffith at the end of the day, watching footage and learning how to improve her editing skills.

Dorothy, who was never as actively employed as her sister, was spending more and more time with James Rennie, her leading man from *Remodeling Her Husband*, which Lillian had directed so successfully.

Time had not been kind to Bobby. Lillian and Dorothy were leading ladies. Bobby was still a nice boy.

When Lillian, at the insistence of Mr. Griffith, was examined by his insurance brokers and given a perfect bill of health, he was satisfied. She only had to take care of herself ... and be in the same good health for the blizzard.

To offset the costs of the costumes for the society ball at the home of Anna's relatives, Griffith wisely asked socialite Mrs.

Morgan Belmont of New York's "400" set if she wished to have a small role in the production. Of course, Mrs. Morgan Belmont accepted, and her presence lent an air of prestige and authenticity[16] (as well as providing an "in" to wealthy people who could easily invest in future productions).

Other ladies attending this party, at which Anna will have her first meeting with the scoundrel who will successfully woo her to Schubert's *Serenade* (coming from a phonograph skillfully concealed near the sofa), were played by models from Lucille's of New York, and Follies girls. Four years earlier (in 1916), Follies girls had appeared with Lillian in *Diane of the Follies*.

Lillian's choice of prim and prissy clothing for her initial entrance at the party was deliberate, a conscious attempt not to blend with her new, finer surroundings. Her city cousins, shocked at her appearance, immediately whisk her upstairs and clothe her in a gown designed by Henri Bendel. That she emerges as much better dressed than any one of the attendees is only natural. She is the prettiest lady there — and the most vulnerable.

On March 6, 1920, the blizzard arrived.[17] With it came a "snowstorm" and a "ninety mile an hour gale." Lillian, who had trained herself for this moment, was not that eager to battle the elements and be filmed. No amount of rehearsal time could have totally prepared her for the actuality.[18]

Now it was here, right out of a Jack London story. The Yukon had come to Mamaroneck, New York. Long Island Sound was "frozen over," and eight foot drifts all but camouflaged Griffith's studio.[19]

The waiting was over. The moment of truth had arrived in full blast. Nobody in the company was really ready for what was going to happen.

What was of paramount importance to cameramen Billy Bitzer and Hendrick Sartov, and the *Way Down East* troupe, was

the unspoken question: could this blizzard be filmed, and would it look real on the screen?

At her temporary residence on Orienta Point (once the home of architect Stanford White), Lillian and her mother readied themselves for work. Underneath their heavy coats were layers of clothing. They could barely walk. Getting to the studio car would be as dangerous as trying to stand on the ice.[20]

The studio car had trouble staying on the road. It was too early to hope for any help. Anyone with common sense would have stayed inside until the storm ceased.

Neither Lillian nor her mother could make that luxurious decision to sit at the window and watch like little children. Studio time was money. Nobody could predict how long this blizzard would last, or if there would be additional snow to compensate for what Billy Bitzer's camera failed to capture.

To Lillian, a veteran of the road since her infancy (when she, her mother, and Dorothy had to crisscross the country in trains and busses, hoping to get to the town on time for the evening's performance in *Her First False Step* and *East Lynne*), this was like an unexpected return to childhood! How many actors could do that?

Lillian's mother, who would rise early with Lillian and repeat the same process for a week until the troupe would go to White River Junction in Vermont for the ice sequences, wasn't as enthusiastic as her energetic daughter.

Filming in the bitter cold wasn't easy. Often Billy Bitzer had to turn his cameras away from the force of the constant gusts of wind. Lillian didn't have this privilege. Either she stood alone, or had somebody from the crew pull her on a sled to a hastily assembled shelter that was little more than a shed with available blankets, hot tea, and a fire coming from an oil drum. A cot was available for Lillian until the shooting could resume.

For the baptism of the newborn baby, Griffith selected a warm corner of the living room in the Henry M. Flagler mansion that served as the Mamaroneck studio. Flagler, a railroad magnate, had gone to Florida for the winter. Although the mansion was more than adequately heated, the crew had to throw blankets over the cameras.

Hanging from Lillian's eyelashes were small icicles which formed when she remained unprotected outside for too long a duration. Often her face was covered with snow. On such occasions, in an effort to save precious time, Griffith instructed cameramen Bitzer and Sartov to take as many close-ups as possible for future use.

Out of the range of Griffith's hearing, Lillian and Bitzer would remark that the presence of Bobby Harron would do much to lessen the tension brought about by the weather. The working days and nights would have been livelier. His last "big" role had been in *Hearts of the World* two years earlier (1918).[21] True, Griffith had used him in the succeeding *True Heart Susie* and *The Greatest Question*, but the former was really a programmer, and the latter a failure.

Richard Barthelmess, the son of an actress, was only a year younger than Bobby, but he was more sophisticated. He had a "suave" quality that Griffith felt stood him well in his first film, *The Girl Who Stayed at Home* (1919). That he could make an effective transition in his portrayal of a Chinese curio shop owner in love with Lillian in *Broken Blossoms* justified Griffith's reasoning in uniting him with Lillian again. In more perilous circumstances their screen chemistry would be stronger.[22]

Although Lillian, in later years, sometimes liked to convey the impression that the famous rescue from the ice floe was accomplished in one continuous take, it was filmed in sections.

Writer Edwin Wagenknecht has documented the various locations utilized for this often exhibited section of celluloid. The blizzard was filmed in March 1920 at Orienta Point, New York. The ice scenes were filmed at White River Junction, Vermont. The falls that are shown for a brief moment are the Niagara Falls.

With skillful cutting and editing, Griffith made Richard Barthelmess's rescue of Lillian Gish an eternal classic.[23]

Lillian thought she would add to the intensity of the scene if she allowed her hair and hand to trail in the water heading toward the falls. It was a suggestion that Griffith quickly accepted, a suggestion that increased her chances of getting pneumonia. For the rest of her life, she would suffer from the aftereffects of frostbite.

Asked to explain why she subjected herself to dangerous, life-threatening situations, Lillian's answer was one word: dedication. If one accepted and believed in Mr. Griffith's commitment to the picture, "no sacrifice was too great to get it right, to get it accurate, true, and perfect."[24]

Richard Barthelmess, recalling *Way Down East*, was less enthusiastic:

> Not once, but twenty times a day (for the two weeks of shooting the ice floe sequence), Lillian floated down on a cake of ice, and I made my way to her, stepping from one ice cake to another. I had on a heavy fur coat, and if I slipped, or if one of the cakes cracked and let me through, my chances would not have been good...
>
> I would not make that picture again for any money that a producer would be willing to pay for it.[25]

Way Down East had its New York premiere at the 44th Street on September 3, 1920. Opening night tickets were a record-high ten dollars, a price Griffith felt justified the prestige of the picture that was

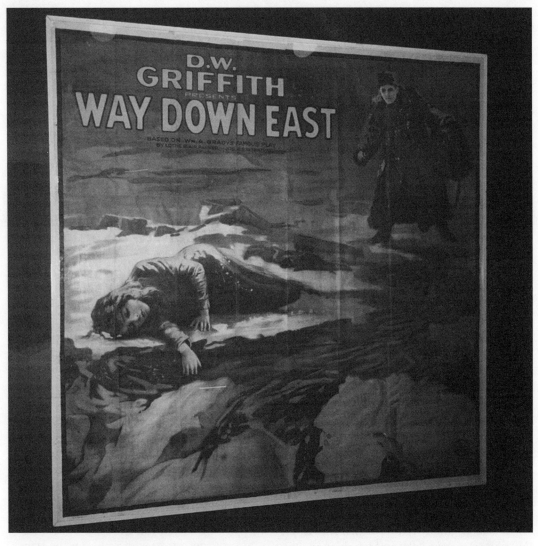

The original poster for D. W. Griffith's successful *Way Down East* (1920). Note Lillian on the ice floe and Richard Barthelmess's attempt to rescue her.

thirteen reels long. While critic Alexander Woolcott, in an unsigned review appearing in the following morning's *New York Times*, complained that Griffith "selected the picture ... not for it's fame ... it's heroine ... or for the wrong done her," but "for the snowstorm," he could not deny the impact the thirteen-reeler had on the first-nighters who rose to their feet and cheered loudly at the conclusion of the rescue of Lillian Gish. "Any audience would have cheered it, and all audiences will."[26]

Robert Benchley's more cynical review for the September 22nd issue of *Life* was more scathing:

> The whole problem of the drama ... is whether or not Anna [Lillian Gish] was it. A straw vote shows an overwhelming sentiment in the negative. Number of votes cast, one. Number in favor of saving Anna, one. Number in favor of letting her ride over the falls, one.[27]

Edward Wagenknecht, praising the thrilling scenes of the last reel, criticized the demands Griffith made on Gish and Barthelmess:

> No director has the right to ask... what Griffith asked, and no film can be worth such risk and suffering.[28]

Examining *Way Down East* in the 1970s from a feminist point of view, critic Marjorie Rosen saw the production as filled with "hackneyed Victorian ideals," and labeled it a sermon against the female transgressions of a woman whose bearing of an illegitimate child was justification to punish her for her sexuality."[29]

At a Metropolitan Opera Guild luncheon, Lillian Gish could not understand the application of contemporary mores when viewing the plight of a barely educated, unemancipated young country girl trying to survive in a man's world of 1879. One cannot cavalierly dismiss the importance of women's lives because they had the misfortune not to be living on the Upper East Side of New York in our enlightened twentieth century!

Way Down East played to capacity houses in New York for over a year when it was originally released. Griffith's intention to make a "plain old-fashioned story for plain everyday human beings" succeeded.[30]

Lillian's performance as Anna Moore, the girl on the ice floe, was reviewed in *Photoplay* magazine by critic Burns Mantle and was considered "thoroughly competent."[31]

The Perils of Pauline serial director Donald Mackenzie (who also appeared in the 1914 film as Blinky Bill, "the terror of the Seven Seas"[32]), fully understood Griffith's logic in wanting to film the popular melodrama for the sake of inserting a thrilling ice floe sequence.

In 1970, at a fiftieth anniversary showing of *Way Down East* at a New Jersey film society, Mackenzie remembered the impact of Griffith's thirteen-reeler, watching it with the opening night audience at the 44th Street theatre:

> It's very easy for younger viewers and film historians watching *Way Down East* nowadays to assume a condescending attitude when they watch these filmed melodramas.
>
> You have to remember that Griffith, and a lot of us in those old days, were fugitives from the theatre. There wasn't enough work to keep us going, and we got tired of living out of a suitcase which we unpacked and then packed sometimes every day, depending on the bookings. So we went into the making of motion pictures, which didn't have and will never have the prestige given "live" theatre. But we had to survive, and hope that one day we would return to the theatre. Some returned, and most didn't — once we got a steady paycheck.
>
> When Griffith made *The Adventures of Dollie* (1908), those of us in the business knew he was using a prop eagle to carry that baby. On film, it worked! You forgot it was a prop eagle, because you were caught up in the action, and those audiences believed that bird was real! You couldn't achieve that effect on the stage, because on the stage everything is smaller, depending on your seat in the theatre, where you only have one point of view. On film, everything looked bigger.
>
> If you were present in the first or second row in those nickelodeons when they originally ran *The Great Train Robbery* in 1903, I guarantee you would have jumped out of your seat when that train came charging at you or when Bronco Billy Anderson, at the end of the film, aimed his pistol at the camera and fired.
>
> Griffith knew the power of the camera, and he knew how to tell the story visually.

Some of those sequences in *Way Down East* are laughable, and they were laughable and they were just as funny when the film was originally shown: the old maid and the country bumpkin were stock characters you always saw on the stage. That opening night audience laughed and laughed — until Lillian was on the ice! And then the laughter suddenly stopped!

In Lillian's films, all of her audiences always rooted for her. She was a professional waif, and she always played that little match girl for Griffith in all kinds of situations. Audiences knew to expect something to happen to her. And Griffith knew it when he bought the rights to *Way Down East*!

He was no fool. Lillian had never been put on the ice! She could have frozen, she could have drowned. You could see her hand in the cold water. You could see her hair in the water. You can't fake that!

Nobody knew if [Richard] Barthelmess, with those daring leaps from ice slab to ice slab, would rescue her from the falls. Pure melodrama! Melodrama at its best.

Griffith knew *Way Down East* would work as a film because it had all of the elements of a good story.

Lillian Gish was the perfect choice for the heroine, and Griffith knew how to keep those audiences sitting at the edge of their seats until she was saved from going over the falls.

The cheers on that opening night were deafening. And I was told every audience had the same reaction: they loved Lillian, and they loved the film.

When you can involve an audience like that, and be able to get almost the same reaction fifty years later, that is master movie-making![33]

The general excitement of the opening night of *Way Down East* was somewhat dampened by the events of the previous evening. While Lillian and her mother were readying themselves for the premiere, Robert Harron, alone in a hotel room near the theatre, died unexpectedly. Whether the self-inflicted gunshots were intentional or accidental, one can only speculate. He had been despondent since the roles he wanted in *Broken Blossoms* and *Way Down East* were given — without any explanation — to Richard Barthelmess, a newcomer. He was painfully aware that Dorothy's increasing involvement with James Rennie was serious and not the "childlike"[34] friendship he had with her. If he had any intentions of proposing marriage, he never voiced them.

Anita Loos, more astute than Lillian in recognizing what Lillian always failed to acknowledge, always called Bobby and Dorothy "pals," not unlike Booth Tarkington's pre-adolescent boys Penrod and Sam, or Mark Twain's equally famous Huck Finn and Tom Sawyer. With Bobby, Dorothy had always been the tomboy. The more experienced James Rennie knew twenty-two-year-old Dorothy was more than that.

Dorothy had matured into a young lady right before Bobby's eyes, but he didn't know what to do about it.

Or maybe he was afraid.[35]

To Billy Bitzer (who was working at Biograph in 1907 — the year that twelve-year-old Bobby applied for an after-school job as a prop boy), Bobby's death marked "the end of an era." Bobby was a "thread of unity." Now that the thread was broken, things would no longer be the same.[36]

The reception given to Lillian and Griffith after the London premiere was wilder than the American one, confirming the opinion that Griffith's latest film would be a greater moneymaker than *The Birth of a Nation*.

After the usual round of parties, the three Gishes returned to their suite at the

Ritz Hotel. Dorothy, dressed like a "flapper in waiting," and wanting to find another party, was depressed James Rennie wasn't with them. She would always be the good-time girl.[37]

Lillian was quite the opposite (as usual), pensive and wondering about her next film assignment. She pondered what her mother thought of the entire evening, particularly what she thought of her film performance. Did she like it a second time?

Mrs. Gish's answer was predictable. "Well, my dear, you're going to have to work hard to keep up a performance like this."

It was a typical response Lillian had come to expect. She wasn't a little girl anymore. First her mother would praise her; then she would warn her. She would never allow her daughter to get "pig-headed."[38]

Mr. Griffith was going to resume work on a new film the moment everyone had returned to America. Using a new pseudonym, Roy Sinclair, he would combine two stories from Thomas Burke's *Limehouse Nights*, the collection from which he chose *The Chink and the Child* to fashion into the successful *Broken Blossoms* the previous year (1919).

He already had a working title for the new film: *Dream Street*.

It would be a wonderful vehicle for Carol Dempster.

CHAPTER 11

Storms and Partings

Do you know that I am leaving Mr. Griffith? *Way Down East*, that we are on, will be my last. I go with the Frohman Amusement Company, between the first and 15th of August. I am to make five pictures a year for two years. If I make successful pictures, I shall make a lot of money. If I don't well, kismet — it's all a gamble anyway.

— Lillian Gish
Letter to Nell Dorr
June 1, 1920[1]

Aware of the continuing popularity of fellow Biograph player Mary Pickford, and the increasing screen presence of Gloria Swanson, Viola Dana, and the vampy European import, Pola Negri, Lillian believed her screen career was finished. More important than worrying about Carol Dempster was her need to be in front of the camera, to be accepted and loved by the audiences she and her sister Dorothy had been developing on the stage during her barnstorming in 10–20–30 melodramas at the start of the century, and on the screens in one-reelers in nickelodeon parlors across the country. The motion picture performance could be preserved. It was eternal and always available for all to see. Its impact could never be calculated.

When her sister Dorothy suddenly married James Rennie on September 26, 1920, Lillian was taken complete unawares.[2] Dorothy had done the unthinkable: she had walked out on her sister and her mother!

Dorothy Gish's friend, actor's agent Alan Brock, who was responsible for as-sembling summer theatre touring packages of plays with star players, recalled what Dorothy had told him in the 1940s about her decision to marry:

> Dorothy's marriage to Jim Rennie was done on a dare. She was always the rebel of the two sisters, always partying, always staying out late for a good time, yet somehow managing to always be on time for rehearsals, or the show, and not looking the worse for it.
>
> Dorothy wasn't in the John Barrymore league, but she liked to raise a glass or two or three when her sister and her mother weren't around. Dorothy was a drinker, and so was Jim Rennie. They both liked to drink.
>
> She and Jim and their pals Connie [Constance Talmadge] and John Pialoglou were having a grand night on the town; dinner and dancing and drinking. Prohibition had already been on the books [July 1, 1919], but it would never matter to people in the entertainment business. They made their own rules!

Both Connie and Dorothy had very domineering mothers who used their daughters as meal tickets. Dorothy was never the meal ticket that Lillian was, but she contributed the same amount of money for their mother's upkeep.

Dorothy openly resented it. Lillian didn't. Dorothy always had dates and boyfriends. Lillian didn't. Lillian was always on hand to take care of Mrs. Gish every time she got sick.

And she always got sick when she thought Lillian's friendships with men were taking a turn for the serious. She would say something, and Lillian would stop seeing him, whoever he was. Robert Harron, Richard Barthelmess, and others.

Lillian would always defer to her mother. Whenever a man liked her too much, she would ask her mother what she thought of him, and the answer was always the same: "No!"

Dorothy told me she once said to Lillian, "Don't you see what she's doing to you? Don't you see the same pattern over and over again? She's not sick! There's nothing wrong with her! She's killing your chances!"

But Lillian always believed what her mother told her. "Didn't mother sacrifice everything for us?"

What did our mother give up?" Dorothy would ask me. "What did she give up? Demonstrating vacuum cleaners in a Brooklyn department store?"

Only Mr. Griffith was Lillian's steady beau. True, he was married, but that placed the kind of controllable Mrs. Gish could understand. It was a relationship that could go nowhere. She was under contract to him, you get the idea....

Dorothy would have broken away sooner or later.

A few good drinks that night. Good food, good company. Why not get married? Dorothy dared Connie. Connie dared Dorothy. John dared Jim. Jim dared John. A crazy idea? This was the twenties, and eloping was the most daring thing you could do. You thought it would keep the party going.[3]

With Dorothy married to James Rennie, and Lillian frustrated and helpless in the wake of Griffith's continuing relationship with Carol Dempster, the Gish sisters, for the first time in their professional and personal lives, seemed to be moving in different directions.

Neither *The Idol Dancer* nor *The Love Flower* nor *Dream Street*, vehicles purposely tailored for Carol Dempster in 1920 and 1921, did anything to increase Carol's following. Nor did they make anyone believe that the younger Carol had — or would ever have — the talent and ability to rival Lillian Gish. Newspaper critics praising Griffith for his lyricism, atmosphere, and brilliant photography, dismissed Carol's acting as a continuing poor attempt to become another fluttering heroine. In *Dream Street*, whose exterior were filmed in Florida while Lillian directed Dorothy in Mamaroneck, not only was Carol miscast but she completely lacked any screen charm!

The mounting negative criticism of Carol Dempster meant nothing to Griffith, who stubbornly insisted his newest discovery had genuine star quality, and would often squire her around New York to the fanciest restaurants.

To those who knew him from his Biograph days when he was fawning over every pubescent teenaged girl who came off the streets asking for a job in "the pictures," this constant attention given to a "no-talent dolly" had everyone mystified.

Anita Loos, present from Griffith's Biograph beginnings, remarked:

> Here, right in front of him, was Lillian Gish, who had given him almost ten years, to be tossed aside for someone he thought he could make into another Lillian Gish!

Why would he want another Lillian Gish, when the real one was still available?[4]

Rumors that Lillian was going to Germany to play the role of Marguerite to Emil Jannings's Faust in a production directed by F. W. Murnau went no further than the early meeting stage. While Murnau considered her a possibility, he would have to have the film made at his studio and not Griffith's. Fellow German director Ernest Lubitsch saw little merit in the Griffith-dominated Gishean school of acting, describing her performances as a "veritable paroxysm of blinks."[5]

Allan Dwan, who had joined Griffith at Triangle in 1915 and had "helped with the camera movements" during the shooting of *Intolerance*[6] (and had gone on to direct five Douglas Fairbanks and two Marion Davies films at the dawn of the twenties), told this biographer that

> Griffith was trapped in his own mythology. He had very fixed ideas. Those of us who worked with him learned the basic craft of moviemaking.
>
> Lillian used to call him "the father of film," and he was, but he wasn't able to keep up with his children. He adored Charles Dickens, and Dickens will always be wonderful, but Dickens lived in another century, not ours.[7]

While filming *Way Down East*, Griffith was approached by a delegation of Russians with an offer from Vladmir Lenin. Lenin, after viewing the modern story portion of *Intolerance*, was convinced Griffith was a Communist by the manner in which he depicted the conflict between capital and labor.[8] Since Griffith had made propaganda films for the Americans (*The Birth of a Nation*, 1915) and the British (*Hearts of the World*, 1918), why not make a propaganda film for the Russians which would glorify the Russian Revolution?[9]

Griffith refused the offer, not telling the real reason: that he didn't want to make only propaganda films that would only preach the Communist party line. Were he to go to Moscow, he would want to make regular features, not picturizations of leftist political tracts. Until something inspired him to make motion pictures of the dimension of *The Birth of a Nation* or *Hearts of the World*, he would live on the profits of *Way Down East*[10] and try to develop projects for Carol Dempster.

Lillian, believing that there were no further projects with Griffith, listened to Albert Grey, Griffith's brother and general manager, about the possibilities of making five features for the Frohman Amusement Company. Although she had never heard of the Frohman Amusement Company, the name "Frohman" was a highly prestigious name in the theatre. The new studio, she reasoned, must be under the sponsorship of a family relative.[11]

She accepted this new proposal and signed their contract. She then recruited a small company of Griffith players, who also signed Frohman contracts, to film *World Shadows*, the first of the five planned features. It was understood that since the former Griffith players were now Lillian's players, she would assume the financial responsibilities of paying their salaries. It was a company within a company, much as Lillian's arrangement with Griffith had been under the Biograph banner.

The scriptwriter was Madame de Gresac, the god-daughter of playwright Victorien Sardou,[12] whose career dated back to the Charles Frohman company in New York in the last 1870s.[13] Sardou had written *La Tosca*, a successful vehicle for Sarah Bernhardt. *La Tosca* later achieved greater acclaim as an opera (*Tosca*) with music by Giacomo Puccini.[14] Madame de Gresac's husband was Victor Maurel of the Metropolitan Opera. Maurel had introduced Giuseppe Verdi's *Falstaff*.

Lillian couldn't have found greater allies. They complemented each other: the worldly and uninhibited de Gresac and the innocent and pure-of-heart Lillian.[15] It was the perfect mating of the sybarite and the cenobite.

Madame de Gresac fashioned a script, and the company immediately started rehearsals. The promised salaries did not come immediately, however, Lillian assumed the responsibility, as promised, and hoped she would be reimbursed within a reasonable length of time.

The only check she received from the Frohman Amusement Company bounced. The bank where she deposited the check informed her that there were no funds to cover it. No Frohman Amusement Company ever existed!

Lillian, in signing the Frohman contract, had automatically removed herself from Griffith's payroll.[16] Whether this was D. W. Griffith's wish, or his manager-brother Albert Grey's wish, was never learned. Certainly Lillian was too horrified to think that someone who had been a father figure, mentor, companion, and employer would dismiss her so casually.

She was stunned. She was professionally and personally humiliated. Was this promise of continued employment at a bogus studio part of an elaborate scheme to calm her growing insecurity as the presence of Carol Dempster in D. W. Griffith's life grew more domineering? If so, at whose instigation?

Not since her early days of touring on the road with her sister in stock companies — whose producers sometimes ran off with the night's receipt — had she felt so helpless or been so shabbily treated.

Was her mother right again? Was she, like her mother, always going to be a victim of men she trusted?

Seeing her plight, Victor Maurel (who had been enthralled with Lillian's performance in *Way Down East*), made her an offer: Would Lillian be his model and pose for him while he put her beauty on canvas? In exchange for thirty minutes of posing she would receive thirty minutes of vocal training. Should she ever think of returning to the stage, she would want the audience in the last rows of the orchestra and those in the uppermost reaches of the balcony to be able to "hear her consonants,"[17]

To study voice with a member of the Metropolitan Opera was a privilege given to very few. An artist of Maurel's status never took students.

Lillian pondered the offer. Of what benefit could Maurel be to somebody whose acting career (at this time) didn't rely on a voice? She was a pantomimist, not a stage actress.[18]

Yet...

Lillian began her singing lessons. Recitatives and arias: she would learn them all, just to get those consonants right.

Depending on who was doing the speaking, both Lillian and Griffith would lay claim to being responsible for bringing Adolphe D'Enery and Eugene Cormon's stage success of 1874, *The Two Orphans*, to the screen as *Orphans of the Storm*, the last film in which Dorothy and Lillian would appear together for the man who first put them in front of the cameras in the 1912 one-reeler, *An Unseen Enemy*. *Orphans* was their 62nd film.

For Lillian and Griffith, it was a logical choice. Griffith was long familiar with the French Revolution and Charles Dickens' *A Tale of Two Cities*. *Orphans of the Storm*, like the Dickens classic, was "a mixture of high life and low, of virtue and dastardly, of tears without laughter." Kate Claxton, who played the blind orphan Louise, toured the United States in various productions of *The Two Orphans* for twenty years.[19]

Lillian was prepared to accept the fact that her relationship with Griffith could never be as it once was. It was an undeniable reality. Still, she saw no reason to sacrifice a working, successful professional team. Her future in front of the cameras would depend on her ability to choose roles of classic types within the range of her special talent. Her genius would sustain itself in her ability to bring to life heroines of an earlier generation. A role like Henriette Girard was meant for her to play. And she was prepared to fight for it.

She presented her ideas to Mr. Griffith very professionally, not neglecting to add that she and Dorothy were the right two sisters to cast as the two sisters in *Orphans of the Storm*.

At the Mamaroneck studio, fourteen acres of land were set aside for the construction of Paris at the end of the 18th century. Replicas would be built of Versailles, the Bastille, and Notre Dame. Griffith wanted a look of total authenticity for this, his first spectacle since the 1915 *Intolerance*. (Critics of the day may have carped at some of the production's aesthetics, but few could deny the awesome visual power of the Babylonian sequences.)

Cecil B. DeMille, whose *The Ten Commandments* would be released the following year (1923) and go beyond his studio's projected million dollar budget,[20] was boundless in his enthusiasm for his mentor, Griffith. At a time when directors believed the drug and/or sex scandals involving Olive Thomas, Roscoe "Fatty" Arbuckle, Mabel Normand, Barbara LaMarr, and William Desmond Taylor would be the downfall of the motion picture, D. W. Griffith and Cecil B. DeMille were taking risks, spending tremendous sums of money in an effort to lure the dwindling audiences back to the movie theatres. Both men were masters of the spectacle, and knew that audiences would want to see motion pictures at their best: lots of action with lots of people on a well-filled screen.[21]

In Griffith's *Orphans of the Storm*, two sisters, Henriette (Lillian) and blind Louise (Dorothy), are on their way to Paris to find an eye doctor with a cure. Henriette is abducted by a marquis, and blind Louise is seized and held by a beggar/woman.

The film is pure excitement and spectacle: an attempted rape, mob scenes, duels and chases, and a thrilling last-minute-just-in-the-nick-of-time rescue of Lillian on the scaffold and ready to be guillotined (when Pierre, a peasant, suddenly rushes up and stabs the executioner in the back). Of course, blind Louise regains her sight, too.

Despite the film resembling a "twin *Perils of Pauline*," it is a "wonderfully sentimental piece of tripe," which derives much of its strength from having two sisters play two devoted sisters.[22]

To prepare for her role — and justify the $1,000 a week she was earning (her largest salary under the Griffith contract)[23] — Lillian researched her character with more concentration than she had ever utilized in any of her previous films. What did Henriette (Lillian's character) wear? What type of food would she eat? Where did she go on holidays? What were her favorite colors?[24]

On the set, Thomas Carlyle's *History of the French Revolution* was a hand's reach away for consultation. If Dickens wrote *A Tale of Two Cities* with Carlyle, Griffith would film *Orphans of the Storm* with Carlyle. Not since he had filmed *Judith of Bethulia* (1914), utilizing the *Book of Judith* from the *Old Testament*, would he have such fidelity to the original material![25]

Orphans of the Storm thrust Lillian's persona of virginity and innocence into the most calamitous of circumstances. The Griffith "symbol of feminine daintiness"[26] who was trapped in a small room in her first film, *An Unseen Enemy* (1912), was

With sister Dorothy in D. W. Griffith's *Orphans of the Storm* (1922). Dorothy plays the blind sister. "Dorothy is the *better* actress," Lillian always said.

now finding herself, ten years and sixty-two films later, still trapped. This time, she was "strapped to the guillotine!"[27]

Has there been any tribulation in the Griffith-Gish melodramatic canon that hasn't threatened Lillian? *Orphans of the Storm* was a return to the romance, drama, and spectacular thrills that audiences loved. The film had no innovations. It was just solid moviemaking, as if Lillian and Dorothy and Mr. Griffith were saying, "Let's give it to them one more time and show them what we can do!"[28]

Trusting her sense of period, Griffith allowed Lillian to design the costumes she and Dorothy would wear.[29] She had always made suggestions about her wardrobe, and Griffith saw no reason to reject any of her suggestions.

His rehearsal period remained the

same. He would rehearse with anyone available in any kind of space. He instantly created props from the immediate surroundings. Chairs became horses. Tables were suddenly thrones. With his penchant for constant repetition until he felt his actors gave him what he wanted, mumbled threats of murdering him could be heard.[30]

Lillian remembered:

> during rehearsals the actors, in order to get into the mood, said whatever words they felt would be appropriate to the action. Often Griffith called the film cutter to take down some of the actors' talk to be used for subtitles on the finished print.[31]

When Lillian and Dorothy were announced as the stars of *Orphans of the Storm*, it was assumed that Lillian, because of her sympathetic roles in *Broken Blossoms* and the recent *Way Down East*, would be playing the blind sister, Louise. Wisely, the role of the blind sister went to Dorothy. The devotion to each other that Lillian and Dorothy had away from the cameras would be easy to film. Wasn't Lillian always waiting for Dorothy to come home from parties? In *Orphans of the Storm* Lillian would look after a blind Dorothy, helping her as they tried to make their way through the Paris streets.

Orphans of the Storm, following the Boston premiere at the Tremont Theatre on December 28, 1921, had its New York opening at the Apollo Theatre on January 2, 1922.[32] The film was a cinematic valediction presenting Lillian, Dorothy, and Griffith at the zenith of their creative powers. All of Griffith's innovations that he had introduced to filmmaking were on the screen for everyone to see in the course of twelve reels: the close-up, the cross-cutting, the changing point of view, the panoramic sweeps of the cameras. Never would Lillian look so radiant. Never would Griffith have another cinematic opportunity to pay tribute to his literary mentor, Charles Dickens.[33]

The public, who had marveled over *The Birth of a Nation* and *Intolerance*, would once again be awestruck at Griffith's handling of crowd scenes. For the guillotine sequence he used hundreds of Mamaroneck residents as witnesses at the executioner's block. They were paid $1.25 (and a box-lunch) for the day's work.[34]

Critics who had been less than kind to Griffith's films with Carol Dempster were praising his return to the kind of film he should have kept making. The critic of *The New York Herald* wrote that Lillian "has a way of reaching right in and straining at one's heartstrings."[35]

To help publicize and increase the returns at the box-office, Lillian and Dorothy appeared with Griffith when the film opened in larger cities: Minneapolis, St. Paul, Chicago, New Orleans,[36] and Washington, D.C. (where they were invited to lunch at the White House with President and Mrs. Warren G. Harding).[37]

Lillian's reaction to all of the honors and festivities was not totally enthusiastic. While she was outwardly gracious and professional, one can detect the impending melancholia and loneliness at being "on" in the crowd.

To her childhood friend and confidant, Nell Dorr, she wrote:

> I would rather do anything else, but if it helps Mr. Griffith, of course, I could not refuse... You can't be a hermit all your life, though I do not enjoy crawling out of my shell ... I was never made for this life — if they would only let me go unnoticed.[38]

Lillian knew there would be no more Griffith film work once this tour was completed. Her relationship with Griffith throughout the tour was professional and polite. He had told her she could learn no more from him, and he couldn't afford to pay her the salary she was worth. So long as she remained with him, she would forever be the "damsel in distress," a type that audiences would soon find predictable and tiring as she and they both grew older. If she wanted to grow as an actress and survive in a very competitive profession, she would have to leave the nest, to break away. It was time for her to go. It was only natural that Trilby leave Svengali.

Director Frank Capra, who began his career in 1923 as a chemical engineer and prop boy for Harry Rapf at Warner Bros. before becoming a gag writer for Mack Sennett the following year, shared his thoughts on the ending of the Gish-Griffith relationship. Capra, in New York to publicize his autobiography, *The Name Above the Title* (1971), appeared with this biographer on *The Joe Franklin Show*.

The Griffith-Gish collaboration was a perfect example of author and creation during the early days of moviemaking. But motion pictures, like any new art form, has to progress if it is going to have any appeal or meaning to younger audiences.

When the twenties arrived, the Gish sisters, particularly Lillian, who was always the total virgin, had little appeal to a generation of flaming youth more interested in bootleg hooch, free love, going to all night parties in speakeasies, or Charleston dancing at some society person's swimming pool.

Moviemakers in the twenties were now saying you don't have to bring every girl home to mother, and that a little innocent petting was acceptable. The flapper, like the girls after the war, still yearned for true love and marriage. Heroines played by Joan and Viola Dana — and I directed both of them — knew when the kissing had to stop, and when the time had arrived to settle down with the man who loved them.

Neither Lillian nor Griffith knew how to deliver that kind of heroine. Away from the camera, Lillian was not a very social person who went to parties the way Dorothy did.

And Griffith was quite Victorian in that he never had Lillian kiss her leading man. Lillian's leading men held her hand very chastely, and were so virtuous you sometimes wondered exactly what they would do when they married.

Audiences in the 1920s knew what Joan Crawford and Clara Bow were all about. You just didn't give them a quick peck on the cheek and walk away grinning.

America had suddenly matured. It had taken a World War to make people realize that nobody would remain young and innocent forever. Newsreels had filmed the casualties. Those dead bodies you saw on the battlefields after the skirmishes were real.

The veterans returning home wanted women, and Lillian's heroines were still little girls. Lillian's screen persona had suddenly become terribly old-fashioned in a very short time.

It was time for the two of them — Griffith and Lillian — to grow up and move with the times. Lillian's audiences weren't young anymore. And neither was she.[39]

CHAPTER 12

In Italy: I

1922: While bootleg liquor made with questionable ingredients in bathtubs was being consumed behind closed doors at the ends of darkened alleys or at private clubs in record amounts for high prices, literature and the theatre were undergoing a renaissance of their own. No longer were domestic comedies and operettas going to be the only Broadway fare. With the steadily emerging naturalism and acceptance of the frankness in the plays of Eugene O'Neill, barriers were broken regarding what themes could be presented on a stage. The heavy hand of the censors was being lifted. To be "banned in Boston" meant an almost guaranteed New York success.

It was a good year for two of Lillian's Biograph contemporaries, Blanche Sweet and Mary Pickford. Blanche was filming *Quincy Adams Sawyer* at Metro, and Mary, playing a mother and son in the very successful *Little Lord Fauntleroy* at her own studio, would be named top female box-office star, based on a Quigley Publication exhibition poll.[1]

Lillian, for the first time in her adult life, was "at liberty," the term used for being out of work. Offers of employment did not come to her as she anticipated. Because of the years spent with Griffith, she had typed herself as a Griffith actress, which in the liberated twenties was a

metaphor for a glorification of the Victorian ideal, a heroine still dwelling within the confines of a very chaste terrain. The younger directors, while admiring Griffith's and Gish's accomplishments, were becoming "increasingly impatient with moralists."[2] They were reluctant to cast her in anything that didn't have a "classic nature." The classics were always worthy of respect on the local library shelves, but they didn't always bring in huge box-office returns. A twenties heroine was expected to go speeding on roadways, dance a mean Charleston, and smoke. With the exception of listening to Schubert's *Serenade* on a party phonograph in *Way Down East*, Lillian's films did not utilize music as a means of seduction. The dance party in *True Heart Susie* was attended by Lillian's former boyfriend's *wife*, not by Lillian.

Lillian was an orphan of a Griffith storm, a casualty of her master's creation. Rival Carol Dempster, noticeably short on talent, was working for Griffith in the provocatively titled *One Exciting Night*. Although the film wasn't successful, Lillian's screen persona would not tolerate such a suggestive idea!

Years later, Lillian recalled how she felt at the time her Griffith persona was believed to be her real self, and the inability of the producers to separate the two:

My pictures were never personal. I saw myself as a painter. I had a canvas. Instead of brushes and paint, I had this — my face and my body — but I painted with emotion or laughter to affect the people who saw my films, so that they would believe what I was trying and never catch me acting.[3]

Of equal, and perhaps greater, concern to Lillian was her mother's sudden hospitalization. An emergency goiter operation set aside any further contemplation of future film work. Mrs. Gish was in intensive care at New York Presbyterian, and afterwards removed to Lillian's apartment, her medical costs to be borne equally by both daughters. That Lillian — who earned more money than Dorothy — expected her sibling to pay equally for their mother's maintenance was something Dorothy greatly resented.[4]

Money was always a source of quarrels and arguments between the two sisters. Lillian, unlike Dorothy, tended to save almost every dollar she earned, remembering (and being constantly reminded by her mother) how husband and father James Gish had squandered his salary and became penniless far away from home.

"We are sisters," Lillian would say to Dorothy, "and mother cared for us equally without favoritism, and we should do the same."

There was no room for discussion. There was nothing to discuss. Since Dorothy's childhood, Lillian's word was law. Like mother, like Lillian.[5]

To Nell, her childhood friend in Ohio, Lillian had written:

My next picture, if all goes well, will be made by myself, so if it makes money I will get some of it.[6]

While caring for her mother, Lillian began to fear that the more prolonged her absence from the screen, the greater her chances of not just being remembered as old-fashioned but being remembered not at all!

Dorothy, unlike Lillian, never had to contend with the stigma of being called a "Griffith heroine," even though she and Lillian had signed with Griffith's Biograph at the same time (1912). Dorothy, never as aggressive as Lillian or as versatile (as Griffith sometimes remarked), seemed not to mind being called "the other one" or "Lillian's sister." Lillian, Dorothy would tell her friends, "lived to work," while she (Dorothy) "worked when she felt like it."

Dorothy, now that she was married, had a husband — not a mother — to take care of. Dorothy's husband, James Rennie, shared the James Gish habit of having a "tendency" to "drink a little," something that occasionally happened during the shooting of *The Country Flapper*, a Paramount film they made together after Dorothy completed *Orphans of the Storm* with Lillian.[7]

With Mrs. Gish's medical costs constantly spiraling upward, it seemed only natural that Dorothy keep working while Lillian continued providing the necessary home care and searched for a vehicle that would guarantee good reviews and future employment. After working for Griffith for eight years, she knew she couldn't appear on the screen in a routine programmer which would temporarily pay the bills before winding up as a second feature in the hick towns.

Lillian's *Way Down East* co-star, Richard Barthelmess, had just completed *Experience*, a less than successful Griffith-like allegorical drama of Youth meeting Temptation in the big city. Barthelmess was also having post–Griffith problems.

When former road show actor and Pathe' film director Henry King offered Barthelmess the chance to become a partner and leading actor in his recently-formed Inspiration Pictures, he seized the opportunity. Henry King, like his mentor, Griffith, shared a "nostalgic love of the wide open spaces and a strong fidelity to rural America of earlier days."[8] Henry King's *Tol'able David*, a project in which Griffith was originally interested but set aside (at Lillian's suggestion) to film *Orphans of the Storm*,[9] was a masterpiece hailed by Soviet director Pudovkin as a model of classical film technique.[10]

Encouraged by Griffith, a wary Barthelmess approached Lillian and asked if she would be interested in joining his Inspiration Company. Barthelmess's method of presentation and logic were sound. Both he and Lillian had worked well together and had mothers to support. Neither he nor Lillian knew when they would be working.

Unbeknownst to Barthelmess, Lillian had been thinking of signing with Robert Z. Leonard's newly-formed Tiffany Company at a salary of $3,500 a year to make four pictures. It was certainly more than she had ever made working for Griffith, but Tiffany already had their major star: former Follies dancer Mae Murray, who was Leonard's wife. Though Mae had been glorifying the American girl in one of the Ziegfeld presentations on the New York Theatre Roof Garden on June 15, 1908,[11] she had clearly aged in the fifteen years since.

The still vibrant Mae, three years older than Lillian, had become very demanding in the way she should be photographed. She was no longer an ingenue, and to photograph young required the use of a camera covered with gauze. At Biograph and with Griffith, Lillian had been able to make these same demands. Could she make these demands at a new studio, given the competition of an equally aggressive Mae — whose husband was in charge? Probably not.

Barthelmess' offer of employment at a lesser salary had its advantages, even though she would be starting all over again at a new studio. Not wanting to reject the offer, Lillian's reluctance to sign was understood by her former Griffith co-worker. Lillian couldn't leave her sick mother and feel totally secure while concentrating on a new role. Like Barthelmess, her method of refusal was logical and sound.

But Lillian, not wanting to totally alienate any future chances or opportunities, had a perfect solution. Sister Dorothy, whose husband James Rennie was playing on Broadway in *Shore Leave*,[12] was available. Why not utilize Dorothy while Lillian spent time at her mother's bedside? By the time Dorothy's film was completed, Mrs. Gish could easily be recovered, and Lillian would be available to step before the cameras.

It was a brilliant decision, and Dorothy knew why she had been corralled into being the subject of experimentation. As masterful and commercially successful as *Tol'able David* was, it was a first film. Had it been a second or third film, it would have been easy to trace the success of the new studio. A first film was only a first film. What guarantee was there of a second or third success? In the creative arts, whether literary, on the stage, or in motion pictures, it was quite common to have a first success and then fold...

Suppose Lillian's initial Inspiration venture failed? She had never appeared in an unsuccessful film under Griffith's aegis. Griffith had tailored everything to her talents. Griffith films were Gish vehicles. Could Lillian appear in young roles if her first film failed? Or would Barthelmess, out of professional courtesy, let her have continued employment in scenes as another older character player?

Dorothy would appear in anything, Lillian knew, so long as she received a salary. She could sustain a failure, which was why Griffith always said she was the better actress. Dorothy spent almost everything she made. So did her husband.

Dorothy's talent would always be greater than her ambition. She would take the first step. It was what Lillian wanted.

In *Fury*, Dorothy played Barthelmess's sweetheart in a sea drama of revenge and redemption. *Fury* was a programmer that was a success. It earned its costs and paid the bills while Lillian continued to search through piles of original stories, novels, and plays to find something suitable.

No wasting time after the completion of *Fury*, Dorothy and Richard Barthelmess left for Cuba to film Joseph Hergesheimer's novella, *The Bright Shawl*. Hergesheimer, a popular author of the day, had been friends with both Lillian and Dorothy. To see one of his works on film would not only bring him closer to the two sisters, it would also bring additional funds to the coffers. With the exception of Willa Cather, most writers saw motion pictures as another source of revenue. Sometimes the motion picture even approached their original intentions.

In *The Bright Shawl*, Dorothy played "La Clavel," an Andalusian dancer who wore a carnation in her hair while gathering information as a spy for Cuban independence. Barthelmess was the visiting American who took the information. For her treachery, La Clavel made the ultimate sacrifice, dying in the arms of her lover, the American.

With the exteriors filmed in Havana guaranteeing its authenticity, the film was a success. The Cuban Republic presented Dorothy with a $25,000 Cuban shawl, and Richard with a $1,000 gold Malacca cane.[13]

Lillian had been away from the cameras for over a year when she decided in 1923 that she had to return to work. Without Griffith to make decisions for her, she was at a total loss. Because of his involvement — professional and personal — with Carol Dempster, he was unable to give her the help she so desperately needed. Mrs. Gish's illness had only served to increase the gnawing fear that Lillian's fame and fortune were only temporary. One mistake, and everyone would be back in Ohio on Aunt Emily's farm. Who would take care of them? Dorothy had a husband. What did Lillian have now that Mr. Griffith was out of her life?

Lillian sent back script after script. Who could believe her as a cigarette-smoking cabaret girl? Could any audience accept her as a society girl who took midnight swims at the homes of irresponsible playboys?

When one of her readers, Lily Hayward, showed her Marion Crawford's novel, *The White Sister*, she brought it to Inspiration's attention. The search was over! Lillian's choice was approved. She signed with Inspiration for $1,250 a week and an additional 15% after the picture had earned a specified amount. The Inspiration salary was considerably less than the Tiffany offer of $3,500, but Lillian knew that *The White Sister* was a story Tiffany would never film. She instinctively knew her audiences would accept her in *The White Sister*, her first film since leaving Griffith.[14] By not pandering to fickle popular tastes, she had achieved a personal victory. She had maintained her standards and lived her life on her own terms. Not anyone else's. Not even her mother's.

The story-line of *The White Sister* was tailored to her talents. Angela (Lillian), a young Italian heiress, is left without any money or a place to live when her father dies and her wicked half-sister destroys the will. When she receives the news that her sailor-fiancé has been killed in the war in Africa, she renounces the world and joins a convent — only to learn that her former lover is still alive.

Angela was the kind of heroine Lillian knew she could play: the highly desirable yet unattainable virgin.[15] Once again she would be rejecting worldly happiness. This time it would be in favor of the veil.[16] Like *Way Down East* and *Orphans of the*

Storm, The White Sister was first dramatized on the stage and had toured successfully. (Its New York cast included Viola Allen, William Farnum, and James O'Neill — father of playwright Eugene.)[17] The three plays had credentials. Two had been great Lillian Gish successes on the screen. *The White Sister* would be another.

Backing, Lillian soon learned, was not immediately forthcoming. Despite its credentials as a successful play, religious films were anathema at the box office. *The White Sister* was a Catholic story, albeit a modern one, but there was enough fear of an anti–Catholic sentiment to keep a sizable amount of people away.

Still, Lillian persisted. *The White Sister* reminded her of the short time she had spent at the Ursuline School of St. Louis.

> I had thought of the nuns as earnest women, hard-working and kindly. My memory of them is an affectionate one — romantic. There had been a time when I fancied I might have a vocation for the veil. The cloister has appealed to so many who later became actresses. I have regretted sometimes that I did not follow that early inclination.[18]

For added dramatic and pictorial value, Lillian inserted a scene that had not been fully developed in the original novel or on the Broadway stage: the taking of the veil. Because the screen could "open" the play and the novel, Lillian felt the film would have a greater impact on the audience.

To author-critic Anthony Slide, she said:

> I worked on the script... And I somehow got hold of the ritual, which was a beautiful and sensuous poem. I'm not a Catholic, but I thought it was so dramatic to say "the bridegroom" and then flash to the crucifix.[19]

Director Henry King, who had earned critical praise with *Tol'able David*, wasn't totally impressed with *The White Sister*, despite Lillian's determination to "tour it in a tent"[20] if a distributor couldn't be found. Still, he accepted the assignment. *The White Sister* would give him the opportunity to go to Italy at someone else's expense. It was an offer he couldn't refuse. That he would be directing Lillian Gish did not impress him. Miss Gish was a Griffith actress, and *The White Sister* could not even remotely resemble a Griffith film.

What must have been a greater worry for director Henry King was the lack of a leading man. Nobody had been cast, and Inspiration Pictures had booked 24 tickets on a Fabre Line steamer, the S.S. Providence, bound for Naples. Dozens of actors had been seen, but none were satisfactory. How were they going to start to film once they had arrived? Neither Lillian nor Henry King could speak one word of Italian.

Less than a week before the sailing, portrait photographer James Abbe, who had agreed to give up a lucrative portrait photographer's job on New York's Fifth Avenue to shoot "stills" in Italy for the film at $150 a week, thought he found someone.

The actor was appearing on stage in *La Tendresse*. He was handsome enough to photograph well on film, even though his motion picture experience had been limited to one very small role in the Selznick Pictures production of *Handcuffs or Kisses* (released two years earlier), and the actor hadn't appeared on the screen since that time. With time narrowing, there was no time for discussion. A frantic Henry King suggested to James Abbe that the unknown quantity report to Abbe's studio immediately.

His name was Ronald Colman, and when Lillian and Henry King saw his face on the Abbe studio screen, they knew they had found their leading man. In the midst of congratulating themselves and Colman, they were reminded that Colman still had a Broadway run-of-the-play contract to fulfill.

Lillian personally telephoned Colman's producer, Henry Miller, and explained the situation. A new film studio, the sailing date for Italy — all were dependent on Colman's release. Without Colman, there would be no film. Was it possible to release him for the sake of the film and Lillian's first job in over a year?

Colman was released from his contract. Everything was readied for sailing. Acting as chaperon for Lillian would be Mrs. Marie Kratsch, a friend of Lillian's Aunt Emily in Massillon, Ohio. Also on board was Charles H. Duell, an attorney with a strong interest in films, who would act as studio supervisor in addition to handling any unexpected legal complications.[21]

The company's first problem wasn't legal. It was professional, and there was nothing anyone could do. Lillian was literally and figuratively at sea.

What was obvious within the first days after the sailing was Ronald Colman's lack of experience playing before the motion picture camera. In his hastily-made screen test, he photographed well and he moved well. James Abbe's portrait studio was not a motion picture studio. One didn't have far to walk in a portrait studio. One came and sat until you were instructed to change positions.

Replacing Colman when the company arrived in Italy was impossible. The time element would discourage looking for a replacement. Could a stage actor learn the rudiments of motion picture acting on a sea voyage? Colman's face, especially in close-ups, was too handsome to waste. And Lillian knew it. As she helped Richard Barthelmess in *Broken Blossoms*, she would help Ronald Colman in *The White Sister*.

She instructed the ship's captain to enclose an area of the deck in canvas for the purpose of rehearsing some of the scenes which were easy to block and didn't require too much playing space. Never one to relax, even on a leisurely sea voyage when immediate grueling work in the hot sun for long hours awaited them once they disembarked, Lillian's compulsion for thriftiness was legendary. Shooting time could be saved, and there would be less wasting of precious film. Daily rehearsals also removed Colman from frequently arguing with his wife, Thelma. Rehearsing in the open air was infinitely better than being in the close quarters of a stateroom.

Also onboard the Providence was Monseigneur Bonzano, a high prelate of the church, who was on his way to the Vatican to be installed as a cardinal. In the company's free time, he was always available to answer questions about church policy and attitudes. Highly impressed with Lillian's education at the Ursuline School, he offered to serve as the link between the church and the Fascisti, in addition to helping Lillian and the director scout for locations. He would also provide advisors for every religious scene.

The company was registered at two hotels on Rome's Via Veneto the Excelsior and the Majestic. Lillian's room at the Excelsior had a window that overlooked Mt. Vesuvius. The dome of St. Peter's could be seen in the distance. To look out of the window, no matter what time of day or night, there was always something to see. In the morning, she was awakened by the sounds of church bells. It seemed as if they were right in her room!

While director Henry King and attorney Charles H. Duell scouted locations, Lillian set out for the studio, located on the outskirts of the city. She had seen the mosaics and the jeweled robes at Palmermo, but Rome was a twenty-four hour wonder. Some of the convents she had been able to visit greeted the idea of filming any ceremony — or even allowing the presence of motion picture cameras — with mixed feelings. Convents were sacred ground. To have an invasion with motion picture cameras that would photograph everything for the outside world to see... No.

Instead of the fully equipped studio Lillian had been led to believe she would find, she was ushered into a huge empty room with two kleig lights.

Lillian's mind was reeling. Had she travelled thousands of miles for an Italian replay of what had happened at Griffith's when she was directing Dorothy in *Remodeling Her Husband*?

Immediately, someone was sent to Germany on an evening train to find suitable equipment. It was a decision that Lillian made on her own. With three groups to deal with (Mussolini and the Fascisti, the Vatican, and the King and his followers), there was no time to waste.

She had to prepare for her role as a nun. She had to master walking in a nun's habit, how to gesture and maintain serenity, and to know the city as her character would have known it: the social aspects and the religious ceremonies and feast days. It had to be second nature: Rome at Easter, the ascending of the Sancta Steps on one's knees, the Gregorian chants at St. Paul's on Good Friday, St. Peter's on Easter Monday. She would have to know the streets and market places — all in character as Angela.

As herself, Lillian the American actress, she knew she had to established a friendly relationship with an Italian crew, whose methods were often at odds with what she had known at Biograph.[22]

She had, in the days that followed, studied Italian, hoping to engage the people in conversation and know them better. She had become a familiar sight around the city, watching day-to-day life lived by people in an international metropolis. What she could not fathom was the Roman reluctance to work on an American time schedule and adhere to deadlines. Taking orders from a woman, an American woman, was not without its problems. The Mediterranean male was not accustomed to being bossed by a foreign woman. The joy of living was more important, and reporting to work was a social occasion, as were the breaks from work, which had to be spent with wine, cheese, and happy talk. If work resumed a few minutes later than desired, what of it? Everything would be done. Why rush? This was Italy, a country thousands of years old. Italy was still here, and would always be here. America, in 1923, wasn't even a century-and-a-half.

Lillian joined the crew whenever she found free moments. She would sit and eat with them, discovering simple food: sardines, cheese, red wine, and Italian bread. Sometimes she allowed herself time to relax as herself, not the nun she was playing.

She watched the building of beautiful interiors, the construction of a chapel, and the use of solid carved wood for the walls of the library. The movie set barely resembled a movie set. It looked like the actual locations in Rome and Florence.[23]

A friend of Mussolini was able to provide transportation to 30 cloistered orders, where Lillian lit candles and offered prayers for her mother's continued recovery. At the Order at Lourdes, Lillian decided she had found the perfect location to film the ceremony of the taking of the veil.[24]

The inclusion of the veil-taking scene was not without its problems. Before *The White Sister* troupe had left the United States, director Henry King had a conference in Washington, D.C. with the papal delegate, an archbishop who wanted the scene excised. King refused to cut any scene he believed was necessary to the film. The veil-taking scene, he informed the archbishop, would be filmed with or without the technical expertise of the Vatican.

A compromise was eventually reached. For the scene involving the veil, a priest would be on the set to act as an observer.

The priest reported to the Order at Lourdes, as promised, on the day of the shooting of the veil-taking sequence. When it was discovered that his assistance and advice was needed and that he spoke no English, King was forced to communicate his wishes through an interpreter. It was time consuming, as King realized the questions had to be translated into two languages before they could be answered.

To insure the success of the scene, King was told, it was necessary that the priest direct the sequence for the Inspiration cameras. King viewed this as a surrender of his authority, but there was no alternative. If he wanted to complete the scene, he had to let the priest take charge. The final editing would be done after the priest had left. The shoot, King estimated, would take eleven hours.

At eight in the morning, the priest, assuming full control, began directing the holy ceremony. He worked quietly, showing great assurance and command. He knew precisely what should be done. He wasted no time. King, who had been relegated to an area from where he could sit or stand and watch, was quite impressed. The priest gave his orders crisply and in a clear, conversational manner. There was little difficulty in understanding what he wanted to be done.

Afterwards, when King reported what had happened to the archbishop in Washington, D.C., he learned why the priest had been so skillful. The priest did have a lot of experience directing. The last show he had staged had a cast of 16,000 people. The quiet priest who had taken charge was the "head ceremonial director" at the Vatican![25]

The White Sister showcased Lillian's "star quality" without bypassing or denying the years of her commitment to D. W.

Griffith.[26] Working at a new studio in a vehicle of her own choosing gave her the long-awaited chance to react as a "mature actress with a face and character that corresponded with her true age."[27] For the first time, Lillian's acting was outward rather than inward. The fluttering hands, a familiar mannerism so often on display in *Broken Blossoms*, were gone. In *The White Sister*, she dealt with objects. Most noticeably, this was in evidence in the hospital scene where, after emerging from a coma, she would notice a photograph of her fiance (Colman) near her bed. She would rise to kiss it before realizing he wasn't in the room with her, and that her new existence had become meaningless and devoid of any worth.[28] Only by joining a convent would she find redemption and salvation.

The White Sister was clearly a showcase of Lillian's talents against a variety of Italian locations: Sorrento, Capri, Rome, Lago Montana, and Tivoli.[29] For the first time, Lillian was clearly the star, and not just an outstanding member of a formula Griffith ensemble. To photograph her against Neapolitan palaces would emphasize the "picturesque rather than the filmic" aspects of the story.[30]

To be sure, the film was replete with the Gish trademarks, the hardship and trauma that Lillian's audiences knew to anticipate: receiving the news (false) that her fiancé had been killed in the war in Africa, being trapped during an eruption at Vesuvius, avoiding being raped by her fiancé who wants her to surrender the veil and return to the outside world, and a flood.

The flood was filmed in Rocca di Papa, a small town outside Rome. For extras, Henry King, like his mentor Griffith in *Orphans of the Storm*, hired the townspeople. It was a final attempt at building a bridge to friendship with many who had looked at the eight month occupation (November 1923 to August 1924) as an invasion by foreign crazies whose daily presence had continually interrupted the tranquility of their lives. That quite a sum of money had been spent in their immediate area (and salaries provided to many local inhabitants) had no meaning. Many of the townspeople had never left their area, or seen a motion picture. Cinema houses were strictly a big city attraction.

The residents of Rocca di Papa disliked the presence of the huge airplanes with their nightmarishly loud propellers that, once started at the command of the director, would blow dust that hadn't been moved in five hundred years. With the addition of the lightning effects and the increasing element of collective panic, it would be impossible to distinguish between actual fear and movie-scene fear. Director Henry King would have to yell commands to an already panic-stricken crowd.

Viewed today, *The White Sister* is hardly a triumph. Lillian's behavior was dictated by her uniform. A volcanic eruption, an earthquake, and a flood were what the film needed to bring everything to a dramatic, though not necessarily logical, ending.

The White Sister was advertised as an audience picture: "A love story that will live forever... You dare not breathe during its tense moments lest you dispel the charm which has been woven around you."[31]

The elegantly dressed audience entering the 44th Street Theatre in New York for the world premiere on September 5, 1924 was observed by Lillian and Dorothy, who were standing behind the curtain on a soap box (which would be utilized for the speeches at the conclusion). Henry King and Lillian had spent the final weeks of August editing the film from twelve to nine reels, which was a more acceptable length.

The tragic ending was decided to be the wiser choice. There was no purpose in having both lovers survive a series of calamities if one had already dedicated herself to the religious life. Heated discussions regarding the kind of catastrophe which would be the most effective ended in a stalemate. Nobody could decide which would be the most effective: an explosion, an eruption, or a flood.

Finally, they decided to use all of the choices. Audiences loved spectacular effects. An expensive picture had to look like an expensive picture to justify the price of admission.

For the premiere, Lillian wore a new gown, a velvet ivory dress made especially for the occasion. The new gown was bought at Dorothy's insistence. Lillian always needed to be prodded into spending money for new clothes. Dorothy was buying new clothes all the time, whether she was working or not. Dorothy was a frequent diner at expensive restaurants. Looking one's best for the occasion was obligatory.

Lillian truthfully didn't enjoy premieres, but she knew they were necessary. She would have preferred to remain in her apartment, away from the lights and the crowds. She wished her mother were in the city, but mother was in the country.

Mother had sent Lillian a telegram.

Mother wishes you all success possible in your new picture. I know you will be sweet and dear in it.[32]

As the distinguished crowd continue to file into the theatre, Lillian looked at her new dress. It was a new gown for a new film which could be the start of a new life without being supervised by Mr. Griffith (on *or* away from the set). The success of the film would offset the cost of the new gown and mother's telegram.

The phone at Lillian's apartment at the Hotel Vanderbilt had been ringing[33] since the conclusion of the film and the necessary thank-you speeches. Lillian had to acknowledge the people who were very prominent in the life of New York: distinguished politicians, famous authors, screen and stage celebrities, and heads of the motion picture industry.[34]

The film critic for *The New York Times* noted in a review dated September 6, 1924, that *The White Sister* was

> notable ... an artistic effort on which the producers seem to have leaned backward to cling to the sterling worth of the picture...a difficult task to undertake as it is a love story with little or no comedy relief, and one in which the heavy part is taken by a woman.
>
> A remarkable and successful effort at characterization by the players...[who] actually appear to live the parts they enact on the screen.
>
> Miss Gish's acting is always restrained. She obtains the full effect in every situation, being, as Italians say, simpatico in all sequences.[35]

The telephone kept ringing at Lillian's hotel apartment, but friend Nell Dorr, who had come to the opening from Ohio, decided not to wake her and let her have a few precious minutes of sleep before the private supper. Nell didn't recognize the voice of the caller, who declined to identify himself and would only ask to "speak to Miss Gish. It is most urgent. It is most urgent..."

Nell cut him off when he repeated his request without bothering to say his name. It was no time to be mysterious.[36]

Few people knew that during the filming of *The White Sister* the previous summer, Lillian had fallen in love. The courtship had taken place away from the watchful eyes of the chaperon.

The young man was the son of the president of the Chase Bank of New York, in Italy enjoying an extended holiday. They had spent her free hours together, sailing on his boat or meeting on the beaches. They had planned to be married when the shooting of the film was completed.

The young man had cabled an announcement of his intentions to his family in New York, hoping that when he and Lillian returned they would be happy for him, and Lillian would be accepted into the family.

His family was not receptive, and he was summoned to return to New York immediately. The matter was not a subject for any kind of discussion. Despite Lillian's prestige, which could easily have matched their family's social standing, marrying an actress was not what the son of a bank president was expected to do.

Becoming involved with an actress sometimes happened to young men of high social standing, but these involvements were nothing more than a momentary diversion. At best, a flirtation. One never fell in love with an actress. Certainly not to the point of ever contemplating marriage. After the honeymoon was over, what would they have in common? What could they talk about?

No actress will ever be welcomed in this house![37]

Perhaps the last paragraph of *The New York Times* review of *The White Sister* presented more than a striking parallel to Lillian's ill-fated summer romance:

> We do not wish to have happy endings to all films, but in this instance such a finish would have strengthened the picture and shown, as is expected, natural human frailty when it comes to a great love.[38]

Lillian had been cheered by the opening night audience and praised the following morning in the newspapers, but, once again, she was alone in the crowd.

CHAPTER 13

In Italy: II

I wish to nominate *The White Sister* for a high place on the White List of dramatic performances... It is religion struggling with human passions, as in real life and gaining its victory after storm and stress.
— Father Duffy, The Fighting Irish
69th Regiment of New York[1]

To film George Eliot's *Romola* in the wake of the success of *The White Sister* seemed a logical decision to make. It would be filmed with co-star Ronald Colman in Italy, where the two had just finished working, and have the advantage of authentic locations. Unlike Eliot's classics *The Mill on the Floss* and *Silas Marner*, which both made an easy screen transition in the versions filmed at Long Island's Thanhouser studios in 1915 and 1916,[2] *Romola* was always viewed by the literary community as very minor Eliot. Still, the work was in public domain, and there would be no traditional haggling for rights. The novel was long out of copyright. Eliot, the male pseudonym for the female writer born Mary Ann Evans, never had the large readership of a Charles Dickens, but her works were highly regarded by more sophisticated readers. *Romola*, with Lillian Gish, would be a prestige production. Devotees of the novel would recognize the authentic locations when seen on the screen. This would not be a Hollywood backlot duplication. In this, Lillian's second film for Inspiration, audiences would see 15th century Renaissance Italy.

As Romola, the daughter of a blind scholar, Lillian would once again be playing a victim. This time, the villain would be her husband Tito, a ruthless magistrate who had no qualms about cheating on her and entering into a mock marriage with Tessa, a peasant girl with whom he has a child. Tito, prior to his own death by drowning, also condemns the priest Savonarola to death at the stake. At the film's conclusion, Romola and Tessa would be united. Carlo, the loyal sculptor, would pledge himself to watch over them.

The supporting case was a strong one. Dorothy was cast as Tessa, providing another chance to appear with Lillian in the same film. Ronald Colman was playing Carlo. The more dramatic role of Tito was given to William Powell.

Because of Mrs. Gish's complete recovery, *Romola* was also the occasion for a grand reunion. Mother, Lillian, and Dorothy were together again "on the road," this time in Florence, Italy at the Grand Hotel — a far cry from the dimly lit rooming houses in towns nobody knew existed, or on the top floor of

Greenwich Village's Hotel Marlton on Eighth Street.

From the Grand Hotel balcony they could see the Ponte Vecchio across the Arno, in addition to many shops and restaurants. Florence was the cradle of the Italian Renaissance. The Uffizi Palace had one of the largest collections of paintings in the world. It was a natural source which would be constantly consulted to verify the authenticity of the costumes. To further steep themselves in research, the Gishes had access to the Boboli gardens on the grounds of the Pitti Palace, once the residence of the Medici family. There, Dorothy and Lillian would be able to walk in the footsteps of Florentine statesmen and rulers from centuries past.[3]

Director Henry King, acknowledging the excellence of the Italian technicians who worked on *The White Sister*, knew he would have only minor problems supervising the building of the 17 acres of sets[4] that would recreate and comprise the world that was Renaissance Italy in the 15th century.[5]

Plans to film *Romola* began during the last weeks of *The White Sister*. So authentic looking were the sets that it was virtually impossible to tell the difference between the real location sites (which included the Duomo, the bridge at Ponte Vecchio, and the Piazza Signoria) and the studio product (involving the building of 15th century streets, complete with shops that sold costumes, harness, basketry, hats, footwear, and furniture). Woodcarvers working on the church and banquet hall interiors were a common sight for twentieth century daily strollers.

For the wedding feast sequence, art director Robert Haas, who had worked with Lillian on *The White Sister*, had to have period glasses blown in Venice.

After securing the actual robes worn by the priests during the time of Romola, four detectives had to be hired to guard them. Four robes, four detectives.

Unlike the town of Rocca di Papa, where citizens were quite reluctant to participate in the filming of *The White Sister*, the more sophisticated citizenry of Florence were willing to work around the clock—in any aspect of moviemaking![6]

To simulate the texture of the stonework, plaster casts were made from the walls of the Davanti Palace.

As the flames surrounded Savonarola's body during his execution, a cloud (it was recorded at the time) enlarged and became a miraculous thunderstorm. To duplicate the historical event, King employed men on high ladders, instructing them to pour buckets of water.[7]

Lillian was always available and on call whenever she was needed. Often she took the liberty to authorize purchases of technical equipment and had to make quick decisions regarding which material would photograph best on camera. One had the impression, watching her examining painting after painting, that she, not art director Robert Haas, was making all of the decisions regarding what would be seen on the walls of the palaces. In effect, Lillian was duplicating her final days with Griffith, who granted her carte blanche to do anything which would speed the production along.[8]

Perhaps Lillian's constant, almost compulsive involvement justified, according to *Motion Picture Classic*, a salary that fluctuated between $8,000 and $10,000 a week—quite a large sum to be paid from a studio that wanted to maintain a low budget.[9] That Lillian often acted as peacemaker was to be expected, given the varying temperaments of her high-powered supporting cast.

Rain was almost a daily occurrence during the winter. The shooting sequence of the day, much to the punctual Lillian's chagrin, was often interrupted.[10] Shots involving extras were often cancelled. New scenes, which could be filmed inside, were hastily assembled to take advantage of the day players, who had reported for work knowing that something would be done that needed their presence. What footage was shot on rainy days sometimes yielded some lovely, usable, honest moments, but there was the constant risk factor. Film stock was limited, and what was improvised could rarely be duplicated, given the cost of successive takes. Little time was given to formal blocking and the precision that was a hallmark of Griffith's methods.

The work continued, and Lillian continued to be unhappy. The relationship with Henry King was deteriorating.[11] King, who had once jokingly remarked that he would film the telephone to get to be in Italy, was no longer exercising the tight control he had previously demonstrated when he directed his initial *Tol'able David* with Richard Barthelmess or the recent *The White Sister* with Lillian.

It is interesting to note that, upon the completion of *Romola*, King was never granted the opportunity to work with an actress of Lillian's stature again. Lillian also learned that she had to choose her directors more carefully.[12] What was happening with Henry King was not far removed from what she thought would happen had she signed with Mae Murray's husband, director Robert Z. Leonard. King wanted to complete the picture. Leonard wanted to constantly appease his wife. Both directors, unlike D. W. Griffith, would place Lillian's career and security second. *Romola*, for all of its pictorial beauty, was little more than a parade of attractive views in an Italian setting.[13] Dorothy, Lillian would say, always believed *Romola* was infrequently shown because it was little more than "an impressive travelogue."[14]

Perhaps Lillian's increasing power on the *Romola* set was granted her because of the constant attentions of her employer, Charles H. Duell, one of the founders of Inspiration Pictures. Duell, recently divorced in Paris (January 24, 1924, on grounds of desertion) from actress Lillian Tucker (who had played the lead in a Chicago production of *Three Faces East*[15]) had known of Lillian's unfortunate relationship with the son of the president of the Chase bank. He was also aware that the additional time needed to complete the film had made her unable to accept the leading role in Paramount's version of *Peter Pan*, although she was playwright James M. Barrie's first choice. The role was consequently played by newcomer Betty Bronson, whose film experience was limited to a small role in *Java Head*, adapted from James Hergesheimer's best-selling novel. So successful was Betty in *Peter Pan* that Barrie insisted she be cast as Cinderella in his film version of *A Kiss for Cinderella*.[16]

Lillian was floundering in a sea of responsibility regarding the daily production decisions, heightened by her personal frustration at being unable to play *Peter Pan*. She never forgot that, many years ago, she was rejected as a candidate for a supporting role by Maude Adams, who played Peter Pan in the New York stage version. Lillian was only slightly taller than Maude. That Maude was forever trapped in the role was a story Lillian loved to tell years afterward.

Her own lot, at that moment, was not that much better than Maude's. It was only natural that Charles Duell, whose association with Lillian on the set of *The White Sister* with Lillian was strictly professional, function as a company advisor. Now he was always present when Lillian was involved with the doings of the day: watching the cameramen, supervising the lights and the crew, checking to see if everyone knew the blocking for the scene to be shot.

Long a seasoned veteran, Lillian rarely deferred to him, and only acknowledged his presence during the few minutes of respite between takes. Even Mr. Griffith knew better than to attempt to socialize during the day, and Duell was wise to emulate him. Only away from the set, away from any possible gossip, was the Gish-Duell association less formal.

While Duell's recent, and some believed sudden, availability after his divorce may have been an occasional source of concern or worry to Mrs. Gish (who was constantly counselling Lillian that men were always after a woman's bankbook), he did possess an impressive set of credentials that overrode any lingering doubts. He was related to Elihu Root, who had served as Secretary of War for Presidents William McKinley and Theodore Roosevelt, and was also a United States Senator from New York and a Nobel Prize winner in 1912.[17] Politically, Lillian, her mother, and Charles Duell were well-suited. All three were interested in Republican politics. Duell was the former Treasurer of the New York State Republican Committee. Lillian could trace her ancestry back to Zachary Taylor, the twelfth President of the United States.[18]

The Duell-Gish association was a carefully orchestrated strategy that skillfully evolved into a courtship. In the beginning, Duell only had to be there — to be present — to give Lillian the assurance that he was a man in whom she could confide. He was literate, and he had money, something which was very important to her. And he would show her how to acquire more.[19]

Hearst newspaper columnist Adela Rogers St. Johns explained:

> Money was very important to the Gish girls. Dorothy liked to spend it. Lillian tended to hoard it. Poverty affected the two of them in opposite ways, and when money came their way, Lillian was the thriftier.
>
> Dorothy liked to go out with men. Lillian, when she had the approval of her mother, liked to go out with men who had money. I think Lillian inwardly frowned on men who spent too much money on what she considered the wrong things, but she liked to have the security that the money was there. Then she'd go to bed with you — until somebody came along who had more money.
>
> Don't misinterpret what I'm saying. Lillian was never easy that way. And she was never a gold-digger. No sex symbol or Hollywood glamour girl ever had as many marriage proposals as Lillian. She had friendships and close friendships, and we always heard rumors of possible engagements to men we knew about, but nothing ever came to be.
>
> I think she was afraid, after spending so much time with Griffith, to completely surrender herself. She felt she was too important to be trapped, like a lot of those girls were. She didn't want to play second fiddle to anyone, especially a man.
>
> But she liked to have men come calling. She liked that kind of attention very much. It gave her a sense of power. She liked to be in control. Of everything.[20]

Romola was completed near the end of May — but not without its complications. Lillian, standing too close to the location where the burning of Savonarola at the stake was filmed, was badly scorched.[21] She had also accepted an engagement ring from Charles Duell, which revived the rumor that Duell's Paris divorce earlier in the year was because of his involvement with Lillian. Both Charles and Lillian vehemently denied any connection between the divorce and the engagement.[22] For the two of them, important work lay ahead: the editing of the film and its preparation for the premieres in New York and Los Angeles.

The critic from *The New York Times* attending the New York premiere at the George M. Cohan Theatre on December 1,

1924 made note of the "constantly changing scenes of wondrous beauty and players in medieval costume" and of the villain (William Powell), who dominated the film more than the hero or heroine (Ronald Colman and Lillian Gish). Lillian's performance was "graceful, restrained, thoughtful, and spiritual" with "never a false move or expression." Her gowns made her look like some "wistful beauty who had come through modern shadows."[23]

On hearing the adjective "wistful" after a performance of *All the Way Home* at the Belasco Theatre in June 1961, Lillian had her own reaction:

> Wistful?
> Perhaps that *Times* reviewer was the first to write it, and Bob (Robert E.) Sherwood read it and later called me "Wistful Lillian" when he would mention my work when he was doing film reviews for *Life* magazine.
> It was nice to read it the first time, but being Wistful Lillian came to haunt me. I lost roles on stage because some producers thought Wistful Lillian could only be wistful.
> I was never wistful! I was fragile![24]

The Los Angeles premiere at Grauman's Chinese Theatre took place on December 6. The three Gishes made the trip by train, arriving at a train station reception that resembled a political convention. From their windows, they could see people wearing large red badges with their names emblazoned on them. Cheering on the station platform were students from the Military Academy, "bathing beauties" from the Ambassador Hotel, and a coterie of film stars (John Gilbert, Norma Shearer, and Eleanor Boardman) and executives from Metro-Goldwyn-Mayer, whose studio was distributing the film. Even the Los Angeles Police and Fire Department were on hand to greet them and escort them across the city.[25]

Waiting for Lillian, Dorothy, and their mother at the Ambassador Hotel was Mary Pickford. The drawing room was filled with flowers. It was all part of what Mr. Griffith described as "selling the product." All that was left to be done was to view the film with the audience and hope for an appreciative response.

Harry Carr covered the opening for *Motion Picture Magazine*:

> The Gish sisters came out on the stage together when the picture was over, and Lillian made a frightened but sincere little speech. They were dressed in quaint, lovely gowns that somehow gave the impression that they were quite not of this world. Out there, behind the footlights, they looked like two fragile and beautiful little flowers.[26]

Film scholar and historian William K. Everson, commenting on *Romola*'s failure to garner an audience despite the presence of Dorothy and Lillian Gish, observed:

> It [*Romola*] wasn't a very cohesive film. It had great pictorial beauty and the use of actual locales, and some nice performances by Dorothy and Lillian, but there are great stretches where nothing happens dramatically to advance the plot. The film doesn't really move. It tends to plod. You can't have that on a screen. You can skip a page or two in a book that bogs down with description, but you can't have that in a motion picture.
> Obviously much time and money were spent to insure the authenticity and historical accuracy, but the success of a film of this type depends on the audiences' prior knowledge of 15th century Renaissance Italy, a period of history I don't think is taught in depth very much in American schools, except for some references to known names like Leonardo Da Vinci, or Boccaccio, or Dante. I rather doubt if anyone except those with a

parochial school background ever heard of the priest Savonarola. *Romola* doesn't explore a period of history that is familiar.

Most Americans were familiar with the period of the French Revolution either in history classes or English classes, where they must have read Charles Dickens' *A Tale of Two Cities*. Griffith's *Orphans of the Storm*, Lillian and Dorothy's last film before *Romola*, contained enough excitement to sustain anyone's interest, even if they weren't aware of the Dickensian parallels.

Romola, despite the obligatory disaster scene we've come to associate with Lillian's films, never acquired an audience of art lovers, who should have rejoiced at seeing so much of the city of Florence in so little time. The film wasn't shown very much after its initial release, and prints over the years became mysteriously hard to find. I wouldn't go as far as to say it's a forgotten film, but its showings are rare and are probably sponsored by a film society of diehard buffs who sit at conventions in motels in the heartland of America.

Remember: the original Eliot novel never enjoyed the popular or critical success of *Silas Marner* or even *Middlemarch*.

[Henry] King was a competent director who made wise choices in taking advantage of the availability of Lillian and Ronald Colman, who had played so well together in *The White Sister*, which also used actual locations — some of which were seen in *Romola*. Unfortunately, the characters in *Romola*, the Eliot novel, never had a life of their own outside the printed page of the original text. Unlike a Quasimodo, or a Scrooge, or a Heathcliff, Eliot's *Romola* characters didn't make it to a twentieth century audience.

Sad, because *Romola* was the last film Dorothy and Lillian would make together.[27]

Romola did not earn its production costs. Missing, but essential to any costume picture, was the heightened drama needed to propel the action ahead to an exciting conclusion.[28] One only has to watch Lon Chaney as Quasimodo, laboring under seventy pounds of rubber harness that prevented him from standing erect, to realize that his character was the center of the action in *The Hunchback of Notre Dame*.[29] Lillian's Romola is more of a spectator than a participant. It is Tessa, the peasant, not her, who has the baby. It is Savonarola, the priest, who dies at the stake, not her.

Critic Edward Wagenknecht was quite enthusiastic about the film, although he was decidedly in the minority.

From Lillian Gish he had received a letter stating:

> I hope you will like *Romola* when you see it. It caused me so much trouble and there are so many things in it that I would have different from what they are that I can never think of it now without a great feeling of sadness for what we might have done with that beautiful story.[30]

While Wagenknecht laments the absence of the "old time violence and the hysteric quality" found in her Griffith period, he is rhapsodic about Lillian's "more self-contained, inward" reactions:

A twitch of her expressive mouth, a shift of expression in her eyes, and she had accomplished what in the old days it took all of the resources of her body to achieve less perfectly.[31]

Lillian's greatest triumph of self-restraint occurs when she discovers that her husband, Tito, has been unfaithful to her at Tessa's house, and that he fathered Tessa's baby that she is holding.

The tears welled up in her eyes, but they did not overflow. Amazement, incredulous wonder, wounded pride, and the pure woman's instinctive recoil from an unchaste man — they were all there in that look; yet beneath and above them all were love and pity — for Tito, and for Tessa, and for the child.[32]

Wagenknecht wisely asks his readers:

> I suppose everybody, now and then, feels that the careers of his favorite artists are being less intelligently managed than he himself could manage them... What difference does it make that Lillian plays so long as she is Lillian?[33]

Lillian's future never looked brighter.

She had become engaged to the man she loved, and she knew he was looking out for her best interests. Charles Duell had selected *The Outsider*, a hit Broadway play of the season that starred Katherine Cornell, as Lillian's first film to be made under his auspices.[34]

Lillian had also signed a two year, six picture contract at Metro-Goldwyn-Mayer studios for which she would earn one million dollars.[35]

Everything seemed to be perfect...

CHAPTER 14

Betrayals

Lillian in Florence, Italy, and Charles, somewhere in mid-ocean, communicated with each other in unsigned letters and radio messages, using a color code to express their feelings and conceal their identities from possible publicity leaks. "Blue" could mean unhappy, sad, or lonely. "Red" meant love. A typical letter from Lillian always began "Carissimo," and lamented missing him "very much."

Its ending used their personal code:

> When are you coming back–
> Love,
> Blue, Red, Blue, Red.

A radio Message from Lillian also ended with the color code.

> Not feeling well. Think you have heart trouble.
> Love,
> Blue, Yes, Blue,[1]

Even the hard-to-please Mrs. Gish approved of Charles Duell as a prospective son-in-law.

In an early letter to Charles, sent during the filming of *The White Sister*, she expressed her feelings (as well as taking time to write about her medical condition should he not have been made aware of it from either Dorothy or Lillian):

You are so thoughtful and sweet to take any part of your valuable time to write to me. I cannot express to you how pleased I was to hear from you and to know that Lillian is so well and happy.

This is the first time that I have ever gone away from the children feeling that there was someone who had a deep personal interest in them and had their interests at heart. You cannot imagine what a satisfied feeling I have. I am very happy to have Jamie [Dorothy's husband, actor James Rennie] as a son, and I am very much afraid that my ego will be overdeveloped when I have the joy of welcoming you as a son, too. Dorothy writes me glowing reports of *The White Sister*, which makes me very happy for both you and Lillian.

My improvement has been a hundred per cent, since coming here. I think that a couple of months will find me in a perfect normal condition. Tell Lillian not to worry about me. I am feeling and looking better than I have for years. If Lillian makes as good a wife as she has been a daughter, your life together is going to be perfect, and there is every indication that she will. Naturally, she is perfect in my eyes.

Love and hug my children, not forgetting Petty. Lots of love and kind wishes to your own dear self.

> Lovingly,
> MRS. GISH

Perhaps Mrs. Gish's observation of Charles' "deep personal interest" was a less than subtle reminder of Lillian's disregard of his admonition: do not try to hide any jewelry when returning to New York from Italy. Charles had done his best to clear the way for her to pass through Customs with maximum ease and a minimum of waiting time. Upon Lillian's arrival, the authorities made sure there was no unnecessary waiting time, but they had seized her luggage and, upon inspection, found a concealed diamond and aquamarine necklace worth $6,540 and three smaller pieces of jewelry which had to be redeemed for $12,000 the following day by Dorothy and James Rennie. Lillian dismissed the potentially embarrassing incident as "forgetfulness."[2]

In the period Lillian had been employed by Inspiration Pictures, Duell had become her financial advisor as well as her companion and had suggested he assume the power of executor of her estate, adding that their marriage would be very advantageous from a business point of view. With a base of operations in Rome, both he and Lillian would be independent of Hollywood studio competition, politics, and the American tax system, which was beginning to make its presence felt in the final take-home pay of the higher salaried actors. Chaplin had never kept all of his money in United States banks. He was a British subject, free to come and go as he wished. Why shouldn't Lillian, an American, have that same privilege?

Lillian, who had never worked under the terms of a paper contract for all of her years with Griffith,[3] signed all of the papers Duell had presented her, never bothering to read them. When she was told that the studio hadn't received all of the moneys due them, she gallantly returned the engagement ring on April 20, 1924[4]—only to learn the ring—the symbol of their forthcoming betrothal—wasn't purchased by Duell the suitor using his own money, but by Duell the studio supervisor using company funds![5]

Thankfully, Lillian, who was becoming increasingly wary of all of the plans and schemes Duell was proposing, had rarely worn the ring during the day in public. Surrendering it meant little to her. Her engagement had never been officially announced, and if anybody knew about it, it was never a topic of discussion. Everyone was close-mouthed. You could do anything as long as the press wasn't aware of it. Whatever the nature of Lillian's relationship with Duell, it was over.

But a letter did exist that documented that Lillian and Charles Duell were engaged. It would surface later.[6]

Instead of reporting to Hollywood on December 6 to film *The Outsider* (which Duel had purchased for $55,000), Lillian left for New York, allegedly to work for another company. It was an action, Duell felt, that was in defiance of a contract signed with Inspiration Pictures on September 1, 1922—a contract that had been transferred to Duell's company on July 31, 1924. Lillian's contract with Duell stated that she would make 24 pictures within a period ending January 31, 1930, at a salary of $1,250 a week (eventually rising to $2,500 a week) as well as a percentage of the gross receipts of the films. If she married, Mr. Duell could terminate her contract 20 days after the ceremony if he wished to do so.

Lillian condemned the contract and considered her association with Charles Duell a fait accompli.

Her attorney, Louis S. Levy of the law firm Chadbourne, Stanchfield and Levy, issued the following statement:

> This latest move is part of a design to force Miss Gish to support Mr. Duel...[It] is impossible to live under his business arrangement.... Mr. Duell assumed to act as her lawyer, her trustee, her manager, and at the same time to contract with her as the executive head of a company to produce her pictures.... He apparently hoped to

bind her to him for a period of years under an arrangement by which he would share the fruits of her artistic efforts without any danger of liability upon him whatsoever. "Heads I win and tails you lose," is not yet recognized as the basis for a legal agreement.[7]

Duell, shocked by Lillian's response, claimed he was looking out for his fiancée's best interests. Lillian responded that it was an "unwarranted presumption," adding that she was never given legal counsel when she signed Duell's contracts.[8] A London cable, dated December 10, 1924, stated that Lillian's percentages (she was to have received 15 percent of all gross receipts in excess of $600,000 for her work in *The White Sister*) were reduced from $3,000 to $1,250, a reduction that saved Duell's company $130,000.[9]

Whether Miss Gish consented to these reductions wasn't known. Trusting the judgment of Charles Duell, she had signed a series of papers without taking the time to read the fine print. She certainly must have been aware that the future of Inspiration Pictures (and possibly her employment) were in jeopardy.

Rather than see Inspiration Pictures face liquidation, ambitious secretary J. Boyce Smith told Charles Duell that he could convince Lillian to sign a paper waiving two months' salary ($42,000) by suggesting that if she didn't "sign on the dotted line" she would never be paid. Her money would be deposited in Guarantee Trust and never issued, except on a direct order from Charles Duell.[10]

Lillian, dismissing Smith's threats, fully intended to begin employment at Metro-Goldwyn Pictures at a salary of $8,000 a week.[11] She continued to read and consider possible scripts.[12] With the constant influx of younger stars who could qualify for flapper roles and appeal to a younger generation whose attendance would bolster the box-office receipts, she knew that too long a second absence from the screen could damage any future screen career. She was over 30 years old, and she knew she didn't have the business acumen of a Mary Pickford. How much longer could Mary last, playing little girls?

On January 30, 1925, Lillian was made a defendant in a suit filed in federal court by Charles H. Duell, who was still trying to enforce his contract. Any delay in preventing Lillian from returning to the cameras would be a victory.

The tiny confines of a courtroom in the Woolworth Building[13] contained 200 seats arranged in four rows of 50 each. Fans and interested spectators, who wanted to catch even a brief glimpse of Lillian, had crowded the corridor and were standing on the steps leading to the sidewalk hours before the proceedings were to have begun at 10:30 a.m. One marshall was bodily seized, lifted, and passed over the crowd like a "chip on the crest of a wave." Disorder seemed to be the order of the day. How often would anyone have a free opportunity to see their favorite movie star, who rarely made appearances unless they were in conjunction with a film?

After the room was cleared of the overflow, Federal Judge Julian Mack, who managed to secure seats for three reporters, issued the following statement:

> This is not a show. Those who want to see the defendant perform must go to a theatre. This court is not going into a larger courtroom for the sake of curiosity hunters.[14]

Lillian, wearing a blue suit trimmed with a Persian collar, sat at the counsel table, unmoved and seemingly unaware of the commotion she was causing by her presence. Not acknowledging anyone, and not looking in the direction of Charles Duell, her hand remained closed against her cheek.

An astute fan remarked in a whisper everyone could hear, "That's the pose she took in *The White Sister*, lookin' out the window at the soldiers."[15]

What the astute fan — and nearly everybody else except a few reporters — failed to notice was a raw carrot concealed in Lillian's palm that she nibbled as her lawyer, Max Steur, painted a picture of her as "a fade out" and "helpless in business." Lillian would later jokingly remark that she was nervous and she would never bring a carrot to court again.[16] A current edition of an off-Broadway revue that featured topical material drawn from the newspapers inserted a sketch of Miss Gish nibbling the carrot in the *Grand Street Follies*, much to the delight of the audience and Miss Gish, who attended an evening performance.[17]

Lillian wasn't the only person subjected to the wrath of her former partner and unwelcome suitor.[18] Charles Duell, "weeping" before Magistrate Norman J. Marsh in the Yorkville Court, also had a summons issued to James Rennie, claiming that Dorothy's husband had threatened to "get him" on February 19 at 2:15 outside his law office on 9 East 46th Street.

Stated a distraught Duell:

> [Rennie] caught me by the arm and said, "Duell, situation is dangerous and must be stopped."
> ...And he further added, "You know what that means ... I will go the limit... This is your only warning, and act quickly. I am giving you this chance to save yourself."
> My secretary, Miss Brigham, at the time of the theatre, was passing out of the building on her way to the Lincoln Storage Warehouse.... She saw Rennie talking to me, and he was extremely tense and white.[19]

Under Steur's cross-examination, Duell admitted that no crowd had gathered outside his office, and that Rennie had struck no blows. For lack of evidence, the charge against Rennie was dismissed.[20]

To Lillian's delight, Judge Goddard also denied Duell's injunction restraining her from appearing in films not under his jurisdiction.[21]

Still trying to damage Lillian's character, Duell revived the incident of the hidden jewelry Lillian had forgotten to declare when she returned from Italy.

Included in the exhibits was a letter that had been written by Thomas Koons, a Massillon, Ohio, resident and friend of Lillian's, to his brother mentioning the engagement of Charles to Lillian, alluding to difficulties that may possibly occur. The family of the writers also received two affidavits to sign, verifying that such an arrangement existed.

Lillian had telegraphed Koons, requesting that he stay out of the case. Koons, knowing that Duell could have a commission appointed to secure testimony which could be damaging to Lillian, hoped all would end peacefully, as any statements he made might be misconstrued as disloyalty. Lillian, for a short time, did accept Duell's ring, but she never wore it for anyone to see.[22]

In a courtroom packed with mostly business girls, Max Steur, counsel for Lillian, painted two differing portraits of her on March 25. One was of the beloved Griffith heroine who could survive being trapped on an ice floe in *Way Down East*, and the other — away from the screen — was of a little girl who was at a total loss with contracts and mathematics.

While the spectators may have been overwhelmed with the business end of show business and the labyrinth of negotiations, they clearly sympathized with Steur's portrait of a "little girl" dominated by a Svengali-like individual who, without any hypnotism, managed to control her life away from the studio. Duell was a "God in her eyes" who also had drawn wills for

Lillian, Dorothy, and their mother in which he was sole executor![23]

On March 26, Lillian could not conceal her smile as she watched Max Steur cross-examining her former attorney, George W. Newgass.

> STEUR: You advised her [Lillian] to consent to raising the amount to $700,000 before she could get any percentage of the profits, which meant a loss to her of about $60,000. [The original contract called for $600,000].
> NEWGASS: I think there were benefits far in excess of that amount … continuation of her relations with the corporation.
> STEUR: Did Duell tell you that he had already obligated himself to procure such a paper to be signed by Miss Gish?
> NEWGASS: Absolutely not.[24]

Steur then placed in evidence a paper which he described as an "obligation" by Duell to obtain Lillian's consent to forfeit $60,000.

When Newgass mentioned Duell's engagement to Miss Gish, Steur saw another opportunity. And he seized it.

> STEUR: Now that you've dragged that in, who told you about it?
> NEWGASS: It was general knowledge.
> STEUR: Did Miss tell you?
> NEWGASS: No, sir.
> STEUR: Did Mr. Duell Tell you?
> NEWGASS: No … yes. [After Deull and Miss Gish had become estranged.]
> STEUR: So all the time he was engaged he never told you about it?
> NEWGASS: He did not.[25]

Later, Newgass testified that Lillian told him she wasn't being treated fairly, and that he had charged her $6,000 for legal services on November 23, 1924. Still, she would complete her contract.

> STEUR: Did she not say she would never have anything more to do with him?
> NEWGASS: She did not.
> Newgass further explained his relations with Charles Duell. When he was Miss

Gish's attorney, he also acted like a "broker" in seeing that money was contributed to the company called Duell Inc.[26]

During the cross-examination of J. Boyce Smith on March 27, the subject of Lillian's salary came up. Once again, Lillian sat at her counsel's table, her hand against her face. This time there was no carrot. She looked away from Charles Duell and made no effort to establish any eye contact.

Steur had pointed out that his client had signed away her salary and percentages of receipts without questioning what she was doing. It gave credence to the "fade-out" moniker he had used to describe her the previous day.

> STEUR: Did not Mr. Duell actually claim that her [Lillian Gish's] salary had been reduced from $2,500 to $2,000?
> SMITH: My understanding is that Miss Gish claimed $2,500 and Mr. Duell thought it ought to be $2,000. He paid her $2,500 with the understanding that the matter was one for discussion.[27]

Steur relentlessly proceeded with his questioning, emphasizing that Duell always stood to gain, while Lillian was going to lose.

> STEUR: Isn't it a fact that he [Duell] did not pay her [Lillian Gish] $2,500 until the first check for $2,000 had been refused and returned?
> SMITH: That is so.[28]

To get a waiver from Lillian for the amount of $42,000 during the time Duell's Inspiration Pictures was facing liquidation was the trust of Max Steur's second day of cross-examination of J. Boyce Smith, former studio secretary, on March 28.

> STEUR: Didn't Mr. Duell say [to you], "I'll guarantee to get Miss Gish to sign a paper giving up this $42,000, and I want half of it?"
> SMITH: That was the effect of it.

STEUR: Lillian Gish was the one out of whom the money was to come. It was not to come from Inspiration Pictures, but he [Duell] was out to trim this little girl out of $42,000. Isn't that it?

SMITH: Well, I couldn't exactly be expected to answer that as a matter of fact.

STEUR: And that was not the first time this weapon was used. It was used last July.[29]

Smith knew to what Steur was referring: the earlier attempt to withhold Lillian's salary by placing it in Guarantee Trust until permission was granted by Charles Duell.

SMITH: We held up the money.[30]

Lillian sat unperturbed. Those hoping to see her take the stand were once again disappointed.

March 30: The day had arrived for Charles Duell to testify. Like in a vaudeville show, the audience who had patiently sat through and applauded the opening acts was aware that Duell, while not a headliner, was someone worth watching. Even Judge Mack, who had been hearing about Duell's "unofficial engagement" which had been characterized by Lillian as an "unwarranted presumption" was looking forward to what Duell had to say.

On the stand, Duell made it seem logical. The "engagement" was "unofficial" because he was married (though separated from his wife, who was suing him for divorce). When the divorce would come through, he and Lillian would make a formal announcement. What he didn't anticipate was Lillian's change of attitude when the divorce became final. Now that he was free, Lillian no longer wanted him. It was like a popular saying of the day: "When you want 'em, you can't get 'em. When you can get 'em, you don't want 'em."

Until Duell had taken the stand, Lillian had never once looked at him nor made the effort to acknowledge his presence. During his testimony she watched him as if he were a case study. Her expression of neutrality never changed. Even when she heard his version of their "unofficial engagement," there was no reaction.

In his opening, Charles told his brother, attorney Holland Duell (who was handling his defense), that he had made loans to Miss Gish in May 1922 but had not asked to be paid back. He was able to charge it to the studio.

He further added:

> "Miss Gish wanted her personal affairs in the best possible shape.... Her personal affairs were not in good condition and the size of her personal holdings, at that time, were very limited. I knew she had worked many years, and had reached the conclusion that what she had made in the past had been very largely spent."

Holland Duell decided not to call Lillian to the stand, preferring to continue his direct examination of his brother, Charles.

HOLLAND: Do you remember the date when you became engaged?

CHARLES: Unofficially toward the end of June 1923, directly after I had been separated by a formal instrument from my wife.

Hearing Charles' answer, a smiling Judge Mack looked down at him and asked:

JUDGE: And officially?

CHARLES: Following my divorce.

STEUR: When was the divorce?

CHARLES: It was a Paris divorce granted, I think, at the end of January 1924.

JUDGE: What do you mean now by officially and unofficially?

CHARLES: The time when we could publicly announce the engagement.

JUDGE: And was it?

CHARLES: No.

JUDGE: And why wasn't it officially announced?

CHARLES: Because in April the engagement was broken.

The judge was heard to mumble, "Well, I never heard the language."

Charles Duell continued his testimony, adding that his company, Inspiration Pictures, had they not gone into liquidation, had plans to star Lillian and Richard Barthelmess in *Romeo and Juliet*.[31]

That same afternoon, after court was adjourned, Lillian attended an art reception honoring Russian painter Nicolai Fechin and herself at the Grand Central Art Galleries. Among his portraits and landscapes was a portrait of Lillian as Romola,[32] which was purchased by the Chicago Art Institute.[33]

Lillian's constant shifting in her chair at her counsel's table during Max Steur's blistering cross-examination of a reluctant Charles Duell revealed, for the first time since the start of the trial, signs of a nervousness she had so far been able to conceal from the spectators who would try to catch a glimpse of her or hear something they could tell others before the press had reported the events of the day.

That Charles Duell was not a good witness was proving itself evident with the continued questioning of how he conducted his business relationships. What mattered was his insistence on his engagement, which was an "unofficial engagement that would become official" once he was divorced, and that he had given Lillian a ring that she had accepted but never displayed. Nobody had ever been able to learn anything of her private life away from the studio. She had never seen the waivers of the percentages of receipts and hadn't any knowledge of what she was being told to sign.

Had Lillian made a mistake in believing that Charles Duell was a good potential husband — as her mother had believed that James Gish was the right person for her?

In his first words to Charles Duell, Max Steur warned him to expect no mercy. Judge Mack, in whose court the trial was taking place, admonished Charles Duell to answer the questions directly without "wandering into interpretations."[34]

STEUR: When you refer to Inspiration Pictures, Mr. Duell, you mean yourself, don't you? You were its President, its general manager, its treasurer. You constituted its Board of Directors and you held the voting power. So that Inspiration Pictures was you.
[And] when the agreement by which Miss Gish was to waive her right to $74,000 was drawn up, did you not take it to her hotel for her to sign.
DUELL: I did.
STEUR: And you told her that it was a fair and just agreement, didn't you?
DUELL: I did.
STEUR: Then were you deliberately intending to deceive the Court when you swore that you did not advise the defendant to sign?
DUELL: No.[35]

In the afternoon session, Steur had painted a portrait of Charles as a Jekyll and Hyde who had been toying with Miss Gish's emotions and her complete lack of business sense. Studio supervisor Duell had consciously been chiseling a helpless little girl out of money coming to her from her contractual agreements and, acting as her attorney-advisor, had been telling her to approve of what was taking place.

Pathetically, Duell had attempted to explain that "business and affection" were interminably intertwined.

STEUR: Don't you recall that you wrote out in your own hand a letter given out for publication, signed by Lillian Gish and written by you?[36]

Duell claimed he had no memory of such letter.

Steur then read from a copy of the letter: "I am not engaged to marry Charles Duell or any other man. [Signed] Lillian Gish."[37]

STEUR: Didn't you write the body of that, and then hand it to her to sign and then didn't you give it to the newspaper to publish, and didn't they publish it?[38]

Again, Duell claimed he had no memory of this. Judge Mack then intervened and said he could not understand how Duell could not recall such an incident.

STEUR: Am I to understand that at one moment you were sitting there as her lawyer, acting in her interests, and the next moment you were sitting there — in the same chair — as President of Inspiration Pictures to gouge her out of money?
...When was she to know that you were her friend and when was she to know you were her enemy? Was she to believe up to 4:10 you were her friend, and that at 4:15 she was to be on guard against you? What was this, a sort of Jekyll and Hyde affair?[39]

Steur then produced a check issued to Lillian Gish when there were no funds to meet it...

But a check had been received at the studio the next day. The entry in the checkbook had been adjusted to show the check had been issued when due and not three days later.

Steur had forced Charles Duell into making too many contradictions. Holland Duell later met with Judge Mack and attorney Max Steur and requested permission to withdraw the case.[40]

At 10:30 on the morning of April 2, Judge Julian W. Mack dismissed Duell's injunction and held him under $10,000 bail on a charge of perjury, threatening him with disbarment. Duell was remanded to the custody of his brother, attorney Holland Duell.

Judge Mack, who had prepared nothing in writing, announced that the court

...in addition to finding the actions of Inspiration Pictures and of Charles

Duell as its President in connection with the employment or alleged employment of Newgass to protect the interests of the defendant were fraudulent, intentionally and knowingly so, and on the testimony of Newgass alone, with nothing further ... that Newgass was not informed of the true situation that he was supposed to be acting on behalf of Miss Gish, as he himself testified, he would not have advised or sanctioned the transactions in question depriving her of moneys due under the contracts ... had he known the entire situation.
...In fact, in 22 years of judicial experience, it has not been my fortune or misfortune to have had before me any case of more flagrant, outrageous breach of trust....[41]

The action of Judge Mack left Charles Duell senseless.

In the hallway outside the courtroom, copies of Mrs. Gish's letter approving Charles Duell as a potential son-in-law, and a letter written to him from Lillian in Florence, Italy, using their personal color code, were distributed to those present. Lillian returned to her apartment at the Ambassador Hotel. Her lawyer, Max Steur, had issued a statement that they were "out."[42]

On May 7, Lillian gave twenty minutes of testimony against Charles Duell in a closed hearing, as reporters armed with cameras waited in the hallway. On the advice of her counsel, Chadbourne, Stanchfield and Levy, she refused to answer any questions or pose for photographs. What she had said to Judge Mack was not revealed.

Charles Duell was indicted by the federal grand jury on May 20. There were three counts and 24 separate accusations in the bill. Colonel William Hayward, acting as Duell's counsel, requested that bail be reduced from $10,000 to $1,000 as Charles Duell was "penniless" and his legal fees were assumed by the American Legion.

United States Attorney Buckner agreed to the reduced fee. Buckner would be conducting the government case against Charles Duell in the fall.[43]

On November 11, 1925, Duell had another court date, not in connection with Lillian Gish, but to answer why he didn't pay $650 to actress Mae Murray for the lease on her apartment on 1 West 67th Street for the month of April while he had been appearing in federal court.[44]

After a few minutes of deliberation, the jury awarded $1,600 to Mae on the grounds that Duell "destroyed certain coverings, upholstery, and furniture, broke china and glassware, damaged bedspreads, covers and other linens, and scratched and damaged the walls, floors, and ceilings"[45]

Nearly a year would pass before Duell would be tried. Lillian knew she needed time to rest—but not for very long. People might forget her.

CHAPTER 15

Mimi

To a visiting American, the Paris of 1925 was the cultural capital of the world. Ernest Hemingway, Gertrude Stein, Ezra pound, *The Transatlantic Review*, black jazz bands: they all were there to be appreciated. You could be free or excessively rude, perhaps indulge in a few quick, impersonal love affairs without any consequences, drink unlimited gin, and pass out under or on top of a table in the Café du Dome.[1]

The Lillian Gish who visited Paris was hardly one to be a *boulevardier* and sit at an outdoor table exchanging a bit of philosophy over a glass of wine. She was in Paris in search of a vehicle that would showcase her talents at a new studio. Said vehicle would preferably possess a French background that would translate well on both sides of the Atlantic. As successful as Hemingway's *The Sun Also Rises* had been with world-wide audiences, she knew she could never be the promiscuous Brett.

Wisely, Lillian knew to look to pre-twentieth century material. Literature and the opera always provided a wealth of subjects that could be filmed, but she shied away from *Nana* and *Madame* Bovary on moral grounds. Both the Zola and Flaubert novels had been viewed as scandalous on their initial publication. Would turning their words into a Lillian Gish picture provoke a similar outrage with audiences?

She renewed her friendship with playwright Madame de Gresac, with whom she had once collaborated on the never-filmed *World's Shadows* for the non-existent Frohman Company five years previously in 1920.[2] One new possibility was *Louise*, an opera written by Gustave Charpentier. Lillian would be playing the title role, a nineteenth century dressmaker in love with Julian, a painter of whom her parents didn't approve. In defiance, Louise would go to live with Julian at his quarters in Montmartre with his bohemian friends, only to return home when she hears that her father is dying. At his deathbed, Louise would continue to defy her father's wishes and leave to return to Julian, as her weakening father hurls a chair at her back.[3]

The idea of conjugal love without marriage, long a *raison d'être* in opera, was something Lillian found distasteful and felt it should not be presented on film to her Griffith-developed audience, who wanted to protect her virtue and shield her from the evils of a corrupt world. Meetings with the composer, during which time she tried to convince him to change the ending and to have the lovers, Louise and Julian, living apart, were futile. *Louise* was already a successful opera the way he wrote it. To insert a happy Hollywood ending would ruin its intention. Didn't a married Nora walk out on her husband in Ibsen's *A Doll's*

House? If Miss Gish wanted to develop an international, sophisticated audience, she would have to stop thinking like a provincial American.

Still wanting to utilize a nineteenth century Parisian milieu, Lillian recalled Henri Murger's 1849 novel, *Scènes de la vie de Bohème,* which was dramatized in 1851 and later turned into an opera, *La Bohème,* with music by Giacomo Puccini, in 1896. As a motion picture with Lillian playing Mimi, the rejected seamstress wrongfully accused of infidelity who dies in her lover's arms on the evening of his successful play's opening, American and European audiences would be seeing a perfectly balanced blending of tragedy and romance.[4]

Madame de Gresac, not wanting to be influenced by the Giuseppe Giacosa and Luigi Illica libretto or Theodore Barriere's stage adaptation, located a copy of the original novel and, with Lillian's suggestions, began to develop a script they could present to the newly formed Metro-Goldwyn-Mayer studio when they returned to Los Angeles.

The process which resulted in the forming of Metro-Goldwyn-Mayer Pictures had taken almost ten years of mergings. It started as Metro Pictures in 1915,[5] and remained as such until 1923, when Loew's theatre magnate Marcus Loew[6] merged Metro with the Goldwyn Company. Now the studio was called Metro-Goldwyn. Still unhappy, Loew consulted lawyer J. Robert Rubin, who recommended including Louis B. Mayer,[7] who had been associated with William Randolph Hearst's Cosmopolitan Pictures.[8]

The final result, Metro-Goldwyn-Mayer, was not devoid of internal anxieties. The creative side (the writers, actors, producers, and directors) resided in the West. The backers (the money people), who viewed any and every suggestion strictly in terms of dollars and sense, were in the East.

The acquisition of Lillian Gish had not been without its doubters. While Louis

B. Mayer's shrewd purchasing of the New England distribution rights for D. W. Griffith's *The Birth of a Nation* in 1915 had yielded him a personal profit of $250,000,[9] he was well aware that ten years had passed and public tastes in femininity had changed. Lillian wasn't Greta Garbo, a recent import who was earning a lesser salary and making motion pictures with more realistic themes. In *The Joyless Street* she had succumbed to making love for money as a means of survival in post World War I Berlin. Would the proper, perpetually virginal Lillian dare to depict this in one of her films? Or would she continue to tiptoe through the same formula Griffith-type story in defiance of the screen's new ruthless honesty?

Was the final scene in Charpentier's *Louise* the real reason she refused to be in a film version? Did Louise's rejection of her dying father's wishes have any real-life parallels still lingering from Lillian's childhood? Was Lillian reminded of her mother's refusal to visit her dying husband, Lillian's father?

Never had Lillian thrown herself into a project with such dedication and verve. While the British reviews of Romola praised Lillian's looks, the film was dismissed as a "turgid failure."[10] To turn *La Bohème* into a Parisian travelogue or a Toulouse-Lautrec–type fashion show would immediately end Lillian's career.

In a magazine article, Dorothy, always a realist, tried to shatter the attitude that Lillian was perpetually ethereal, cerebral, and angelic:

> Lillian is not soft and dreamy. Nothing matters to her except her work and career. Mother and I tease her about her remorseless activity. One of our pet names for her is The Iron Horse [a popular film of the day about the building of the transcontinental railroad]. We hope neither of us dies while she is doing a picture.[11]

As Mimi in *La Bohème* (1926, MGM, directed by Vidor). A clash of temperaments was evident. Lillian fought with her director, costumer and leading man regarding how the Puccini heroine should look and act. But nobody was prepared for the death scene which proved how right she had been from the start!

Like fellow Metro-Goldwyn-Mayer actress Aileen Pringle, who was often called a "Darling of the Intelligentsia,"[12] Lillian was one of those screen actresses who liked to read books — complete books, not a Sunday newspaper synopsis for the purpose of name-dropping at a cocktail party. Lillian moved with ease, assurance, and confidence in literary circles populated by the successful writers of the day: F. Scott Fitzgerald, Dorothy Parker, Theodore Dreiser, Edna Ferber, Sinclair Lewis, Dashiell Hammett, Carl Van Vechten, Fannie Hurst, Joseph Hergesheimer, and *American Mercury* editor and founder H. L. Mencken.[13]

Mencken, Lillian's frequent escort when dining in New York (until he had become more involved with Aileen Pringle), once remarked to Lillian's friend, Anita Loos (with whom he had had once had an affair), that he found Lillian amusing and well-informed."[14] Anita viewed her friend Lillian as someone who knew how to surround herself with men of intelligence by keeping quiet, listening, and smiling when they took a breath.[15]

Both Aileen and Lillian were unofficial ambassadors, always on hand to smooth the way for the important incoming writers hired to develop screenplays, and bestselling authors whose works and services Mayer wanted to acquire at the lowest possible rates. A pattern was established. The more chatty Pringle would greet them as they arrived at the train station and whisk them over to the studio in a chauffeured limousine to Mr. Mayer, who would greet them with Lillian at his side. Sometimes a photographer from the publicity department would be there.

Aileen Pringle recalled:

> There is nothing more distracting than having to be charming during the course of the day when you are shooting. Garbo, who became my tennis partner, would never allow herself to be anything but an actress. That, she felt, was enough. To play hostess, as Lillian sometimes did, was quite annoying. I hated doing it, if I didn't know the person.

But Lillian didn't seem to mind. She had learned from Mr. Griffith to be aware of the public. It was part of her day's work.

Unlike Garbo, who learned how to demand and get a closed set, Lillian had a mother to support. Lillian wouldn't do anything that might stop that support.[16]

One of Mencken's *The American Mercury* compatriots who frequently dined with Lillian in New York was *The Saturday Review of Literature* and *Vanity Fair* magazine critic George Jean Nathan. Nathan's disdain for motion pictures was well known. He preferred the stage, and always made theatre reservations for two when assigned to review an opening night performance of a new play. He often went alone and placed his hart and coat on the second seat.[17]

Both Nathan and Mencken were very confirmed bachelors and notorious womanizers. If the relationship with any woman began as a sexual one, that was all it could ever be, and it ran its course with no regrets. With the constant availability of young chorus girls who wanted to be seen with them and possibly be introduced to producers who might offer them a job in an upcoming revue or musical play, there were plenty of potential partners. Chorus girls were passed around and shared like hors d'oeuvres and good wine. There was never any emotional involvement. It was advantageous to both sides and only a matter of time before they "solved the mystery."[18]

Depending upon who is telling the story, Lillian met Nathan in one of several ways. She might have been introduced to him when Joseph Hergesheimer, covering an interview assignment for *The American Mercury*'s April 1924 issue, asked him to accompany him.[19] Anita Loos, however, always believed she was present, not Nathan, at the Hergesheimer interview, because she and editor H. L. Mencken had known Lillian and Hergesheimer.[20]

Lillian told actor O. Z. Whitehead, a juvenile appearing with her onstage in the 1939 production of *Life with Father.*

> We [George Jean Nathan and Lillian] got acquainted in London. We only saw each other for just a few days. After that, we were separated for more than a year. During that time he wrote me beautiful letters. I think that his best writing was in those letters...[21]

A second, more propitious meeting occurred accidentally during a train ride from New York to Philadephia. Lillian was on her way to spend a weekend with the Hergesheimers at their West Chester Home. It was one of her last opportunities to spend time with friends before leaving to film *La Bohème* in Los Angeles.

The train ride was only 75 minutes, but it was long enough for Nathan and Lillian to engage in conversation. Nathan was less than kind about motion pictures, but he managed to find something nice to write about her work in an article for *Vanity Fair*:

> Her technique consists in thinking out a characterization directly and concretely and then executing it in terms of semi-vague suggestion....
>
> She is always present, she always dominates the scene, yet one feels somehow that she is ever just out of sight around the corner. One never feels that one is seeing her entirely. There is ever something pleasantly, always alluringly missing, as there is in the case of women who are acting artists.

Acting artist? George Jean Nathan had possibilities. He could flatter Lillian in print.

Lillian Gish, the former Biograph player and leading lady at the insolvent Inspiration Pictures, standing at the Culver City gates of the mammoth Metro-Goldwyn-Mayer Studios that had "more stars than there are in the heavens," had good reason to be apprehensive. When she began with Biograph in 1912, there was no need of affixing her signature to a formal contract. Everything was conducted on a handshake, and then the commitment was honored. Her short stay with Inspiration was formalized with a Duell-written contract, and then another (and another) "agreement" to which she had to give her written consent.

Still bitter because she hadn't bothered to read the fine print on the contract, she signed with Metro-Goldwyn-Mayer because contracts had become de rigeur, whether working under a strict studio regimen or on a picture-to-picture basis for an independent company. She hadn't wanted to turn out a guaranteed number of films a year, but this was a new Hollywood, where everything was budgeted — from acquiring the property to casting the leads, supporting players, and day-extras. Moviemaking, whether done behind an East 14th Street tailor's shop in New York or behind the gates at Culver City, was still moviemaking. Metro-Goldwyn-Mayer, where terms like "production values," "lavish," and "big budget" were a matter of course, was just a little better than the others. Lillian only had to consider their recent successes (Alice Terry in Rex Ingram's *Scaramouche*, John Gilbert in Erich von Stroheim's *The Merry Widow* and King Vidor's *The Big Parade*, and Ramon Novarro in Fred Niblo's *Ben-Hur*) to realize that the choicest of directors worked there, and they were matched with the best of the current crop of actors. The

Metro-Goldwyn-Mayer product was packaged. Other studios made movies, but Metro-Goldwyn-Mayer was the movies.

Despite *Romola*'s disappointing box-office returns, a stern but sentimental Louis B. Mayer felt he had a moral obligation to include Lillian as part of his studio family. Lillian was a reminder of an earlier period of his life when he cannily pooled his and his family's money to purchase the New England distribution rights to a film of unprecedented length, the 12 reels of *The Birth of a Nation*, starring Lillian Gish.

More than a decade later, that same Lillian Gish, in the post–Griffith *The White Sister* and *Romola*, was still the cinema's little match girl, miraculously weathering an earthquake, a flood, and a volcanic eruption while maintaining her innocence and enough strength to face a corrupt world with faith and optimism.

The Lillian Gish entering through the Culver City gates was entering her thirties. She could still project an aura of innocence and vulnerability. Mayer wanted to protect her. She had been indirectly responsible for his first fortune.

She was received on her first day of arrival with the fanfare and respect afforded visiting royalty. A huge banner across the streets of Culver City proclaimed that LILLIAN GISH IS NOW AN MGM STAR. There were bands, flowers, and lines of executives to welcome her.[22]

And then — nothing.

Fortunately, Lillian had been developing her *La Bohème* project on her own with Madame de Gresac. The contract, still in its "honeymoon"[23] phase, gave her complete approval of her director and leading man. She was MGM'S most prestigious resource. Soon, she would become their greatest salaried expense.[24]

Twenty-seven-year-old production supervisor Irving Thalberg, to whom she would submit her requests, suggested running some of the studio's recent output.

Among the films were two reels of King Vidor's *The Big Parade,* featuring John Gilbert and Renée Adorée in the now classic chewing gum sequence and the departure of the soldiers.[25] The mammoth production of a poignant wartime love in France that utilized Griffith-like panoramic sweeps of the camera and hundreds of soldiers may have reminded Lillian of *The Birth of a Nation* and *Hearts of the World.*

The Big Parade had cost $245,000 to make and had grossed in excess of $15,000,000.[26] Twenty-eight-year-old John Gilbert had scored positively with female audiences, playing opposite vampish Aileen Pringle in Vidor's romantic *His Hour* and Mae Murray in *The Merry Widow.*

Before the conclusion of the second reel of *The Big Parade,* Lillian knew she'd found not only *La Bohème*'s director in King Vidor and leading man in John Gilbert, but also much of the supporting cast: Renée Adorée, Roy D'Arcy, and Karl Dane.[27] She would also have, as her photographer, Hendrick Sartov, who had photographed her with his soft lens in Griffith's 1918 feature, *The Greatest Thing in Life.* Sartov's invention, which he now called the "Lillian Gish lens," had been improved, and would be used with panchromatic film for *La Bohème.*

Having been working in Italy for two years on *The White Sister* and *Romola* prior to her return, Lillian was unaware of the changes that had occurred at American studios. No longer was everything the sole responsibility of the director. A Griffith-created art form, at which she had been present in its infancy, was now an industry that functioned with machinelike precision. No longer did actors move props when requested, or apply their own makeup. The emergence of a union prevented directors from making actors work far into the night for the same pay. What directors had done

Lillian with Renée Adorée and company in *La Bohème*. *Bottom row* (from left to right) Catherine Vidor, Valentina Zimina. *Second Row* (from left to right) Renée Adorée and Lillian Gish.

alone was now accomplished by assistants. Now there were wardrobe managers and hairdressers.[28]

Metropolitan Opera patrons accustomed to seeing a rather substantial Enrico Caruso and Nellie Melba or Marcella Sembrich appearing as Rodolpho and Mimi, must have been overjoyed at the publicity department's release that John Gilbert and Lillian were going to be in the film version. Lillian was a "perfect incarnation of the doomed little grisette."[29]

The Griffith heroine, who had survived an ice floe entrapment, was now making a comeback — by heading for the Latin Quarter and consumption.

The filming, originally slated to begin in June 1925, had to be postponed because director Vidor and several of the actors Lil-

lian wanted weren't available. Lillian, who was staying at the Beverly Hills Hotel, alternated her free time between visiting Douglas Fairbanks and Mary Pickford at Pickfair, their Beverly Hills home near the hotel, and driving down the seacoast and stopping at little fishing villages with George Jean Nathan, who would spend part of his time on the West Coast when not reviewing plays in New York. Occasionally they would be joined by Aileen Pringle and H. L. Mencken.[30]

On one weekend, when neither Nathan nor Mencken were available for a quiet dinner, Lillian drove three hours to Laguna, where she went camping with Mary and Doug. Fairbanks camping was not done in the rugged style one associates with being close to nature in a scenic area.

The Fairbanks "camp" consisted of 14 individual sleeping tents in a secluded beach area. There was a dining tent and a sitting room.[31]

In August, the *La Bohème* company was ready. It remained for Lillian to set the pace and determine what would happen next. Not since the 1920 *Remodeling Her Husband,* which Lillian directed for Dorothy, had she ever been given such control.

King Vidor would be directing *La Bohème,* but Lillian would have the final word. It was her turn now. She had waited long enough.

Lillian's *La Bohème* sticks closely to the opera, rather than the Murger novel, and provides an admirable vehicle to showcase Lillian's talents for portraying long-suffering heroines. Mimi [Lillian], a seamstress, is going to be evicted because she is unable to pay her rent. Rodolpho, a newspaper journalist and aspiring playwright, notices how cold she is and takes her inside his quarters, introducing her to his bohemian friends. Neither Rodolpho nor Mimi has much to live on, but their simple, unconditional love overcomes any vestiges of poverty. When Rodolpho is fired from his newspaper job, Mimi, pretending not to know what has happened, continues to pretend to submit his material. Paul, a boulevardier, suggests she take one of Rodolpho's plays to a theatre manager. Mimi disguises herself in her friend Musette's clothes and goes with him. Rodolpho, thinking she is being unfaithful, makes her leave him. Later, after his play has opened, a now consumptive Mimi braves the elements to return to him and die in his arms.

The filming did not begin smoothly. Although miniatures of the sets had been submitted to Vidor and his staff, Lillian disliked the miniature of the attic where her character was to live.

> It wasn't right. Mimi was a poor seamstress in the year 1830, not a vacationer who was renting a large room in a cheaper section of Paris for a few months. To show poverty, you have to have cramped quarters — a garret, not a loft out of Greenwich Village. These characters were of limited means, not society types who wanted to slum. You could have the cameraman just as easily pan a small room. The establishing shot has to show just how limited Mimi's life was by those walls.
>
> Mr. Thalberg listened and told me that living in an attic was a sign of poverty, and the type of clothing I would wear would indicate how poor I was.[32]

Lillian also rejected costume designer Erté's sketches. Erté had designed the costumes for the *Folies Bergère* in Paris, covers for *Vanity Fair* magazine, and for Aileen Pringle in MGM'S *The Mystic* the previous year (1924).[33] Lillian disdainfully characterized him as a "small dainty man who seemed to have designed [her costumes] for himself." Erté saw Mimi as a vamp, and his Mimi costumes were closer to those he had designed for Aileen Pringle than what Lillian had in mind for an 1803s Paris.

There was a definite clash of wills. Erté wanted tattered and heavy garments to indicate the coldness of Mimi's surroundings,[34] while Lillian wanted to use "old silk," claiming it was more authentic than wool and would photograph better.[35]

With the exception of Lillian's costumes, Erté designed all of the costumes for the film and told the press at a newspaper publicity session that Lillian was uncooperative by refusing to wear anything but silk. Mimi would never have the money to buy silk. It did not fit her character.[36]

In the opening scenes of the opera on which the film was based, Rodolpho, reaching for her hand, says that her hand is frozen. Earlier, Marcello has remarked that his fingers are frozen, whereupon Rodolpho reaches for some of his manuscript pages and tosses them into the fire. The roofs are snow-covered, and it is Christmas Eve.

Snow-covered roofs, Christmas Eve, Mimi's frozen hand, Marcello's cold fingers, a fireplace: Wouldn't it be more practical to be wearing wool? Still, strong-willed Lillian would not yield. Her Mimi would wear silk.

With the assistance of Mother Coulter of the wardrobe department, a costume was created out of available material that would be in keeping with the ensemble of the company. Only Lillian's picnic costume was new.

Lillian had won an early battle, and Erté never spoke to her again. She never knew if he saw the completed picture.[37]

Lillian's method of rehearsing harkened back to her Griffith days. Although Vidor thought this type of rehearsal was more aligned to the theatre (out of which Griffith and Lillian came), he allowed her to exercise her contractual rights. He was also curious, as he knew he would never have — even in the mid-twenties — such an opportunity to watch an old-style approach to filming (an approach which made Griffith an anachronism in his own lifetime).

Rejecting the "few bare walls with openings for doors and windows," and the inclusion of kitchen chairs and tables to act as furniture, Lillian asked for a bare stage, having failed to acclimate herself to Vidor's suggestion that the props he supplied were his method of knowing where the characters were.

A script girl was present to take notes on what Lillian was doing as Mimi: opening and closing imaginary doors and drawers, combing her hair, and walking to imagined places where there would be a dresser and a door. Without the actual props, she was able to move around in a much freer manner. If the actors would be able to follow her methods, they would learn their blocking quicker and actually shorten the rehearsal process.

On the second day, the company moved outdoors at her suggestion. They repeated the process on a bare lawn. Still working without any props, they rehearsed the major scenes, including the café scene and Mimi's death, in full view of anybody who happened to be in the area.[38]

Vidor, overwhelmed at Lillian's drive and commitment, didn't understand her concept of the love relationship between Mimi and Rodolpho. In the Griffith era, the idea of love was expressed by holding hands while walking down a country lane or quickly exchanging a chaste kiss on the cheek when nobody was looking. Rodolpho and Mimi were lovers on the grand scale. And the audience, particularly John Gilbert's audience, wanted to see that. John Gilbert was publicized as The Great Lover.

So began another clash of wills — this time between Lillian and Vidor.

Lillian saw Mimi as a playful tease, the direct opposite of woman-crazy Rodolpho. If Mimi yielded too easily, where was the tragedy? To build the audience's anticipation of the first kiss from Rodolpho, she suggested keeping the lovers as far away as possible: Mimi in an overhead window with Rodolpho looking up from the street in the manner of a Parisian Romeo and Juliet. Lillian also thought having Mimi kiss Rodolpho with a windowpane between them would further heighten the anticipation.

While Lillian's reasoning seemed logical, Mayer, Thalberg, and Vidor knew what the moviegoing public wanted to see: John Gilbert, The Great Lover, living up to his reputation.[39]

Aileen Pringle, John Gilbert's leading lady in King Vidor's 1924 *His Hour*, offered a humorous reason why Lillian didn't want to have close contact with her leading man, who had now become completely enamored of her:

> John Gilbert almost constantly smelled of liquor. I'd find him in the morning sleeping on my chaise lounge on my porch in Santa Monica on Adelaide Drive.
>
> When we filmed *His Hour*, there was a dance sequence, and he lifted me up while he was drinking champagne and laughing and swaying to the waltz music. And I said — and lipreaders must have howled — "If you drop me, you son of bitch, I'll kill you!"
>
> That's why the proper Lillian didn't want to kiss him.
>
> Her loss![40]

Colleen Moore, a friend of Lillian's and a companion of King Vidor late in his life, offered a more plausible explanation concerning Lillian's reluctance to do any passionate love scenes with John Gilbert:

> How could Lillian play a love scene convincingly on the screen when she never had one in real life? I know that's a terribly catty thing to say, and I love her, but that's the truth. Her sister Dorothy liked the men, but Lillian had all of that repressed emotion.
>
> If they had cast Dorothy as Mimi, I think we would have had a more natural French girl, who lived as a bohemian.
>
> Lillian liked to suffer on film, and she did it very well. She knew how to make your cry, but in *La Bohème* she had to play a genuinely passionate woman.
>
> John [Gilbert] was wonderful. Who couldn't be passionate with John Gilbert? The line goes around the block.
>
> Lillian knew how to "die for love," but in *La Bohème* she had to "live for love," and I think she found this difficult to play. She never had to tap those emotions.
>
> Suffering is easy. Loving is harder"[41]

The filming continued and the Gish-Gilbert "kiss controversy" developed into an in-house studio feud with specific lines of battle. On one side was Lillian, her contract, and her constant cry of "artistic integrity." In the opposite camp were a most concerned Irving Thalberg and Louis B. Mayer. While Thalberg found Lillian's work "brilliant," he was coming to the realization that her attitudes were "dated," and she was "unbending" in the face of modern reasoning.[42] Director King Vidor had no choice but to accede to her demands. *La Bohème* was filmed without even one kiss or physical embrace. Lillian had turned the Mimi-Rudolph relationship into something "ethereal," in alignment with Gish's persona of the unapproachable virgin, the eternal innocent.

What neither Lillian nor Vidor anticipated was the death of Giacomo Puccini, the composer of the *La Bohème*. It had been hoped that his music could have been used, had the studio been able to enter into negotiations. Because the licensing of film rights was complicated and time-consuming, Metro-Goldwyn-Mayer had resident composers William Axt and David Mendoza supply melodies that would invoke — but never consciously copy — the Puccini themes. (In the following year [1927] they performed a similar service by providing melodies that sounded like — but never were — Romberg themes for Metro-Goldwyn-Mayer's *The Student Prince in Old Heidelberg*, thereby saving the studio from having to enter into negotiations with Sigmund Romberg, who was still living.)

Lillian admiringly spoke of Axt and Mendoza:

> What those men did in a couple of weeks when they saw that the Puccini estate wouldn't cooperate was sheer genius. They used the Puccini harmonies and wrote melodies around them. They would use one or two easily identifiable introductions and

make adjustments, while still maintaining Puccini's time signatures and rhythm.

When George [Jean Nathan] heard the Axt-Mendoza score with the film, he said it was better than the original![43]

The *La Bohème* preview audience lauded the aesthetic tone and beauty of the film, but the John Gilbert fans were very disappointed. Where were the love scenes? How could a John Gilbert film not have at least one love scene?

Vidor tried to explain the audience's written response on the preview cards they had filled out at the conclusion of the film on the following morning to Mayer and Thalberg, but both men remained unconvinced that Lillian's concept of no kissing would only heighten their desire and the inevitable tragedy.

Lovers require — demand — physical contact. Actors Gish and Gilbert barely touch. Women, a major segment of the movie audience, went to see John Gilbert films for the love scenes. The presence of a Lillian Gish was of secondary importance. Lillian was just John's leading lady. A leading lady should kiss the leading man, especially if he is John Gilbert.[44]

Louis B. Mayer, convinced that John Gilbert's career (which was on the rise as his popularity increased) would fizzle if this non-kissing policy of Lillian's weren't changed, ordered Vidor to insert love scenes before the New York premiere. Without love scenes in a John Gilbert movie, there was no John Gilbert movie.

Vidor told Lillian what Mayer demanded. The windowpanes were removed. No need for glass barriers.[45] A "chaste peck" was not enough for the legions of John Gilbert fans.[46]

It was not an easy, nor desirable, task for Lillian to kiss John Gilbert. She never had to play a love scene in any Griffith film. In three days of shooting, perhaps one kiss

was printable after much maneuvering and coaxing. Lillian found it almost impossible to relax.[47]

To her chauffeur, Lillian was alleged to have remarked on her way to the studio: "Oh dear. I've got to go through another day of kissing John Gilbert."[48]

Silent film actress Leatrice Joy, once married to John Gilbert, offered a possible explanation regarding Lillian's problem playing a love scene with her former husband:

People think that love scenes are easy. All you have to do is move your heads together, pucker up, and kiss.

Love scenes are easy if you're in love with somebody, or maybe just like him a little.

John [Gilbert] never had any problems with love scenes. I heard reports all of the time. The director called for "Action!" and John went ahead and *acted* until he was told to "Cut."

Sometimes with some leading ladies, John kept right on *acting*, especially with Miss Garbo. Both of them kept on *acting*. They were so involved with their *acting*, I was surprised nobody called the fire department to hose them down, once they stopped *acting*!

Lillian, I heard, had problems with her love scenes. I can understand why, I think. As an actress, she didn't have anything to draw upon, if you know what I mean. Everything she did was technical.

Love scenes have to be properly lit. The camera is going to film every motion you make: how you turn your head, when you close your eyes, or move your lips. You can't "fake" a love scene the way you can "fake" a crying scene by reaching for a towel, or a "death" scene by merely taking a deep breath and closing your eyes.

I think Lillian was afraid of love scenes because she never had to do any when she worked for Mr. Griffith.

I don't know what Lillian did away from the studio. I don't know if

Lillian had any kind of social life. I never saw her. I do know that Dorothy, her sister, was always at parties.

Lillian was an aging innocent, and after a certain age, that isn't always the best thing to be. A lady creates her own atmosphere anyway.

A lot of men were in love with Lillian. I know John was in love with her for a short time. Maybe Lillian didn't know how to accept love from a man. Maybe she didn't know how to return love to a man. Or maybe she was afraid of returning it. That would mean you might be interested.

Lillian, you see, always had to be in control. No man could tell her anything. Sad...[49]

Lillian asked to be notified well in advance when Mimi's tragic death scene would be shot. She wanted to be ready for it. To lie on her back and close her eyes would be too reminiscent of what she had done for Griffith in *Broken Blossoms* seven years earlier in 1919. She didn't want to be accused of repeating herself. An acting artist, as Mr. Nathan once described her in a *Vanity Fair* article, has to grow.

Lillian was also quite aware of the younger Gilbert's huge popularity as a matinee idol. She was competing for the audience's attention, not against a younger lady but against a younger man, whose popularity, she believed, stemmed from his ability to play a love scene. Maybe that was why she chose him. He was certainly more of a strongly masculine presence than Richard Barthelmess or the gentle Bobby Harron.

Had audiences forgotten how she moved them to tears in *The Mothering Heart* (1913) after the death of her child? She would do it again in *La Bohème*. *La Bohème* was her picture, not John's. *La Bohème* was Mimi's story, not Rodolpho's. Mimi's death would remind the audience how important she is.

I knew I would have to prepare myself the way I had prepared for *Way Down East* [1920].

I read about tuberculosis. I spoke to several doctors. I visited tubercular wards in hospitals to see the faces of the patients and watch their breathing. Every illness has its own breathing pattern. It's very subtle, and it isn't taking deeper breaths or quicker breaths.

I told Mr. Vidor I wanted the camera to stay on my face in full close-up as much as possible. I didn't want any panning around the room and then coming back to me, and I'm in another position. It was my scene.

Luckily, this was a movie, not an opera. I know in an opera they always have the soprano sing a final aria, and, to great applause, she staggers to the bed, lifts her arms to the ceiling, and then falls and dies.

If I did that "opera blocking" on film, it would get laughs, and everything I had tried to do would be destroyed in less than a second.[50]

To the astonishment of her fellow cast members and crew, it was a wraithlike Mimi they saw on the shooting day of her tubercular death scene. It was almost canceled on the day before the shooting, but, seeing her, Vidor knew nothing else must take precedence, so impressed had he become with her work drive and total commitment to the film.[51] Lillian was an actress "bred to the manner of pain," and he had only recently photographed her holding onto the back of a cart and actually being dragged over the cobblestones in her effort to be reunited with Rodolpho.[52] She had been granted three days in which to prepare for her final scene. And prepare she did.

By refusing any liquids and sleeping with wads of cotton between her teeth and gums, she had removed any traces of saliva from her mouth, which had turned outward and was parched with dryness. Her throat was dry. Her eyes were bleary and devoid of any expression. Her voice was barely audible, and she spoke in tones barely above a whisper, preferring to sit in silence and wait until cameraman Hendrick Sartov and King Vidor were ready to begin.[53]

Action!

Mimi was carried into her room by her bohemian friends and cautiously placed upon her bed. They said their farewells, and then Rodolpho entered and played the final scene.

But something unexpected happened — something for which none of the cast members were ready.

Gilbert, after seeing Mimi die in his arms, didn't remain in her room for a few moments and then take his exit as rehearsed. He forgot what he was supposed to do! Like the other actors in the scene, so stunned was he by the impact of Lillian's acting that he was unable to move.

Vidor, pinned between Sartov's camera and a slanting wall in a corner of the attic, was aware that Lillian

> had completely stopped breathing and the movement of her eyes and eyelids was absolutely suspended.... The moments clicked out, but still Miss Gish had not moved nor breathed...
> The cameras ground on — moments turned into minutes.... After an untold length of time ... everyone was fearful of what might have happened ... [she] could now take breath and open her eyes. But this she did not do.... I fearfully walked over to where she lay and touched her gently on the arm. Her head turned slowly, and her lips formed a faint smile.[54]

Despite the enormous amount of effort put into *La Bohème*, not all of the European audiences (whose following Lillian wanted to gain in order to be considered on a level with Garbo) voiced the same opinion. While the film ran for years in Germany under the title *Mimi*,[55] the British critics' opinions were split. *La Bohème* was either a "triumph for MGM" or a "dismal entertainment."[56]

The American premiere at the Embassy Theatre in New York on February 24, 1926, was a double occasion: a Lillian Gish film and Lillian Gish in person! The capacity audience included socialites, studio executives, fellow professionals, and a large delegation of women who were on hand to cheer John Gilbert.

Mordaunt Hall, film critic for *The New York Times*, praised the film by calling it a "production that is virtually flawless" and "one that will do its share to bring the screen to a higher plan." Lillian's performance was labeled "marvelously clever." It was not the sort of accolade she had anticipated. To be clever meant she was skillful, and nothing more. She had been dismissed as a technician — a good technician, but nothing more.

Even King Vidor, who had followed all of Lillian's suggestions, admitted that her performance was "artistic and delicate, but never believable."[57]

It was John Gilbert who earned the critical kudos from *The New York Times* critic:

> [It] shows throughout his portrayal that he is thinking the part. You can detect it in his eyes.
> In an earlier sequence where he pretends to be fighting a duel with foils, his falling to the floor, pretending to be wounded, aroused great applause.[58]

Truly, it was John Gilbert who was the opening night audience's favorite.[59] Lillian was of secondary importance to the audience, who preferred to watch John Gilbert kissing, instead of Lillian, the Griffith actress, suffering and dying once again. Her formula was wearing thin. Its age, perhaps, was beginning to show.

John Gilbert would not disappoint his female fans. *Flesh and the Devil*, with its brilliantly lit erotic love scenes involving a sultry Greta Garbo, was less than seven months away.

Why, in the passage of time, has *La Bohème* become a Lillian Gish film and not remained a John Gilbert film?

Aileen Pringle, Gilbert's leading lady in King Vidor's *His Hour*, offered a theory about her co-star:

> With the exception of *The Big Parade*, John Gilbert was a Garbo prop, in the manner that Fred Astaire's female partners were props. Garbo and Gilbert were a marvelous screen team in the way Astaire and Rogers were a screen team.
>
> But John had a problem Astaire's partners never had: He wasn't ever sure of himself. He always had doubts beneath that boisterous personality.
>
> Perhaps that was why he drank. And he drank to the point where it was known outside the studio gates the way it was known about Fields and Barrymore. And you could see it! He was well lit, but if you look closely at him in *La Bohème*, you can see the puffiness under his eyes at certain angles and when he turns his head.
>
> When sound came in, his voice was too soft for his very masculine physique. The two didn't match. The voice was too sensitive. It wasn't that falsetto that television comedian Sid Caesar used in that sketch when he was portraying a silent film matinee idol petrified of "talkies."
>
> John Gilbert, in his own time, was a symbol for all of the silent film stars who couldn't make a transition into sound.[60]

A Los Angeles reporter interviewing Lillian was surprised at her lack of interest in the divided critical opinion of her work in *La Bohème*. As the interview progressed, Lillian "sat quietly toying with the folds of her dress, betraying no sign of annoyance or concern" (a pattern she would maintain for the rest of her life in the face of any negative review). In a moment of silence, Lillian looked up at the reporter and asked, "Has someone been criticizing me?"[61]

Colleen Moore spoke of the revised critical opinion of Lillian's performance when the film began to resurface at film societies and conventions in the late sixties (due to Lillian's lecture tours):

> There was a tendency for people and critics during the 20s to believe that anything that came to prominence in the teens was hopelessly outdated and old-fashioned.
>
> Lillian's persona was the proper Victorian type, the menaced virgin whose villains were right out of the penny dreadful stories. The fact that she made a habit of always being seen with her mother also contributed to that helpless image.
>
> What I find fascinating today [1967] is the young people's fascination with Lillian when she speaks at colleges and universities. Here is the lady from another generation — the time of their grandmothers — who survived and is still active, but also maintains that other generation outlook while living in this period of the hippies and the protest movements. These young people find different values in her films, and they seem to get something out of it, and out of her.
>
> *La Bohème* was a period piece when it was an opera, and the opera was written almost 60 years after the book. What sustained the appeal of the book was its honest emotion: two lovers living in poverty with all of their jealousies and regrets.
>
> What is literature all about? Will people in the next century call any book about Viet Nam or *Hair* a "period piece?"
>
> Lillian has outlived her detractors. She is saying forty years after the original release, "I AM STILL HERE!"
>
> Quite Frankly, I still cry over that film, and it's good to have it back. I

know its technique. Chaplin had technique. He still makes us laugh. Lillian still makes us cry. That's why these young people go to see her.

You have to take her at face value. She's my friend, my good friend, but when Helen Hayes, Lillian, and I get together, Lillian is never a bundle of laughs.[62]

Lillian's lack of humor may have intensified during the final weeks of shooting *La Bohème*. Charles Duell wanted to return to court to answer the perjury charge against him. Judge Knox assigned the first Monday in May as the trial date.

Until then, Lillian would be making another disappearance. She had planned to vacation in Europe[63] — with George Jean Nathan.

CHAPTER 16

Hester

There are two kinds of actresses: working and non-working. I like to be working.

— Lillian Gish
Conversation with author
October 1958

The European vacation with George Jean Nathan lasted two weeks. By the end of February Lillian and George had to return to New York. George had plays to review, and Lillian had picture work in California. Apparently the MGM executives, eager to use her in anything before the expiration of her two-year contract, were open to suggestions. Classics were given top priority. They were out of copyright, so only a screen-writer had to be paid. While films starring other studio players might mean big box-office and large grosses, Lillian's films meant prestige. She was the personification of the studio motto: *Ars Gratia Artis* (Art for the Sake of Art). With George Jean Nathan in her life, she now had entré to the intellectuals, artists, and writers. Only Charlie Chaplin had that mobility. And Chaplin was a man.

March 1926: When Lillian proposed filming *The Scarlet Letter*, Nathaniel Hawthorne's 1850 novel of adultery and redemption in the days of Puritan New England, Louis B. Mayer was shocked. Was this proposer the same young lady whose virginal portrayals of Griffith's Victorian

heroines had endeared her to moral men and women alike? What had happened to the only Metro-Goldwyn-Mayer actress whose good name, reputation, and well-publicized devotion to her mother were above reproach? How could Lillian Gish, who had played a nun so convincingly in *The White Sister*, lower herself to playing an adulteress? Had she fallen under the influence of certain younger studio players, whose outside antics were always being hushed up with well-placed, generous secret payments? Was the character of Hawthorne's Hester Prynne Lillian's idea of being fast and loose while maintaining her virginity within her fastidious parameters?

To many American families, *The Scarlet Letter*, despite its classic status, represented the kind of moral effrontery they wouldn't allow to be kept on their home library shelves. That it had been a moderately successful Fox Film Corporation five-reeler in 1917 was not the issue. *The Scarlet Letter* dealt with the aftermath of an adulterous affair that produced a daughter and the downfall of the village clergyman.

Corruption in the clergy has always been a subject of sordid fascination with the reading public since Matthew Lewis' 1795 shocker, *The Monk*. The 1921 publication of W. Somerset Maugham's *Rain* (followed by a successful dramatization on Broadway with Jeanne Eagels and the motion picture version starring Gloria Swanson) proved there was still an audience for the tried-and-true formula of sin, suffer, and repent. Novelist Sinclair Lewis, a keen chronicler of the American landscape, was completing *Elmer Gantry* (1927), which examined the public and private life of a Billy Sunday–type traveling preacher and revivalist.

Lillian was puzzled. Exactly what was Mr. Mayer's problem? Was it because the dose of sin was heavier than previous films had dealt with and that one of the repenants was a man of the cloth? Or was it Lillian Gish?

Lillian, appearing on Broadway n the 1975 revue *A Musical Jubilee,* recalled her initial meeting with Mr. Mayer to discuss his reluctance to film *The Scarlet Letter:*

> Mr. Mayer sat at his desk and looked across at me as if I had gone mad. Then, he stood and pointed at me. "You?" he screamed. "You? You? In a story like that?
>
> "Miss Gish, would you feel comfortable making a motion picture about such a woman like Hester? How are we going to show that on the screen without running into the censors? We can't show you and that minister just holding hands and staring into each other's eyes? This isn't *Way Down East!*
>
> "Motion pictures have grown up. This is the twenties, not D. W. Griffith! Audiences have grown up! They want a real love scene, especially since they know the book, as you say.
>
> "They know a baby's going to come of this lovemaking! How do you propose to show that?"
>
> I told him they could do it with titles, the way they did in the earlier Fox version.

> My Mayer threw his hands up. "Titles? They can get words from the book. We make pictures, not titles.
>
> "Today's crowd wants women to act like women, not like little innocent school girls. How do you think the churches are going to take this film? Do you think they'll recommend it? They'll think that Lillian Gish has betrayed their trust! 'You'll be the subject of sermons across the country! Maybe the world!' And what will happen to us."[1]

Lillian, who had been fashioning a *Scarlet Letter* script with screenwriter Francis Marion[2] during the final weeks of shooting *La Bohème*, knew what she had to do: write personal letters to prominent clergymen and women's organizations across the country and enlist their support.[3]

> It was a very simple letter, honest and direct. I wrote that Hawthorne's *The Scarlet Letter* was long an American classic, and should be brought to the screen tastefully. I thanked them for their response to *The White Sister*, in which I played a nun, and I told them I would be personally responsible for the production.[4]

She had also met with Will Hays, former postmaster-general during the Warren G. Harding administration, now in charge of the recently created Motion Picture Producers and Distributors Association of America (known simply as the Hays Office), a Hollywood-created committee that would patrol the industry in an effort to supervise the morality of the product.[5]

In Lillian's eyes, Hester Prynne in Hawthorne's novel was not a far cry from the heroines she had played in *Broken Blossoms, Way Down East, The White Sister,* and recently in *La Bohème*. Hester was another doomed woman. The studio's resistance centered on Hester's adultery, and that she was forced to wear the letter "A" for her transgressions.

Critical discussions of the novel have always concentrated on two questions: Why did Hester knowingly commit adultery, and why did she refuse to name the father of her child?

The answer, Lillian felt, rested not with Hester, but with Chillingworth, the older, cruel doctor Hester was forced to marry. It was Chillingworth who sent her to America to live until he could join her.

Lillian presented her conception of Hester and *The Scarlet Letter* to interested listeners.

Hester was a trapped woman because of her loveless marriage. Her sin was not any act of adultery, but the natural wanting to be loved. She was motivated by her heart. Throughout the novel and the film, Hester's actions are the actions of someone who has reconciled herself with herself and with God.

It is the Reverend Dimmesdale who has committed the unpardonable sin. Reverend Dimmesdale cannot acknowledge nor forgive his own desires. Hawthorne has given him the right symbolic name: a dim dale, a valley where little light shines. He cannot accept forgiveness.

Hester's husband is named Chillingworth. Chilling. What is this man of science worth? Chilling refers to a state of numbness, or cold, or without feeling. Remember, this is a man of science, and men of science, as Hawthorne well knew, were devoid of compassion. To them, the heart was just another part of the body.

Hester never repents. She doesn't feel that she has sinned. She never says she is sorry. What Hester has done is to make honest love acknowledged in a town of hypocrites who have suppressed their feelings.

The Scarlet Letter is a woman's story, and the price women have to pay for wanting to be loved. A husband rejects her, and a minister cannot acknowledge his own feelings because of the strong Puritan ethic.

By the end of the novel, Hester has been forgiven. Her "A" that she has been forced to wear shines even brighter, because her adultery symbol has become awe. The same women who once condemned her now willingly visit her for advice.[6]

Lillian also knew that the role of Dimmesdale had to be played by an unknown actor, or a new film actor with little reputation. *The Scarlet Letter* was Hester's story, not Reverend Dimmesdale's. Lillian didn't want to be forced into playing love scenes with another matinee idol like John Gilbert. Gilbert's name and performance were the main reason that droves of women attended *La Bohème* across the United States and set the dominant tone of the newspaper reviews — despite Lillian's fine performance.

Names were submitted and rejected. If a young, new actor captured reviewers' attention, where would that leave her? Would MGM finish her contract in programmers that were ignored? What studio would employ her? She knew it was Mayer's sentiment that had secured her this contract. As much as he respected her, she knew she couldn't compete against this new Swedish import, Greta Garbo.

When Louis B. Mayer screened the 1923 Swedish film, *The Story of Gosta Berling* with Greta Garbo and Lars Hanson, and directed by Mauritz Stiller, Lillian knew she had found her Dimmesdale.[7] Stiller, who had brought both Garbo and Hanson,[8] would not be asked to direct Lillian. Lars Hanson had been active in Swedish cinema under Stiller's direction for ten years.[9] Would Lillian be able to control the non–English speaking Hanson as well as his Swedish compatriot, Stiller?

The director of *The Scarlet Letter* would be of Lillian's choosing. Director approval was also part of Lillian's contract.

As Hester in *The Scarlet Letter* (1926, MGM, directed by Victor Seastrom). Nathaniel Hawthorne's classic was still on some restricted reading lists when Lillian wanted to bring Hester's story to screen audiences.

Said Lillian:

> I was asked which director I would like, and I chose Victor Seastrom, who had arrived at MGM some years earlier from Sweden. I felt that the Swedes were closer to the feeling of the New England Puritans than many Americans.
>
> Victor Seastrom's direction was a great education for me. In a sense, he put me through the Swedish school of acting. I had gotten rather close to the Italian school in Italy with *The White Sister* and *Romola*. The Italian school is one of elaboration. The Swedish is one of repression.[10]

There was a genuine professional rapport between Lars Hanson and Lillian. Hanson, whose conversational English was at best limited, acted his scenes in Swedish while Lillian played in English. The intensity of the drama displayed in their performances registered so strongly that neither player experienced any language barrier. When such problems occasionally arose, director Victor Seastrom was an able translator.[11]

> "Lars Hanson," noted Lillian, "is a wonderful actor. We used to improvise our spoken lines before the camera (even though sound never registered). Lars Hanson's scaffold speech was so eloquent and affecting that we were all tremendously moved by it."[12]

Hawthorne purists may have carped at the scene in which Lillian's Hester meets Lars Hanson's Dimmesdale the minister, and there is a sense of attraction that will intensify. After one of their tender walks in the woods, Hendrick Sartov's camera shows a set of Hester's underwear that she has washed and left drying on the bushes. Perhaps it was censorship that dictated this,[13] but even without any censorship policy, one doubts if Lillian would have allowed any filming of lovemaking,

particularly in *The Scarlet Letter* with its Puritan ethos that emphasized a "God-fearing, life-denying repression of sexuality."[14] One has to remember that Lillian, in her personal letter-writing and campaigning, promised to be personally responsible for the film.

Sartov's camera also provided the cinematic answer for readers who always wondered if Hester's "A" was also on Dimmesdale's breast when he stepped onto the scaffold toward the end of the Hawthorne novel and "tore away the ministerial band from before his breast. But it were irreverent to describe the revelation."[15]

Hawthorne was too wise to keep the secret to himself:

> Certain persons who were spectators of the whole scene, and professed never once to have removed their eyes from the Reverend Mr. Dimmesdale, denied that there was any mark whatever on his breast....[16]

Does the audience watching the motion picture see the "A" on Dimmesdale's breast? Most definitely yes.

Lillian explained:

> We tried to stress that Dimmesdale, not Hester, has committed the unpardonable sin, because his own nature has been wrecked. He cannot accept any forgiveness. It was he who acted upon Hester, and that was what we were trying to show.
>
> I think Hawthorne was trying to do that, too.
>
> That is also Hawthorne's genius: that *The Scarlet Letter* is a very consciously balanced, structured novel, allowing each generation of readers to bring their own values to it.
>
> We tried to do that with the film, and it was highly endorsed by church groups.[17]

While Lillian and Lars Hanson were doing retakes, James Rennie, playing the lead on Broadway in Owen Davis' stage adaptation of F. Scott Fitzgerald's novel, *The Great Gatsby*,[18] telephoned with an urgent message: Lillian's mother, visiting her daughter Dorothy in London, had had a stroke and was dying.[19] Lillian cabled Dorothy immediately that she would be leaving New York when the next ship was available.

What Lillian didn't want to tell Dorothy was that the retakes would take at least two weeks to complete — unless something drastic could be done.

The next three days were virtually a re-play of the time in 1914 when D. W. Griffith kept his company at Biograph for five days and nights to shoot *The Battle of the Sexes*, a program picture needed for a suddenly vacant theatre. In 1926, film technology had advanced, and if director Victor Seastrom and producer Irving Thalberg could ask *The Scarlet Letter* company to temporarily waive the union contract long enough to work around the clock on a non-stop twenty-four hour schedule, the completion of *the Scarlet Letter* would take three days.

The company cooperated. Filmmaking history for Lillian once again repeated itself. The final shots were made at the evening's end of the third day. Two weeks of work![20]

Without changing her costume, and with the help of a motorcycle police escort to the train station,[21] Lillian was able to board the Los Angeles Limited on the evening of April 15 for the four day cross-country journey to New York. The publicity department had done its job well.[22] As the train arrived at the Albuquerque, New Mexico, and Topeka, Kansas, stations on its journey East, people had been gathering on the platform to wish Lillian well. Some had driven one hundred miles to see her and say they were praying for her mother's recovery. One of the women at the Topeka station held up a baby and asked Lillian to touch it for luck.[23]

In New York Lillian went directly to the pier where the Majestic was docked. There was no time to spare for an hour's visit at her apartment to pack some clothes for her mother. An unexpected traffic jam could ruin everything. She didn't know of the next sailing, and it could be too late. This was a twelve day journey, a luxurious time to relax under any other circumstances. When someone is dying, however, even one day is too long.

She boarded immediately. Once again, in the midst of all of the ship's splendor, she was the center of attention.

And once again, she was alone.

From Dorothy, Lillian had learned what had happened.

Dorothy had spent an evening at the theatre. Returning to their hotel, she kept the bedroom lights off, not wishing to awaken her mother. Moments later, she felt something touch her. Nothing was spoken. Again, she felt something touch her. Nothing was said. The room was silent.

Turning on the light over her bed, Dorothy saw what had happened. Her mother, unable to speak, had somehow reached across the space between their twin beds and tried to speak. She had no voice, and her right side was useless. Luckily, her bed was at Dorothy's right. Otherwise Dorothy would have been unable to detect that anything was amiss.

Lillian knew there was nothing to do but wait until conditions had improved or worsened. Both Gishes had employment. In London, Dorothy was set to film *Tip Toes*, a British adaptation of George Gershwin's American musical, co-staring with Will Rogers. Lillian had to return to New York and settle the problems with Charles Duell, who was still under indictment. Then she could return to California.

Mrs. Gish's illness was a subject of great concern in the English papers. Lillian's race across the United States and Atlantic Ocean had been given large headlines. Gifts, flowers, and cards were left at her door every day.[25] Mrs. Gish had taken ill during a great strike, and nothing requiring the use of wheels was being delivered. Fortunately, the King's personal doctor was available, and Lord Beaverbrook had visited several times, always bringing a bag of eggs from his farm.[26]

It was up to Mrs. Gish to show some signs of healing before she would be deemed safe to return to New York. Within a few days of Lillian's arrival, her condition began to improve with the enlarging of her eyes in appreciation of her presence. She recognized Lillian, but she could not tell her. Even so, Lillian was grateful.

Despite Mrs. Gish's stroke, being together in London was a happy occasion. Dorothy's *Nell Gwynne*, which opened the Plaza Theatre on Lower Regent Street, was playing to capacity audiences.[27] Playwright Eugene O'Neill, a friend of George Jean Nathan, was enjoying a moderate success with his controversial *The Great God Brown*, and Sigmund Romberg's operetta, *The Desert Song*, was keeping Londoners merrily humming after they left the theatre.[28]

It was a matter of watching and waiting. The show would go on.

CHAPTER 17

Other Matters

You cannot strip a man of everything he has in life, brutally and un-
fairly challenge every ideal, and then to shield and protect others, pros-
ecute him, and think he is not going to fight. I have been battling since
the end of last summer for a trial and have tried to act with the courage
of my convictions.

I came into the movies to do my best. It's a difficult business and at
times a hard road to travel. Sinister influence has been at work. And
now, jail or freedom, I am ready.

> — Charles H. Duell,
> Statement to the press
> March 30, 1926

A defeated Charles Henry Duell, former president of the now bankrupt Inspiration Pictures, was back in Lillian's life to
haunt her. With a vengeance. Bitter, frustrated and, unable to earn a living as an
attorney, Duell was fully aware of Lillian's
two year $800,000 contract that had begun
with the filming of *La Bohème*.

Now it was his turn at bat, but there
was no pitcher on the mound, and the ball-
park was empty. Nobody had cared to see
him play. Lillian, still in Europe with
Dorothy and their mother in London, gave
every indication that she might remain
after Judge Knox had posted the trial date
for the first Monday in May. Lillian's presence as a witness was not considered crucial.[1]

Mrs. Gish's condition had been
steadily improving, although she had lost
the power of speech. Still, she had been
able to attend a performance of Dorothy's

Nell Gwynne at the Plaza Theatre as part of
a distinguished audience that included
Prince and Princess Arthur of Connaught,
and Princess Helena Victoria.[2]

Dorothy's performance (cheered two
London papers — *The Sunday Pictorial* and
Daily Telegraph, in addition to Scotland's
Glasgow Herald) had dominated the screen
for almost the entire duration of the two
hour film, with moods that "ranged from
low comedy to high tragedy" and showcased her ability to use her comedic talents in establishing Nell (who began as an
orange seller outside the Drury Lane Theatre only to later become a prominent actress and the most famous of Charles II's
mistresses) as a "living, vibrant personality."[3] Dorothy's Nell was considered her
best work.[4]

In the wake of such praise, Dorothy,
who once remarked that British filmmakers
were unable to keep up with the American

product, now said they could easily win in a world competition.[5]

Dorothy was always ready with a quick answer to any question. When a newspaper interviewer remarked that Mrs. Gish, who was always present, always wore her hair bobbed while the modern Dorothy wore her hair unbobbed, Dorothy responded: "We have no explanation to offer, except that mothers are getting awfully young."[6] Echoing a policy of Lillian's, when asked about meeting some of her British fans, Dorothy answered: "We believe in personal disappearances."[7]

Dame Anna Neagle, the widow of Henry Wilcox, who directed the Dorothy Gish silent *Nell Gwynne* and her sound version opposite Cedric Hardwicke, shared her impressions of both versions when she spoke to the biographer at a 1985 Museum of Modern Art showing of her award-winning *Odette*.[8] With her was Lillian Gish.

> Dorothy — and I know that Lillian will agree with me — always had a wonderful sense of humor. She was always a joy to work with. She had a quick wit, and in *Nell Gwynne* there were ample opportunities to display it.
>
> Maybe it was a blessing that sound hadn't come in, because some of Dorothy's ad libs that couldn't be recorded wouldn't have escaped the censor's scissors. She would have been the voice on the cutting-room floor.
>
> I don't want to say in front of Lillian that I copied Dorothy's performance. I'll just say that I learned from it! One bawd to another![9]

Dame Anna laughed. Lillian placed her hand in front of her lips and blushed.

May 27, 1926: It had taken less than thirty minutes to choose the jury. Asked if the presence of Lillian Gish as a witness for the prosecution would have an undue influence on their decisions, all responded in the negative.

The indictment charged that Duell had lied under oath when he said that Lillian had approved the assignment of her contract with Inspiration Pictures, and that she had not paid Duell any part of the $6,000 charge for his services (she claimed to have paid $3,000) and had been represented by counsel.

The indictment further stated that Mr. Duell had sworn falsely that he was unable to pay his debts. It was the corporation that had been financially irresponsible. The entries in Duell's books were an effort to deceive the court.[10]

What must have further rankled Mr. Duell was Lillian's conscious choice of J. Boyce Smith, Jr., as her attorney. Smith was Duell's former law partner!

Nathan Burkan, counsel for Charles Duell, did not want the contract submitted as evidence, stating that Miss Gish's contract and her failure to consent to the contract in writing was not the issue.

Assistant United States Attorney George S. Leisure read Lillian's contract to the jury, while J. Boyce Smith was on the stand. There was an exchange afterwards.

> LEISURE: Were Duell and Smith paid for legal services by Miss Gish?
> SMITH: Duell and I had talked over that matter and decided that $6,000 was a fair amount for our services. Duell said he would collect the money from Miss Gish, and asked me if he could keep it for the time and pay me out of his salary at the end of the month. I suggested he give me a check, and that I could take the amount from his salary. That was done.[11]

A good portion of the afternoon of June 1 was spent in disputes between Leisure, conducting the prosecution, and Nathan Burkan, counsel for Duell, regarding the admissibility of letters in affidavits submitted by the Government as evidence. United States Attorney Buckner demanded that J. Boyce Smith be allowed to answer questions regarding the letters, because they were the equivalent of contracts.

Miss Gish, contrary to what Duell had sworn, did not have counsel. In a letter from July 1924 she had agreed to terms awarding 15 percent on all gross receipts in excess of $600,000 but she waived these and had lost money. Her percentages went down from a weekly $3,000 to $1,250. She saved Inspiration Pictures the sum of $130,000.

Burkan immediately objected, claiming that the jury was receiving a false impression. Lillian, he insisted, "made thousands!"[12]

On the following afternoon, Nathan Burkan tried to force J. Boyce Smith to admit that he and trustee Walter Camp, Jr., were pressuring Lillian Gish during the filming of *Romola* in Italy, and that attorney George W. Newgass was hired as a protective measure. Smith objected to the term "protect," and said he would agree if the word "protect" were changed to "represent."

The Duell trial, characterized by the newspapers as a "debate on legal technicalities," became more dramatic when J. Boyce Smith was being cross-examined by Burkan.

> BURKAN: Do you mean to tell the jury you don't know who furnished the financial backing?

Earlier the silent backer for Inspiration Pictures had been disclosed as William Averill Harriman, with both Walter Camp, Jr., and J. Boyce Smith claiming they were nothing but Harriman dummies. Smith had denied any knowledge of Harriman's $250,000 investment.

Angrily, Burkan yanked a piece of paper from his table and pushed it into a nervous Smith's hand.

> BURKAN: Is that your handwriting, Mr. Smith?
> SMITH: Why, yes. This is my handwriting.

Smith identified two of the signatures, his own and Walter Camp, Jr.'s, but he could not identify Harriman's, as it was a signature with which he was not familiar.

> BURKAN: Harriman ought to be called as a witness.

But nothing further was said or done. 34-year-old polo playing William Averill Harriman, chairman of the Merchant Shipbuilding Corporation, was the scion of a multi-millionaire industrialist who owned controlling interest in the Union Pacific Railroad.[13]

William Averill Harriman had approximately $400,000 in Inspiration preferred stock, and his loans yielded $600,000. Two meetings attended by Duell and Camp had been held in Harriman's Washington Square home for the intention of raising the necessary funds for *Romola*, Duell's second production for Inspiration starring Lillian.[14]

Smith, during his cross-examination by Nathan Burkan, additionally made it known that Inspiration's preferred stock was issued in Duell's name, but it was held for Camp who, in turn, held it for Harriman.

Smith also admitted that Lillian's forfeited percentage of $60,000 was within reason, because there was a miscalculation in the production expenses.

And then Burkan, without any warning, took a different tack.

> BURKAN: Did you not in your previous testimony tell the Court that Mr. Duell was robbing and cheating the company in favor of Miss Gish?
> SMITH: I said something like that.... It was evident Mr. Duell was favoring Miss Gish at the expense of the company. It looked very bad going out and hiring Newgass to act against the company.

In Smith's view it wasn't fair of Duell to ask Lillian to eliminate the gross receipts from road shows in determining her percentages due her, as road shows were "publicity and exploitation."[15]

That Charles Duell was the "tool" of J. Boyce Smith and Walter Camp, Jr., was the thrust of Burkan's continuing cross-examination, Nathan Burkan said on June 3. Burkan also inquired of Smith if there had been a "trade" after Duell had left Inspiration Pictures and had formed Charles H. Duell, Inc., with Lillian Gish as its chief star. Did Miss Gish and Walter Camp, Jr., try to obtain a loan of $50,000 from the Fifth Avenue Bank? Smith did admit that he would try to secure a complete release by Miss Gish against any claims she might have against Inspiration while negotiating with Metro-Goldwyn for the distribution of *Romola*.

The cross-examining of J. Boyce Smith continued.

> BURKAN: Did Duell ever get a penny for those services?
> SMITH: No.
> BURKAN: Did Inspiration ever get back the $30,000 in percentages or the $12,000 in salary from Miss Gish that Duell said he would try to get?
> SMITH: It did not.[16]

Attorney George W. Newgass, who had negotiated Lillian's original contract with Inspiration, testified on June 4 that she had failed to pay him $500 for personal services provided between March 6 and April 24, 1924, adding that he did not think he had been retained when Charles Duell asked him to protect her interests during the modification of her contract. He also added that Lillian's box-office appeal was doubtful after she had stopped working for Griffith, and that his firm had spent more than six months trying to find a studio who would hire her.

Lillian's services included helping write the titles, assisting with the editing, and appearing with the film at road show performances — for which she would be paid, although she had said she was volunteering them.

Romola was in deep financial trouble, J. Boyce Smith added to his testimony. The filming of *Romola* was never smooth. On more than one occasion, the production would have ended had it not been for the additional funding provided by Walter Camp, Jr., through the backing of William Averill Harriman.[17]

As the *Mauretania* docked in New York during the trial proceedings on June 4, Lillian, returning from London with her mother (and accompanied by English physician Dr. Henry Rowan and a nurse), told reporters that she would be willing to testify at Duell's trial if called. She had planned to return to Hollywood to assist in the editing of *The Scarlet Letter*. The condition of her mother warranted that she remain in New York until Dr. Rowan felt that such a cross-country journey wouldn't place Mrs. Gish at risk.

Lillian added that she had never met William Averill Harriman, and that she knew nothing concerning his financial assistance. Harriman's contracts were strictly with Charles Duell.[18]

June 7: It was a day characterized by contradictions.

George W. Newgass, whose testimony was responsible for Duell being indicted for perjury, took the stand and said he had given inaccurate testimony the previous year, and that he had had "very little time to prepare as a witness."

Burkan seized the opportunity.

> BURKAN: And as a result, what you said was subject to considerable inaccuracy.
> NEWGASS: Yes, and I answered to the best of my ability; but the testimony included some inaccuracies.
> BURKAN: Inaccuracies, yes; and inconsistencies?
> NEWGASS: And inconsistencies.
> BURKAN: And inconsistencies. Quite a number of inconsistencies, Mr. Newgass?

George W. Newgass remained silent. Nathan Burkan did not press for a response.

Newgass was the second lawyer associated with Charles Duell whose evidence was contradictory. J. Boyce Smith, at first denying he had dealings with William Averill Harriman, had admitted not only to have met him, but to have helped draw up the contracts for Inspiration Pictures. Attorney Nathan Burkan later asserted that had the witness in Duell's injunction suit been given a more thorough hearing, Duell would never have been indicted for perjury.

It was learned in the afternoon that Lillian would be called as a Government witness, because Judge Goddard refused to admit her affidavit as evidence. Burkan had objected to the affidavit, and Leisure said that Lillian was being kept in readiness.[19]

On June 9, Burkan was still adamant about Leisure's failure to call Lillian to testify. He was quite upset when he was told the Government was resting its case. Burkan stood and said:

> I want it to go on the record that the Government might have called Miss Gish to testify to its allegations, but did not do so, although she is stopping in this city at the Hotel Ambassador and was available.

Burkan then motioned that the indictment against Duell be struck void on the grounds that Duell had not been shown to have made the false statements he was accused of making, and that the Government had not established the "falsity of statements" he said he made: that Lillian was without legal counsel when she signed the Inspiration contracts, that Duell hadn't received any moneys for his services, and that he had not acted as her legal advisor.

The motion was denied.

Still, Burkan was able to delay the Government's decision to rest, offering the reasoning that he (Burkan) should be allowed to read from earlier Duell testimony from the previous trial as the Government's attorneys, Leisure and Buckner, had done. This time there would be no conscious attempt to deceive the jury by emphasizing the wrong words.

Burkan proceeded to imitate Lillian's attorney's (Max D. Steur) delivery in the earlier trial: a shouted question to his client Duell, followed by Duell's calm and soft answer. After one of the questions had been asked with a decidedly increase in vocal power, a smiling Judge Goddard interceded.

> GODDARD: Is that question underlined, Mr. Burkan.

Burkan replied that the court records were not written in that manner. He could only safely say that it was the "manner in which Mr. Steur had delivered it."[20]

A pathetic Charles Duell was only able to testify for 12 minutes on the following morning of June 9 before court was adjourned. In that short period of time, United States Attorney Buckner raised seven sustained objections, arguing that Mr. Duell's age, his father being a Judge of the United States Court of Appeals, and Duell's navy record were not relevant to the case. Neither was the letter from Colonel Theodore Roosevelt, stating that he knew Charles Duell and his father.[21]

Burkan's loudest protests were heard when it was disclosed that William Averill Harriman's investment of "upward of $1,000,000" might have been predicated upon "some interest in Miss Gish."[22]

Burkan then called upon Frank Wilson, President of the Motion Picture Corporation, and Metro-Goldwyn-Mayer official Nicholas Schenck to speak on Duell's behalf. Wilson stated that Lillian's contract was not his concern regarding the financing of motion pictures. Schenck testified that Metro-Goldwyn-Mayer acted strictly as distributors of Mr. Duell's properties. An assistant cashier of the Bowery East River National Bank said that, in

October 1924, when Inspiration was formed, the bank was willing to advance $200,000.

The Government continued to maintain that what Duell had was contract a with Lillian Gish.[23]

Buckner then charged Burkan with attempting "to make the defendant [Duell] out as more stupid than he really is," and stressed that the adjustment of Lillian's contract, which was to her advantage, had been made while Duell and Lillian were engaged.

Duell responded that he had spent little time in actual law practice, and that he had not actually advised her but had only "declared his belief."

Buckner answered that this "belief" had been tantamount to "advice" and that, in swearing in an affidavit that he had not given such "advice," Duell had committed perjury.

Outside the courtroom, Duell told reporters that in the three days he had answered over 2,000 questions from two attorneys, and that he had not been given a fair trial.[24]

On June 14, the Government and the defense presented their summations.

Nathan Burkan, hitting the rail of the jury box as he spoke, characterizing the trial as a "desire for revenge by William Averill Harriman, who lost $500,000 in Inspiration Pictures," and a desire of Lillian Gish to get publicity and have her name splashed across the front pages of American newspapers. Her failure to testify was because she could not find any guilt in Charles Duell's actions.

United States Attorney Buckner opened his summation:

> We have tried to try one case, and Mr. Burkan has tried to try another. We are trying the case against Duell; he is trying Duell against Gish. He has tried to confuse the issues by trying the Gish case over again. It is of the highest importance to the courts, to the profession of the law, and to all citizens that this man should not be allowed to come into the courts and perjure himself and get away with it.

Duell had reasons to commit perjury, Buckner concluded.

> He [Duell] saw millions of dollars slipping from his grasp if he lost his contract for the services of Miss Gish.[25]

It had taken Judge Goddard approximately 25 minutes to instruct the jury on June 16, but after eight hours of deliberation they were locked up for the night, not having reached any conclusion.

Duell and Burkan were in the corridor of the Federal Building, their minds remembering the words of Judge Goddard:

> Perjury is one of the most insidious of evils. It is of the highest importance to keep our courts clean of perjury if our courts are to remain courts.[26]

From the jury room it was learned that on the first ballot, eight were for acquittal and four for conviction. One juror changed his mind, and the second ballot showed nine for acquittal.

On the following morning at 10:15, a slip of paper was handed to the foreman on which was written:

> We have deliberated long and carefully and find ourselves absolutely and unalterably unable to agree upon a verdict.

The jury had been dismissed, but Duell's indictment had not. United States Attorney Buckner was undecided about the possibility of a retrial. Duell, while not totally satisfied, viewed the jury's verdict as a vindication.[27]

On November 26, the Government dropped its case against Charles Duell. United States Attorney Buckner had filed a nolle prosequi, an entry on the record signifying that neither the prosecutor (the Government) nor the plaintiff would continue in this action or suit.[28]

Although she won, Lillian felt no urge to celebrate. Her private life had been made public, and that was something she had never wanted to happen. Fearful of the press and of answering questions that were not related to her latest film, Lillian cautiously left the Hotel Ambassador via the back door.[29]

Back doors she knew, were always perfect for disappearances.

CHAPTER 18

Unkindest Cuts

Even though James Rennie was living with his wife Dorothy, his sister-in-law Lillian, and his invalid mother-in-law at New York's Ambassador Hotel, it was the three Gishes at home once again. It was just like the old days when Lillian and Dorothy were barnstorming across the country in 10-20-30 melodramas, and they would plan for a grand reunion when they would be playing in the same city. James Rennie was still doing his eight performances a week as Jay Gatsby. Fortunately.

Dorothy would soon be returning to England to begin filming *Tip Toes* with Will Rogers. The only presence at Mrs. Gish's bedside—apart from the full time nurse—was Lillian. Next to Lillian was George, the name she had bestowed upon the wire-haired terrier, a gift from George Jean Nathan. George the wire-haired terrier had only one problem: He liked to chew on the expensive chairs in the drawing room.[1] While both Georges were always available, the drama critic George wasn't very fond of trying to carry on a relationship in a now-crowded apartment whose inhabitants were constantly trying to cater to the demands of a sick mother. Mrs. Gish's room was next to Rennie and Dorothy's and on nights when Rennie didn't have a Wednesday or Saturday matinee, it was difficult to predict when he would arrive after the curtain came down.

Lillian's mother wasn't always the perfect patient. When Lillian wasn't maintaining a constant barrage of chatter, she would turn on the radio, for no other reason than to have a sound in the room. Mrs. Gish didn't like the radio when Lillian was sitting next to her.

But Lillian only had so much to say to her. No matter how much she adored her mother, there were only so many topics to discuss with someone who couldn't answer.

At first, Lillian kept the radio time to a minimum. Then she rebelled. The radio continued to play. By voluntarily choosing to stay at her mother's bedside, Lillian now realized that she had become her mother's captive. Mrs. Gish had never known what it was to not have every request satisfied.[2]

Still, it was a devoted Lillian who would speak about caring very willingly for her convalescing mother: "I think Mother is a happy woman. She hasn't got a care. There is little life left for me when I have to be with mother so much."[3]

Anita Loos, who visited Lillian often during the first stages of Mrs. Gish's illness, recalled Lillian's subtle changes in her relationship with her mother:

> I can't pinpoint the exact moment when Lillian's feelings for her mother

went from genuine love to sickeningly close. Lillian would never say this, but I think she may have felt guilt that she had allowed her mother to constantly travel back and forth between Dorothy and herself, without ever considering the toll that all of that mileage had taken on her.

Mrs. Gish, now that I think about it, may have been in her early fifties, which is still reasonably young. She had always traveled, ever since their beginnings, to be with one or both of them. Lillian and her mother were always together when we were together at Biograph. It was an accepted package. We were younger, and a mother acted as a chaperone. I, of course, didn't have a chaperone. I knew what to expect around the corner....

Mary [Pickford] always had her mother, but Mary was able to get married. The first was Owen Moore. That was an elopement. The second — and her mother was there for that — was to Douglas Fairbanks.

Lillian and her mother were like that Ivor Novello song, *And Her Mother Came, Too*. Mrs. Gish was always there: at work in the early days at Biograph doing wardrobe, playing a "bit" part, at lunch, going out with Lillian and Mr. Griffith.

We had lives of our own, but it was always Lillian and her mother. Lillian's life was dedicated to her mother. Lillian and her mother were a team. Both of them seemed to be responsible for each other's welfare. Even now, all of these years later, it's strange to talk about it. We never thought of one without the other.

It was never that way with Dorothy. Wait! Let me correct that! Dorothy was always her own boss from the time I met her, even though she was younger. It's ironic that it was Dorothy, not Lillian , who was in London when Mrs. Gish had the stroke.

I don't know if Dorothy would have come quickly if it were Lillian who made that telephone call. Dorothy

once told me that the mother and daughter roles should have been reversed. Lillian became the mother, the way she looked after her mother.

There was a full time nurse living with them, but it was Lillian, not the nurse, we would see pushing Mrs. Gish in the wheelchair on Fifth Avenue when the sun was shining. Lillian wanted everyone to see how much she loved her mother, and Mrs. Gish wanted everyone to see that although Lillian was a world-famous movie star, she was still her mother's little girl!

To make sure Mrs. Gish didn't catch cold, Lillian made sure her mother's legs were covered with a sable laprobe, not an ordinary blanket. A sable laprobe![4]

Dorothy Gish's agent, Alan Brock, remembered how Mrs. Gish's medical expenses caused friction between her two daughters:

Dorothy had to return to England, and Lillian asked her to pay half of their mother's expenses. Dorothy balked at paying half, and she said so.

Lillian said their mother had raised them equally, had loved them equally without any favoritism or partiality, and that it was only right and correct that the two of them should equally share the cost.

Now you and I know that Dorothy never made as much money as Lillian, but that was Dorothy's own fault. Lillian also told Dorothy not to ask [James] Rennie for money.

Whatever Dorothy contributed — with or without her husband's help — made up half of their mother's bills.

Whatever Lillian wanted for her mother, Lillian got for her mother.[5]

July 1926: There was never any question of leaving Mrs. Gish alone with a nurse or Jim Rennie while Lillian returned to California to help edit *The Scarlet*

Letter for the August premiere in New York. Dorothy had already left for England.

It was one of those occasions for which Lillian was grateful she had saved her money. To avoid the hazards of the constant heat while crossing the desert or the reduced oxygen over the mountains, Lillian hired a railroad car, which was fastened to the end of a rapidly moving mail train. This was in the era before the availability of air-conditioning. Cool temperatures in passenger trains were non-existent in certain parts of the United States.

On the advice of Dr. Rowan, the English physician who had accompanied Lillian and her mother on the Mauretania from Southampton (and would travel with Lillian and her mother to Los Angeles), large tubs of ice were installed beneath constantly blowing fans. Beds and comfortable chairs were also available.[6]

Even with all of these attempts to provide comfort, the three travellers still experienced considerable heat crossing the desert. There was some comfort in knowing that the temperatures would have been considerable higher had they not taken such precautions.

Instead of remaining on her back for the whole trip, there were times when, to Lillian's satisfaction, Mrs. Gish was able to sit up and smile at the passing scenery.

By the time they reached Los Angeles, there was a slight, but significant improvement. She was able to take very limited steps, and to speak a few words.[7]

For the rest of the month, Lillian and her mother lived at Mary Pickford's Santa Monica beach house. In the morning and the evening they were surrounded by the sight and the sound of the waves.

Among the visitors Lillian remembered seeing were Zelda and her husband, novelist F. Scott Fitzgerald,[8] whose novel *The Great Gatsby* was about to go into production at Paramount with Warner Baxter and Lillian's friend, actress Lois Wilson.

Years later, in 1968, Lois would understudy Lillian's role of Margaret Garrison in the New York production of Robert Anderson's autobiographical play, *I Never Sang for my Father*.

Neither F. Scott nor Zelda Fitzgerald, paid much attention to Lillian or her mother.[9] Both preferred to watch the ocean and to "drink their whiskey as if it were water, with seemingly no effect, in tall tumblers."[10]

Still, it was necessary to overlook the free-wheeling habits they constantly paraded in front of anyone who would watch. F. Scott Fitzgerald's stories were often purchased as screen material. Indeed, on one occasion Scott mentioned that he wanted to write something original for her.[11]

Perhaps he had conveniently forgotten that six years earlier (1920) Dorothy had rejected an original scenario he had fashioned for her, in the wake of the success he had with his first novel, *This Side of Paradise*.[12] His friend, poet and short story writer Dorothy Parker, had been more successful with her original, *Remodeling Her Husband*, in which Dorothy had starred under Lillian's direction.

The recovery of Lillian's mother was slow, but by the end of July she had shown sufficient progress so that she was able to be leave the beach house to sit at the edge of the ocean, or be taken for short drives to the city during the week that George Jean Nathan and H.L. Mencken had come to call. Lillian, still editing *The Scarlet Letter*, was grateful to see friends from the East.

What Lillian found professionally frustrating—because of her mother's illness—was the inability to scout new projects. In the last weeks of completing any previous film, it had always been her habit to begin reading scripts, plays, and novels and, after selecting a possible project, to enlist a collaborator who would structure the project into the form she could present to Mr. Thalberg and Mr. Mayer. (Francis Marion, who prepared the titles for *The Scarlet Letter*, had gone to London to begin Dorothy's *Madame Pompadour*, following Dorothy's completion of *Tip Toes*.)

Although Lillian might quibble years later that *The Scarlet Letter*'s heroine, Hester Prynne, was a little beyond her age range, the film contained some of her "most subtle and graceful underplaying."[13] *The Scarlet Letter* was a serious film with little comic relief. Lillian had been as faithful to the Hawthorne novel as was possible. Aware that the film might not appeal to a Saturday night audience out for a "thrill or a laugh or a cry,"[14] it had the potential to garner an international following, and be viewed seriously by the academic community, which was beginning to consider the American cinema as a legitimate art form.

Lillian was very fond of Swedish director Victor Seastrom, whose "integrity of vision, full use of decor, lighting, camera placement, sensitivity to landscape and texture"[15] contributed to making *The Scarlet Letter* a director's — as well as actor's — film. Seastrom understood the dour quality of the New England sensibility and saw the parallel in the Scandinavian.

Like Griffith's *Orphans of the Storm*, Seastrom's *The Scarlet Letter* is rich in crowd scenes and scenes of intimacy, most notably those set at the town square: A solitary Lillian elicits our sympathy when she sits alone in the stocks; then a two character exchange takes place between Lillian and Lars Hanson; and then comes the finale (much like the finale in Griffith's *Orphans*) showing hundreds of extras amidst the "privacy of the scaffold" as it becomes a stage from which Dimmesdale [Hanson] will deliver his confession.[16]

The Scarlet Letter was a big film, lavish in production. It had a "non–MGM quality" which both Lillian and Seastrom hoped audiences would be quick to realize.

There was no effort to be slick. The film was truly American, but it had been executed with a Swedish sensibility.

Throughout its filming, Lillian had conducted herself like royalty — and indeed she was, having been given privileges no other actress at any studio could hope to receive. In fact, no other actress would have been allowed to film the Hawthorne novel. It remained for the critics and the public to respect the achievement.

The premiere of *The Scarlet Letter* at New York's Central Theatre on August 9, 1926, was well attended, as was any Lillian Gish film.

The New York Times critic, Mordaunt Hall, praised the integrity of the film in its fidelity to the original Hawthorne novel:

> Louis B. Mayer, head of the Metro-Goldwyn-Mayer studio, could not have chosen a better director than [Victor] Seastrom for Nathaniel Hawthorne's narrative. He is painstaking in studying his characters, and it was to his advantage to have Lillian Gish in the principal role, that of Hester Prynne. Miss Gish has a strong inclination for such parts, and in this vehicle she gives an excellent conception of the courage of a young woman in the face of sneering, scorn, and tittle-tattle.[17]

The critic for *The New York Sun* wrote that

> Miss Gish, for the first time in the memory of the oldest inhabitant of the cinema palaces, plays a mature woman of depth, of feeling, of wisdom, and noble spirit....
>
> She is not Hawthorne's Hester Prynne, but she is yours and mine, and she makes *The Scarlet Letter* worth a visit.[18]

While *The Scarlet Letter* was a popular success, there was a sizable segment of the American audience who continued to view Lillian as "too old-fashioned for the Jazz Age,"[19] despite the total silence before the sustained thunderous applause that came from British audiences long after its premiere.[20]

The most vocal of Lillian's detractors in the United States was, surprisingly, *Photoplay* editor James R. Quirk. Quirk's influential publication (whose circulation was in the millions) had built up Lillian's reputation a decade earlier when she was working for D.W. Griffith. Now her post–Griffith performances contained mannerisms, and she was merely a technician, not an artist.

In the March 1926 issue of *Photoplay* (which appeared on the stands concurrent with the release of *La Bohème*), Quirk was dismissing her as "The Enigma of the Screen":

> Examining [her] characterizations, you will find she achieves greatness of effect through a single plane of emotion, namely hysteria.[21]

The October issue of *Photoplay* continued the caustic criticism with a piece written while *The Scarlet Letter* was still being exhibited in major theatres across the United States:

> Lillian Gish wears the red letter of sin with her stock virginal sweetness.[22]

Stock virginal sweetness.

The body of Lillian's screen work had become the stuff of which gossip column jokes were made.

> Who is your choice for Lorelei in *Gentlemen Prefer Blondes*? Ours is Lillian Gish. But failing to get Lillian, we suggest that Paramount borrow the services of Harry Langdon.[23]

What had happened to Lillian Gish?
Aileen Pringle offered the following answer:

What was happening to Lillian had happened to me. Her fall was greater. I was an Elinor Glyn heroine [1924: *Three Weeks, His Hour*] and was not as successful afterwards. Lillian was a Griffith heroine, and to her credit, the appeal of Griffith's films with her were superior to what came afterwards.

I think she did better work at Metro-Goldwyn-Mayer because she was able to pick her own material, but she was also older. She couldn't have played those parts at Biograph. She would have been too young, and Griffith would have never suggested to Lillian that she play Hester in *The Scarlet Letter*.

What neither Mayer nor Thalberg realized was the fact that Lillian matured. She was older, and the roles she played were older parts.

She was quite aware of who she was. And she knew the parts she could play. The had signed an ingenue, they thought, from their younger days. That wasn't what they got. Lillian couldn't be Garbo, anymore than Garbo could be Lillian. Even Garbo knew she was getting older, and she knew when to walk out.

Nobody would say it, but Quirk and *Photoplay* were at the mercy of Metro-Goldwyn-Mayer. Anything Mr. Mayer wanted, he got. James Quirk knew he had to listen or lose the chance of being the first publication to cover the latest MGM news.

Mayer didn't get the returns he thought Lillian Gish was capable of bringing in. But he didn't want to look like the evil man. He let *Photoplay* do the job. Then he could call in Lillian and show her what was being written about her.

Movies have always been about money. The investment has to be smaller than the return. She no longer justified the investment. She wasn't bringing home enough bacon.

And she still had time on her contract."[24]

Silent film actress and author Louise Brooks spoke candidly at her Rochester, New York apartment about Lillian's changing status after the release of *The Scarlet Letter*:

She [Lillian Gish] had control of everything: leading men, supporting casts, directors, and salary. But she was unable to control the box-office.

Mr. Mayer couldn't fathom what was wrong. He had given less to newer players like Garbo, who was getting only $16,000, but he knew Garbo's returns with *Flesh and the Devil* would far surpass Lillian's grosses. And Garbo's leading man, John Gilbert, had worked with Lillian first!

Now Garbo and Gilbert were an on-screen and off-screen team, and the fan magazines couldn't print enough about them. The public wanted to see more of them. In anything!

There was talk of putting Lillian in *Anna Karenina*, but Garbo pushed all of those thoughts aside. *Anna Karenina* became a Garbo and Gilbert film called *Love*. Not a particularly subtle title, but with Garbo and Gilbert, that was all their public wanted to see: kissing! They didn't see much of that when Lillian worked with him. And John loved Lillian, too.

Those executives were aware of that, but they were beholden to Lillian's contract. If Garbo had made *La Bohème*, there wouldn't be enough theatres to play it. A story like that?

Lillian was without peer as an actress, but as the twenties moved ahead it was obvious that she hadn't made commercially successful transitions. Her MGM films, *La Bohème* and *The Scarlet Letter*, like *The Birth of a Nation* and *Way Down East* she made for Griffith, were period pieces. She had effectively transitioned backwards with Parisian bohemians and New England Puritans — as the twenties were moving ahead with flappers and short skirts!

Mr. Mayer knew that the only one really getting any benefits was Lillian, not the studio. When it came to business, Lillian wasn't ethereal anymore. She knew how to project that angelic innocence on the screen very well.

When the time came to draw up a contract or to make requests regarding what she wanted to have in her next film, she was an angel of iron![25]

Lillian was being pulled in three different directions by the demands to come up with a commercial success, the demands of her mother in her time of convalescence, and the demands of George Jean Nathan for time alone. Time spent at mother's bedside could be regulated. George was more demanding. A day or two at the Suburban Hotel in Summit, New Jersey's countryside was not enough.

Nobody was happy. Lillian would have loved to make a disappearance. But from whom?

CHAPTER 19

Miss Gish Is Miss Gish

Nathan confesses that La Gish has floored him.
— H.L. Mencken
Letter
July 7, 1927[1]

The Lillian Gish and George Jean Nathan friendship that had originally begun with a simple meeting in London was followed by a steady flow of letters. After a period of silence, the friendship resumed during the course of a train ride to spend a weekend at the home of the Joseph Hergesheimers in West Chester, Pennsylvania. Nathan, who never seemed to be able to commit himself to any woman, and whose involvement's were little more than a sexual encounter with any available chorus girl for an evening's duration or two, had told his friend, H.L. Mencken (with whom he edited *Smart Set* magazine), that he was in love for the first time in his life, and not with a chorus girl, but with Lillian Gish! He was obsessed with her to the point that actress Sylvia Sidney, appearing on Broadway with James Rennie in *Crime*,[2] would remember, years later, that the walls of Nathan's home were covered with photographs of Lillian Gish.[3]

In Hollywood, Nathan, who had expressed on several occasions, no great fondness for film actresses, was Lillian's frequent escort at Pickfair, the palatial estate of Mary Pickford. There he hob-nobbed easily with Lillian's Biograph contemporaries Richard Barthelmess and Constance Talmadge, as well as stage favorites Lois Moran and John Barrymore[4] (who had compared Lillian's work in *Way Down East* to Duse and Bernhardt at the height of their powers).[5]

Aileen Pringle, also present at Pickfair, recalled being part of the Gish-Nathan-Mencken "frequent foursome" when they dined at restaurants in Los Angeles and New York:

> Lillian and I weren't friends. We were friendly only because Henry [H.L. Mencken] and George [Jean Nathan] were friends and business associates. When the four of us went out together it was more of a man's evening. They paid more attention to each other, talking about their magazines and deadlines, and which writers were reliable and unreliable, than they did to us.
>
> I knew both men were fond of Lillian, or they wouldn't have allowed her to be with them. They also liked Anita Loos, and if she didn't bring a man with her we didn't mind. You wouldn't think of her as a fifth wheel,

because she could hold her own anywhere. She knew how to blend.

Lillian didn't have to do anything but sit there, and she knew how to do that very well. She knew how to listen and occasionally say something. George and Henry were great talkers, and the talk often centered on literature and the new books and plays.

Lillian took in everything — short of taking notes like you do in school. A book or a play could be a future film for her. She was very smart that way. She scouted her own material by attaching herself to the greatest sources possible, after she had left D.W. Griffith. Who better than Mencken or Nathan?

Lillian wasn't anything out of *Gentlemen Prefer Blondes*. She clearly wasn't a gold digger or flapper type. Both men could find those types, and did, all the time.

Lillian was someone — for a night owl like Nathan — who would easily be a good theatre companion, and someone to come home to after the curtain fell and the review was written.

Her problem, which Nathan soon found out, was her mother. If Lillian didn't have to be at the studio, she'd stay home and watch her. She loved being with her mother, and now that her mother was a stroke victim, and the best doctors and round-the-clock nurses were available on both coasts, she still wanted to be with her. Dorothy wasn't like that, but Lillian and her mother came as a package, sick or well.[6]

While some believed that the Jazz Age began in 1920 when the Fitzgeralds (Scott and Zelda) chased each other in the Biltmore Hotel revolving door in a drunken spree for over half an hour,[7] the rest of the world was not as joyous. Seven years later, in 1927, Great Britain had severed diplomatic relations with the Soviet Union, and Leon Trotsky was thrown out of the Communist Party.[8] America and American thought continued to travel on its well-worn isolationist path. The Greta Garbo, who was standing on *The Joyless Street* two years ago (in 1925), was still reaping the success stemming from the love scenes (with cigarettes) she had played on the floor in the 1927 American-made *Flesh and the Devil* with John Gilbert, Lillian's former leading man.

Clearly, both Lillian and Metro-Goldwyn-Mayer knew that there would be no love scenes on the floor — with or without cigarettes! While she, her mother, and George Jean Nathan had spent a brief interlude with Dorothy in England, the studio was busily preparing her next assignment: *Annie Laurie*, an action film about the feud in the Scottish highlands between the Campbells and the MacDonalds. That she hadn't chosen this for her next project, nor given her approval of the studio's choice of leading man (Norman Kerry) and director (John S. Robertson), didn't seem to faze anyone. Was Metro-Goldwyn-Mayer planning this film purposely at a time when she wasn't available for any consultation? Was she being cast in a programmer as a punishment because neither *La Bohème* nor *The Scarlet Letter* yielded large returns from the box-office?

The May 11, 1927, premiere of *Annie Laurie* at New York's Embassy Theatre was covered by Mordaunt Hall of *The New York Times*:

> [Audiences] ... will undoubtedly be sorely disappointed with the picture.
>
> On several occasions Mr. [Norman] Kerry has an opportunity to show how easily he can carry Miss Gish across ravines.... Sometimes Ian [Kerry] is décolleté, and in other episodes, like his brothers, he scorns to wear a stitch above his waist.
>
> Miss Gish is Miss Gish.... A lassie who went to the Embassy Theatre last night prepared with quite a good-sized handkerchief for weeping

purposes found to her dismay she did not have to use it at all....

Despite the slaughter in this photodrama, it hardly stirs one to the core. Annie [Lillian Gish] evades a pursuer and manages to arrange matters so that the signal light blazes forth.

Annie is safe, and so is Ian MacDonald, the gallant wearer of the MacDonald tartan, who marched bare-chested through the blades of many men....

The story of *Annie Laurie* is not especially dramatic.... As far as Miss Gish goes, the poet might have written that her face is not only "the fairest that ere the sun shone on" but also the palest. And, after all, you do not see many pale lassies north of the Tweed.[9]

It seems obvious that in using the very masculine Norman Kerry, MGM was attempting to develop him into a star along the lines of a John Gilbert. A constantly working actor since his motion picture debut as Mary Pickford's leading man in 1917's *The Little Princess*, Norman Kerry was best known as a supporting actor to Lon Chaney in *The Hunchback of Notre Dame* and *The Phantom of the Opera*. Off screen, Norman Kerry was part of the hard-drinking, womanizing crowd headed by director Marshall (Mickey) Neilan, whose cronies included Matt Moore, Jack Pickford, and sometimes Charlie Chaplin and John Barrymore.[10]

For Lillian, the *Annie Laurie* set must have been fraught with tension, both professionally and personally. Norman Kerry, unlike John Gilbert, was quite outspoken when he was rejected by any woman, and he often berated any woman with whom he may have had a temporary liaison and who denied knowing him later.[11]

Lillian would never comment on her work in *Annie Laurie*, except to dismiss it as a blur, adding that it was impossible to give her full concentration on the project because of her mother's stroke.[12]

Perhaps the presence of director John S. Robertson was the underlying cause of her uneasiness. Although he had directed Dorothy in the 1923 *The Bright Shawl* for Inspiration Pictures, *Annie Laurie* was his first picture for Metro-Goldwyn-Mayer. Robertson's former supervisor at Inspiration was the troublemaking Charles Duell.

At whose suggestion was Robertson hired to direct an already distraught Lillian?

With Robertson on the Metro-Goldwyn-Mayer lot, could Charles Duell be far behind?

Away from the camera, Lillian's life continued to be involved in the supervision of her mother and a continuing relationship with George Jean Nathan, who tried to visit as often as his schedule would permit. The geographical distance that kept Lillian and George separated for long periods made their cross-country correspondence more urgent, so that it often took the form of telephone calls and telegrams signed in code.

Phyllis Moir, Lillian's secretary, had the responsibility of attempting to put Lillian's life on a daily regimen: morning exercises, a quick swim in the ocean, and honoring a few requests for signed photographs. Marriage proposals that occasionally cropped up, in addition to the requests for money for any number of reasons, were disregarded.

Lillian's penchant for disappearances was broken in the early weeks of July when former film producer Charles Duell brought suit against Lillian's mother! Justice Teirney of the New York Supreme Court had signed an order striking out the allegations.[13] Ten days later, on July 17, the suit against Mrs. Gish was dropped at the request of Mr. Duell, who couldn't file a complaint without the allegations.[14] In the ten days that had elapsed since Duell's filing date, Justice Tierney had ordered the papers sealed and not to be opened by anyone without his permission.[15]

On June 22, Lillian's name again appeared in the newspapers. Rumors of an intended marriage to George were incorrect, as they had been for the last three years. Not only was an impending marriage denied, but so were all references to any engagement.

To the press in Santa Monica, Lillian released the following statement:

> Mr. Nathan and I are very good friends, but that is all. We have never been engaged.

Nathan added words of his own, prior to returning to New York:

> Miss Gish and I are good friends, but no announcement such as that published in New York is true.[16]

It was time for Lillian to avoid the spotlight and return to the cameras, but the train bearing Mr. Duell from New York to Los Angeles had already left.

Within hours of his arrival on June 23, Duell filed a $5,000,000 suit at Los Angeles Superior Court against Lillian, her mother, and the executives of Metro-Goldwyn-Mayer, charging that Lillian's defection from Inspiration to Metro-Goldwyn-Mayer had been a planned conspiracy to ruin him financially and professionally within the artistic community. Not only did Lillian romantically estrange herself from him, she was also earning an $8,000-a-week salary that he was in no position to match.

The suit was broken into actual damages of $3,000,000 and punitive damages of $2,000,000.

Hoping for a quick trial, Duell released the following statement to the newspapers:

> My complaint speaks for itself of three years of corruption and hypocrisy of every kind. An exposé of consequences as far-reaching as the film industry ever faced will be the outcome. It will shock the country and reach every self-respecting home in the land.[17]

Lillian knew there was no stopping a jilted lover and executive who had been disgraced on several different levels. Had she forgotten that after she walked out on Griffith she had no offers of employment from any studio for six months — or that she had been described and dismissed by members of the motion picture industry as a "sexless antique?" It was Charles Duell who sought to rescue her from sudden obscurity. Was this the thanks he was getting?

Fearing that Duell would be encamped at her door, Lillian sought legal protection[18] via the offices of William McAdoo, the former California senator and secretary of the United States Treasury who had put in an unsuccessful bid for the presidential nomination of 1924.[19]

To threaten Lillian's mother, who was still trying to recover from the effects of a debilitating stroke, was something only the lowest form of human being would do! It called for the highest protection she could secure!

McAdoo readily complied with Lillian's request, but it was the offices of Louis B. Mayer that would provide the unkindest cut.

She paid the rumors little attention. Insisting on rehearsals before shooting made for a better product and saved the studio the cost of wasted, unnecessary footage.[20] Did Mayer and Thalberg naively think that Lillian Gish was another assembly line mannequin? Was rehearsing the reason stage performers had difficulty adjusting to this motion picture medium? Was West Coast Hollywood intimidated by East Coast New York stage actors?

While it was certainly true that few of Lillian's films, with the possible exception of the not very successful *Diane of the Follies* (in which she was cast as a showgirl), ever reflected trends that were au courant, exactly how were the actresses who were jazz babies faring?

Gloria Swanson's pictures were regarded by Lillian as little more than a fashion show with a plot that served merely as another reason for trying on different clothes.[21] What dates quicker than current clothing?

Friend Colleen Moore, enjoying great success in *Ella Cinders* and *Irene*, soon would regard herself — when she wanted to break away from typecasting — as a trapped flapper![22]

Lillian knew that a real actress, an actress of the caliber of a Duse or a Bernhardt, would never allow herself to become a prisoner of the moment. Artistry must be constantly evolving and could only be acquired if one took chances and played roles that were challenging.[23]

To critics who still referred to her as a Griffith heroine, she responded:

> The women I played were all different types. They also came from different time periods.
> Mr. Griffith was like Shakespeare. Are Shakespeare's women the same?[24]

The overhead July sun at the Mojave Desert, 230 miles from the safety and security or the Culver City Metro-Goldwyn-Mayer studio, registered 120 degrees every day at 11 a.m. The temperature was too hot for the cameras.[25]

Was it this hot when Von Stroheim had his actors filming *Greed* in Death Valley? The answer is meaningless. Everyone who agreed to work for Von Stroheim knew that his quest for perfection was somewhere between fanatic and demonic.

Director Victor Seastrom, who had worked with Lillian on *The Scarlet Letter*, was part of the short–lived Swedish colony headed by Greta Garbo (whom he would direct in *The Divine Woman*). Like Garbo, he was austere and professional. He rarely socialized. The quality of his direction, which had endeared him to Lillian during the filming of *The Scarlet Letter*, was minimal, consisting of softly spoken commands in the Griffith manner. His Swedish temperament, which blended so well with Hawthorne's Puritan community, had effectively been transferred to the "Texas" locale he was attempting to evoke in California for *The Wind*.

The repressed emotions that dominated the lives of the characters in the Scarborough novel had visited themselves upon actors working daily under the unrelenting heat of the sun. There was no party atmosphere that characterized the working conditions of a Mack Sennett–Keystone Kop set with Chaplin and Arbuckle. Seastrom's troupe knew the energies had to be devoted to the grimness of the task. There was no filming between the hours of eleven in the morning and one in the afternoon. The cameras could not tolerate the heat. Rather than return to the Pullman cars that served as living quarters a few miles away, it was more practical to stand near a hastily erected tent, drink iced lemonade, and wait.

On one of the shooting days, two rattlesnakes had been captured and put inside a box. It was a minor interruption. What was a bigger problem was the constant noise from the whirring of the overhead planes that were used for the wind effects and the movement of the hot sand, which often got into everyone's eyes. The shooting had to continue. One could not stop the action of the scene. The actor stayed in character.

The presence of the wind in the novel was the factor that suggested that this was a story to be filmed. The wind was the star of the film. The wind carried the picture.

As Letty in *The Wind* (1928, MGM, directed by Victor Seastrom). The studio "didn't think the wind was enough, so they added sawdust ... and smokepots to the mixture...."

The wind was present when Letty (Lillian's character) makes her first entrance. The wind was present when Letty's husband, Lige (Lars Hanson, her co-star from *The Scarlet Letter*), has to go away to corral some wild horses. The wind was present when Roddy, another rancher (Montagu Love), forces his way into Letty's home when Lige is away, and spends the night with her. The wind was present when Letty refused to go away with him in the morning. When Letty shot Roddy and buried him outside in the heat of the overhead sun and the constantly shifting sand, the wind was there.

Miss Gish told a reporter:

> You see, out here the wind blows the sand all the time, but they didn't think the wind was enough, so they added sawdust. And then that didn't give the desired effect, so they added smoke pots to the mixture. I'm glad to report that one of the cinders hasn't gotten into my eyes yet, although a few have burned my hands.
>
> It [*The Wind*] is without the slightest doubt the most unpleasant picture for me that I have ever made. It's so uncomfortable.
>
> I don't mind the heat so much, but working before the eight wind machines all of the time is nerve-wracking. It isn't hard for me to enter into the state of the mind of the character I'm playing.[26]

The austerity depicted in the film was also evident in the accommodations given to the cast. The Pullman cars that housed the actors also doubled as a makeshift motion picture studio. Nightly screenings of each day's work held in the baggage car that served as the projection room. The refrigerators, in addition to holding the food, also stored the film in order to prevent melting.

Men not involved in any acting capacity (in addition to the actors not in the scene being photographed) wore goggles to protect their eyes.

Only Lillian, because she was always on camera, had no safeguards against the hazards of the desert. Her costume consisted of low shoes and slovenly clothes. Between takes she would run into the shack adjacent to a corral holding thirty head of cattle to escape the noise from the overhead airplanes and the wind machines that constantly blew wind, sand, and sawdust into her face.

Her answer to inquiries regarding why she couldn't be as well-protected as her fellow actors reflected her continuing professionalism in the wake of the most adverse circumstances"

"That's the lot of an actress."[27]

While Lillian was battling the sun, sand, and wind in the Mojave desert, Dorothy, in England, was battling her increasing weight. Upon completing *Madame Pompadour*, which garnered personally satisfying reviews, she agreed to film Margaret Kennedy's best-selling novel, *The Constant Nymph*.

Producer Basil Dean, noting Dorothy's tendency to gain weight when not employed in front of the cameras, inserted a clause that required her to "weigh in" at 130 pounds in London. Upon arriving from New York, it was noted that Dorothy's constant nymph did not have a constant weight, and was therefore not eligible to fulfill her agreement. Dorothy insisted that she was the required weight before she sailed from New York.

Her protests were in vain once she stepped on the British scales.[28]

The Constant Nymph was filmed with Mabel Poulton as the nymph, and co-starred British matinee idol Ivor Novello as the composer.[29]

A problem that continued to plague *The Wind* was the ending. Scriptwriter Francis Marion maintained strict fidelity to the novel,[30] emphasizing how the wind conditioned the emotions of the characters, as well as molding their lives. Although the Metro-Goldwyn-Mayer executives Mayer and Thalberg carped at the book's conclusion, and believed the ending would send the audiences into a depression (which would affect the grosses), Lillian insisted the ending be filmed as written. After Letty murdered and buried Roddy, the intruder who forced himself upon her, she went insane and surrendered to the elements that were dominant throughout the picture. The final shots would show Letty wandering without purpose into the wind.

At an executive showing prior to the official release, Lillian recalled Thalberg's reactions.

> Mr. Thalberg said we had a very artistic film, which I knew was a veiled punch. It meant he had doubts about its commercial success.
>
> "We had a preview audience view it," [he said] "and weren't pleased with the ending."
>
> Now remember, Stuart, that all of us were aware of the threat of *The Jazz Singer*, which we considered a novelty on the surface. But we knew, novelty or no novelty, it was a novelty that was being repeated with increasing success. Audiences wanted to hear spoken films, and we knew that what we were doing wasn't going to be around much longer. We knew that sound was going to be a part of all of our futures, and many of us had voices that didn't match our faces.
>
> Once we were hired for our faces. Now we needed to have voices that were compatible if we wanted to have a career in films. You very well couldn't have someone playing an Arabian princess if she sounded as if she came out of the deep South or the docks of New York. Audiences would laugh.
>
> Mr. Mayer heard about the reactions and he rushed us into a happy ending. Dramatically it didn't make sense—that after all that happened the husband and wife would be reunited, and the two of them would fling open the door, face the terror of the wind, and see it as something romantic as the sunrise.
>
> I jokingly asked when would the wife do the floors. All of that sand blowing in, and the debris, would drive anyone out of that house.
>
> Yet, this was how Mr. Mayer, who happened to be passing by, saw it. He agreed with Mr. Thalberg.
>
> Mr. Thalberg kept saying how artistic the film was, and Mr. Mayer kept shaking his head, repeating over and over like a broken record, "Change the ending. Change the ending. Change the ending."
>
> Remember, sound was beginning to be heard, and Mr. Mayer always had tow eyes: one, for the audience's reaction, and the second, on the cash register.
>
> With a reshot ending and a quick release, the studio might get back the cost of the production.[31]

On September 27, 1927, Lillian was ordered by Superior Court Judge Walter F. Gates in Los Angeles to show cause why she should not answer questions for a deposition sought in the $5,000,000 suit brought against her by Charles Duell.[32]

The Wind, like the Lillian Gish–Lars Hanson–Victor Seastrom production of *The Scarlet Letter*, had all of the elements of a European film. Victor Seastrom was relentless in omitting nothing that showed the bitterness of existence on the plains.[33] *The Wind* should have extended Lillian's career. She certainly had given her most dedicated performance under Seastrom's direction.[34]

The omnipresence of the wind, from Lillian's first entrance, served as counter–melody—from the brushing aside of a few particles of earth on a sleeve to the crescendo of fury that climaxed with her murder of the man who raped her.[35]

Poster for *The Wind* (1928, MGM, directed by Victor Seastrom). Lillian found the novel by Dorothy Scarborough and brought it to the attention of the studio.

the setting, nor designating any year in time, the characters were made subservient to the timelessness of the laws of nature and its eternal disregard for human life.

At the time of its original release in New York, *The Wind* should have been hailed as an American masterpiece of cinema, an example of American silent filmmaking to give the proponents of sound second thoughts. Yet, there were still doubts within Metro-Goldwy-Mayer's offices regarding its audience and their ability to see Lillian Gish, the Griffith heroine on the ice floe, in a role that didn't place her on the same virginal terrain on which she had been traveling so brilliantly since her entrance into motion pictures in 1912.

Sometime, somewhere, after leaving Griffith, between the Massachusetts of *The Scarlet Letter* and the "Texas" locale on the Mojave Desert in California, Lillian had acquired fortitude. Before she would surrender to the wind, she would try to fight it. She would try to save herself, even if it meant killing to survive.

Yet the release of *The Wind* was withheld for almost a year. For what reason? A second, happier ending had been shot. Lillian had complied with Mr. Thalberg's and Mr. Mayer's suggestion.

After the second out-of-town preview, Mr. Thalberg again sent for her. Their relationship had gone, in the wake of her studio employment, from cordial

John Arnold's camera made strong use of visual imagery: the dust, the wind, and the punishing skies, all of which emphasized the desolation of the lives of the characters. By not specifically fixing the geography of and supportive to reservedly respectful. He was aware that Louis B. Mayer had hired Lillian because he believed she had been responsible for the fortune he had made from his acquiring the New England distribution rights of *The Birth of a Nation* a dozen years ago.

Lillian remembered the second meeting with Mr. Thalberg after *The Wind* was seen with the alternative "happy" ending.

Changing the ending, Mr. Thalberg, the more literate executive, explained, wasn't the same as tampering with a classic to avoid censorship problems.

The Wind was a contemporary novel that was issued anonymously when it first appeared. I don't know how it came to my attention. Maybe George [George Jean Nathan] or Henry [H.L. Mencken] sent it. Both of their magazines, *Smart Set* and *The American Mercury*, reviewed new books, and I think they were fascinated by a writer who didn't take credit.

It was a good publicity stunt, but it was also a good story with a strong female character fighting nature and human nature.

I had signed a two year contract, promising to make six pictures. *The Wind* was my fourth. I had chosen it. It was mine.

The third film, *Annie Laurie*, was not a success. I didn't ask to make it, and I certainly had no control over any part of it.

The Wind was mine. I chose it. I was willing to fight for it.

Suddenly, Mr. Thalberg said, "We don't know what to do about you. Your work is very artistic, your choice of material is artistic, and you are a very dedicated artist, but we think you should be talked about more."

I thought he was going to ask me to appear with the film, something I occasionally did for Mr. Griffith. But I was wrong. He wanted me to have a scandal!

I couldn't believe what I had just heard! I didn't know what he was talking about! I was still taking care of my mother, who still needed my help. Dorothy was in England. It was in the newspapers. Where was there time for a scandal?

Before I could say no, Mr. Thalberg smiled and said he would arrange one for me. Nothing special. Just something for the magazines. Something to knock me off my pedestal.

I didn't know what pedestal he was talking about. I spoke to everyone on the set. I made friends with the crew ever since I was in pictures. If I had made enemies, wouldn't these enemies have refused to put in those extra hours when my mother had the stroke in London, and I had to rush over there?

Mr. Thalberg tried to convince me that a scandal sold movie magazines and it would give me the publicity that would get more audiences to see *The Wind*.

And then he started naming people whose popularity had increased, because they were involving in real scandals! Their audiences got bigger, and their films made money! More money because of the magazines wrote about them! Garbo [Greta Garbo] and Gilbert [John Gilbert] had lines around the corner to see their films all over the country!

I rose from my seat, and I told Mr. Thalberg very politely that I had to discuss this with my mother before I made my decision.[36]

The release of *The Wind* was withheld. Lillian was shuttled into *The Enemy*. She had no say in the matter.

The Enemy was a long held "dreary studio property"[37] that served as Lillian's said valedictory to her employment at Metro-Goldwyn-Mayer. To her it was a programmer like *Annie Laurie*, which she wouldn't discuss and dismissed as a "blur."[38]

The Enemy was a return, albeit a final one, to the fragile, weepy-eyed type Lillian had played so well in the previous decade. The heroine, Pauli Arndt, was a type she hoped to avoid playing in the future, had *The Wind* been released at its originally scheduled time.

Was placing an older Lillian Gish in *The Enemy* a concerted studio effort to subtly remind audiences how long this Griffith Victorian heroine had been making pictures? Were the Metro-Goldwyn-Mayer executives showing how remoted their $800,000 property had become?[39]

The Enemy was set in Austria at the beginning of the First World War. Lillian was playing the granddaughter of a professor who had been imprisoned for voicing his opposition to the war, and a wife whose husband has been taken into military service the day after they were married. Thinking her husband has been killed, Pauli [Lillian] becomes a prostitute to keep herself and her starving baby alive. The baby dies, and the husband returns, his death having been mistakenly reported.

Her sufferings in *The Enemy*, wrote the critic of *The New York Times* after the New York premiere at the Astor Theatre on December 8, 1927, were "hammered home with a bludgeon." The battle scenes were almost parallel to those in *The Big Parade*.

"Lillian," the review concluded, "is acting on her own familiar lines," and, "should not be held responsible for the hysteria of this picture."[40]

Nothing in *The Enemy* was very subtle: Lillian surrendering herself for a half a bottle of milk for her sick baby, a soldier handing over a spoonful of meat for some cigarettes.[41]

Audiences had seen similar moments before in other films. They had seen Lillian Gish many times before. The war had ended nine years ago. Why was she still hopelessly out of sync?

The long delayed New York opening of *The Wind* took place at New York's Capitol Theatre on the afternoon of November 4, 1928.

The opening sentence of *The New York Times* review couldn't have been more devastating:

> Yesterday afternoon's rain was far more interesting than the Capitol Theatre's current screen offering....[42]

The rest of Mordaunt Hall's review paid great attention to the wind, rather than the performance of Lillian Gish and Lars Hanson, or the direction of Victor Seastrom.

> In this picture, the wind, whether it is a breeze or cyclone, invariably seems a sham, and Lillian Gish, the stellar light in this new film, frequently poses where the wind is strongest; during one of the early episodes she does her bit to accentuate the artificiality of this tale by wearing the worst kind of hat for a wind.
>
> Victor Seastrom hammers home his points until one longs for just a suggestion of subtlety.... Mr. Seastrom's wind comes in a strict continuity, with seldom the impression of a gust. And instead of getting along with the story, Mr. Seastrom makes his production very tedious by constantly calling attention to the result of the wind. If it were realistic, it would all be very well, but it isn't....
>
> Miss Gish acts in very much the same way she did in the haphazard days of films. She rolls her eyes, stares, twitches, and then notices the revolver placed nicely on a table....
>
> In some of the sequences Miss Gish is dainty and charming and she succeeds in giving the impression of repressed hysteria.[43]

Even the advent of sound, which had been introduced within the previous month in *The Jazz Singer*, gets a drubbing:

The sound effects with this production [*The Wind*] are not calculated to increase the demand for such ideas. There are a couple of songs which come forth as if they were being sung by someone behind the screen.[44]

The damage had been done. Despite Lillian's superb control over potentially flamboyant theatrics (the shooting of the man who raped her, the attempts to bury his body in the constantly shifting sand outside her home, the increasing insanity, the wandering aimlessly in the wind), the story of *The Wind* was perhaps "too old-fashioned" and without much of a period sense to be considered seriously. What sustains our interest is Lillian's performance, a triumph of "talent over scenario."[45]

The Wind cast Lillian as a virginal heroine, to be sure, but it was a virginal heroine "facing up to the sexual realities" of life. It was a conscious attempt to answer the criticizers who believed she could only portray the Victorian heroine. Under Seastrom's surrealistic direction, *The Wind* was Lillian's "transitional metaphor."[46] As Letty wandered off (in the original ending) to die, Lillian was bidding farewell to the years at Biograph and a persona that had kept her in front of audiences for 16 years. She was wandering to an unseen future.

Lillian remembered telling Irving Thalberg:

> I died in *La Bohème*, but he said we couldn't change an opera without being ridiculed by the opera world.
> After the panning *The Enemy* received, I had no choice. They became the final arbitrators. They had allowed *The Wind* to be filmed, but they wouldn't take chances.
> I told him I was proud of my work, despite the second ending.[47]

She had every right to be proud of her work. As the *National Board of Review Magazine* observed, *The Wind* marked one of the most interesting productions in which Lillian Gish had appeared:

> Anyone who knows how effectively Miss Gish with her fugitive hands and agitated mobility of bodily gesture, at times so strikingly effective and so peculiarly hers among screen actresses, can do this sort of character, will perceive that *The Wind* gives her an opportunity to act, which she is able to take full advantage of.[48]

From European film critics and the director of the Moscow Art Theatre, Lillian Gish and *The Wind* had won high words of praise. But praise from Europe and Moscow meant nothing to Mayer and Thalberg, who saw Lillian as an American product. *The New York Times* review and the negative criticism from *Photoplay* magazine hit harder — right at the box-office.

"By mutual consent,"[49] Metro-Goldwyn-Mayer terminated Lillian's contract with one picture still to be done. The failures of *Annie Laurie*, *The Enemy*, and *The Wind* did not justify keeping her employed at $400,000 a year. It simply wasn't good business. Had Lillian agreed to an arranged scandal, perhaps she might have made that final film and completed her contract. But "artistry and integrity" came first.[50]

Anna Karenina, the project once discussed with Lillian in mind, would be given to the lower salaried Greta Garbo, whose accent in the private tests she had secretly been making might not be understood once sound had established itself as the method which would replace pantomime in screen-acting's future. Could Garbo talk?

Anita Loos recalled Lillian's last days at Metro-Goldwyn-Mayer:

> Although Lillian would never directly admit it to me, I think she was intimidated by Garbo from the moment Garbo was signed.

Garbo used to stand in back of the cameras and watch Lillian whenever she could. She worshipped Lillian, and both of them were very courteous to each other.

Victor Seastrom had directed them both, and he knew how to get good performances from them.

Lillian would do anything to publicize a film. Griffith taught her that. Garbo wouldn't. Ever. Garbo wanted to maintain the mystery. There was nothing mysterious about Lillian. Sometimes we wondered if she had a life away from the studio, now that her mother's illness seemed to take up a lot of her time.

What good would an arranged scandal be for Lillian? If the newspapers knew about her relationship with Griffith, who was still married, that would be a scandal! Anything else would be of secondary importance. Of course, a scandal with a married man, in those days, could quickly end a career.

Lillian had an image to maintain. And she did. She had purity and principles!"[51]

Lillian had the last laugh. On December 6, 1927, she signed a two year contract with United Artists, where she would make only one or two pictures a year. The first would be under the direction of her mentor, D.W. Griffith, if a story could be found that was suitable to both of their talents.[52]

Lillian's salary would be $50,000 a film, and would receive 50 percent of the profits.[53]

No matter which studio would employ her — Biograph, Inspiration, Metro-Goldwyn-Mayer, or United Artists — Miss Gish would always be Miss Gish.

CHAPTER 20

Travels and Tribulations

Lillian was starting all over again at the very beginning, as she had learned to do when she, Dorothy, and their mother were touring the country in 10-20-30 melodramas. It was a pattern with which she had long been familiar. When the tour was over, one looked for work.

Even though she had signed a lucrative contract with United Artists, there was no guarantee of security. Didn't Inspiration Pictures go bankrupt? Wasn't she released from her contract at Metro-Goldwyn-Mayer before the contract was completed? Why wouldn't United Artists do the same if the box-office returns were unsatisfactory?

Nothing in the performing arts was permanent — except being unemployed. You finished one project and, with luck, you had the opportunity to begin another. You either had a job, or you didn't. If you had no work, who cared about your talent?

One of the continuing benefits of Lillian's relationship with drama critic George Jean Nathan was the mobility accorded her amongst playwrights and actors eager for good notices. Lillian wanted to be associated with the theatre. With the coming of sound, she knew that Hollywood would be looking to the Broadway stage as a source to draw upon for actors to put in front of the cameras. Broadway

theatre actors could talk. They knew how to use their voices and sustain a two hour performance eight times a week in front of an audience. All of the Barrymores came out of the theatre.

One of Nathan's close friends was playwright Eugene O'Neill, who had become a proven mainstay of the American theatre. Lillian, in Nathan's company, had dined with O'Neill on several occasions. O'Neill told her she had a "good bean," which was tantamount to high praise from somebody who wasn't overly fond of actors and their egos. To Dr. Alvin Barach (the diagnostician he would consult when he felt his bodily disorders were increasing because of his "nerves") he confided that Lillian was "the exact opposite of all you imagine when you say 'movie queen.' " Lillian was "quiet, had real brains and fine eyes."

When Nathan hinted that Lillian might be a good choice to replace Margalo Gillmore in the part of twenty-year-old Princess Kukachin in *Marco Millions*, O'Neill agreed and said he would put her name before the Theatre Guild hierarchy.[1]

The O'Neill and Nathan friendship went back to 1917 when Nathan printed O'Neill's sea play, *The Long Voyage Home*, in *Smart Set* magazine. At the time Nathan accepted the unsolicited manuscript, O'Neill's name and talent were strictly local. He was known only to a few people in Provincetown. Nathan's sophisticated magazine had given the struggling young playwright his first taste of the recognition that was to come. Nathan's intuition about O'Neill was later validated when *Smart Set* published the young writer's *Ile* and *The Moon of the Caribbees*.[2]

The Theatre Guild rejected O'Neill's proposal that Lillian go into *Marco Millions*. O'Neill offered no explanation. Nathan wouldn't want to hear one. A suggestion was either listened to or ignored.

To his wife, Agnes Boulton, O'Neill confided a real reason: Lillian's presence would "wreck their company with jealousy and dissension."[3]

It was time for Lillian to look elsewhere.

One of the reasons Lillian signed with United Artists was the promise of an opportunity to star in a film based on a story created for her, and which would be directed by Max Reinhardt of the European stage. Reinhardt's theatrical productions were always innovative. His revolutionary approach to staging sometimes went beyond the traditional proscenium arch and often caused as much post-performance of *Sumrun*, a play without words at New York's Casino Theatre, was viewed as an "oddity."[4] His $400,000[5] sec and sadism spectacle, *The Miracle*, cloaked in a religious theme[6] (a straying nun leaves her calling to return to the world and sample its pleasures, causing a Madonna to step down from her pedestal and assume the nun's duties),[7] was the oddity of the 1923-24 season.

For *The Miracle*, scenic designer Norman Bel Geddes transformed the Century Theatre into a veritable cathedral,[8] complete with pillars, stained glass windows, and no curtain between the scenes or acts. 700 extras were used for mob scenes. The main appeal of *The Miracle* was its use of pageantry and lavishness.[9]

Had Lillian not been filming *Romola* in Italy, she would have gladly accepted the part of the nun.[10]

She met with Reinhardt in 1927, while she was still under contract to Metro-Goldwyn-Mayer, and he was in California with *The Miracle*. Neither spoke the other's language. (The German Reinhardt spoke no English, and Lillian spoke no German.) Reinhardt's traveling companion, Rudolph Kommer, acted as interpreter. With Karl von Mueller, the two men lunched with Lillian at her home in Santa Monica, prior to a private studio screening of *Broken Blossoms*, *La Bohème*, and *The Scarlet Letter*.

At the conclusion of the last film, Reinhardt, who had spent 35 years in the theatre and was bored, suggested that he and Lillian collaborate on a film. That he had never made a motion picture was of the least importance.[11] Reinhardt was an international name. His theatres in Berlin and Vienna were considered the best in Europe.

Lillian wanted to work with him, even if it meant risking her mother's health taking her to Germany. If the patient could handle the sea voyage, German's medical facilities were considered the best.

Lillian's attempt to replace Margalo Gillmore in *Marco Millions* was unsuccessful. There was no reason for her to remain in California. Perhaps it would be wise to set her sights on Europe, where silent films were not yet threatened by the advent of sound.

In the early months of the winter of 1928, Reinhardt was in New York presenting his troupe in productions of *A Midsummer Night's Dream*, *Everyman*, and *Danton's Death*.[12] At the Drake Hotel, he and Lillian conferred on possible material for his film directorial debut. The *Faust*, project in which she would have played Marguerite, was rejected again.

Reinhardt believed the story of Theresa Neumann, the peasant miracle girl of Konnersreuth, had possibilities. Her case had been studied by scientists in Germany and Austria. She was still being watched. On Fridays, except feast days, Theresa Neumann enacted the entire sufferings of Christ, with the blood falling from stigmata on her forehead, hands, and feet.

Its possibilities interested Lillian. Unless she could go to Konnersreuth and actually see Theresa, she would not commit herself. Such an undertaking needed a more than casual familiarity with the village peasantry, something she was aware of when she made *The White Sister* in Italy.

Reinhardt, who lived in Leopoldskron, assured Lillian there wouldn't be any problems. With the success of *Mimi* (the German title given to *La Bohème*), Lillian was a star of international renown. *The Miracle Girl of Konnersreuth*, filmed in the actual German locations, already had an audience proud to see their area photographed for the screen.

For Lillian, the film was a needed opportunity to film a twentieth century story which, properly marketed, could garner the same respect given to *The White Sister*.

The project excited her. Max Reinhardt could be her new D.W. Griffith!

Lillian, her mother, and a resident nurse set sail for Hamburg from New York in April, arriving at Cuxhaven, where they were met by Reinhardt and his staff. In Hamburg Mrs. Gish was put to bed for a few hours, then everyone departed by train to Berlin.

The reception at the Berlin train station, like other train station welcomings whenever Lillian arrived on behalf of a motion picture, was not without the usual noise and commotion. Dozens of newspaper reporters and cameramen, in addition to hundreds of spectators (who had been waiting before dawn for her arrival), crowded each other.

Berlin, while seemingly like the others, had its unexpected moments of sadness in the midst of all the excitement. When Lillian wasn't in a convenient area to pose for photographs, the cameramen stationed themselves around her mother, who was imprisoned in a chair that had to be lifted and carried everywhere with poles. Unable to voice any protests against the unwarranted attention, she stared helplessly at the cameras and wept, as the shutters clicked and the flashes continued. When the crowd dispersed, she and Lillian were driven to their hotel, only to have their car followed by other cameramen and reporters eager to have a picture of the occasion for their newspapers and magazines.

Reinhardt was thrilled that Lillian's arrival had been given such an overwhelming reception. Lillian, aware that her mother was going to be hospitalized at the Kaiser Wilhelm Institute before being transferred to Dr. Sinn's Sanatorium at Neubabelsburg, didn't agree. But she knew it was useless to say anything.[13]

Present at the first meeting at Reinhardt's castle in Leopoldskron was German poet Hugo von Hofmannsthal, famed collaborator of composer Richard Strauss. Hofmannsthal's librettos for Strauss' operas were often described as "two sides of the same fabric," because their matching of words and music was so seamless.[14]

For the next three weeks, von Hofmannsthal, Reinhardt, and Lillian worked on the Neumann story, before Lillian took a two weeks' leave to be with George Jean Nathan in Paris.

Aware that his continuing relationship with Lillian was subject to the inquiries of ambitious and curious reporters anxious to obtain an "exclusive" story for their front pages, Nathan did everything he could to avoid destructive gossip. That he was in love with Lillian was a well-hidden secret. Lillian and he were close friends with a common interest in theatre and the arts.

Lillian would answer the often repeated questions with often repeated questions of her own:

> What kind of wife would I make if I am never home?
>
> Can you show me a successful actress who is also a successful homemaker?

When the questions continued, Lillian would include her mother in the patented answers:

> If my mother, who is the most perfect mother in the whole world, couldn't have a good marriage, how could I? I've worked too hard and too long to accomplish what I've done.[15]

At the end of her Paris stay, the matter of taking Mrs. Gish to Neubabelsburg still remained. It was something neither she nor George relished doing. As frustrating as his relationship with Lillian was, the constant priority of "Mother's health and welfare" would always be a further barrier. Lillian's friend, actress Colleen Moore, would often say Lillian was "married to her mother, and her career."[16]

From Max Reinhardt's castle at Leopoldskron outside Salzburg, Lillian gave her views on the motion picture as a legitimate art form:

> Art is beauty idealized. And there are minutes-only minutes probably—when film meets the requirement. And there are hours-unfortunately many hours—when it falls quite outside the borders of the requirement, just as do drama, or painting, or music. If the film is not art because of the many thousands of trashy films that are turned out, then maybe painting isn't art either because of the many thousands of 'Greenwich Village' trashy paintings,

and music isn't art because of the many thousands of 'Yes, We Have No Bananas' that are produced.

> The film, like the theatre, is not a school for morals. Just as little as the drama is supposed to educate men and women, it could only make them think about things they know anyway. It ought to show the difference between lofty thoughts and feelings. This is the goal of the best films. The battle for the film will not be easy...Finally, we must remember that the film is at present dumb [silent].[17]

Having secured written permission from the Archbishop of Regensburg, Lillian saw Theresa Neumann, the subject of her proposed film, after making a second trip to Salzburg.

Theresa, at the time of Lillian's visit, was 30 years old, the eldest of eleven children, and living in a tiny bedroom that was always inundated with sunlight. Konnersreuth was not a wealthy village, and the church had been responsible for maintaining the family. To be sure, Theresa had brought an unwanted fame and notoriety to the area, but she was protected as much as possible from exploitative tourists who would gladly photograph her as if she were one of the famous "white horses of Vienna" at the Salzburg Festival.

Lillian saw a Theresa in a blood-soaked nightdress, neither sitting nor lying but "giving the appearance of being suspended halfway with her hands held before her."[18] The priest, who had admitted her after examining her credentials, stood at the bedroom door and watched Lillian's every move, for only members of the clergy or those with special permission were allowed so near.

Theresa Neumann had not eaten any food for two years. She had gone without water for eighteen months.

In her very limited German, Lillian asked if she might examine Theresa's hands, which were covered with black mittens.

On the backs of Theresa's hands were scars the shape and approximation of quarters. On her palms the scars were long and narrow.

The Bishop of Lisbon, seated at the head of Theresa's bed and acting like a sentinel, explained that Lillian was watching Theresa undergoing her "passion ecstasy."[19]

Lillian recalled:

> It was the most amazing sight in the world. Her ecstasy begins about one o'clock Friday morning, and lasts until noon. The wounds, which are closed and black between times, open, and blood flows from them — from those on her hands and feet, from the spear wound in her side, and thorn wounds on her forehead. Tears of blood drip from her eyes, run down from her cheeks, and stain her white gown. I was within three feel of her and saw all this...If this is trickery, it is beyond anything of the sort I have ever heard of. I asked her to pray for Mother, and I believe she did...[20]

A slightly improved Mrs. Gish and her nurse from New York were still at Dr. Sinn's Sanatorium in Neubabelsburg when Lillian sailed on the Ile de France for New York. Days later, Max Reinhardt and Hugo von Hofmannstahl followed, their work completed on the script for *The Miracle Girl of Konnersreuth*.[21]

In New York, the movie made on the Warner Bros. Lot featuring an actor who never made a silent film in his career was still playing to capacity crowds eager to hear singing and a few words of spoken dialogue coming at them directly from the screen. His name was Al Jolson and the film was *The Jazz Singer*, a heart-wrenching story of a "Jewish boy who prefers jazz to the songs of his race" but returns to the synagogue to sing *Kol Nidre* when he learns that his orthodox Jewish cantor father is too ill to sing on the Day of Atonement, a sacred holiday.[22]

Although no known print of the scenes Jolson filmed for D.W. Griffith's *Mammy Boy* exist, Jolson did attempt to have a career in silent films. Griffith naively signed the Broadway singer to a written contract, and Jolson, so appalled at what he had shot in blackface and whiteface, walked away a few days after he had begun filming. The motion picture was never completed.[23]

Al Jolson was not the first choice for *The Jazz Singer*. The actor who played the part on the Broadway stage, George Jessel, saw no reason to play the part on film in relative silence (except for a few songs). Like many theatre actors of the period, Jessel saw no reason to give "half a performance" and sacrifice his speaking voice to a "novelty that hadn't proven its worth."

Even Jolson, the second choice, was doubtful that this thing called sound would work. But he needed the money. He took a larger salary instead of a minimal wage and stock in the company.[24]

Years later, a cynical George Jessel gave a characteristic philosophical shrug of the shoulders when asked to explain the mistake he had made in 1927:

So, who knew?[25]

At the conclusion of a filmed musical sequence in which Jolson sang "Dirty Hands, Dirty Face" to the extras serving as the audience in a nightclub, the entertainer waved away the applause and ad-libbed what he would say to the Wintergarden audiences who had attended his New York performances: Wait a minute! Wait a minute! You ain't heard nothing yet![26]

Jolson's ad-libbed eleven words heralded the death of silent films.

An additional scene, featuring dialogue between Al and his mother (Eugenie

Besserer), further convinced the executives at Warner Bros. That titles were no longer needed to tell the story. Like newborn babies, the motion picture had learned how to talk.

The Jazz Singer opened in New York as a $3.00 picture. *The Birth of a Nation*, the most important photoplay of the previous generation, was a $2.00 picture. By the time the Ile de France, carrying Lillian Gish, docked in New York, *The Jazz Singer* had earned over $3,000,000.[27]

Recalled Lillian: "It wasn't the movie world I knew when I left. It had changed overnight. So quickly."[28]

A hit song of the day summed up very succinctly what had just taken place in Hollywood: *If I Had a Talking Picture of You...*

Every silent film in production rushed to finish shooting before the impact of the novelty of sound threatened the impending fox-office returns. If the least satisfactory film was within a few days of completion, a few spoken words of dialogue[29] (qualifying it as a "part-talkie") made it a bigger commercial success than the best of the silents.

Actors were not the only ones affected by the new rage. Big city theatres using symphonic-sized orchestras were closed until a sound system could be installed. Rural theatres still playing the "old" silents continued to do so until the increasing demand for sound pictures made employment for local pianists and organists impossible.

With the advent of sound, the American Federation of Musicians Union had its first meeting with wholesale technological unemployment. By 1930, 22,000 moviehouse musicians across the United States were out of work. Those who were able to record musical soundtracks on the remaining completed silent films (issued in an effort to retrieve some of the production costs) numbered less than 200.[30]

Lillian knew it was too late to film *The Miracle Girl of Konnersreuth*. The Hollywood she knew from the D.W. Griffith days was gone forever. Everything in the creative arts — literature, theatre, musical composition, or motion pictures — depended on timing. The product had to be there when there was a call for it. Perhaps a "talkie" could have been made, but that required a technique neither Lillian nor Max Reinhardt understood. She had never made any tests for sound, and Reinhardt had never made any films at all! Who would be leading whom?

Lillian was still in Santa Monica when a telephone call from George in New York notified her that the Theatre Guild was in the process of assembling a touring company of Eugene O'Neill's *Strange Interlude*. Never averse to going on the road, Lillian immediately packed her bags for the train ride East.

The part was practically hers, Nathan assured her. Eugene O'Neill who had great respect — personal and professional — for her agreed to coach her. Lillian felt confident. With the playwright on her side, she might be able to return to the theatre, her first love, with a hit assured of large audiences. A touring company would show audiences just how talented she was.

And then Hollywood would have something for her.

Dorothy, coincidentally, had been planning a return to Broadway in *Young Love*, a light comedy directed by George Cukor and co-starring James Rennie. With Mrs. Gish due to return from Germany, wouldn't it be wonderful to have everyone together again, even if only for a short time? And wouldn't it be even better to have Dorothy and Lillian back "on the boards?"

In March 1960, Alfred Lunt, co-starring with his wife Lynn Fontanne in a two week City Center revival of *The Visit*, recalled Lillian's attempt to play the part Lynn created in *Strange Interlude*:

It was an accepted theatrical tradition that the best plays always toured the provinces. We used to joke that it was the only way you could see an America you thought never existed. The audiences loved and waited for those touring productions from New York. They brought subscription tickets, and we were grateful for the work.

Dear Lillian wanted to return to the theatre very much. Her film career at Metro-Goldwyn-Mayer did not turn out well. Lynnie and I were once under contract to Metro-Goldwyn-Mayer and we only made one film [*The Guardsman*], so we knew what she was going through, even though she signed a contract with another studio.

Lynnie's part in *Strange Interlude* was very demanding. She had doubts about whether she could do it. Five hours. Nobody had ever done anything like that. It was very challenging for its length alone. So many side [pages] to learn. She couldn't tour, because we were getting ready to go Caprice at the end of the year.

Lillian thought if she could get the chance to tour in it, it would be a good way to show Hollywood what they had lost, and they would ask her back. I told her Hollywood never cared what they lost. They only cared about what they could gain, and at what low price.

Lynnie met with Lillian several times. She sent her her coach to help her learn how to pace herself, and how to project. No microphones in those days. You had to know how to pitch your voice up to the second balcony without electronic assistance.

Gene [Eugene O'Neill] himself worked with Lillian. I'm sure he didn't tell the Guild what he was doing. It was better to keep that a secret, but everyone knew he and Lillian and George Jean Nathan were great friends who respected each other's talents. Nathan took Lillian to see the play several times, and Lillian, to Gene's delight, memorized her entire role.

Gene took Lillian to [theatre Guild founder Lawrence] Langner's office and she went through some of the longer speeches by memory. Lillian was aware that she wasn't the only actress trying to win the part.

Whoever landed the part was going to play it in New York first, which was a good thing, because it was good for advertising. Starring so and so, Direct from Broadway.

Lillian wasn't signed. They took Judith Anderson instead. Gene was upset. So were we.[31]

When Lillian, during a later visit to New York, told Alfred Lunt that she planned to purchase the film rights to *Strange Interlude*, his response was less than encouraging.

> Lillian didn't realize that, although it was possible to purchase the rights, it didn't necessarily guarantee that the film would get studio support—no matter what she was told.
>
> If that were the case, and I would never have said this to her, we should have purchased the film rights as a way to get Lynnie to repeat her role on film.
>
> Hollywood is at one end of the map, and Broadway is at the other. The miles between are as extreme as the thinking.[32]

Lillian was still under contract to United Artists and had to make one more picture under the terms of her contract. Nothing had been written about the proposed film being a "talkie" or a silent.

She was prepared to pay $75,000 for the opportunity to film Eugene O'Neill's *Strange Interlude* on her terms: choice of supporting cast, director, and leading man. If she were granted control in the same way she had had control when she was under contract to Metro-Goldwyn-Mayer during the filming of *La Bohème*, she might have been able to sustain a career in motion pictures.[33]

Fate was in Lillian's corner in Los Angeles on the day she was able to sign the papers. A lady in New York named Lewys had filed suit against Eugene O'Neill, charging that the plot of her privately printed 1924 novel, *The Temple of Pallas Athenae*,[34] had served as the basis of *Strange Interlude*. Paramount, who (unbeknownst to Lillian) had been eyeing the O'Neill play for their studio, immediately withdrew their interest.[35]

Judge Woolsey, in whose chambers Lillian had once appeared during an early Charles Duell action, listened to the arguments before dismissing Lewy's claims as "wholly preposterous," ordering her to pay

$7500 to Eugene O'Neill, $5000 to the Theatre Guild, and $5000 to Horace Liverwright, O'Neill's publisher.

None of the three mentioned in Woolsey's decisions — O'Neill, the Theatre Guild, or Liverwright — received any monies. The author dropped out of sight.[36]

The greatest loss was, of course, to Lillian. She didn't get the part for the stage. She couldn't buy the rights for the film.

Once again, she was at the mercy of a studio who would want to put her in anything to finish her contract.

Her professional future, once again, was dependent upon the whims of men.

CHAPTER 21

Novelties

Talkies are a novelty. Sound will never last.
— D.W. Griffith
Conversation with Lillian Gish
(1928)[1]

1930: It had been three years since Lillian made a motion picture. The era had changed, and Griffith's hasty pronouncement was no longer taken seriously. The "novelty" was here to stay. To market Griffith's last silent, *Lady of the Pavements*, sound sequences were hastily inserted toward the end of the film to qualify it as a "partial talkie," thus making it playable in both old-fashioned movie-houses and those that were equipped to show the more modern, innovative version.

William Bakewell, playing a pianist in *Lady of the Pavements*, recalled Griffith's last minute efforts to keep up with changing times and attitudes:

> Mr. Griffith was quite outspoken about sound, but he had no choice. He wasn't the money-maker he had been when Lillian Gish worked for him.
> Irving Berlin was a very popular composer, and Mr. Griffith used Berlin's *Where Is the Song of Songs for Me?* for the star, Lupe Velez, to sing.
> With the addition of a few lines of dialogue, he was able to send it out. It wasn't top drawer Griffith."[2]

Neither was Griffith's earlier release that year. *The Battle of the Sexes* was a more sophisticated remake of Lillian's 1914 version which, ironically, received better reviews for its Victorian attitudes.[3]

After the release of *Lady of the Pavements*, United Artists president Joseph Schenck terminated Griffith's contract and had him removed from salary.[4]

Frank Capra, discussing the actors, their features, and his fellow directors trying to survive this transitional period, remarked:

> Some could talk, some couldn't, some shouldn't.[5]

Lillian Gish was still wary of the new medium of sound, as were her contemporaries Charlie Chaplin and Greta Garbo.

London-born Chaplin had been taking elocution lessons in a conscious effort to permanently shed his working class, East End accent. With the advent of sound, the poetry of silence and pantomime was permanently removed. If he had to talk, it would be wiser to have a new persona. His tramp had become a thing of the past. The new Charlie would maintain a position of elegance. That his speaking voice wouldn't be heard until the 1940 film, *The Great Dictator* (although he still made the silent *City Lights* and *Modern Times* in the thirties) was not something he could have predicted. True, his voice was heard in *Modern Times*, but he was singing a nonsense song in no identifiable language. His added speech at the end of *The Great Dictator*, in which he portrayed a character modeled after Adolph Hitler, was delivered in perfect Mayfair-accented English![6]

By her own decision, Lillian had remained out of the new sound films, hoping that the public would come to its senses and call for a revival of silents. Still, her name was good news copy, although what was printed wasn't always to her liking.

During the previous August (1929), she was embarrassed on the *Île de France* by the presence of Charles Duell who, learning of her solo departure from Paris on the liner, had somehow been able to purchase a ticket for himself on the following day. He told reporters that it was sheer coincidence that he and Lillian were traveling on the same ship that was met in New York by George Jean Nathan.

Lillian didn't quite agree when she spoke to reporters:

> I can go nowhere but what he [Charles Duell] is either present or has his process servers hounding me. For five years he has been doing nothing but bringing suits, and all have been thrown out in the lower courts. This is his idea of vengeance.[7]

In California, Lillian continued to maintain her residence in Santa Monica with her mother. Occasionally Mr. Griffith would visit, and the three would have dinner together, as they had done many times in New York during Lillian's days at Biograph. Predictably, the talk was centered on making motion pictures and possible projects on which they might collaborate.

Lillian was polite, but she knew any professional association with her former mentor was impossible. Griffith's last efforts were a far cry from Griffith at his prime, which ended when he and Lillian filmed *Orphans of the Storm* a decade earlier.

Griffith's relationship with Carol Dempster ended with the completion of the 1927 release, *The Sorrows of Satan*, which *Photoplay* dismissed as "old-fashioned" while deeming Carol's performance "excellent."

Carol, noting Griffith's unemployment, and seeing no future in motion pictures without his support, married New York banker Edwin S. Larsen and retired.[8]

Instinctively, Lillian knew not to encourage any projects with someone whose career went back even farther than hers. She knew if she wanted to continue, her future depended on being associated with the new, younger directors who would keep her name above the title.

A frequent fourth person at the Gish dinner table was French director Jean Renoir, who was a next door neighbor.[9] Renoir hoped, on the basis of his successful *Nana* and *Le Grande Illusion*, to have a career in Hollywood.

In his 1974 memoir, *My Life in Films*, Renoir recorded his impressions of those evenings over four decades ago: She [Lillian Gish] was a woman of incompatible youth, but she belonged to another age. She was no longer given interesting roles.[10]

Lillian's problem was persona and a lack of suitable properties. At the age of 37, she was hardly the type or age to play supporting roles, having been a leading lady since her debut in films. What was happening to her, as a pioneer, would continue to happen to other film actresses up through the present day.

Character actresses like Marie Dressler were always in supporting roles. As much as Lillian admired her, she knew she couldn't be used in only a few scenes, like Marie, and "steal" it. Lillian's affect was cumulative. She had to grow in the part as the film progressed.

When United Artists offered Lillian the leading role in *One Romantic Night*, a film based on Ferenc Molnar's play, *The Swan*, she accepted, although she had doubts regarding the ability of what Griffith called "the ninety per cent of the world's ability to understand English, which would lower the potential returns at the box office."[11]

The part Lillian was playing was Alexandria, the daughter of a dowager princess (Marie Dressler) who is forced, because of political convenience, to marry a prince (Rod La Rocque) she does not love.

It was this sort of part that a cynical Aileen Pringle described as:

> Passive. The poor actress just stands there in a ballroom gown and, for the first part of the play, has to gracefully acknowledge everyone's bows. Then she sees the handsome, but equally dominated prince, and she either likes him or hates him. Somehow, before the final curtain, there is a Grand Ballroom scene, which gives the princess a chance to put that gown to good use. Before the end of the first waltz, and God knows how many whirls, the two hopeless ones realize they are somehow in love, and they have to acknowledge everyone's bows and curtsies again. It's all very nice to watch, if you like that sort of thing, but very boring for any actor worth his salt to play."[12]

One Romantic Night was the sound remake of the 1925 silent, *The Swan*, that had starred Frances Howard (the actress who married mogul Samuel Goldwyn) and Ricardo Cortez. The Gish–La Rocque version utilized cameras in booths called "iceboxes."[13]

Cameraman Arthur Miller, whose long career began at the Bison Company in Fort Lee, New Jersey, in 1909 and steadily progressed from *The Perils of Pauline* into sound (culminating in an Academy Award in 1946 for *Anna and the King of Siam*), would still laugh when "iceboxes" were mentioned in discussions of the early days of sound.

> Iceboxes? Those little booths were hot boxes. They had to put the cameras inside these walled confinements because of the inability of anyone to totally control what sounds were being recorded besides the spoken dialogue.
>
> In the silent days, Mr. Griffith could shoot three film sequences simultaneously, side by side — watch the action, give commands, and somehow tell the crew what to assemble as soon as one of the scenes finished. Everything was organized chaos, but it made no difference, because the pictures were dumb [silent], and there was no concern about sets being hammered together and furniture being rearranged a few feet away.
>
> In sound films in those early days, you didn't have that luxury. Nothing could be touched once the film started rolling. A creak in the floor was even picked up. A cameraman couldn't last for more than ten minutes without contracting heat prostration.
>
> Not all of the sound films were total sound. They only used sound when they had to, for the two or three character "intimate" or "close" scenes. The ballroom scenes requiring dancing or many actors were still shot in silence. The orchestra sounds or "crowd" movements were added afterwards.
>
> We would shoot the dialogue with hidden microphones and hope that our voices weren't being recorded as shouts instead of natural conversation.

Some actors had terrible voices with accents that were out of place when we saw the "rushes" at the end of the day.[14]

Making a sound film was a risky business. For Lillian it was the equivalent of making a debut in another medium. She had no choice but to try and succeed. Silent films were a thing of the past. The sound novelty was here to stay, despite Griffith's pronouncement.

Fortunately for Lillian, Rod La Rocque, her leading man, was a stage-trained actor. In the course of his work in Chicago stock companies, he had learned to perform in one play while memorizing the lines for the part he was going to play the following week.

It was a great strain, but it was the way stock companies functioned. When an actor signed for the season, he worked for the season, appearing in as many productions as possible.

Lillian and Dorothy were touring juveniles, often playing the same part in different cities. It was a toss-up: changing cities sometimes twice a week, or learning a new part each week and remaining in one theatre.

Studio president Joseph Schenck had no cause for worry. The cast of *One Romantic Night* (Lillian Gish, Rod La Rocque, Marie Dressler, and Conrad Nagel) were seasoned stage veterans.

On the *One Romantic Night* set in California, Lillian recalled:

> I always was an early person going back to my touring days. You somehow got to the theatre no-matter-what.
>
> I was very concerned about this film, and I often left after everyone had gone. We had an excellent cast, but I was carrying the picture.
>
> Mary Pickford had a bungalow that she graciously allowed me to use as a dressing room. If I had an early call, I would sleep overnight and let the nurse look after mother.

> I kept hoping that Professor Reinhardt [Max Reinhardt] would somehow contact me and announce that he would attempt a sound version of the Theresa Neumann film we had planned. But he didn't.
>
> While he was in Hollywood, he had been neglecting his theatres, and they were suffering for it. He had to return to Salzburg, if he wanted to salvage something for the season.
>
> That's the nature of this profession. You can only hope that work will get you more work. When it doesn't come to you, you have to look for it.
>
> Max Reinhardt, Professor Max Reinhardt, was like every director or actor. You have to work if you want to have a career.[15]

To their delight, a shared love of Clos de Vougeot, a French wine from the 125 acres of a monastic vineyard in the Nuit-St-Georges region of France,[16] was responsible for the Ruth Gordon and Jed Harris friendship, which now included George Jean Nathan and Lillian. Manipulator Ruth was well aware of the benefits Jed Harris could reap if he were friends with an influential, powerful critic like Nathan, whose words were often responsible for the success or failure of a production. Harris was aware that the presentation of a classic needed a bankable presence to attract an audience who only wants to see a star. Lillian had a long career that was praised and respected. That she was returning to her roots, the theatre, after a 17-year hiatus was news in itself. Curiosity would lure even the most casual moviegoer to the Cort Theatre eight times a week.

If the venture failed, Hollywood pundits would say she was someone who had turned her back and had gone "high-hat." But if Lillian succeeded...

Beneath the polished veneer of Ruth Gordon's elegant dinners, complete with sophisticated exchanges among Harris, Nathan, and Lillian Gish, was the underlying motive: everyone would benefit. Anton Chekhov's 1897 infrequently-staged *Uncle Vanya* was work. Lillian needed work. Her last film, *One Romantic Night*, did not yield the box-office returns that would justify the $50,000-a-film and 50 percent-of-the-profits contract she had signed with United Artists. She had learned from her experience at Metro-Goldwyn-Mayer that while her presence was prestigious, she no longer had the ability, as a leading lady, to bring in the profits.

Nathan's continuing relationship with Lillian was beginning to show signs of wear. She was still devoted to her ailing mother, a factor that would always frustrate his intentions of getting a permanent commitment.

Lillian truly enjoyed Nathan's company, but there was something mysterious about him, something about him that wasn't very clear. There were things about his background he wouldn't discuss.

On a professional level, Lillian was aware that while Nathan's friendship with Eugene O'Neill almost landed her parts in *Marco Millions* and *Strange Interlude* (and had been the reason she was playing Helena in Jed Harris' revival of *Uncle Vanya*), her voice was never a powerful instrument, although it had registered clearly in *One Romantic Night*. Thanks to her constant vocalizing, a habit she had maintained since trying out for *Strange Interlude*, she had hoped she could project to the balconies for eight performances a week.[17]

Nathan was intimidated and perhaps jealous of Jed Harris' ability to make himself attractive and desirable to actresses. Lillian was not an exception:

Anita Loos observed:

> Jed Harris was a very powerful man in the theatre, the way D.W. Griffith

had been powerful in motion pictures in the World War I era [1914–1918] and for a short time afterwards until the start of the twenties.

> I don't think Lillian ever pursued Jed Harris except professionally, to get his approval. Jed was too involved with Ruth [Gordon] who was her friend and was responsible for Lillian being considered.

> This was not a great time in Lillian's life. She didn't know where her film career was going, and she had the additional pressure of taking care of her mother, who, in a wheelchair, was still dominating her.

> Dorothy was another matter, which I'll explain.

> Jed was also talking to her about a proposed revival of Gogol's *The Inspector General.*

> Dorothy was having problems with Jim [James Rennie] whose drinking had gotten worse. Occasionally she would let a sentence drop, but nothing more than that. One sentence, if you were closely listening, and nothing more than that. We wouldn't ask for details, and we'd never let on to Lillian that we knew.

> Dorothy was under triple pressure: the incoming play, Jim's drinking, and having to pay half of the bills of her mother's maintenance, whether or not she was earning as much as Lillian. I always thought Lillian helped Dorothy out once in a while.

> Jed Harris was a shrewd one. What better showmanship than to present both Gishes on Broadway in Classic plays under his banner: Lillian in *Uncle Vanya*, Dorothy in *The Inspector General.*

> Lillian would say it was like touring in the old days. Two sisters in the same town appearing at two different theatres![18]

In 1961, Lillian, appearing in *All the Way Home* at the Belasco Theatre (where she had appeared with Mary Pickford in the 1913 production of *The Good Little Devil*), remembered that first day of rehearsal in 1930 with the *Uncle Vanya* company:

> It was a brilliantly picked ensemble: Kate Mayhew, who had been celebrating 50 years in the theatre, Osgood Perkins, Walter Connolly, Eduardo Ciannelli.... All of those people had wonderful careers in the theatre. Some had made a few films, but they always went back to the stage, because they truly loved it. They loved doing eight performances a week.
>
> I loved the theatre, too, but I was going back, frankly, out of necessity. I needed to work. I was never a vaudevillian like Will Rogers, who could do his act anytime he wasn't in front of a camera. He could tell jokes and do rope tricks.
>
> At that first *Uncle Vanya* rehearsal I didn't think I was good enough. I was quite scared. I hadn't done theatre work in years, and here I was, in the midst of all of these professionals who didn't worry about mistakes, which would stop the action.
>
> That was all that was on my mind during that first line-reading, that I would stumble, although I had memorized what I was going to say.
>
> It was the total ensemble of it all that frightened me. They knew how to make jokes, even on that first day, and how to make everything seem of one piece. They knew, by virtue of their experience, how to blend. I never knew how to blend.[19]

Jed Harris also sensed Lillian's insecurity that first day. Quietly taking her aside, he instructed her:

> Just do this as if you were in a movie. Don't worry about projection. Don't worry about the size of performance. My advice is the woman you're playing [Helena] is the pivotal figure in the play. If they believe her, everything else will be believed.
>
> You're playing every man's idea of a woman. Try and keep that in the back of your mind. You're going to be wonderful.[20]

Going to be wonderful...

And indeed Lillian was wonderful.

John Anderson, writing in the January 1931 issue of *Theatre Arts Monthly*, remembered: "The contrivance of Lillian Gish's [initial] entrance: she merely fluttered across the stage without speaking to anyone and vanished."

Uncle Vanya celebrates all of life's boredom as shared by its gallery of Chekhovian types: an omnipresent country doctor, an ostentatious professor, a rejected spinster, a man for hire to perform the most menial of tasks. It is a society with could easily lend itself, except for the twice attempted shooting (unsuccessful) of the brother-in-law, to audience despair at the play's lack of dramatic action. Yet, properly directed, the despair of the play's inhabitants is an occasion for high comedy.

In Jed Harris' hands, the audience attending the April 15, 1930, opening saw *Uncle Vanya* as a "very actable drama under sensible direction." To the play, Harris brought "luminously beautiful performances," an "old confidence in Chekhov's uncanny perceptions..." and an ability to see the "high comedy where most observers merely see the gloom of futility."[21]

Of Lillian's performance, Brooks Atkinson in *The New York Times* wrote:

> Although judging by the storminess greeting her entrance, Lillian Gish is the star of the production, the performance has a unity that takes no account of personality. A coherent design in monotone, it includes every part on equal terms. Individually the parts are exquisitely acted — Miss Gish, fragile and pliant.[22]

On May 30, *One Romantic Night*, Lillian's debut in a sound motion picture, opened at the Rivoli Theatre, a few streets away from where she was appearing on stage in *Uncle Vanya*.

Mordaunt Hall, motion picture critic for *The New York Times*, reviewed the film, taking note of the sound qualities as well as the performances:

> This is Miss Gish's debut in vocalized pictures and it is gratifying to note that her voice records so effectively that it causes her screen work to be far more interesting than it was in silent productions.
>
> There is a splendid performance by Marie Dressler, who creates no end of fun in the part of Princess Alexandria's [Lillian Gish] mother...
>
> Mr. La Rocque [Rod La Rocque] frequently appears trying to be suave, but he misses being successful at it. His voice issues much too loudly from the screen...: At the particular showing the reproduction of sound was much too boisterous.
>
> There is a sensitive and gracious interpretation by Miss Gish.[23]

Miss Gish voiced her opinion of *One Romantic Night* years afterward:

> I don't like the film. I don't know if I could watch it today. It was a first effort at acting in a sound film, and I was a veteran of silents.
>
> It's primitive, but not primitive the way the early silents were. The earliest silents had fluidity of motion, no matter how it registered on the screen. And they had beautiful music.
>
> It seems everything in *One Romantic Night* has to come to a stop to "act" a scene using dialogue.
>
> The problems were technical, because of a lack of mastery of sound equipment. It wasn't the actor's fault.
>
> It was work, but work that I didn't like to talk about then or now.[24]

Lillian spent the summer of 1930 in France with George Jean Nathan, visiting the home of Eugene O'Neill and his new wife, Carlotta Monterrey. She returned to New York at the end of August for rehearsals of *Uncle Vanya*, in which she was going to play for two weeks prior to a road tour which included Newark, Boston, Chicago, Philadelphia, and Pittsburgh.[25]

The tour would have been more appreciated had Lillian not been aware that the Theatre Guild had mounted a second touring company of *Strange Interlude*, which had just concluded its New York run of 18 months.[26] The second touring company was headed by Pauline Lord, who had originated the title role in Eugene O'Neill's 1921 success, *Anna Christie*. This company would be playing in lesser cities, including a week's engagement in Jackson Heights and Jamaica at Brandt movie houses less than an hour away from Times Square.[27]

Lillian would have worked for nothing to do *Strange Interlude*, even in a suburban movie house on the subway circuit.

If she were asked.

CHAPTER 22

Integrity

On the *Uncle Vanya* tour, the sight of Lillian and a book had become commonplace. Her choosing to remain by herself in her dressing room between performances on matinee days rather than go with one of her fellow troupers to a restaurant for a quick meal was no longer a topic for conjecture. When not on stage, she rested. What is she reading now was no longer asked. Thanks to George Jean Nathan, Lillian always had a steady stream of books waiting for her at each new city.

It was no secret that she had made a request to United Artists president Joseph Schenck that she be released from her contract. Schenck, reluctant to do so, complied, although he believed that Lillian had an acceptable speaking voice and there was a future for her in sound films.[1]

The *Uncle Vanya* tour, for all of the newspaper publicity and radio hoopla that preceded it, was not a national tour in the tradition of the Threatre Guild successes starring the Lunts. But it was work, even if only for a month. How many opportunities does an actor have to tour in something artistic rather than the usual musical or drawing room comedy? There would always be an audience for musicals, but who would cast Lillian in a musical? Musicals were for singers and dancers. Lillian was neither. A Jed Harris tour of *Uncle Vanya* was theatre with a capital T.

Unlike Lillian's early days when, given the blessings of anonymity, she and her mother and Dorothy would always find a room somewhere, Lillian, as a member of the *Uncle Vanya* tour, stayed in suites in the best hotels and dined (when she had to) in the most expensive restaurants. It was something columnists expected when she was going to be interviewed. It was part of what Mr. Griffith used to call "selling the product." The product, in *Uncle Vanya*, was Lillian.

Although her role was small, Lillian was regarded as the star. Her name, because of her previous association with D.W. Griffith, could always engender a combination of nostalgia and curiosity amongst fans who would want to see her — even in a Chekov comedy (a far cry from the ice floes of *Way Down East*). The image of "the girl on the ice floe," while always a subject interviewers would mention, was something she expected. Sometimes, when business could be improved, she even spoke about it in full sentences: where it was filmed, the temperatures, and how she survived. If being a survivor was how audiences saw her, there was nothing she could do. Like her stage performances, her interviews were, in a sense, well-rehearsed one-act monologues that began with the Griffith days (including, of course, "how I survived that freezing weather") and concluded with the importance of the current product, the play.

In her younger barnstorming days, Lillian, because of her extreme youth, would never socialize after a performance, but would head back to her room. She still maintained the habit, unless George Jean Nathan happened to be in town.[2]

Books, Nathan had taught her, could always be presented to any studio executive interested in employing her. It was always safe to suggest a classic. A classic could always be found in a school and public library. A classic, with rare exception, meant family viewing.

Throughout her life, Lillian would tell interviewers that being an actress was not a career she would have chosen to follow. She had wanted to be an elementary school librarian in her hometown of Massillon, Ohio. Her films, since the beginning with D.W. Griffith, were projects in which she could take pride.

Her mother and Mr. Griffith had encouraged her to read. She had brought Hawthorne to the screen with *The Scarlet Letter*. Perhaps audiences would warm to *Jane Eyre* or *Wuthering Heights*, and discover the Brontes.

H.L. Mencken had told her to look into the realistic writings of feminist novelists like Willa Cather and Ellen Glasgow. Lillian knew that the failure of Cather's *A Lost Lady* as a screen vehicle would forever seal her chances of securing *My Ántonia*. Cather wrote words to be read, not to be diluted into moving images for illiterates.[3] Edith Wharton, who never saw a motion picture, had no qualms about her works being turned into moving pictures — as long as she received a nice sum.[4]

Knowing it would be more advantageous to be associated with a literary property, Lillian was reluctant to personally approach Edith Wharton, although Mencken and Nathan, as editors of two respected magazines (*The American Mercury* and *Smart Set*), certainly could have set up such a meeting. Lillian had never forgiven Nathan for suggesting that she accept Molnar's *The Swan* as the motion picture in which she would make her sound debut. Retitled *One Romantic Night*, the grosses were less that $400,000 — a good enough reason to cancel her contract (even though she had one remaining picture to make). She didn't want to be forced, as she had been during her Metro-Goldwyn-Mayer contract, to be shoved into unsuccessful programmers and let the studio have the last word. By leaving of her own volition,[5] she would be able to tell interviewers that she had come to films out of the theatre, and now she wanted to return to the theatre.

Not every audience on the *Uncle Vanya* tour was a sophisticated New York group of Chekov devotees familiar with the plot of the play (usually as a reading assignment from their university days). The reception in Boston was cool, and the theatre was like a barn. There were "paid-for empty" seats.

In Chicago, Lillian was the bigger hit than Chekov.[6]

Lillian, with distance between her and the unsuccessful Boston engagement, reflected on the business end of show business, and how she viewed her profession:

> I have never been an actress who enjoys working just for the love of doing it. I only like to work when there are customers out there to watch. I am interested in knowing how much money is coming into the box-office. It is embarrassing to try and act when hardly anyone is out in front.[7]

The *Uncle Vanya* tour was coming to an end. And then what would Lillian have? Her only offer of employment came from Max Reinhardt, still anxious to work with Lillian, but only if she would come to

Germany. What Professor Reinhardt had in mind for Lillian wasn't an acting job, but an offer to serve as production manager of a sound motion picture version of *La Vie parisienne* with Emil Jannings, once her proposed co-star in a never-made film version of *Faust*. *La Vie parisienne* would have three versions: German, French, and English.

Lillian rejected the offer. Was this the same Professor Reinhardt who, when he was in Hollywood, was afraid to attempt a sound version of *The Miracle Girl of Konnersreuth*?[8] Wasn't Max Reinhardt one of the reasons she had originally signed with United Artists? Was he preparing to work in Germany because he was afraid to fail in Lillian's American studio, a studio with whom she had canceled her contract?

Lillian knew from her one directorial experience with Dorothy in *Remodeling Her Husband* (1920) that her career depended on what she could do in front of a motion picture camera, not behind it. To learn how to master the technique of performing in a sound film, having spent all of her cinema days emoting in silents, would be traumatic enough without the additional burden of being personally responsible for the worth of the entire production while worrying about Reinhardt's reception of her efforts! He might dislike the second version and fire her! He also might terminate his promise to complete the three-picture assignment!

Lillian offered a very logical, albeit convenient, excuse for rejecting the Reinhardt offer: her mother's illness now required that she be in the immediate vicinity. While Lillian was aware that full time medical assistance was excellent in Germany, Mrs. Gish always felt better when Lillian was within arms' reach at her bedside. To bring Mrs. Gish back to Germany and Dr. Sinn's Sanatorium at Neubabelsburg was too emotionally draining. It was also a waste of hard-earned money![9]

A telephone call from George Jean Nathan the following May to Lillian, vacationing alone in Bad Nauheim and taking the rest cure, jolted her into remembering what Eugene O'Neill had tried to explain to her the previous summer. O'Neill had shown her a bulky, incomplete manuscript consisting of three plays to be presented in a single evening, with a dinner break for the actors and the audience.

The manuscript (entitled *Mourning Becomes Electra*), Nathan informed her, had been finished, and O'Neill, impressed with Lillian's "earnestness" in memorizing the roles in *Marco Millions* and *Strange Interlude* (for which she had unsuccessfully auditioned in the offices of Guild president Lawrence Langner), had suggested Lillian once more.[10]

Perhaps the Theatre Guild was hoping to have the same results Jed Harris reaped when he had used Lillian and Dorothy on Broadway the previous season in *Uncle Vanya* and *The Inspector General*. Unfortunately, duplicating a success in the theatre is never a sure thing. Dorothy's earlier appearance under the Guild aegis in George Bernard Shaw's *Getting Married*, presented in March 1931, had received one of critic John Mason Brown's most negative comments: *Getting Married* is … one of the most trying and interminable bores that the present season has produced.

Brown then criticized Phillip Moeller's direction as slow, the production as "heavy-handed," and the casting, in some instances, as "unfortunate."[11]

The same Phillip Moeller, at O'Neill's insistence, was to journey to Bad-Nauheim, Germany, with actress Helen Westley, an actress who had been with the Theatre Guild since its 1914 beginnings as the Washington Square Players, to provide a second opinion.[12]

What Lillian hadn't realized was the amount of pressure the failure of *Getting Married* had placed on the Theatre Guild.

To have a commercial success with an un-orthodox play, the leading actor has to be a commanding presence whose very name would sell tickets. A bankable actor always guaranteed a percentage of fans willing to pay for the ticket just to see that person onstage. The theatre, like the opera world, always had its own aristocracy. Names on marquees always sold tickets in advance of the opening night: Katherine Cornell, Helen Hayes, Alfred Lunt, Lynn Fontanne, the Barrymores, Helen Menken, Eva LeGallienne, Ina Claire… Could Lillian Gish do the same?

A fact of which Lillian was unaware was the list of actresses who didn't want to star in *Mourning Becomes Electra*, including Lynn Fontanne and Katherine Cornell.

Phillip Moeller was willing to audition Lillian only as a personal favor to O'Neill. Moeller had directed O'Neill's *Marco Millions* and *Strange Interlude*.

From Bad Nauheim, where he and Helen Westley acted as a "committee of two," an appraisal was sent to Lawrence Langner's offices:

> She [Lillian Gish] is marvelous in type, but practically inexperienced as an actress — but very, very intelligent and with marvelous pantomimic projection which of course was to be expected. Her voice, while somewhat monotonous in range, I think could be worked and what encouraged me was the amazing way in which she understood and reacted to the directions I gave her.
>
> [I] would obviously prefer [Judith] Anderson [who toured in *Strange Interlude*] because I know her work and know what she could do … but Gene seems opposed to her and calls her a "ham."

At the Theatre Guild offices in New York, Lillian auditioned again. And again, she was rejected. Her voice was "too weak for a ramrod character as Lavinia."[13]

The role of Lavinia was played by Alice Brady, who was one of the actresses who rejected the part of Nina in *Strange Interlude*, which Lynn Fontanne played and which Lillian had wanted to assume for one of the touring companies.[14]

Weeks later, when Jed Harris approached the Theatre Guild to produce *Othello* (which he would direct with Paul Robeson in the title role and Lillian as Dedesmona), the idea was rejected. Lillian, in the shared opinions of Lawrence Langner, Phillip Moeller, and Helen Westley, was not a stage actress. That her recent *La Dame aux Camelias* had closed after 15 performances was justifiable proof that she was not a commercially viable name to risk placing above the title. The 48-performance failure of Dorothy's Shavian venture did not endear either Gish to the Guild.[15]

Lillian, determined to have a career in the theatre, sought the advice and help of Margaret Carrington, who had been Walter Huston's voice teacher and had worked with John Barrymore for a strenuous ten week period before he appeared on stage as *Hamlet*, one of the highlights of the 1922-23 Broadway season.

Lillian wanted stage work, preferably in a classic vehicle which would confound her Theatre Guild detractors who believed she lacked the experience and stamina to be able to sustain a full-bodied performance as a leading lady eight times a week.

When the opportunity arose to play Marguerite Gautier in *La Dame aux Camelias* in a just-restored 1860 Central City Opera House in Colorado, Lillian didn't need to consult with George Jean Nathan for advice before she signed the contract, which also name her casting director. Like the *Uncle Vanya* engagement, Lillian would have offered her services for nothing to be associated with so ambitious a project.

The Dumas play was a crowd pleaser. The part of Marguerite was actor-proof. What was good enough for Sarah Bernhardt was more than good enough for her.

Amongst the supporting cast she had auditioned and chosen was Raymond Hackett, as Armand Duval, Marguerite's lover. Hackett was the husband of Lillian's long-time friend, actress Blanche Sweet, who reminisced about the production in Colorado:

> Robert Edmond Jones, an important set designer, found enough standing of the Central City Opera House, built in 1860, to want to restore it, thinking it would be a nice place to present plays and develop a regular theatregoing audience, as well as a tourist trade. He presented his idea to some sort of council, and they went for it.
>
> Immediately all of the citizens in the area went digging in their cellars and attics, looking for anything they could contribute, when they heard the first production was going to star Lillian Gish. Everybody knew *Camille*. It was a very popular melodrama. Sarah Bernhardt had toured in it for years. She also filmed it.
>
> That theatre was loaded with things people were glad to get rid of: furniture, rugs, lamps, little insignificant things like old antimacassars that must have covered the arms of their grandmother's sofa.
>
> What was finally chosen for the sets became a matter of local pride. It certainly brought in people who must have attended just to see their furniture come to life on that stage. That sofa Miss Gish is sitting on belonged to our aunt, sort of thing.
>
> By the dress rehearsal, when everything had been assembled, we didn't believe that anything had been recreated. What we saw on that stage had simply been maintained and dusted before they rang up the curtain. That's how authentic it looked. You only had to look at that set and you

> yourself were back in 1860, and it was the current day!
>
> People came from miles away to attend the opening: on horseback, in haywagons, stagecoaches. And they were dressed in the clothing of the day!
>
> Even with all of the help, we were told the cost of the restoration was over $200,000. A hefty sum for those days.
>
> What better choice for a Marguerite Gautier than Lillian Gish? Who could be better? Lillian certainly knew how to play a death scene. Everybody always said *Broken Blossoms* after her name was announced. That's how she had fixed herself in everyone's mind out there.
>
> There wasn't a dry eye in the house, that opening night — or during any of the performances that followed. Even the ushers wept. You saw them at the beginning of the play, and then they came back for the last minutes, just to watch that death scene. Marguerite was a role Lillian was born to play.
>
> I wish I had the handkerchief concession![16]

At the conclusion of the Central City engagement, Lillian returned to New York to spend a week with her mother, Dorothy, and George before returning to Bad Nauheim, Germany, to spend a few weeks at the mineral springs.

In September she sailed back to New York on the liner *Europa*. On the same ship were actress Margalo Gillmore, whose princess role she had wanted to assume in *Marco Millions*, and the distinguished husband and wife team of E.H. Sothern and Julia Marlowe.[17]

To inquiring reporters, Lillian announced that she had planned to bring her successful Central City production of *Camille* (an easier title to remember, and the name given to the play by audiences in America), to New York (opening at the Morosco Theatre on November 1) after additional engagements in Albany (October 18),

Utica (October 19, 20 and 21), Newark, New Jersey (at the Broad Street Theatre October 24-30).[18]

Blanche Sweet remembered the "out-of-town" reviews before the production opened in New York:

> The critics weren't as ecstatic as they had been in Colorado, but those Colorado people were also praising the restoration of the theatre to its former days of glory in the 1860s when they had some touring company pass through. The Colorado engagement was a double package: the restoration of the theatre, and then the play.
>
> Lillian's *Camille* was a real "ticket printer" as they used to call a success. A real "ticket printer."
>
> I don't think anybody would consider the play in the same league as a Eugene O'Neill evening. That would be impossible.
>
> The pre–New York reviews contained words we had anticipated: old-fashioned, which it was; melodrama, which it was; creaky, it was; and the phrase that spelled doom — showing its age. The older reviewers called it solid theatre. Everyone praised Lillian's performance.
>
> What New York audiences were going to see was grand old theatre, the kind of theatre our grandparents saw. Of course, by modern standards, it wasn't sophisticated. Dumas, like any writer, was writing for the audiences of his generation.
>
> That the play survived his generation, and spoke to generations afterward was the reason the play became a classic. Nothing becomes a classic if it only has limited appeal.[19]

In the wake of the Newark riots and civic disturbances during the summer of 1967, Lillian recalled the *Camille* engagement in a much calmer city thirty-five years earlier:

> The *Camille* booking was the second time we had played there. I was in New York previously as part of the Jed Harris tour of *Uncle Vanya*. We played Newark, because the Philadelphia engagement fell through, and Newark was the available city at short notice. It was also Jed's hometown, and I think he wanted to show what he had done.
>
> Newark was a nice city. There were two theatres: the Shubert, where they had the musicals, and the Broad Street Theatre, where they ran the straight shows, the name given to dramas and comedies.
>
> The Broad Street Theatre was under the management of a man named Schlesinger. It was a good-sized theatre. Wonderful acoustics, and a good stage for large casts. Bob [playwright Robert] Sherwood told me his first play, *The Road to Home*, with Jane Cowl, had its world premiere in Newark [1929].
>
> To get there, I'd take the Hudson Tubes to the Newark station, cross the street to this wonderful 24-hour-a-day pharmacy [Petty's, still in existence] that had the longest soda fountain I'd ever seen in my life: one full block. It ran across the store to the rear entrance. There were always people at that soda fountain waiting until their prescription was filled. It was good business, and it made the waiting time seem shorter.
>
> I'd leave my prescription for mother when I arrived, walk on Broad Street to the theatre by myself, play the performance, return to the pharmacy afterwards at eleven or so, pick up the prescription, have a wonderful ice-cream soda or a sundae, cross the street, and take the midnight or one a.m. train back to New York.
>
> For the week we played Newark, I really stocked up on prescriptions. What I saved on those prescriptions, I spent on ice-cream sodas and sundaes.
>
> I know Newark has changed, but whenever I hear the name "Newark," that is the first thing I think of: ice-cream sodas and sundaes.

When Dorothy and I played in *The Chalk Garden* at the Bucks County Playhouse in the 50s, there also was a good ice-cream place in the vicinity. That is one of the joys of touring. You meet nice people, and you find good places that have ice-cream. I love ice-cream![20]

La Dame aux Camelias opened in New York on November 1, 1932. Brooks Atkinson of *The New York Times* reviewed the production:

The *Camille* in which Lillian Gish is acting has a strange, quaint sort of magic.... If it is not Camille, it is Lillian Gish who remains one of the unworldly mysteries.... Miss Gish moves delicately and quietly through the part. She is frail and her features are exquisitely modeled. Her voice is as innocent as a star of the evening. In the death scene her voice is pathetically childish. Her gestures are limp. Throughout her performance her miniature chaste little Camille seems quite unaware of a courtesan's perquisites, duties, and prerogatives. She is as detached from worldly turmoils as a vagrant wisp of cloud. And yet when you have noticed all of these aspects of Camille you still have the idealized spirit of Miss Gish to contend with. Even in the part to which she is unsuited, she can still silence a first night audience.

Her company is of no great assistance. Some of them overact to the point of burlesque. Some of the make-ups are bad.

Camille has a sort of distant charm.... And Miss Gish has reminded us that the tenuous quality of her acting is not to be imprisoned in a midnight review.[21]

The role of Marguerite in *La Dame aux Camelias* was a double-edged sword for Lillian. While attempting to play it "added to her stature and local reputation as a dramatic actress,"[22] the opinion that it was "a part to which she was unsuited" may have been the reason the play closed after 15 performances.

The sudden reappearance of Charles Duell with a $5,000,000 suit against Lillian filed on December 30 in San Francisco for breaking her contract with Inspiration Pictures studio in 1924 certainly couldn't have been a source of joy. Once again, Duell was being a nuisance. And once again, this time in San Francisco, the District Court of Appeals, following the Los Angeles Court, had thrown it out.

Lillian's biggest disappointment had occurred the previous September when *Strange Interlude* had finally made it to the movie screens. A condensed Metro-Goldwyn-Mayer 110 minute version, it still retained all of the force and fury of the stage version in which she had so desperately wanted to play. Had there not been an earlier plagiarism suit, she would have been able to bring the play to the screen and cast herself in the leading role!

The much rehearsed film had been produced by her former employer, Irving Thalberg. Starring in the role she wanted was Thalberg's wife, Norma Shearer.

Wrote motion picture critic Mordaunt Hall in *The New York Times*: "Norma Shearer has given several noteworthy performances in recent motion pictures ... but in this present offering she excels anything she has done hitherto."[24]

The leading man, Clark Gable, was someone opposite whom Lillian believed she could have played. Gable, like herself, had done plays in New York. How many people knew he had first appeared on the screen in a 1924 silent film in a small role in *Forbidden Paradise*, starring Pola Negri?

Depending on who was doing the talking, the Thalberg-Shearer union was a brilliant one of mutual convenience: the powerful studio executive and the steadily ascending star. Or vice-versa.[25]

How long was Norma Shearer going to last? Hadn't she taken speech lessons to shed her Canadian accent? Would she have been able to make the transition from silents to sound if she still had an accent and did not have a Thalberg?

Lillian knew better than to settle for being a studio wife. Had she been able to marry Griffith, what would have happened to her once his contract with United Artists had been terminated? Would her film work suddenly have ended because of the association? Even not being married to Griffith, newspapers still referred to her occasionally as a Griffith actress. Weren't they aware that she hadn't worked for Mr. Griffith in 13 years?

Lillian knew that whatever would happen to Lillian, Lillian would live Lillian's life on Lillian's terms! With tenacity, there would be integrity!

CHAPTER 23

Games, Favorites, and Politics

With the help of George Jean Nathan and H.L. Mencken, Lillian continued to be seen at parties where she would have the opportunity to meet the leading authors of the day and build professional friendships which might result in a suggestion that she portray their heroines on stage or on film. By 1931, the additions to her library shelves included works by Ruth Suckow, Waldo Frank, Fanny Hurst, Conrad Aiken, Louis Bromfield, Glenway Wescott, and Sinclair Lewis.[1]

Her friendship with Edna Ferber was actually more of an acknowledgment of mutual respect between two strong–minded single women who were constantly trying to maintain a firm foothold in their branches of the arts dominated by men. The two ladies were formally introduced on the set of *So Big* in 1924, which starred Lillian's friend, Colleen Moore. Ferber's Pulitzer Prize novel had a strong female lead which Lillian could have played: a wife of an inarticulate vegetable farmer, whose sudden death forces her to assume full responsibilities for the running of the farm and providing for her son's education. It was a heroine both Lillian Gish and Edna Ferber understood. Lillian's mother assumed responsibilities for her two daughters after being abandoned by her husband, and Edna's father, claiming he had no head for business, gave his wife

rein on decision-making while he read the newspapers.[2]

In 1925 Lillian had read Sinclair Lewis' medical novel, *Arrowsmith*, upon a recommendation from H.L. Mencken, who had published Lewis' earlier short fiction in *Smart Set* and was his confidante during the writing of the book.[3] The sympathetic character of Leora, the first wife of Dr. Arrowsmith, was a part Lillian could play. Unfortunately, Warner Bros., who had filmed Lewis' *Main Street* and *Babbitt* without any success, did not want to risk losing money a third time on another Lewis novel. Other studios, seeing Warner Bros.' reluctance, followed their example.[4]

Lillian was too embroiled in contractual problems with Charles Duell to suggest staying with his Inspiration Pictures studio might be possible if *Arrowsmith* were purchased. Regretfully, *Arrowsmith* had to be passed over and, for the time being, forgotten.

Six years later, at a reception given by Lewis' publishing house in honor of his winning the Nobel Prize, Lillian observed Lewis sulking in the corridors mumbling to himself, "This is the end of me. I cannot live up to it."[5]

His lack of confidence had to be dispelled a few days later when United Artists purchased the still available *Arrowsmith* and successfully filmed it with stage actress

206

Helen Hayes playing the role Lillian wanted. Ronald Colman, Lillian's former leading man from *The White Sister*, played the title role.[6]

Lillian's inability to find any stage or picture work, the persistent pressure from George Jean Nathan to marry her, the fact that her invalid mother's condition would worsen and she would die, and Dorothy's continuing problems with — and separation from — her alcoholic husband must have created an atmosphere fraught with tension in her two-bedroom apartment.

Dorothy, never one to actively pursue work like her sister, was having problems paying half of Mrs. Gish's medical bills. Most of the Gish's household expenses had been handled by a more solvent Lillian. Even in the best of times, Lillian and her mother had lived rather frugally, rarely seen dining out together. Mrs. Gish's medical expenses, with the addition of a live-in nurse, were more than what Lillian and Dorothy had earned in the early days of touring in melodramas and as day players in their first weeks at Biograph.

The Depression had confirmed Lillian's worst fears: that nothing good lasts forever, and one had to be prepared for hard times.

Younger Dorothy never listened to her mother's nor her sister's warnings. Now, living at Lillian's, she was beginning to buckle under the pressure of encroaching calamity. Her last engagement (at a converted barn in Westport, Connecticut) with the New York Repertory Company did not attract significant audiences in great numbers, despite the high quality of the productions. Playing in Ibsen's *The Pillars of Society*, while prestigious, wasn't the type of commercial fare that would provide enough salary to pay the rent.[7]

What was the actual relationship between Lillian and George? Were they lovers, or were they just an American version of England's Noel and Gertie? Was their friendship nothing more than traveling together and being photographed at piers during arrivals and departures? Wasn't their constant response of "We're just good friends" beginning to wear thin and sound overly coy? Or did both Lillian and George have hidden fears they were afraid to acknowledge?

Were Mrs. Gish's early warnings about men (in view of her own disastrous marriage) emphatic enough to instill in Lillian a permanent distrust of men?

What was in George's background that precluded any mention of his beginnings (other than his initial writing experiences with H.L. Mencken) from becoming a topic of discussion? Why did he always try to divert Lillian's attention when she wanted to know about his family? It was no secret that Chaplin's British childhood was one of Dickensian poverty. Exactly what were George's Philadelphia origins?

1933: American movies continued to reflect what was happening in society. The twenties Charleston-dancing heroine was no longer in vogue after the stock market had crashed in 1929. With spiraling unemployment affecting the lives and fortunes of everyone, motion pictures now concentrated on mobsters and their showgirls, struggling Park Avenue socialites, and hopeful shopgirls and secretaries waiting for the right man to come along, marry them, and take them away from the daily drudgery of existence. Films like *Three on a Match*, with Joan Blondell, Ann Dvorak, and Bette Davis, brought all of these worlds together and provided a "moral commentary on the times."[8]

Joan Blondell knew the difference between the twenties and the thirties actor:

> In the twenties, you were a face. And that was enough. In the thirties, you also had to be a voice. And your voice had to match your face, if you can imagine that.

Jimmy [James] Cagney and Eddie Robinson [Edward G. Robinson] had voices that were as important as the characters they played. You knew what you were getting even before you paid for the ticket.[9]

For Lillian, who had started with Griffith and miraculously survived the twenties with only nine pictures to her credit, motion pictures had undergone another change while moving from silents to sound. With the exception of Mary Pickford, she was the only former Griffith player to make a reasonably successful transition. Lillian's twenties period may not have earned what her producers anticipated, but her name and presence was synonymous with prestige.

Now, at the age of forty, what type could Lillian play? What director in the sound era would be willing to take a chance directing an actress who still existed in the mind as the girl on the ice floe in *Way Down East*?

Paramount was willing to take a chance on Arthur Hopkins, a stage director who, like Max Reinhardt, had never made a motion picture. Hopkins, unlike Reinhardt, was not one to retreat from the challenge. In the twenties he had hit his stride as the producer-director of Eugene O'Neill's Pulitzer Prize play, *Anna Christie*.[10] There followed a trio of Shakespeares with various Barrymores: John as Richard III, Lionel as Macbeth, and John's famous Hamlet.[11] Hopkins also cast an unknown Clark Gable and Zita Johann in *Machinal*, a dramatization based on the much publicized Snyder-Gray case.[12]

At the Eastern Service studios in Astoria, Hopkins directed Lillian and Roland Young in an updated version of Arnold Bennett's 1908 novel, *Buried Alive*, which he had presented in 1913 as *The Great Adventure*.[13] Now it was retitled *His Double Life*.

His Double Life, a delightful piece of whimsy, suffused the premise of switched identities with gentle humor, relying on literate dialogue rather than spectacular effects to make its points.

Priam Farrel (Roland Young), a famous and much harried artist tired of constant attention, allows the world to believe he has passed away. He then takes the name of his valet, Leek, whose body is interred in Westminster Abbey. (Priam had hidden out in London with his valet who, upon arrival, came down with pneumonia.)

When an attending physician mistakes Priam for his valet, the artist naturally goes along with the error. Cousin Duncan Farrel, who has not seen Priam in many years, hands a sum of money to the "valet," which allows him to go to the Great Babylon Hotel. There he meets Mrs. Alice Young (Lillian Gish), with whom Leek has been carrying on a long-term correspondence.

Neither party has ever met, but Alice recognizes Priam immediately, because Leek has sent her a photograph of himself and Priam. Alice believes Priam is really Leek, and when Priam says she is mistaken, she dismisses this as delusion brought on by the shock of his master's death.

Priam and Alice marry, and he resumes his painting, not signing his canvases and frustrating art dealers who are at a loss to account for the sudden spate of work done by an artist who is allegedly dead.

Lillian enjoyed making *His Double Life*. Making the trip every day from her apartment in New York to Astoria must have been reminiscent of the days when she, her mother, and Dorothy would report from their Greenwich Village room on West 8th Street to Griffith's Biograph Studio on East 14th Street. Working in Astoria gave Lillian more time to spend with her mother, something she had wanted to do.

Once again, George was of secondary importance to mother and the movies.

Spoon-feeding Roland Young in *His Double Life* (1953, Paramount, directed by Arthur Hopkins and William C. DeMille). Critics praised her naturalness in a difficult role.

Lillian's next choice of heroine to play was a brilliant one. Effie Holden, in John Colton's and Carlton Miles' stageplay *Nine Pine Street*, was clearly patterned on Lizzie Borden, the Fall River, Massachusetts ax murderess accused of killing her father and stepmother on the morning of August 4, 1892. Although Borden had been acquitted by a jury, she never left the area and remained a subject of curiosity.

She was immortalized in a taunting rhyme for future generations:

> Lizzie Borden took an axe
> And gave her mother forty whacks.
> And when she saw what she had done,
> She gave her father forty-one.[14]

Years later, Lillian recalled the research she had done, and the reactions to the play:

> The Lizzie Borden case was always a subject of endless fascination and conjecture. She had died in 1927, six years before *Nine Pine Street* went into production, so she was even more a topic of conversation than she is now.
>
> Even though a jury didn't find her guilty, there were still people in Fall River when George and I went up there to see where the murders happened and to get a sense of time and place.
>
> Everybody knew where the house was — and we even met people who believed Lizzie Borden literally got away with murder, because she was a local girl who had led a quiet life.

The actual house wasn't an admission-charge tourist attraction yet, but there were people playing amateur detective and taking pictures, and retracing the steps of the killer from the newspaper clippings, and arriving at the most bizarre solutions — which they were more than happy to share with us, whether we wanted to listen to them or not.

The newspapers, especially the local one, had done a very good job. Remember there was no such process as photocopying available to the public in those days, and some of the people we met even had some yellowed clippings they must have received from their grandparents.

All of this attention at that time [1933] wasn't something Fall River wanted or was proud of. Towns in those days didn't see sensationalism as a way of making money.

I believe there were Borden family survivors. We never met any. I don't really remember meeting anybody from the family. But the playwrights made minor adjustments to avoid lawsuits and problems. Sometimes you have to take dramatic license to heighten the play. The actual facts can be too restricting, and the audience, if they find the events dramatized too predictably, can lose interest.

In *Nine Pine Street*, there had to be an interpretation of what actually occurred, since nobody was there who was alive, and there were no reliable witnesses.

I think if what was said in the courthouse had any credibility, there would have been another verdict. But we weren't there to make any sort of plea for or against Lizzie Borden. I was in Fall River as an actress about to go into a play called *Nine Pine Street*. I play from the script.[15]

Lizzie was now named Effie Holden. The setting was changed from Fall River to New Bedford. Effie is sweet and very religious. So upset is she at her father's sudden marriage to a Mrs. Riggs that she smashes her stepmother's head with a flat-iron and then hammers at her father with his knotted walking stick until both are dead.

At her trial, Effie's only line of defense is that she wasn't at home when the murders occurred, but was instead at the home of her fiancée. With the help of the church she is acquitted, and she remains in the home she shared with her parents in defiance of her neighbors, who believe she killed her parents.[16]

The real-life Lizzie Borden, like Effie Holden, shut herself up in her home and lived like a recluse for the rest of her life.

This fidelity to the facts had little dramatic impact and did nothing for the play, according to *The New York Times* writer who drew the assignment to review the play's opening on April 28, 1933, at the Longacre Theatre. Still, *Nine Pine Street*

> is woven together nicely. And then there are Miss Gish and a good cast to move it along.... She gives a fine performance in all its varied details, and they are many, ranging as they do from love to murder. She injects into the whole of the play a feeling of sincerity, and those parts of it that seem most real are due to her.

The play, as the evening progresses,

> grows tedious. The Borden case on which the play has so admittedly been based is too fresh even now to require a further setting.... On the whole there must remain the feeling that *Nine Pine Street* is not quite in the same class with the model of Fall River.[17]

While Miss Gish's portrayal of Effie Holden, the heroine modeled on Lizzie Borden, may have "added to her stature and local reputation as a dramatic actress, following a none-too-successful Marguerite in *La Dame aux Camelias*,"[18] both

Effie and Marguerite were "forget-me-nots in the rain."[19]

Nine Pine Street lasted 28 performances.[20]

George continued to squire Lillian around New York, where they were a familiar sight at play openings and restaurants. Occasionally, Dorothy, still living apart from James, would leave Mrs. Gish at their apartment in the care of the resident nurse and join them. On the weekends, George and Lillian would sometimes take the train to the New Jersey countryside or visit the Hergsheimers in West Chester, Pennsylvania (where they had renewed their friendship — now in its fifth year).

Despite George's repeated proposals of marriage, Lillian was still reluctant to commit herself as a wife. Her reasoning had not changed: If my mother couldn't have a good marriage, how can I?

Dorothy's inability to sustain her marriage to an alcoholic husband only served to strengthen Lillian's fears of being abandoned and helpless. Her alcoholic father had walked out on her mother, and Dorothy never knew when her husband would be coming home. That daughters of alcoholics often married alcoholics only to see the behavior patterns resurface was not a topic to be dealt with or even admitted. Few of Dorothy's friends knew of her father's problems with the bottle. So long as her husband's behavior remained controlled and behind closed doors, there was no reason to divulge this — even confidentially — to anyone.

Certainly Lillian was aware of what had been happening between Dorothy and her husband, but she deemed it wise to watch silently the steady erosion of Dorothy's marriage until Dorothy herself could no longer deny the problem. Lillian, in her maturity as an adult, did not want to become the dominating older sister that she was when they were both younger.

Lillian's hard-earned money, when the work came, was better spent on the best medical care her mother could possibly have. The latest fashions never meant anything to her. She had always regarded herself as an actress, not a clothes horse for the fan magazines and newspapers.

If one honored one's obligations, there was nothing with which to find fault or criticize. One lived a clean life, as shown in the Bible.

It was their mother's ethic. Now it was theirs.

Lillian and George were amongst the guests (that included writers Sherwood Anderson and Floyd and Mrs. Dell) at Theodore Dreiser's home in Mt. Kisco, New York, in October, 1933.[21] Dreiser's long career as a novelist had begun with the controversial bestseller *Sister Carrie* in 1900 and peaked twenty-five years later with *An American Tragedy*. Dreiser, like F. Scott Fitzgerald, wanted to fashion an original story for Lillian.[22]

Dreiser, in the summer before he and Lillian were introduced, started *The American Spectator*, a four page collection of commentary on issues and events of the day that sold for ten cents and had no advertisements (the better to be free from commercial obligations that could determine editorial policy).[23]

At their staff meetings, which were called "Editorial Conferences (with wine)," the founders Dreiser, James Boyd, Eugene O'Neill, James Branch Cabell, and George Jean Nathan bandied about the news of the day, which in 1933 often centered on the rising power of Adolf Hitler in Germany. Nobody present at the meetings of *The American Spectator* staff could foresee the Holocaust that would emerge. Frivolous, and sometimes anti–Semitic, remarks about Hitler's Jewish problem were not something to be taken seriously. Every new leader always had a scapegoat.

Yet Dreiser dwelled on it, claiming that too many Jews had avoided "muscular labor," preferring to be active in law, medicine, and the arts.

To Nathan and O'Neill, the large number of Jews in the arts, particularly in the New York area, was never a threat. Nathan did, on one occasion, admit he didn't like Jewish poetry and music.[24]

Lillian found Nathan's criticisms of any Jewish presence in the arts perplexing. What was threatening about them? The studio magnates who had employed her after her rough times at Inspiration were Jewish: Louis B. Mayer, Irving Thalberg, and George's friend, producer Jed Harris, who was willing to take a chance on her ability to do stage work. Didn't Harris' *Uncle Vanya* start to rebuild her career?

Lillian knew it was wise not to protest too much, lest she not be invited to the meetings and possibly miss the opportunity of being introduced to a writer who might suggest her name when casting started. She went back to following the pattern she had established at previous "literary" evenings: remain silent and let the men voice their opinions. That she had been considered an equal was, for them, a hard concession to make. Politics was fleeting. The arts survived. Lillian's only concern was being able to support her mother and herself, and survive.

Still, Nathan's remarks, while not so vehement as Dreiser's or caustic as Mencken's in the past, were puzzling. Did Nathan harbor any hidden prejudices that were coming to light? Or was Nathan just keeping the conversation going?

His Double Life had its world premiere at the Times Square and Brooklyn Paramounts on December 16, 1933. Mordaunt Hall, film critic for *The New York Times*, wrote of Lillian's performance that she was "thoroughly natural in what was by no means an easy role."[25] While Lillian's role was important, it was of lesser importance than Roland Young's comic turn as Priam, which turned the film into a vehi-

cle for himself. It was easy to see why his light touch would make him a natural for the *Topper* series co-starring Billie Burke four years later.

Ballet dancer and choreographer Agness DeMille, daughter of stage and silent film director William DeMille (who assisted Hopkins on *His Double Life*), commented years later:

My father [William DeMille] always thought Lillian's name always evoked a sense of nostalgia for the earlier, much simpler, days of movie making. She was a name when most of the moguls like Mayer and Selznick were just getting started. No matter how hard she tried to distance herself from the Griffith *Orphan-of-the-Storm* image of that *Way Down East* ice floe, that was what immediately came to mind when you heard the name Lillian Gish.

She kept on going. The others stopped. But she kept on going. She stayed with Griffith, and her loyalty stood her in good stead. For a while. Then her loyalty was misbegotten.

My father always said that Lillian had gumption and stick-to-it-iveness. She knew when she didn't complete the terms of her contract at Inspiration and couldn't complete the terms of her contract at Metro-Goldwyn-Mayer that she had to get out. Had she stayed, more than likely her contract wouldn't have been renewed. What would she have gained for that one remaining picture? No more work.

It was better to sacrifice the salary. That way she saved face. It enabled her to return to the theatre where she first began.

She had drama critic George Jean Nathan helping her. He took her around to people she would never have met. And it was done socially.

She was smart that way, too. Meeting someone at a party is better than shaking hands with someone on an opening night. You're at the theatre to

Lillian in a countryside portrait.

see the play. George was there to review it.

Lillian never did anything that didn't help Lillian. She was a single woman. She knew if she didn't look out for herself, nobody else would.

When Theda Bara and Mabel Normand tried to rescue their faded careers by going into the theatre, never having had any real theatre experi-

ence, the results for both were disastrous.

Lillian was a success in *Uncle Vanya*, and that upset a lot of people in Hollywood, particularly the columnist Hedda Hopper, who was a failed actress before she turned to journalism, if you want to call it that. When Lillian very courageously turned her back on Hollywood and returned to

New York theatre, Hedda wrote that Lillian had gone high-hat.

When Lillian returned to picture-making, it wasn't done in Hedda's territory. It was done in Astoria on the East Coast. I know she was taking care of her mother, but she was also not making herself available to her detractors.

His Double Life was directed by theatre people: Arthur Hopkins and my father! To Hollywood and people like Hedda Hopper, the theatre world and theatre people were very intimidating. My father, unlike his brother, my Uncle Cecil [Cecil B. DeMille], was a theatre man.

His Double Life was a very funny, literate, sophisticated comedy. It was a film theatregoers in New York and Chicago would and did enjoy. It wasn't "opened up" to include many visuals, the way films sometimes did when they were adapted from stage plays. Both of the characters in *His Double Life* were fully developed.

His Double Life was a moderate success, and I say that with great love for my father and respect for Arthur Hopkins' integrity. I think Hopkins, my father, and Lillian would have been a good team, if there were other opportunities. But they never came.

Arthur Hopkins went back to New York stage work, and Lillian didn't want to wait around for the verdict on her. Maybe out of kindness or nostalgia, they might have let her make programmers or second features, which were the bottom half of the program. Rather than do that, Lillian went back to the stage. Somehow she always managed to stay ahead, however precariously.

The theatre was always talent. Hollywood, if you wanted to survive, was always games, favorites, and politics. Lillian had been in the business too long, and there was no need for her to learn the new games.[26]

Lillian's 1933 ended with a whimper. It would be ten years before she would return to motion pictures.

It was not the best of times for anyone. America was in the throes of the Depression. Europe was gearing itself for a war.

Lillian was looking for work and wondering how she would get through the coming year. Mr. Griffith had once told her the reason she had fared so well in his films was due to the parts she played. They were "conspicuous in their importance," and they required "no additional build-up" other than her presence.[27]

Lillian made her New Year's resolution. Being there was not enough. She promised herself to be conspicuous.

Chapter 24

Back on the Boards

All you need for a theatre is four planks, four trestles, two actors, and a passion.

— Lope de Vega, playwright
(1562–1635)

1934: The consequences of the Depression continued to bear down on the American economy. Nobody escaped untouched. A loaf of bread was viewed as a precious treasure.[1] Movie theatres, hoping to bolster their declining mid-week attendance, were offering free dinnerware to the ladies, and holding "bank-nites," awarding prizes to lucky ticket stub holders. On Broadway, legitimate theatres lowered their admission prices. Escapism and social realism, in accordance with the times, had found their way on Broadway with productions as varied as Cole Porter's musical mayhem at sea in *Anything Goes* and Elmer Rice's *Judgment Day*, an ideological drama which dealt with the ever-increasing Nazi menace and the Reichstag building fire trial. Both drew audiences, although, understandably, Cole Porter's was much larger.

The new year began quietly for Lillian, with relatively little to disturb her beyond her constant concern for her mother's health and welfare. The sight of Lillian pushing her mother in a wheelchair on sunny days no longer drew glances from pedestrians long familiar with their walks on Fifth Avenue early in the day. The Gishes were long established New York residents enjoying the neighborhood. Grocers and newspaper vendors treated them with respectful familiarity. Unlike Greta Garbo, who lived a few streets away, the Gishes were very approachable.

George had proposed again, and again Lillian would not consent to surrendering her Gish identity and become a Mrs. Male. Work had again taken precedence. Being someone's wife, no matter who that man was or how distinguished or important that man was, meant being a second fiddle. Lillian, having worked all of her life, was not about to enter into any competition with a man who would want to exercise control over everything she did. Her mother had allowed her husband to exercise control until he walked out while she was at work and cavalierly abandoned two little girls. Lillian saw no merit in committing herself to somebody who, this long in the relationship, was still evasive about his familiar past.

While taking the rest cure the previous summer at Baden-Baden, Germany,[2]

Lillian had learned that Charles H. Duell had become engaged to Josephine Smith of Charleston, South Carolina. Miss Smith's family was one of historical distinction. Her great-great-grandfathers, Edward Rutledge and Arthur Middleton, were two of the signers of the Declaration of Independence.[3] Lillian must have laughed at Duell's quest for impressive family genealogies, having President Zachary Taylor as part of her ancestry. The disbarred Mr. Duell and his fiancée were married in October.[4] Duell was now vice-president of a New York publishing house. Perhaps Duell's marriage and employment would put an end to his nuisance suits.

Dorothy's last appearances on Broadway were in the 22-performance run of *Foreign Affairs* (playing an Austrian countess escaping from her husband with her lover for a week's vacation)[5] and as replacement for the female lead (playing a 35 year old spinster) in *Autumn Crocus*, which enabled the play to last for 210 performances[6] and provided enough funds to help Lillian maintain a resident nurse for Mrs. Gish's round-the-clock care when her daughters were away.

Both Lillian and Dorothy, newspapers announced, were returning to Broadway. Dorothy would be starring in *By Your Leave*, a domestic comedy about a middle-aged couple agreeing to take a two week hiatus from each other to wander without later questions or recriminations.[7] Lillian's Broadway return was as Sister Christina, visiting her family's Beacon Street Boston home during a spiritual crisis, in Phillip Barry's *The Joyous Season*.[8] Playwright Barry had fashioned the part originally for Maude Adams, who turned it down.[9] Dorothy and Lillian's last return to Broadway, observers noted, had occurred in 1930, when they were appearing in *The Inspector General* and *Uncle Vanya*.

Long in Eugene O'Neill's shadow because of their Irish origins, Barry, unlike O'Neill (who used Irish characters to dramatize powerful themes), preferred poignancy and whimsy to make his points.[10] Barry wrote about the rich and the wealthy via amusing dialogue delivered by glamorous performers in luxurious surroundings. Often dialogue was glib, but it was honest and sometimes piercing.

"When the Irish arrive, they turn British."[11]

In *The Joyous Season*, Barry was finally turning to Irish material, whose strength of characterization depended on an acknowledging of one's Irish roots. Phillip Barry was once more in O'Neill territory, but on a wealthier plane. This was no "Long Day's Journey into Night."

Lillian was playing Christina, a daughter who had become a nun many years ago, and who was returning to her Beacon Hill Boston home for a short visit at Christmas, the joyous season. She has the option of choosing the family home or an old farm to be designated a boarding school, in accordance with her father's will. At the play's conclusion, the decision-making is left to the family, but for the duration of her visit she had restructured their lives.[12]

The Joyous Season reunited Lillian with Arthur Hopkins, with whom she had forged a good working relationship on the movie set of *His Double Life* the previous year.

Neither Gish effort, *By Your Leave* nor *The Joyous Season*, was successful. *By Your Leave*, opening at the Morosco Theatre on January 24 to almost uniformly negative reviews, closed after 37 performances.[13] *The Joyous Season*, opening at the Belasco Theatre on January 29, confounded and confused the audiences. Was this new Barry play a religious one? Or was he once again cloaking potentially dramatic issues of family loyalty and responsibility under a veil of Irish whimsy?

To Brooks Atkinson, drama critic for *The New York Times*, the religious issue of

Sister Christina's character seemed to place a hindrance on Barry's imagination. Perhaps *The Joyous Season* was better suited to a Boston audience more familiar with the milieu of the Boston Irish.

Still, there was much to praise in Lillian's performance:

> As Christina Miss Gish is superb. Apart from the aura of her presence which illuminates the sort of part she is playing, she has created a character with the imagery of her gestures and the inflections of her passionless voice.[14]

Phillip Barry's *The Joyous Season* was not the great religious play Mr. Barry was capable of writing. Nor was it "flooded with imagination."[15] It closed after 16 performances.[16]

Phillip Harry's religious conscience[17] was often at odds with the Phillip Barry who could write what John O'Hara called "New Yorky"[18] dialogue in his comedies about the "foibles and inadequacies of the rich."[19] Barry was still five years away from establishing Katherine Hepburn in *The Philadelphia Story*.

Dorothy would often tell people that treating Lillian as if she were a defenseless woman was the biggest mistake one could make. It was like the vaudeville comedian's trick of kicking the hat under which a brick was hidden.[20] Lillian possessed great stamina. What other explanation could be offered for her ability to live through all of the hazardous circumstances she endured while she worked for D.W. Griffith?

Under George Jean Nathan's continuing guidance, she was exposed to the best of current literature and drama. At this time she was introduced to the plays of Sean O'Casey, with whom she wasn't very familiar. Next to Eugene O'Neill, Nathan considered O'Casey one of the great playwrights of the twentieth century. Nathan had been in part responsible for the 1926 New York production of O'Casey's *Juno and the Paycock*. In the following year, 1927, the play was revived in New York by the Irish Players, imported at Nathan's suggestion. The troupe also presented O'Casey's *The Plough and the Stars*.[21]

Lillian discussed the Nathan–O'Casey relationship:

> George [George Jean Nathan] was very similar to O'Casey in that they both respected the written and the spoken word. There was music in words, and music in the way some actors could speak them if they were well-written.
> He called Sean O'Casey "Irish Irish." He felt O'Casey was the real thing compared to Gene O'Neill, who was an American of Irish descent.
> O'Casey's plays came out of Ireland with Irish actors who emotionally invested more of themselves in their roles. They knew the city streets O'Casey was writing about. An O'Casey evening wasn't drawing room Noel Coward.
> George and Sean O'Casey were great letter-writers, who constantly kept in touch even before they met, and afterwards throughout their lives. George was constantly giving O'Casey encouragement, as very few purely Irish plays had long runs here. British plays were here all the time. It was a much politer theatre.
> The Irish plays, particularly O'Casey's, were closer to the soil.[22]

Sean O'Casey's writing was a blend of "downright humor and unrestrained horror." O'Casey, not a devotee of "contrived theatricality's" or the formal techniques of dramaturgy, believed in scenes from the streets and their ability to be shown on the stage via good observation.[23] *Within the Gates*, set in London's Hyde Park, was a combination of realism and abstraction.[24]

Lillian played the role of a nameless character described as "Young Whore." It would cause problems in the minds of some New York theatregoers when they read the names of the characters in their Play bill. *Within the Gates* did not come to New York without its pre–opening night gossip and raised eyebrows.[25]

The original London production had lasted one week. The British reviews called *Within the Gates* "anti-moral and anti–Christian, with cheap irony for making the Bishop and father of the woman" (Lillian's character).[26] *Within the Gates* was dismissed as "pretentious rubbish," and "O'-Casey's charade."[27]

In its defense, *Within the Gates* was also called a very Christian play, as it attacked celibacy in the ministry, which did not exist for the first three centuries. What O'Casey was doing was "attacking a church that was unable to relate to natural, sexual energies."[28]

Within the Gates marked a radical departure from the realism of O'Casey's *The Plough and the Stars*, which concerned itself with the uprising during Easter Week 1916 and its effect on the residents living in the tenements of Dublin. *Within the Gates* centered on people from the city streets, but the setting of the play was the Hyde Park section of London. The characters served as a representation, a microcosm of society: a Dreamer representing the idealists, a Bishop who is confused by some of the church's teachings, and a Young Whore who pleads for the more vulnerable.

By themselves and in groups they gravitate to the park to express themselves. There are debates and discussions about the existence or non-existence of God, and a yearning for fulfillment in religion. It all comes to an end when the Young Whore dies in her father's (the Bishop's) arms.[29]

O'Casey, who came to New York for the rehearsals and stayed at the Royalton Hotel (where George Jean Nathan lived in two dingy, book-cluttered, rarely cleaned rooms),[30] often sought shelter from questions about the play in Lillian Gish's dressing room. Often he would answer that he didn't know what to say. He had no answer about the "plot" of the "story" of the play. The play *Within the Gates*, he would say, "simply is."[31]

While Lillian and O'Casey acknowledged that the play would not have been produced in New York if not for the efforts of George Jean Nathan, Lillian would also add that George was not the reason she was cast in the play. She had landed the part herself.

Within the Gates opened at New York's National Theatre on October 22, 1934. It was received with respect by a divided press,[32] but a press that was generally kinder and more tolerant than the original London reviewers.[33]

Brooks Atkinson of *The New York Times*, perhaps in anticipation of a public who might attack the play on grounds without ever having seen it, opened his review by announcing his intention in the first sentence: "Let us face this thing boldly. Sean O'Casey has written a great play."

No mention was made of the play's problems since its inception, or the controversy and discussions that had taken place in London prior to the New York production starring Lillian.

> *Within the Gates* ... [is] a testament to Mr. O'Caseys abiding faith in life. Nothing so grand has risen in our impoverished theatre since this reporter first began writing of plays....
> This is a great play. There is iron in its bones and blood in its veins and lustre in its flesh, and its feet rest on the good brown earth. In fact it is a humbling job to write about a dynamic drama like *Within the Gates*.

Lillian came in for special praise:

As the tortured young woman, Lillian Gish give the performance instinct with the spirit of the drama. Never did an actress play a part with more sincerity or deeper comprehension.[34]

It was a dream review for the actress Lillian Gish and the playwright Sean O'Casey. Yet the prospects of a successful touring production were bleak. Early reactions centering on the handling of the relationship between the Bishop and the Young Whore, and the alleged anti–Catholic bias, made the likelihood of audience acceptance in less cosmopolitan cities very remote. That the play was banned in Boston was a fait accompli, and perhaps a portent of things to come.

Recalled Lillian about the Boston mayor's action:

> Theatre people used to say when a play was banned in Boston before it came to New York it meant that producers had a possible hit on their hands because the newspapers would give it free publicity, and some non-theatregoers might want to see it out of curiosity.
> To ban a play in Boston after it had been in New York for over 100 performances sometimes had an adverse effect. Plays on the road sometimes could recoup the losses in New York. In the case of *Within the Gates*, it might not attract a Boston audience willing to go into the suburbs. We didn't want to lose money.
> *Strange Interlude* was banned, but it found an audience because of its notoriety. It was different. It was a novelty because of the dinner hour intermission.
> *Within the Gates* had a conventional length, but it had other problems because of the portrayal of the Bishop. If any member of the clergy were depicted as anything but sacrosanct and inviolable, there were grounds for demonstrations and protests.

The Bishop in *Within the Gates* fathered an illegitimate child.

American literature certainly wasn't without its book-banning and even book-burning in some areas the United States. Hawthorne's [*The*] *Scarlet Letter* had it problems. Harold Frederic's *The Damnation of Theron Ware* [1896] was considered immoral. Sinclair Lewis' *Elmer Gantry* was denounced from the pulpits.

Those ministers and preachers were Protestant! The Bishop in O'Casey's *Within the Gates* was an Irish Catholic!

Boston had a significant Irish Catholic population and *Within the Gates* was a very Catholic play.

Attacking or questioning or challenging the legitimacy or validity of the policies within the Catholic Church wasn't permitted or even tolerated. The Church was infallible.

That O'Casey would even hint or suggest that anything in the Church was immoral was out of the question. Did O'Casey think this kind of questioning would be tolerated in the United States?

Had anybody in Boston known Sean O'Casey wasn't a Catholic, but and Irish Protestant and a Communist...?[35]

The playwright's wife, Eileen O'-Casey, believed the play might have been accepted in Boston if the Mayor had seen the Bishop the was Sean O'Casey had created him: a symbol, and part of the fantasy of the play.[36]

Within the Gates, after a Philadelphia engagement, returned to New York for an additional 40 performances, making a total run 141 performances.[37] Its success was more artistic than commercial.[38]

On November 13, Dorothy opened at New York's Vanderbilt Theatre in Vincent York's and Frederic Pohl's Brittle Heaven, playing poetess Emily Dickinson tragically in love with Major Edward Hunt, the husband of her best girlfriend. Her wish to follow him into the Civil War is crushed when she receives news that he has been killed.

Although critics warmed to Dorothy's interpretation of Emily, the reviews weren't strong enough to keep it running beyond 23 performances.[39]

On March 25, 1935, Dorothy, in Bridgeport, Connecticut Superior Court, filed for divorce from James Rennie.[40] Although Lillian would claim Dorothy and Jim were still on friendly terms,[41] there was no reason for either of them to remain legally tied to each other if they were still living apart: Dorothy in Connecticut, James in New York. The marriage was over. Ultimately it hadn't worked. His drinking was considered intolerable cruelty, for which she suffered a nervous breakdown. She wasn't seeking a divorce in order to remarry. She wanted no alimony. She wanted to resume being Dorothy Gish.[42]

Lillian, witnessing the event, was no stranger to heartbreak. First, there was her mother's. Now there was Dorothy's. Once again it made her wonder if she should accept George's latest marriage proposal. She was free, and there weren't any indications of work in the offing. What kind of excuse could she give now?

Dorothy wanted to take an ocean voyage to get away from the publicity. Lillian thought about it.

Maybe it was time for the two of them to make a disappearance!

CHAPTER 25

The Road to Elsinore

Not since 1917 and the filming of D.W. Griffith's *Hearts of the World*, which required the utilization's of black sails as a protective measure against sudden German torpedoing during a hazardous ocean crossing, had Lillian taken such precautions not to call attention to herself. In New York, her apartment had become her world, which was being subjected to George Jean Nathan's constant phoning and questioning about other men. Even Lillian's mother was being demanding, asking that the radio should be shut off. There was entirely too much talking being broadcast. In the evenings, when Lillian wanted to listen to a concert, her mother complained there was too much noise.[1]

Dorothy's reports were now starting to make sense. She wasn't lying when she called her mother unbearable. Something had to be done. Both Dorothy and Lillian had to get away.

On Dorothy's spur of the moment suggestion, she and Lillian sailed from New York in early April 1935, not on the usual or even first available luxury liner, but on a cargo ship used to transport furniture, automobiles, and foodstuffs. In addition to the spartan cabins for the captain and the crew, there were cabins available for up to 12 passengers who were willing to forgo the customary amenities and carry their own bags, maintain the cleanliness of their own quarters, and dine on the same food as the captain and crew in sometimes less than first-class surroundings.

In later years both Dorothy and Lillian were regulars on tramp steamers, which did not have a regular route or schedule and traveled on the ocean like a taxi-cab, picking up whatever freight came their way.

For Dorothy, who always saw "dressing up" as work, not to have to look constantly elegant was something she greatly treasured.

Lillian, who always opted for anonymity when not appearing on stage or film and later television, found herself succumbing to Dorothy's penchant for wanderlust.

> We were always afraid of the consequences if anyone would say, "I saw the Gish sisters, and they weren't dressed!" Even doing simple morning marketing in our own neighborhood required dressing up, as if we were en route to a fancy restaurant.
>
> Did people actually think we lived like the society type actors played in the movies? We're actresses, not mannequins! Not everyone dresses unless you are entertaining.
>
> I didn't entertain very much...
>
> Being on a cargo ship or a tramp steamer was like being on the road in our touring days. Except we were on

the ocean, and we didn't have to arrive at the theatre by half-hour.

We were part of the baggage, and we went with the tide. It's a great luxury to be able to wander aimlessly.

What a thrill to be able to lose yourself and just look at the constant blue water, and not have to worry about time or responsibility.[2]

It was the first time Dorothy returned to England in five years, the last occasion taking place in 1930 when she and stage actor Charles Laughton filmed *Wolves*, a partial-talkie for director Herbert Wilcox, who had used her so effectively in the 1926 silent *Nell Gwyn*. Lillian claimed Dorothy was so frustrated with her performance in *Wolves*—because of the changes from silence to sound during the filming—that she never saw the completed released version in England or America.

Film critic and historian William K. Everson explained:

> Depending on whose account you read, *Wolves* was either the last of the British silents or the first British "talkie."
>
> Actually, *Wolves* was a combination of both, which in 1930 was quite unfortunate. The British film industry was undergoing the same kind of transitional problem Hollywood had undergone a few years earlier with *The Jazz Singer* [1927].
>
> But *The Jazz Singer* was a musical, and the dialogue, even the few words ad-libbed by Al Jolson, was minimal. *Wolves* needed words.
>
> Operating in England at the same time was a director named Alfred Hitchcock, who was rushing to complete a thriller entitled *Blackmail*. Hitchcock, like D.W. Griffith, was becoming a household word since his recent critical and popular success, *The Lodger*.
>
> I think, because of the material, that circumstances were not as favorable to *Wolves* as they had been to *Blackmail*.

> Hitchcock, whether in a silent or a sound film, knew how to use silence and sound to create tension and atmosphere. As limiting as the emergence of sound could be, Hitchcock knew how to make the best use of both. Silence in a sound film could always create tension. In thrillers, silence works brilliantly if used at the right time.
>
> It's a pity *Wolves* didn't fare better, because both Dorothy Gish and Charles Laughton had an interesting on-screen chemistry between them. Dorothy was a fine dramatic actress.
>
> When *Wolves* was released in the United States a few years later with a new title [*Wanted Men*, 1934] because of Laughton's popularity in American films, so much technical progress had been made in Hollywood that many thought the film looked primitive. What was originally a vehicle for Dorothy was now ironically a showcase for Laughton. Dorothy's work was by-passed. She didn't return to motion pictures for 14 years! Just like Lillian, she was thrown aside by the medium she helped create. Sad...[3]

While Dorothy remained in England, Lillian journeyed ahead for a short vacation and rest cure at the spa in Baden-Baden, Germany. With the rise of Nazi aggression, it was rumored that Dr. Niehans, under whose guidance the spa operated, was the illegitimate son of Kaiser Wilhelm.[4] Still, Lillian was willing to continue to controversial treatment of receiving injections of lambs' embryos and sleeping each night with a bandage saturated with water around her waist.[5]

That a noted film and stage star was on the continent was soon the topic of gossip, although no mention was ever made of Lillian's name, or any specific locale, or whether she was traveling alone or with anyone.

The underground news reached Lillian Gish's friend, actress Helen Hayes, vacationing on the island of Mykonos near Greece, with amusing results:

> Charlie [husband and playwright Charles MacArthur] and I wanted to get away for a few weeks before I went into rehearsals for *Victoria Regina*.
>
> When we checked into the hotel, the owner told us how happy she was to meet the star of *Broken Blossoms*, because she lived that film. When she saw it, she was pregnant, and she hoped that the baby would look just like me. She gave birth to a daughter she felt was just like the way I am.
>
> Needless to say, Charlie and I did our best to avoid her. I didn't know how to tell her I wasn't Lillian Gish![6]

Although most European motion picture houses had converted to sound systems by the mid-thirties, there were still silent films being exhibited in more remote areas unable to afford such expensive renovations. With such a vast amount of silent films readily available, it seemed foolish to import films in different spoken languages. Music, in silent films, was the universal language.

John Tzortzakis, director of the Municipal Band and Orchestra for the city of Iraklion, Crete, remembered:

> My father conducted an eight piece theatre orchestra in the silent film days. We weren't what Europeans or Americans would call "symphonic," but in our theatre we had very full sound that went well with those pictures.
>
> You would never know that we were in the nineteen thirties, if you went to that theatre. Lillian Gish and Charlie Chaplin films were still popular. A lot of the audience had seen them when they were originally released, and now they were taking their children to see those same pictures: *Way Down East* and *The Gold Rush*.
>
> People on Crete are very emotional. They react to everything they see on the screen. Often things that in America may cause no comment can be a source of discussion over here.
>
> With someone like Lillian Gish or Charlie Chaplin you only had to look at the faces.[7]

To look at the faces of Lillian and Dorothy outside a hut on the Albanian frontier was all that a barefoot, stoutish woman, the head of the household in a black dress held in place by a thick rope, had to do. Even in that mountainous wasteland the impact of silent films lingered, even though there were no movie theatres for miles.

Years earlier a Catholic priest, in an effort to exhibit a testament of faith to his parish, had somehow managed to secure a print of Lillian's *The White Sister* and project it on an interior wall of his humble church. The film and a projector were miraculously delivered to the poor village on an ox.

The Albanian woman, years later, recognized Lillian on the road and wept tears of joy. The motion picture had made the world a little smaller, and one of the world's international stars had stepped out of the screen and was standing next to a very grateful viewer.[8]

At the end of the summer, both Lillian and Dorothy returned to New York. Lillian then headed for California for a visit with Mary Pickford, hoping she could use her influence to secure work for her at Paramount.[9] Dorothy remained in New York. Mrs. Gish needed to be assured that one of her daughters was present, and Dorothy needed to prepare for her September 27 divorce hearing in Connecticut.[10]

Lillian's visit was short-lived, and she returned to New York, stated a publicity release, to begin preparing for a play to be directed by George Abbott.[11]

There were no further releases concerning the production with Mr. Abbott.

When he and Lillian did work together in the theatre, it was thirty years later in the musical *Anya* in 1965.

On October 12 Dorothy obtained her divorce from actor James Rennie on the grounds of intolerable cruelty exacerbated by his drinking, which caused her to suffer hysteria and exhaustion. Judge Ernest A. Inglish also granted Dorothy permission to use her maiden name in future employment.[12]

Dorothy Gish returned to Broadway in the winter of the following year. *Mainly for Lovers*, an English import, opened on February 22, 1936, at the Forty-eighth Street Theatre. Drama critic Brooks Atkinson, covering the production for *The New York Times*, noted that the customary tradition of the 8:40 curtain was delayed for ten minutes, as the theatre was half empty.

When the curtain rose and the theatre was almost filled, his review indicated why so many had stayed away. *Mainly for Lovers* was a "teapot tale" of a married couple unable to get along, and another married couple with the same problem. There was "chit-chat over sherry" in the second act, and more of the same over bacon and kidneys in the third.

Mainly for Lovers showcased the talents of Leo G. Carroll, but Dorothy's work in a supporting role did not go unnoticed by Mr. Atkinson, who spent the previous afternoon watching her on the screen in the 1915 feature *Old Heidelberg* opposite Wallace Reid:

> She [Dorothy Gish] has more spirit now, which is becoming to an actress of her intelligence....

In *Mainly for Lovers*:

> She gives an animated and shrewd performance as the astringent wife of a singing Egyptologist.[13]

The play, Mr. Atkinson concluded, was "mainly for torpid minds," and closed after eight performances.[14]

If Lillian showed any signs of distress over Dorothy's last theatrical venture, they were minimal. Her mind was considering a proposal made by Guthrie McClintic to tour in a production of *The Old Maid*, Zoe Akins' Pulitzer prizewinning adaptation of the Edith Wharton novella that was enjoying a successful run starring Judith Anderson and Helen Mencken.[15]

Lillian was familiar with McClintic's work in connection with his wife Katherine Cornell, a disciplined actress whose career in the 1920s consisted of playing the sullen sophisticate in plays far beneath her ability. In the subsequent decade, a more mature Cornell emerged, and she was playing in *The Barretts of Wimpole Street* and George Bernard Shaw's *Candida*, surrounded by excellent supporting casts under Guthrie McClintic's aegis.[16]

The Old Maid production McClintic had in mind for Lillian would not be touring the United States. Lillian would be the sole American actress in an English troupe touring the provinces prior to a London opening.

On the advice of actress-friend Lynn Fontanne, she accepted. Miss Fontanne, wife of actor Alfred Lunt, had toured the provinces for years before she had emigrated to the United States. Touring the provinces was a respected theatrical tradition in England. It was an opportunity for the new, aspiring actor to learn his craft and play the classics, as well as the last stronghold of the older professional to receive assurance that his audiences haven't forgotten him. Even if success never came, an actor willing to tour could sustain a career in the provinces.[17]

The Old Maid cast Lillian as Charlotte Lovell, who promised to marry her sister's rejected beau upon his return from his military obligations in the Civil War. What Charlotte didn't anticipate was the death of her suitor and, at the same time, discovering she was pregnant with his child. Lillian's part was later portrayed on the screen by Bette Davis.

The opportunity for Lillian to play a "psychically deprived unmarried mother"[18] was the chance to show a dramatic flair she hoped would allow producers to give her meatier parts in the future. She may not have been the type to Charleston on the tabletop like Joan Crawford in the '20s, but in the '30s she was certainly more than eligible to play an older embittered society woman.

While Lillian was pleased with the company of British players that Hugh (Binkie) Beaumont assembled, she was unable to satisfy the woman director who constantly berated her dialogue delivery and the way she moved onstage. At first she listened to the director's criticism, believing it was the way things were done. After all, she had never worked in British theatre, and she was the outsider, the only American. Maybe, in an effort to take her down a few pegs, this would make her a company member, not a star soloist.[19]

Singer Linda Lee, featured in *Knights of Madness*, a British revue of the 1950s that starred The Crazy Gang (a revue troupe whose stage and screen antics began in the '30s), offered a possible explanation of Lillian's feelings of insecurity at the time of *The Old Maid*:

Lillian Gish was a film actress of another generation. To my father and to the people of his day, she was the girl on the ice floe in *Way Down East*. *Way Down East* was in 1920, and the memory still lingered.

In 1936 Lillian Gish, like many Brits, was out of work. The Depression was on, and she was unemployed. But Lillian Gish wasn't an ordinary person who was out of work. You wouldn't ever see her standing in line for bread.

She could look for work. Anyplace in the world. Even in England.

Producer Charles Cochran, who was called "the British Ziegfeld," knew that with a straight American play he needed an American star, a major American star whose name always got a smile and could bring in the audiences.

Movies cost pennies, and people always went to the movies. Good times or bad times. But theatre in England was always a special occasion. That was why you paid a little more money.

Lillian Gish came over here to get work. She was probably taking a cut in her salary demands, but she was still earning more than the other members of the company. There were theatre people who had spent all of their lives working, and Lillian, the film actress from America, was probably the reason they had this tour. She was the reason they were working.

We never heard anyone ever say a bad word about Lillian, and I'm sure she earned the respect of her fellow players.

Her sister Dorothy had worked here in films, and Lillian had filmed parts of *Hearts of the World* here with a very young Noel Coward.

British people, no matter what their financial situation, always flocked to "live" theatre.

The theatre is the real test of the artist. Eight shows a week.

I think the problem Lillian might have had with this female German director was due to a resentment of Lillian's name and prestige as a drawing card. What this director didn't know was that Lillian had begun her career in the theatre, went into movies in their infancy, made a few sound films, and then returned to the theatre.

Lillian Gish was always a great pro. If she could survive all of those years, it was a testament to her resiliency. Griffith or no, she wouldn't get on the ice if she couldn't swim.

"Malcolm, my West Highland white terrier, was a gift from Sir Ian Malcolm. He stayed with me (the terrier) for 16 years. I was *his* pet!"

> The quiet types are the ones who surprise you. They have hidden strength.[20]

Apparently Lillian's harsh treatment was noticed by the members of the company. They sent a telegram to Binkie Beaumont in London, who went up to Glasgow immediately,[21] where the troupe had begun to perform the play in the traditional pre–London circuit of Glasgow, Manchester, Liverpool, and Birmingham.[22]

Guthrie McClintic, arriving from New York, saw some of the performances. Not satisfied with the costumes designed by Gladys Calthrop, the sets, and some members of the supporting cast, he pulled the play at the end of the run and did not allow it to open in London.[23]

Perhaps Lillian was upset by a tiny article she had noticed in an imported edition of *The New York Times* of March 3, the day after *The Old Maid* had premiered at the King's Theatre in Glasgow.[24] It read: "D.W. Griffith Wed."

A 56-year-old Griffith, divorced from Linda Arvidson (from whom he had been separated in 1915), married 26-year-old Marjorie Baldwin in Louisville, Kentucky. After being separated from Linda Arvidson for a five year period, there were no legal barriers to obtaining the divorce.[25]

Aware of this, why didn't Griffith file for divorce in 1920, the year after Carol Dempster entered his life (and appeared in a minor role in Lillian's feature, *True Heart Susie*)?

Did Carol turn out to be like Lillian, another willing innocent, too?

The British experience wasn't a total loss. Guthrie McClintic, who had suggested Lillian's name, had had the opportunity to observe her stage work. He would remember her.

When Lillian sailed home at the conclusion of the tour, she had another passenger with her, one that was to remain at her side for the next 16 years: a 5-month-old West Highland white terrier, a gift from Sir Ian Malcolm, the British representative in the Suez Canal.

Malcolm, the name Lillian had given to the white terrier, traveled with her everywhere, recalled actress Frances Tannehill:

> Malcolm was a perfect darling, and perfect for Lillian.
> She was appearing in stock, summer stock, in the 50s, in a trifle of a play called *Miss Mabel*.
> There was a booking in the Bahamas. Lillian was going by plane. Don't you think Malcolm had the adjacent seat? And without occupying his little cage? I don't know how she convinced the airlines to allow it. But then again, she had two seats. Maybe the little dog charmed them. Certainly Lillian knew how to charm.[26]

Less than six months after her return from the unsuccessful tour of the provinces, Guthrie McClintic asked Lillian to read for Ophelia in an upcoming production of William Shakespeare's *Hamlet*, starring John Gielgud, who would be making his first trip to New York since appearing in a minor role in *The Patriot* in 1928.[27]

In light of Sir John Gielgud's acquired near-mythic status as one of the foremost interpreters of Shakespeare, it is hard to conceive of the courage it took director Guthrie McClintic to ask him to come to New York to play Hamlet. Perhaps the fear

that another production of the play starring Leslie Howard planned to open around the same date served as a reasonable motivator.

Howard, who was also a British import, made his Broadway debut in the 1920 production of *Just Suppose*.[28] Howard, unlike Gielgud, remained and had become a Broadway mainstay, triumphing in Robert E. Sherwood's *The Petrified Forest* (and repeating the role in the film version with Humphrey Bogart). Howard also had established himself as a film star of presence opposite Bette Davis in the film adaptation of W. Somerset Maugham's *Of Human Bondage*. That Howard had long cherished an ambition to play Hamlet, the Prince of Denmark, was no secret in the theatrical community.[29] What was most unfortunate for both actors were the inevitable comparisons that would crop up, and the attempts from the press to create a rivalry for public and critical favor.

John Gielgud, whether portraying Somerset Maugham's spy-chasing Ashended in Alfred Hitchcock's film, *The Secret Agent*,[30] or the elegant but frosty Jack Worthing in Oscar Wilde's *The Importance of Being Earnest*,[31] was regarded within the acting community as the consummate actor, capable of acting in any style or period. Prior to his arrival in New York on the *Normandie* on September 1, he had just completed a 185-performance run of *Hamlet* in London. It marked the second time he had played the Prince of Denmark. He had even directed the production in which he starred.[32]

The 32-year-old actor was fully aware that he was under a lot of pressure, and at a September 6 press conference he spoke frankly and honestly about the upcoming engagement in New York, sharing his feelings about the character he was going to play. Gielgud's opening remark was not an apology or plea, but it faced the problem:

On the stage as Ophelia in *Hamlet* (1936, directed by Guthrie McClintic). The New York box-office record was set with 122 performances.

To represent the English theatre is a terrible ordeal.

I was never mad about the character. You have to pick out of the character that which corresponds with something in yourself, a sort of selectivity of emotion, and then convey that to the audience. Because you can't fool them with *Hamlet*.

I have always found it difficult to be my real self in normal life, but let me put on a costume and walk out upon a stage...[33]

Guthrie McClintic, the director of John Gielgud's upcoming *Hamlet* production, telephoned Lillian Gish after he read the interview.

Lillian remembered:

Mr. McClintic and I discussed the press conference, and suddenly he made this confessional statement: "You know, Lillian, John Gielgud has done the part twice and directed one of the productions. I've never directed a Shakespeare play in my life!"

I laughed and answered, "Don't worry! I've never acted in a Shakespeare play in my life!" [34]

McClintic sent word calling for a 9:00 rehearsal. It was an hour earlier than Mr. Gielgud's reporting time.

Lillian remembered:

Naturally, some of us were there before 9:00. We were quite self-conscious of our own insecurities and limitations. Mr. McClintic told some of us he knew well, that he was at a loss how to direct someone of John Gielgud's stature, and how Mr. Gielgud would respond to being directed in a play he had already done twice. Would he take suggestions, or would he become the director?

We were making small talk and trying to look relaxed.

John Gielgud arrived on the precise hour, impeccably dressed. Everyone waited to see if he would be announced, or would he take the initiative and announce himself.

There wasn't much time for us to think too long about it. John Gielgud announced himself. "Good morning, everyone!"

And while we responded with something resembling a greeting, Mr. McClintic announced very theatrically, "Mr. Hamlet has arrived! I'd like to introduce him to everyone he eventually will be seeing at the castle. You know a lot has happened around here since he's been away at school!"

John nodded in my direction, and Mr. McClintic commented, "I see you already know Miss Ophelia..."[35]

William Roehrick, best known as Henry Chamberlain in the long-running television soap opera *Guiding Light*, was playing the part of Guildenstern in the McClintic production of *Hamlet*. Inside the entrance of New York's St. Bartholomew's Episcopal Church, where Lillian Gish regularly worshipped, he shared his memories of the *Hamlet* production after the conclusion of Miss Gish's Service of Celebration on March 11, 1933:

The director in this, Guthrie McClintic, not the actor who has the lead, has to set the tone of the rehearsal process on the very first day. Everyone knew that John Gielgud had done the play twice, and had directed a production, but Mr. McClintic was in full charge.

John Gielgud approached the role as if he were playing it for the first time. Of course, he knew his lines ahead of us, but conducted himself like the great gentleman he is, allowing the director to make the suggestions and give the necessary criticism.

John Gielgud was well aware that this was his first time in New York in almost a decade. We had New York credits, and no matter what would happen, we would survive and get work in New York again.

But what would happen to John Gielgud, a British actor, if his much heralded performance failed to impress the critics, who were familiar with John Barrymore's *Hamlet*, or preferred the rival *Hamlet* of Leslie Howard?

For us, every moment John Gielgud made, every word spoken, was a lesson in acting from the Master. He was the visiting soloist who had played the piece before, and we were the members of the accompanying orchestra. We constantly watched him, and he knew it. There was never any question of us going up on our lines. We didn't want to embarrass ourselves in front of him.

John Gielgud would constantly experiment with the sound of the words, and try difference interpretations of a line, and then look at Mr. McClintic and ask if each new reading was an improvement.

We were curious about the stage presence of Lillian Gish, whose films were all part of our childhoods. We knew it was her first time acting in Shakespeare, and she was quite aware of it, and in awe of the material. We were in awe of her.

When Lillian practiced her scenes with John, everyone sat and watched. There was no applause, because we weren't an audience for them, and I don't think either one would have wanted us to be. We were all in this together, and they were getting accustomed to each other's timing and adjusting their different acting styles.

I guess you could say we were fans of Lillian Gish and John Gielgud, but that was for offstage. The minute we reported for rehearsals, we were fellow actors. We were members of an ensemble who had to work well with each other. There wasn't any time for egos.

On some days we rehearsed on the roof in hot weather. I don't know who suggested it, Mr. McClintic or John Gielgud, but rehearsing outside in all kinds of weather improved our pro-jection. Shakespeare was originally performed out of doors, you know.

As the formalities wore away, and the scenes were becoming part of the whole play and flowing naturally into each other, some of the company whispered to me during a "break" and they saw that Lillian was by herself, "Ask her! Ask her! You'll never have the opportunity again."

"How did you survive those cold outdoor temperatures, and being on the ice all of that time in *Way Down East*? Did Richard Barthelmess rehearse on the ice? How many times did they shoot that part of the scene where he arrives just in time to scoop you up?"

Here we were: professionals! And we were acting like little children at a Saturday matinee waiting at the stage door with autograph books...

So I asked her, and everything stopped. It was quiet, like the silence every actor wants to have before the great moment he is going to play. He is in full control, and he knows it!

Lillian smiled, because she knew who she was, and she was aware of her importance in the early days of moviemaking. But this was 1936. Sound had been in use almost ten years, and I think Lillian was trying consciously to distance herself from those Griffith days. She wasn't ashamed of her Griffith work, but in 1936, when you spoke of the silent days, you were pushing actors back into the Stone Age. You were calling them old-fashioned.

Now Lillian was never any *Perils of Pauline* type, but how can anyone not forget she was the girl on the ice floe and an orphan of the storm? Whoever watched those films wanted to save her. Whoever worked with her wanted to protect her: to wait for a taxi with her, or to walk her home.

She answered those questions as if she had never heard them before. But this was praise from her fellow professionals, not a producer who would see her as archaic and not want to employ her.

She had done a few plays in New York. She didn't need any protection. Still, Lillian would look at you during a scene and focus those big blue eyes on you and you'd want to...[36]

In later years, John Gielgud would often tell people of the kindnesses shown to him from Lillian Gish. "She took me under her wing and became a lifelong friend."[37]

Lillian took John Gielgud with her to visit President and Mrs. Franklin Delano Roosevelt at the White House. It wasn't Lillian's first occasion to visit the White House, but it was John's. It was an opportunity he might not have had, had he not been a friend of Lillian's.[38]

Toronto: Prior to the New York premiere, Guthrie McClintic decided not to take the play to the usual pre–Broadway tryout towns (Philadelphia, Boston, or New Haven) where new plays were rewritten and polished — or closed. In Toronto there was a significant British population whose enthusiasm could easily fill the theatre. With a major box-office star of John Gielgud's caliber, a success seemed almost assured.

Lillian Gish explained:

As Ophelia in the stage production of *Hamlet* (1936, directed by Guthrie McClintic). "I was a member of the ensemble, part of a very distinguished company."

The British, whether in England or Canada, have always viewed Shakespeare as one of their own. And rightfully so. When other nations were still in the dark, the British were going to the theatre and listening to beautiful words that had appeal and could be understood by kings and commoners.

You can't ad-lib Shakespeare. You can't leave out words and substitute new ones. You play the text as it was set down.

I think Mr. McClintic wanted to try this production of *Hamlet* in front of an audience who already knew the play and would listen to it, and not just sit and wait for the "To be or not to be" speech — the way some people only know one aria from an opera and nothing more. There are many beautiful lines in *Hamlet*, and Mr. McClintic wanted total audience involvement in the total play.

The British who settled in Canada still observed high and low tea, and often became more British than the British![39]

No opening of any play is a relaxed affair, whether in London, New York, or

Toronto. There was the usual pre-performance tension characteristic of any opening, but the burden of the evening rested on the shoulders of John Gielgud.

William Roehrick remembered:

> The play was referred to as *John Gielgud's Hamlet*, although there was never any billing like that. Actually it was John Gielgud's *Hamlet*, but John is not a flamboyant actor in the John Barrymore manner. John Gielgud is a very quiet, modest person, almost shy.
>
> We wanted to get it over with. We'd rehearsed. We knew our entrances and our exits. We just wanted to do it. I never met an actor who liked opening nights.
>
> The audience was naturally very dressy. This was a Theatre, instead of a play, evening. Shakespeare was going to be played by an actor who, by virtue of the publicity, was so closely associated with the role you would have thought he originated it.
>
> We were excited. A good review, even from as far away as Toronto, would always get back to Broadway in advance of our arrival.
>
> The collective adrenaline level was very high.[40]

The premiere of *Hamlet* ran three hours, with one intermission. While the general opinion of the Toronto critics was that John Gielgud's Hamlet was the "finest Hamlet of our times," there were dissenters who felt that, while the Gielgud portrayal was better than the other Hamlets they had seen, Gielgud had "too many mannerisms" and he "lacked the strength to be a great Hamlet."[41]

Lillian was listed as a member of the company. Her performance as Ophelia went unnoticed.

The New York opening of *Hamlet* on October 8, 1936, at the Empire Theatre was one of the great theatrical events of the season. Drama critic Brooks Atkinson, noting John Gielgud's "prodigious reputation in London," wrote a criticism that almost mirrored the Toronto critics, calling Gielgud's Hamlet portrayal not "roaring or robustious" but "brimming over with grief," displaying the actions that would be demonstrated by a "cultivated youth." Ranking Gielgud's characterization with the best, he noted that the ferocity of Hamlet's character shown in other productions was downplayed, and that other actors with less knowledge of Hamlet's motivations made their Hamlet's horror "more harrowing" and his tragedy "more deeply felt."[42]

Clearly, the Gielgud Hamlet was a Hamlet to which few critics were accustomed. Perhaps this was the reason the two productions of *Hamlet* were so hailed in London. There were no carbon copies of other actors' performances. John Gielgud had treated the Shakespeare classic as a modern play, and had created an original characterization without sacrificing the classic quality of the text.

Lillian's Ophelia indicated:

"What any actress can do for Ophelia Lillian Gish has done with innocence of perception, but that disordered part contains some of the sorriest interludes that ever blotted paper."[43]

While director Guthrie McClintic's direction did not reflect the "forcefulness he previously displayed in other productions,"[44] the impression was created that *Hamlet* may have been guided rather than directed, perhaps in deference to John Gielgud who had played the part in two previous productions, the last running for 185 performances.

Guthrie McClintic's production of *Hamlet*, starring John Gielgud, set a New York box-office record of 122 performances, breaking the record previously held by John Barrymore, who had played the part 101 times.[45]

The Leslie Howard production opened and closed within a month.

One hundred twenty-two performances of a straight play was considered creditable. For *Hamlet*, the number was hailed as magnificent! Classics often lost money, and were often, in an effort to ensure maximum attendance, booked for "limited engagements." That McClintic's production was so huge a success more than justified the risk that was taken in asking John Gielgud to make the Atlantic crossing, and casting Lillian as his Ophelia.

Sixty years later, Sir John Gielgud wrote to this biographer from his home outside London:

"Lillian [Gish] was indeed one of my most treasured and unfailing friends.... We were immediate friends when we played together in *Hamlet* in 1936-7.... Her professional expertise as well as her simplicity and integrity in private life will always be a most cherished memory for me."[46]

CHAPTER 26

Changes and Adjustments

1936: Even with the success of her Ophelia performance in *Hamlet*, there were no offers from Hollywood for Lillian to return to the screen. In answer to reporters' questions regarding her future plans, the former silent star stated repeatedly that now that she was a stage actress, she could not think of considering talking pictures with any degree of seriousness, despite the fact that the incorporation of sound had been a success since *The Jazz Singer* revolutionized picturemaking almost a decade ago. She had appeared in two sound films, the less than successful *One Romantic Night* (1930) and *His Double Life* (1933), but neither film, she felt, had utilized the gifts she had brought to her Griffith efforts. Sound had limited the path of the camera. No longer could anything be accomplished visually and with music. The actors had to say what they were thinking and doing.

Incidentally, she would add as an afterthought, the continually circulating rumor that she had once toured as Little Eva in any stage production of *Uncle Tom's Cabin* were untrue.[1]

In Hollywood, Lillian's caustic remarks were seen as further examples of New York snobbery, but Lillian stood her ground. She had begun as a stage actress when she was a child, and she would remain a stage actress as an adult. She had

never owned property in Hollywood during her time at Metro-Goldwyn-Mayer in the late twenties. She had rented.[2]

Dorothy, whose efforts in the sound medium were also unsuccessful, may have entertained similar opinions about how Hollywood had bypassed her after Griffith, but, ironically, she remained silent. She would voice her opinions at parties after she had taken a few drinks and no longer felt encumbered by her former alcoholic husband, James Rennie.

Fortunately, stage actress Lillian had maintained her friendship with her *Hamlet* director, Guthrie McClintic. In the summer of 1937, she was cast opposite Burgess Meredith in Maxwell Anderson's dramatic fantasy, *The Star Wagon*. Anderson, one of the theatre's most gifted and prolific playwrights, had won the Pulitzer Prize for *Both Your Houses* during the season of 1932-33.[3]

The Star Wagon, one of the 1937-38 Broadway season's early entrants, had none of the social messages of the Sacco and Vanzetti–inspired *Winterset* (1935) or the Shakespearean elegance of the playwright's poetic *High Tor* (1936), both of which starred Burgess Meredith. This latest effort was strictly escapist fare. A middle-aged couple (an inventor and his patient and understanding wife) are given the opportunity to transport themselves in a time machine back to the days of their youth in the Age of Innocence. There they repeat their courtship, only to realize that they would still fall in love with each other and marry for love, not money.

It was a variation, given the device of the time machine, on the theme of James M. Barrie's *Dear Brutus* of almost two previous decades, but the Depression audience of the thirties didn't seem to notice or char.[4] The play offered the audience the opportunity, even for a short time, to return to a gentler era and the security of a healthier atmosphere. The qualities of human life, no matter the time frame, were still the responsibility of the individual.[5]

Film actor Edmond O'Brien, then a young stage actor, played a minor role in the production. Years later, in Brentwood, California, he laughingly recalled one of his first jobs to this writer, who had written a college term paper on Maxwell Anderson in the early sixties as an undergraduate.

> We always thought Buzz [Burgess Meredith] was sweet on Lillian Gish, even though she was a few years older. You still thought of her as someone you watched on the screen in the silent days when you were a kid. She still had that persona: the damsel in distress. She wasn't–not by a long shot. But I think we kept seeing her that way.
>
> Here I was, working with someone I had grown up watching.
>
> Lillian Gish was very professional. I never saw her offstage. I only saw her at the theatre. She was always on time, and line perfect, which was a lesson to all of us.
>
> She knew our names, and she always said good night to us, as we were leaving. I know this might seem like an odd thing to say, a star to remember the names of the minor players. I always thought she was royalty.
>
> What I still remember were the costume changes she made in what

seemed like seconds. Think of how the audiences reacted! There was a "flashback" to an earlier generation that occurred when they dimmed the lights. We were afraid, although nobody would ever say it, that when the next scene started, the "flashback," and Lillian Gish had to appear in costume fifty years younger, that she wouldn't have completed her changes. And then what?

> A stage play isn't a film, where you can stop the action by yelling "cut." In a stage play the action has to keep on going. There's an audience out there watching, you know. You make a mistake, you go up on your lines....
>
> But Lillian did it! She did it eight times a week! When the lights came up, and the audiences saw her as a young girl, they applauded! At every performance! It lifted the production ever further.
>
> You could sense the love in the audience right from the very start: an inventor wants to have control of time! Who doesn't? And, in those days, who didn't?
>
> None of us knew when our next job was coming from, or how long the current job would last....[6]

The Star Wagon opened at the Empire Theatre on September 29, 1937. While some critics believed the play was "patched together" for Anderson's friend and neighbor, Burgess Meredith, they conceded its "popular values" were sufficient to have a respectable run of 223 performances until it closed in April of the following year.[7]

In 1967, thirty years after the original production, Lillian still had fond memories of the production. She recalled:

> In the Anderson canon, *The Star Wagon* was never regarded or given the respect granted to his earlier *Elizabeth the Queen* or *Mary of Scotland*, both of which were critical and popular successes for my friends, the Lunts and Helen Hayes.

When the opportunity came to play in *The Star Wagon*, I took it, knowing that Burgess Meredith had starred in Mr. Anderson's *Winterset* and *High Tor*. Burgess Meredith was an Anderson actor in the way that, years later, Jason Robards was called the O'Neill actor.

Early in the rehearsals I could see how Burgess Meredith could say Anderson's lines and make them work.

There were nights during the run when I found myself still as moved as the audiences were, when I heard those last lines in the play about what was out there in the dark beyond the window. It was pure poetry that called to be spoken. Get a copy of *The Star Wagon* and read those last lines aloud, and you'll understand what I mean.

The Star Wagon was a light comedy that I thought Mr. Anderson must have written as a holiday from his heavier works, in the way that Gene [Eugene O'Neill] wrote *Ah, Wilderness*.

All of the writers I've ever known always wrote about what was important to them at that moment in their lives.

If *The Star Wagon* had been a first play, there might not have been the rumors that it was a trunk piece that was quickly mounted by Guthrie McClintic to fill a vacant theatre.

Maxwell Anderson was a real theatre man, who knew how to write full parts for actors that put them through their paces. His characters changed costumes in seconds, aged, and made physical changes with their body movements. Actors and audiences love to watch that when it's done "live." You could hear their reactions across the footlights. When that happens, you know you've connected.

I'm glad that I played in *The Star Wagon*.[8]

Prior to *The Star Wagon* tour, which would have a three week engagement in Chicago at the Grand Opera House,

Lillian told George Jean Nathan, who was still squiring her around the city, that she would have to make an unexpected train trip to Philadelphia for a day or two. George, who had hoped he would marry Lillian one day, and always said that he came from a Main Line Philadelphia Episcopal family, let it slip that his mother was in the hospital.

His mother? In a Philadelphia hospital?

Accomplished actress that she was, Lillian's face betrayed no emotion or surprise. It remained immobile.

It was the first time George had ever mentioned that his mother was alive, and the she was sick in a hospital. The moment he had mentioned mother, she could see that he regretted it. She didn't pursue the matter by asking any questions or showing any signs of concern. But she was even more curious about his background.

Perhaps during the course of the day she would visit George's mother by herself. If this courtship/relationship/friendship were to continue, wouldn't such a visit to Mrs. Nathan be more than warranted? George had met Lillian's mother many times. Wouldn't it be perfectly natural to visit Mrs. Nathan and have a nice informal chat? People confined to a hospital bed would welcome anyone who would cut through the monotony of the day. Lillian was someone who might be part of the Nathan family one day.

The visit was a revelation and a disaster. Mrs. Nathan, to be sure, was polite to her famous unexpected visitor who came alone and without any advance notice.

Before the drama critic's mother could complete her first sentence, Lillian immediately knew that George could never have been the son of Main Line Philadelphia Episcopalians, and that his mother was unable to qualify as a society Christian.

Present at Mrs. Nathan's bedside was George's sister-in-law, who confirmed Lillian's gathering suspicious over the years. In answer to a direct question from Lillian regarding George's background, his sister-in-law replied, "If George's brother is Jewish, I suppose George would be, too!"[9]

George would be, too?

At that moment in the Philadelphia hospital, Lillian's relationship with George was shattered. Permanently. That George was a Jew meant nothing. That in the course of ten years he had mentioned a Cornell University education, and a University of Bologna education, and had never mentioned that his mother was still alive was unconscionable. She would retain a sense of animosity toward him for the rest of his life.[10]

Aileen Pringle later explained why Lillian felt she was betrayed:

> George never said much about his family in all of our evenings together with him. And this was *before* he started going around with Lillian!
>
> George was Henry's friend. They worked together on Henry's magazine. I, too, came in later.
>
> George never discussed anyone but himself. In the writing profession, being narcissistic and self-centered is de rigueur.
>
> But somehow an occasional reference to a parent, no matter how quick or slight, is sometimes made. It doesn't have to be a criticism. It could be a song you heard on the radio that was a favorite of your mother's, or a book that might have been a family shelf when you were growing up. Everyone starts from a family, whether we like the family or not.
>
> The moment Lillian heard George's mother, she knew he had been lying about his background. George Jean Nathan was a Jew. He created a background and a family tree that never existed. It was a subterfuge.
>
> There are no secrets in the arts. It all turns up.

Lillian left George because he had denied his mother's existence!

Lillian adored her mother. George, very obviously, was ashamed of his. He kept his mother a secret. Lillian hated secrets. About anything.

When she was involved with Griffith, Griffith kept his marriage a secret. Griffith also kept his sneaky relationship with Carol Dempster a secret. And now George Jean Nathan was keeping his family origins a secret.

Lillian hated dishonesty. In an actor's performance, and in life.

I don't know what happened after she returned to New York. Henry just said, "Lillian and George are having problems," and nothing else. Maybe Lillian's mother saw Nathan's deception as the perfect opportunity to pull the parental strings and rein her in.

I do know that Nathan's deception made her even more fearful of getting involved with anybody.[11]

Anita Loos, discussing the demise of the Gish-Nathan relationship, reflected:

> Ultimately, none of these men — Griffith, Charles Duell, Nathan — ever did anything for Lillian.
>
> And you must not quote me!
>
> Griffith used Lillian until Carol Dempster came along. Duell used her name to bring in money for a studio he didn't know how to run. And Nathan — I don't know. I don't think either one was capable of any commitment.
>
> If — and I say "If" — they had married, and that never could have happened, but if it had, it would have been a disaster. Nathan wouldn't be able to share the spotlight with her. They were both very insecure, and very, very competitive.
>
> I don't think Lillian ever, ever forgot seeing the furniture people come in and remove almost all of their household goods when her father took off with the rent money her mother had left before she went to

work. Maybe she thought Nathan would take off while she was doing a play.

Nathan's denial about his Jewish origins was his problem, not Lillian's. But I think Lillian felt if he was going to be dishonest about one thing, he would be dishonest about other things.

Dorothy would have shrugged the whole thing off and quickly found another man. She was resilient. She always bounced back.

This Nathan involvement proved her mother was ultimately right:

Never totally trust any man. If Lillian had to admit this, it meant that she was helpless and unable to survive on her own. How would she survive after her mother died? By being a recluse?

The only thing Lillian knew how to do was act. The only time she was ever in total control of her life was onstage. Onstage, she knew how everything would end.

Fortunately, Lillian had a tour coming up. A tour meant work.

She always like to work. It kept her busy.[12]

CHAPTER 27

Choices: Right and Wrong

1937: It was not a happy time for Lillian or George Jean Nathan. George continued to review the latest openings, keeping the seat next to his reserved for his coat. Sometimes the adjacent seat was occupied by his lady-of-the-moment. News of his breakup with Lillian had quickly circulated within the theatrical community, and was greeted with the traditional shrug. Nothing lasts forever. The best plays come to the end of the run. In the case of Lillian and George, cynics grinned, the prospects for any revival were quite low. That their relationship had lasted so long was a surprise, knowing both Lillian's and George's fear of permanent commitment. Lillian often spoke making disappearances. Why should George be any different?

Anita Loos commented:

> Unless there was a klieg light present, Lillian couldn't react emotionally. Rather than face any crisis, she would choose to withdraw and stay inside her apartment instead of talking about it. No matter what it was.
>
> We knew her, so we didn't push the issue. If what had happened to her were dramatized in a play or a film, she would have played it brilliantly and had audiences in tears, which she knew how to do very well.
>
> In her real day-to-day life, away from the stage or screen, she was lost. She was a slave to fantasy. She went

from one role to the next, knowing just which button to press to achieve the desired effect.

In her own life, she was like Mickey Rooney. She never had a childhood. And she would say that, the way Mickey would. Her only sad times, and this was reinforced by her mother, were the times she was unable to earn enough money to put the bread on the table.

Now that her mother was ill and required attention, Lillian realized that she was even more needed, and her bedside presence was even more required.

I'm not saying Dorothy didn't do her share. She did. Lillian saw to it, but Dorothy saw it as something that had to be done, like the day's washing. With Lillian, taking care of her mother was also a labor of love.

It made Dorothy frustrated, but not frustrated enough to even refuse any help from Lillian when she needed it occasionally.

Lillian was handy to have around. Luckily, she wasn't ruined by the Depression or by her inability to maintain her career. Some of her high-living Biograph contemporaries from her Griffith days were flat broke. Lillian would never allow that to happen to her. She would always be a survivor.[1]

In their two-bedroom apartment, the three Gishes were an affectionate, close little unit, bravely battling the outside elements of a cruel world. Nothing had really changed since their days when they were rooming on West Eighth Street and walking to Griffith's Biograph on East Fourteenth Street as five-dollars-a-day players.

If Dorothy would sometimes behave as if she didn't know where the next meal was coming from, it was meant to be the next expensive meal. Dorothy always liked to dine out, and to be seen dining out, preferably with a man. If she dined solo, it was her reward for the time she had to spend taking care of her mother, although a live-in nurse was always present.

The little family unit was enlarged with the addition of two Siamese cats and a masculine looking parrot they named John. John, to everyone's amusement, could imitate Jed Harris and George Jean Nathan. Lillian had been John's patient teacher. To Lillian's surprise, John, at the age of 30, laid an egg![2]

Columnist Sheila Graham, a companion of author F. Scott Fitzgerald, then in Hollywood trying to eke out a living writing screenplays at the time Lillian made her allegedly "anti–Hollywood" remarks, told this biographer:

Scott [F. Scott Fitzgerald] knew where Lillian was coming from. Lillian created all of this, the movie business, and they threw her away because her persona wasn't in alliance with the new breed of moviemaker and the new styles. They only saw Lillian as a Griffith heroine on the ice floe.

The same thing would happen to Garbo [Greta Garbo] a few years later when she made *Two Faced Woman*. Being aloof and mysterious, when World War II was at our front door, was no longer desirable. The boys at the front wanted a younger, more American type like Betty Grable.

Lillian, like Garbo, who followed her out the door soon afterwards, was also an MGM victim.

I know you see it as a pattern and I suppose it is, but the overworked cliché is true. You're only as good as... You know the rest.

What did those executives expect Lillian to do, get on her knees and beg for work, or sit around the swimming pool and talk to whoever would listen about the good old days? Even in the good old days, Lillian was never one to sit around.

She was smart from the beginning. It was nothing more than work. Employment.

She had the courage to go back to the theatre and look for work. She was willing to start all over again.

She was almost 40, and she was very lucky. At the age of 40, Garbo packed it in. At the age of 40, everything Scott wrote was out of print. He was out of print in his own lifetime! How do you think he felt?

It wasn't any secret that Lillian wanted a part in *Gone with the Wind*. Everybody wanted to be in that picture. Any part.

In Hollywood, which was never a theatre town, you can't say you prefer stage work to picture work and then expect studio executives to forget what you said to the papers and offer you a job in a picture. I always thought that Selznick offered Lillian a part in *Gone with the Wind* after she signed to do a play [*The Star Wagon*] in New York. It wasn't the Belle Watling role that she wanted, the lady who ran the sporting house. She was offered the role of Scarlett's mother — a completely thankless part.

Lillian had already played a prostitute in a play on Broadway [*Within the Gates* 1934]. What was the problem? Ironically, the actress who did play Belle Watling [Ona Munsen] committed suicide, because she claimed she had been typecast and couldn't get the parts she wanted!

This is a business of complainers. First, you want the part and the work, and when the part and the work comes, you don't like it. You want something else, something different!

Scott was that way. He was the leading writer of the twenties, and when the thirties came, he was painfully out of fashion. His heart was never on the breadlines.

In the long run, Lillian was very lucky. She instinctively knew what to do, and she made the right choices. She kept right on going.[3]

Lillian's mentor D. W. Griffith wasn't faring very well since the failure of his last film, the 1931 sound feature, *The Struggle*. Like his protégée, Lillian, he, too, had embarrassed himself when he, reacting to the disastrous panning given *The Struggle*, had bemoaned the current sound era and longed for a return to the universal purity of silents, the kind of silents he had made with Lillian Gish.

Allan Dwan (Griffith's former assistant), who had recently directed 20th Century–Fox's latest phenomenon, child star Shirley Temple, in two successful features (*Heidi* and *Rebecca of Sunnybrook Farm*), remembered a visit to Griffith's hotel suite and

> looking at the walls covered with stills from his films. It looked like wallpaper: one photograph after another. They weren't arranged in any chronological order, or even by year. I don't think he intended his living room to be a museum, but it was.
>
> He'd stare at those stills, and he'd drink. I had the impression that if he could jump inside those pictures and return to the past, he'd do it.
>
> And maybe do the right thing with Lillian...
>
> Lillian and Mary [Pickford] always kept in touch. It was a friendship that dated back to their childhoods of touring in melodramas before they entered films. Both had a sentimental attachment toward their former boss, even though they no longer worked for him and had left him in less than pleasant circumstances.
>
> Mary no longer saw Griffith, but Lillian would try to find an excuse to see him when she came to visit Mary.
>
> This is what I heard from Mary: Griffith wasn't in the best financial shape, and he always thought if he and Lillian ever got the right financial backing, they could return to films together.
>
> Now remember, neither Lillian nor Griffith believed in sound. They didn't like it. I was never threatened by it. I was an engineer. We make progress all the time.
>
> I don't know who instigated it, Lillian or Mary, but there was a lunch meeting someplace. I don't know where. It was a good opportunity for the three of them to get together, swap a few memories, and laugh.
>
> Of course, both Lillian and Griffith knew that Mary, if she could make a profit, might possibly approve of a project for the two of them.
>
> They met and, after the usual Hollywood hugs, they had their lunch. And when there was a lull in the conversation, Lillian began to talk about a project.
>
> Griffith, who was probably told in advance by Lillian to let her do the talking, was still drinking. He was, according to Mary afterwards, drinking from the time they sat down at the table.
>
> Mary, who was known for raising her elbow a few times on more than one occasion, never drank when she sensed any kind of business deal was in the works. When she saw Griffith's condition, she steeled herself to expect a favor, and she didn't order any drinks for herself.
>
> Lillian was never a drinker, so there weren't any problems. Only Griffith drank ... and drank ... and...
>
> He began complaining about the then-current state of the motion picture business. Nobody knew how to make a film the right way, and production offices—rather than the directors—were calling the shots and telling people what to do.

I could imagine Lillian cringing. Mary had become part of the production.... Hell, she was the production office she was railing at, and he wasn't even working. He wasn't even offered a job!

Lillian saw the chance to end Griffith's babbling by launching into an idea for a possible film which Mary might find interesting: the Lizzie Borden case. It was a play Lillian had done [Nine Pine Street] and it was part of American history, of which Mary and D. W. Griffith were fond. It was also an unsolved mystery.

Griffith, who liked everything planned, wasn't too crazy about anything unsolved, but somehow Lillian was able to quiet him while she continued.

It must have been embarrassing for her. She was almost pleading for herself to get back to films. I could just see Mary looking across the table at this stubborn, perverse old man and thinking to herself: Lillian, why are you wasting your time? It's all over for him. Mary was polite, but it was obvious that nothing was going to happen of any benefit for anybody. Especially Griffith.

When David Selznick invited Griffith out to his studio to watch the shooting of Gone with the Wind, Griffith was just an arrogant old fool living in the past. Selznick, whose father was a contemporary of Griffith's, wanted to do something for him, maybe some sort of consultant's job, just to show some respect.

Griffith watched the shooting and afterwards said, "I did the same thing years earlier in The Birth of a Nation [1915] and I did it without sound!" Here was this arrogant son-of-a-bitch, who was living on nickels and dimes, and refusing a job!

Believe me, the Selznicks never gave any handouts to anybody!

Griffith refused to realize, or maybe he didn't realize, at that moment, that time had passed him by. For Lillian to stay with him and try to save him,

was to lower herself in quicksand, or go back to the ice floe. She had already broken with him professionally in 1920, and now she was realizing [in 1937] the break had to be total!

No matter how important Griffith's contribution was, and it was important by anyone's measure, Griffith, the man, was this own worst enemy.

Lillian and Mary remained friends, of course, but Griffith's name was never a topic of conversation. He was from the past, a past Mary had no desire to recall.[4]

The Lillian Gish who returned from her annual visit to the health spa at Baden-Baden was an actress still in search of a project. Being at liberty was always a source of great concern, but at this moment in her life and career she needed to prove to her West Coast detractors and herself that her name above the title on a New York theatre marquee was capable of selling tickets at the box-office and insuring a respectable run. Thankfully, her embarrassing lunch with Mary and D.W. Griffith had never been reported to any of the Hollywood gossip writers, who would have been only too eager to print something less than flattering about an ungrateful actress who had deserted them.

It was time to look for work. But where? There were no plays going out on the road in which Lillian had any interest. What had been submitted for consideration was of little merit. Her friendship with Guthrie McClintic had landed a leading role for Dorothy in the short-lived production of Missouri Legend, in which she played Jesse James' wife during a scant 48-performance run.[5]

For Lillian to appear onstage just for the sake of being seen was foolhardy. Dorothy had just done that.

Lillian glanced across the bed, on which her mother was sleeping, to the nightstand. One of the stations was broadcasting a "live" concert on the radio. She listened to the applause for a few moments, followed by the voice of the commentator.

There was work. One only had to know where to look for it.

The popularity of the radio in American homes since the 1920s was due not only to its portability, but to it being a source of music and the latest news bulletins of events around the country. The presidential election returns were heard from Pittsburgh. Pittsburgh's radio station WDKA once broadcast in 1936 a dramatization of *Jane Eyre*, in which Lillian starred. It was strictly experimental, but Lillian was never one to shy away from taking artistic chances. What were the early silent films?

Radio had unlimited opportunities. The Chicago Civic Opera's 1921-22 season of "live" performances under Mary Garden's direction was responsible for increasing that area's sale of receivers from 1300 to 20,000 within that season. Drama was introduced in Schenectady with *Great Moments in History* and *True Story*. *Amos 'n Andy*, the comedy series first heard at the end of the decade, was radio's first national success, paving the way for variety shows and serials.[6]

Not every member of the theatrical profession wholeheartedly embraced the new medium that made their performances heard and not seen. Working in radio was given the same disdain that was given to the actors who worked in the early days of one- and two-reelers. A stage actor working in silent films sacrificed his voice. On the radio airwaves, a stage actor became a voice without a face.

It took stage actress Ethel Barrymore, of the distinguished acting family, to break through her theatrical profession's resistance to being heard in any room of a listener's house or hotel room without said listener having to pay the price of admission. In 1923, while appearing on Broadway in *The Laughing Lady*, she ventured behind the microphone with her troupe and broadcast the production. At the touch of a dial, the world of the theatre came into people's homes, developing future audiences for other plays on the Great White Way.[7]

Lillian's decision to seek radio employment in 1938 and accept a co-starring role in *The Couple Next Door*[8] was greeted with surprise. She paid it little matter. Having worked since babyhood in touring melodramas before she had acted in one- and two-reelers, silent features, and sound films, and then returned to the legitimate theatre once again, had always produced cries of surprise. While some of Lillian's contemporaries bewailed their fate and their inability to make smooth transitions, Lillian simply kept on going. Wherever there was possible work, there was Lillian.

Discussing her venture into radio, Lillian recalled:

> Everything I ever did was always greeted with a raised eyebrow from the moment my mother put Dorothy and me on the stage when we were children. My father had walked out on us, and my mother certainly didn't have any money to support the three of us. Do you realize the chance she was taking, leaving Dorothy and myself alone in that apartment early in the morning to take a subway to Brooklyn everyday to work? We only had a next-door neighbor to look after us to feed us lunch. I think if any mother did that today, she'd be in jail for abandoning her children!
>
> Where else could we go, but the stage? That we succeeded was very lucky. Once I started to become prominent, my detractors became envious.
>
> I always considered radio, in any form, a Theatre of the Mind. In many instances, if utilized to its fullest potential, radio is even more powerful because it requires using your imagination.

I've always been an actress who likes to work. Acting has always been my profession, and radio was always another source of work.

I was also on *Information, Please!* I always wanted to be an elementary school teacher or librarian. Radio let me be an educator, too![9]

Jerry Devine, producer-director of *This Is Your F.B.I.*, the only series dealing with life in the Bureau that J. Edgar Hoover personally endorsed for its authenticity, recalled Lillian's radio days:

She wasn't a pioneer in radio. She was a regular who was on a weekly series. She was a member of the cast.

Everyone couldn't help but know who she was. How could you not know? She wasn't working on radio like a Barbara Stanwyck or Marlene Dietrich did on those guest shots on *Lux Radio Theatre* for the glamour. Lillian was working for the salary.

The Couple Next Door was a nice easygoing series that had an audience. It was the kind of thing she could do well. Using just her voice, she blended in well. That was probably the reason they hired her. She could act casual and hold back the histrionics she used in silent films. Her role wasn't a star turn like Agnes Moorehead's role in *Sorry, Wrong Number.*

When Arthur Hopkins, the producer, went into radio for a short time with adaptations of Broadway plays, he used Lillian, who had worked for him before. He knew he could count on her to come through.

Lillian always had a no-nonsense attitude about what she did, and that was what had earned everyone's respect. It's probably the reason she lasted so long. She had no illusions.[10]

1939: When the opportunity came for Lillian to return to Broadway, she took it, opening at the Broadhurst Theatre on January 11 in *Dear Octopus*, a British family comedy that had been a success in its Lon-

don production with John Gielgud and Marie Tempest. In its American production, directed by Glen Byam Shaw, Lillian played Fenny (full name: Grace Fenning), a long-suffering companion of an aged matriarchal employer, whose son, during the festivities of a golden wedding anniversary, discovers he is in love with Fenny.

Dodie Smith's characters, in the course of exchanging pleasantries and having the obligatory tea and crumpets at a long dining room table, emphasize — while the outside world is readying for a gathering crisis that will be World War II — the durability of the British family. Unfortunately, the humorous and touching aspects of the play, which delighted British audiences, failed to solidly register with their American cousins across the sea.

Drama critic Brooks Atkinson of *The New York Times* called the play "bountiful and affectionate," and praised Lillian's "aura of maidenly reserve" and her "considerable expertness as an actress." He also noted that "none of the emotions run deep," and that the play was too rooted in English conventions to really succeed on Broadway.[11]

Dear Octopus lasted for 53 performances before closing.[12]

Both Lillian and Dorothy were part of the New York opening night audience who attended the premiere of *Life with Father* on November 8, 1939, at the Empire Theatre. Before the end of the first act, they looked at each other and nodded in agreement. *Life with Father* was the kind of play they could do, and bring to audiences across the United States.

Lillian remembered:

Dorothy knew the Lindsays [actress Dorothy Stickney and her husband, playwright Howard Lindsay, who, in collaboration with Russel Crouse, dramatized the Clarence Day stories that made up *Life with Father*], and we went backstage to congratulate them. It was also done out of professional courtesy. Howard and Dorothy were playing Clarence and Vinnie Day, the main characters in the play. And they were truly, truly wonderful.

I told Howard that Dorothy and I would like to tour in *Life with Father*. We thought it was a wonderful play, the kind of play our audiences, who remembered us from our Griffith films, would like to see us do. We didn't have to explain that the Victorian era setting and our Griffith films had period settings from that era…. He understood immediately.

I could head one company, and Dorothy another.

Please remember, Stuart, I was doing all of this talking and the Lindsays were still in makeup, the curtain had barely come down ten minutes ago, and the play hadn't been reviewed for the morning papers. And there was the usual post-performance bedlam that always happened on opening night. Everything was in chaos! I'm sure Howard must have thought I was quite mad. On opening nights backstage you only hear congratulations and exchange hugs and kisses. And I'm making a salespitch, asking for the chance to tour!

Howard didn't say anything. There wasn't any reaction, positive or negative, at all.

We didn't stay backstage very long, although I felt it was an eternity with all of the talking I did. There were other people coming and going. It was a big cast. Actors are any actor's best audience.

When we were outside on the street, beyond the range of anyone who could overhear us, Dorothy whispered that she was still rehearsing for *Mornings at Seven*, which hadn't opened yet! How could I offer her services for any touring production?[13]

On November 30, Dorothy opened at the Longacre Theatre in Paul Osborn's *Mornings at Seven*, a close examination of the lives of small town middle-aged inhabitants. Dorothy's performance was criticized by Brooks Atkinson as having only a "notion of character." Had the play been a little sturdier, he continued, perhaps those who were present would have been warmed by the production rather than the excessive amounts of heat steaming from the theatre's radiators.[14]

Mornings at Seven closed after 44 performances.

Alan Brock recalled Dorothy's reaction to the play's unexpectedly short run:

> Dorothy stopped by my office and said, "We closed." She didn't say anything else. She didn't have to.
>
> I saw no reason to say that I disagreed with *The Times* review. What good would it have done? Any actor is only as good as the lines and the material presented to them.
>
> The curtain had fallen, and the play was history. A stage actor, regardless of the reviews, has to go on.
>
> I had a feeling in those days that Dorothy wanted to get out of town. The sooner she did so, the better she would feel. The review of her performance, had that been written about anyone else, would have destroyed them. Unless you are a major, major star, you don't recover that quickly.[15]

If any play can lay claim to being one of Lillian's personal favorites, the honors would have to fall upon *Life with Father*, Howard Lindsay and Russel Crouse's dramatization of Clarence Day's memories of his New York Victorian childhood as the son of a lovable, pompous stockbroker father in the final decades of the nineteenth century.

Vinnie Day, Clarence's wife, was a character both Lillian and Dorothy understood. She was someone whose presence was sufficient to give strength to the Day family unit. She wasn't supposed to be an equal, or a competitor for anyone's affection but her husband's.

Publicity shot for the play *Life with Father* (1939, directed by Bretaigne Windust). "We played for over a year in Chicago with this play," said Lillian. "Dorothy played Vinnie on tour. She was wonderful."

To Clarence, Vinnie was an ornament, a little dolly whose wishes and desires had to be acquired through deviousness and persistence. She knew not to be aggressive, for that would accomplish nothing. In asking "Don't you think, dear" she was able to defeat her autocratic husband, whose word and decisions seemed to be final.

Lillian explained the appeal of the play that opened when the effects of a gathering war were being felt on European soil:

> *Life with Father* created a nostalgia for a period of time when life and living seemed to be less complicated. It was a wonderful audience play that created a yearning for an America whose values, no matter how strict and limiting they may gave been for a woman, were easily identifiable and understood.
>
> It was the perfect escape from the issues of the day, and the headlines that only seemed to forecast doom and death.
>
> Vinnie's character, by today's standards, liberated as we ladies are seeming to be, might be classified as "victim," and her husband might be called "domineering." You have to realize that it was a man's world in those days. He had to be the provider. Very few women broke that mold, and those that did paid heavily.
>
> Feminism and women's issues were never a subject for the dinner table. I don't think they were ever a topic at all. I don't ever believe my mother said anything about the women's right to vote. When Dorothy and I were growing up, we were concerned about having food put on the table, and she did the best to provide for us. She devoted her life to us.
>
> Vinnie Day was living in an opulent era. The Day family didn't have any of our problems. My mother went to work. She had no other choice if she wanted to survive and support two children. I'm sure she would have wanted to stay at home.
>
> When a woman worked in those days, it meant her husband's income was inadequate. That was considered a disgrace. My mother had no husband after my father walked out on us. Dorothy and I had no father.
>
> Vinnie Day gets what she wants! was how the script played to me. Vinnie Day was shrewd enough to let her husband think he originated everything!
>
> When Howard Lindsay asked me to head the Chicago company, and Dorothy to take the play on the road to Boston, Philadelphia, and Detroit, we both agreed immediately. Dorothy's play [*Mornings at Seven*] had closed, and I had been giving lectures at college auditoriums and stock houses with a program of some footage from our Griffith films and reminiscences about the days of working in silents.
>
> Some of the people from the audiences who came back-stage afterwards during the Chicago engagement of *Life with Father* told us how they identified with the values of the Day family, and how they remembered going with their family to see *Way Down East* when they were children. They still remembered seeing me on the ice floe! Did they think I would still have frostbite after all of those years?[16]

Alan Brock explained the necessity for the lecture tour:

> Lillian, more than Dorothy, always had a fear of poverty. She never lived beyond her means. She liked her East Side, Upper East Side, address. It stood for something she had accomplished by herself. Without any help.
>
> I'm also sure that she thought the audiences who went to her presentations might engender an interest in reviving the career of D. W. Griffith, and ultimately reunite them in a sound film. It didn't happen...
>
> Frankly, I never thought of Griffith and Lillian as a screen team in the way that I thought of Fred [Astaire] and

Ginger [Rogers], but the phrase sometimes used to ballyhoo Fred and Ginger wouldn't have disappointed Lillian if it were used about her and Griffith!

Dorothy never said anything about Lillian's lecture series. When I would ask about Lillian, Dorothy would say, "She's on the road again," and laugh.

In her free time, Dorothy dated men. Lillian stayed by herself and looked after her mother.

I changed my attitude about Lillian and her mother when I saw them together. Lillian would wheel her around the block and talk to her the entire time, like an interminable monologue.[17]

Lillian had to work, because she didn't know how to do anything else."

Lillian's Chicago company of *Life With Father*, after a short tryout tour, was booked at the Blackstone Theatre for a three week engagement, beginning February 19, 1940.

The play had a run of an incredible 66 weeks.[18]

She never missed a performance!

September 1940: It was no longer impossible for the world to ignore the encroaching Nazi menace. For 57 consecutive summer nights, 2800 German bombers were attempting to pound London into submission — without success.[19] Thousands, whose homes and streets were horribly devastated, were somehow able to get through the ravaged city to seek shelter in the dampness of the Underground, only to be subjected to the constant cold and the sound of rhythmically dripping water that never stopped. Young children, fortunate to be classified as "Vaccies," were evacuated from their families and sent to safer places many miles out of the cities.[20]

What politically astute actress Myrna Loy had reported to MGM executive Louis B. Mayer years earlier, when she had returned from Munich to publicize *Test Pilot*

with Clark Gable in 1933, could no longer be ignored. The broken windows, the painted slogan Juden Raus! (Jews Get Out!) could no longer be ignored, or its implications denied. Hitler's inflammatory speeches at torchlight parades could no longer be dismissed as mere showmanship.

Mayer informed Myrna Loy that, while he was well aware of what she said, retrieving the box-office receipts was more important for the moment than an oncoming global conflict.[21]

Aviator-hero and Germanophile Charles A. Lindbergh's four trips to Germany between 1936 and 1938, in an effort to develop a friendly relationship with Germany and the incoming Nazi leaders,[22] had served to enrage President Franklin D. Roosevelt. Roosevelt had remained uncommitted, maintaining a policy of official indifference to the pleas of Jewish leaders who sought to allow selected refugees to be granted entry into the United States.[23]

Roosevelt, aware of an election coming, knew that the America First Committee of 800,000 Americans believed any involvement in a war with Germany, and any aid to Britain, was foolhardy. Forty percent of the American public, according to a Gallup poll, supported their policy of isolationism.[24]

Included amongst the members of the America First Committee were Lillian Gish, Charles A. Lindbergh, World War I quartermaster-general Robert E. Wood, World War I flying ace Eddie Rickenbacker, General Hugh Johnson (who supervised President Franklin D. Roosevelt's National Recovery Act), Alice Longworth Roosevelt (President Theodore Roosevelt's daughter), corporation magnate Sterling Morton (of Morton Salt), automobile pioneer Henry Ford, and writers Kathleen Norris and Irving S. Cobb.

Opposing the America First Committee was the nationwide Committee to Defend America by Aiding the Allies, and the New York–based Century Group.

Until something happened which would give Roosevelt no other alternative but to enter a war, it was to his advantage to maintain a middle ground[25] and concentrate on building America's own strength from within.[26]

Although Lillian had returned from the battle fields of France horrified and haunted by her firsthand sightings and observations of the consequences of war while filming *Hearts of the World* (a World War I propaganda film for D. W. Griffith) in 1917, she had never made any public statements nor committed herself to any causes of a political nature. The Griffith film, she felt, was the antiwar sentiment's best spokesperson. The message was there. Griffith, like President Woodrow Wilson, was antiwar and antiviolence.[27]

With Griffith ignored in 1940, and the public's memory dimmed, Lillian felt it was time to speak out and urge American non-involvement: "If I could save one American life and ruin my career in doing so, I would consider my career well lost."[28]

So antiwar was Lillian that she had written letters to President Franklin D. Roosevelt urging him to keep his campaign promises and keep our boys home.

During the Chicago run of *Life with Father*, she continued delivering isolationist messages, along with 24-year-old Douglas Stewart (son of the vice-president of the Chicago office of Quaker Oats) and Sears, Roebuck and Company President General Robert E. Wood. Lillian's message was always the same: There was nothing to be gained from fighting. Whether one wins or loses, a life is lost too young and for no reason. The Nazi aggression was far away from American soil.[29]

While Lillian's antiwar and pro-isolationist speeches may have given her favorable publicity among Republican politicians in Chicago, the manager of the Blackstone Theatre, where *Life with Father* was still playing, felt her alliance with any political cause was going to give unfavorable publicity to the play's box-office potential.[30]

Aware that any negative publicity could hasten the closing of the play before its rightful time, Lillian resigned from the Chicago chapter of the America First Committee.[31] The play ran until May 24, 1941. It was a record for a production done on the road.

When Dorothy's recurring intestinal problem forced her to go to the hospital for treatment during her Southern tour, Lillian quickly joined the company and played with them for a few weeks until Dorothy's recovery allowed her to resume her assignment.[32]

Playing opposite Lillian in Dorothy's company was Louis Calhern, an actor with whom Dorothy was having an affair. Calhern's capacity for alcohol when offstage was a subject of great concern among the company, although it did not seem to show during the performances. To Lillian, Calhern's drinking was a replay of the frustration Dorothy had with her former husband, actor James Rennie.

To O.Z. Whitehead, a supporting actor who had worked with Lillian in the Chicago company, Lillian remarked: "I only did it for Dorothy. He [Louis Calhern] was not agreeable to work with, and he wasn't good to my sister."[33]

Columnist Sheila Graham, residing with author F. Scott Fitzgerald in one of the bungalows that made up Alla Nazimova's Garden of Allah complex (a property the silent film actress purchased on Hollywood's famed Sunset Boulevard in 1918),[34] remembered the stormy Dorothy Gish-Louis Calhern relationship:

> Louis Calhern was a very charming man who drank. Dorothy also liked to lift a glass or two, and it drew them together.
> It also drew them apart. And then they'd get back together — until it got out of control.

You get the pattern: promises and broken promises.

Scott was like that: good days and bad days.

They were very professional, Louis Calhern and Dorothy Gish. Whatever problems they had offstage stayed offstage.

They shared a bungalow, and they tried to keep their battle royals quiet, but nothing was a secret. Everybody knew everything about everybody.[35]

Of her relationship with Louis Calhern, Dorothy said to O. Z. Whitehead:

I could never have married him [Calhern]. He had 3 living wives. I tried to help him, but I wasn't able to do much. I always had to be the strong one, and that is hard for a woman.[36]

On June 20, 1941, the United States closed their consulates in Germany and Italy.[37]

On June 21, 1941, Lillian was the final speaker at an antiwar rally held at the Hollywood Bowl. She followed Senator D. Worth Clark from Idaho and popular novelist Kathleen Norris.[38]

On July 1, 1941, in the wake of the German capture of two Red armies, the destruction of 2000 tanks, 4000 airplanes, 1000 armored cars, and 800 heavy guns, Lillian delivered an antiwar speech with Charles A. Lindbergh and Ex-President Herbert Hoover to an enthusiastic audience at San Francisco's Civic Auditorium, while a crowd estimated between 10,000 and 30,000 stood outside.[39]

And then the tide changed.

There is only one form of work that matters — resistance — blind, dogged, desperate resistance.
— Robert E. Sherwood, playwright
There Shall Be No Night (1940)[40]

Perhaps the audience reaction to Sherwood's lines acted by Alfred Lunt

needed time for its implication to sink into the minds of those who attended the play's performances since the opening night on April 29, 1940.[41] It was the playwright's third Pulitzer Prize–winner, but what was significant was the shifting of his antiwar stance to the inevitability of a necessary battle.

That his slogan STOP HITLER NOW!, reprinted in newspapers and magazines, had won such immediate acceptance was also a shock to the once ardent pacifist, whose first play, *The Road to Rome*, preached the futility of war. Now young men would soon be awakening to an "ugly responsibility." Students at his alma mater (Milton Academy in Massachusetts) agreed.[42]

Across the Untied States, motion picture studios began to film stories which preached anti–Nazism (beginning with *Confessions of a Nazi Spy*).[43] Hollywood was taking up the fight by raising funds to support relief needed in Greece, Russia, China, and England. Joan Crawford set aside her $112,000 fee to make a film for the Red Cross, and Cary Grant divided $100,000 of his own money between British and American war charities.[44]

The America First Committee, in the voice of gathering opposition, continued to preach an isolationist philosophy. When Lindbergh, appearing in Des Moines, Iowa, told an audience on September 11, 1941, that the "British, Jewish, and the Roosevelt administration" were only a "small minority trying to use a tremendous influence" in pressuring the United States to go to war, it was a big mistake, an error in timing and judgment that would bring about their downfall.[45]

The New York theatre and the Hollywood studios were very significantly influenced by Jews, both on the creative side and as a large percentage of audience members. To continue to support the America First Committee's policy of virulent anti–Semitism was tantamount to professional suicide.

At the imploring of her friend Burgess Meredith, Lillian resigned from the America First Committee at the right moment.[46] On December 7, 1941, the Japanese bombed Pearl Harbor. It was called by President Roosevelt a "Day of Infamy." That the United States would enter into the war with Germany and Japan was a foregone conclusion.

The America First Committee was disbanded without fanfare four days later on December 11.[47]

Lillian's former isolationist stance was now being interpreted as anti-patriotic, in the wake of instant revisionism. To gain the public favor, she would have to do public penance.

The girl on the ice floe had slipped, this time, into the water.[48]

CHAPTER 28

The Road Back

I was never *out* of style, because I was never in style.
— Lillian Gish
Conversation with Dr. Ralph Wolfe, curator
The Gish Film Theatre and Gallery
Bowling Green State University
Bowling Green, Ohio
October 9, 1982

While nobody would dare to say that Lillian Gish, in the aftermath of the events of December 7, 1941, had suddenly become persona non grata, she certainly was a political liability, as were many members of the America First Committee whose former opinions were now suspect. Isolationism was no longer desirable. America was now involved in another Great War, and patriotism was the order of the day.

One month before the surprise Japanese attack on Pearl Harbor, Lillian admitted her mistake in "I Made War Propaganda," a confessional article she wrote for *Scribner's Commentator*, hoping the public would forgive her mistake in judgment, and the studios from which she had been absent for the last decade would employ her.[1]

Anita Loos explained Lillian's situation:

> Lillian, even in her D. W. Griffith days, was never a social animal. Now that the war was on, she wasn't, at her age, going to suddenly change and go

to the Hollywood Canteen to dance with the soldiers before they went overseas. She wasn't that type.

Neither was Garbo, but Garbo wasn't a member of the America First Committee, and Garbo never publicly aligned herself with the pre–German Charles Lindbergh, who now had problems of his own because of politics.

It was important for Lillian to be seen. She had to be easily accessible. She, more than ever before, had to be way out front.[2]

Being out front meant being in a film. A motion picture, unlike a stage play, meant being seen on movie screens everywhere. Lillian's last film was the not very commercially successful *His Double Life* in 1933! Because of the unexpectedly long engagement (66 weeks) in the Chicago company of *Life with Father* (which ended on May 24, 1941), she had been unable to consider appearing in *Ladies in Retirement*[3] and in Samuel Goldwyn's *The Little Foxes*,[4] both of which would have provided successful comebacks and rekindled her screen career. To her amusement, she was also being considered for a possible role as a goose in *The Snow Goose*! In rejecting the latter, she questioned Gabriel Pascal's intentions. Did he really think she was suited for the goose part?[5]

In January 1942, at the behest of Mary Pickford, Paramount tested Lillian for the leading role in *Mrs. Wiggs of the Cabbage Patch*.[6] She didn't get the job. The studio wanted her to look padded, hoping this would look motherly. Lillian defended her dramatic choices, claiming that if the Wiggs family were always hungry, being padded would work against her character.

She still harbored a silent film prejudice against sound. It was believed that Lillian might not have been able to handle the great amount of dialogue and the camera. Dialogue, Lillian had always said, was spoken on a stage, not from a screen.[7] It was not the attitude to embrace, as sound had been the medium that had been utilized for the screen since 1927.

Still fighting the latest technical advances, she was trying to make the case for a return to silents with a script she had developed on the life of her mentor, D. W. Griffith, called *Silver Glory*. The studios weren't interested, even though she had offered her services as a producer. The name D. W. Griffith no longer meant a box-office success. Griffith was from another era, a silent film era.[8]

The studio executives who had once vied for her services in any capacity were no longer interested in her. What her mother had once warned her to expect had finally happened. It had just taken a little while longer.

Lillian herself liked to quote her mother as often as possible:

> Mother taught us "Men might leave you."
> I was the little pet out there once.

Everyone did as I said. I made fine pictures that I like, and they made money....
> Mother said, "You may feel secure to be making so much money now, but break your leg and then see how much you have left...."[9]

Thinking it was Lillian's former isolationist stance that was the underlying cause of Hollywood's reluctance to giving her employment, a very courageous Mary Pickford took Lillian to the offices of Louis B. Mayer, Lillian's former boss.

Mary never wasted words or time on social amenities. She spoke her mind:

> This lady is as you and I are. She was merely against war.[10]

Lillian went back to New York. There was no work for her in Hollywood.

In July, director John Farrow offered Lillian a small part in *Commandos Strike at Dawn*, an anti–Nazi film being shot on the coastline of Victoria, British Columbia, although the scene of the action was a Norwegian village.[11] Eager to be seen in anything anti–Nazi, no matter how small the part, Lillian agreed, not knowing anything about the plot, or even the name of her leading man.[12]

When she learned her leading man was Paul Muni, she was thrilled. Mr. Muni, as he was called by his fellow professionals, was a perfectionist who stayed by himself between takes and didn't socialize with anyone while he was on the set. Muni preferred to remain in character as much as possible.[13] He would be playing a Norwegian patriot whose village was suffering under the invading Nazis. During the filming, Canadian troops would be utilized, as they always had to be on hand should there be any attacks from the real Germans![14]

Commandos marked a return to the screen after a considerable absence for both Lillian Gish and Paul Muni. Happily,

Lillian told *The New York Times*, her spoken dialogue was minimal.[15]

Working under tight wartime security during the summer of 1942 must have reminded Lillian of the risks she and Dorothy and their mother must have taken when they crossed the Atlantic on a ship fitted with black sails in 1917 to film *Hearts of the World* for D. W. Griffith.

Lillian explained:

> Both *Hearts of the World* and *Commandos Strike at Dawn* were made during two different World Wars in countries open to air attacks.
>
> We never had a work schedule we could depend upon when we were shooting in Vancouver, as the Canadian troops were always on call to practice drills and maneuvers. Canada was open to the threat of constant attacks, which I am glad to say never occurred.
>
> We learned never to ask questions regarding their availability. Matters regarding wartime security were serious business. We knew why scenes we had rehearsed were suddenly dropped in favor of other scenes.[16]

Prior to the film's January 14, 1943, New York opening, screenwriter Irwin Shaw announced that he "would not assume full responsibility for the film, as it had been tampered with by persons unknown."[17]

Lillian, responding in the late 50s to Shaw's remark, had no comment, except to state that *Commandos* had not been a critical success, but was one of many war films made quickly for audiences who wanted to see them.[18]

Film critic Bosley Crowther, covering the picture for *The New York Times*, noted that Lillian had a "few fleeting moments in which to look like a Norse housewife."[19]

While not pleased with the critical reactions to her film, Lillian felt being in any anti–Nazi film had vindicated her honor

and erased her former association with the misguided America First Committee.

In November 1942, both she and Dorothy were back on the boards, opening in different plays within days of each other. Ketti Frings, who would earn a Pulitzer Prize in 1957 for her adaptation of Thomas Wolfe's *Look Homeward, Angel*, was making her playwriting debut with *Mr. Sycamore*, opening at the Guild Theatre on November 13. The play, which co-starred Stuart Erwin, was Lillian's first association with The Theatre Guild,[20] whose doors during her attempts to be involved in O'Neill's plays had been closed to her.

Dorothy was co-starring with Louis Calhern in Frances Goodrich and Albert Hackett's comedy, *The Great Big Doorstep*, opening at the Morosco Theatre on November 26.[21] To observers, Lillian and Dorothy were appearing together but separately.

Mr. Sycamore was a "whimsical failure."[22] Lillian played the wife of postman Stuart Erwin who, tired of seeing his life "vegetate into passivity,"[23] asks to be planted in his backyard, later to become a tree.

Mr. Sycamore, wrote *Journal-American* reviewer John Anderson, was a "forest of faults" containing "plenty of corn and marshmallow" which turned into a "coy idiocy" that was "slightly embarrassing."[24]

Drama critic Brooks Atkinson, writing for *The New York Times*, took the opportunity to praise Lillian's acting achievements in the theatre: "[Lillian Gish is] … a remarkable actress who can penetrate a character with remarkable insight."

He was not impressed with *Mr. Sycamore*, and noted how the lack of workable material affected the quality of her performance: "There is nothing spectacular about her acting of this part…. The play is not written with sufficient imagination to give the part wings."[25]

Mr. Sycamore lingered for 19 performances before closing.[26]

Lillian was still wary of Dorothy's continuing offstage relationship with Louis Calhern, a relationship she believed was placing Dorothy's health in constant jeopardy. Alan Brock, Dorothy's friend, noticed an obvious parallel in the marriage of the Gish parents and Dorothy's former marriage to actor James Rennie. Both James Gish and James Rennie were alcoholics.

Dorothy had once confided to Lillian that she never knew if Calhern would report to the theatre on time, draw a sober breath, and be able to remember his lines well enough to sustain a performance. Calhern's behavior was a definite link to Dorothy's recurring intestinal problems that often required hospitalization.[27]

The Great Big Doorstep, which premiered at the Morosco Theatre on November 26, 1942, involved a Cajun family who finds a doorstep placed against their cabin after a flood. Could the Cajun couple, Dorothy and Louis, raise the necessary funds to acquire a house to go with the door?

Such a premise could not be taken seriously by the reviewers, and the play closed after 28 performances.[28]

In a season whose productions included the innovative Thornton Wilder play, *The Skin of Our Teeth*, and Richard Rodgers and Oscar Hammerstein's first musical collaboration, *Oklahoma!*, Dorothy's effort hadn't a chance.

Doorstep director Herman Shumlin, speaking at the State University at New Paltz (N.Y.) as part of a noontime lecture series during the summer of 1965, had very little to say about the production. But he did have kind words to say about its star, Dorothy Gish, to this biographer afterwards:

> Can I be honest? Dorothy's work always impressed me more than Lillian's. Dorothy had a greater breadth. Lillian always played the perennial handwringer in those Griffith films. But she did it better than anyone else around.
>
> Calhern was a boozer, and Lillian wouldn't have tolerated it. Both Dorothy and Louis knew how to empty a bottle, but Louis' drinking was a real problem.
>
> Dorothy always took up for him, no matter how difficult things would get. Dorothy was loyal.[29]

What Herman Shumlin was alluding to was recalled by Lillian in her book, *Dorothy and Lillian Gish*:

> During one performance Louis Calhern arrived far removed from himself. In spite of black coffee he couldn't remember a line, so Dorothy as his wife played both parts, prefacing each line with a "you said" or "you told me" and saved the play for the audience.[30]

Had *Commandos Strike at Dawn* been a success, perhaps Lillian might have been cast in 20th Century–Fox's adaptation of John Steinbeck's *The Moon Is Down*, which utilized the talents of *Commandos* player Sir Cedric Hardwicke in another film about invading Nazis and Norwegian villages. Even Warner Bros. had their version of a Norwegian village under Nazi occupation in *Edge of Darkness*.

In all of the aforementioned films, the Nazi and Norway theme didn't totally succeed. Production offices at the three studios who made these films (Columbia, 20th Century–Fox, and Warner Bros.), believed audiences were becoming tired of pictures about war,[31] particularly war films involving only the Norwegian aspect.

Seeing the slightly declining grosses, musical films might be the solution to boost the morale of the military and promote patriotism.

Universal, aware of the musical talents of young Donald O'Connor, saw him as a possible competitor to MGM's Mickey Rooney. To that end, the studio fashioned *Top Man* as a blatant imitation of Rooney's Hardy family series. With the thinnest of plot lines, *Top Man* cast the eager O'Connor as a son who wanted to put on a show at his father's factory to help raise money for the war effort.

Lillian played the kind but puzzled mother, with Richard Dix as her husband.

Film critic Bosley Crowther, seeing *Top Man* as "plenty of Donald," perhaps out of kindness made no mention of Donald's film parents in his review.[32]

The performance, the presence of Lillian Gish in a patriotic film had been ignored! Since her resignation from the America First Committee, she had vainly been trying to rekindle a demand for her services, but it hadn't worked. Dorothy would be replacing Ruth Gordon in *Over 21* and taking the play to military bases under the sponsorship of the USO.[33] For Lillian there was nothing. Was the Military punishing her for her association with the America First Committee?

Lillian was aware that the war had created a demand for younger stars. Hadn't Garbo retired without fanfare the previous year (1942)?

Perhaps it was time for another disappearance, one that would last until the war was over, whenever that would occur.

Then it would be the right time to rebuild her career.

There would always be a tomorrow.

CHAPTER 29

None but the Lonely Heart

For the rest of the war Lillian remained out of public view, preferring to stay in her apartment taking care of her mother and venturing out in the sun to wheel her around the block. Local residents, long accustomed to seeing the two of them, showed their respect and maintained their distance. What Lillian had always sought was finally granted: privacy. Unlike Greta Garbo, who travelled around the world obsessively seeking solitude, Lillian only had to close the door of her apartment.

Dorothy had finally returned to Hollywood and the Paramount lot in 1944 to make what she called her "talkie" debut in *Our Hearts Were Young and Gay*, hoping audiences had forgotten her 1930 partial-talkie, *Wolves*, which she had made in England under the direction of a young Alfred Hitchcock.[1]

In December 1944, the curtain rose in a Chicago theatre on *The Glass Menagerie*, a new play being tested for a possible Broadway opening a few weeks later. So unsure were the producers of getting a full house when the streets were snow-covered and the playwright, Tennessee Williams, was unknown, that extra tickets were distributed at the local USO canteen, hoping that some of the servicemen would fill the theatre.

Tennessee Williams recalled years later that

Lillian [Gish], who was one of the first choices to play Amanda, had turned down the play, claiming she had a sick mother who needed constant care.

Fortunately, we were able to secure the services of Miss Laurette Taylor, who wanted to work in the theatre. She turned the role of Amanda into a personal triumph.

A few years later [1947], when we were looking for possible actresses to play Blanche in *Streetcar* [*A Streetcar Named Desire*], Lillian made it known she was interested. Again, we were fortunate to have Miss Jessica Tandy play Blanche.

What I am saying is that Miss Gish and her mother were a mutual aid society by this time. I was an unknown when *Menagerie* was done, even though I had already had a New York production of an earlier play [*Battle of Angels*]. Now that I had some sort of name after the *Menagerie* success, perhaps Lillian thought she could take a chance.

You see, her mother's illness was no longer a problem. She could push that illness aside and have somebody else supervise her mother for the round-the-clock care Lillian said she needed.

Don't misinterpret what I am saying! Miss Gish is a fine and gifted artist, but when *Menagerie* was first mounted in Chicago, she couldn't

257

afford to be associated with an unknown, and especially an unknown whose first effort wasn't a success.

Any artist's career, any writer's career, is always subjected to acceptance. It goes on all of the time. All creative ventures, whatever they may be, always begin at square zero.

Lillian's last play on Broadway [*Mr. Sycamore* 1942], was a first effort which closed quickly. She had always done plays written by proven masters: Chekov, O'Casey, Shakespeare, Maxwell Anderson.

Now [1980] I could say I understood her feelings. Maybe she didn't like the play, and she didn't want to hurt my feelings. Her mother's illness was an acceptable convenience for her. It wasn't for me.

An actor or actress either takes the role or turns it down. The reason isn't important. Being available is part of the business.

Lillian is always available when it is to her advantage. She was absolutely wonderful in *Portrait of a Madonna* when it was done in West Berlin [1957].

I still love her. I always will.[2]

In July 1945 Dorothy returned to Hollywood to play a supporting role in *Centennial Summer*, a Jerome Kern musical based on the novel by Alfred E. Idell, and directed by Otto Preminger, who would later use a much ailing Dorothy in 1964's *The Cardinal*, her last film.

Centennial Summer recreated a romantic America of the 1870s. To war-weary audiences tired of motion pictures with battles and stories about lonely factory girls whose men were fighting for a violence-free world, the innocent America depicted on the techinicolor screen actually did exist. *Centennial Summer*, like its predecessor, *Meet Me in St. Louis*, was set in a city where a World's Fair had taken place.

The setting of *Centennial Summer* was Quaker Philadelphia in 1875.[3] None of the film's principal actors (Linda Darnell, Jeanne Crain, Cornel Wilde) were singers, a concept that delighted Jerome Kern. To compensate for the lack of singers of professional caliber, the vocals were dubbed. Dorothy and Constance Bennett's songs, however, used their actual voices, as they were playing character parts.[4]

Cornel Wilde remembered Dorothy Gish and *Centennial Summer* with great fondness:

One of the benefits, if you want to call it that, of a studio contract was the teaming. You hoped for a chemistry that would work well on screen, and the public's response would pair you in another film. I knew both Jeanne [Crain] and Linda [Darnell], and they were nice girls.

Centennial Summer was Fox's attempt to duplicate the success of MGM's *Meet Me in St. Louis*, another period musical. We didn't have a Judy Garland, who could sing her way through anything.

None of us had ever worked with Dorothy Gish. She's been away from pictures a long time, and we only knew her as "the other one, the sister." We thought we were going to be working with Lillian.

One of the crew said they were quite different. Lillian was serious and professional, and Dorothy would come on the set and ask, "Well, what are we going to do today?"

Dorothy knew all of her lines, and between takes she kept us in stitches. Both Dorothy and Connie [Constance Bennett] were very funny ladies. Connie could be very raunchy, but Dorothy gave her a good run for her money.

Between takes, Dorothy just plain hung out. She wasn't the type of person who, because they had been in the business so much, had come to regard herself as royalty, the way those silent stars sometimes did when they were playing supporting roles. That was the way the fan magazines had written about them, and the public believed it.

> Dorothy was fun. She was perfect for the film. Even Otto [director Otto Preminger] would laugh.
>
> Working with Otto is an experience every actor should have...only once."[5]

The conclusion of Lillian's latest disappearance almost coincided with the signing of the treaty on the battleship Missouri on September 2, 1945.[6]

Like many Americans, she was grateful the war had finally ended. Perhaps this would signal a return to steady employment. She wanted to be a working actress once more, not someone who was merely recognized on the streets of the city. Her social life, since the dissolution of the relationship with George Jean Nathan, was less than active. Her previous pro-isolationist statements and later public apology, she hoped, were things of the past.

Still, she had doubts about a quick return to the stage or screen. What more did she have to do? She hadn't given away any atomic bomb secrets. Nor had she espoused any Communist party causes.

Nobel Prize–winning author Sinclair Lewis, whom she had met through *The American Mercury* editor H. L. Mencken, a mutual friend, was probably her most frequent companion.[7] The relationship was platonic. Writers, beginning with F. Scott Fitzgerald and Joseph Hergesheimer in the twenties, knew Lillian was always a good listener.

Lewis, like Lillian, was also opposed to American involvement in the war,[8] and told her, "If Dorothy comes out for war, I'll take Madison Square Garden and come out against war."[9]

But Lewis did not suffer the same consequences for his isolationist views. Nor was he shunned. Literature and politics sometimes intertwined. It was permissible for writers to go against the grain. Writers were always bold dreamers, and it

was easier to later claim they were seduced by the pervasive atmosphere. An actor on-stage said someone else's words, not their own.

Listener Lillian had provided the shoulder for Lewis to cry upon when his marriage to columnist Dorothy Thompson was disintegrating.[10] Later she had received Lewis and his young companion, actress Marcella Powers, backstage in Chicago during the engagement of *Life with Father*.[11] Now she was playing host to him in New York. He was another lonely old bachelor who was desperate for female companionship.

As fond as Lillian was of Lewis, she still had her own views regarding matrimony. She was 53, still single, and even more set in her attitudes: "A woman who rushes heedlessly into matrimony for the sake of her own social security, is selfish."[12]

After Dorothy finished *Centennial Summer*, she began rehearsing in New York for a January 22, 1946, opening as Fanny Dixwell Holmes, the wife of Justice Oliver Wendell Holmes, in Emmet Lavery's *The Magnificent Yankee*. The play, directed by Arthur Hopkins, co-starred Louis Calhern.

Set in 1902, *The Magnificent Yankee* was a story of a man, his wife, and his great love for the United States of America.

John Chapman, drama critic for *The New York Daily News*, wrote that Dorothy and Louis Calhern were giving the finest performances he had ever watched.[13]

Alan Brock had even more to say about the acting:

> The two of them, Dorothy and Louis, had broken up. It was all over. Finished. Done.
>
> I had asked, in a conversational manner, of course, how things were going. I knew they had had some rocky times, but I knew it was par for any relationship Louis had with a woman. He was never easy going.

And Dorothy was always honest with me. We were always honest with each other.

This time she said, "Okay," and nothing more.

I knew not to ask anymore questions, and I immediately started talking about which plays were going into rehearsal. Anything to fill the sudden gap in the conversation.

I could name a lot of reasons their friendship had ended: his drinking, Lillian's constant resentment, and the fact that he was still married to Natalie [actress, Natalie Schafer].[14]

Sheila Graham further elaborated:

Lillian Gish disliked Calhern. She felt he was treating her sister badly. After they had starred together in Los Angeles in *Life with Father*, Dorothy suffered with ulcers. When I heard he could not get a divorce because Natalie was refusing to give him his freedom, I mentioned this in my column. The next time I saw Natalie she said, "Thank you," and she promptly divorced Calhern. But he never married Dorothy.[15]

From Alan Brock:

The two of them, Dorothy and Calhern, were magnificent in that magnificent play. You wondered how they were able to get through those love scenes, especially the one where she is dying.

I wondered, seeing that play a few times, just how much of those were her own, or was she just playing the scene very well and doing all of the tricks.

It doesn't really matter, when you think about it. All that matters is whether the scene works. It certainly did, every time I saw it. And I knew what was coming. There wasn't a dry eye in the house, including my own.

Dorothy knew Louis was seeing somebody else, and that she would probably marry him. It was sad for her. She had stood by him.

Lillian was probably right. But it was Dorothy who paid the price.[16]

A war is not forgotten with the mere signing of a treaty. There is the aftermath for both sides: the period of adjustment that accompanies the return to normalcy. Movie studios, operating within the framework of providing entertainment, had to provide a product that acknowledged and attempted to deal with post-war problems: the physical and emotional crises combatants returning from the battlefields, jungles, and internment camps were facing in civilian life. Studio chiefs were also aware that post-war films couldn't use the problems of amputees and shattered marriages to attract and sustain a significant audience interest over a long period of time.

Of equal importance was the spate of comedies and musicals that provided a panacea for the recent horror. Comedies and musicals were soothing, reassuring escapist fare that would bring family audiences back to their neighborhood moviehouses week after week.

Miss Susie Slagle's, Augusta Ticker's nostalgic look at life in a Baltimore boarding house inhabited by medical students in the first decade of the twentieth century, returned Lillian to movie making. The running time was less than ninety minutes, but it was enough time to cover four years of student high-jinx, love interests, and personal problems, and occasionally nod at the reason they are in medical school. Lillian played the boardinghouse resident mother, and, while the role was "decidedly limited," she managed to give an impression of respectability and pride personified."[17]

The film opened at the Paramount theatre in New York on February 6, 1946. While *The New York Times* film critic, Bosley Crowther, noted "there was nothing exciting about it," he did say *Miss Slagle's* was a "personally engaging little picture of fabricated life."[18]

Between the two Gishes, Lillian was the greater box-office attraction on the stage and screen. Fellow professionals (including D. W. Griffith and Lillian herself) always believed it was Dorothy, however, who had the greater depth and versatility.[19] No stage role ever demonstrated Dorothy's range to greater advantage than the short-lived *The Story of Mary Surratt*, John Patrick's post–Civil War tragedy of a woman who was hanged for her alleged complicity in the assassination of Abraham Lincoln.[20]

Lillian wrote of Dorothy's performance:

> [It] had such an emotional impact…. I would have to leave the theatre, so as not to disturb the theatre with my sobbing. When I looked for an easy exit [there were] others in the same state…. Dorothy's gift for tragedy was as great as her gift for comedy.[21]

What was upsetting were the reviews. Dorothy's performance was praised, but the play's reviews were almost evenly divided. The producers didn't want to sink any additional monies into a play with so non-commercial a topic. There were those who believed that Dorothy's good performance might have given the play a respectable run, but …[22]

When Lillian learned that Warner Bros. had purchased the screen rights for *Life with Father*, she began to lobby for the role of Vinnie Day that she had played so successfully in Chicago for 66 weeks. Never reluctant to chase after a part she coveted, she knew she was competing against Dorothy Stickney (who created the role in the original New York production), Bette Davis, and Mary Pickford.[23]

Securing the stage roles in *Life with Father* proved no problem for Lillian and Dorothy. Both sisters had offered their services directly to the author, Howard Lindsay, who was playing Clarence Day opposite his wife, Dorothy Stickney. When it was announced that *Life with Father* would have two touring companies, each sister headed one.

Post-war Hollywood was another matter. One didn't cavalierly approach a producer or a director. One depended upon an agent. And then you waited and hoped.

Mary Pickford was tested. Lillian Gish wasn't.

Still eager to play Vinnie Day, Lillian invited Peg Day, the real wife of Clarence Day, to watch a private screening of *Miss Susie Slagle's* at Mary Pickford's home. Mary had tested for the Peg Day role for sentimental reasons. Mary, afraid of photographing too old, had no real interest in returning to face the cameras, having been away from the cameras for over a decade.

Lillian had hoped that Peg's influence might help her.

At the end of the screening, Peg turned to Lillian and said, "I'm very fond of you, dear, but you haven't got quite the warmth Mary Pickford has."

Lillian answered, "No, I haven't," and did not dine with Peg that evening.[24]

Realizing that she had possibly embarrassed herself, Lillian had a dinner party the following evening at her home. Among the invited guests were Peg Day, D. W. Griffith (and his new young wife), and Richard Barthelmess and his wife.

After a quick cross-country telephone call to New York for the latest news on Dorothy's play, *The Magnificent Yankee*, and for news on the health of Mrs. Gish, Lillian screened D. W. Griffith's *Way Down East*, hoping that when Peg Day watched the ice floe sequence, she would change her opinion of her work. The ice floe sequence always thrilled audiences. How could Peg not be impressed?

Jennifer Jones in *Duel in the Sun* (1947, Selznick International, directed by King Vidor). "Mr. Selznick wanted to make another *Gone with the Wind*. It wasn't, but it was a top-grossing successful film.

When the lights came up, D. W. Griffith, who had been drinking too much, remarked to the guests in full view of Lillian, "It's a lot of malarkey, isn't it?"[25]

The Vinnie Day role in the Warner Bros. screen version of *Life with Father* was played by Irene Dunne.[26]

Although Lillian was reluctant to admit she was embarrassed at the less than professional respect shown to her by the studio, her spirits were greatly lifted when David O. Selznick asked her to be part of the distinguished cast of *Duel in the Sun*, an outdoor epic Western that would eventually cost over $5,000,000 to make.[27] Her salary would be $5,000 a week for 30 weeks.[28]

The basic story of the picture, devoid of all the spectacular effects, involves an Indian girl (Jennifer Jones) who is torn between two brothers: one who is honorable (Joseph Cotten) and one who is not (Gregory Peck). Set on the Spanish Bit, the Texas ranch of a wheelchair ridden Senator (Lionel Barrymore) and his wife (Lillian Gish), *Duel in the Sun* is a combination of the Cain and Abel story with a dash of Eugene O'Neill in Western garb, a Wagnerian horse opera that owes a considerable debt to *Gone with the Wind*.[29]

Lillian recalled filming *Duel in the Sun*

as a kind of reunion with the people I loved: Lionel Barrymore from my Biograph days with Mr. Griffith, King Vidor, who directed me in *La Bohème*, and Walter Huston, who was the leading actor when I was billed Baby Lillian in *In Convict's Stripes* and we played in Risingsun, Ohio.

I loved watching Walter rehearsing. I wish I had been older when we first met. He had the type of role that could easily be acted over the top. The frontier preacher always was a melodramatic character, and Mr. Selznick had to cut some of Mr. Huston's lines from the final print. Some people, when the film was previewed in California, objected to the type of character a man of God was being shown.

Mr. Selznick removed some of his lines. Mr. Selznick also cut some of my scenes!

On one of the shooting days, Mr. Griffith visited the set. Both Mr. Barrymore and I felt inhibited, doing our scenes. Mr. Griffith had created us. Because of him, our faces were on the big screen. And now we were working in his creation, and he wasn't. Nobody wanted him.[30]

Still hoping to play a Eugene O'Neill heroine, Lillian and Dorothy, at the close of the *Duel in the Sun* assignment, went to England, Ireland, and Sweden to scout actors for three contemplated Theatre Guild productions.

They returned to New York on the Gripsholm. Among the 1395 passengers arriving in New York on September 4, 1946, were Mrs. James Forrestal, wife of the Secretary of the Navy, and actress Greta Garbo.[31]

The official New York premiere of *Duel in the Sun* took place at the Capitol, but 38 Loew's moviehouses in New York–New Jersey area also had their own heralded openings.[32]

Man versus Nature, a popular theme in Vidor's films, was quite evident in *Duel in the Sun*. Man in the persona of a wheelchair trapped Senator, fights Nature, in the form of the invading railroad affecting the future of his ranch.[33]

The film is resplendent in glorious technicolor, with eye-dazzling scenes of wide open vistas enhanced by fitting musical backgrounds. The film's only problem was the lack of congruency between the dramatics and the technical. Lillian's performance, though on the heavy-handed side, was neither better nor worse than the script allowed.[34]

Although the critics generally were unkind to the film, and there were jokes that the title, because of Jennifer Jones' sexy performance, would be more appropriate if it were renamed *Lust in the Dust*, such remarks attracted audiences.[35]

It was not a thoroughly happy set. Selznick's constant hovering over his wife, Jennifer Jones, and fussing over her every move created such tension between himself and director King Vidor that Vidor walked out on the production before its completion. Vidor still received solo director's credit, however.[36]

Still, Vidor had to admit that Selznick was right. With all of the disagreements and differences of opinion, *Duel in the Sun* was one of the biggest box-office attractions of all time.[37]

Lillian was nominated for a best supporting actress Oscar. She lost to Anne Baxter.

Actress Constance Collier suggested to Lillian that she try out for the role of Roxanne opposite Jose Ferrer in *Cyrano de Bergerac*.[38] Lillian instead decided in favor of playing Katrina Ivanna, the second wife of Marmeladov (a poor government clerk who drinks), in *Crime and Punishment*. A British success of the previous season the play was based on the classic Dostoyefsky novel.

John Gielgud would play the dual-natured Raskolnikov, the student who believes he is superior enough to commit murder and rise above moral law. He would be repeating the role he had played previously in London and he would be performing with Lillian. They had last worked together in *Hamlet* in 1936.[39]

The Rodney Ackland dramatization of *Crime and Punishment* was set for a December 1947 opening. Boris Marshalove would be working with Lillian at the end of the summer.[40]

To provide summer income, Lillian signed an engagement to play in stock house. Touring with her was Mary MacArthur, the teen-aged daughter of actress Helen Hayes. The vehicle was Noel Coward's *The Marquise*, which was set in eighteenth century France and offered good roles for an older woman and a young girl.[41]

The play had but two productions on record: the original 1926 London production starring Marie Tempest (for whom the play was written),[42] and an American production the following year starring Billie Burke.[43]

Every literature student knew *Crime and Punishment*. The Russian novel had never gone out of international print since its original serialization in 1866. Dramatizing a classic was nothing new to the theatre. In the twenties there had been two adaptations of Dostoyefsky's *The Brothers Karamazov*: one in Russian with the Moscow Art Players (1923),[44] and an English version (1927) with Alfred Lunt and Edward G. Robinson.[45]

Originally, it was believed that Lillian had been signed to act the role of Sonia, the 18-year-old girl who became a prostitute. Lillian knew that she didn't look 18 years old and requested the role of Katerina, who was 30 and married with 3 children. It was a role Edith Evans had done in London.[46]

Crime and Punishment, presented in London and directed by Anthony Quayle, was the most popular play of the season. The production in New York would star John Gielgud, but it would be directed by Theodore Komisarjevsky.

When the new director began to work on the play, he quarreled about Ackland's adaptation during the early weeks of rehearsal. Only one week was left to bring everything into shape for the December 22 opening.[47]

What the audience saw at the National theatre on December 22 was a large cast in a visually overwhelming drama. John Gielgud's Raskolnikov was "superbly acted." Lillian's Katerina "reveals once more her remarkable range as an actress."[48]

The production had its problems. A play is not a novel. "Two pound Russian novels cannot be serviceable eight ounce dramas."[49] Dostoyefsky can be overwhelming on any level, page or stage. Many of the individual scenes were very exciting. What was lacking was a company trained in a uniform manner. *Crime and Punishment* was more of an actor's holiday. The play needed a finality.[50]

Costume designer Lester Polakov remembered *Crime and Punishment* years later:

> It [*Crime and Punishment*] wasn't the success we had hoped for. It was a big success in England. They've always liked literary plays. John Gielgud coming over here, we thought, was a bonus.
>
> Working with Lillian Gish was a real treat. She was line perfect from the first day of rehearsal, and she continued to work very hard.
>
> She was very friendly, but she was all business. She gave everything to the play.
>
> I remember we had some bad weather: blizzards and snow, and public transportation was limited. But the show went on, and Lillian was able to trudge through the streets to the theatre, like an *Orphan of the Storm*.
>
> Her performance was part of a very wonderful ensemble: Sanford Meisner,

Dolly Haas, Alexander Scourby, Marian Seldes ... Lillian was part of the company, unlike Judith Anderson, who thought Medea was written for her.

I don't think anybody who worked with Lillian would ever call her their buddy. Lillian was always professional. Her life existed only on the stage.[51]

Crime and Punishment closed after forty performances.[52]

Lillian returned to the summer theatre circuit in 1948 with another touring production of Noel Coward's *The Marquise*. The company was a new one, later to acquire other supporting actors as the play went from theatre to theatre.

Lillian had hoped to convince Mr. Coward that a second summer of presenting *The Marquise* would prove the play's potential for a New York run. Mr. Coward tabled the idea, telling Lillian once again that the play, no matter how well it was received, wasn't strong enough for New York. *The Marquise* was written as a vehicle for Marie Tempest. It would remain that way, on the shelves.[53]

Word reached Lillian while she was touring on July 23, 1948, that D. W. Griffith passed away earlier that morning. He hadn't made a film since 1931. Director Cecil B. DeMille was the only member of the film profession paying his respects in the small group of local people stopping at the funeral parlor. Everyone in the industry would attend the more austere service at the Hollywood Masonic Temple,[54] which would be easier to take. Strength in numbers. In true Hollywood tradition. It doesn't matter what you really thought of the deceased — or if you knew him at all. The most important question the industry will ask is, "Were you there?"

Lillian didn't attend the Masonic service. Doing the performance was more important. That was the way she was trained.

One honors one's commitments. The show must go on.

Nobody at the Masonic service wanted to produce her story of Griffith's achievement, but she knew she would always sing his praises.

Griffith and his wife had separated, and he had been hospitalized in sanitariums before their marriage ended.[55]

His last days were spent alone at the Knickerbocker Hotel, where he spoke to nobody and had no visitors. He wandered through darkened hallways without stopping. Nobody wanted to hear what he had to say anymore.

Years later, at the Motion Picture Country Home outside the Hollywood Griffith created, Donald Crisp, who had begun his career for Griffith,[56] told this biographer: "D. W. Griffith? They used him up, and then they spit him out!"[57]

In August 1948 Lillian acted in J. M. Barrie's *The Legend of Leonora*. The play drew its inspiration from another Barrie play, *What Every Woman Knows*. "The complexity of a woman's nature is beyond man's simple powers of comprehension."[58]

The story-line was simple: a bachelor, terrified of facing women, finds himself with seven different women. Each has her own personality: an unspeakable darling, a politician, a comedian, a coquette, a murderess, a mother, and a clinging woman. When the bachelor is asked to select the woman most suitable to his personality, he learns that all seven are actually the same woman, and she is a marriageable widow.[59]

In early September, Lillian was in Seattle rehearsing *Mrs. Carlyle*, an original play written for her by Professor Glenn Hughes when a phone call came from Dorothy in New York. Mother was ill. At fist the doctors thought everything was under control. Now they wanted to operate. It was appendicitis.[60]

Lillian was on the first plane bound for New York. She recalled:

> After the stroke, Mother wanted the nurse to go, but I wouldn't let her. If I had let her make the effort to walk and take care of herself, she might have recovered....[61]
>
> Dorothy stayed right beside Mother when she got sick. Dorothy was the strong one....

> I couldn't get there in time...[62]
>
> I hope I was a good daughter to my mother....[63]
>
> I'll miss Mother dear. She was my only child.[64]

Mary Robinson McConnell Gish died on September 16, 1948.[65]

CHAPTER 30

Tubes in a Box

The death of Mary Gish brought Lillian and Dorothy closer together. They were all they had left. Lillian didn't need a script to instruct her how to continue. What was most important was the work ethic. It was the way her mother had raised her, and her mother had never been wrong. Otherwise they'll hire another little girl...

She returned to Seattle in October 1948 to honor her commitment to the professor and his play. That it was a university production and not a professional one was immaterial. Lillian had given her word, and her word was always good.

Dorothy wanted to move to another apartment. The apartment she and Lillian had maintained at 444 East 57th Street was actually their mother's. Dorothy never wanted a home,[1] and there was no longer any need for extra rooms. She preferred living in hotels, where she could be served and there was someone to clean the room. Perhaps it was a reaction to the time when actors couldn't stay in hotels, because many of them would often slide down the pipe at night to avoid the morning desk clerk who would want the room fees when the show was closing.[2]

Lillian moved to an apartment building located at 430 East 57th Street, while Dorothy took a furnished hotel apartment (sitting room, bedroom and kitchenette) a few streets away at the Hotel Elysee.[3]

Lillian, who bought the East 57th Street residence and stayed there for the rest of her life, told a magazine interviewer:

> Of course, in a sense, this apartment is only a base. I travel all over the country.... I'm still a nomad at heart....
> At my mother's teas we used to have everybody: Mary Pickford, Kit [Katherine Cornell], people who knew that if they dropped by on a Sunday, mother would serve them tea and just sit and listen while the conversation went on all around her.[4]

Portrait of Jennie, Lillian's next film assignment, reunited her with Jennifer Jones and David O. Selznick. Her convent scenes were filmed at the Cloisters in New York.[5] Like Selznick's *Duel in the Sun, Portrait of Jennie* was an "over produced" film[6] made at what Selznick claimed was an "absurdly high cost."[7]

Its storyline was slight: an artist (Joseph Cotten) painting the portrait of a dead girl proceeds to fall in love with her. The film offered fine views of New York in the winter and gave Lillian a chance to commute to the location from her new apartment with a minimum of difficulty. She also avoided having to pay extra fees for a room, had the production been filmed in California. She would always be thrifty.

Although she would still hear that she had gone "high-hat" because she had defected to the East, she was never more grateful to be living in New York than in December 1948 when she received an unexpected telephone call from television producer Fred Coe, who headed *Philco Television Playhouse*.[8]

Television was still relatively new on the entertainment scene. Television was test patterns during the day, and evening newscasts, wrestling matches, roller derbies, quiz shows, and "B" westerns that no longer had any drawing power in movie theatres. Variety shows, like Milton Berle's *Texaco Star Theatre*, were just starting to develop. In 1948 there were 36 television stations broadcasting in various capacities across the United States. The boom had started.

Like her career in motion pictures, Lillian wanted to be present at the birth.

She was not totally unfamiliar with the concept of this new medium. In 1929 D. W. Griffith had travelled to Schenectady, New York to deliver a 15 minute speech on how actors like Rudolph Valentino, Mary Pickford, and Lupe Velez attained success and popularity in motion pictures. Television, Griffith believed, was the "last miracle of miracles."[9]

While Griffith understood the principles of television, he was clearly intimidated by it,[10] as he was by sound. Audiences paid to see a motion picture or to attend a stage play. Television was free. He did nothing to pursue the cultivation and development of this new medium.

Almost twenty years later, Lillian was one of the first actresses to recognize television's power and potential.

On February 6, 1949, she made her television debut on *The Philco Television Playhouse* in a 60 minute adaptation of the 1932 Broadway hit, *The Late Christopher Bean*.[11] She played an exhausted housemaid who was left a fortune because of her kindness to her employer.[12]

Years later, Lillian recalled the prevailing attitude of her fellow artist regarding this new entertainment medium:

The attitude expressed by theatre and motion picture people on the possibilities of television was not that far removed from the earliest reactions to the flickers in another time, or to radio drama.

Television was entertainment you saw on a ten inch or twelve inch black-and-white screen in your living room for nothing. It would distract people from doing their jobs, and who was going to pay the salaries of the actors? In the theatre, you sold tickets.

It wasn't much different than the radio reaction. Radio programs, like television, you also heard from a box in your living room. There were commercials, of course, but nobody thought of commercials as a way to defray expenses.

Television broadcasts, in those early days, also ran the risk of being interrupted by announcements of technical difficulties beyond our control…

How would you know if what you were doing was even being seen? How can you cover your mistakes when a camera is always right on top of you? In movies, you could shoot the scene again. What do you do when you are being seen "live"?

It took courage to appear on television in those days. It was a medium even more intimate than you realized. Your acting techniques had to be adjusted. You only had one chance, and if you made a mistake, there was nothing you could do, and you were seen by millions of people in their homes! The home audience could laugh at you, and you wouldn't be aware of it. Or they could change the program!

When Dorothy and I worked for Mr. Griffith at Biograph, the flickers were considered inferior. Now television was considered inferior.

What was this "television" anyway? Tubes in a box!

Stuart, both Dorothy and I went into television for the same reason our mother took us to Biograph: to earn a living. Nobody ever gave us handouts or supported us. Television was work. And work could create work. Even on television![13]

On March 30, 1049, *Portrait of Jennie* opened at New York's Rivoli theatre. A visual triumph with its varying color, sepia, and black-and-white images, it climaxed with a tinted green seacoast storm on an enlarged, curved, circular screen. Many now believe this was Selznick's best film.[14]

Such was not the initial critical reaction.

Wrote film critic Bosley Crowther of *The New York Times*: "Assuming you want to see it … we advise you to take a mental recess and have some cotton ready to stuff in your ears."[15]

Lillian's performance was "substantially the same as the whole thing, which is deficient and disappointing in the extreme."[16]

Lillian would always extol the "timeless" quality of *Portrait of Jennie*. But the success of the film was as elusive as its subject matter.[17] *Portrait of Jennie* was only a poignant trip into fantasy.[18]

Lillian's second film for David Selznick was not a commercial success, and she would not return to the motion picture cameras for seven years.

Dorothy was always known for her quick wit and wicked sense of humor. Lillian, when she would compare her personality to that of her sister's, would always remark: "When I go to a party, the party stops. On the other hand, Dorothy *is* the party."[19]

In November 1949 Dorothy jumped at the opportunity to return to the theatre to play in Mel Dinelli's thriller, *The Man*. She had taken her turn in the classics of Ibsen, Shaw, and Gogol. Now she wanted to have fun onstage and leave the "literary theatre" for the critics and the intelligentsia. *The Man* was a vehicle that would keep her friends and audiences at the edge of their seats, and give everybody a good scare while the curtain was up. If the play succeeded, it might have an extended life for her in summer theatre, like the popular melodramas *Seven Keys to Baldpate* and *The Cat and the Canary*. A good audience pleaser was an actor's annuity.

The Man was a '50s return to the old fashioned melodrama, but it was done in modern dress. The formula was the same: someone living alone, and widowed, was suddenly thrust into a terrifying situation. In *The Man* the someone was Dorothy Gish, living alone in her country house, a middle-aged widow who hired a handyman to do some home repairs. That the handyman was a fugitive from a nearby mental home was something she would soon discover.

The play opened at the Fulton Theatre in New York on January 19, 1950. While Dorothy, "one of the theatre's most cultivated ladies,"[20] made a "very fine victim,"[21] and the play itself was ingenuous and interesting,"[22] her good performance wasn't strong enough to overcome the weakness of the writing and carry its run beyond 92 performances.[23]

Recalled agent and friend Alan Brock:

Dorothy never regretted doing *The Man*. When she went into rehearsal she said, "I've heard them laugh and weep. Now I'll hear them scream. This show is strictly harum-scarum."

There's always been a tendency on the part of some snobs and critics to lessen this type of play. It's a genre that is very predictable. But when something happens they didn't expect, they scream. Maybe they're embarrassed afterwards, so they downplay it.

In a play like *The Man*, something has to be happening all of the time. The writing has to be very tight. There can't be any lapses. Every action has to produce a more horrifying reaction.

I've seen audiences shout, "Watch out!" to the actor on the stage, and the actor has all he or she can do not to hear this and break character.

Movie audiences did this at the screen when Martin Balsam went up the stairs in Hitchcock's *Psycho*.

I was there at *The Man* when audiences during the run stamped their feet and yelled "Boo!" when Dorothy was being menaced by the crazy handyman. It was thrilling, that collective reaction, and quite scary.

Dorothy was brilliant. She played the role dead seriously. She didn't listen to the audience. She didn't allow the audience to unnerve her. She didn't give in and camp it up.

The problem with *The Man* was that it ran out of steam. Dorothy, however, didn't.[24]

For her tour of stock theatres during the summer of 1950, Lillian selected British playwright R. C. Sherriff's comedy-mystery *Miss Mabel*.[25] The play was strictly fluff about a housekeeper under suspicion of murder. It was perfect fare for the summer audiences who didn't like their theatre too heavy or demanding.[26] Sherriff was better known for his more successful anti-war play, *Journey's End*, which had a respectable Broadway run during the 1928-29 season.[27]

Produced by Joel Schenker, the play toured with a nucleus cast and used resident actors at each different theatre, much in the manner of Lillian's summer tours of 1947 and 1948 with Noel Coward's *The Marquis*.

Alexander Clark was part of the nucleus cast for the run of the play, whose engagements included bookings of a week or two in theatres in Hinsdale, Illinois; Stock-

bridge, Massachusetts; Skowhegan, Main; and the Royal Colonial Theatre in Nassau, Bahamas.

Actress Frances Tannehill, wife of actor Alexander Clark and president of the Twelfth Night Club (a society of actresses whose existence dates back to 1891), recalled the *Miss Mabel* tour and Lillian:

Lillian was always friendly and always professional. You knew from the very first day of rehearsal that *Miss Mabel* was her show and that she was carrying it. She was the star, and she was the person that audiences were coming to see.

But that doesn't mean she wasn't supportive of the rest of the actors.

She was very nice to Alex [husband-actor Alexander Clark] and me. Both of our families, Alex's and mine, had deep roots in the theatre. My grandparents ran a repertory theatre in Memphis during the Civil War, and Alex's family were touring before the twentieth century. His father was a very popular musical comedy star and comedian.

We were theatre kids, like Lillian an Dorothy. I was on the road with Florence Reed in *Purity*, and I was one of the children in Jerome Kern's *Music in the Air* on Broadway.

Alex appeared on Broadway for The Theatre Guild in *Biography* with Ina Claire, and in *Victoria Regina* with Helen Hayes. Both actresses were close friends of Lillian's.

Lillian knew to surround herself with good people who would be able to have her noticed by other good people.[28]

In the supporting cast for part of the tour was Clarence Derwent, the president of Actor's Equity and the president of the American National Theatre and Academy. He was also the establisher of the Clarence Derwent Award, whose recipients included a young Judy Holliday, Tom Ewell, and Barbara Bel Geddes. Derwent, whose

Lillian at Helen Hayes' home in Nyack, New York, with actress Frances Tannehill, 1973. Frances accompanied her husband, actor Alexander Clark, who appeared with Lillian in the 1950 summer tour of *Miss Mabel*.

career began in Weymouth, England, in 1903, came to New York to play in the first American production of George Bernard Shaw's *Major Barbara* in 1916.[29]

Frances Tannehill remembered:

Rehearsals for *Miss Mabel* went smoothly, once we learned to anticipate interruptions over which we had no control, like the noise and whistling from the trains. We had an idea of their schedule, so we could time when we were going to have our words drowned during the matinees and evening. Whoever was talking would just remain in place and not say a word until the train had passed.

Clarence [Clarence Derwent], for all of his impressive British training and background, was a very casual actor. He had a very relaxed delivery, and he didn't like to wear any makeup other than his costume.

Once, on a matinee day, he came to the theatre from a long walk in the woods just before half-hour. He put on his costume and he took his seat on a soft chair onstage as the curtain went up, which he was supposed to do. A few minutes into the performance, he fell asleep.

The audience didn't know what was happening, but those onstage, including Lillian, did. Clarence wasn't snoring. He had leaned back and closed his eyes.

Lillian looked over in his direction, and very casually, during the course of the scene, tiptoed behind the chair where Clarence was sitting. She placed her hand on his shoulder, leaned over, and blew on his neck!

She might have whispered something which only he could have heard, but Clarence opened his eyes and said his line as if the action were rehearsed!

Whether she gave him a dressing down afterwards we never knew. But he never took any morning walks on a matinee day. And he never closed his eyes in that chair for the rest of the run![30]

When the *Miss Mabel* company flew to the Bahamas to play an engagement at the Royal Colonial Theatre, Lillian made a star's demand: to allow Malcolm, her West Highland terrier who had been with her since *The Old Maid* [1936], to ride next to her on the plane.

Frances Tannehill remembered:

A reservation for two was made in Lillian's name. Seats were reserved for Miss Lillian Gish and Malcolm. Two seats. No further explanation.

On the day of departure, in walks Lillian Gish carrying Malcolm. Someone behind the counter looked quite surprised! But Lillian acted as if everything were within reason.

"Here we are," she announced, "Lillian Gish and Malcolm." And before there was any kind of response, "The seats were confirmed for the two of us."

The airline staff looked at each other and they didn't know what to say. Perhaps if Miss Gish had forgotten to bring a protective cage...

Lillian shook her head. "Two tickets were purchased. Two seats were confirmed. We are here on time. I don't understand the problem. I'll be on one seat. Malcolm will occupy the other. He was a gift to me when I toured Glasgow and the provinces. He is fully trained."

That sweet little dog was easily 15 years old, and she was holding him in her arms like a newborn baby.

Then the dog looked right into her eyes. Those big blue eyes, and she played the scene...

That Malcolm boarded with Lillian, and he sat on the seat next to hers.

Lillian got her way.[31]

Miss Mabel completed its summer tour successfully, but the play didn't come to New York. Lillian was afraid of the critical reaction to a play that didn't have very much depth. Perhaps they would fault the playwright, R. C. Sherriff, for not writing something weightier, like *Journey's End*. Summer plays fared best in summer theatres.[32]

Never one to lament any lost opportunities over a long period of time, Lillian, at the start of the 1950-51 Broadway season, rushed into rehearsal (under Peter Glenville's direction) for an October opening of John Patrick's comedy, *The Curious Savage*. John Patrick was no stranger to the Gishes. Dorothy had acted in his respectable *The Story of Mary Surratt* during the Broadway season 1946-47. Lillian wasn't the original choice for the new play. Patricia Collinge, unhappy with the play, quit after the Wilmington, Delaware pre-Broadway tryout, claiming line changes made it impossible for her to continue.[33]

The Curious Savage opened in Boston with the understudy, Marie Carroll, playing the leading role until Lillian went into the play during the second week of the engagement.[34] That she was taking over someone else's part meant nothing. In the twenties, she would gladly have assumed Margalo Gillmore or Lynn Fontanne's role in O'Neill's *Marco Millions* and *Strange Interlude*, had The Theatre Guild asked her. Lillian had last worked for The Theatre Guild eight years ago (1942) in the unsuccessful *Mr. Sycamore*. It was time to work for The Theatre Guild again. Work begets work. Even for The Theatre Guild.

In *The Curious Savage*, Lillian played an elderly lady with a philanthropic bent. Recently widowed with an inheritance of $10,000,000, she gives the money to people who wish to indulge their fantasies. Fearing she will exhaust her bank account too quickly, her three stepchildren have her committed to a mental home. There she decides the inmates are nicer than her stepchildren and more sensible than the outside world. In a court victory, she is allowed to maintain her fortune.[35]

Neither Lillian nor the author antici-

pated the negative reactions of the critics. While Richard Watts of *The New York Post* viewed her opening night performance on October 24, 1950, at the Martin Beck Theatre as "appealing," and thought the play "mildly favorable entertainment," he questioned using the mentally ill as a subject for comedy.[36]

Seemingly in agreement was Brooks Atkinson of *The New York Times*, who viewed the premise of *The Curious Savage* as an exercise in bad taste, and the poking fun at psychopathic people embarrassing.[37] Lillian's performance as a wealthy lady who is legally sane was a "trifle kittenish."[38]

The Curious Savage closed after 31 performances.[39]

As close as they could be as sisters, both Lillian and Dorothy knew that to maintain the closeness they had to live apart.

Occasionally, their differing attitudes would come to light, as reported in a *Life* magazine article of August 20, 1951.

On the motion picture *Sunset Boulevard*:

Lillian:

> A fine job of Hollywood fouling its own nest.

Dorothy:

> A fine job by Gloria Swanson.

On evaluating each other:
Lillian (cool and managerial):

> I'm Dorothy's ulcer.

Dorothy (warm and inefficient):

> I'm just a slob.[40]

Dorothy returned to face the motion picture cameras in New England as a mill-owning widow in *The Whistle at Eaton Falls*.

Filmmaker Louis de Rochemont, utilizing the documentary style that was so successful in his *The House on 92nd Street* (1945), now concentrated on a labor-management dispute in a mill town.

Unfortunately, the film's intentions were better than the results.[41]

1952: With no prospects of work that would engender any newspaper or magazine publicity, Lillian began to make an occasion out of being seen at restaurants, the theatre, and the opera. No matter where she was, a camera could always record the event. Being seen was now of foremost importance. It would give the public the opportunity to see her as she saw herself: aware, disciplined, and an actress proud of her profession.[42]

Mr. Griffith would have given his approval. She was selling the product to the public. This time, it wasn't a Griffith film. It was herself.

When she was under contract in her MGM period, she had no regular agent. Work was gotten simply by telephoning Adolph Zukor, Joseph Schenck, or Louis B. Mayer, and playing one executive against the other in the hopes of a better offer.[43]

Those days, she now realized, were gone forever. Now she had to wait for the telephone to ring.

The year 1952 marked her 40th year in motion pictures. It was like the beginning, when she was hopeful. She was on the verge of 60.

In February she spoke to an audience of 98 women and two men at the cosmopolitan Club of New York on behalf of the New York Women's League for Animals. Both she and Dorothy, she told the audience, were dog lovers and had had many dogs over the years. Some were gifts from Mary Pickford, another dog lover.

Dogs, Lillian advised the audience, should be bathed twice a year. To keep their bloodstream clear, a pinch of Epsom salts should be placed in their drinking water.[44]

Both Lillian and Dorothy hoped that Truman Capote's influence would help them land the roles of the Talbo sisters, Dolly and Verena, in his stage adaptation of his novel, *The Grass Harp*. Director Robert Lewis refused to listen to him.[45]

The Grass Harp opened on March 27 and closed after 36 performances. Capote always believed that the presence of Lillian and Dorothy would have extended the run of the play.[46]

When a telephone call came from CBS television with an opportunity to play famed American primitive painter Grandma Moses on a March 28 broadcast of the *Schlitz Playhouse*, Lillian was grateful. It was her first job in two years.[47]

Lillian remembered Grandma Moses as

> a very simple country woman. Not very worldly. She had that rural wisdom that comes with living near the soil. If she were a writer, I would think she would have been a female Robert Frost.
>
> She didn't understand all of the attention, and thought New York was all noise and crowds, and how could anyone live here?
>
> We spoke about our families, and how they lived and struggled just to survive...
>
> I told her all about Mother, and what she had done for us. She thought that was beautiful. She saw beauty all around her. Even in New York.
>
> She gave me one of her paintings.[48]

1953: Later it would be called The Golden Age of Television. During their inception they were merely television plays: thirty, sixty, or ninety minute weekly dramas created specifically for the new medium by a cadre of writers willing to have their efforts televised only once (and who would not balk too loudly at the commercials that sometimes destroyed the mood between the acts).

Among these new dramatists was Horton Foote, whose *A Trip to Bountiful*, directed by Fred Coe and presented on NBC's *Goodyear Television Playhouse* on March 1, would later have other incarnations beyond the small screen in the living room. When first seen, the president of CBS had telephoned the president of NBC to say that television had finally come of age.[49] An alliance, not totally congruent, had been formed between television and the theatre. The talents of Lillian Gish, the sensitive words of Horton Foote, and the intimacy of the small screen were at one.[50]

A Trip to Bountiful offered Lillian the chance to play Mrs. Carrie Watts, an old woman who wants to return to the small town of her past because she can no longer live with her passive son and domineering daughter-in-law in their cramped city apartment. Carrie is fully aware that she left her small town because of the changing times that hastened its decay, but that is of little matter. It was in the small town of Bountiful that she once had her own identity.

During her journey she meets a war bride (Eva Marie Saint), who becomes her temporary companion. When she reaches the area where Bountiful once existed, she sees only woodland. Her beloved Bountiful is no longer there, but this doesn't phase her. In trying to recapture her past she has regained her personal worth, and she can face her future without any fears.

A Trip to Bountiful was the first television film to be included in the archives of New York's Museum of Modern Art.[51]

During the last week of the Summer, *A Trip to Bountiful*, now a full length play in three acts, was presented as one of the final offerings of a Connecticut summer stock theatre, the Westport Country Playhouse, prior to its New York opening in November under the auspices of The Theatre Guild and Fred Coe.

Playwright and Arthur Sullivan biographer John Wolfson was in the opening night audience in Westport.

Decades later he still remembered that

> Lillian Gish emitted sympathy the moment you first saw her. You just wanted to get out of your seat to help her. She looked so vulnerable.
>
> One of the great moments occurred in a bus scene with Eva Marie Saint, someone she just met and befriended. You were so happy that someone, a total stranger, took time to talk to the old lady. When Eva Marie Saint's character left and Lillian waved her hand in this gesture of acknowledgment, the audience broke into applause. I can still close my eyes and relive that moment.
>
> There was another heart-wrenching moment when Lillian kept saying "Bountiful! Bountiful!" over and over again when you didn't think she was ever going to get there. The audience was weeping. She knew how to play that scene brilliantly! Such power! And only saying that one word: Bountiful!
>
> When she went to pieces, you just went with her.[52]

Eva Marie Saint stayed with *A Trip to Bountiful* from its original television production and the subsequent Westport engagement to make her Broadway debut with the play on November 4, 1953, at Henry Miller's Theatre.

At a tribute given to Lillian Gish by the American Film Institute on March 1, 1984, at the Beverly Hilton in Beverly Hills, California, Eva Marie Saint told the capacity audience of Lillian's generosity. She had just finished the bus scene with Miss Gish and had exited, when

> I heard thunderous applause. I wondered, "What had I done?" I asked the stage manager, and he answered, she [Lillian Gish] raises her hand and holds her back to the audience.

Miss Gish had given the scene to the Broadway newcomer.

While *Christian Science Monitor* critic John Beaufort hailed Lillian's performance as "one of those rare performances that touch at the heart of human existence,"[53] Brooks Atkinson of *The New York Times* noted

> that [Lillian's performance] does not make a very substantial play for a whole evening.
> ...*The Trip to Bountiful* is Miss Gish's play.
> The theatre has a whole bagful of tricks for describing old ladies. But Miss Gish never uses any of them.... [She] is at the peak of her career in the leading part. It is a triumph of skill and art.[54]

Although decades later (in 1985) *A Trip to Bountiful* earned success as a motion picture with Geraldine Page, the original Broadway production starring Lillian Gish closed after only 39 performances.[55]

Lillian had received the most professionally and personally gratifying reviews of her theatrical career. She had appeared under the auspices of The Theatre Guild a second time. That neither *Mr. Sycamore* nor *A Trip to Bountiful* were commercial hits was no fault of hers.

What she didn't realize was that *A Trip to Bountiful* would be the last New York play in which she played the leading role. Her future New York stage roles would be supporting ones.

CHAPTER 31

The "Comeback"

Lillian Gish? One of the toughest women I ever met. Why do you think she lasted so long?

— Robert Mitchum
Conversation with author (1975)

1954: The fragility of Dorothy's health precluded Lillian's plans of considering any stage assignments early in the new year. The unanticipated short run of *A Trip to Bountiful* may have been a blessing, as Dorothy had to be hospitalized for an undisclosed illness. Among Lillian's friends, rumors of Dorothy's diagnosis, never mentioned to them, included chronic ulcers and bouts of alcoholism and depression. All of these illnesses were the result of Louis Calhern's recent marriage.

To those brave enough to inquire, a close-mouthed Lillian gave the same statement: "She [Dorothy] is the only person left whom I have to take care of."[1]

On February 22, Lillian received an honorary Doctor of Fine Arts degree at Rollins College in Winter Park, Florida.[2]

Seeing no reason for Dorothy to remain home, Lillian took her to the spa at Baden-Baden. Having watched over their mother for so many years, having Dorothy as a companion would be a most welcome change. In Germany they would be away from the prying questions of reporters and the flashing lights of their cameras. She and Dorothy had visited Baden-Baden so many

times they were practically regarded as residents rather than tourists. Their privacy had been respected, and the local inhabitants knew how to maintain a respectful distance. Their presence at restaurants only occasionally would turn a head or raise an eyebrow.

On the ship headed for New York at the end of their stay they saw Rita Hayworth's latest film, *Salome*, for which Lillian had no comment.

Regarding the top talents of 1954, she told reporters she most admired "Disney, the only one who even touches Griffith in conception and freshness. *Cinerama* is something special, too. I've seen it three times… And Olivier's *Henry V.*"[3]

She found herself back in Hollywood in May, not employed in front of the cameras. Now she was a roving ambassadress speaking for Mary Pickford on behalf of the 35th anniversary of United Artists, the studio Mary founded in 1919 with D. W. Griffith and Charlie Chaplin in an effort to realize greater profits from their films. That Lillian happened to be in Griffith's moneymakers was just a matter of luck. Lillian was more than happy to recall those halcyon days to whoever would listen, but now she was primarily a stage person.[4]

Former film actress Lillian Gish was unaware that theatrical producer Paul (*The Caine Mutiny Court Martial, Don Juan in Hell, John Brown's Body*) Gregory, during the summer of 1953, had acquired the film rights to Davis Grubb's Southern Gothic novel, *The Night of the Hunter*, a story of Good and Evil involving a fake evangelist, orphaned children, and hidden money in a swampland.

Charles Laughton, who had directed Gregory's *Court Martial* production in Santa Barbara, California, prior to its successful Broadway run, was asked to direct the filming of the Grubb novel. It would mark Laughton's film directing debut.

Laughton had definite ideas about casting. For the role of the children's strong-willed spinster protectress, Rachel Cooper, Laughton naturally envisioned his wife, actress Elsa Lanchester.

Elsa Lanchester, for reasons unknown to him, declined the role, suggesting that Lillian Gish play it.[5]

Lillian Gish?

Fragile, wistful Lillian Gish?

A doubtful Charles immediately flew to New York for the express purpose of seeing all of Lillian's films, the one-and two-reelers, and the silent features she made for D. W. Griffith, from the very first *An Unseen Enemy* (1912) to the 1922 *Orphans of the Storm*.[6] Although Lillian was well aware that Laughton, cinematographer Stanley Cortez, and screenwriter James Agee were at the Museum of Modern Art almost every day watching specific sequences over and over again, she felt it wise not to be present unless her presence was requested. If her performances could not speak for themselves after all of these years, being in the seat next to them would not do anything to enhance what was being shown on the screen. Her filmwork had to speak for itself. Otherwise it was worthless.[7]

Watching film after film, Laughton was more than aware of the immediacy of Lillian's responses to the requirements of Griffith's direction without resorting to superfluous gestures or trickery. Her work had a purity and an innocence that transcended the limitations of the camera.

When he viewed the classic ice floe sequence in *Way Down East*, his response was radically different from others who saw Lillian as a victim in another melodramatic situation.

How could anybody have viewed Lillian as a victim? Didn't they see that she overcame every obstacle that was placed in her path? A victim would have been quickly defeated.

Lillian wasn't a victim. She was a damsel in distress who fought back. Lillian didn't go over the falls. She was a survivor![8] Silent films. Sound films. The legitimate theatre. Radio. Television. He wanted Lillian to play Rachel Cooper, the guardian of the orphaned children in *The Night of the Hunter*.

Both Charles Laughton and James Agee were great admirers of the Griffith silent films, particularly the way they showcased the talents of Lillian Gish. Griffith's films, viewed after an interval of more than thirty years, still "made you sit up in your chair in anticipation of what was coming."[9]

Agee's eulogy, written immediately after Griffith's death, perhaps said it all: "There is not a man working in movies, or a man who cares for them, who does not owe Griffith more than he owes anybody else."[10]

In fashioning a script for *The Night of the Hunter*, both Laughton and Agee agreed to remove the Depression Era setting and strive for a Griffith-type pervasion: timeless, with long white fences and tall churches.[11] The film opening with Lillian Gish reading to the children could suggest a Mother Goose speaking to her captive flock.[12]

Film critic William K. Everson explained the brilliance of the opening scene with Lillian Gish:

> The opening scene, in addition to establishing the tone necessary to a Southern Gothic melodrama, shattered any pre-conceived notions or memories you ever had of a Lillian Gish you might have seen in her Griffith days. She wasn't being beatific.
>
> Director Charles Laughton was consciously forcing the fifties audience, who had been familiar with her earlier work, to look at her in a different light. The sequence is dreamlike, with quite a lot of underlying suspense and mood shifts.
>
> The Bible, always a source of comfort in motion pictures, is now, with the use of night sounds, contributing to the slowly mounting tension. You know, with the night sounds that are always present, something bizarre is going to happen.[13]

Laughton's perfect casting resembled a "tapestry": Lillian Gish, Robert Mitchum, Shelley Winters, Evelyn Varden, James Gleason. If one thread were pulled, everything would unravel.[14]

The Night of the Hunter was Laughton's film directorial debut. There could be no loose ends. Everything had to be tightly structured. Laughton knew from his experience with *Galileo* in the theatre that he could not act and direct at the same time. Joe Losey, following Laughton's dictations, was given credit as "director."

For *The Night of the Hunter*, Laughton knew he would be on his own. There would be no assistant to whom he could voice his demands. If he wanted to continue as a film director there could be no mistakes.[15]

Although James Agee was given full credit as screenwriter, what eventually became the finished product was written by Charles Laughton. Agee, in one of his drunken disagreements with Laughton had returned to Paul Gregory's Santa Monica home, where he proceeded to consume even more alcohol. There he remained on the *floor*—for two weeks, unable to do any kind of writing or rewriting.

After Agee was moved to a motel, Laughton completed the screenplay. Agee was paid the agreed upon sum of $30,000, but what he had submitted was never examined or considered. Agee later claimed that Laughton refused to have any dealings with him, but Laughton, in rebuttal, answered that Agee was never in any approachable condition.

The completed script was sent to Lillian, who immediately accepted.[16]

Lillian Gish, an almost sober James Agee, and Charles Laughton[17] met for afternoon tea at the Algonquin Hotel in New York.[18] In the mid-twenties the Algonquin was the meeting place of the Algonquin Round Table, a publicly secret club of prominent literary personalities of the day: Marc Connelly, George S. Kaufman, Alexander Woollcott, Edna Ferber, Dorothy Parker, Peggy Wood, Anita Loos, Robert E. Sherwood, and Louis Bromfield. Over lunch, they would exchange caustic opinions on literary and theatrical matters, issues of the day, and problems with their works-in-progress. Outsiders, like Lillian Gish (with George Jean Nathan),[19] Margalo Gillmore, Aileen Pringle, and Katherine Cornell were permitted to join.[20] A receptive audience was always needed.

While James Agee may not have recognized everyone's name, their significance was not lost on Charles Laughton. Agee, during the tea meeting, sat in silence, having been drinking since the orders were placed. Soon he was too drunk to contribute anything of importance.[21]

Laughton, always the consummate gentleman, was being professionally courteous to Agee, who would be receiving full credit as screenwriter.

Lillian, well aware of who comprised the Algonquin Round Table, was able to talk to Laughton of literary matters, hoping that Agee might open his eyes and add a word or two. There was no need for Lillian to prove her intelligence by literary namedropping, but she didn't want to be regarded as a visiting novelty like Gloria Swanson, whose *Sunset Boulevard* did not create an anticipated second career in films.

Lillian, who made her film debut in 1912, didn't want the press to see her return to the cameras as the polishing of an antique to compete with the latest fad.

She recalled the Algonquin tea with James Agee and Charles Laughton.

> He [Charles Laughton] said he wanted to meet with us individually before we began filming, because he wanted to talk about the film and get our opinions. He also wanted us to hear his insights before we were an ensemble.
>
> With any first meeting in professional circumstances, and this Algonquin tea was certainly professional, you have a certain uneasiness. You just try not to show it.
>
> It happened when we had our first meeting with Guthrie McClintic, who had never directed Shakespeare, and there he was: directing Sir John Gielgud in *Hamlet*.
>
> I could sense Charles Laughton's nervousness. He had never directed a film.
>
> Listening to Charles was like listening to Mr. Griffith, a man whose films he deeply admired, and had rediscovered them when he saw them again. Mr. Griffith would have meetings, too, to show the actors what he wanted them to do when he began shooting.
>
> Poor James Agee sat at the table in absolute silence. He said absolutely nothing. No comments. No interruptions.
>
> Charles was doing a monologue of ideas, because I was quiet, too. He was

> so nervous, and I could do nothing to calm him, because to do that would have meant I knew he was nervous.
>
> We're all a little bit like that. It's a matter of knowing that everybody started the same way. You have to cover your insecurities. Act confidently!
>
> Charles was so honest!
>
> I knew what he was talking about, but poor James simply kept that glass in front of his mouth and kept drinking. When it was empty, he'd signal the waiter for another refill. Charles and I continued talking as if James Agee weren't with us.
>
> I didn't know about the script problems until much later.[22]

Shooting began on September 14, 1954.[23] Lillian enjoyed being directed by Charles Laughton, whose approach to every scene was thoughtful and methodical in the Griffith manner. Her portrayal of Rachel Cooper, a character who could be "tough and saintly, forbidding and adorable," was "flawless."[24]

Discussing Laughton's directorial methods to a reporter from *The New York Times,* she recalled years later:

> He [Charles Laughton] wanted me to do a dozen takes of one scene. I kept pitching my acting higher and higher and then I said, "Is that what you want?" Laughton said, "The first take was fine. I just wanted to see how many different ways you could do it."[25]

To questions from this biographer concerning the presence of, or any problems with, James Agee on the set of *The Night of the Hunter,* Miss Gish answered:

> I really don't remember. I never had any dealings with him. All of my direction would always come from Charles Laughton.
>
> James Agee was a sick man. If he were present, it wouldn't have made many difference to me. It wasn't James Agee's set.

As Rachel Cooper in *The Night of the Hunter* (1955, United Artists, directed by Charles Laughton). "A film that was unappreciated, but has grown in stature over the years," Lillian observed. "Sad that Charles Laughton was not given more films to direct."

He had demanded too much of himself, like all great artists, but he was already dying. We didn't know it.

He just wasn't able to turn out the material when it had to be done. Ultimately that is what any writer has to do: turn out the material.

O'Neill [Eugene O'Neill] could do it. Scott Fitzgerald could do it. James Agee couldn't — after being trapped so long in the bottle.

He died a few months later [May 16, 1955], but I wasn't surprised. Just saddened. The film hadn't opened yet.

I'm sorry he couldn't pull himself together, and we didn't develop a friendship. I read his published letters. What a gifted man.

A few years later [1961] I appeared on Broadway in a dramatization by Tad Mosel of James Agee's *A Death in the Family*. The play was called *All the Way Home*.

The novel was also unfinished. He was working on it.

Sometimes you don't know what to say about artists. You can only admire their work and wonder how they created it, or what inner desire made them play so recklessly with their lives.

With James Agee, his life was his tragedy, and his tragedy was his life.

What can be salvaged from it is art. Sometimes...[26]

Producer and friend John Houseman (who always maintained that Hollywood never used Lillian's talents correctly since the demise of the silent film era) put forth Lillian's name for the role of Victoria Inch, an autocratic hospital administrator, in MGM's *The Cobweb*, a dramatic film based on playwright William Gibson's first and only novel (inspired by his wife's long stay working with the Menninger Clinic staff). The studio acquired the rights for $54,000 after the book's 1954 publication. Big plans were made to utilize color and the Cinemascope process for this non-musical. Directing this ambitious all-star film, whose cast would include (in addition to Lillian) Richard Widmark, Gloria Grahame, Lauren Bacall, Charles Boyer, and Broadway newcomer John Kerr, was veteran Vincent Minnelli.[27]

Houseman's previous suggestion to utilize Lillian in *Miss Susie Slagle's* (produced at Paramount in 1945) resulted in a pleasant enough programmer, but it failed to eradicate Lillian's Griffith/ice floe image and make her an American Mrs. Chips.[28]

Filming *The Cobweb* would begin in early December and would last for approximately seven weeks.[29]

Set on the grounds of The Castle, a private psychiatric hospital based on the Austin Riggs Center in the Berkshires,[30] *The Cobweb* was a "Grand Hotel in a loony bin,"[31] where the patients were encouraged to pursue their individual creative dispositions, and were of sounder minds than the doctors and other members of the administrative staff.

The film's drama centered on two dallying head doctors (Richard Widmark and Lauren Bacall) and the problems of choosing suitable new drapes for the library. Indeed, the disturbed were looking after the disturbed.

The Cobweb, Lillian would tell Anita Loos, was her "comeback"[32] to the studio where she had last worked in 1928 and, by mutual agreement, had terminated her contract at the end of the silent era. That she was returning, almost three decades later, represented a personal victory. She had triumphed over the then reigning executives who thought her box-office appeal could be increased if a studio-arranged scandal could coincide with the releases of *The Enemy* and *The Wind*, which didn't receive good reviews.

Metro Goldwyn Mayer wasn't the same studio in 1954 that it had been in 1928. True, it still occupied 167 acres in Culver City, and still had executive buildings, star bungalows, a private zoo, schoolhouse, hospital, and park,[33] but the era had changed. After Lillian had gone, they had lost Garbo. Thalberg had died. And Louis B. Mayer, the last of the old guard, would soon be deemed useless, and phased out.

Lillian was over 60. Her return brought no fanfare (such as there had been when she had begun her first employment at the studio in King Vidor's *La Bohème* in 1926). Hollywood had changed, and her Hollywood had especially changed. She wouldn't have script approval. She wouldn't have cast approval. She wouldn't have director approval. In 1954 she was just another studio player, which she had been at the time she began working for Griffith at Biograph in 1912. Now she was an older studio player. Her career had come full circle.

She smiled at the new younger executives who would be sitting and watching her dailies. Would they know who she was? It was a new regime, but she would always be the professional.

1955: Lillian returned to New York in March. Neither *The Night of the Hunter* nor *The Cobweb* had been released. She knew it wasn't wise to remain out of the public eye after her recent return to Hollywood. If neither studio would send any pre-release publicity to the newspapers, she would create her own. In this instance she would be the product.

She spoke at a Columbia University Student Council Conference at the Low Memorial Library on March 27. Her subject was the necessity for creating a "Ministry of Fine Arts" in the President's Cabinet

or some Court of Appeals for the creative arts in Washington.... Dogs get blue ribbons, heroes get iron crosses. Hemingway writes a fine book like *The Old Man and the Sea*, and he goes to Scandinavia to get a prize for it.[34]

Although the newly created post would be government supported, Lillian continued, it was also to be understood that it would not be subject to any government scrutiny or censorship.[35]

The Cobweb opened at New York's Loew's State on August 5.[36] Although it was conceded that the film had fine production values and the sincerest of intentions to present an honest portrayal of the patients and staff at a psychiatric clinic, the entertainment appeal was considered too narrow for any chance of a commercial success.[37] No matter the use of Cinemascope, color, and the plush look created by director Vincent Minnelli, *The Cobweb* was little more than a "shrill and slightly horrifying peep at a streamlined isolated rest home"[38]—despite the all-star cast.

The performance of Lillian Gish as the "abominably tempered spinster auditor was neither panned nor praised by Bosley Crowther, reviewing the film for *The New York Times*. She was part of the ensemble, only a little meaner.[39]

It remained for writer Lawrence J. Quirk to single out Lillian's performance as "coming off best ... forceful, authoritative, no nonsense, cynical."[40]

The Night of the Hunter opened in New York at the Mayfair Theatre on September 29.[41] Like Lillian's 1949 *Portrait of Jennie*, time and a reevaluation has been kinder to the film, bestowing upon it a cult-like status. While a motion picture's initial success depends on the first box-office returns, its artistic worth requires additional viewings at much later dates. Great operas at their original premieres are often failures and are frequently dismissed or panned. So it can occur with some motion pictures. A cult status depends on a group of devotees who will constantly discuss the film's worth. The values they will find in a motion picture are often overlooked by mainstream critics.

The Night of the Hunter was an attempt to refashion the Southern Gothic genre: to add something to the standard formula of abandoned children in the clutches of a terrorizing monster. The Grubb novel was a morality play of Good versus Evil: of innocent, orphaned children held in the grip of a fake evangelist preacher who is after hidden money that was secreted by their now dead father.

Director Charles Laughton magnified the horror of the novel's rural atmosphere, concentrating on the ignorance and sometimes ugliness of small-town life when it is so far away from regular human existence. His debut film is a series of stark visual images.

What went wrong with the film, wrote critic Bosley Crowther, was Laughton's departure from the terror he strove so hard to establish in the early sections. After the children have managed to escape from the menacing preacher to find shelter in the home of "sweet, wispy" protectress Lillian Gish, the viewer knows the ending is not far away. The children will be safe and, "God bless them, will endure."[42]

Because general audiences did not flock to see *The Night of the Hunter* when it was originally released, it wasn't a commercial success.[43] While some sequences seemed to depart from the theme of the film, everything was resolved at its conclusion. Credit director Charles Laughton with giving the production a form.[44]

Why did it take "ten years, fifteen, twenty,"[45] to consider *The Night of the Hunter* an important film, one that would be studied in university film courses?

Film critic and teacher William K. Everson explained to a group of cinema history students at New York University:

> *The Night of the Hunter* owes its importance to film students and cultists, who saw it as more than your general horror film programmer.

It's probably one of the few films that will introduce a silent film actress to generations of people who never saw a silent film.

Its cult status is probably due to the excellent combination of poetic visuals and Charles Laughton's skillful manipulation of the book's Gothic narrative.

Some of Laughton's imagery is blatantly derivative of the best of D. W. Griffith and Erich Von Stroheim. Laughton knew more than most about the potential of silent film. He adored both Von Stroheim and Griffith.

What he rediscovered when he watched their films in privacy in one of the screening rooms of The Museum of Modern Art was how Lillian's presence and acting ability under Griffith's direction made those films so successful that you wanted to view them again. You always found something new. Lillian's Griffith silent film work spoke.

The impact of *The Night of the Hunter* didn't depend on language. Laughton was a long-established stage actor, and he knew he was directing a film, not a play.

A film is pictures, moving pictures. You tell your story in visuals. And Laughton knew that was what Griffith and Von Stroheim did. The camera was your voice. Your eyes heard what the camera revealed.

Laughton also wisely used Robert Mitchum in a definite Von Stroheim type characterization. Mitchum was the man you love to hate. He was so thoroughly malevolent that young audiences discovered a very sexually appealing heavy whose screen presence in the later *Cape Fear* made them react with a mixture of fear and glee. Mitchum's evil was a delicious evil.

I know Lillian [Gish] told me she felt Laughton didn't want to push Mitchum too far, because he didn't want other producers to see him only as a criminal type. Laughton knew something about being typed, having played Captain Bligh in *Mutiny on the*

Bounty and always being imitated by nightclub comedians for a long time afterwards.

Both Mitchum and Laughton were rebels, but they were different types of rebels, and they instinctively knew how to give each other space. If pressured, Mitchum's character would have lapsed into caricature and possibly destroyed the film's very delicate balance.

It didn't do well at the box office, because audiences had pre-conceived notions of a Mitchum type: the trenchcoat tough guy, the cowboy drifter, the soldier. His character in *The Night of the Hunter* wasn't a personality. He's doing good solid acting in a character he's never had to play.

The Night of the Hunter isn't Lillian's picture, but she more than holds her own as a tough backwoods type. She, too, wasn't playing her personality from the silent film era.

It might have been too much for general audiences used to predicting what the film was about on the basis of the actors' names.

The Night of the Hunter wasn't a moneymaker, and Laughton never directed another film. Given a second chance, he could have made a name for himself behind the camera.

You only get one chance in Hollywood.

The Night of the Hunter showed audiences another side of Lillian's acting ability.

She wanted another chance, too.[46]

Work came — but in television. On October 19 Lillian appeared on NBC's *Kraft Television Theatre* in a production of Paul Crabtree's *I, Mrs. Bibb*. Lillian played Mrs. Bibb, a senator's widow who assumes his office and learns, moments before her first televised appearance in her new capacity, of her late husband's possible involvement in a bribery scandal.

Television reviewer Jack Gould, writing for *The New York Times*, praised Lillian's performance as "gripping in its simple intensity [that] ... lifted the drama beyond the commonplace."[47]

The drama itself did not fare so well. When, at the end, it was revealed that the deceased senator was blameless, and the mistake had been made by a secretary who wasn't in total control of her senses, what "would have been a stimulating play on morality in politics [was turned] into a trite whodunit."[48]

Lillian's complexion, which had been the envy of Griffith contemporary Miriam Cooper during the shooting of the 1915 epic *The Birth of a Nation*,[49] was extolled in print 40 years later by Lydia Lane of *The Brooklyn Eagle* on December 12, six days after Lillian's appearance on a *Playhouse 90* dramatization of part three of William Faulkner's *The Sound and the Fury*. Beauty within, she told the interviewer, was the necessary ingredient for making the face lively. What she had mastered during her Griffith days, she was continuing to uphold.[50]

1956: The work in television continued. Although she hadn't owned a television set when she made her debut in *The Late Christopher Bean* on the *Philco Television Playhouse* in 1949, she immediately bought a set after "waitresses and cab drivers" during the days that followed told her they had seen the program. Television, because it came into one's home, had an even greater potential than films.[51]

Coming from the theatre, where one worked "live," she naturally gave unbridled support to "live" television:

> I don't like filmed TV. When it's on film, I turn it off. A film is a film, and it's kind of embalmed. If I want to see a film, I believe in seeing it in a theatre. But when it comes to live TV, I'm an addict.[52]

Lillian's long interest in Abraham Lincoln and his wife may have been the reason she was chosen to play Mrs. Lincoln in the dramatization of Jim Bishop's best-seller, *The Day Lincoln Was Shot*, on CBS's *Ford Star Jubilee* on February 11. The network had paid $600,000 for the rights, a record-high sum at the time.[53] Raymond Massey, who had immortalized himself as Lincoln in Robert E. Sherwood's Pulitzer Prize–winning play *Abe Lincoln in Illinois*, a hit during the 1938-39 season,[54] was once again portraying the president. John Wilkes Booth was being played by Jack Lemmon. Charles Laughton, who wasn't very solid financially in the wake of the failure of *The Night of the Hunter*, was hired to narrate and give the presentation a sense of solidity.[55]

Lillian, who had played many ladies in fact and fiction, had never recreated Mary Lincoln.

She had definite ideas about her character:

> I know she [Mary Lincoln] was a lady who went mad because of grief. By the time I do her I hope I'll know as much as I need to know about her. When you do anyone well-known or authentic, you're torn between making her as well as she should be, or as you'd like her to be.[56]

Rehearsals for the February 11 "live" broadcast went smoothly until Jack Lemmon, playing John Wilkes Booth, suffered a sprained ankle in a dress rehearsal leaping from the Presidential Box to the stage, ten feet below. History was repeating itself, for the real John Wilkes Booth also suffered a similar sprain when he leapt to the stage moments after assassinating President Lincoln on April 14, 1865.

The telecast, it was announced, would go on, but the leap would not be repeated.[57]

The Day Lincoln Was Shot was a heroic attempt to compress 24 hours and 22 minutes into the limitations of television's allotted 90 minutes. Even though the viewing audience knew the outcome of the events that took place on April 14, there were still moments of genuine suspense.

What was most disconcerting to television critic Jack Gould were the commercial interruptions which tended to break the mood of the drama. To insert a commercial as John Wilkes Booth is approaching the Presidential Box prior to the assassination demonstrated a complete lack of dramatic awareness.

Lillian's domineering Mary Lincoln may have been historically accurate, but on the home screen her emotions during Lincoln's deathbed scene were too overwhelming.[58]

Still interested in the creation of a Fine Arts Commission, Lillian spoke at an April 15 session at the United States Court House at New York's Foley Square, called by Senator Herbert H. Lehman. Hoping to be forgiven for "being greedy," she also coyly requested "A Secretary of Fine Arts Commission in the Presidential Cabinet, a national theatre, and government assistance in the arts." Of course, she added as an aside, the government assistance would have to be "free of government control."[59]

In the spring Lillian began to give some thought to the upcoming summer and how it would be spent. Although Dorothy had played Lillian's screen role in a television production of *Miss Susie Slagle's* the previous November (*Lux Video Theatre*, November 24, 1955),[60] Lillian felt her sister needed something to keep her busy and her mind alert. Aware that there were no relatives who could assume the burden of responsibility for their care in case of any unexpected emergency, Lillian was constantly watching her diet and exercising daily. Dorothy, who needed "five people to take care of her," as her mother said,[61] tended to be more laid back.

When they were working together at Biograph, Lillian achieved her results after much study, concentration, and sustained effort. Dorothy's results seemed to be attained with a simple snap of her fingers. Fearful that Dorothy's casual approach was beginning to affect her lifestyle (with her increasing withdrawal from any kind of socializing), Lillian suggested they do a summer tour together.

Before Dorothy could voice even the mildest of protests, Lillian had quickly pointed out the positives: They loved to tour when they were younger; this tour was only for the summer; people would gladly pay to watch them "live" onstage; and they would have some needed revenue.

What Lillian tactfully neglected to say was that she was fearful of leaving Dorothy to her own devices if she were on her own too long. With Lillian away on tour and unable to watch Dorothy, the drinking might start and possibly become dangerous. Better to have Dorothy on tour. Audiences would love to see them.[62]

Choosing a play for a summer tour requires special thought and care. Nothing too heavy or demanding would do. Summer theatre audiences were non–New York based people who lived away from the city. The play Lillian and Dorothy needed had to give audiences a good chance to see them in different costume changes, as well as providing good individual scenes for each sister *and* a few good scenes of them together.[63]

Wisely, Lillian acquired the rights to Enid Bagnold's British high comedy, *The Chalk Garden*, which had been a recent success on Broadway, achieving a run of 182 performances in a season which also presented other quality plays: *Tiger at the Gates* and *The Lark*.[64]

Both characters in *The Chalk Garden*—the socialite with the Lady Macbeth–like wish to dominate people as if they were flowers in her garden, and the ex-convict hired to supervise the socialite's

granddaughter (who likes to set fires)— were well-drawn. Originally, it was thought that Lillian and Dorothy would alternate playing the parts, but those plans were dropped.

Dorothy had problems learning her lines almost from the very beginning.[65] At first, Lillian thought Dorothy, who had not played on a stage since *The Man* (1950), was having temporary "blocks." Dorothy would stop in mid-sentence and, if Lillian were onstage, look to her for help.

Lillian, by virtue of the play's construction, could not be onstage when Dorothy suddenly went "blank." She knew something was amiss, but she couldn't identify the source of the problem. Dorothy wasn't drinking. Her lines were easy enough to say. Lillian knew Dorothy's timing well enough to sense when something was wrong. She would "feed" her the line in the same way Dorothy supplied Louis Calhern his lines during *The Great Big Doorstep* (1942).

Although Lillian had the showier role, it was important that Dorothy be able to hold the stage in her scenes. Without her lines, the scene would come to a dead stop. Dorothy had the leading role. The play revolved around her. The audience wanted to see the two of them.

Lillian took matters into her own hands before the play went on tour. She "adjusted" Dorothy's part by removing some of the sentences from the longer speeches, hoping a shorter part would be easier to learn.[66]

Somehow Dorothy managed to learn her lines, but the insecurity among the supporting cast was always there. Hopefully they would be able to steer her through the performances.

The opening night in Toronto wasn't very successful.[67] In Niagara Falls, Dorothy's mastery was still shaky.[68]

The "adjustments" Lillian made in Dorothy's role angered author Enid

Bagnold's office. No adjustments were to be made without her approval, and she threatened to stop the production.

Lillian disclosed that she was not using the printed Bagnold script. She had secured a copy of Sir John Gielgud's script for the production he directed in London. His script already contained adjustments![69]

She said to producer Charles Boeden, "You bought the rights to the play for a tour of the summer theatre. She [author Enid Bagnold] has no control over what changes we might make!"[70]

Actor Neil Fitzgerald, who toured with Lillian and Dorothy in *The Chalk Garden*, remembered Dorothy's problems. Appearing on Broadway with Jessica Tandy in Edward Albee's *All Over* in 1971, he reminisced:

> A summer theatre tour isn't as easy and casual as it looks. You play seven or eight shows from Monday to Saturday, pack the scenery after the curtain falls, and then drive, or bus, or sometimes fly, to the next place on Sunday. You have to run–through or a brushup on some scenes before you have time to unpack, settle in, and try to get some sleep. And then you open on the next night.
>
> Sometimes you may get the luxury of a free day or two, depending on the tour and the frequency of the bookings.
>
> *The Chalk Garden* wasn't your standard lightweight summer fare. This was high comedy, which is very hard to play. And it's a hard sell.
>
> The star is everything. The star is what attracts the people, not the play.
>
> Not every British play crosses the ocean well. The audience's sensibilities are different, which can often mar the play's reception. *The Chalk Garden* is a very sophisticated, literate comedy, and a very risky choice for summer theatre.
>
> Lillian, in *The Chalk Garden*, was doing double-duty. She had two responsibilities. She had to look out for the welfare of the play and do the necessary publicity for each booking, and — and this is a very important — she had to watch over Dorothy.
>
> Dorothy was having 'in and out' periods of awareness. They didn't last long — just long enough, if you're doing a scene onstage, to unnerve you.
>
> There were short moments where she'd seem to lose sight of where we were in the play. She'd shake her head, or temporarily stop speaking in mid-sentence and pretend she forgot what she was going to say. And then she'd go right on as if nothing unusual had taken place. She was enough of a pro and she knew how to cover. Sometimes.
>
> It didn't happen in every performance. Sometimes she was line perfect, and we'd breath a long sigh of relief.
>
> Everybody was polite, because of Lillian.
>
> We had some good nights, after Lillian rehearsed alone. The play was able to sail somewhat smoothly.
>
> Still, there were some potentially dangerous voyages...[71]

The final engagement of *The Chalk Garden* took place at Millburn, New Jersey's Paper Mill Playhouse. Frank Carrington, the theatre's producer, took advantage of his status and played one of the minor roles.

Laughingly, he recalled the assignment:

> It was one of the great joys of my life, just to be on the same stage with Lillian and Dorothy Gish.
>
> It was a small role. I had to serve something in a formal manner, and then bow and leave.
>
> It wasn't listed in the program. On their tour it would have been done by a young actor from the theatre where they were playing.
>
> I wanted to do it. And the audience, of course, loved it. And the

three of us did all we could not to break character. It was probably the only time that "bit" got a laugh and applause.

I could feel Lillian shooting a look at me sometimes, because it did stop the action of the play, but I didn't milk what I had to do. We knew there would be a reaction, but we didn't know how much!

Before the founding of the Playhouse I was an actor.

Both ladies were delightful. Lillian was the more domineering offstage. She made all of the decisions about where the two of them would go, but she would put the suggestion to Dorothy in a very charming manner.

"Dorothy dear..."

And Dorothy would go along with her.

Lillian was always guarding her. You know why, of course. I don't have to explain.

Lillian always had Dorothy with her for the press conferences. Lillian was in total control, and she would defer to Dorothy. "Don't you think so, Dorothy dear?"

They had behaved like this so often in the old days, it was easy to keep up. They were like a team, and I think the reporters liked the illusion. They were interviewing the Gish Sisters.

Lillian left nothing to chance. She gave them what they wanted: a little show after the show.

She was always a perfectionist, and a thorough professional at all times. Before, during, and after the show. You never caught them off guard.[72]

Dorothy wasn't always silent when Lillian was around. In praise of her sister, she would sometimes say, "I have nowhere near what Lillian has."

Lillian would respond, "Listen to the audience laugh at Dorothy. She has so much charm on the stage. I have a definite tendency to draw away from people. I can feel myself doing it."[73]

Now Dorothy was doing it. What neither Lillian, nor Dorothy, nor their closest friends and associates could predict was just how far it would go for Dorothy. If there were any ideas about a stage team of Lillian and Dorothy, they were crushed. *The Chalk Garden* was their first and final attempt.

The spool was slowly beginning to unravel.

CHAPTER 32

Just Her Name

Lillian Gish ... was such a gorgeous actress.... I made a terrible mistake once. My partner and I produced a play called *A Swim in the Sea* and she wanted to play the lead. Instead we took Fay Bainter, who, while good, was not as exciting as Miss Gish would have been. I've been carrying those regrets around 38 years!

— Harold Prince, Producer-director
Letter to author, June 12, 1995

Beginning September 20, the New York Public Library on 5th Avenue and 42nd Street saluted the Broadway Theatre season of 1956-57 with an exhibit of promptbooks, scripts, portraits, and stage designs of theatre highlights from 1673 to 1956. Lillian, the first actress consulted, offered her portrait of herself in *Camille* from the season of 1932-33. Impressed with the care and dedication shown by curator George Freedly and library director Edward Freehafer, she returned to the library bringing Robert Edmond Jones, who designed the sets for *Camille*.

After Lillian and Robert Edmond Jones donated the *Camille* promptbook, photographs, and reviews from the successful production of the play at the Central City Opera House in Colorado (which had preceded the New York engagement), Lillian happily told the enthusiastic crowd that she now knew that her life would be forever documented and on record for all to see.[1]

1957: At the request of the State Department, Lillian was in West Berlin, Germany, with a company of actors (including Burgess Meredith, Ethel Waters, and Eileen Heckart) and playwright Thornton Wilder to present an evening of seven American one-act plays by Wilder, Tennessee Williams, William Saroyan, and Eugene O'Neill on September 20 at Congress Hall, a just-completed cultural center that stressed the importance of the city as a post-war symbol of the free world.[2] Among the audience of 1200 were several East Berliners who were able to obtain tickets from the United States information Service at America House.[3] That West Berlin was a "living symbol of the West" in its own traditions was highlighted in speeches by David K. E. Bruce, United States ambassador to West Germany, and Mrs. Claire Booth Luce, the former ambassador to Italy, who spoke as the representative of Secretary of State John Foster Dulles prior to a recital by the American soprano Eileen Farrell on the previous evening.[4]

Congress Hall was less than one-quarter of a mile away from Communist East

290

Berlin. The war had ended a dozen years ago, but the barbed wire and metal fences were not a thriller film set. They were a constant reminder that the road to recovery had been thus far only structural. A new building could not replace what the war and post-war generation had known once existed in their lifetimes. Nobody won the war. It just stopped. There were too many dead people on both sides.

Lillian starred in the premiere of Thornton Wilder's *The Wreck on the 5:25*, which concerned a man who wanted to stand outside life and ended with his standing outside the window of his house to watch his wife and daughter. She also played in Tennessee Williams' *Portrait of a Madonna*, a character study of a woman living in romantic dreams of another time.[5]

For Lillian, whose trips to Baden-Baden were a way of life, the opportunity to act in Germany before a "live" audience was one she could not turn down. The year 1957 marked the 30th anniversary of *The Jazz Singer*, the first sound film. Sound did not become the novelty D. W. Griffith had predicted. That ninety percent of the world was not English speaking was no longer a studio concern.

For Lillian 1957 marked 45 years since her motion picture debut. While contemporaries Mary Pickford, Clara Bow, and Greta Garbo had fallen by the wayside, Lillian had miraculously ridden out the storm. Being relegated to heirloom status in the early days of sound in the 1930s was topic of discussion only for the film historians. In 1957 she was a lovable heirloom, the only major silent film star still working in an age of television! She was an unofficial living cultural landmark, and she intended to take full advantage of it! Her name alone created an inherent problem for any director who wanted to use her.

Richard Griffith explained:

because of her [Lillian Gish's] personal magic and the magic of her association with Griffith and all the high traditions of the screen ... Lillian Gish is big medicine [who] will draw attention off the leading players unless she appears only in a sequence in which they are not present.... It doesn't make a great deal of economic sense to pay her thousands a week for the purpose of being invisible, especially if her name in advertising and publicity matters has aroused expectations in older moviegoers which are not fulfilled on the screen.[6]

To the surprise of many in the theatrical community, it was announced that Dorothy Gish would be returning in October to costar with Peggy Wood in Howard Teichmann's *The Girls in 509*. Whatever rumors had been circulating about Dorothy's problem (or problems) had been set aside. Both she and Lillian would be working in theatre again, together but separately as before.

Dorothy's rehearsals (as long as they were involving the script) had worked moderately well. She could deliver a line and get the laughs. When the company went "off-book," the difficulties she had had with *The Chalk Garden* were resurfacing. This time Lillian wasn't there to help her, and the supporting cast wasn't as tolerant or sympathetic. Dorothy was up there on her own. Broadway wasn't summer stock.

Howard Teichmann, teaching playwriting at Columbia University during the summer of 1963, explained:

Dorothy Gish? A sad sweet lady who hadn't been able to hold her lines.

With any play you have rewrites, and she hadn't been able to completely master the original lines. It wasn't anything we could put our finger on. Some days she was okay. But she was a little slow to pick things up.

She didn't argue with any of the revisions. She had been in enough plays to know about rewrites.

It seemed her fight was gone.

I heard about *The Chalk Garden* tour, but we had Peggy Wood, who had known Dorothy for years, with us. We hoped she could help.

Dorothy was playing a lovable old lady living in an old hotel room in New York.

Sometimes she simply froze up there. It was more than just going up on her lines. You could sense the problem she was having just concentrating.

I know Lillian covered for her when she could, but this was a different situation. We were bringing a play to Broadway that was going to be toured at the end of the engagement.

I knew we couldn't bring Dorothy Gish to New York. We had to replace her, or we didn't have a chance. It was embarrassing, and very sad.

But that's the way it is. You know your lines or you don't. You deliver or leave.

She had to go. She didn't know her lines. Or her blocking.

After a lifetime in the theatre, this was a sad way to go, but that happens sometimes.[7]

There would be no more plays for Dorothy. The pressure was too much for her. Pressure had been the reason Lillian, who had purchased *The Barretts of Wimpole Street* for Dorothy in 1930, released the rights to producer Guthrie McClintic, who saw the play as a perfect vehicle for his wife, actress Katherine Cornell.

In her more lucid moments, Dorothy would occasionally mention a "chance missed" but never elaborate. Was she referring to the recent mishap with *The Girls in 509* or to the more distant *The Barretts of Wimpole Street*? Could it have been the failed marriage to James Rennie or the problems in her relationship with Louis Calhern?

Perhaps the bouts with the bottle had lessened her confidence, and the occasionally "going up" on her lines was the end result. The term Alzheimer's was not part of anyone's vocabulary at that time.

Whatever condition Dorothy had was part of Lillian's life. Lillian had to care for her the same way she did for her mother. Care required money, and one only made money if one continued to work. This time the decision was made for Lillian.[8]

Lillian's return to the theatre in the fall of 1958 marked her off–Broadway debut in the American premiere of T. S. Eliot's *The Family Reunion*. Eliot, despite the success of the 1936 production of *Murder at the Cathedral*[9] and the 1950 production of *The Cocktail Party* (starring Alec Guiness and Irene Wroth),[10] was never considered a commercial playwright whose plays brought large audiences to the theatre for long runs. Eliot, to be successful in New York and save these works from permanent resting places on the library shelf, required "actor's actors" willing to play at lower salaries for professional prestige.[11]

The Family Reunion, written in 1939,[12] with its message that man's hope for salvation lay in organized religion,[13] was not your standard Broadway fare, no matter what day of the week. A well-heeled Broadway audience, fed a diet of musicals and comedies, might not be willing to plunk down their dollars for an evening, no matter how affirmative, of a verse play concerned with guilt and redemption prior to ascending to a state of holiness.

And yet this is what Lillian, appearing in the Phoenix Theatre production in New York's Greenwich Village hoped would happen — that *The Family Reunion*, like the uptown Broadway productions of *Murder in the Cathedral* and *The Cocktail Hour*, would be a success. *The Family Reunion* was opening the Phoenix Theatre season on October 20, 1958, with a series of plays written by Nobel prizewinner.[14]

The Family Reunion was the story of a man's return to his family to celebrate his mother's birthday eight years after the mysterious drowning of his young wife.

Drama critic Brooks Atkinson, citing *The Eumenides* of Aeschylus as the basis of Eliot's drama, praised the fine cast but gently castigated the author for "not writing a play about people, only ideas, form and ritual." Lillian, as the sister, delivered a "particularly fine performance that catches the other-worldliness of the part, but never sacrifices reality."[15] The play, however, was a "wordy drama about uninteresting people engaged in a struggle that they are not eager to explain."[16]

Lillian explained why she chose to be associated with *The Family Reunion*:

> This is actor's theatre, and it could never be performed uptown, where the overhead is very high and the box-office receipts are everything.
>
> It's the reason the Phoenix Theatre operates off Broadway. The actors work for mini-wages in a play they are proud to do.
>
> These plays have a short run of a few weeks. Not every actor can afford to spend a total season working for Equity off–Broadway minimum.
>
> When someone in England wants to be an actor, he trains in the classics, and the classics are always being performed in London or the provinces. You always have an audience for the classics, and they don't rely on name actors to bring in the people. The play's the thing!
>
> In New York, the actors train on the classics at some universities, but it ends there in most instances. How many classics are being revived in any season? Where can you find an Ibsen or a Shakespeare at a Broadway house?
>
> Here you've mastered all of the techniques, and you have no opportunity to put them to use. Why study the classics if, when you are finished, you're going to be working in a detergent commercial or on a television soap opera?
>
> In an off–Broadway theatre like the Phoenix you can perform what you've been trained to before an audience: the classics. You only hope your play can attract a serious audience.
>
> We need a government-supported theatre that plays the classics.
>
> In England, T. S. Eliot is revered like Shakespeare. T. S. Eliot used language, a different kind of language than we are accustomed to hearing in the theatre.
>
> It's not conversational. You have to listen. You have to pay attention. Eliot's language is richly textured like the Elizabethan classics.
>
> The American contribution to the world theatre is the musical. Nobody will ever match us.
>
> The British contribution to the world theatre is words.
>
> *The Family Reunion* is words, beautifully written words.[17]

Lillian made her British motion picture debut the following year (1958) in *Orders to Kill*, a thriller whose cast included good friend Irene Worth. The premise of the Anthony Asquith production was that only the toughest, emotionally secure people were able to see things through on important counter-espionage assignments. A young American airman hired to kill someone who was betraying resistance agents to the enemy completed his mission only to learn he killed an innocent victim.

The film opened at the Fine Arts Theatre in New York on November 18, 1958. Reviewers found the picture riddled with contradictions. Eddie Albert as the American airman didn't have the pre-requisite tough look of a gunman for hire. One also couldn't help but notice that only the most precise English was spoken by the members of the French underground. Where were the French accents? One was also at a loss to explain why such a well-trained resistance group would even think of recruiting an American to help them.[18]

Lillian's cameo appearance, perhaps out of recognition for her longevity in motion pictures, wasn't mentioned in most of the reviews.

Film historian William K. Everson offered his reactions to the picture, and to Lillian's brief appearance:

> *Orders to Kill* didn't set itself to be a great work. It's a well-directed effort, perhaps a trifle slow in places, a thriller that is little more than a pleasing programmer, a well made second feature.
>
> What's surprising is that it was directed by Anthony Asquith, who was best known for his very civilized and entertaining literate stage-to-screen transformations of George Bernard Shaw's *Pygmalion* in the late 30s, and Terrence Rattigan's *The Winslow Boy* and *The Browning Version* of the late 40s and very early 50s.
>
> Some people might take offense that an American, out of every group in the world, is the only one who can help the French resistance. I'm sure it occurred many times, but in the cinema world it doesn't seem logical.
>
> Not using French accents, or what Americans would understand to be a French accent, is possibly an oversight, although I don't see how. This film was made by a British company. English audiences, I assure you, wouldn't have had this problem.
>
> I'm sure English audiences would be covering their ears if they had to listen to hysterical shrieking Germans for an entire film.
>
> Using Lillian, I thought, was a very nice touch. Even though she isn't on the screen for more than 5 or 6 minutes. You wouldn't have paid attention if the mother's role were played by a lesser player. Yet with Lillian, audiences sat up and paid closer attention.
>
> The British have always had a fond regard for the older stars they saw at the height of their popularity. Lillian Gish was no exception.
>
> Just to see her looking well on the screen in an English film was more than enough reason to see it. Usually English go to America, and stay there. An American star, like Lillian Gish and a year or two later, Judy Garland, coming over to England was a reversal.
>
> I'm sure if the current generation of film buffs saw *Orders to Kill* on PBS-TV late at night, they'd love it.[19]

The Lillian Gish, who registered at the Hotel Casablanca in Durango, Mexico,[20] in early January 1959 prior to beginning the filming of John Huston's adult western, *The Unforgiven*, was not a stranger to the Huston family. John's father, actor Walter Huston, appeared in a touring production of *In Convict's Stripes* in Risingsun, Ohio, where he carried Baby Lillian (billed as "Little Florence Niles") on his shoulders during a curtain call on the night of her stage debut in 1902.[21]

In 1947 Walter and Lillian were reunited in David O. Selznick's *Duel in the Sun.*

Rather than use Texas locations, John Huston chose Guadiana, a remote Mexican village, to shoot his film. There were no telegraph poles, no aircraft vapors, and the traffic under the virtually cloudless blue skies moved at an absolute minimum.[22]

In some ways the winds[23] were a replication of the atmospheric conditions of Lillian's *The Wind*, filmed over three decades earlier (1927), but Lillian, unlike the rest of the cast, knew how to make the necessary adjustments. She knew a John Huston set was a man's set,[24] rugged and uncompromising and outdoors, where a constantly blazing sun would supply her with more than one opportunity to demonstrate the same kind of pioneer fortitude[25] she would be enacting as the family matriarch struggling for survival on the Texas Panhandle and fighting the Kiowa

Indians in the 1870s. Huston knew that when the actor shouldered a lot of the responsibility, it was like a challenge. The actor would give more to prove the director was right.[26]

Lillian, Huston knew, was more than capable of meeting the challenge.

The Unforgiven was the story of an Indian girl rescued as a baby and raised by a frontier family, headed by matriarch Lillian Gish, who keeps the baby's real identity a secret as long as possible.

Lillian would always tell interviewers that she loved her film daughter, Audrey Hepburn, as if she were her own real daughter.[27] Lillian had little to say about Audie Murphy, with whom she refused to ride in the cab between the hotel and the shooting locations. Murphy, a World War II hero who had attained fame in Westerns, was under a serious charge of cattle rustling. Only his Hollywood studio connections prevented a prison sentence.[28]

Murphy, Lillian would often state, was trigger happy, shooting any animal that crossed his path. Often he would shoot a beer can tossed in a bar. Lillian, an animal lover, found his behavior and professional demeanor abhorrent.[29]

On the first day of shooting, Lillian appeared on the set in full costume and white pancake makeup, which scriptwriter Ben Maddow said made her look like a clown. Removing it took quite a long time.

Production secretary Jilda Smith, observing Lillian filming a long scene in which she speaks about how she came to adopt the Indian child raised as her daughter, recalled:

> She [Lillian Gish] must have been good in 1912, but [in 1959, on the set of *The Unforgiven*] she was absolutely … awful.
>
> [In the scene] she said she had a baby of her own, and it died after birth, and then she heard this crying and found this Indian baby and she

had to say, "And my breasts were hurting with all that milk, and I took the Indian baby and I fed it."

Lillian is a very fastidious lady, and John knew she didn't like the line, and he'd say, "very good, Lillian, not too heavy on the breasts, honey." And he made her do that take God knows how many times. It was agonizing.[30]

Huston spent the entire day shooting Lillian's scene, determined to break her down.

Lillian kept repeating, "D. W. wouldn't do it this way," but Huston ignored her. He wanted this scene done his way. Lillian quietly groused, defending her answer, adding that she had been with Griffith for years and knew more about picturemaking, and had more successes, than Huston.[31]

Despite the constant retakes, Lillian's eyes were so expressive, she didn't require any dialogue.[32] Her "mad scene" in which she pushes a horse forward carrying a lynching victim being punished for revealing the origins of her adopted daughter[33] is almost a replay of her flower beating scene when she is grief-stricken after the death of her newborn child in Griffith's 1913 *The Mothering Heart*.

Albert Salmi, playing a rancher in *The Unforgiven*, explained why John Huston was seemingly putting what he thought was an inordinate amount of pressure on the veteran actress:

> John Huston, more than anybody, knew Lillian wasn't this innocent prissy type she had been playing in those Griffith films, and he did his damnedest to get to that undercurrent he knew she had. He wanted her to become the character internally, and not have to rely on the tricks she had used when she was working Griffith.
>
> We, who were a younger generation, just hung around to watch. It

was an acting lesson from somebody who was there almost from the beginning. How many opportunities like that come your way?

What she did was amazing in take after take. Those thousands of feet of film could be a documentary.

Huston also grew up in the movies. He knew that he wanted to take the Griffith out of her. She was playing Griffith, because this was a period film, and it was the same period Griffith used in his films. [Huston] didn't want *The Unforgiven* to look like a Griffith film with sound.

Lillian could turn the emotion off and on like a light switch, which is probably the reason she lasted so long. She knew which buttons to press and when to press. That's all acting is, and it takes a lifetime to learn.

Lillian made it all look easy, but don't let her little old lady demeanor fool you. She could take it, and give it back equally. She's a tough, solid actress.

Huston was afraid she would overact if she filmed the death scene which was in the original novel. She had done so many, I think audiences wouldn't pay much attention to it.

He had gotten to her tough side. She was compassionate and gritty. When she plays Bach and Mozart on the grand piano outside during that Indian uprising, that was tough! He showed another side of her, that tough side. And I think she liked it![34]

On March 28, 1960, a week before the New York premiere of *The Unforgiven*, Lillian appeared on television in David Suaskind's production of Truman Capote's *The Grass Harp*, the play she had wanted to do on Broadway with Dorothy in 1952.

Playing the same role in a shortened television adaptation was a bittersweet triumph. Dorothy wasn't stable enough to work with her.

Lillian was proud that, at the age of sixty-one, she could work with the same

determination she had shown at the beginning of her long career. "We had twelve days to learn it. The last day we worked twenty-two hours. I'm still the iron horse if I can work twenty-two hours."[35]

The Unforgiven opened on April 6, 1960, at the Capitol Theatre in New York. Film critic Bosley Crowther noted Huston's attempt to try to make another "different" Western in the manner of his successful *The Treasure of the Sierra Madre* of 1948. For a major portion of this two-hour wide-screen color film, it appeared that a statement on racism was going to be made.

The viewer's anticipation was wasted on a programmer in which Lillian was merely utilized as part of the cast. Huston's Western did not erase anyone's good memories of his earlier Western success of *Shane*.[36]

In wake of *The Grass Harp* and *The Unforgiven*, Lillian discussed her image, her acting choices, and personal decisions she had to make.

The image? I'll tell what we tried for: the essence of femininity. Mostly in those movies [for D. W. Griffith] I was a virgin. We tried for virginity — in mind, in looks, in body, in movement.

Not that I enjoyed this. To attract and hold the interest of an audience with nothing is difficult; goodness becomes dull so quickly. It's so much easier to win an audience with a little wickedness....

That virginal character hadn't anything to do with me. I tried to make my character a Grant Wood: strong in spirit, strong in body. She carries a gun, and yet is maternal....

I think being a good wife is a 24-hour-a-day job. I certainly haven't lacked for male companionship. I've had much more than I deserve: wonderful men and wonderful minds. I'm greatly indebted to George Jean Nathan. Through him I knew Mencken and all the American writers of the twenties as friends, and later on the writers of Europe.

I'm always interested in new things. If it's new or different, I want to know about it. I was born with a terrific curiosity.[37]

Playing Catherine Lynch, a character modeled on author James Agee's grandmother, in Tad Mosel's *All the Way Home* (a play based on Agee's unfinished autobiographical novel, *A Death in the Family*), Lillian returned to the Belasco Theatre for a respectable run on November 30, 1960.

Assigned a catty-cornered dressing room at the topmost floor brought back all sorts of memories. Lillian had shared this same room in 1913 with Mary Pickford in *A Good Little Devil*.[38]

Lillian greeted this biographer in the hallway, then entered the cramped quarters and drew aside the curtains that covered the dusty window.

The same brick wall is here. I still can't tell what kind of weather we're having, rain or snow. The plays come and go, and the theatre dressing room always remains the same.

Had a better room when I was here with *The Curious Savage* [1950], but I was the lead in that play.

Now I'm back as a supporting player, and upstairs is where the supporting players go: the same dressing room, the same flights of steps...

It's full circle, isn't it?[39]

All the Way Home was a "simple and searching play about commonplace things like love and death and the need to go on living," wrote Howard Taubman of *The New York Times*. The death is the death of Agee's father in a car accident that occurred in May 1915 when Agee was a youngster living in Knoxville, Tennessee.

Colleen Dewhurst, playing the author's mother, spoke to the biographer a few years later when she was working opposite her husband, actor George C. Scott, in Eugene O'Neill's *Desire Under the Elms*:

When we began rehearsals, we had read the Agee novel, so we knew what was beneath the script.

Tad Mosel did a wonderful job putting everything into dialogue: all of those thoughts which were unspoken in the novel. You know *All the Way Home* won the Pulitzer Prize, don't you?

Lillian told us about her experience with James Agee and Charles Laughton during the making of *The Night of the Hunter*. That phase of Agee's life was nowhere to be found in the novel, but it was useful to know.

Agee, had he lived, couldn't have written a stage adaptation. He was gifted with words, as you can see in the novel, but he wasn't a theatre man.

Alcoholism had gotten the better of him. Eugene O'Neill, and I've played my share of O'Neill, was also an alcoholic, but he was still able to turn out a playable script. But he was trained in the theatre. Agee wasn't....

I used to stand in the wings and watch Lillian when I could, and there was enough time. She was amazing. Everything was clean. Nothing varied from performance to performance.

She didn't chew the scenery as many stage people of that generation did. Her gestures were quite minimal, but they were minimal in a lot of her silent work.

In our play, she played a grandmother everyone the audience wished they had. You couldn't take your eyes off her.

It was a dainty part, but Lillian was as dainty as a steel road![40]

On April 22, 1962, Lillian guest starred in *Grandma TNT*, one of the episodes of *The Defenders*, a weekly series on CBS-TV.

Television, theatre, and motion picture actor Lou Jacobi, thirty-five years after working in the same episode, could still recall

> being intimidated, and Lillian Gish did absolutely nothing to intimidate anyone. I had no scenes with her, and I have to confess that just seeing her sitting alone in the corner by herself, when she wasn't on camera, was intimidating.
>
> I would have loved to have gone up to her and introduce myself, but I honestly would have to admit that I was a little shy. After introducing myself, what was I going to say to her?
>
> She did her scenes and then went back to that corner. She picked up her script and went over her lines, and waited to be called for the next scene.
>
> Maybe it was her longevity that was intimidating. She worked in every phase of the business, and she made the transitions from one medium to the other so naturally.
>
> How many actors can do that? And succeed? And keep getting called back?
>
> A lot of us wanted to talk to her, but we didn't. We did our job, and she did hers, which is what we're supposed to do.
>
> Now I'm sorry I didn't speak to her. She was all by herself.
>
> Maybe she was shy, too.
>
> You wouldn't think that, would you?[41]

Running with African American actor Frederick O'Neal, Lillian polled 1,656 votes as first vice-president of the Actors Equity Association on April 26. She was the only one of 14 independent candidates to be elected. As a counselor, she would be serving on the Union's governing board.[42]

Following a short engagement in January 1963 as Mrs. Moore in a student production of Sama Rama Thau's adaptation of E. M. Forster's novel, A Passage to India, at Chicago's Goodman Theatre,[43] Lillian returned to New York to begin rehearsals as Mrs. Mopply in an all-star revival of

George Bernard Shaw's Too True to Be Good. The play had not been mounted since its original Theatre Guild production in 1932.[44]

Shaw's satire, set in a bedroom in a wealthy suburban English villa and on a beach in a mountainous unnamed locale, offered a message that 1932 Depression audiences didn't find humorous: the capitalistic system was burdensome on the idle rich.[45]

Whether the more financially secure audiences of 1963 would come to sit through an evening of Shaw's collection of sermons remained to be seen. Certainly the cast was an impressive box-office lure: Robert Preston, Glynis Johns, Eileen Heckart, David Wayne, Ray Middleton, and Sir Cedric Hardwicke.

To give the rarely-staged lesser play a modern pacing, some of the lines were cut. Shaw, Lillian informed high school students after some of the Wednesday matinees, was real theatre, not Broadway. Although his messages were universal, his plays were infrequently revived.

Too True to Be Good, wrote drama critic Howard Taubman of The New York Times, reviewing the March 12 Opening Night, was "hardly prime Shaw, but are there any second-rate Shaws to comfort us in these arid days?"[46]

Lillian's performance drew little mention, other than Taubman noting that she was a "fussy old mother."[47]

Lillian, reflecting on the 94 performance run (longer than the original run of 57 performances in 1932), remarked:

> When I did Eliot's The Family Reunion downtown, we had lower prices, and not as many young people as we thought we would get.
>
> Now, here we are uptown, at higher prices, and we're getting people from the colleges and universities!
>
> I have to smile when we speak to the high school students after the

Wednesday matinees. They remember Robert Preston in *The Music Man*, which they saw when they were younger.

What a relief not to have to answer questions about the ice floe and "Did you catch a cold when you made *Way Down East*?"

I feel so young![48]

The Dorothy Gish who reported to the Columbia lot to play the mother of a priest in Otto Preminger's *The Cardinal* was a far cry from the actress and "delightful woman"[49] whose wit had been so engaging between takes during the filming of Preminger's *Centennial Summer* in 1946, and who later visited the Middleburg, Virginia, race track, where she so easily mingled with the horsey set.[50]

The Cardinal was the story of a Boston Irish priest who rose through the ranks to become a cardinal. The film, like the original novel by Henry Morton Robinson, was not without its controversial aspects. The sister of the priest had a baby out of wedlock and died in order that the baby might live.

Cardinal Francis Spellman, of the New York Archdiocese, believing the priest and his sister were modeled after himself and his sibling (although his sister was in fact unmarried), pressured Columbia Pictures not to film the novel. He wrote letters to every bishop, urging their support.[51]

With the cooperation of Cardinal Cushing of Boston, the pastor of the Catholic church in Stamford, Connecticut, and Cardinal Franz König of Vienna, the motion picture was able to be filmed at authentic locations, including the Pope's summer residence. All of these locations were beyond the jurisdiction of Cardinal Spellman.[52]

What Preminger did not anticipate was Dorothy's inability to hold her lines for a complete scene. Unlike a "live" performance in a theatre, where an actor could quickly ad lib another actor's lost line without the audience being aware of what had happened, the camera recorded everything — including the mistakes. Dorothy was making far too many,[53] and the locales Preminger had scheduled for scenes had limited availability.[54]

Because of Dorothy's many good years in films and on stage, Preminger flatly refused to replace her. Rather than embarrass her, he had her lines cut for the additional scenes where her presence was absolutely required. The camera would merely acknowledge her presence in the scene as a necessary family member, and the dialogue she had been required to learn was now removed.[55]

Bosley Crowther, reviewing the film's opening in New York on December 12, 1963, at the DeMille Theatre, made no mention of her.[56]

In January 1965 Lillian was doubly busy. She was rehearsing her role as the Nurse to Juliet in William Shakespeare's *Romeo and Juliet*. The play would officially open on June 20 in repertory at the American Shakespeare Festival at Stratford, Connecticut.[57] In March there would be school matinees for students.

Lillian was also aware that Dorothy's "premature memory loss" had jeopardized her ability to do any film work. Her conversation no longer made sense. Words were strung together without any congruity. In May Lillian was forced to admit that Dorothy could no longer be left alone. She required constant supervision at all times.[58] To her friends Lillian was now admitting that Dorothy had lost her memory — the worst thing that can happen to anyone.

Romeo and Juliet was Lillian's Shakespearean debut. It was a long time coming, as Anita Loos recalled:

Lillian wanted to play Juliet when she was working with Dick Barthelmess in her D. W. Griffith days. Griffith thought it was a good idea, even though he was more of a rural Americana director. He would have done almost anything Lillian suggested.

The project was shelved because the production office said Shakespeare wasn't a money maker.

Griffith agreed. How can you film only the story and not include some of the text. To him, movies were not words. Words belonged in a theatre, where they would be heard.

The balcony scene, the most famous part of the play, required words. Griffith did not want to be attacked by the purists, who would take him to task for not including all of the words used in the balcony scene. That balcony scene would be terrible without those words.

So they shelved the project, even though Lillian would have been heartbreaking as Juliet.

Years later, when Lillian went into *Romeo and Juliet* as the old Nurse, she would joke and say, "Shakespeare is an actor's dream. There are parts for all ages!"[59]

In a letter to this biographer, actress Mary Hara, who was Lillian's understudy and completed the run of the play, wrote:

> I remember telling her [Lillian Gish] how beautiful she looked at a rehearsal one day, and asked [for] her secret.
> She said, "Oh those Swiss doctors!"[60]

Speaking directly to the biographer one month later, she continued:

> Lillian Gish was always in a state of total serenity. I never knew how she could be so outwardly calm in the midst of all of those problems.[61]

Playwright Milan Stitt, then handling press relations for the American Shakespeare Festival, explained:

When Lillian began rehearsals, Dorothy was totally infantile and had to be constantly supervised. At fist Lillian would leave Dorothy alone in her dressing room. Not wanting to frighten Dorothy, Lillian would keep the door open.[62]

Rehearsals for *Romeo and Juliet* were proving to be difficult. Mary Hara, understudying Lillian's role, recalled:

> Lillian was always acting. She knew how to "play" this "sweet old lady" to get whatever she wanted.
> She didn't want to say some of the words she thought were vulgar, and she'd say—in that very quiet, disarming way she must have mastered from her Griffith days—"Oh, I can't say those words…"
> She made the director, Allen Fletcher, cut them. "Now by my maidenhead—at twelve years old—I bade her come," became, "Now I bade her come."
> She didn't like saying, "Thou wilt fall backward when thou comest of age," the words her dead husband used to say. She had problems with "Taste the wormwood on the nipple of my dug."
> The director didn't make or alter everything she wanted. The husband's words were crucial. She explained that they were bawdy, and that schoolchildren would get wrong ideas about Shakespeare, and they associate them with her.
> Do you think she told Sean O'Casey when she played the Young Whore, as the role was called in *Within the Gates* (1934), that she wanted the name description changed?
> Not if she wanted work!
> When I took over the role of Juliet's Nurse after Lillian Gish left, it became Shakespeare's Nurse, not Lillian's Nurse. I said those lines as they were originally written!
> But I have to be honest. Even though Lillian diluted the character, the audiences weren't aware of it.

She was wonderful, no matter what she did. She was history, living history. And that's why she's a star![63]

Milan Stitt also had rehearsal and performance memories of Lillian:

Miss Gish told us that she researched the role, and concluded that the Nurse couldn't be older than 30. So to give the impression of being young, she skipped sometimes!

I never saw anyone dominate the stage the way she did in Act 4, scene 5: Juliet's chamber. Lillian, seeing Juliet asleep, tries to waken her. She calls her name. No response. She leans over the bed and tickles her. Still no response. You can sense what is going to happen when the Nurse discovers Juliet is dead.

The way Lillian used her face! You could see her facial muscles slowly contort, and then her body and her hands. Every motion was made, one after the other, like a continuous balletic movement.

And then, in one swoop, Lillian yanked the bedsheet away from Juliet, and she lets out this blood-curdling scream that filled the theatre. This moment of revelation that she had been moving toward!

Afterwards she came way downstage and sat on this box or trunk. The spotlight was right on those big beautiful blue eyes, and you could see the tears of grief streaming down her face. Tears! Great big tears! And then she seemed to freeze. No movement at all. That spotlight stayed right on her eyes the entire time.

Some of us were lucky to see those eyes almost every performance.

She was ethereal. In that scene you were watching the Art of Lillian Gish: a lifetime of craft in pantomime.

She had such total concentration. Once, during one of the performances, Dorothy, who was thought to be locked in Lillian's dressing room, somehow got out. Maybe someone who was assigned to watch the door forgot to lock it.

Lillian was onstage, and Dorothy just wandered into the scene, calling Lillian's name over and over. By the second time Dorothy called Lillian's name, Lillian, without breaking her concentration, quickly glided to where Dorothy was standing and glided Dorothy to whoever was in the wings.

I don't know if the audience sensed what was happening. It could have been one of those school audiences, but it was a potentially dangerous situation. Dorothy was very much watched afterwards.[64]

Lillian's eyes were also singled out for recognition — in addition to her overall performance — by reviewer Howard Taubman of *The New York Times*: "Lillian Gish is capital as the Nurse; her eyes have a baby stare as she recalls her late husband's old witticism, and they turn cool and shrewd as she guys poor Juliet."[65]

Now that the play had officially opened, what remained for Lillian to insure its continued success was to sell the product. With Milan Stitt acting as chauffeur, she went to a radio station to personally publicize the production and to answer any questions listeners might ask during a "call-in" segment.

Milan Stitt recalled

sitting next to Lillian with a set of books with information about her career, a list of her films — and Griffith films — with complete casts and credits and a one or two line synopsis. The listener would ask the question, and while it was repeated, I would thumb through the reference books to search for the answer, if Lillian would raise her head to look at me or shake her head. A few seconds later, I would point to a sentence, and Lillian would answer the question. She knew her Griffith films and her other films, and she had anecdotes she could tell if I couldn't find the answer quickly.

She was very generous to the rest of the cast, always mentioning their names whenever possible.

She was wonderful to Eileen Herlie, who was starring in *Coriolanus*, one of the other productions, which wasn't doing as well as *Romeo and Juliet*. Lillian told the listeners to see *Coriolanus* as well as *Romeo and Juliet*, and to pay close attention to Eileen Herlie's wonderful performance.

How many actors, given the chance to be the only guest on a radio interview, would take the attention away from themselves and, on the spur moment mention another actor in another show?

But that was Lillian Gish.[66]

As the summer wore on, the relationship between Milan Stitt and Lillian grew beyond that of press relations manager and actress.

Milan remembered

> driving Lillian to New York after some of the matinees, or picking her up on the day of the show.
>
> She would serve tea on Thursdays to her friends: Blanche Sweet, Claudette Colbert, Greta Garbo…
>
> No, I never saw Greta Garbo, and I didn't hear about it until after the fact. Just her name was said. Nothing more.
>
> I once drove Lillian and Blanche back to New York after a matinee, and, even though I had the radio on, I frankly tried to eavesdrop on what two Griffith actresses would talk about. Maybe I would hear something nobody ever heard.
>
> I heard nothing but general conversation, but Lillian brought up

something she read about Griffith and racism, which angered her. She saw herself as the keeper of the Griffith flame, and was quite adamant if something were written that, in her mind, was nonsense.

"If Mr. Griffith were a bigot," Lillian asked Blanche, "would he have a white soldier kiss a dying black soldier on the lips in full view of the camera before he died in *Hearts of the World*?"

And then the conversation stopped.

Lillian was very much in the present. What was happening at the moment that she thought was important, and what affected her always got her attention. She was not a nostalgia lady.[67]

Once Lillian noticed that Milan seemed a little sad during one of their automobile trips. She inquired, and Milan answered:

> I was getting divorced, and I told her.
>
> I was surprised at her response. Everybody had been sympathetic and kind, and understanding, et cetera.
>
> Lillian Gish wasn't.
>
> "You have no business feeling sad. You have no business getting a divorce, anymore than you had any business getting married.
>
> "You have no right to tell someone they are second best.
>
> "That's why I never got married! I won't be second best to anyone!
>
> "I worked very hard for what I have!"
>
> She held her script up for me to see. "This is everything!"[68]

CHAPTER 33

The "Singing" Empress

They were just adding words and taking longer to do the same things we had done better with pantomime. We had to be articulate and let audiences know we were people. It was a new art form and it's lost, and it's a pity.

— Lillian Gish
The New York Herald Tribune
June 13, 1965[1]

Frankly, it was the juiciness of the part that attracted her to the role of the Empress. She had seen the 1954 production of *Anastasia* (starring Eugenie Leontovich as the Empress and Viveca Lindfors as the amnesia victim who claimed to be the escaped Romanov princess, daughter of the last Czar) and the subsequent film version with Helen Hayes and Ingrid Bergman in 1956.[2]

A personal telephone call from director and longtime friend George Abbott was all that was necessary to clinch the deal.

Abbott recalled:

I'd known Lillian Gish for years, but we never worked together. It was something we would always say in passing to each other whenever we'd meet at the Theatre or at someone's party: "We must do something together," etc. Talk like that. It happens all the time, but the projects we were interested in doing just never got beyond the talk stage. Something else would come up, we we'd go in different directions, still good friends.

The role of the Empress has one of the most exciting and moving confrontational scenes in the theatre. Lillian and I both knew it, and she said a definite yes.

This wasn't a revival, what we were doing. It was an all-out musical, but her role was strictly dramatic. It was almost a repeat of what had been done in the original production a decade earlier. The scene of the interview between the young girl claiming to be the princess, the last surviving member of the royal family, and the Empress who wanted to meet and test her and expose her as a highly skilled pretender, reduced audiences to tears.

Lillian would not be required to sing. I knew she had never done any singing in her life, either on Broadway or when she and Dorothy were touring as children in those dreadful melodramas that were so popular in those days.[3]

The score for *Anya* was written by the popular songwriting team of Robert Wright and George Forrest, based on themes by Sergei Rachmaninoff. No strangers to the

303

limitless possibilities of classical music, they had successfully adapted the melodies of Edvard Grieg and Alexander Borodin for their long-running musicals *Song of Norway* (1944)[4] and *Kismet* (1953).[5]

Confidences ran high with the announcement that playwright Guy Bolton, who had co-authored the original *Anastasia*, was working in collaboration with the director to turn the drama into a "musical musical."

Guy Bolton told this biographer during the previews in New York (for this production was too expensive to try out of town):

> Here we were with these glorious melodies being snug by beautifully trained voices, and the moment this wonderful scene with Lillian and Constance Towers [as Anya] begins, it's a thud.
>
> Everything we've worked toward just came to a sudden halt. On its own, the scene was brilliant, well played, good for a handkerchief or two, if the audience goes along with it.
>
> But here — nothing. Dead.
>
> What went wrong?
>
> And then George [George Abbot] said what the scene needed.
>
> I thought about it. I had hoped it wouldn't happen, but it did, and we had no choice.
>
> How do we tell Lillian, whose scenes didn't require much revision beyond a little tightening, that she has to sing?[6]

George Abbott:

> When I approached Lillian to sing, she was very doubtful. I knew what her reaction would be even before she voiced it. This wasn't what she expected. She thought she would have a non-singing role, and that her scene with Constance worked very well.
>
> I listened and nodded and gently reminded her that *Anya* was a musical that was being publicized as a "musical musical," and in musicals people sing.
>
> In a straight play, lines are added or removed, and in musicals songs are added or removed. Some of the songs from *My Fair Lady* were removed and put into *Gigi*.
>
> I told her, very gently, that she was quite wonderful in her scene, and that audiences loved what she was doing, and so did we. But audiences were being cheated if she didn't sing.
>
> We've had non-singing actors who did very well when they had a song to deliver. Robert Preston in *The Music Man*, Rex Harrison in *My Fair Lady*, Richard Burton in *Camelot*. Walter Huston stopped the show with *September Song* way back in *Knickerbockers Holiday*.
>
> She would do the same with one song.
>
> Audiences loved her, no matter what she did. I knew she had rhythm. I've danced with her. A song during her scene would be a bonus. I knew she could do it.
>
> Only one song. We would orchestrate it to have the pit orchestra violinist play the melody underneath her talking the lyrics, and Constance on the second chorus would hum the melody softly. The moment would be even more poignant.
>
> Lillian did very well with "Little Hands," a melody Wright and Forrest adapted from Rachmaninoff's *Vocalise* that took about two minutes.
>
> Audiences loved it. Granted, Lillian is no Mary Martin or Ethel Merman, and never will be, but when an actress of Lillian's caliber signs to do a musical, the audiences would like her to sing somewhere during the play. Even if only one song. And that is just what Lillian did: one song.
>
> Vivian Leigh was carrying *Tovarich*, the musical, two seasons ago. And she really couldn't sing.
>
> Lillian was self-conscious at first, but the cast was very encouraging, and Lillian and I still remain good friends.[7]

Anya, the musical musical, opened at the Ziegfeld Theatre on November 29, 1965. The first night audience, familiar with the original stageplay and film, knew the plot. What was a matter of curiosity among some theatregoers was Lillian's ability to sing. Could she sing? The insertion of a specially-written song during previews was mentioned in more than one newspaper column.

Howard Taubman, reviewing the musical musical for *The New York Times*, wrote that Lillian was

> looking marvelously old world and regal in a taffeta suit with ample skirts and a jeweled choker....[8]

Lillian's musical debut, the singing of "Little Hands,"

> creates the affecting moment.[9]

What was troublesome was that

> [director] George Abbott's tempo is occasionally sleepy....[10]

Anya, despite the wonderful singing of beautiful melodies, wound up resembling "a turn of the century operetta."[11]

Although Lillian's performance was "worth noting,"[12] the "musical musical" closed after 16 performances.[13]

Next to D. W. Griffith, Lillian always regarded Walt Disney as the most imaginative and innovative filmmaker. When she was asked to play a wealthy eccentric in Disney's *Follow Me, Boys*, a Boy Scout film adapted from MacKinlay Kantor's novel, *God and My Country*, she quickly accepted.

William K. Everson commented:

> *Follow Me, Boys* is probably the only "family film" geared toward young children that Lillian ever made. Disney was a solid filmmaker with a good reputation. His name alone could be trusted.
>
> Like Alfred Hitchcock, Disney was known by the man on the street. He employed many of the same actors from film to film, like Fred MacMurray. MacMurray's career began in the thirties, and the Disney films introduced him to a new generation.
>
> I think that Lillian might have been investigating the possibilities that would put her name in front of a young generation.
>
> The Disney comedies tended to be silly and not very sophisticated, but they had their own particular audience.[14]

Follow Me, Boys had its premier on December 1, 1966, at New York's Radio City Music Hall.

Film critic Bosley Crowther was present, and noted that the early morning audience was composed of "older people chuckling all through the film."[15] He called it

> painful and embarrassing ... a clutter of sentimental blubberings about the brotherhood of the Boy Scouts.
>
> Who is the rich old lady with the eccentric ways but Lillian Gish, offering her land for a Boy Scout camp because that's where her two deceased sons used to play.[16]

Dorothy's condition steadily worsened to the degree that she required round-the-clock supervision. As devoted as Lillian had been, by virtue of her age (74), she was unable to physically cope with Dorothy's demands. Rather leave Dorothy in New York, the two of them flew to Italy, where Dorothy was registered at the Villa Chiara, a resort in Rapollo.[17]

Lillian's next film, *Warning Shot*, brought her back to the big screen in a mystery that opened on June 8, 1967, in neighborhood Theatres throughout the New York metropolitan area.[18] Her last film to open "all over town" was the prestigious *Duel in the Sun* two decades earlier.[19]

Warning Shot, released through Paramount, was hardly as weighty or significant. The title refers to a decision or choice an officer of the law (David Janssen) has to make in a sudden crisis: to shoot or refrain from shooting a fleeing suspect, and then justify that decision.

The film was episodic in its construction, like a huge jigsaw puzzle. In an effort to resemble the Italian verissimo school of filmmaking after the Second World War, actual locations were utilized, rather than Hollywood-built sets. Documentary in style, *Warning Shot* was a "garishly solemn tough private eye noir melodrama"[20] with an all-star cast including Joan Collins, Steve Allen, Carroll O'Connor, Stefanie Powers, Keenan Wynn, and George Sanders.

Quickly shot by television director Buzz Kulik, *Warning Shot* was a most agreeable few days' work.[21]

Putting her philosophy of at least "one new horizon a day"[22] into practice, Lillian delivered a positive message of hope when she spoke to the members of the Actors Fund of America meeting in New York at the Helen Hayes Theatre on the afternoon of June 10. A suggestion that performers should produce a television show, turning the profits over to the Actors Fund, was well received.

Still lobbying for the addition of a Minister of Fine Arts position to be included as part of the Presidential Cabinet, she also stressed the need for government support of the arts, but not if it included governmental interference.

Reminding the audience that she was a former child actress, Lillian offered her belief that children should be raised with insecurity, as it helps in the formation of their personalities and makes them stronger and able to cope with life's problems when they are older.

Her entrance into the theatre wasn't a choice she made. It was done because her family, having been abandoned by her father was "very poor, and the job paid $10 a week. We learned to read and write in dressing rooms all over the country."[23]

About to leave for Italy, where she would work on a biography of her mentor, D. W. Griffith (scheduled for a September or October publication), Lillian rejected any ideas about retiring after a career of sixty years: "Retire? If you want to die, retire and die of boredom."[24]

One doesn't quit after recently being honored with fellow actress Peggy Wood at the Whitney Museum of American Art the previous month by the National Council on the Arts for a "significant contribution to the high quality of the American Theatre." By continuing to work, one proves that a right choice was made for the honor.

Lillian was going to continue working.[25]

The Villa Chiara, where Dorothy was living in Rapollo, Italy, was a short drive from Nice, where Lillian would be completing location shots for her next film, *The Comedians*, a motion picture version of Graham Greene's novel. Earlier location shots would be made in Dahomey, West Africa, in an effort to duplicate the unnamed Caribbean country that bore more than a passing resemblance to modern day Haiti under the terroristic reign on "Papa Doc" Duvalier."[26]

The Comedians reunited Lillian with Peter Glenville, who had directed her in 1950 in *The Curious Savage*.[27] In *The Comedians* Lillian would be playing a naive American liberal. The film's all-star cast

Lillian played Mrs. Smith, here up against Paul Ford (left), Roscoe Lee Brown (second from left), and an unidentified character in *The Comedians* (1967, MGM, directed by Peter Glenville). "A film dealing with political unrest. The world is smaller than anyone realizes," said Lillian.

included Elizabeth Taylor, Richard Burton, Alec Guiness, Paul Ford, Peter Ustinov, Gloria Foster, Roscoe Lee Browne, Raymond St. Jacques, and James Earl Jones.

Director Peter Glenville recalled being in awe of

> Lillian's amazing strength and endurance. She's a great pro, and her professionalism was a lesson to all of us.
>
> The weather in Africa was quite, quite hot. Not real shade area. We had a constant sun all day, and we began shooting just after sunrise.
>
> One of the sequences involved Lillian being pushed onto the ground, which was covered with pebbles and little stones.
>
> I was worried about her. She was quite frankly up there, and I was concerned. But I would never bring up the matter of her age as the reason we should do her scene on another day. Having directed Lillian on stage, I knew she would be quite insulted and hurt that I thought of her as this frail old lady who required that special adjustments be made. She was very adamant about people trying to make things easier for her. She had been able to take good care of herself since she had been on the road as a child.
>
> And you would hear about it in no uncertain terms.

Richard Burton, who was in the scene with her was also concerned but Lillian said she didn't want to have the shooting schedule adjusted for a few falls — falls, she had learned to do in her Griffith days. So we worked until sundown and finished the scene.

You would have thought that after so many years Lillian would have graciously accepted the free time. She more than earned it. But she wouldn't do that. She had a very strong work principle the two times I worked with her. I think she was afraid word would get back that we had to stop shooting because she was too old and couldn't do it anymore.

She was just as vital on the set of *The Comedians* as she had been when we did *The Curious Savage*. She reported on time, line perfect and ready.

Everything was her career, and her career was everything.[28]

Despite Glenville's efforts to make American audiences apprehensive about Haiti's close proximity, *The Comedians*, with it's impressive and oppressive atmosphere, has for its main characters people whose actions are predictable, no matter how well they are played.

Premiering at the Coronet and the De-Mille theatre in New York on October 31, 1967, *The Comedians* emerged as a motion picture with a message of horrible implications, and at the same time only a moderately engaging portrait of indifference on the part of its character to the crisis at hand. Lillian's character leaves when the going gets too rough. Richard Burton's American Ambassador, although well played, is a stock character whose actions were ones we expected, even if enacted with the Burton gestures that have become so familiar.

What lingers afterwards makes us realize that political unrest, although seemingly far away in another country, is much closer than it seems. The world is smaller. Nobody can exist or survive in isolation. Not even America.[29]

One only had to examine the list of plays mounted on Broadway during the 1967-68 season to observe that it was a golden age for straight plays. Usually the musicals have greater grosses than the comedies or dramas, but it was generally conceded that the quality of the musicals was inferior to the new plays by American playwrights Arthur Miller, Frank Gilroy, Tennessee Williams, Neil Simon, and Robert Anderson, as well as the imports of Great Britain's Tom Stoppard, Joe Orton, and Harold Pinter.[30]

Lillian had returned to the Broadway theatre after a 3 year absence to appear in Robert Anderson's *I Never Sang for My Father*, which concerned itself with the animosity between a father and son, and the son's lack of feeling as the father dies alone, wheelchair-ridden and filled with hate.[31]

The play opened in New York on January 25, 1968, after having done good business during its pre–Broadway engagement in Boston.[32]

Lillian told an interviewer from *The Boston Herald Traveler* how she prepares:

> When I work on a part, I don't have a pat formula. I wait for the director to tell me what he wants — then I do it. A strong director like Alan [Schneider] pulls all the performances together. In any medium you need a Boss Man, whether it's films or theatre or on TV. I learned that early with Griffith.[33]

Clive Barnes, reviewing *I Never Sang for My Father* for *The New York Times,* slaughtered any potential the play might have had for a successful run with his opening line: "A soap opera is a soap opera whichever way you slice the soap."[34]

While citing the acting as often admirable, and acknowledging the believable poignancy of the situation, Barnes complained that the playwright's intentions were "betrayed by its over obviousness."[35]

Lillian and the author backstage at the Longacre Theater in New York, 1968, during the run of *I Never Sang for My Father*.

Lillian's performance was singled out for special mention:

> Lillian Gish's delicately fluttering mother, warm and attractive, is another performance worthy of a more productive cause.[36]

Lillian spoke to this biographer during the first week of the play's 124-performance run.[37]

> I Never Sang for My Father, like All the Way Home, is a work with autobiographical overtones. Both plays aren't what you would call happy Saturday night fare. The lack of communication between father and son is a mighty theme that will forever be constantly explored.
>
> Many things in I Never Sang were stated, as if that should be enough. This is not an Arthur Miller play with a lot of shrieking and fingerpointing accusations and somebody not being there during hard times. Robert Anderson is obviously not a New York thirties protest writer. He writes with restraint and grace and he doesn't skirt the issues. It took courage to mount this play in a Broadway theatre instead of an off–Broadway house.
>
> Hal Holbrook, playing the son who doubles as narrator, does a splendid job of holding everything together, like the Stage Manager did in Our Town.
>
> I always felt, when I read the script for the first time, that Anderson's play should have been a novel, too. So much of the narration plays like prose. I think the play would have a larger audience.[38]

Although the play kept Lillian living and working in New York while Dorothy was in Rapollo, Italy, there were weekly visits.

Lillian's understudy, former silent film actress Lois Wilson, who had starred in Miss Lulu Bett, The Covered Wagon, and The Great Gatsby, recalled Lillian's often repeated pattern after the Sunday matinee:

> We were playing 3 mats a week — Wednesday, Saturday, and Sunday. As soon as the curtain comes down: boom! Lillian dashes down the stairs and right into the taxi waiting to scoot her to Kennedy for a flight to Rome.
>
> She'd arrive early the next day, get to Rapollo and stay a day with Dorothy, and then fly back here. Somehow she'd grab a few hours of sleep on the cot in her dressing room and manage to do her show. Thank God for time zones.[39]

Playing eight shows a week were demanding in themselves, but the visits to Dorothy were beginning to sap her strength.

During one of her visits to Rapollo, Lillian was invited to co-star with her longtime friend, actress Helen Hayes, in a television production of Joseph Kesselring's hit homicidal comedy, Arsenic and Old Lace.[40] Lillian and Helen would be playing two sweet, elderly ladies, sisters, who murder lonely old men after extending an invitation to them to visit and sample their special elderberry wine.

Helen Hayes jokingly told this author at their first meeting that she and Lillian had known each other forever.[41] In actuality, their friendship, according to close friends, started around 1930. When Lillian had become frustrated with Hollywood after her sound debut in One Romantic Night and decided to return to New York, stage star Helen Hayes had just signed a film contract and was on her way to the coast to begin shooting what was later released as The Sin of Madeline Claudet.[42]

Helen Hayes said:

> Lillian and I both came up the same way: touring in shows when we were children. Lillian went into films, and I kept on doing stage work.

Helen Hayes, Lillian, Bob Crane and an unidentified player in *Arsenic and Old Lace* (1968, ABC-TV). "The only time I worked with my longtime friend Helen Hayes."

Lillian came back to work for Jed Harris in *Uncle Vanya*, which was her Broadway debut, although she had done stage work many years earlier.

She said her voice didn't record right [on film], and not to expect very much. In those early days of sound, if the studio felt your voice didn't match your look, you had no future, no chance.

Luckily, I came from the stage, and I have no previous silent film career. There were no preconceptions on the part of any producer regarding how I sound on film. I knew that stage people were in demand, and they took us as we were.

I spoke 8 shows a week. No amplification. If producers or their scouts could hear us in the last row of the balcony, we were approached with a contract. Voices were what landed the contract. Faces were what maintained them.

Lillian's voice didn't register then or now as the sound of a damsel-in-distress, the type she played in those Griffith films. Lillian in those days was a face.

I was never a face. I was a stage character.[43]

Lillian's three weeks of rehearsals for *Arsenic and Old Lace* required that she rise before eight in the morning, report to the television studio at ten, rehearse until six, have something to eat, and get back to the theatre by seven, the required half-hour before the curtain went up. It was well after midnight when she would arrive home. With Sunday rehearsals, it meant she was working without a day off.[44]

Working straight through the week was nothing unusual for Lillian. A 7-day workweek was commonplace when she began acting in one-reelers for Mr. Griffith in 1912. A full day in a full week in 1968, more than half a century later, made Lillian realize she had come full circle.

As long as work was available, she would take it!

During rehearsals for *Arsenic and Old Lace*, Lillian preferred to dine at Longchamps because of their flattering lighting. Lillian had maintained her annual overseas trips for injections of lamb embryos in an effort to keep her looking young. Longchamps had low lights, which didn't throw too much attention on anyone. Lillian was fearful of looking older and not being able to get any work.[45]

Helen observed:

> Sometimes she [Lillian Gish] is so closely in tune with her own drummer she misses the beat of what is going on around her.... All her

clothes date from 40 years, but the dresses are still elegant ... and they still fit.

> When it came to work, she's still sharp as a tack.[46]

For the final week of rehearsals, prior to the actual taping, Lillian was rising at five to be ready for makeup at seven. Because the taping went beyond the usual time, Lillian missed two performances of the play. Lois Wilson played them.[47]

I Never Sang for My Father ended its run on May 11. Shortly afterwards a telephone call from Rapollo informed Lillian that Dorothy had contracted bronchial pneumonia. Three hours later, Lillian was on a plane bound for Italy.

With Lillian at her bedside, 70-year-old Dorothy died on June 5, 1968. Next to the passing of her mother, Lillian would regard Dorothy's death as the second greatest tragedy of her life.[48]

Lillian had been raised by her mother to always look after Dorothy because she was younger and more playful. Now that Lillian was alone, she would only have to look after herself.

Otherwise they'll hire another little girl...

CHAPTER 34

Full Circle

I think movies must be preserved, because they're such an important part of our heritage ... nobody knew it was an art form except Lillian Gish.

— Roddy McDowall
The New York Times
December 2, 1997[1]

It had taken Lillian almost twelve years to complete a *Reader's Digest* proposal to write a "Most Unforgettable Person I Ever Met" article. Lillian thought she could submit something on her years with D. W. Griffith.[2]

That's what I thought it would be — a simple remembrance and tribute to Mr. Griffith, the father of film, the man who gave motion pictures its grammar and structure.

I was naive to think that a career like Mr. Griffith's could be summarized or covered in a few pages.

Then they wanted me to include some little anecdotes about Mr. Griffith's contemporaries: Chaplin [Charlie Chaplin] and Mary [Mary Pickford].

I sent in a few more pages, and they called and asked me, "Where are you in all of this?"

I frankly didn't want to say much about myself. The article wasn't supposed to be about me. It was supposed to be about Mr. Griffith.

I told them so, but they answered, "We want something about you in all of this. Otherwise, it doesn't make

any sense. You were there when all of this was happening."

The Night of the Hunter had just been released, and Mr. Laughton [Charles Laughton] had given interviews about being influenced by Mr. Griffith, and I had worked for Mr. Griffith, and here I was working, still working, and you know the rest.[3]

The once simple article was no longer a pleasant divertissement, a few pages to be read on the bus or at the barber shop or beauty parlor. What Lillian was asked to write was the story of motion pictures, which, of course, would include the beginnings of her own career.

After three vacations in Switzerland *The Movies, Mr. Griffith, and Me*, written in collaboration with Ann Pinchot, was a reality.

Lillian had kept her promise.[4]

Film historian Arthur Mayer (author of *The Movies*, written in collaboration with Richard Griffith), reviewing Lillian's autobiography for *The New York Times*, detected her reluctance to disclose very much about her personal life, and how she

313

only concentrated on the external facts and events and how they affected her career.

What was most impressive and important about Lillian's book were

> her descriptions of the mechanics of the rehearsal system on which his [D. W. Griffith's] achievements were so largely based and which his successors so ill-advisedly abandoned.[5]

That she was praised for setting down Griffith's methods of filming in an articulate manner was what mattered most to her. She had been present and active in every aspect of the process. Millions were going to the movies and paying for what she did on the screen. Her private life, Lillian had maintained from her very beginnings, was private. Her film and stage work were professional appearances. Everything else was a disappearance.

William K. Everson, who furnished Lillian with his personal files on D. W. Griffith during the writing of her autobiography, explained:

> Lillian, from the very start, didn't want to write a kiss-and-tell book about herself. She certainly didn't live that kind of life, and even if she had, she certainly wasn't going to discuss it with anyone.
>
> Her friend Paulette Goddard, who was married to Charlie Chaplin, Burgess Meredith, and Erich Maria Remarque, returned her publisher's advance when she was told to include her sex life in addition to her recollections of working with Chaplin in *Modern Times* and *The Great Dictator*.
>
> Lillian's book was supposed to be about Griffith — his contributions and her recollections — since she was there when it happened. That she had remained active only served to make whatever she wrote more credible.
>
> She saw no reason to include anything else. Her association with

George Jean Nathan was important because he provided the entrée to the important literary personalities of the day. We'll never really know what the true nature of their relationship was, anymore than we'll learn about D. W. Griffith when he wasn't near a camera. She was quite hurt by all accounts when he began to spend more of his time with Carol Dempster than with her.

What ultimately mattered most to Lillian about the Griffith-Dempster relationship was how it affected his art: it suffered and declined. I'm sure Lillian was quite hurt when nobody wanted to use him, because it meant they wouldn't use her.

Work was what mattered most to Lillian. It had been ingrained in her by her mother since she was a child when her father abandoned them. I was amazed Lillian wrote anything about her life away from the studios.

Lillian's autobiography is quite revealing in that she consciously distanced herself from human experiences. She preferred to watch or listen, rather than participate.

It had a definite affect on her art. Her range was narrow, but it was very, very deep. No other silent film actress could portray loss as well as she.

On the other hand, Dorothy was the opposite and she paid the price, as some of us do. Maybe that was what Lillian was hinting at when she and Griffith called Dorothy the better actress. Dorothy had experiences, and she went into them with her eyes open.

If you want to find out anything about Lillian's private life, you would have to ask her contemporaries, and I'm not so sure they know very much.

Both of her books, *The Movies, Mr. Griffith, and Me* and *Dorothy and Lillian Gish,* are the recollections of a working actress and still-working actress who was there when it all began.

She wrote it for future generations. Her acting is her *self* and her *self* is in those books. There isn't anything else.[6]

What finally evolved into the formal presentation known as *Lillian Gish and the Movies* had begun as informal Griffith lectures Lillian had been occasionally presenting in the '30s and '40s in stock theatres and universities when there wasn't any stage or film work. Armed with a few reels from *Way Down East, Broken Blossoms, The Lady and the Mouse*, and her debut film, *An Unseen Enemy*, she would provide commentary.

At the program's conclusion, if the mood of the audience so warranted, Lillian would answer a few questions afterwards. Certainly there were people who wanted to tell her how the ice floe sequences in *Way Down East* and the scenes with her sister Dorothy in *Orphans of the Storm* had made an indelible impression on their childhood when these films were originally released.

Now her program, created and produced by Nathan Kroll and edited by Miriam Arsham, was going to be reaching yet another generation of filmgoers and film buffs. The presentation would include, in addition to the first flickering of film, scenes of Charlie Chaplin, Buster Keaton, and Rudolph Valentino, as well as sequences from her films of the twenties away from the Griffith studio: *The White Sister, La Bohème*, and *The Wind*. There would be no question and answer period.

Rather than do only a standard book signing tour with appearances limited to influential bookstores and department stores with large book sections, Lillian saw this presentation as a great opportunity to show herself and her work, accompanied by her own unique commentary. She often jokingly said that she had been present at the birth of the film and had seen the "baby" grow and mature. The twentieth century was the first century to record its history on film, and D. W. Griffith was a vital part of the twentieth century.

Instead of occasionally being accompanied by Dorothy (as was the case decades earlier), Lillian was now blessed with James E. Frasher, who was hired to serve as Lillian's manager. Until now, Lillian, who had been quite independent all of her life and career regarding assistants and assistance, had always preferred to handle her own responsibilities.

At their first meeting, James was warned, "I wear out managers," but Lillian had more than met her match. For the rest of her life she had someone who, if such were possible, was more dedicated to her career and welfare than she was. Jim was Lillian's confidante, advisor, and, when the occasion warranted, a terrific chef.

On their cross-country and European tours, entailing hotel accommodations, Lillian and Jim often did a reversal after being shown where they would be staying. A quick exchange and transfer of luggage was discreetly transacted. Jim took Lillian's more luxurious accommodations, and Lillian went to the single standard room![7]

1969: New York City: Columbia University, McMillan Theatre. Against the turmoil and background of campus unrest (an adjacent building had been occupied by several student dissenters) it was business as usual. *Lillian Gish and the Movies* was presented by the film division of the School of the Arts for the benefit of the newly established D. W. Griffith Scholarship Fund.[8] The audience of 1200, unable to hear any outside sounds of protest or cries for academic freedom, included Katherine Hepburn, Lauren Bacall, Truman Capote, Anita Loos, Aileen Pringle, and the biographer.

Lillian, gowned in white and standing erectly behind a lectern, a spotlight of her for the entire duration of the program, spoke from a prepared script, pausing only to watch the action on the screen. "Do you realize that film is our only native art form?...There's a form and immediacy about film today, almost like a car wreck."

The audience hung onto every word, applauding at the opening shots of the classic ice floe sequence in *Way Down East*.

That little spot on the ice is me.[9]

For ninety minutes, without an intermission, the capacity crowd sat spellbound, witnessing an icon whose career began before the twentieth century, and who, during her silent film years, had valiantly battled screen crisis after screen crisis: windstorms, a search for a blind sister, consumption, and an earthquake.

The evening's presentation, like the years of Lillian's career, had gone by too quickly. The audience rose in concert when it was over and applauded loudly for several minutes.

The presentation would be going on the road. At the age of 76, Lillian was just entering another phase of her amazing life. *Lillian Gish and the Movies* would be presented anywhere and everywhere there was an audience.

William K. Everson, who researched and compiled the films for the presentation that would occupy Lillian for several transcontinental crossings and tours around the world for more than a decade, commented:

> Lillian Gish's Griffith touring show was an annuity and a testament to herself. It was her valedictory and a farewell reminder to the world of who she was and with whom she worked. She wanted to be forever linked in cinema history with D. W. Griffith — her mentor, the master, the father of film, the man who gave motion pictures its grammar.
>
> To many she still was the Griffith heroine. She had arrived on the Biograph lot after Mary Pickford and Blanche Sweet, who were the reigning stars. By virtue of dedication to her craft and intense work ethic, Lillian became the Griffith star that audi-

ences would remember in years to come.

Lillian's presentation, which she would be doing for years, crystallized her as living history — her history, if you will, as she saw it.

What was conveniently forgotten, or perhaps consciously omitted, was that she had been forced to leave motion pictures in the twilight of the silent era, and take a great chance that when she returned to the theatre, she might be unsuccessful.

By virtue of having made these transitions quite successfully as each challenge presented itself and was met, Lillian was now able to compartmentalize her life and career. She could reinvent herself to a younger generation on her terms while not missing the opportunity to remind older generations that for the better part of the twentieth century, there has always been a Lillian Gish who was part of their lives.

She created her own demand, and to her amazement, the demand to see her in the flesh was greater than she had ever anticipated.

That she could proudly stand next to a screen on which images from 50 years were projected was her way of saying to the audience, who recognized them and applauded them, Look what we've come through![10]

Aileen Pringle, whose silent film career had begun in 1919 (seven years after Lillian's), cynically encapsulated Lillian's achievement to the biographer after the applause had stopped:

> Lillian Gish was a professional orphan of the storm who knew when to come in out of the storm. Sheer luck … but I envy her.[11]

In newspaper interviews, Lillian stated the purpose of *Lillian Gish and the Movies: The Art of film, 1900–1928*:

> To reach the young in colleges, universities and schools who will make

our future pictures, and to impress upon them the power they leave on the world, and to take the responsibility of where they leave this power.[12]

Unable to visit Russia in 1928 with Mary Pickford, Douglas Fairbanks, and Charlie Chaplin because of her mother's illness, she went to Leningrad and Moscow for 15 days in 1969[13] to present her program at the Kremlin Palace of Congress on July 7. In attendance were representatives from over 70 countries.[14]

Her lecture was also presented at the Palais de Chaillot in Paris by famed historian and film preservationist Henri Langlois, director of the Cinémathèque Française.

Langlois, in the summer of the following year (1970), presented a series of silent films at the Metropolitan Museum in New York.

He summarized his impression of meeting Lillian Gish to this biographer, who was hired to provide musical accompaniment for the series: "Monsieur, Lillian Gish is the cinema!"[15]

In Los Angeles, California, Lillian had been honored with an honorary Academy Award "for Superlative Artistry and for Distinguished Contribution to the Progress of Motion Pictures"[16] at the 43rd Academy Awards on April 15, 1971, at the Dorothy Chandler Pavilion.[17]

What Lillian said in her short acceptance speech humbly summed up a lifetime of dedication to the art that is the motion picture:

> It was our privilege for a little while to serve that beautiful thing, the film. And we never doubted for a moment that it was the most powerful thing, the mind and heartbeat of our technical century.[18]

With headlines ranging from the highly laudatory "Lillian Gish Creates Magic" (*The Denver Post*, June 28, 1971) to the more informal "Dignified, Delicate and an Absolute Gas" (*Philadelphia Daily News*, September 29, 1971), it was obvious that Lillian, no matter how the headlines were written, earned the respect of another generation.[19]

The Denver Post:

> Her audience ... will need no special markers of Oscar statuettes to signify their feelings about Miss Gish. She will forever be carried in their hearts.[20]

A student quoted in the *Philadelphia Daily News*:

> Frankly ... I thought she'd turn me right off. She's really something out of the past and all that stuff just doesn't hold up anymore. But she gassed me. I think I love her.[21]

Lillian, in the wake of having just received the Handel Medallion in New York for her achievement in the arts (her other awards were honorary degrees from Rollins College and Mt. Holyoke College), recalled her impressions of her cross-country tour and some of her post-performance visitors backstage:

> I didn't know how much film collecting actually went on until I met some of the collectors. Because of them, so much of Mr. Griffith's work is available on video!
>
> Imagine that! Films I had made over 50 years ago are being reissued on video in good condition, and they're being rediscovered by young people!
>
> They show the same excitement and enthusiasm as their grandparents did when those films were first released!
>
> In those days, I'd be stopped for an autograph. Now I'm stopped for information! They want to know more

about *The Birth of a Nation*, which some of them might have seen in their university film history classes before they ever saw my *Art of Film* presentation. They want to know what attitudes Mr. Griffith had about the period after the Civil War, and What do you think of them?

The Birth of a Nation, I always tell them, has been misinterpreted since its original release [1915]. That it still gets the same reactions all of these years later [1973] only continues to indicate to me how aware Mr. Griffith was of the times.

Remember, Mr. Griffith was a very proud Southerner, and when the film came out the Civil War had only been over for fifty years. There was still bitterness on both sides. He was very courageous to put a Southern viewpoint, since they lost the War, on the screen.

I've learned to adjust myself to seeing 2 or sometimes 3 generations of the same family visiting me, and hearing them talk about when they saw some of these films. I know they didn't see them at the same time.

Some of the younger people, who are eager to show off their knowledge, usually begin their questions: When you made such and such, and they give the year...

I try not to wince, but it's true. Their years are quite accurate. I don't like to think of the year of the film as anything else but a date. I can see their minds subtracting the year of the film from the current year. When you're young, you do that, I guess. I don't like to think of years. Art is eternal, and the camera has made us live forever.[22]

1973: Lillian's return to Broadway, playing Marina the nurse in an-star cast, Mike Nichols directed revival of Anton Chekhov's *Uncle Vanya*, had to give Lillian a sense of déjà vu, even though the play was given a new, modern translation.

The Nichols production, which in-

cluded George C. Scott, Julie Christie, Cathleen Nesbit, Barnard Hughes, Nichol Williamson, Conrad Bain, and Elizabeth Wilson, was going to be played in the round, rather than the traditional proscenium manner to which Lillian was accustomed.

While each new production of any play was a new experience, the new staging of a play she had done before, albeit 43 years earlier, was at first unnerving.

Lillian explained her temporary uneasiness:

I had seen theatre-in-the-round productions, and of course my perspective as an actress wasn't the same as that of the audience. When I first stepped onto that circle stage and saw those empty seats on all four sides of me, I thought I would be constantly turning with every speech and acting as if I were on a merry go-round or spinning around and around like a top.

It wasn't that way at all.

Mr. Nichols [director Mike Nichols] made me feel very secure and relaxed.

Very few actors, unless you're James O'Neill, who played *The Count of Monte Cristo* virtually all of his life, or Yul Brynner, who played the King in *The King and I*, have the opportunity to be in another production of the same play.

When I was asked by Jed Harris to act in his *Uncle Vanya*, the play that brought me back to the theatre years ago [in 1930], I naturally said yes. I played Elena. It was a wonderful experience. It made me want to do more theatre.

For Mr. Nichols' production, I wasn't playing the same role. Putting aside my memories of the earlier production was very easy.

I approached this production in the round as if the play and the new staging were a totally new package. And it is. The translation which Mr. Nichols worked on, along with the new staging, brought to mind what Sir John [Gielgud] had told me when he played in *Hamlet* [1936] over here. Play it as if this is your first time with a new play.

Which is what I was doing. It's like returning to a familiar neighborhood you once visited before. The area is the same, but some of the houses are different and newer.

Mr. Nichols' *Uncle Vanya* is being played for comedy, the way Chekhov should be played. Chekhov wrote human comedy, but in the American theatre, playing Russian anything, unless it is outright slapstick, has come to mean gloom and doom. *Uncle Vanya* is not *The Lower Depths*.

It's ironic, isn't it, playing the role of the nurse. Mr. Griffith had once thought of filming *Romeo and Juliet*, with me as Juliet. It never happened. I would have loved to have played Juliet.

When I finally did play in *Romeo and Juliet*, it was many years later [1965] and I was the Nurse.

Here I am, back in *Uncle Vanya*, and I'm playing a Nurse — Marina, the Nurse.

I guess this is what happens to actresses if you are fortunate to have a long career. You start playing juveniles, then ingenues, and you finish as a nurse![23]

The Mike Nichols production of Anton Chekhov's *Uncle Vanya* opened in New York at the Circle in the Square Theatre on June 4, 1973.

Of the production and Lillian's performance, Clive Barnes, for the next morning's edition of *The New York Times*, wrote:

Uncle Vanya ... represents the kind of classic theatre we need in New York. This is a very special brand of theatrical excitement....

It is to Mike Nichols' credit that the stars don't get in your eyes and conceal the classic....

Lillian Gish proved to be a soft-toned delight as the old nurse.[24]

Greeting this biographer, a jubilant Lillian Gish exclaimed:

I'm glad there are parts for me to play. Both Shakespeare and Chekhov were playwrights who didn't limit themselves to writing for just one age group.

Did you have to memorize Shakespeare's *All the World's a Stage* when you were in school? I know I must be in one of those stages.

Isn't Mr. Nichols' staging wonderful? With this production there are no bad seats. You can see and hear everything! That's important, especially in a classic where the language is important.

This round staging works well with this play. The audiences are very involved. They are so close, you can hear them listening!

Being in the theatre with a good play, a good cast, and a good director is still thrilling. We can't wait to get onstage, and that is what matters most![25]

In a season of revivals, the Mike Nichols production of *Uncle Vanya* was the "masterful" revival, chalking up 64 performances.[26]

CHAPTER 35

Honors and Surprises

I'm not a feminist. I like to think I used common sense most of the time.

I don't know how I'd manage if I were starting out today.... I guess I would do what I've always had to do: to decide on what meant more, and go after it all the way.

—Lillian Gish
Conversation with author,
January 1976

1974: In March Lillian curtailed her social activities. She no longer was a familiar face at opening nights, and her presence at restaurants was limited. It was time for a disappearance, something to which her friends had become accustomed. She had paid her visit to Baden-Baden.

William K. Everson revealed what was occurring in Lillian's still-active life:

> Lillian's secretly been taking singing and dancing lessons. Apparently she's going to be doing musical comedy now, or at least some sort of revue.
>
> She's done everything but an opera. But I wouldn't put it past her.[1]

A month later, Lillian, with John Raitt, Cyril Ritchard, Tammy Grimes, Dick Shawn, and Patrice Munsel, boarded the SS *Rotterdam* to perform nightly in *Theatre at Sea*, a series of 11 evenings of plays, lectures, and scenes from musicals, vaudeville, and cabaret. The final evening was a celebration of the American musical

contribution to the world, from frontier songs and dances of America's nineteenth century to excerpts from operettas, and the beginnings of American musical comedy. Because of the success of *American Jubilee*, the production was slated for a future Broadway engagement.[2]

Lillian, in England that September with her *Art of Film* lecture, told British readers of *The London Times* that D. W. Griffith's lack of business sense was legendary. Fifty-eight years after the filming of *Intolerance* (1916), she could still bewail how frustrating this was at the time, and how devoted she still remained to her mentor's memory, and the preservation of his artistic visions and conceptions that kept her steadily employed for ten years: "If he [D. W. Griffith] kept just half the profits of *Intolerance* he could have made all the films he ever wanted instead of dying broke."[3]

1975: With Biograph contemporaries, actress Blanche Sweet and writer Anita

Loos, Lillian was present at the Museum of Modern Art in January of the occasion of D. W. Griffith's 100th birthday, celebrated with the unveiling of a reproduction of a stamp issued in his honor.

Lillian's performance in those early Griffith potboilers, noted film critic Vincent Canby of *The New York Times* (while considering Griffith's 1913 short, *The Lady and the Mouse*), were as "complex as any she would give in Griffith's later features *Way Down East* [1920] and *Orphans of the Storm* [1922]." Additionally, Canby concluded, the making of 500 of these one- and two-reelers in a period of four years is a major achievement.[4]

In preparing for her resumed *Art of Film* lecture tour, Lillian researched herself as if she were another person. She didn't want to disappoint her interviewers, be they newspaper journalists, film historians, or interested university students. The younger they were, the more disappointed they were apt to be if she couldn't recall the name of the supporting player, director, or plot line. There were things she had forgotten, and things she definitely didn't wish to remember. Evading a personal question might somehow give the impression that she was old.[5]

The television generation, naturally, asked about her television, even though her presentation had only covered her years in the silents that ended in the late '20s, just before the birth of sound.

I don't remember everything I did on television. I was amazed that somebody asked me afterwards about Elmer Rice's *Street Scene* [1951] and some of the plays from *Campbell Anthology*. That was a summer series [1952 and 1953] which I had all but forgotten.

It's amazing what people remember, and how powerful the media can be, and obviously was, even back then. Those programs were only aired once.

You know, Mr. Griffith was one of the first directors to be exposed to television in its early development, and he chose not to be involved with any part of it. Television is just as personally involving as motion pictures, but I think he was reluctant to take any responsibility for a product that went directly into your home that was so accessible for free.

Free entertainment was something Mr. Griffith associated with no salary. He had begun as a stage actor, and there were times he didn't always get all of his salary he was promised by those theatre managers. Some of those managers and producers sneaked away with the receipts, and those actors had to make their way on their own.

Mother, Dorothy, and I knew about things like that.

A film was something you paid to see, and if you liked it, you saw it more than once. How many people have told me they saw *Broken Blossoms* more than once? Or *Way Down East*?

It's very gratifying to be remembered by so many people from towns all across the country. This tour has taken me to areas I haven't seen since I was on the road with Dorothy and mother.

I remember split weeks: two or three days in one place, and then we travelled by train to the next town and hoped the hotel or rooming house knew our date of arrival, and the room was available, and neat, and clean, and decent.

That part of touring hasn't changed. Jim [manager James E. Frasher] still has to telephone ahead to make sure everyone knows he'll be there.

We travel by airplane now. It doesn't take as much time. Everything is so streamlined. The world has gotten smaller.[6]

With the addition of Larry Kert, who was unable to join the company the previous spring, the expanded Morton Da Costa production, now retitled *A Musical Jubilee*, opened at the St. James Theatre in New York on November 13, 1975.

Drama critic Clive Barnes' jubilant review appeared the following morning in *The New York Times*:

> There is so much that is smashing about the new musical entertainment, *A Musical Jubilee*....
>
> Seven stars of genuine stature performed with consummate skill and grace....
>
> ...and as for Miss Gish ... it would be difficult, perhaps impossible, for anyone not to love her. She glistens. So does the show.[7]

Lillian was assigned a large basement dressing room with a curtained window that shut out any possibility of outside light. A large sign, written in magic marker and prominently displayed on an ironing board, informs all who enter that at the opposite end of the hall "The Madam is practicing her arias."

Everyone knows the identity of The Madam. The voice is that of Patrice Munsel, the youngest American singer ever to star at the Metropolitan Opera.

Lillian listened, and began:

> This show is fun to do. It was fun to do when we were onboard the *Rotterdam* as part of the ship's entertainment. We are really having a good time on that stage. I hope it comes across that way to the audience.
>
> I'm not a stranger to the musical theatre. I always went to the opera, and to the musicals, whenever I had the chance. The American musical is a valid contribution to world Theatre.
>
> Were you surprised to hear my contribution to "I Wanna Be Loved by You"? It wouldn't have been as effective if I had to carry the song alone. It needed the good voices of Pat [Patrice] Munsel and Tammy Grimes to sing it the right way, so I could add my contribution.

> "I Didn't Raise My Boy to Be a Soldier" is a pure dramatic recitation. It was very often heard during the First World War. It was a mother's sentiment of the times, but no mother would ever tell her son to shirk his patriotic responsibility and obligation. Those lyrics are timeless, and they still have directness and relevance that speaks to the Viet Nam generation.
>
> Some of these old songs recreate some wonderful moments.... What better way to celebrate 200 years of America than in its music, which is still heard all over the world![8]

With its seemingly inexhaustible energy. *A Musical Jubilee* ran for 92 performances.[9]

1976: *Twin Detectives*, starring the Hager Twins of television's "Hee Haw" fame, marked Lillian's television film debut on May 1, 1976. The film, intended as a pilot for a television series, utilized the identical twins who would confuse their opponents by appearing in two places at the same time as they attempted to solve the murder of a beautiful psychic.[10] The series was never developed.

When D. W. Griffith asked Lillian and Dorothy, prior to hiring them for their first film *An Unseen Enemy* in 1912, where they came from, Lillian answered, "The theatre ... but we come from Massillon."[11]

Throughout her entire career, Lillian, whenever she was interviewed, always mentioned her Ohio origins, referring to herself as a "buckeye," the nickname given to the state of Ohio.[12]

On June 11, 1976, the loyalty of the Gish sisters to their native Ohio was formally acknowledged with the dedication of The Gish Film Theater at Bowling Green University in Bowling Green, Ohio.

Lillian, present for the dedication, accepted the honor for her late sister and herself.

On the following day, Lillian was awarded the honorary degree of Doctor of

The Gish Film Theater, Bowling Green State University, Bowling Green, Ohio. *(Courtesy of the office of Public Relations, Bowling Green State University, Bowling Green, Ohio, 43403.)* "Now I have a home!" Lillian exclaimed.

Performing Arts. With the dedication and honorary degree came a film studies program in the College of Arts and Sciences.

Lillian, who always realized the importance of film as a legitimate art form, noted:

> Technically, film is providing us with constant miracles; emotionally, it has brought the world closer together. It is far more powerful than the printed world. It is how we know each other. It is our greatest form of communication.[13]

The hopes and wishes of Dr. Ralph Haven Wolfe of Bowling Green University's English Department had become a reality:

> I had always admired the work of both Lillian and Dorothy Gish. I was in the audience when Lillian pre-

sented her *Art of Film* lecture at Findlay College in 1971. She was not only presenting film history, she was presenting American history, of which she had been a very vital part.

> When I heard and saw clusters of students actively discussing what they had been privileged to witness, I knew we had to have Lillian Gish at Bowling Green. She and Dorothy had made permanent contributions to twentieth century America and the world. They needed a permanent home at Bowling Green in their native state that would recognize their importance.

> Nobody at any college or university could accomplish this alone. I had support all the way.[14]

1977: Director Robert Altman, in Palm Springs, California, after the completion of

With John Cromwell in *A Wedding* (1978, 20th Century — Fox, directed by Robert Altman).

Three Women, responded caustically to a question regarding plans for a future project. He would film a wedding and everything a wedding entailed. After thinking over what he had said in jest, Altman discussed the idea at lunch. That same evening he outlined a story on which he would collaborate with John Considine.[15]

In the spring, Altman personally brought a script of his proposed wedding film to Lillian's East 57th Street apartment in New York. Sitting on a sofa in Lillian's living room, where once Mary Pickford and Katherine Cornell met for Sunday afternoon tea poured by Lillian's mother,[16] Altman discussed Lillian's pivotal role of Nettie, the grandmother, a character with the same name as Altman's own grandmother.[17] Lillian would be part of an impressive cast of 48 that included Carol Burnett, Mia Farrow, Geraldine Chaplin, Desi

Arnaz, Jr., Viveca Lindfors, and Lauren Hutton.[18]

An Altman experience, Lillian had heard from an actress who had once acted in an Altman film, was definitely not a Griffith experience. Where Griffith held tight reins and everything was practically choreographed, Altman was the very opposite. His players worked "free," and they improvised situations, some of which went into the final script. Altman's players were given their actual lines on the night before shooting.[19]

In *A Wedding* each character was given a "secret" about their background. Lillian's "secret" would be that her character dies during the wedding ceremony, a "secret" that could not remain a secret during the wedding reception.[20]

A Wedding was her 100th film. That certainly wasn't a secret.[21] Viveca Lindfors, who played the catereress,[22] told this biographer:

> I wanted to work with Robert Altman for a long time, and I wrote to him and I told him I would always be available. Altman's eyes were never on the commercial marketplace. He had ideas, which he discussed.
>
> I see nothing wrong with going after something if you really want it. Hollywood actors always wait to be approached. In New York, in the Theatre, you don't work that way. At least I don't. I never did.
>
> I'm like Lillian: a working actress, an actress who likes to work. This is my chosen profession![23]

Robert Altman's *A Wedding* involves two disparately different families: the bride's (the Brenners) whose fortune was made from operating a truckstop in Louisiana, and the groom's (the Corellis) who are "old money" from Lake Bluff, Illinois. Every family has secrets, and these families are no exception.

At the reception held at the groom's family home, some of these secrets are revealed: the bride, a former high school cheerleader, has a sister whom the groom impregnated. Someone was a morphine addict and girlfriend of Fidel Castro. Another has planned a love tryst with the groom's uncle.

When somebody in the reception line begins insulting the guests, all sorts of pandemonium break loose. The reception is constantly interrupted by arguments, deaths, sexual encounters, and a tornado. Nobody remains unaffected.

The big secret, which nobody wants to discuss, is the unexpected death of the grandmother (Lillian Gish) during the wedding ceremony.

Budgeted at $4,000,000, the shooting began on June 15, 1977, at the Grace Episcopal Church in Oak Park, Illinois. With many of the cast committed to other projects, time was limited. Television star and comedienne Carol Burnett, for instance, was committed to her variety show and had to report no later than August 10.[24] A benefit premiere in Chicago had been announced for April 1978, a chancy thing to promise, since the film was scheduled for an October release. Any delay was subject to different explanations, none of which would be satisfactory.

The success of *A Wedding* would depend, like the French society satire *The Rules of the Game*, upon characterization.[25]

Actors discussing working in an Altman film always mention fun. *A Wedding* was no exception. Carol Burnett called the *Wedding* set a "happy Saturday matinee family atmosphere."[26]

Miraculously, the *Wedding* shoot was completed by the planned deadline and opened in New York, Chicago, and Los Angeles.[27]

Not everything would go well in New York.

Lillian, in addition to her supporting role in *A Wedding*, had also returned to act in front of the television cameras in the second of two pilots which would hopefully become a series.

Sparrow, the title of the proposed series, was the last name of Jerry Sparrow, a New Orleans insurance mailroom clerk turned detective. Episode number one had aired that winter on January 12.

That Sparrow's character had been given an added dimension was obvious when the second episode, the one with Lillian in the supporting cast, was filmed. Now Jerry Sparrow was a private investigator with a large detective agency in New Orleans. Lillian's episode, in which she was cast as a wealthy woman whose valuable rare bird has gone missing, was aired on August 11.

Neither episode of *Sparrow* impressed the network executives. Like Lillian's earlier *Twin Detectives* pilot, the *Sparrow* series was canceled.[28]

With no prospects of future television work in the offing, all of Lillian's hopes rested on good notices for the upcoming Altman film. She had not appeared on the big screen since *The Comedians* in 1967.

What nobody anticipated was the decision of *The New York Times* printers to go on a strike that lasted from September 23 to November 5, the early weeks of *A Wedding*'s release. The unavailability of this major metropolitan daily severely hampered the production's box-office potential. Many New Yorkers only read *The New York Times,* from which they drew their opinions, despite the easy access to other New York newspapers and magazines.

Hardest hit would be the incoming Broadway and off–Broadway plays and latest film releases, whose success depended upon positive word-of-mouth.

Film and drama critic Walter Kerr, to publicize *A Wedding* playing at the Sutton Theatre, utilized the wire service of *The New York Times and The Associated Press* to disseminate his review.

> You have to be able to count to get through Robert Altman's *A Wedding.* So do the characters who drift in and out of corners, bathrooms, sickrooms and cellars during the reception following the ceremony....
>
> Lillian Gish appears as the matriarch of the bridegroom's family, lying ill in an upstairs room.... She dies before the wedding party assembles, and her doctor goes to extreme lengths to keep news of her demise from family and friends ... which means that one after another various daughters, caterers ... must go to Miss Gish's chamber and carry on conversations with her corpse. One daughter does become concerned enough to ask how Miss Gish's temperature is; the doctor replies that it is somewhat below normal, but that is usual in the circumstances. The others either assume she's playing possum or talk so much them-

selves that they don't notice a body turning slowly to stone.

> ...The film doesn't know how to balance out its serious-comic shift of style ... any mourning which we indulge must be for the half-hearted film itself.[29]

In discussing her role in *A Wedding*, Lillian told William K. Everson: "I don't know. I slept through it!'

"She would say no more," added Everson. "She hoped she had aroused enough curiosity to get people to see it."[30]

Although Robert Altman's *A Wedding* ran for four months in New York and was a success,[31] one offended fan wrote a letter to the editor asking why "some little model" (Lauren Hutton) was cast in a movie with "the great Lillian Gish."[32]

Lauren Hutton was unaware that someone had written such a letter until a fan informed her. She was also surprised when she learned that Lillian had taken the time to answer the incensed letter writer.

> Lillian immediately fired off this letter saying in fact she thought I was a very good actress — something she knew something about.
>
> After that I wrote to Lillian and she wrote to me.[33]

Lauren Hutton further elaborated on her relationship with Lillian in "A Portrait of Lillian Gish," her part of the tribute program *Lillian Gish Remembered* presented on March 15, 1997, at the Bruno Walter Auditorium of the New York Public Library for the Performing Arts. In recalling when she and Lillian had their pictures taken together, Lauren Hutton remarked:

> I was at some opening with her [Lillian Gish], sitting on a couch, and a photographer crouched down in front of us. She quickly put her hand over her face and told him, "Get up,

young man, right now! Don't you know I have jowls." That taught me a lesson; I never let photographers take me from that angle anymore.

There was this exquisitely beautiful thing about Lillian ... her skin just glowed. She had this sweetness.... But you couldn't shock her; she'd seen everything.[34]

As Nellie Sloan in *A Wedding* (1978, 20th Century–Fox, directed by Robert Altman). "I slept through it! It was a welcome change from what happened to me in my D.W. Griffith films."

Lillian returned to Washington in June 1979 to make an appeal to the House Government Operations that they realize the implications resulting from the loss of 12,600,000 feet of 1930 and 1931 newsreel film in nitrate state that was destroyed at a National Archives storage warehouse fire in Suitland, Maryland. Nitrate film is highly flammable.

There also were other reasons to take steps to preserve newsreels: "[The newsreel is] a powerful history, and we should preserve a living record of it."[35]

In October, Lillian, with 48 others (including playwright Phillip Barry and actor-director Sir John Gielgud), was selected by the New York drama critics for the Theatre Hall of Fame.

One month later, Lillian, with her friends Anita Loos, Hermione Gingold, and agent Milton Goldman, attended a 1920s party hosted by Blanchette Rockefeller (the widow of John Rockfeller III) and Richard Oldenburg (president of the Museum of Modern Art) at the museum, marking its 50th anniversary. It was a black tie evening. Many of the ladies attending saw this as an opportunity to dress in '20s period,[36] even if their dresses had to be specially created.

Anita Loos wryly observed:

It's good to see Lillian at a party that isn't connected with film preservation and making sure her name is included.

Isn't that dress she's wearing getting a lot of compliments?

It certainly says something for dieting, doesn't it?

What Lillian saves on clothing she spends on mothballs![37]

In December Lillian and Anita Loos were among the guests in the lounge of the Ethel Barrymore Theatre to honor the late Miss Barrymore's 100th birthday and the 50th anniversary of the theatre named in her honor.[38]

1980: When the Museum of Modern Art honored Lillian with a 19 film retrospective in September, Anita Loos was the most obvious person to write the tribute.

Lillian and I have been friends for almost 50 years....

When I first arrived at the studio [Griffith's Biograph Company in New York] Lillian was away on location, but I met Dorothy. She was a bit of a clown, both on-screen and off, and we became cronies, but it was some time before I really got to know Lillian. I never worked on her pictures. My stories were largely satires in which Lillian would have been out of place.... Dorothy and I loved to tease her by pretending she was "stuffy."

...Her viewpoint on films has been unique; she considers them as Power; a power that generates energy as great as that of Arab oil or the nuclear stations. "There's no question that films influence the entire world as nothing has since the printing press. But impact of the printed word is nowhere near as strong as a visual experience."

Looking back on those early days, I remembered that Lillian had a premonition about the importance of films that few of us shared. It was Lillian alone who took those silent flickers seriously. We others looked on them as a fad that would soon lose public interest.

Her experience [working with Griffith, assisting on lighting, cutting, and editing of scenes] served to increase her awe of the medium and her respect for its infinite capabilities "which ... we haven't yet even begun to realize.[39]

While 81-year-old actress Gloria Swanson announced at a press conference that the segment of her autobiography to be printed in the November issue of the *Ladies' Home Journal* would concentrate on the late Joseph P. (father of President John F.) Kennedy's efforts to get official permission from the Catholic Church to allow him to live apart from his wife Rose,

and maintain a second household with Gloria,[40] Helen Hayes, celebrating an 80th birthday — her 84th.

Lillian's birthday party luncheon at the Four Seasons restaurant, hosted by Douglas Fairbanks, Jr., was attended by several of her friends, including Helen Hayes and actress Joan Fontaine.

Lillian's cake had only one candle. The message was on the icing: "Happy Birthday, Diamond Lil."

To her guests, Lillian announced she wasn't ready to retire. She had just completed filming *Thin Ice*, a television movie for CBS, and she was flying to California to film a *Love Boat* episode.[41]

1981: Lillian, serving as guest preacher at St. Andrew's Episcopal Church in Murray Hill, New Jersey, had a good reason to be happy on Saturday, April 5. At Aqueduct, a 3-year-old chestnut mare named Lillian Gish won her first race, paying $3.40. She had come in second in a previous race.

Jerry Brody, a restaurateur who breeds horses, needed a name for his filly whose sire was "Silent Screen," and whose dam was "Birth of a Nation." When a friend suggested "Lillian Gish," he telephoned Lillian and asked her permission, hoping she wouldn't be offended.

Her response was joyful:

> I've always loved horses, even learned to read with the help of the book *Black Beauty*. By the time I was six, I could ride bareback. And besides, with the horse's parents names, it was only natural that she took mine.
>
> I've never seen Lillian, but now she's a star, and I'll have to pay my respects. My back elevator man has bet on her before, and if he didn't bet to win Sunday, he's going to have a fit. I'm ready to bet on her myself.[42]

CHAPTER 36

Taking Stock

I was supporting myself from the age of four.

I look forward to new places, new people.... Life is just taking somebody's hand, walking a little way with them, dropping it, and taking another hand. And that's the way it should be. You can't ask for anything more than is given.

— Lillian Gish[1]
October 1981

To the audience attending her *Art of Film* lecture performances across the United States, Europe, Australia or New Zealand, Lillian Gish was far removed from the heroines in perpetual distress she played on the screen. She was on a roll, stopping only to receive an award or attend the opening of a recently renovated movie theatre that had been built in the silent era. She was "clear-eyed, hard-working," and quite aware of what was happening in the world.[2]

In interview after interview connected with each appearance, she and manager Jim Frasher limited the time for questions and answers to 45 minutes. The questions, however phrased, were predictable variations on the same themes: touring as a child in the early years of the twentieth century; the wonderful, perfect mother who had surrendered her identity and given up everything to raise two daughters; the relationship with and working habits of D. W. Griffith; the longtime association with drama critic George Jean Nathan; and how she, a single woman operating in what was essentially a man's world, had been able to survive.

She answered the questions patiently, as if nobody had ever asked them before.

On touring:

> Life on the road was incredibly hard for a child. There were oatmeal meals, hard floors and benches to sleep on, uncomfortable trains, and being stranded far from New York and friends. It was difficult to maintain friends. I never learned how to play with other children.
>
> I never had an acting lesson. I was simply told, "Go out there and speak loud and clear or we'll get another little girl." It was also drilled into us that when an audience pays to see a performance, it is entitled to the best performance you can give. Nothing in your personal life must interfere, neither fatigue, illness, nor anxiety....[3]

On how her mother handled her daughters' success:

Early in life Dorothy and I came home to mother and said that people had turned around on Fifth Avenue [New York City] to look at us, that they seemed to know who we were.

She said, "Well, if you walked down Fifth Avenue with a ring in each of your noses, they'd do the same thing!"[4]

Regarding George Jean Nathan, who was always asking Lillian to marry him — even though he openly resented her family closeness:

I never met anyone I liked better than mother or sister. I was really never happy away from them. I certainly wasn't going to marry anyone who would take me away from my mother, if I could help it.[5]

On surviving:

I was allowed to come near him [playwright Eugene O'Neill] because [his wife] Carlotta knew I wasn't looking for a husband or a man.

I was an intellectual snob. I didn't want to be with people who knew less than I did.[6]

Before boarding an airplane at Kennedy Airport headed for London in July 1981, where she would attend a performance of *The Biograph Girls*, a British musical comedy about D. W. Griffith's early silent film heroines, Lillian gave the real reason she and Dorothy entered moviemaking after spending months as touring stage actresses:

We had to do something to live in the summertime because theatres were closed down. No air-conditioning.[7]

She also couldn't forego the opportunity to ruminate on filmmaking and the future:

Whatever the condition of the world, we in films have to take some responsibility for it. We have troubles, but the human race is living longer and doing more. I don't think any century has been as exciting as this one.[8]

Lillian and Helen Hayes attended the November 8 New York opening of *Ned and Jack*, Sheldon Rosen's play about playwright Edward Sheldon and actor John Barrymore.[9] Edward Sheldon, at the age of 22, had a huge success with Mrs. (Minnie Maddern) Fiske in *Salvation Nell* (1908),[10] and five years later with *Romance* (1913), starring Doris Keane, who played Mme. Cavallini, the prima donna modelled on Lina Cavalieri. (Keane played the role in America for two years and then took the play to London, where it had an unprecedented four year run.)[11]

Both Lillian and Helen Hayes had fond personal memories of playwright Edward Sheldon, whose crippling arthritis kept him virtually bedridden while still in his '30s.

Lillian, who frequently visited Sheldon to ask for his advice, recalled:

We called Edward Sheldon the Pope of the theatre. You'd have dinner with him at seven and you'd swear you'd go home by midnight, but you never would — he was so entertaining. Anyone who had a problem that had to do with the theatre went to him for help.[12]

Director Colleen Dewhurt, who had acted with Lillian onstage in *All the Way Home* (1960), remembered how she felt when she was told that Lillian and Helen Hayes were in the audience:

Both ladies were very supportive and very sweet, but I didn't want to be on the premises when they were there. I was that nervous.

Lillian's reputation preceded her. So did Helen's, but Lillian's earlier career was documented on film.

Lillian was a friendly, sweet lady, and a wonderful actress, but you always were aware of who she was. She didn't have to remind you.

I was honored they came. I didn't know if they actually would. We were playing at the Hudson Guild, a theatre not exactly on or off Broadway. We were trying to make ends meet. It didn't look like anything around Lincoln Center. It looked like a place where real theatre, true theatre was, without the plush seats.

Both Lillian and Helen couldn't have been more gracious, and I was quite moved when Lillian said, "You brought Ned Sheldon back to us. We'll tell some people who remember him."

And they *did*![13]

Following an earlier 1982 appearance at Wolf Trap, where she hosted a showing of her silent *La Bohème* (1926) that included an informal lecture on the making of the motion picture, Lillian returned to Washington, D.C., a second time, on August 15, to receive honors at the Kennedy Center with director George Abbott, clarinetist Benny Goodman, dancer-choreographer-director Gene Kelly, and conductor Eugene Ormandy for their high achievement in the arts.[14]

All of the honorees were presented with laurel-designed gold plated brass medallions in a ceremony in the Benjamin Franklin Room of the Department of State. Cary Grant announced the citations, which were bestowed by Roger L. Stevens, board chairman of the Kennedy Center.[15]

Lillian, dressed in a creamy Grecian gown, was told by violinist Issac Stern, "You do the honors honor."[16]

President and Mrs. Reagan extended greetings to the sparkling crowd of 400, amongst whom were Helen Hayes, Jose Ferrer, Claudette Colbert, and Douglas Fairbanks, Jr.

Nancy Reagan, who stayed at Lillian's home during the time she was seeking a film career, said of Lillian: "She's an amazing and darling woman whom I've known since childhood."[17]

At the Opera House, the segment of the evening devoted to Lillian's achievements was presented by Eva Marie Saint, who made her Broadway debut in Horton Foote's *The Trip to Bountiful*, starring Lillian.

Following the performance, a crowd of 1700 dined on veal and beef tenderloin in the Grand Foyer. Moments before, they had cheered as Lillian was rescued just before going over the falls in *Way Down East*.[18]

The ceremony in the Benjamin Franklin Room, and the receptions at the White House and the Kennedy Center Opera House were all beautiful and impressive to Lillian, but, she would tell reporters as 1982 came to an end, it wasn't the first time she had been at the White House. She had been attending White House functions since President Harding had invited D. W. Griffith to present his *Orphans of the Storm* in 1922.[19] Could 60 years have passed so quickly?

Lillian would claim to be 83, and she had no problems about her age. She was, in fact, 89, but she also realized that nobody would ever get it right.

She wouldn't care, she told interviewers

if they said I was 100. It would probably make me more interesting.

You know when I was first making films, Lionel Barrymore played my grandfather. Later he played my father, and finally he played my husband. If he had lived longer, I'm sure I would have played his mother. That's the way it is in Hollywood. The men get younger and the women get older.[20]

Her age, whatever it was, never slowed her down. Nor did it dampen her enthusiasm for meeting people and working. Since 1975, her *Art of Film* tour had taken her around the world three times, and had been presented at 387 colleges in 36 states across America.

In Australia she waived her salary and was paid in opals.

Never caring about current fashions, Lillian's interest in clothing centered on classic designs with meticulous workmanship.[21]

Her mother, Lillian would brag, had made their total wardrobe:

> We could be hungry, but we always had real Alcenon lace on our panties. Mother made everything — our hats, coats, everything but our shoes and stockings.[22]

After Mrs. Gish had died in 1948, a safe-deposit box was discovered. What did it contain?

Lillian recalled: "We were intrigued. We though it was full of money, but it was full of handmade Alcenon lace.[23]

Lillian, who wears clothes from Vera Maxwell, could remember when Mainbocher's evening dresses could be purchased for $75 at his tiny Paris workshop. Regretfully, she gave most of them away. The dresses she wears that were made by Valentina 50 years ago have never been cleaned or altered. She is still the same size. The Grecian gown many found so startling at the Kennedy Center was made by Valentina between 1925 and 1930.

In Lillian's closets could be found hundreds of evening bags, her mother's Russian ermine coat, and her own Blackglama mink coat, the payment she received for allowing herself to appear with it without any name identification in the advertisement, "What Becomes a Legend Most."[24]

Lillian's frugality regarding clothes, frequently commented upon by Helen Hayes and others, now had become a virtue. What Lillian had worn over the decades that many had considered old, now was described by young journalists as classic. Lillian's clothing, like her life and career, had come full circle. Styles had come and gone, but Lillian had continued to maintain her integrity.

In April 1983, she was among the Lincoln Center audience of 2500 honoring Lord Lawrence Olivier for half a century of accomplishment. The evening had been hosted by Douglas Fairbanks, Jr.[25]

In June Lillian was in the midst of Times Square traffic. Hard-hatted construction workers sat high up on girders watching barmen below in tuxedos pouring champagne as Lillian together with Mollie Parnis (there on behalf of Marilyn: *An American Fable*, an upcoming off–Broadway play on the life of actress Marilyn Monroe), cut a ribbon dedicating Marilyn Monroe Hall, an area of 20 flowering cherry trees and 1000 pink and white wax begonias. The ceremony coincided with what would have been Marilyn Monroe's 57th birthday.[26]

Lillian recalled the occasion — and Marilyn Monroe:

> It was almost like the time we were shooting Dorothy's *Remodeling Her Husband* [1920], and we used an actual New York street. The same congestion for both occasions, but we made no effort in those days to get any clearance. We just went there, shot our little sequence, and hoped for the best.
>
> I couldn't help thinking how many telephone calls were made for today's effort, and how much Marilyn Monroe would have appreciated this attention. This event is a far cry from those Hollywood premieres she attended. What relief this would have been. She never owned much, and here is a piece of New York covered with flowers....

She was such a skillful comedienne in *Some Like It Hot* [1959] but such a tragic person. Now that she's gone, they call her a legend. She paid a terrible price to earn the title legend. Sad...[27]

For the CBS television broadcast of *Hobson's Choice*, the original Lancashire locale of Harold Brighouse's 1913 stage success was changed to New Orleans, complete with a toe-tapping musical score (rousingly played by an ever-present Dixieland band).

The plotline remained essentially the same: Hobson, a domineering fixer of shoes who is reluctant to admit he is dependent on his daughter Mollie, opposes her wish to marry Will Mossop, a depressed employee who doesn't appear to have much of a future.

But Mollie is not easily dissuaded by her father's abuses. She sees herself as perfect for the reluctant Will, and justifies their relationship quite succinctly when she tells her bashful beau, "Nobody can make the shoes the way you can, and nobody can sell the shoes the way I can."[28] They are a perfect match.

While the ending of the television production, directed by Gilbert Cates, is more positive than the original stage version, John O'Connor, television critic for *The New York Times*, had definite reservations about the December 21, 1983, broadcast. Not all of the scenes hung well together.

The casting also seemed to be against type. Jack Warden, more often associated with the rough streets of New York, Chicago, and Los Angeles, looked out of place as Hobson in New Orleans.

Richard Thomas, an actor not afraid to take chances, definitely made a wrong decision to portray Will Mossop as a wimp.

What was thoroughly approved of—and rightly so—was the casting of Lillian Gish as Miss Winkle, a wealthy customer who is interested in Will's shoes and believes in his abilities. Miss Winkle was a role that Lillian handled beautifully and in which she was "twinklingly delightful."[29]

Lillian had fond memories of *Hobson's Choice*:

> *Hobson's Choice* is a British working class play about the acquiring of mobility and respect and how each plays a major role in nineteenth century industrial England.
>
> I saw the Charles Laughton film [1954], which came out around the time Charles was lobbying for me to be cast in *The Night of the Hunter*. I thought his performance and the film were delightful.
>
> Our television producers, when they decided to bring this play to New Orleans before we entered the First World War, hoped that the essence and sensibility of the play could survive, and its message would appeal to a younger generation.
>
> When the script was sent to me, I gladly accepted. It gave me the opportunity to work with Gilbert Cates, who had produced *I Never Sang For My Father* [1968], which I did. This time Mr. Cates was directing.
>
> All plays, to be successful, have to have a universal message to truth if they are going to ring true to an audience. Certainly there have been European productions of Tennessee Williams plays performed in front of audiences who have little familiarity with his locales.
>
> Setting *Hobson's Choice* in New Orleans and including the right music gave the play a lightness Americans mightn't have realized if they were to have heard the lines spoken with the Lancashire accent.
>
> Unless the play is downright slapstick, Americans don't understand the wordplay in English humor. Americans are mesmerized by accents. I couldn't have played my role with the authenticity it deserved if I had to deliver my lines with a Lancashire sound. There is English regional

writing, as there is American regional writing.

No matter what the locale, good literature and theatre must tell the truths of the human heart. And that is what *Hobson's Choice* does. I was happy to have been given the chance to do it, no matter how some critics may have carped about the lack of fidelity to the original.[30]

When Lillian returned to the small screen in March 1984, it was not to show her talent in another adaptation, but to be recognized for seven decades of brilliant work in motion pictures. Her screen work and career longevity had survived changing acting styles, transitions, and the comments and envy of whatever few detractors she may have acquired. Both she and her work had stood the test of time. For this, at the age of 90, she was going to Hollywood to receive the coveted American Film Institute's 12th Life Achievement Award, following the likes of John Ford, James Cagney, Orson Welles, William Wyler, Bette Davis, Henry Fonda, Alfred Hitchcock, James Stewart, Fred Astaire, Frank Capra, and John Huston.[31]

To interviewers she would announce that her day began at 7:00 with a round of sit-ups and lying upside-down on a collapsible slant board she had been using since 1940.

Aljean Harmetz, who interviewed Lillian in Hollywood before the awards ceremony, recorded Lillian's philosophy — an outlook that supplied her with the spiritual strength to endure and survive the sentimental silliness of some of her early silent one- and two-reelers:

Time is your friend … vanity is a virtue. How can you let yourself weigh 300 pounds? The human body is a wonderful thing, and it's the only house you get to live in…
I couldn't ever be ill.
I've never had my hair cut, nor have I ever plucked an eyebrow. I don't wear glasses, and I have all my own teeth.
There's never been a more exciting century. As I get older, I believe in what I cannot see and understand.[32]

Like the tributes paid to the 11 previous American Film Institute honorees, Lillian's evening (televised on April 17) adhered to the formula. She was given a black-tie dinner at a Los Angeles hotel. Some of the guests scattered around the hotel ballroom at large dining tables were immediately identifiable. At the sound of the fanfare, Lillian entered to a standing ovation and headed toward her designated table to listen to friends, colleagues, and co-workers tell of her achievements and milestones. Her program included screenings of scenes from her Griffith-directed classics, *The Birth of a Nation, Way Down East,* and *Orphans of the Storm*, in addition to Victor Seastrom's *The Wind*. All of the films were exhibited on special projectors and were accompanied by an orchestra conducted by Carl Davies, who composed the wonderful music for the presentation.[33]

Douglas Fairbanks, Jr., who hosted the evening, proclaimed Lillian "the first lady of the American screen."

Among the speakers who extolled Lillian's professionalism and work ethic were John Huston, Jeanne Moreau, Sally Field, Eva Marie Saint, Robert Mitchum, Mary Martin, and Richard Widmark.

Lily Tomlin, injecting humor into the presentations, told the audience that after the premiere of her own film, *9 to 5*, Lillian ran up to her saying, "Tell me you have a piece of it."

Richard Thomas, with whom Lillian had appeared in the recently televised *Hobson's Choice*, told the audience of Lillian's unhappiness at the low positioning of a camera before the shooting of a scene. Lillian looked down at the camera person and

At the American Film Institute tribute in Washington, D.C., 1984: a lifetime honor for the first lady of film.

said: "Young man, if God wanted you to see me that way he would have to put your eyes in your button."[34]

In the wake of AFI director George Stevens' plea calling for the preservation of old films (they are "our collective memories, our dreams, our myths, our heritage"[35]), Lillian rose to acknowledge the tributes and to thank the speakers. Her simple statement, spoken so eloquently, was the perfect way to conclude the evening.

Thank you for my life.[36]

Within a month of Lillian's televised American Film Institute tribute, Lillian was granted the fulfillment of a long held fantasy. During the celebration of the 100th anniversary of the Metropolitan Opera, patrons (who paid up to $1000 a ticket to be present for the final performance on May 14 of Cuban ballerina Alicia Alonso) witnessed the debut of a ballet lover whose career was spent in the theatre and motion pictures.

Patrick Dupond, of the Paris Opera Ballet, in a costume of rose petals, whirled around a chair on which a dreaming girl was sleeping in a scene from *Le Spectre de la Rose*. The "dreaming girl," much to the audience's delight, was Lillian Gish, the surprise of the evening.

Her balletic abilities, at the age of 90, scored a big hit with the audience.[37]

If Lillian had any professional disappointments at this period, they had to center on the still unreleased film, *Hambone and Hillie*. It was her first leading role in a motion picture since her ill-fated "talkie" debut in *One Romantic Night* (1930). Her subsequent film, *His Double Life* (1933), was not one in which her name alone was above the title.

William K. Everson explained what had gone awry:

In *Hambone and Hillie*, Lillian

played an elderly lady named Hillie, who is separated from her dog, a mixed breed named Hambone, at the Los Angeles Airport en route to New York. I know I'm not softening the film's possible impact if I tell you that the dog, after traveling a distance of 3000 miles, is reunited.

Hambone and Hillie is a very charming little programmer, and Lillian heads a very competent cast that includes Timothy Bottoms and Candy Clark.

I shouldn't say this, but the film is Lillian's and to succeed with a young audience, the film needs an actress who is instantly recognizable — like a Margaret Hamilton, who played the Wicked Witch in *The Wizard of Oz*. I mentioned Margaret Hamilton only because she is instantly recognizable. She would have been dead center wrong for this film, and it would require considerable marketing to publicize that she was not playing another witch!

Lillian, throughout a very long career, never had a young following.

Maybe the idea of being separated from a dog in so large an airport was considered too nightmarish for young children, who are the film's intended audience. The Disney film Lillian made [*Follow Me Boys!*, 1966] was not a success, despite the presence of Fred MacMurray, who certainly wasn't a stranger to young children — who were familiar with his other kiddie films.

Lillian certainly was receiving a lot of well-justifiable publicity for her work, but it was for work done in the past. What the film's well-intentioned producer mightn't have realized was that her new recognition wasn't going to put her name on the minds of children, for whom this film was geared. The children who saw her in *Follow Me, Boys!* were not, for the most part, children. They were grandparents. That was almost 20 years ago!

Moviemaking was always about making money. The senior citizen of the '60s who went to see *Follow Me, Boys!* Might have seen Lillian's silent film work. The senior citizen of the '80s only had Lillian's stage work to refer to. None of her recent plays went on tour....

We live in a television generation, a television series generation. You have to keep bombarding the television all of the time if you want to make an impression.[38]

Lillian had no desire to remain alone in her apartment. She wanted to work. She needed attention. Attention meant publicity. Publicity meant work ... sometimes.

In November 1984 she went to New Haven, Connecticut, as part of a 50 member committee to help plan a Museum of American Theatre. New Haven was the "pre–Broadway" birthplace. A museum in New Haven could provide an additional source of revenue from speaking engagements.

Among Lillian's distinguished fellow committee members were Helen Hayes, Mildred Dunnock, John Houseman, Ossie Davis, and Ruby Dee.[39]

Lillian's presence at functions was no longer a rarity. At a March 15, 1985, Museum of Modern Art reception for veteran British film star Dame Anna Neagle (in connection with an upcoming British film series), Lillian's presence was noted along with that of *Upstairs, Downstairs* television series star Jean Marsh and actor-director Sir Richard Attenborough. While everyone wanted to meet Dame Anna, *The New York Times* reporter Georgia Dullea, covering the evening for her column "The Evening Hours," observed:

An exception was a silent film pianist named Stuart Oderman, who only had eyes for Lillian Gish.[40]

Lillian, drinking champagne with Blanchette Rockefeller, told *The New York Times* reporter:

They [the eyes] tell the story. What gets the eyes is low lights and a high camera.[41]

To Stuart Oderman, who had seen Lillian on the Radio City Music Hall stage as one of the participants in *Night of 100 Stars* (a benefit for the Actors' Fund) earlier that same week, Lillian said:

I think we, who were crowded backstage in that limited space, had more fun than the audience, if that's possible. We were three and four in a dressing room, trying not to crowd in front of a mirror to put on our makeup.

For a lot of us, it was a grand reunion. We had worked together years ago and had lost touch. There was lots of picture-taking. We brought our own cameras. You won't see these pictures in the newspapers. They went right into our own albums.[42]

Wisely, this biographer didn't solicit Lillian's opinion of the video format of the 1933 abridged version of D. W. Griffith's *The Birth of a Nation* in which an hour had been excised. A constant defender of the film, Lillian, in 1933, felt the editing of the picture had undermined her integrity, as well as the purity of Griffith's original vision. To witness the availability of a cut version on the market again after more than 50 years of suppression was the repeating of old wounds that hadn't completely healed.

Now a younger generation would be getting a negative impression of an acknowledged masterpiece, and Lillian, once again, would be put on the defensive, as she had been for 70 years:

The Birth of a Nation [1915] has always been the subject of two constant judgments — its technical accomplishments, as it tells the story of two families, North and South, before, during, and after the Civil War — and the questionable nature of the original.

This version from 1933 cuts an hour out of the original scenes sensitive to the charges of racism without changing attitudes.[43]

Was the cutting of scenes an admission that certain critics had been right in calling the Griffith film racist and prejudicial to blacks? Would a more liberal, sophisticated generation of the '80s cry censorship?

If Lillian's career were to keep coming full circle, she preferred that it involve less controversial topics. She was happy that Grandma Moses, a painter who was the subject of a 1952 *Schlitz Playhouse* dramatization in which she starred,[44] was now to be included in *In Celebration: An American Portrait*, which Lillian narrated.

In June Lillian was part of the 50th anniversary celebration of the Museum of Modern Art's acquisition of what has become an impressive collection of 8000 films from practically every film-producing country in the world. The museum collection dated back to Edison's 1894 film, *Chinese Laundry*, and the 1895 *Leaving the Factory* made by the Lumière brothers in France.

The Museum of Modern Art's priceless archive, whose influence has been acknowledged by countless film scholars, actors, and directors, almost never came into being.[45]

The conception of a film library was a mere idea mentioned at a Pickfair (the palatial home of Mary Pickford and her husband, Douglas Fairbanks, Sr.) party in 1935 whose guests included D. W. Griffith, Charlie Chaplin, Samuel Goldwyn, Mack Sennett, Walt Disney, Mervyn LeRoy, and Ernst Lubitsch.[46]

A few days after the Pickfair gathering, Iris Barry, the founding curator of the museum's film department, acting on a suggestion from Alfred Barr, the museum's first director (who believed that motion pictures were a vital part of visual arts), made a trip to Hollywood.

She returned to New York with more than one million feet of film. It was an impressive start, but vital to the collection's credibility was the involvement of D. W. Griffith, who, even though he could no longer afford to pay the costs for storing his collection, was unwilling to surrender his material.[47]

If Lillian could possibly prevail upon the reluctant Mr. Griffith...

Lillian, who had always advocated the preservation of films, went to California and convinced her mentor to donate his collection of negatives, prints, papers, and 325 films to the Museum of Modern Art.[48]

At the 50th anniversary celebration, Mary Lea Bandy, the director of the film department, acknowledged the importance of Lillian's efforts. Because of Lillian, Griffith's film collection

> really became the foundation of the museum's collection. Griffith's films were seen all over the world, and the influence he had on filmmakers in every country is incalculable.[49]

Acquiring the collection was simply a matter of time and tenacity.

Time and tenacity were important factors in the broadcasting of Mark Twain's *Huckleberry Finn* the following winter (1986) on educational television stations.

There is no doubt that Twain's *Huckleberry Finn* is an important American novel. Whether it is *the* American masterpiece will always be a topic of debate. Twain's compelling portrait of two dispossessed souls (Huck, a poor, beaten white boy, and Jim, a black man on the run from the degradation of slavery) is a powerful image.

The television adaptation of *Huckleberry Finn* in four episodes over a month's duration was not necessarily the most convincing way to bring this classic to the small screen. Although the story was approached with care and sensitivity, Jim, no matter how clean cut and sanitized, is still believed by many black Americans to be a cultural stereotype.[50] That he is articulate and does not rely on dialect does not raise his station.

In the second episode, Lillian appeared as Mrs. Judith Loftus, an elderly lady who lives in a shack away from the town and senses that the young girl who calls herself Sarah Mary Williams or Mary Sarah Williams doesn't catch a tossed lump of yarn like a young girl would.

While the production utilized the top-drawer talents of Richard Kiley, Barnard Highes, Sada Thompson, Jim Dale, and Geraldine Page in supporting roles, their appearances, wrote television critic John O'Connor for *The New York Times,* "fell into the category of standard guest shots, mildly interesting and looking a bit hurried."[51]

That the face of writer-director-actor Alan Alda mirrored his soul[52] was only one of the reasons Lillian gave for working in Sag Harbor, Long Island, during the summer months of 1985 in *Sweet Liberty,* her 104th film. In this spoof of Hollywood attitudes, a motion picture company, hoping to make a screen version of a college professor's historical novel about the American Revolution, finds themselves embroiled in small town politics.

The actual shooting of the film couldn't have taken place at a more inopportune time. The villages of Sag Harbor and Southampton on Long Island's East End are heavily saturated with tourists.[53] Much of the location shooting would be involving Sag Harbor's Main Street, municipal building, fire house, and the American Hotel. All of these structures would be slightly changed to resemble buildings at the time of the Revolutionary War. At the conclusion of the shoot, they would have to be restored to their former look.

The *Sweet Liberty* company also agreed to provide $4000 worth of public benches, donate money to the ambulance and fire department, and pay a $500-a-day fee to the village of Southampton.

One of the motels happily agreed to allow 50 of its 66 rooms to be used from Mondays through Thursdays to accommodate the crew (representing a 20 percent increase in occupancy over the previous summers).[54]

Because public relations play so important a role in any negotiation, Alan Alda made a personal visit to the Southampton Elementary School, where he shook hands with the students and presented a $1200 check for playground restoration.

In the film, a professor's (Alan Alda) teaching schedule is disrupted by a movie company's arrival. Fearing a similar disruption would occur when Alda's actual shooting took place, the school sequence involving an 80 person crew was shot in August.[55]

Lillian played the professor's belligerent mother, a woman who has slept in the living room for 11 years because "the devil is in the bedroom."[56] The actress was not eager to play such a character.

Her anxiety at playing truly offbeat comedy disappeared immediately, however, because of Alan Alda's considerate, charming direction.

> My scenes were all amusing, and I had great fun playing the off-center woman. The film was easier to make than most because it was shot in beautiful summer weather, and nearby, around Sag Harbor, Long Island.[57]

The distance between Southampton and Sag Harbor was minimal, thus lowering the cost of transporting the heavy film equipment. Many of the technicians working out of New York City were within reach,[58] something Lillian could

As Cecilia in *Sweet Liberty* (1986, Universal City Studios, directed by Alan Alda). This was Lillian's 104th film. The face of Alan Alda "mirrored his soul," said Lillian. A good reason to appear on camera once again.

Sweet Liberty means to be a sendup of Hollywood manners and methods when a movie company invades a small college town to shoot the screen version of a college professor's book which, to his horror, has suddenly become a Revolutionary War comedy.

It's possible that *Sweet Liberty* is exactly the sort of movie that ... Alan Alda set out to make....

The great Lillian Gish appears briefly (and to the film's advantage) as Mr. Alda's nutty old mom....

Sweet Liberty rolls along in stately fashion when it's supposed to be rollicking.... Instead of laughing, as one expects to do at a comedy, one smiles at isolated incidents.

I liked Miss Gish's flat announcement that she never eats anything that hasn't been sitting on the television set for at least 24 hours. The radiation kills what "they" have put in it.[60]

understand, having directed her sister Dorothy in Mamaroneck in 1920 in *Remodeling Her Husband*.

> Making *Sweet Liberty* reminded me of D. W. Griffith in 1912. There was no place we could go that was as happy as when we were shooting, and this film was just like that.[59]

Sweet Liberty opened on May 14, 1986, at Loew's Theatre in New York City.

Vincent Canby reviewed the film for *The New York Times:*

In a letter to the biographer, Alan Alda recalled directing Lillian Gish:

> The one striking moment I remember in shooting *Sweet Liberty* was shooting a scene in a hospital bed and while they were touching up the lighting, she started to reminisce about D. W. Griffith. Everyone on the set (carpenters, grips, everyone) stopped in their tracks and listened. We all knew we were in the presence of a living history of our profession. I've always regretted that I was so taken with the moment it didn't occur to me to tell the operator to roll film on the moment.[61]

CHAPTER 37

The Last Reel

I'll never forget the time we decided to put on a production of
Brigadoon here at the church, and I was to take the part of the school
teacher. Miss Gish was away on tour, but I received a telegram from
her. It said, "Real work at last!"
— The Rev. Terence J. Findlay
St. Bartholomew's Episcopal Church, New York
March 11, 1993

The discipline Lillian had shown throughout her professional life was also rigorously maintained when she was not facing the camera or the audience. Her weight since the '20s was the same 115 pounds, as were her dietary habits when she was in New York.

I've never dieted. Breakfast is a muffin with Smucker's jam, two pieces of bread, homemade apple-sauce, boiled eggs, three cups of coffee and pancakes. Lunch is fruit. Dinner is a glass of stout and takeout Chinese food or something sent over from restaurants — or my manager [James Frasher] does me some meat and vegetables.[1]

Her day, which started with rising at 7 a.m. and a round of exercises, gets into full swing with a 10 a.m. telephone call from Jim, who will announce he will arrive at noon. The afternoon, if there are no film, stage, or television projects, is dedicated to dictating answers to the constant arrival of mail from around the world.[2]

The correspondence falls into 3 categories: letters of compliment over a past performance, requests for specific information on her past films that are rarely shown, and questions on other directors from the silent era. Somehow, perhaps due to her longevity, she had become a historian.

Requests for signed stills (8 × 10 glossies) were not answered, unless the sender enclosed the photograph and a self-addressed envelope with correct postage. When Lillian was employed by the studios, photographs with a stamped signature were handled by the publicity department.

Lillian's spartan lifestyle did not make any provision for a housekeeper. All of her life she had picked up after herself, something she had been taught to do by her mother.

She would tell interviewers:

Can't afford it [a housekeeper]. I've never been financially comfortable. My sister Dorothy discovered Valentino, and I established a film company in 1923, but we never seemed to get real money.[3]

An absence of a dresser at the theatre had been noted by this biographer in 1958, the year he began attending Lillian's stage performances (starting with *The Family Reunion* when he was 18 years old).

Her reasons for not having a dresser were made evident in 1975, when he visited Lillian after a performance of *Uncle Vanya*.

Barefoot, devoid of any makeup, and wearing only a slip, she was raising and lowering her heavy Russian costume and concentrating on a hook on the wall when she told him to enter the room.

"I can hang that up for you," he said.

Lillian shook her head and whispered, "Shh!"

After 3 more raisings and lowerings, she lunged forward, raised her arms and placed the costume on the hook.

"I could have done that," he said.

She shook her head again. "You're not here every night, and if you were, I would become dependent on you. That's not good, to be dependent on anybody. Nobody can be there all the time, except those connected with the production. If I became dependent on other people, I'd lose my will to live."

Her desire to continue to work and remain active as long as possible was quite obvious in September 1986 when, dressed in four pairs of leg-warmers under a

With Mary Steenburgen in *The Whales of August* (1987, Alive Films and Circle Associates, directed by Lindsay Anderson).

summer dress, she took the 40 minute ferryboat ride to Cliff Island in Casco Bay off the coast of Maine to film her 105th motion picture, *The Whales of August*. It was based on the 1981 play by David Berry, which producer Mike Kaplan (who worked with Lillian in *The Comedians*, 1968) would not option until she agreed to star.[4] She was 93 years old. Her co-stars, Ann Sothern, Vincent Price, and Bette Davis, were all veterans with over 50 years of performing experience.

Lillian and Bette were playing elderly sisters who spend what possibly might be their last summer together[5] in a cabin, battling over a picture window and reflecting on lost childhoods, deceased husbands, the aftermath of the wars, and children who abandoned them. That the whales they had come to watch every year are no longer present symbolizes that the end is near.[6]

The film's plot was slight. Only the casting of a Lillian Gish and a Bette Davis could give the film a small chance at commercial success.

Bette, who was 15 years younger than Lillian, was cast as the blind Libby, a role she had rejected six years earlier. Lillian was playing Bette's younger sister, Sarah. Bette was also in the process of recovering from a second stroke. The first had left her in a state of partial facial disfigurement.[7]

Younger Bette's reaction to the older Lillian playing her younger sister was characteristic: "Older? Older? My gosh, Gish has to be in her nineties!"[8]

Asked if she were playing the heroine or the bitch, Bette answered:

> Let's say I'm the tough one, and Gish is softer. I'm bitchy, but not a bitch. Gish is frail, but is strong underneath. Until you read the script, you won't know what I mean. It's all underplayed, how we react.[9]

While Harry Carey, Jr., found it "astonishing" that he was acting in a movie with Lillian Gish 75 years after his father had played with her in Griffith's 1912 *The Musketeers of Pig Alley*, Vincent Price lamented that he was "surrounded by wind and wet" in a location without any of the usual conveniences: a dance hall, a motion picture theatre, or a bar to patronize.[10] Price also noted that at the age of 76, he was the youngest of the company, and that he was playing the ingenue.

Of interest to the cast were the ways Lillian and Bette related to and took direction from Lindsay Anderson, the film's director.

Mr. Anderson made a quick comparison:

> Lillian's first instinct is to try to give the director what he asks for. Her professional attitude comes from those days with D. W. Griffith. Bette tries to dismiss the director.[11]

Ann Sothern recalled a precarious moment when she and Lillian were standing at the edge of a cliff looking out to the sea.

> It was a long shot, so no one could hold us, so I held onto Lillian's apron strings when she turned around. Here was this 93-year-old woman pulling me back like a sturdy horse. Lillian got to the porch and said, "That's the last time I'm doing that damn scene!"[12]

Both Lillian and Bette commanded respect. While Lillian used quiet strength, Bette butted heads with director Lindsay Anderson everyday, generating arguments that invariably ended in a draw.[13]

Bette's battles included how she and co-star Lillian would be billed. Bette, who threatened not to make the film unless she received top billing over Lillian's, settled for having her name first on the left-hand side of the advertisements, while Lillian's name would be slightly higher on the right.[14]

William K. Everson, hearing stories of the on-and-off-the-set problems, told this biographer:

> The only way to silence Bette Davis is not to back down. Her William Wyler days were long over, and there wasn't any great demand for her.
>
> She knew, more than anybody else, how sick she was, and that she was an insurance risk. If the insurance company believed your illness could jeopardize the film, you were pulled out.
>
> Bette was in constant fear. It was very sad. To remind everyone who she was meant constantly barking commands.
>
> Lillian would only have to lightly touch a man's arm and softly whisper, I wonder if... And she got even better results. What man would refuse a request from Lillian Gish?[15]

Working together was not a happy experience for Lillian or Bette.[16] Bette, who was renowned for disliking her female co-stars (with the exception of Olivia de Havilland, Anne Baxter, Mary Astor, and Gena Rowlands), did not like Lillian.[17] Even the crew sensed there was a constant enmity between them.[18]

Bette articulated:

> Let's just say that we don't particularly like each other personally — and let it go at that. But we respect each other a lot. The location is murder and doesn't help anyone's feelings.[19]

Bette's feelings were quite evident during the first two weeks of shooting when she had to stay in a summer cottage that failed to have the central heating she required.

Vincent Price told an interviewer from *The New York Times*:

> Bette does have her dukes up![20]

Ann Sothern, who was very fond of Lillian, commented on the lack of camaraderie between the two leading ladies:

> Bette wasn't very nice to Lillian. Lillian's a great lady. Bette was jealous.[21]

Bette, by virtue of her longevity, had become adjusted to the growing generation gap between herself and her co-workers, who referred to her admiringly as "the old pro." Now she found she was in competition with someone who was an older pro. Lillian was starring in D. W. Griffith's *The Birth of a Nation* in 1915, the year Bette was a sever-year-old girl in elementary school. It intimidated her.[22]

The Whales of August was Bette's long awaited chance to return to motion pictures, albeit in a supporting role (as she had done in *What Ever Happened to Baby Jane?* Always a trouper, Bette, whose weight had sunk to less than 90 pounds, reported for work with the vigor of a young actress about to make her motion picture debut. Eager to succeed, she had learned all of her lines, and everybody's else's.

Bette's trouper-like dedication and urgency wasn't lost on Lindsay Anderson:

> That half of Bette is the victim of some temperamental compulsion. She's difficult because she's Bette Davis, not because she's a star. She has an initial hostility to life and people that she has had all her life. But she was never concerned with what she looked like. She came to the rushes and never once said, "Oh god, I look awful." She just wanted to get the character right.[23]

Perhaps their conflicting temperaments were best articulated in the sayings sewn onto their sofa pillows in their respective living rooms.

On Lillian's: "What you get is a living ... what you give is life."

On Bette's: "NO GUTS. NO GLORY."[24]

Just before rehearsals, *My Mother's Keeper*, a book about Bette written by her daughter, B.D. Hyman, was released. Bette was quite upset that her daughter had not one complimentary thing to write about her. Her daughter had nothing for which she was grateful.[25]

Lillian, who continually praised her mother in print and in public throughout her career, observed:

> She [Bette Davis] must be an unhappy woman. That face! Have you ever seen such a tragic face? Poor woman! How she must be suffering. I don't think it's right to judge a person like that. We must bear and forbear.[26]

Lillian was very satisfied with the daily rushes. Watching the rushes was something she had been doing since her film debut 75 years ago. She was able to show more emotion in one glance than most actresses could with pages of dialogue. Her performance in *The Whales of August* was "as clear and simple as a drop of water filled with sunlight."[27]

The pacing of *The Whales of August*, which was released without a rating, was deliberate and careful. Its events were small in scale and commonplace in detail, its benefits unanticipated and quite extraordinary.

After it premiered at the New York's Cinema 2 on October 2, 1987, Vincent Canby of *The New York Times* wrote: "What happens on the screen is not to be underrated."[28]

The film, with its performances by Lillian Gish and Bette Davis, is a metaphor for film acting styles — representing both Cinema's beginnings and its nothing-less-than-perfect visions of women (Lillian), and its golden age when women (Bette) were portrayed as "far less than perfect."[29]

The pleasure of watching *The Whales of August*

> comes from watching [how the director] keeps his two stars working in unison, though each works by totally different methods.
>
> Miss [Gish is] ... still something of the silent film innocent, but there's not a gesture or line-reading that doesn't reflect her nearly three-quarters of a century in front of a camera.
>
> Miss Davis is more than up to the competition, which comes to look like harmony....

Bette Davis' acting, while not trying to

> overwhelm Miss Gish [gives] ... something to act with and against.
>
> When Miss Gish sits in front of a mirror ... doing her hair ... we're seeing ... a demonstration of how a movie works on all the memories we bring to it.[30]

Lillian, the author, returned to her desk to begin writing *An Actor's Life for Me!* The autobiography, told to Selma G. Lanes and illustrated by Patricia Lincoln, was geared for children in elementary schools. The book covered the early years of Lillian's life when she and sister Dorothy were touring juveniles, daughters of an abandoned mother who demanded that they succeed in life on their own[31] — even if it meant short term separations and traveling alone or together on poorly it, cold, less-than-comfortable freight trains to the next town where there was a theatre, a rooming house in which to sleep, and often nobody to greet them in the early hours of the morning.[32] The gypsy life, spent "rattling about in drafty day coaches and on nearly empty milk trains up and down the Eastern Seaboard,"[33] was never a source of frustration to Lillian, who was quite aware that other children her age might be having fun. She was learning very early, in her long life, to find joy in what she was doing.

There were parents who forbade their children to play with them when they were back at their Aunt Emily's farm in Massillon.[34] On the road there was a wonderful world of make believe, a world that would soon come to an end when something called nickelodeons, featuring 10 minute films hand-cranked by a projectionist and shown on a white sheet in semi-darkness, made Lillian and Dorothy aware that it was time to look into the new form of entertainment that was being created on 11 East 14th Street by a man named D. W. Griffith.[35]

After a terrifying audition in which they were asked to play a scene without lines, they were hired, having reacted as two frightened children trapped in a lonely house being attacked by robbers. To get camera-perfect reactions, Mr. Griffith fired a gun into the air.[36]

The 73-page, tightly told tale has a happy ending. Lillian, after a New York engagement at the Belasco Theatre in *The Good Little Devil* (the play in which she had been touring with childhood friend Mary Pickford), is reunited with Dorothy and their mother in Los Angeles.[37]

To readers familiar with Lillian's 1969 autobiography, *The Movies, Mr. Griffith, and Me*, the 1986 watered down children's version seemed a well-conceived effort to widen her appeal to younger generation raised on the television and video media.

Like the picaresque children's stories of an earlier generation, the strength of *An Actor's Life for Me!* lies in the first 58 pages where Lillian is on the road, trying to survive and get work.

To introduce young readers to a D. W. Griffith and Mary Pickford, without any preparation, is meaningless. An unmotivated 10-year-old raised on MTV and CDs is not going to be interested in soundless black-and-white "old things."

While *An Actor's Life for Me!* has authenticity and a tale whose first person narration keeps the story moving at a good pace,[38] it does not seem to be a book children would pick up on their own.[39]

That Lillian could write so candidly

about herself as a young girl trying to survive both as a fatherless child and a child actress in the theatre at the start of the twentieth century is what makes her book a small masterpiece.

Perhaps *An Actor's Life for Me!* was Lillian's unconscious response to the inordinate amount of time it took for *Hambone and Hillie* to be released. Never had any film with which Lillian had been associated been kept in abeyance for so long a period of time. *Hambone and Hillie*, like *Follow Me, Boys!* (1966), Lillian's last release, was entitled to better treatment.

William K. Everson offered a possible explanation:

> All G-rated films hadn't, for a number of years, been the box-office successes the studios anticipated. Some of the older G-rated audience were aware of the meanings of the letter symbols and resented being treated like babies. To give a motion picture a G-rating limited its distribution to the children's section of a video store right after it had been shown on airplane flights that guaranteed a captive audience!
>
> Lillian's *Hambone and Hillie* was a good old-fashioned film that families, in the era of Mary Pickford's *Rebecca of Sunnybrook Farm*, *Pollyanna*, and *Little Lord Fauntleroy*, would have watched together.
>
> All of those films were adapted from long-established classics. I don't think a star's name above the title was even necessary.
>
> In Lillian's case, *Hambone and Hillie* was not taken from a classic. Her name, while worthy of respect, meant nothing to children whose knowledge of performers was confined to people seen on a weekly television series.
>
> Lillian's book was a gallant attempt to introduce herself to younger audiences via print instead of motion pictures. I think she wisely sensed that children weren't going to line up at the box-office to see a film because

she was in it. Even in her Griffith days she was never a Mary Pickford, whose characters appealed to young children, or a Charlie Chaplin, whose antics appealed to everyone.

Lillian's book had a lot going for it. True, it was geared to young readers who, like Lillian, were children of what we would call dysfunctional families.

But Lillian and Dorothy were never home long enough to really be aware of what had happened to what should have been a typical rural American childhood. Lillian and Dorothy were on the road, traveling by themselves, like children in a Dickens novel, to strange cities to act in a theatre and receive applause. It made little difference that their lives outside the theatre, with the ever-hovering fear of being stranded and being penniless, was never secure. Inside the theatre everything was wonderful.

Of course, she and Dorothy loved to travel. No humdrum life for them! Who wouldn't want to be an actor or an actress and have a life filled with constant excitement?

If someone had the sense to film *An Actor's Life for Me!* don't you think someone like Lillian would have wanted to play someone like Aunt Emily, an older woman, who could be in a few scenes?[40]

A sad announcement was made by actress Helen Hayes at the D. W. Griffith Awards ceremony at the Lincoln Center Library of the Performing Arts on February 1, 1988. Lillian Gish, the evening's special guest of honor and the only recipient ever to celebrate a Diamond Jubilee (1912: *An Unseen Enemy* through 1987: *The Whales of August*) on the screen, would not be present. She was to have received two awards: best actress (*The Whales of August*) and Career Achievement.[41]

The reason for her absence followed. In early January she had taken an accidental fall in her apartment. She was standing in the kitchen, made a slight turn, and, without any warning fell onto the floor.

At the hospital Lillian was told that an operation would restore her ability to enjoy a fuller life. To be fully mobile, a hip replacement was necessary.

Lillian shook her head. On the subject of doctors and hospitals she was intolerant. She never liked hospitals.

Doctors?

She had little use for doctors. To whoever would listen, Lillian would say the same words about doctors and hospitals: Doctors killed my mother. Doctors killed my mother. Doctors...[42]

Helen Hayes, the First Lady of the Theatre, accepted the Career Achievement Award for the First Lady of Film.

Telling the audience how hard it was to be understudying Lillian's two roles, Helen Hayes added:

> Lillian wanted to come, and I'm sorry she was bullied into staying home. That doctor, I'm sure, has been dismissed![43]

To this biographer, whom she and Anita Loos met over a decade ago, she privately said:

> When did you ever know Lillian not to show up for anything? Especially an award? It took quite a lot of persuasion to get her to stay away. She thinks a few days of rest will heal everything.
>
> Lillian's spirit, even through the pain, is quite strong. She's always been a trouper, and she's still a trouper.
>
> Unfortunately, nobody can convince her to have an operation. She's never had to have any kind of anesthesia, because she's never been sick. She doesn't even wear eyeglasses.
>
> She doesn't want to lose any work, and I am told, in her present condition she won't get any work unless she has the operation.

October 9, 1982, Bowling Green, Ohio: Lillian in the Gish Film Theater at Bowling Green State University. Behind Lillian is James E. Frasher, her very devoted manager, who was always present. *(Courtesy of the Office of Public Relations, 806 Administration Building, Bowling Green State University, Bowling Green, Ohio.)*

Lillian wouldn't listen. She's spent her life defying the odds, and she'll probably keep defying the odds.

That's why Lillian is so special — for two reasons: her art, and her self.[44]

Lillian defied the odds again. She took part in the first totally complete recording of all of the words, music, and dance music as the Lady on the Levee in Oscar Hammerstein's and Jerome Kern's *Show Boat*.

On July 11 she sat for a straightforward interview,[45] accompanied with film clips of scenes from her films, for "Lillian Gish: The Actor's Life for Me" part of the PBS series, *American Masters*. Still vigorous after her recent fall, Lillian still projected the aura of fragility in the midst of feistiness.[46]

At the age of 95, time would have to catch up with her before it could stop her.

There simply wasn't time to have a hip replacement. It would have to wait.

Readers of the "Letters to the Editor" column in the August 30, 1990, issue of *The New York Times* were treated to a tribute to Sandy, the dog in the musical comedy, *Annie*, who had passed away at the age of 16.

Lillian, hosting a press reception at Sardi's honoring the 1978 Miss America and the members of her court noted Sandy's presence.

Lillian, while being acknowledged by the actors and actresses from the attractions currently playing on Broadway, had a special fondness for Sandy who came immediately over to me and we had a good heart-to-heart pet. Next he shook hands with Miss America and proceeded down the line gallantly shaking hands with each member of her [Miss America's] lovely group....

He then jumped up on one of Vincent's [Sardi] plush banquettes, stretched out and took his pre-evening performance nap to conserve energy for his next audience. Very sensible. Sandy was a true star.[47]

On her birthday in October 1990, the Gish Film Theater at Bowling Green State University, Bowling Green, Ohio, was rededicated after extensive repairs that included the installation of a 35 millimeter projector with surround sound, replaced floor and wall coverings, more Gish memorabilia in the gallery, new lighting, and plush red seats. Each seat had a name plate on the back, acknowledging Lillian's and Dorothy's friends and admirers who helped the theatre Lillian called "a little jewel" glitter with even more warmth.[48]

On February 27, 1993, Lillian, like all good art, became eternal.

Epilogue

"Any artist has just so much to give. The important thing is to give it all. Sometimes it's more than you think."[49]

Lillian was just making another disappearance.

Notes

Introduction

1. Glenn Collins, "Hundreds Gather to Mourn a Friend, Lillian Gish," *The New York Times,* 12 March 1993, p. 19.
2. "Lillian Gish Dies at 99 After a 75-year Film Career," *The Star-Ledger,* 1 March 1993, p. 5.
3. Albin Krebs, "Lillian Gish, 99, a Movie Star Since Movies Began Is Dead," *The New York Times* 1 March 1993, p. 1.
4. Lillian Gish, conversation with author, March 1954.
5. Blanche Sweet, conversation with author, March 1967.
6. Ezra Bowes series, editor, "The Glamour of the Films," *This Fabulous Century: 1920–1930* (New York: Time-Life Books, 1969), p. 228.
7. King Vidor, "Lillian Gish in La Bohème," *A Tree Is a Tree* (New York: Harcourt, Brace, 1953), p. 127.

Chapter 1: Father, Dear Father

1. "Lillian Gish," *Stars of the Photoplay: Art Portraits of Famous Film Favorites with Short Biographical Sketches* (Chicago: Photoplay, 1924).
2. Writers Program of the Work Projects Administration, "Springfield," *The Ohio Guide* (New York: Oxford University Press, 1940), p. 314.
3. *Ibid.,* p. 315.
4. *Ibid.*

5. Writers Program of the Work Projects Administration, "Folklore and Ethnic Groups," *The Ohio Guide,* p. 77.
6. Writers Program of the Work Projects Administration, "Massillon: Tour 7: The Theatre," *Ibid.,* p 160.
7. *Ibid.,* p 162.
8. Albert Bigelow Paine, "A Girl Child, Born with a Caul," *Life and Lillian Gish* (New York: Macmillan, 1932), p. 1.
9. *Ibid.,* p. 2.
10. *Ibid.*
11. Lillian Gish, conversation with author, June 1961.
12. *Ibid.*
13. Lillian Gish, "The Life-Giving Light," *Guideposts: A Practical Guide to Successful Living* (New York: Guidepost Associates, May 1982), p. 2
14. Gish, June 1961.
15. Paine, p. 2.
16. "Dorothy Gish," *Stars of the Photoplay: Art Portraits of Famous Film Favorites with Short Biographical Sketches.*
17. Paine, "Life and a Little Girl," *Life and Lillian Gish,* p. 3.
18. *Ibid.,* p. 5
19. Lillian Gish, *Guideposts: A Practical Guide to Successful Living,* p. 3.
20. *Ibid.*
21. Paine, p. 4.
22. Lillian Gish, conversation with author, June 1961.
23. Anna Rothe, editor, "Lillian Gish," *Current Biography: Who's Who and Why 1944*

351

(New York: H. W. Wilson, 1944), p. 239.

24. Paine, "Theatre People," *Life and Lillian Gish*, p. 12.

25. Gish, June 1961.

26. Lillian Gish, with Ann Pinchot, *The Movies, Mr. Griffith and Me* (Englewood Cliffs, New Jersey: Prentice-Hall, 1969), p. 6.

27. Lillian Gish, as told to Selma G. Lanes, "How Mother, Doatsie, and I went on the Stage," *An Actor's Life for Me!* with illustrations by Patricia Henderson Lincoln (New York: Viking Kestrel, 1987), p. 9.

28. Gish with Pinchot, p. 6.

29. Gish as told to Lanes, p. 10.

30. *Ibid.*

31. Gish with Pinchot, p. 6.

32. Terry Ramsaye, "The Gishes, 'Pink and Blue,' " *A Million and One Nights* (New York: Simon and Schuster, 1964), p. 604.

33. Paine, p. 12.

34. *Ibid.*, p. 13.

35. Gish with Pinchot, p. 7.

36. Rudi Blesh, *Keaton* (New York: Macmillan, 1966), p. 35.

37. *Ibid.*

38. Jerry Devine, conversation with author, July 1969.

39. Gish with Pinchot, p. 7.

40. Paine, p. 13.

41. Gish with Pinchot, p. 7.

42. Paine, p. 14.

43. Lillian Gish, conversation with author, June 1961.

44. Lillian Gish, as told to Selma G. Lanes, "The Awe-Inspiring Rescue of a Child," *An Actor's Life for Me!*, p. 23.

45. *Ibid.*

46. Phillip C. Lewis, "Life on the Road or the Well-Known Strangers," *Trouping: How the Show Came to Town* (New York: Harper and Row, 1973), p. 114.

47. *Ibid.*, p. 113

48. *Ibid.*, p. 115.

49. Devine, July 1969.

50. John Chapman, "Introduction," *S.R.O.:The Most Successful Plays in the American Stage*, edited by Bennett Cerf and Van Cartmell (Garden City, by special arrangement with Doubleday, 1946), p. xiii.

51. Phillip C. Lewis, "Hits! Palpable Hits!" *Trouping: How the Show Came to Town*, p. 97.

52. Mrs. Henry Wood, "East Lynne," *S.R.O.: The Most Successful Plays in the American Stage*, edited by Bennett Cerf and Van Cartmell, p. 99.

53. Anthony Slide, "Dorothy Gish," *The Griffith Actresses* (South Brunswick and New York: A. S. Barnes, 1973), p. 79.

54. John Chapman, "Introduction," *S.R.O.:The Most Successful Plays in the American Stage*, edited by Bennett Cerf and Van Cartmell, p. xl.

55. Lillian Gish, as told to Selma G. Lanes, "An Actor's Life for Me," *An Actor's Life for Me!*, p. 26.

56. Paine, "A Little Trouper," *Life and Lillian Gish*, p. 23.

57. *Ibid.*, p. 16.

58. Gish with Pinchot, p. 16.

59. *Ibid.*, p. 28.

60. Lillian Gish, conversation with author, October 1969.

61. *Ibid.*

62. Time-Life Books Editors, "A Thousand Hits Count 'Em," *This Fabulous Century Vol. 1, 1900–1910* (New York: Time-Life Books, 1969), p. 244.

63. Paine, "Mary Pickford in the Scene," *Life and Lillian Gish*, p. 32.

64. Gish with Pinchot, p. 25.

65. Robert Windeler, *Sweetheart: The Story of Mary Pickford* (New York and Washington: Praeger 1973), p. 19.

66. *Ibid.*, p. 25.

67. Gish with Pinchot, p. 25.

68. *Ibid.*, p. 29.

69. Betty Bronson, conversation with author, September 1969.

70. Gish with Pinchot, p. 23.

71. Paine, "Theatre People," *Life and Lillian Gish*, p. 12.

72. Paine, "Shawnee," *Ibid.*, p. 69.

73. *Ibid.*, p. 70.

74. Gish with Pinchot, p. 32.

75. Anita Loos, conversation with author, May 1972.

76. Paine, "Mary Pickford in the Scene," *Life and Lillian Gish*, p. 32.

77. Adela Rogers St. Johns, conversation with author, July 1973.

Chapter 2: The Road to Biograph and Mr. Griffith

1. Albert Bigelow Paine, "Dorothy's Tree," *Life and Lillian Gish* (New York: Macmillan, 1932), p. 50.

2. Paine, "Where the Road Ends. Nell," *Ibid.*, p. 61.

3. Paine, "A Convent School. Typhoid," *Ibid.*, p. 64.

4. Lillian Gish, conversation with author, June 1961.

5. Paine, "Massillon Days," *Life and Lillian Gish*, p. 57.

6. Time-Life Books Editors, "A New Entry in Show Biz," *This Fabulous Century: Vol 1, 1900–1910* (New York: Time Life Books, 1969), p. 249.

7. Writers Program of the works Projects Administration, "Springfield," *The Ohio Guide* (New York: Oxford University Press, 1940), p. 162.

8. Time-Life Books Editors, "A New Entry in Show Biz," *This Fabulous Century: Vol. 1, 1900–1910*, p. 249.

9. *Ibid.*

10. Robert Windeler, *Sweetheart: The Story of Mary Pickford* (New York and Washington: Praeger, 1974), p. 29.

11. *Ibid.*, p. 28.

12. Robert M. Henderson, "The Background," *D. W. Griffith: The Years at Biograph* (New York: Farrar, Straus, and Giroux, 1970), p. 4.

13. Scott Eyman, *Mary Pickford: America's Sweetheart* (New York: Donald I. Fine, 1990), p. 39.

14. Henderson, p. 9.

15. Windeler, p. 73.

16. Gish, June 1961.

17. Windeler, p. 73.

18. Gish, June 1961.

19. Paine, "Mr. Biograph," *Life and Lillian Gish*, p. 83.

20. Joyce Johnson, *Minor Characters* (Boston: Houghton Mifflin, 1983), p. 129.

21. Gish, June 1961.

22. *Ibid.*

23. Richard Williams, "The Gallant Gish Girls," *Life,* 20 August 1951, p. 115

24. Gish, June 1961.

25. Richard Schickel, "Oldham County," *D. W. Griffith: An American Life* (New York: Simon and Schuster, 1984), p. 16.

26. Schickel, "To the Biograph," *Ibid.*, p. 90.

27. Schickel, "On the Road," *Ibid.*, p. 64.

28. Gish, June 1961.

29. Brigid Berlin, "Lillian Gish," *Interview,* December 1978, p. 42.

30. Henderson, "1909: Cuddebackville," *D. W. Griffith: The Years at Biograph*, p. 71.

31. Edward Wagenknecht and Anthony Slide, "The Struggle," *The Films of D. W. Griffith* (New York: Crown, 1975), p. 257.

32. Adela Rogers St. Johns, conversation with author, July 1973.

33. Henderson p. 71.

34. Miriam Cooper, with Bonnie Herndon, *Dark Lady of the Silents: My Life in Early Hollywood* (Indianapolis and New York: Bobbs-Merrill, 1973), p. 3.

35. Karl Brown, edited and with an Introduction by Kevin Brownlow, "If at First You Don't Succeed, Try Something Else," *Adventures with D. W. Griffith* (New York: Farrar, Straus and Giroux, 1973), p. 204.

36. Anita Loos, conversation with author, May 1972.

37. Brown, p. 204.

38. Gish, June 1961.

39. Cooper with Herndon, p. 56.

40. Loos, May 1972.

41. Gish, June 1961.

42. Cooper with Herndon, p. 57.

43. Blanche Sweet, conversation with author, May 1976.

44. Gish, June 1961.

45. A. Scott Berg, "Dramatis Personae," *Goldwyn* (New York: Alfred A. Knopf, 1989), p. 44–45.

46. Schickel, "Great Expectations," *D. W. Griffith: An American Life*, p. 181.

47. Lillian Gish, June 1961.

48. *Ibid.*

49. *Ibid.*

50. *Ibid.*

Chapter 3: Events Leading to The Birth: I

1. D. J. Wenden, "Movies Developing Style," *The Birth of the Movies* (London: Macdonald, 1975), p. 51.
2. *Ibid.*, p. 50.
3. Lillian Gish, conversation with author, June 1961.
4. Deems Taylor, Marceline Peterson, and Bryant Hale, "Birth and Infancy," *A Pictorial History of the Movies* (New York: Simon and Schuster, 1950), p. 20.
5. *Ibid.*, p. 21.
6. Aileen Pringle, conversation with author, November 1968.
7. Albert Bigelow Paine, "Belasco Delivers a Verdict," *Life and Lillian Gish* (New York: Macmillan, 1932), p. 87.
8. Irving Drutman, "Lillian Gish: Loveliest of Perennials," *The New York Herald-Tribune*, 13 June 1965, p. 25.
9. Anita Loos, conversation with author, September 1972.
10. *Ibid.*
11. Gish, June 1961.
12. Paine, p. 90.
13. "A Good Little Devil," *The New York Times*, 9 January 1913, p. 9.
14. Richard Schickel, "Great Expectations," *D. W. Griffith: An American Life* (New York: Simon and Schuster, 1984), p. 182.
15. Paine, p. 88.
16. Gish, June 1961.
17. *Ibid.*
18. Paine, p. 89.
19. Lillian Gish, with Ann Pinchot, *The Movies, Mr. Griffith, and Me* (Englewood-Cliffs, New Jersey: Prentice Hall, 1969), p. 78.
20. Paine, p. 90.
21. *Ibid.*, p. 89.
22. *Ibid.*, p. 90.
23. *The New York Times*, 9 January 1913, p. 9.
24. Paine, p. 90.
25. Abel Green, and Joe Laurie, Jr., "Pix-Poor Man's Amusement," *Show Biz: From Vaude to Video* (New York: Henry Holt, 1951), p. 52.
26. Mary Pickford, "The Lillian Gish I Know: A Star's Story of a Star," *Movie Weekly*, 24 January 1925, p. 4.
27. Robert Windeler, *Sweetheart: The Story of Mary Pickford* (New York and Washington: Praeger, 1973), p. 79.
28. Robert M. Henderson, "1910: California," *D. W. Griffith: The Years at Biograph* (New York: Farrar, Straus, and Giroux, 1970), p. 111.
29. Paine, "A Studio on Pico Street," *Life and Lillian Gish*, p. 93.
30. Lillian Gish, with James E. Frasher, "First Decade," *Dorothy and Lillian Gish* (New York: Charles Scribner's Sons, 1973), p. 24.
31. *Ibid.*, p. 95.
32. Paine, p. 90.
33. Schickel, "The $100,000 Idea," *D. W. Griffith: An American Life*, p. 187.
34. Henderson, "1912–1913: Spectacle: Griffith Leaves Biograph," *D. W. Griffith: The Years at Biograph*, p. 150.
35. Adela Rogers St. Johns, "The Big Four," *Love, Laughter and Tears: My Hollywood Story* (New York: New American Library, 1978), p. 71.
36. Gish, with Ann Pinchot, p. 96.
37. Eileen Bowser, "Brand Names and Stars," *The Transformation of Cinema: 1907–1915* (New York: Charles Scribner's Sons, 1990), p. 102.
38. Bowser, "Acting: The Camera's Closer View," *Ibid.*, p. 91.
39. Lillian Gish, conversation with author, March 1963.
40. George C. Pratt, "Griffith at Biograph (11): More Experiments," *Spellbound in Darkness: A History of the Silent Film* (Greenwich: New York Graphic Society, 1973), p. 93.
41. Pratt, "Thunder on the Right (1909–1913): Griffith Leaves Biograph, *Ibid.*, p. 95.
42. *Ibid.*
43. Henderson, p. 150.
44. Anthony Slide, "American Biograph and Griffith," *Early American Cinema* (New York: A. S. Barnes, 1970), p. 133.
45. Pratt, p. 105.
46. Henderson, p. 150.
47. Pratt, p. 105.
48. Enid Markey, conversation with author, November 1963.

49. Kevin Brownlow and John Kobal, "Lawful Larceny, *Hollywood: The Pioneers* (New York: Alfred A. Knopf, 1979), p. 56.

50. Richard Griffith and Arthur Mayer, "The Birth of the Movies," *The Movies* (New York: Simon and Schuster, 1957), p. 29.

51. Brownlow and John Kobal, p. 57.

52. Schickel, p. 189.

53. Daniel Blum, "1904," *A Pictorial History of the American Theatre: 1860–1970*, edited and enlarged by John Willis (New York: Crown, 1969), p. 81.

54. Henderson, "The Background," *D. W. Griffith: The Years at Biograph*, p. 10.

55. Henderson, "1912–1913: Spectacle: Griffith Leaves Biograph," *Ibid.*, p. 131.

56. *Ibid.*, p. 152.

57. Blanche Sweet, conversation with author, May 1976.

58. Gish with Ann Pinchot, p. 106.

59. Henderson, p. 153.

60. Paine, "The Path to Stardom," *Life and Lillian Gish*, pp. 101–102.

61. Gish, March 1963.

62. Sweet, May 1976.

63. Gish, March 1963.

64. Wenden, p. 38.

65. Edward Wagenknecht and Anthony Slide, "Judith of Bethulia," *The Films of D. W. Griffith* (New York: Crown, 1975), p. 29.

66. Henderson, p. 155.

67. Billy Bitzer, "Farewell to Biograph," *Billy Bitzer: His Story* (New York: Farrar, Straus, and Giroux, 1973), p. 89.

68. Lillian Gish, conversation with author, April 1963.

Chapter 4: Events Leading to The Birth: *II*

1. Anita Loos, conversation with author, September 1972.

2. D. J. Wenden, "Movies Develop Style," *The Birth of the Movies* (London: Macdonald, 1974), p. 51.

3. Robert M. Henderson, "Conclusions," *D. W. Griffith: The Years at Biograph* (New York: Farrar, Straus and Giroux, 1970), p. 158.

4. Henderson, "1912–1913: Spectacle: Griffith Leaves Biograph," *Ibid.*, p. 156.

5. Allan Dwan, conversation with author, September 1975.

6. Lillian Gish, conversation with author, June 1961.

7. Charles Lockwood, *Dream Palaces: Hollywood at Home* (New York: The Viking Press, 1981) p. 27.

8. Charles Chaplin, *My Autobiography* (New York: Simon and Schuster, 1964), p. 157.

9. Adela Rogers St. Johns, conversation with author, August 1974.

10. Constance Talmadge, conversation with author, May 1968.

11. Dwan, September 1975.

12. Eileen Bowser, "General Flimco and the Pushcart Peddlers," *The Transformation of Cinema* (New York: Charles Scribner's Sons 1990), p. 79.

13. Lillian Gish, with Ann Pinchot, *The Movies, Mr. Griffith, and Me* (Englewood Cliffs, New Jersey: Prentice-Hall,1969), p. 110.

14. Albert Bigelow Paine, "The Path to Stardom," *Life and Lillian Gish* (New York: Macmillan, 1932), p. 104.

15. Billy Bitzer, "The Birth of a Nation," *Billy Bitzer: His Story* (New York: Farrar, Straus and Giroux, 1973), p. 102.

16. Donald Crisp, conversation with author, August 1968.

17. Edward Wagenknecht and Anthony Slide, "The Escape," *The Films of D. W. Griffith* (New York: Crown, 1975), p. 35.

18. Bitzer, "Farewell to Biograph," *Billy Bitzer: His Story*, p. 90.

19. Paine, p. 105.

20. Lillian Gish, conversation with author, April 1963.

21. *The New York Times*, 12 April 1914, p. 5.

22. Wagenknecht and Slide, "The Battle of the Sexes," *The Films of D. W. Griffith*, p. 32.

23. Bitzer, p. 90.

24. Paine, p. 105.

25. Henderson, "1908: The Beginning," *D. W. Griffith: The Years at Biograph*, p. 49.

26. Gish with Ann Pinchot, p. 205.

27. Crisp, August 1968.

28. Bitzer, "The Birth of a Nation," *Billy Bitzer: His Story*, p. 103.

29. *Ibid.*, p. 105.
30. Wagenknecht and Slide, "Home Sweet Home," *The Films of D. W. Griffith*, p. 37.
31. "New Strand Opens, Biggest of Movies," *The New York Times*, 12 April 1914, p. 15.
32. Wagenknecht and Slide, p. 337.
33. Blanche Sweet, conversation with author, October 1968.
34. Gish, April 1963.
35. Gish with Pinchot, p. 103.
36. Crisp, August 1968.
37. Loos, September 1972.
38. Gish with Pinchot, p. 114.
39. Loos, September 1972.
40. Richard Schickel, "Re 'Birth'," *D. W. Griffith: An American Life* (New York: Simon and Schuster, 1984), p. 218.
41. Schickel, "The Curse of the River," *Ibid.*, p. 41.
42. Bitzer, "Broken Blossoms," *Billy Bitzer: His Story*, p. 198.

Chapter 5: The Birth of a Nation

1. Lillian Gish, conversation with author, December 1960.
2. *Ibid.*
3. Robert M. Henderson, "1912–1913: Spectacle: Griffith Leaves Biograph," *D. W. Griffith: The Years at Biograph* (New York: Farrar, Straus and Giroux, 1970), p. 155.
4. Billy Bitzer, "The Birth of a Nation," *Billy Bitzer: His Story* (New York: Farrar, Straus and Giroux, 1973), p. 109.
5. Henderson, "The Background," *D. W. Griffith: The Years at Biograph,* p. 28.
6. Eileen Bowser, "Trademarks, Titles, Introductions," *The Transformations of Cinema* (New York: Charles Scribner's Sons, 1990), p. 143.
7. Bowser, "The Genre Film," *Ibid.*, p. 177.
8. Donald Bogle, "Black Beginnings: From Uncle Tom's Cabin to the Birth of a Nation," *Toms, Coons, Mulattoes, Mammies and Bucks: An Interpretive History of Black in American Films* (New York: The Viking Press, 1973), p. 10.
9. Edward Wagenknecht and Anthony Slide, "The Birth of a Nation," *The Films of D. W. Griffith* (New York: Crown, 1975), p. 46.
10. Albert Bigelow Paine, "The Birth of a Nation," *Life and Lillian Gish* (New York: Macmillan, 1932), p. 111.
11. Gish, December 1960.
12. David Shipman, "1914," *Cinema: The First Hundred Years* (London: Weidenfeld and Norman, 1993), p. 55.
13. Gish, December 1960.
14. Bogle, p. 14.
15. Daniel J. Leab, "The Birth of a Nation," *From Sambo to Superspade: The Black Experience in Motion Pictures* (Boston: Houghton Mifflin, 1976), p. 33.
16. Karl Brown, "Sorcerer's Apprentice," *Adventures with D. W. Griffith,* edited with an introduction by Kevin Brownlow (New York: Farrar, Straus and Giroux, 1973), p. 78.
17. Wyn Craig Wade, "Writing History with Lightning," *The Fiery Cross: The Ku Klux Klan* (New York: Simon and Schuster 1987), p. 131.
18. *Ibid.*
19. Wagenknecht and Slide, p. 60.
20. Leab, p. 33.
21. Lillian Gish, letter to author, 3 May 1961.
22. D. J. Wenden, "Movies Develop Style, *The Birth of the Movies* (London: Macdonald, 1975), p. 51.
23. Brown, "The Great D. W.," *Adventures with D. W. Griffith,* p. 16.
24. *Ibid.*
25. Gish, December 1960.
26. Eve Golden, "Mae Marsh: The Natural," *Films of the Golden Age,* Winter 1996, p. 32.
27. Gish, December 1960.
28. Donald Crisp, conversation with author, August 1968.
29. Lillian Gish, conversation with author, February 1961.
30. *Ibid.*
31. Wagenknecht and Slide, p. 46.
32. *The New York Times*, 3 March 1915, p. 20.
33. *Ibid.*
34. Wagenknecht and Slide, p. 61.
35. "The Birth of a Nation," *The New York Times,* 4 March 1915, p. 9.
36. *Ibid.*

37. Wagenknecht and Slide, p. 60.
38. *Ibid.*, p. 61.
39. Lillian Gish, conversation with author, March 1961.

Chapter 6: Triangle Time

1. Anita Loos, conversation with author, May 1972.
2. Lillian Gish, with Ann Pinchot, *The Movies, Mr. Griffith, and Me* (Englewood Cliffs, New Jersey: Prentice-Hall, 1969), p. 110.
3. *Ibid.*, p. 167.
4. Minta Durfee Arbuckle, conversation with author, July 1969.
5. Lillian Gish, conversation with author, May 1961.
6. Lillian Gish, with James E. Frasher, "First Decade," *Dorothy and Lillian Gish* (New York: Charles Scribner's Sons, 1973) p. 54.
7. Dorothy Davenport Reid, conversation with author, August 1975.
8. Charles Lockwood, *Dream Palaces: Hollywood at Home* (New York: The Viking Press, 1981), p. 43.
9. Albert Bigelow Paine, "There Were No Love Affairs," *Life and Lillian Gish* (New York: Macmillan, 1932), p. 124.
10. Lillian Gish, conversation with author, June 1968.
11. Patricia King Hanson, executive editor, and Alan Gevinson, assistant editor, "The Lily and the Rose," *The American Film Institute Catalogue of Motion Pictures Produced in the United States: Feature Films, 1919–1920, Vol. F 1* (Berkeley: University of California Press, 1988), p. 520.
12. *The New York Times,* 8 November 1915, p. 12.
13. *Ibid.*
14. Paine, p. 124.
15. Kalton C. Lahue, "How Heroes Are Made," *Dreams for Sale: The Rise and Fall of the Triangle Film Corporation* (South Brunswick and New York: A. S. Barnes, 1971), p. 141.
16. Gish with Pinchot, p. 89.
17. *Ibid.*

18. *The New York Times,* 10 April 1916, p. 15.
19. Lillian Gish, conversation with author, November 1972.
20. Allan Dwan, conversation with author, September 1975.
21. *Ibid.*
22. Milan Stitt, conversation with author, February 1996.
23. D. W. Griffith, *The Man Who Invented Hollywood: The Autobiography of D. W. Griffith,* edited and annotated by James Hart, with a foreword by Frank Capra (Louisville, Kentucky: Touchstone, 1972), p. 115.
24. Loos, May 1972.
25. Griffith, p. 115.
26. Gish with Frasher, p. 65.
27. Gish with Pinchot, p. 178.
28. Griffith, p. 116.
29. Gish, June 1968.
30. Gish with Pinchot, p. 167.
31. Patricia King Hanson, executive editor, and Alan Gevinson, assistant editor, "Diane of the Follies," *The American Film Institute Catalogue of Motion Pictures Produced in the United States: Feature Films, 1919–1920, Vol. F 1,* p. 214.
32. Loos, May 1972.
33. Marjorie Farnsworth, *The Ziegfeld Follies: A History in Text and Pictures* (London: Peter Davies, 1956), p. 188.
34. Charles Higham, "Midnight Frolics," *Ziegfeld* (Chicago: Henry Regnery, 1972), p. 117.
35. Ann Pennington, conversation with author, June 1970.
36. Loos, May 1972.
37. George C. Pratt, "Outposts of the Cinema's Advance: THE BIRTH OF A NATION (1915) and INTOLERANCE (1916)," *Spellbound in Darkness: A History of the Silent Film* (Greenwich: The New York Graphic Society), p. 214.
38. Allan Dwan, conversation with author, August 1975.
39. Constance Talmadge, conversation with author, May 1968.
40. Pratt, p. 210.
41. Kalton C. Lahue, "The Late Lamented," *Dreams for Sale: The Rise and Fall of the Triangle Film Corporation,* p. 165.

Chapter 7: Dark Crossings

1. Kalton C. Lahue, "The Late Lamented," *Dreams for Sale: The Rise and Fall of the Triangle Film Corporation* (South Brunswick and New York: A. S. Barnes, 1971), p. 165.
2. Allan Dwan, conversation with author, September 1975.
3. Proprietor of Newark's Old Book Store, conversation with author, December 1959.
4. Lahue, p. 165.
5. D. W. Griffith, *The Man Who Invented Hollywood: The Autobiography of D. W. Griffith*, edited and annotated by James Hart, with a foreword by Frank Capra (Louisville, Kentucky: Touchstone, 1972), p. 121.
6. Daniel Blum, "1917," *A Pictorial History of the Silent Screen* (New York: Grosset and Dunlap, 1953), p. 144.
7. Albert E. McKinley, Ph.D., Charles A. Coulomb, Ph.D., and Armand J. Gerson, Ph.D., "Naval Operations," *A School History of the Great War* (New York, Cincinatti, Chicago, Boston, and Atlanta: American Book Company, 1919), p. 102.
8. Kevin Brownlow, "Lillian Gish," *Films and Filming*, November 1983, p. 25.
9. Griffith, p. 121.
10. McKinley, Coulomb, and Gerson, "The War in 1917," *A School History of the Great War*, p. 118.
11. Ivan Butler, "The Early Years," *Silent Magic: Rediscovering the Silent Film Era*, with a Foreword by Kevin Brownlow (New York: Ungar, 1988), p. 22.
12. Edward Wagenknecht and Anthony Slide, "Hearts of the World," *The Films of D. W. Griffith* (New York: Crown, 1975), p. 95.
13. Butler, p. 23.
14. Billy Bitzer, "Hearts of the World," *Billy Bitzer: His Story* (New York: Farrar, Straus and Giroux, 1973), p. 183.
15. Lillian Gish with Ann Pinchot, *The Movies, Mr. Griffith, and Me* (Englewood Cliffs, New Jersey: Prentice-Hall, 1969), pp. 187–88.
16. Bitzer, p. 182.
17. Albert Bigelow Paine, "The Nightmare of War," *Life and Lillian Gish* (New York: Macmillan, 1932), p. 129.
18. *Ibid.*
19. *Ibid.* p. 132.
20. Lillian Gish, conversation with author, June 1961.
21. Paine, "Under Fire," *Life and Lillian Gish*, p. 132.
22. Charles Castle, "Bursting with Remarkable Talent," *Noel* (Garden City, New York: Doubleday, 1973), p. 30.
23. Sheridan Morley, *A Talent to Amuse: A Biography of Noel Coward* (Garden City, New York: Doubleday, 1969), p. 30.
24. Stuart Oderman, "Lillian Gish: A Friend Remembered," *Journal of Popular Film and Television*, Summer 1994, p. 53.
25. Paine, p. 133.
26. Gish with Pinchot, p. 196.
27. Paine, p. 133.
28. Gish with Pinchot, p. 196–97.
29. Allan Dwan, conversation with author, September 1975.
30. Gish, June 1961.
31. Gish with Pinchot, p. 201.
32. Paine, "Hearts of the World," *Life and Lillian Gish*, p. 137.
33. Gish with Pinchot, p. 201.
34. Gene Brown, "1918," *Movie Time: A Chronology of Hollywood and the Movie Industry from Its Beginnings to the Present* (New York: Macmillan, 1995), p. 46.
35. Jack spears, "The Movies of World War I," *Hollywood: The Golden Era* (New York: Castle Books, 1971), p. 37.
36. Sir Noel Coward, conversation with author, 1969.

Chapter 8: Little Poems

1. Herman G. Weinberg, conversation with author, June 1972.
2. Robert M. Henderson, "1909: Cuddebackville," *D. W. Griffith: The Years at Biograph* (New York: Farrar, Straus and Giroux, 1970), p. 81.
3. Patricia King Hanson, executive editor, and Alan Gevinson, assistant editor, "The Hun Within," *The American Film Institute Catalogue of Motion Pictures Produced in the United States: Feature Films, 1919–1920,*

Vol. F 1 (Berkeley: University of California Press, 1988), p. 435.

4. Frederick Lewis Allen, "Revolution in Manners and Morals," *Only Yesterday* (New York: Bantam, 1946), p. 114.

5. Richard Hefner, *A Documentary History of the United States,* 4th ed. (New York: New American Library, 1985), p. 256.

6. Richard Koszarski, "The Stars," *An Evening's Entertainment: The Age of the Silent Feature Picture: 1915–1928* (Berkeley, Los Angeles, and London: University of California Press, 1994), p. 293.

7. Richard Griffith and Arthur Mayer, "But Flaming Youth Flamed On," *The Movies* (New York: Simon and Schuster, 1957), p. 190.

8. Ann Douglas, "Setting the Stage: White Manhattan," *Terrible Honesty: Mongrel Manhattan in the 1920s* (New York: Farrar, Straus and Giroux, 1995), p. 67.

9. William K. Everson, "A Survey," *American Silent Film* (New York: Oxford University Press, 1978), p. 4.

10. Everson, "Stabilization," *Ibid.,* p. 113.

11. Griffith and Mayer, p. 192.

12. James Naremore, "True Heart Susie and the Art of Lillian Gish," *Quarterly Review of Film Studies,* vol. 6, no. 1, Winter 1981, p. 93.

13. *Ibid.*

14. Sheila Graham, conversation with author, March 1960.

15. Edward Wagenknecht and Anthony Slide, "A Romance of Happy Valley," *The Films of D. W. Griffith* (New York: Crown, 1975), p. 102.

16. Allan Dwan, conversation with author, September 1975.

17. Colleen Moore, conversation with author, September 1967.

18. Lillian Gish with Ann Pinchot, *The Movies, Mr. Griffith, and Me* (Englewood Cliffs, New Jersey: Prentice-Hall, 1969), p. 209.

19. Anthony Slide, "Lillian Gish," *The Griffith Actresses* (South Brunswick and New York: A. S. Barnes, 1973), p. 103.

20. *Ibid.*

21. *Ibid.*

22. *Ibid.*

23. Gish with Pinchot, p. 210.

24. Stanley J. Kunitz and Howard Haycraft, editors, *Twentieth Century Authors: A Biographical Dictionary of Modern Literature* (New York: H. W. Wilson, 1942), p. 221.

25. D. W. Griffith, *The Man Who Invented Hollywood: The Autobiography of D. W. Griffith,* edited and annotated by James Hart, with a foreword by Frank Capra (Louisville, Kentucky: Touchstone, 1972), p. 123.

26. Ruth Wing, editor, *The Blue Book of the Screen* (Hollywood, California: Pacific Gravure: 1923), p. 16.

27. Albert Bigelow Paine, "Broken Blossoms," *Life and Lillian Gish* (New York: Macmillan, 1932), p. 140.

28. Billy Bitzer, "Intolerance," *Billy Bitzer: His Story* (New York: Farrar, Straus and Giroux, 1975), p. 146.

29. Gish with Pinchot, p. 218.

30. Dale McConathy and Diana Vreeland, "...Starring Lillian Gish," *Hollywood Costumes* (New York: Harry N. Abrams, 1976), p. 50.

31. Gish with Pinchot, p. 219.

32. Kevin Brownlow, "Lillian Gish," *Films and Filming,* November 1983, p. 19.

33. Slide, "Carol Dempster," *The Griffith Actresses,* p. 148.

34. Bitzer, "Broken Blossoms," *Billy Bitzer: His Story,* p. 201.

35. Bitzer, *Ibid.,* p. 206–207.

36. Paine, p. 143.

37. Bitzer, "Broken Blossoms, *Billy Bitzer: His Story,* p. 210.

38. Thomas Burke, "The Chink and the Child," *Limehouse Nights* (New York: Grosset and Dunlap, 1917), p. 18.

39. Lillian Gish, conversation with author, June 1961.

40. Gish with Pinchot, p. 219.

41. *Ibid.*

42. Lillian Gish with James E. Frasher, "First Decade," *Dorothy and Lillian Gish* (New York: Charles Scribner's Sons 1973), p. 85.

43. *Ibid.*

44. Everson, "The Early Twenties," *American Silent Film,* p. 150.

45. Griffith, *The Man Who Invented Hollywood: The Autobiography of D. W. Griffith,* p. 124.

46. Bitzer, p. 210.

47. Gish, June 1961.

48. Paine, p. 144.

49. Bitzer, p. 210.

50. Kevin Brownlow, "D. W. Griffith," *The Parade's Gone By* (New York: Alfred A. Knopf, 1968), p. 91.

51. Bitzer, p. 211.

52. Kevin Brownlow, "Lillian Gish," *American Film*, March 1984, p. 26.

53. Brownlow, *The Parade's Gone By*, p. 91.

54. David Robinson, "The Idols," *Hollywood in the Twenties* (New York: Paperback Library, 1968), pp. 178–79.

55. Gish with Pinchot, p. 220.

56. Donald Crisp, conversation with author, September 1974.

57. Paine, "I Work Such Long Hours," *Life and Lillian Gish*, p. 146.

58. Hanson and Gevinson, "Broken Blossoms," *The American Film Institute Catalogue of Motion Pictures Produced in the United States: Feature Films, 1919–1920, Vol. F 1*, p. 103.

59. Gish with Pinchot, p. 221.

60. Paine, p. 146.

61. Slide, "Lillian Gish," *The Griffith Actresses*, p. 100.

62. Gene Brown, "1919," *Movie Time: A Chronology of Hollywood and the Movie Industry from Its Beginnings to the Present* (New York: Macmillan, 1995), p. 50.

63. Allen, "Prelude: May, 1919," *Only Yesterday*, p. 16.

64. Allen, "The Revolution in Manners and Morals," *Ibid.*, p. 120.

65. Allen, "Prelude: May, 1919," *Ibid.*, p. 22.

66. Robinson, "The Nation," *Hollywood in the Twenties*, p. 9.

67. Marjorie Rosen, "Mary's Curls, Griffith's Girls," *Popcorn Venus: Women, Movies and the American Dream* (New York: Coward, McCann and Geohegan, 1973), p. 52.

Chapter 9: A Reward

1. Minta Durfee Arbuckle, conversation with author, August 1968.

2. Lillian Gish, with Ann Pinchot, *The Movies, Mr. Griffith, and Me* (Englewood Cliffs, New Jersey: Prentice-Hall, 1969), p. 225.

3. Lillian Gish, with James E. Frasher, "Second Decade," *Dorothy and Lillian Gish* (New York: Charles Scribner's Sons: 1973), p. 94.

4. Albert Bigelow Paine, "Director Lillian," *Life and Lillian Gish* (New York: Macmillan, 1932), p. 152.

5. *Ibid.*, p. 149.

6. Gish with Pinchot, p. 225.

7. Paine, p. 153.

8. "James Rennie," *Stars of the Photoplay: Art Portraits of Famous Film Favorites with Short Biographical Sketches* (Chicago: Photoplay, 1924).

9. Daniel Blum, "1920," *A Pictorial History of the American Theatre: 1860–1970*, edited and enlarged by John Willis (New York: Crown, 1969), p. 183.

10. Aileen Pringle, conversation with author, September 1970.

11. Anthony Slide, "Dorothy Gish," *The Griffith Actresses* (South Brunswick and New York: A.S. Barnes, 1973), p. 88.

12. *Ibid.*

13. Paine, p. 155.

14. *Ibid.*

15. Gish with Pinchot, p. 226.

16. Slide, p. 89.

17. Pringle, September 1970.

Chapter 10: Ice Floes

1. William K. Everson, "The Early Twenties," *American Silent Film* (New York: Oxford University Press, 1978), p. 157.

2. Lillian Gish, with Ann Pinchot, *The Movies, Mr. Griffith, and Me* (Englewood Cliffs, New Jersey: Prentice-Hall, 1969), p. 225.

3. Patricia King Hanson, executive editor, and Alan Gevinson, assistant editor, "The Greatest Question," *The American Film Institute Catalogue of Motion Pictures Produced in the United States: Feature Films, 1911–1920, Vol. F 1* (Berkeley: University of California Press, 1988), p. 354.

4. Edward Wagenknecht and Anthony Slide, "The Greatest Question," *The Films of*

D. W. Griffith (New York: Crown, 1975), p. 136.

5. *Ibid.*

6. Anita Loos, conversation with author, May 1972.

7. Daniel Blum, editor, "1903," *A Pictorial History of the American Theatre: 1860–1970* (New York: Crown, 1969), p. 76.

8. Gish with Pinchot, p. 229.

9. Richard Griffith and Arthur Mayer, "Screen Art: The Decline of D. W. Griffith," *The Movies* (New York: Simon and Schuster, 1957), p. 208.

10. Lillian Gish, conversation with author, June 1961.

11. Pauline Kael, "A Great Folly and a Small One," *Going Steady* (Boston and Toronto: Little, Brown, 1970), p. 46.

12. *Ibid.*

13. Albert Bigelow Paine, "Way Down East," *Life and Lillian Gish* (New York: Macmillan, 1932), p. 156.

14. Gish, June 1961.

15. *Ibid.*

16. Gish with Pinchot, p. 232.

17. Paine, p. 156.

18. *Ibid.*

19. Gish with Pinchot, p. 232.

20. Paine, p. 157.

21. Billy Bitzer, "Broken Blossoms," *Billy Bitzer: His Story* (New York: Farrar, Straus, and Giroux, 1973), p. 204.

22. Billy Bitzer, "Mamaroneck: The New Master," *Ibid.*, p. 221.

23. Wagenknecht and Slide, "Way Down East," *The Films of D. W. Griffith*, p. 159.

24. Gish with Pinchot, p. 234.

25. Paine, p. 158.

26. Alexander Woolcott, "The Screen," *The New York Times*, 4 September 1920, p. 7.

27. George C. Pratt, "BROKEN BLOSSOMS, and Some Griffith Films in the Twenties," *Spellbound in Darkness: A History of the Silent Film* (Greenwich: New York Graphic Society, 1973), p. 254.

28. Wagenknecht and Slide, p. 159.

29. Marjorie Rosen, "Mary's Curls, Griffith's Girls," *Popcorn Venus: Women, Movies and the American Dream* (New York: Coward, McCann, and Geohegan, 1973), p. 51.

30. Pratt, p. 34.

31. Ivan Butler, "1920," *Silent Magic: Rediscovering the Silent Film Era*, with a Foreword by Kevin Brownlow (New York: Ungar, 1988), p. 34.

32. Kalton C. Lahue, "The Spellbound Multitude," *Bound and Gagged: The Story of the Silent Serials* (New York: Castle Books, 1968), p. 53.

33. Donald Mackenzie, conversation with author, March 1970.

34. Gish with Pinchot, p. 205.

35. Loos, May 1972.

36. Bitzer, "The End of an Era," *Billy Bitzer: His Story*, p. 204.

37. John Kobal, "Dorothy Gish," *People Will Talk* (New York: Aurum Press, 1986), p. 35.

38. *Ibid.*, p. 37.

Chapter 11: Storms and Partings

1. Albert Bigelow Paine, "Sad, Unprofitable Days," *Life and Lillian Gish* (New York: Macmillan, 1932), p. 165.

2. Gene Brown, "1920," *Movie Time: A Chronology of Hollywood and the Movie Industry from Its Beginnings to the Present* (New York: Macmillan, 1995), p. 55.

3. Alan Brock, conversation with author, October 1980.

4. Anita Loos, conversation with author, November 1972.

5. Hubert Howe, "The Film Wizard of Europe," *Photoplay*, December 1922, p. 22.

6. Peter Bogdanovitch, "Galloping Tintypes," *Allan Dwan: The Last Pioneer* (New York: Praeger, 1971), p. 35.

7. Allan Dwan, conversation with author, September 1975.

8. Lillian Gish, with Ann Pinchot, *The Movies, Mr. Griffith, and Me* (Englewood-Cliffs, New Jersey: Prentice-Hall, 1969), p. 182.

9. D. W. Griffith, *The Man Who Invented Hollywood: The Autobiography of D. W. Griffith*, edited and annotated by James Hart, with a foreword by Frank Capra (Louisville, Kentucky: Touchstone, 1972), p. 140.

10. Richard Griffith and Arthur Mayer, "Screen Art: The Decline of D. W. Griffith," *The Movies* (New York: Simon and Schuster, 1957), p. 208.

11. Gish with Pinchot, p. 240.

12. *Ibid.*, p. 275.

13. Daniel Blum, "1904," *A Pictorial History of the American Theatre: 1860–1970,* edited and enlarged by John Willis (New York: Crown, 1969), p. 83.

14. Cornelia Otis Skinner, "La 'Damala' aux Camelias," *Madame Sarah* (Boston: Houghton Mifflin, 1967), p. 203.

15. Paine, p. 166.

16. Gish with Pinchot, p. 240

17. Paine, p. 166.

18. *Ibid.*

19. John Chapman, "Introduction," *S.R.O.: The Most Successful Plays of the American Stage,* edited by Bennett Cerf and Van Cartmell (Garden City, New York: Garden City), pp. xiii-xiv.

20. Anne Edwards, "Carrying the Torch: 1918–1928," *The DeMilles: An American Family* (New York: Harry N. Abrams, 1988), p. 95.

21. Agnes DeMille, conversation with author, November 1978.

22. Marjorie Rosen, "Mary's Curls, Griffith's Girls," *Popcorn Venus: Women, Movies and the American Dream* (New York: Coward, McCann, and Geohegan, 1973), p. 50.

23. Anna Rothe, editor, "Lillian Gish," *Current Biography: Who's Who and Why* (New York: H. W. Wilson, 1944), p. 239.

24. Paine, "Picturing the Reign of Terror," *Life and Lillian Gish,* p. 171.

25. Lillian Gish, with James E. Frasher, "Second Decade," *Dorothy and Lillian Gish* (New York: Charles Scribner's Sons, 1973), p. 109.

26. Charles Affron, "Actress and Author: Gish and Griffith," *Star Acting: Gish, Garbo, Davis* (New York: E. P. Dutton, 1977), p. 54.

27. *Ibid.*, p. 55.

28. Anita Loos, conversation with author, May 1972.

29. Jack Gaver, "Recalls Griffith Film on TV Thursday 'Silents Please' Brings Back Fond Memory for Lillian Gish," *The New York Times Morning Telegraph,* 20 June 1961.

30. Paine, p. 170.

31. Gaver.

32. Edward Wagenknecht and Anthony Slide, "Orphans of the Storm," *The Films of D. W. Griffith* (New York: Crown, 1975), p. 169.

33. Chris Van Ness, "Lillian Gish Remembers the Movies," *The Los Angeles Free Press,* 2 November 1973, p. 6.

34. Gish with Frasher, p. 113.

35. Gish with Pinchot, p. 245.

36. Paine, p. 171.

37. *Ibid.*,

38. *Ibid.*, p. 172.

39. Frank Capra, conversation with author, October 1971.

Chapter 12: In Italy: I

1. Gene Brown, "1917," *Movie Time: A Chronology of Hollywood and the Movie Industry from Its Beginnings to the Present* (New York: Macmillan, 1995), p. 43.

2. Marjorie Rosen, "Mary's Curls, Griffith's Girls," *Popcorn Venus: Women, Movies, and the American Dream* (New York: Coward, McCann and Geohegan, 1973), p. 62.

3. Sheridan Morley, "Interview with Lillian Gish," *Films and Filming,* January 1970, p. 15.

4. O. Z. Whitehead, "Lillian," *Theatre Book,* vol. 1, no. 1., Spring 1978, p. 46.

5. Alan Brock, conversation with author, October 1980.

6. Albert Bigelow Paine, "Italy," *Life and Lillian Gish* (New York: Macmillan, 1932), p. 176.

7. Brock, October 1980.

8. Ephraim Katz, "Henry King," *The Film Encyclopedia* (New York: Perigee Books, 1982), p. 656.

9. Richard Schickel, "A Man's Estate," *D. W. Griffith: An American Life* (New York: Simon and Schuster, 1984), p. 454.

10. David Robinson, "Recruitment," *Hollywood in the Twenties* (New York: A. S. Barnes, 1968), p. 97.

11. Marjorie Farnsworth, "Appendix," *The*

Ziegfeld Follies (London: Peter Davies, 1956), p. 188.

12. Daniel Blum, "1922," *A Pictorial History of the American Theatre: 1860–1970,* edited and enlarged by John Willis (New York: Crown, 1969), p. 195.

13. Lillian Gish, with James E. Frasher, "Second Decade," *Dorothy and Lillian Gish* (New York: Charles Scribner's Sons, 1973), p. 124.

14. Paine, p. 177.

15. Anthony Slide, "Lillian Gish," *The Griffith Actresses* (South Brunswick and New York: A. S. Barnes, 1973), p. 104.

16. Alexander Walker, "All for Art: Lillian Gish," *Stardom: The Hollywood Phenomenon* (New York: Stein and Day, 1970), p. 70.

17. Daniel Blum, "1909," *A Pictorial History of the American Theatre: 1860–1970,* edited and enlarged by John Willis, p. 110.

18. Paine, p. 177.

19. Slide, pp. 104–105.

20. Katz, p. 656.

21. Lillian Gish, with Ann Pinchot, *The Movies, Mr. Griffith, and Me* (Englewood-Cliffs, New Jersey: Prentice-Hall, 1969), p. 252.

22. *Ibid.,* p. 254–255.

23. Paine, p. 181.

24. *Ibid.,* p. 180.

25. Kevin Brownlow, "Henry King," *The Parade's Gone By* (New York: Alfred A. Knopf, 1968), p. 110.

26. Charles Affron, "Before Glamour at MGM: Gish, Vidor, and Seastrom," *Star Acting: Gish, Garbo, Davis* (New York: E. P. Dutton, 1977), p. 60.

27. *Ibid.,* p. 62.

28. *Ibid.,* p. 63.

29. Brownlow, p. 112.

30. Affron, p. 60.

31. Paine, p. 188.

32. *Ibid.,* p. 190.

33. *Ibid.*

34. "The Screen: The White Sister," *The New York Times,* 6 September 1923, p. 17.

35. *Ibid.*

36. Gish with Pinchot, p. 258.

37. Millan Stitt, conversation with author, May 1996.

38. *The New York Times,* p. 17.

Chapter 13: In Italy: II

1. Albert Bigelow Paine, "Romola," *Life and Lillian Gish* (New York: Macmillan, 1932), p. 194.

2. William K. Everson, conversation with author, April 1978.

3. Paine, p. 195.

4. Kevin Brownlow, "Henry King," *The Parade's Gone By* (New York: Alfred A. Knopf, 1968), p. 111.

5. Paine, p. 195.

6. *Ibid.,* p. 189.

7. Brownlow, p. 111.

8. Kevin Brownlow and John Kobal, "Cult of the Personality," *Hollywood: The Pioneers* (New York: Alfred A. Knopf, 1979), p. 180.

9. Marion Meade, "Italian Villa," *Buster Keaton: Cut to the Chase* (New York: HarperCollins, 1995), p. 178.

10. Paine, p. 194.

11. Anthony Slide, "Lillian Gish," *The Griffith Actresses* (South Brunswick and New York: A. S. Barnes, 1973), p. 106.

12. Charles Affron, "Gish, Vidor, and Seastrom," *Star Acting: Gish, Garbo, and Davis* (New York: E. P. Dutton, 1977), p. 66.

13. Paine, p. 197.

14. Lillian Gish, conversation with author, September 1961.

15. "Lillian Gish Sued by Film Producer," *The New York Times,* 31 January 1925, p. 15.

16. Betty Bronson, conversation with author, September 1968.

17. Thomas H. Johnson, in consultation with Harvey Wish, *The Oxford Companion to American History* (New York: Oxford University Press: 1966), p. 694.

18. Lillian Gish, conversation with author, May 1961.

19. Lillian Gish, with Ann Pinchot, *The Movies, Mr. Griffith, and Me* (Englewood Cliffs, New Jersey: Prentice-Hall, 1969), p. 265.

20. Adela Rogers St. Johns, conversation with author, July 1974.

21. Paine, p. 199.

22. *The New York Times,* p. 15.

23. "A Florentine Story," *The New York Times,* 2 December 1924, p. 13.

24. Lillian Gish, conversation with author, June 1961.

25. Paine, p. 201.

26. Slide, "Dorothy Gish," *The Griffith Actresses,* p. 91.

27. William K. Everson, conversation with author, October 1983.

28. Edward Wagenknecht, "Lillian Gish: An Interpretation," *The Movies in an Age of Innocence* (Norman: University of Oklahoma Press, 1962), p. 253.

29. Robert G. Anderson, "The Portrayals," *Faces, Forms, Films: The Artistry of Lon Chaney* (New York: Castle Books, 1971), p. 109.

30. Wagenknecht, p. 254.

31. *Ibid.*

32. *Ibid.*

33. *Ibid.*

34. *The New York Times,* p. 13.

35. Gish with Pinchot, p. 274.

Chapter 14: Betrayals

1. "Court Holds Duell on Perjury Charges, Quashes Gish Suit," *The New York Times,* 3 April 1925, p. 1.

2. "Quarrel Enlivens Lillian Gish Suit," *The New York Times,* 14 February 1925, p. 28.

3. Lillian Gish, with Ann Pinchot, *The Movies, Mr. Griffith, and Me* (Englewood Cliffs, New Jersey: Prentice-Hall, 1969), p. 265.

4. "Duell-Gish Troth Merely Unofficial," *The New York Times,* 31 March 1925, p. 23.

5. Gish with Pinchot, p. 265.

6. *The New York Times,* p. 23.

7. "Lillian Gish Sued by Film Producer," *The New York Times,* 31 January 1925, p. 15.

8. "Duell Summons Rennie in Gish Row," *The New York Times,* 25 February 1925, p. 40.

9. "Says Duell Kept Miss Gish's Profits," *The New York Times,* 2 June 1926, p. 7.

10. "Judge Clears Room at the Gish Trial," *The New York Times,* 28 March 1925, p. 6.

11. "Says Duell Kept Miss Gish's Profits, *The New York Times,* 2, June 1926, p. 7.

12. "Lillian Gish Signs,: *The New York Times,* 25 April 1925, p. 16.

13. Albert Bigelow Paine, "Also, the Intelligentsia," *Life and Lillian Gish* (New York: Macmillan, 1932), p. 205.

14. "Judge Clears Room at the Gish Trial," *The New York Times* 28 March 1925, p. 6.

15. *Ibid.*

16. "Lillian Gish Opens Lawsuit in Person," *The New York Times,* 25, March 1925, p. 25.

17. Leonard Sillman, conversation with author, November 1970.

18. Charles Affron, "Gish, Vidor and Seastrom," *Star Acting: Gish, Garbo, Davis* (New York: E. P. Dutton, 1977), p. 66.

19. "Duell Summons Rennie in Gish Row," *The New York Times,* 25, February 1925, p. 40.

20. "James Rennie Is Cleared," *The New York Times,* 12 March 1925, p. 6.

21. "Lillian Gish Wins Decision," *The New York Times,* 13 March 1925, p. 23.

22. "Quarrel Enlivens Lillian Gish Suit," *The New York Times,* 14 February 1925, p. 28.

23. "Lillian Gish Opens Lawsuit in Person," *The New York Times,* 25 March 1925, p. 25.

24. "Miss Gish at Trial a Study in Emotion," *The New York Times,* 26 March 1925, p. 20.

25. *Ibid.*

26. *Ibid.*

27. "Miss Gish to Take Stand in Duell Suit," *The New York Times,* 27 March 1925, p. 19.

28. *Ibid.*

29. "Judge Clears the Room at the Gish Trial," *The New York Times,* 28 March 1925, p. 6.

30. *Ibid.*

31. "Duell-Gish Troth Merely 'Unofficial'," *The New York Times,* 1 March 1925, p. 1.

32. "Lillian Gish at Art Reception," *The New York Times,* 31 March 1925, p. 17.

33. Gish with Pinchot, p. 265.

34. "Duell Is Tangled on Gish Dealings," *The New York Times,* 1 April 1925, p. 25.

35. *Ibid.*

36. "Gish Betrothal Befuddles Duell," *The New York Times,* 2 April 1925, p. 19.

37. *Ibid.*

38. *Ibid.*

39. *Ibid.*

40. *Ibid.*

41. "Court Holds Duell on Perjury Charge; Quashes Gish Suit," *The New York Times,* 3 April 1925, p. 1.

42. *Ibid.*

43. "Miss Gish Appears Against Charles Duell," *The New York Times,* 8 May 1925, p. 22.

44. "Mae Murray Wins in Court," *The New York Times,* 11 November 1925, p. 16.

45. "Mae Murray Wins $1,600," *The New York Times,* 17 November 1925, p. 11.

Chapter 15: Mimi

1. Frederick Lewis Allen, "The Revolt of the Highbrows," *Only Yesterday* (New York: Bantam, 1946), p. 208.

2. Albert Bigelow Paine, "Sad, Unprofitable Days," *Life and Lillian Gish* (New York: Macmillan, 1932), p. 166.

3. Pitts Sanborn, "Louise," *The Metropolitan Book of the Opera* (New York: Simon and Schuster, 1937), p. 48.

4. Richard Fehr and Frederick G. Vogel, "Music, Music Everywhere; 1928–1929," *Lullabies of Hollywood: Movie Music and the Movie Musical, 1915–1992* (Jefferson, North Carolina: McFarland, 1992), p. 40.

5. Norman Zierold, "The Selznick Saga," *The Moguls: The Power Princes of Hollywood's Golden Age* (New York: Avon, 1969), p. 17.

6. Zierold, "Mayers-Gans-Mispochen," *Ibid.,* p. 276.

7. *Ibid.*

8. David Robinson, "The Industry," *Hollywood in the Twenties* (New York: A. S. Barnes, 1968), p. 32.

9. Zierold, p. 276.

10. Ivan Butler, "1926," *Silent Magic: Rediscovering the Silent Film Era,* with a Foreword by Kevin Brownlow (New York: Ungar, 1988), p. 22.

11. Dorothy Gish, "My Sister Lillian: What One of the Best Known Comediennes of the Screen Thinks of the Art and Character of Her Noted Relative," *Theatre Magazine,* December 1927, p. 31.

12. Richard Lamparski, "Aileen Pringle," *Whatever Became of...?* second series (New York: Crown, 1968), p. 174.

13. Fred Hobson, "A Beautiful Episode,"

Mencken: A Life (New York: Random House, 1995), p. 330.

14. *Ibid.*

15. Anita Loos, conversation with author, May 1972.

16. Aileen Pringle, conversation with author, April 1989.

17. Sydney Sutherland, "Lillian Gish: the Incomparable," *Liberty,* 27 August 1927, p. 54.

18. Pringle, April 1989.

19. Joseph Hergesheimer, "Lillian Gish," *The American Mercury,* April 1924, p. 397.

20. Loos, May 1972.

21. O. Z. Whitehead, "Lillian," *Theatre Book,* vol. 1, no. 1, Spring 1978, p. 21.

22. Peter Harry Brown and Pamela Ann Brown, "But Not on the First Date," *The MGM Girls: Behind the Velvet Curtain* (New York: St. Martin's Press, 1983), p. 76.

23. John Baxter, "An End to Ephemera: The Big Parade to Show People," *King Vidor* (New York: The Monarch Press, 1976), p. 26.

24. Abel Green and Joe Laurie, Jr., "Pix Boff B. O.," *Show Biz: From Vaude to Video* (New York: Henry Holt, 1951), p. 257.

25. Colleen Moore, conversation with author, September 1967.

26. King Vidor, "The Big Parade," *A Tree Is a Tree* (New York: Harcourt, Brace, 1953), pp. 124–25.

27. Lillian Gish, with Ann Pinchot, *The Movies, Mr. Griffith, and Me* (Englewood Cliffs, New Jersey: Prentice-Hall, 1969), p. 279.

28. *Ibid.,* p. 275.

29. "La Bohème," *The Victor Book of the Opera* (Camden: Victor, 1913), p. 37.

30. Deems Taylor, Marcelene Peterson, and Bryant Hale, "The Twenties," *A Pictorial History of the Movies* (New York: Simon and Schuster, 1943), p. 184.

31. Paine, "La Bohème," *Life and Lillian Gish,* p. 211.

32. Lillian Gish, conversation with author, September 1967.

33. Dale McConathy and Diana Vreeland, "1920's: The Flapper and the Waif," *Hollywood Costume* (New York: Harry N. Abrams, 1976), p. 64.

34. McConathy and Diana Vreeland, "1910's:

The Vamp and the Broken Blossom," Ibid., p. 49.

35. Gary Carey, "Star Gazing," *All the Stars in Heaven: Louis B. Mayer's MGM* (New York: E. P. Dutton, 1981), p. 95.

36. *Ibid.*

37. Gish with Pinchot, p. 279.

38. Vidor, "Lillian Gish in 'La Bohème,'" *A Tree Is a Tree*, p. 128–29.

39. *Ibid.*, p. 130.

40. Pringle, April 1989.

41. Moore, September 1967.

42. Roland Flamini, "Irving's Women," *Thalberg: The Last Tycoon and the World of MGM* (New York: Crown, 1994), p. 91.

43. Gish, September 1967.

44. Brown and Brown, p. 77.

45. Vidor, p. 131.

46. Flamini, p. 91.

47. Moore, September 1967.

48. Boze Hadleigh, *Hollywood Babble On: Stars Gossip About Other Stars* (New York: Berkley, 1994), p. 198.

49. Leatrice Joy, conversation with author, November 1970.

50. Gish, September 1967.

51. David Robinson, "Recruitment," *Hollywood in the Twenties* (New York: Paperback Library, 1968), p. 113.

52. Charles Affron, "Gish, Vidor, and Seastrom," *Star Acting: Gish, Garbo, Davis* (New York: E. P. Dutton, 1977), p. 76.

53. Vidor, p. 132.

54. Paine, p. 219.

55. Gish with Pinchot, p. 282.

56. Butler, p. 119.

57. Alexander Walker, "All for Art: Lillian Gish," *Stardom: The Hollywood Phenomenon* (New York: Stein and Day, 1970), p. 77.

58. Mordaunt Hall, "The Screen," *The New York Times*, 25 February 1926, p. 2.

59. Carey, p. 97

60. Pringle, April 1989.

61. Paine, p. 221.

62. Moore, September 1967.

63. "Duell Asks Trial on Perjury Charge," *The New York Times*, 30 March 1926, p. 12.

Chapter 16: Hester

1. Lillian Gish, conversation with author, November 1973.

2. Albert Bigelow Paine, "The Scarlet Letter," *Life and Lillian Gish* (New York: Macmillan, 1932), p. 224.

3. Lillian Gish, with Ann Pinchot, *The Movies, Mr. Griffith, and Me* (Englewoodcliffs, New Jersey: Prentice-Hall, 1969), p. 285.

4. Gish, November 1973.

5. Paine, p. 224.

6. Gish, November 1973.

7. David Robinson, "Invaders," *Hollywood in the Twenties* (New York: A. S. Barnes, 1968), p. 71.

8. Deems Taylor, Marcelene Peterson, and Bryant Hale, "The Twenties," *A Pictorial History of the Movies* (New York: Simon and Schuster, 1943), p. 185.

9. Liam O'Leary, "The War Years: 1914–18," *The Silent Cinema* (London: Studio Vista, 1965), p. 44.

10. Robinson, p. 71.

11. Gish with Pinchot, p. 286.

12. Robinson, p. 78.

13. Alexander Walker, "Art for Art: Lillian Gish," *Stardom: The Hollywood Phenomenon* (New York: Stein and Day, 1970), p. 79.

14. *Ibid.*, p. 78.

15. Nathaniel Hawthorne, "The Revelation," *The Scarlet Letter*, with a new introduction by Willard Thorp (New York: Collier, 1962), p. 242.

16. Hawthorne, "Conclusion," *Ibid.*, p. 245–46.

17. Gish, November 1973.

18. Daniel Blum, "1926," *A Pictorial History of the American Theatre: 1860–1970*, edited and enlarged by John Willis (New York: Crown, 1969), p. 224.

19. Sidney Sutherland, "Lillian Gish, the Incomparable," *Liberty*, 27 August 1927, p. 54–55.

20. Gish with Pinchot, p. 286.

21. Paine, p. 227.

22. Sutherland, p. 55.

23. Paine, p. 227.

24. *Ibid.*

25. Paine, p. 228.

26. Gish with Pinchot, p. 288.

27. Ivan Butler, "1926," *Silent Magic: Rediscovering the Silent Cinema*, with a Foreword by Kevin Brownlow (New York: Ungar, 1988), p. 137.

28. *Ibid.*, p. 139.

Chapter 17: Other Matters

1. "Duell Asks Trial on Perjury Charge," *The New York Times*, 30 March 1926, p. 12.

2. Lillian Gish, with James E. Frasher, "Second Decade," *Dorothy and Lillian Gish* (New York: Charles Scribner's Sons 1973), p. 154.

3. Antonia Fraser, editor, "The Stuarts: Charles II," *The Lives of the Kings and Queens of England* (New York: Alfred A. Knopf, 1975), p. 234.

4. Gish with Frasher, p. 156.

5. "English to Win in Films," *The New York Times*, 28 March 1926, p. 26.

6. Gish with Frasher, p. 156.

7. *Ibid.*

8. Georgia Dullea, "The Evening Hours," *The New York Times*, 15 March 1985, p. 8.

9. Dame Anna Neagle, conversation with author, March 1985.

10. "Jury Picked to Try Duell for Perjury," *The New York Times*, 28 May 1926, p. 44.

11. "Duell's Ex-Partner Aids Prosecution," *The New York Times*, 29 May 1926, p. 16.

12. "Says Duell Kept Miss Gish's Profits, *The New York Times*, 2 June 1926.

13. "Backer of Duell was W. A. Harriman," *The New York Times*, 3 June 1926, p. 27.

14. "W. A. Harriman Lent $600,000 for Films," *The New York Times*, 4 June 1926, p. 25.

15. "Backer of Duell Was W. A. Harriman," *The New York Times*, 3 June 1926, p. 27.

16. "W. A. Harriman Lent $600,000 for Films," *The New York Times*, 4 June 1926, p. 25.

17. "Testifies Miss Gish Did Not Pay His Fee," *The New York Times*, 5 June 1926, p. 7.

18. "Lillian Gish Returns; Brings Mother, Ill," *The New York Times*, 5 June 1926, p. 7.

19. "Erred in Testimony, in Duell-Gish Suit," *The New York Times*, 8 June 1926, p. 14.

20. "Mimics Max Steur 'Bullying' Duell," *The New York Times*, 9 June 1926, p. 12.

21. "Duell Takes Stand to Deny Perjury," *The New York Times*, 10 June 1926, p. 27.

22. "Judge Mack Unfair, Duell Declares," *The New York Times*, 11 June 1926, p. 8.

23. "Duell Takes Stand to Deny Perjury," *The New York Times*, 10 June 1927, p. 27.

24. "Judge Mack Unfair, Duell Declares," *The New York Times*, 11 June 1926, p. 8.

25. "Duell Case Goes to the Jury Today," *The New York Times*, 15 June 1926, p. 27.

26. "Jury Is Locked Up at the Duell Trial," *The New York Times*, 16 June 1926, p. 7.

27. "Duell Trial Ends in a Disagreement," *The New York Times*, 25 June 1926, p. 25.

28. "Government Drops Suit Against Duell," *The New York Times*, 27 November 1926, p. 11.

29. Lillian Gish, with Ann Pinchot, *The Movies, Mr. Griffith, and Me* (Englewood Cliffs, New Jersey: Prentice-Hall, 1969), p. 288.

Chapter 18: Unkindest Cuts

1. Lillian Gish, with Ann Pinchot, *The Movies, Mr. Griffith, and Me* (Englewood-Cliffs, New Jersey: Prentice-Hall, 1969), p. 288.

2. O. Z. Whitehead, "Lillian," *Theatre Book*, vol. 1, no. 1, Spring 1978, p. 57.

3. *Ibid.*

4. Anita Loos, conversation with author, May 1972.

5. Alan Brock, conversation with author, October 1980.

6. Gish with Pinchot, p. 289.

7. *Ibid.*, p. 288.

8. Sara Mayfield, "The Drunkard's Holiday," *Exiles from Paradise: Zelda and F. Scott Fitzgerald* (New York: Delacorte Press, 1971), p. 121.

9. Lillian Gish, conversation with author, June 1968.

10. Mayfield, p. 122.

11. Gish, June 1968.

12. Matthew J. Broccoli, "New York and First Trip Abroad: Fall 1920–Summer 1921," *Some Sort of Epic Grandeur: The Life of F. Scott Fitzgerald* (New York and London: Harcourt Brace Jovanovich, 1981), p. 148.

13. William K. Everson, "European Influences," *American Silent Film* (New York: Oxford University Press, 1978), p. 319.
14. Charles Affron, "Gish, Vidor, and Seastrom," *Star Acting: Gish, Garbo, Davis* (New York: E. P. Dutton, 1977), p. 78.
15. *Ibid.*, p. 83.
16. *Ibid.*, p. 78.
17. Mordaunt Hall, "The Screen: The Scarlet Letter," *The New York Times,* 10 August 1926, p. 19.
18. Albert Bigelow Paine, "The Scarlet Letter," *Life and Lillian Gish* (New York: Macmillan, 1932), p. 230.
19. Alexander Walker, "All for Art: Lillian Gish," *Stardom: The Hollywood Phenomenon* (New York: Stein and Day, 1970), p. 77.
20. Ivan Butler, "1926," *Silent Magic: Rediscovering the Silent Era,* with a Foreword by Kevin Brownlow (New York: Ungar, 1988), p. 119.
21. Walker, p. 77.
22. *Ibid.*, p. 78.
23. Louise Brooks, "Gish and Garbo," *Lulu in Hollywood,* Introduction by William Shawn (New York: Alfred A. Knopf, 1982), p. 90.
24. Aileen Pringle, conversation with author, April 1989.
25. Louise Brooks, conversation with author, May 1967.

Chapter 19: Miss Gish Is Miss Gish

1. Carl Bode, editor, "1927," *The New Mencken Letters* (New York: Dial, 1977), p. 209.
2. Daniel Blum, "1927," *A Pictorial History of the American Theatre: 1860–1970,* edited and enlarged by John Willis (New York: Crown, 1969), p. 231.
3. Jeff Laffel, "Sylvia Sidney," *Films in Review,* vol. XLV, no. 9/10, September-October 1994, p. 19.
4. Arthur Mizener, *F. Scott Fitzgerald* (New York: Thames and Hudson, 1972), p. 79.
5. Albert Bigelow Paine, "Way Down East," *Life and Lillian Gish* (New York: Macmillan, 1932), p. 163.
6. Aileen Pringle, conversation with author, April 1989.
7. Mizener, p. 79.
8. Ivan Butler, "1927," *Silent Magic: Rediscovering the Silent Film Era,* Foreword by Kevin Brownlow (New York: Ungar, 1988), p. 163.
9. Mordaunt Hall, "The Screen: Annie Laurie," *The New York Times,* 12 May 1927.
10. Jack Spears, "Marshall Neilan," *Hollywood: The Golden Era* (New York: Castle, 1971), p. 294.
11. Pringle, April 1989.
12. Lillian Gish, with James E. Frasher, "Second Decade," *Dorothy and Lillian Gish* (New York: Charles Scribner's Sons 1973), p. 160.
13. "Duell Sues Mrs. Gish," *The New York Times,* 7 June 1927, p. 30.
14. "Seeks to Drop Gish Suit," *The New York Times,* 16 June 1927, p. 25.
15. "Duell Drops Gish Action," *The New York Times,* 17 June 1927, p. 23.
16. "Nathan Denies Betrothal," *The New York Times,* 22 June 1927, p. 23.
17. "Sues Lillian Gish for $5,000,000," *The New York Times,* 23 June 1927, p. 4.
18. Lillian Gish, with Ann Pinchot, *The Movies, Mr. Griffith, and Me* (Englewood-Cliffs, New Jersey: Prentice-Hall, 1969), p. 290.
19. "William McAdoo," *Newsweek,* 10 February 1941, p. 17.
20. Ethan Morden, "The First and Greatest Star," *Movie Star: A Look at the Women Who Made Hollywood* (New York: St. Martin's Press, 1983), p. 54.
21. Allan Dwan, conversation with author, September 1975.
22. Colleen Moore, conversation with author, August 1967.
23. Lillian Gish, conversation with author, April 1963.
24. Lillian Gish conversation with author, June 1961.
25. "Trials of an Actress," *The New York Times,* VIII, 3 July 1927, p. 3.
26. *Ibid.*
27. *Ibid.*
28. "Weight Keeps Star Here," *The New York Times,* 26 July 1927, p. 44.

29. Ivan Butler, "1928," *Silent Magic: Rediscovering the Silent Film Era*, p. 187.

30. David Robinson, "The Industry," *Hollywood in the Twenties* (New York: A. S. Barnes, 1968), p. 42.

31. Lillian Gish, conversation with author, December 1965.

32. "Order in Lillian Gish Suit," *The New York Times*, 27 September 1927, p. 18.

33. Charles Affron, "Gish, Vidor, and Seastrom," *Star Acting: Gish, Garbo, and Bette Davis* (New York: E. P. Dutton, 1977), p. 83.

34. Bernard Rosenberg and Harry Silverstein, "Albert Lewin," *The Real Tinsel* (New York: Macmillan, 1970), p. 107.

35. Robinson, "Invaders," *Hollywood in the Twenties*, p. 72.

36. Gish, December 1965.

37. Louise Brooks, "Gish and Garbo," *Lulu in Hollywood*, Introduction by William Shawn (New York: Alfred A. Knopf, 1982), p. 90.

38. Lillian Gish, with James E. Frasher, "Second Decade," *Dorothy and Lillian Gish* (New York: Charles Scribner's Sons, 1973), p. 160.

39. Affron, "Generous Stars," *Star Acting: Gish, Garbo, and Bette Davis*, p. 8.

40. "The Screen: The Enemy," *The New York Times*, 28 December 1977, p. 26.

41. *Ibid.*

42. Mordaunt Hall, "The Screen: The Wind," *The New York Times*, 5 November 1928, p. 26.

43. *Ibid.*

44. *Ibid.*

45. William K. Everson, "European Influences," *American Silent Film* (New York: Oxford University Press, 1978), p. 320.

46. Alexander Walker, "All for Art: Lillian Gish," *Stardom: The Hollywood Phenomenon* (New York: Stein and Day, 1970), p. 79.

47. Gish, December 1965.

48. George C. Pratt, "The American Film: 1925–1929," *Spellbound in Darkness: A History of the Silent Film* (Greenwich: New York Graphic Society, 1973), p. 473.

49. Kalton C. Lahue, "Lillian Gish," *Ladies in Distress* (South Brunswick and New York: A. S. Barnes, 1971), p. 123.

50. Louise Brooks, conversation with author, June 1967.

51. Anita Loos, conversation with author, May 1972.

52. "Lillian Gish Joins with United Artists," *The New York Times*, 7 December 1932, p. 32.

53. Gish with Pinchot, p. 295.

Chapter 20: Travels and Tribulations

1. Louis Shaeffer, "Marco Millions," *O'Neill: Son and Artist* (Boston and Toronto: Little, Brown, 1973), p. 261.

2. Brooks Atkinson, "Two Broadway Promenaders," *Broadway* (New York: Macmillan, 1970), p. 160.

3. Shaeffer, p. 260.

4. Abel Green and Joe Laurie, Jr., "Legit Pre-World War I," *Show Biz: From Vaude to Video* (New York: Henry Holt, 1951), p. 63.

5. Green and Laurie, "Mae West, Young Man, Mae West," *Ibid.*, p. 295.

6. Allen Churchill, "Roundup," *The Theatrical 20's* (New York, St. Louis, and San Francisco: McGraw-Hill, 1975), p. 132.

7. *Ibid.*, p. 127.

8. Daniel Blum, "1924," *A Pictorial History of the American Theatre: 1860–1970*, edited and enlarged by John Willis (New York: Crown, 1969), p. 213.

9. Green and Laurie, p. 295.

10. Albert Bigelow Paine, "Reinhardt," *Life and Lillian Gish* (New York: Macmillan, 1932), p. 246.

11. *Ibid.*, p. 247.

12. Daniel Blum, "1927," *A Pictorial History of the American Theatre: 1860–1970*, edited and enlarged by John Willis, p. 232.

13. Paine, p. 249–50.

14. Stanley J. Kunitz and Howard Haycraft, editors, "Hugo von Hofmannstahl," *Twentieth Century Authors: A Biographical Dictionary of Modern Literature* (New York: H. W. Wilson, 1942), p. 657.

15. Lillian Gish, conversation with author, August 1961.

16. James Watters, with photographs by Horst,

"Lillian Gish," *Return Engagement: Faces to Remember — Then and Now* (New York: Clarkson N. Potter, 1984), p. 50.

17. "As Lillian Gish Views Art," *The New York Times,* VIII, 1 July 1928, p. 4.

18. Lillian Gish with Ann Pinchot, *The Movies, Mr. Griffith, and Me* (Englewood Cliffs, New Jersey: Prentice-Hall, 1969), p. 302.

19. *Ibid.*

20. Paine, p. 252.

21. *Ibid.*, p. 253.

22. Kevin Brownlow, "The Talking Picture," *The Parade's Gone By* (New York: Bonanza Books, 1968), p. 570.

23. Green and Laurie, "Pix Biz Boff B.O.," *Show Biz: From Vaude to Video,* p. 262.

24. George Jessel, conversation with author, June 1972.

25. *Ibid.*

26. Brownlow, p. 570.

27. Green and Laurie, pp. 262–63.

28. Lillian Gish, conversation with author, September 1961.

29. Brownlow, p. 571.

30. "1920s: Economic Influences," *International Musician,* October 1996, p. 24.

31. Alfred Lunt, conversation with author, March 1960.

32. *Ibid.*

33. Colleen Moore, conversation with author, August 1967.

34. Shaeffer, "At the Chateau," *O'Neill: Son and Artist,* p. 343.

35. Shaeffer, "Mourning Becomes Electra," *Ibid.*, p. 366.

36. *Ibid.*, p. 369.

Chapter 21: Novelties

1. Lillian Gish, conversation with author, October 1958.

2. William Bakewell, conversation with author, August 1975.

3. Edward Wagenknecht and Anthony Slide, "The Battle of the Sexes (1928)," *The Films of D. W. Griffith* (New York: Crown, 1975), p. 234.

4. Richard Schickel, "At the Crazy Hotel,"

D. W. Griffith: An American Life (New York: Simon and Schuster, 1984), p. 549.

5. Frank Capra, conversation with author, October 1971.

6. Paulette Goddard, conversation with author, October 1971.

7. "Three Liners in at Once Bring Jams on Piers," *The New York Times,* 21 August 1929, p. 18.

8. Anthony Slide, "Carol Dempster," *The Griffith Actresses* (South Brunswick and New York: A. S. Barnes, 1973), p. 162.

9. Jean Renoir, "D. W. Griffith," *My Life and My Films* (New York: Atheneum, 1974), p. 46.

10. Renoir, "First Days with the Redskins," *Ibid.,* p. 189.

11. Gish, October 1958.

12. Aileen Pringle, conversation with author, November 1969.

13. Bernard Rosenberg and Harry Silverstein, "Rod La Rocque," *The Real Tinsel* (New York: Macmillan, 1970), p. 253.

14. Arthur Miller, conversation with author, August 1968.

15. Gish, October 1958.

16. Hugh Johnson, "The Cote de Nuits-St-Georges," *The World Atlas of Wine: A Complete Guide to the Wines and Spirits of the World* (New York: Simon and Schuster, 1971), p. 63.

17. Martin Gottfried, "No Isotta Fraschini for Jones," *Jed Harris: The Curse of Genius* (Boston and Toronto: Little, Brown, 1984), p. 121.

18. Anita Loos, conversation with author, June 1972.

19. Lillian Gish, conversation with author, September 1961.

20. Gottfried, p. 123.

21. Brooks Atkinson, "The Play: Uncle Vanya," *The New York Times,* 16 April 1930, p. 26.

22. *Ibid.*

23. Mordaunt Hall, "The Screen: One Romantic Night," *The New York Times,* 31 May 1930, p. 19.

24. Lillian Gish, conversation with author, June 1973.

25. "Uncle Vanya Returns," *The New York Times,* 22 September 1930, p. 31.

26. Frederic I. Carpenter, "From Lazarus to

Electra," *Eugene O'Neill* (Boston: Twayne Publishers, 1979), p. 119.

27. *The New York Times,* 22 September 1930, p. 31.

Chapter 22: Integrity

1. Scott Eyman, *The Speed of Sound: Hollywood and the Talkie Revolution: 1926–30* (New York: Simon and Schuster, 1997), p. 263.

2. Joanna Roos, conversation with author, January 1960.

3. Aileen Pringle, conversation with author, November 1969.

4. R.W.B. Lewis, "The Span of Time," *Edith Wharton* (New York: Harper and Row, 1975), p. 7.

5. Eyman, p. 264.

6. Albert Bigelow Paine, "Uncle Vanya Takes the Road," *Life and Lillian Gish* (New York: Macmillan, 1932), p. 289.

7. O. Z. Whitehead, "Lillian," *Theatre Book,* vol. 1, no. 1, Spring 1978, p. 70.

8. Paine, p. 290.

9. Frederic I. Carpenter, "From Lazarus to Electra," *Eugene O'Neill* (Boston: Twayne, 1979), p. 120.

10. Roy S. Waldau, "1930–1931," *Vintage Years of the Theatre Guild: 1928–1939* (Cleveland and London: The Press of Case and Western Reserve University, 1972), p. 125.

11. *Ibid.,* p. 113.

12. Waldau, "Antecedents and Birth of the Guild," *Ibid.,* p. 7.

13. Waldau, "1930–1931." *Ibid.,* p. 125.

14. Louis Shaeffer, "Homecoming," *O'Neill: Son and Artist* (Boston and Toronto: Little, Brown, 1973), p. 383.

15. Martin Bauml Duberman, "Othello (1930–1931)," *Paul Robeson* (New York: Alfred A. Knopf, 1988), p. 138.

16. Blanche Sweet, conversation with author, March 1971.

17. "Lillian Gish Returns," *The New York Times,* 24 September 1932, p. 18.

18. "Lillian Gish Here in 'Camille'," *The New York Times,* 18 October 1932, p. 28.

19. Sweet, March 1971.

20. Lillian Gish conversation with author, January 1968.

21. Brooks Atkinson, "The Play: Lillian Gish as 'La Dame Aux Camelias,' at the Morosco," *The New York Times,* 2 November 1932, p. 23.

22. Burns Mantle, editor, "The Season in New York," *The Best Plays of 1932-33 and the Yearbook of the Drama* (New York: Dodd, Mead, 1933), p. 9.

23. "Higher Court Backs Lillian Gish," *The New York Times,* 30 December 1932, p. 13.

24. Mordaunt Hall, "The Screen: Strange Interlude," *The New York Times,* 1 September 1932, p. 24.

25. Norman Zierold, "Mayer's-Ganz Mespochen," *The Moguls: The Power Princes of Hollywood's Golden Age* (New York: Avon, 1969), p. 310.

Chapter 23: Games, Favorites, and Politics

1. Glenway Wescott, conversation with author, January 1971.

2. Colleen Moore, conversation with author, September 1967.

3. Mark Schorer, "Success," *Sinclair Lewis: An American Life* (New York, Toronto, and London: McGraw-Hill, 1961), p. 387.

4. *Ibid.,* p. 405.

5. Mark Schorer, "Decline," *Ibid.,* p. 545.

6. Deems Taylor, Marcelene Peterson, and Bryant Hale, "The Talking Picture," *A Pictorial History of the Movies* (New York: Simon and Schuster, 1943), p. 244.

7. Alan Brock, conversation with author, October 1980.

8. John Baxter, "The Studios: Warners," *Hollywood in the Thirties* (London: Tantivy Press, and New York: A. S. Barnes, 1968), p. 60.

9. Joan Blondell, conversation with author, October 1971.

10. John L. Toohey, "Anna Christie," *A History of the Pulitzer Prize Plays* (New York: The Citadel Press, 1967), p. 23.

11. John Houseman, "1937," *Unfinished Business: Memoirs: 1902–1988* (New York: Applause Theatre, 1989), p. 139.

12. Houseman, "1902–1930," *Ibid.*, p. 34–35.

13. Daniel Blum, "1913," *A Pictorial History of the American Theatre: 1860–1970*, edited and enlarged by John Willis (New York: Crown, 1969), p. 140.

14. Arnold G. Brown, *Lizzie Borden: The Legend, The Truth, The Final Chapter* (Nashville: Rutledge Hills Press, 1991), p. 12.

15. Lillian Gish, conversation with author, September 1961.

16. Burns Mantle, editor, "Nine Pine Street," *The Best Plays of 1932-33 and the Yearbook of the Drama in America* (New York: Dodd, Mead, 1933), p. 480.

17. "The Play: Nine Pine Street," *The New York Times,* 28 April 1933, p. 24.

18. Mantle, editor, "The Season in New York," *The Best Plays of 1932-33 and the Yearbook of the Drama in America*, p. 9.

19. *The New York Times*, p. 24.

20. Mantle, editor, "Nine Pine Street," *The Best Plays of 1932-33 and the Yearbook of the Drama in America*, p. 488.

21. W. A. Swanberg, "American Spectator," *Dreiser* (New York: Charles Scribner's Sons 1965), p. 409.

22. *Ibid.*, p. 412.

23. *Ibid.*, p. 402.

24. *Ibid.*, p. 408.

25. Mordaunt Hall, "His Double Life," *The New York Times,* 16 December 1933, p. 12.

26. Agnes DeMille, conversation with author, May 1976.

27. Lillian Gish, conversation with author, March 1963.

Chapter 24: Back on the Boards

1. Gail Stewart, "The 1930s," *Timelines* (New York: Crestwood House, 1989), p. 13.

2. "Noted Movie Stars Back from Europe," *The New York Times,* 2 August 1933, p. 8.

3. "C. H. Duell to Wed Josephine Smith," *The New York Times,* 11 July 1933, p. 8.

4. "Josephine Smith Becomes a Bride," *The New York Times,* 22 October 1933, II, p. 4.

5. Burns Mantle, editor, *The Best Plays of 1931-32 and the Yearbook of the Drama in America* (New York: Dodd, Mead, 1932), p. 411.

6. Burns Mantle, editor, *The Best Plays of 1932-33 and the Yearbook of the Drama in America* (New York: Dodd, Mead, 1933), p. 425.

7. Burns Mantle, editor, *The Best Plays of 1933-34 and the Yearbook of the Drama in America* (New York: Dodd, Mead, 1934), p. 485.

8. *Ibid.*, p. 486.

9. Mantle, editor, "The Season in New York," *Ibid.*, p. 7.

10. Brooks Atkinson, "The Giddy Times," *Broadway* (New York: Macmillan, 1970), p. 242.

11. William Shannon, "The Irish in the Theatre," *The American Irish: A Political and Social Portrait* (New York: Macmillan, 1966), p. 287.

12. *Ibid.*

13. Burns Mantle, editor, *The Best Plays of 1933-34 and the Yearbook of the Drama in America,* p. 485.

14. Brooks Atkinson, "The Play: Lillian Gish in Phillip Barry's 'The Joyous Season'," *The New York Times,* 30 January 1934, p. 16.

15. *Ibid..*

16. Mantle, editor, *The Best Plays of 1933-34 and the Yearbook of the Drama in America,* p. 487.

17. Atkinson, "The Giddy Times, *Broadway,* p. 241.

18. Finis Farr, "Malloy in Manhattan," *O'Hara: A Biography* (Boston and Toronto: Little, Brown, 1973), p. 149.

19. Atkinson, p. 241.

20. Atkinson, "Welcome to the Players," *Broadway,* p. 355.

21. Daniel Blum, "1927," *A Pictorial History of the American Theatre: 1860–1970,* enlarged and revised by John Willis (New York: Crown, 1969), p. 232.

22. Lillian Gish, conversation with author, April 1963.

23. E. Bradlee Watson and Benfield Pressey, editors, "June and the Paycock," *Contemporary Drama: European, English and Irish, American Plays* (New York: Charles Scribner's Sons 1961), p. 799.

24. *Ibid.*

25. Gish, April 1963.

26. Saros Cowasjee, "The Exile Plays: I," *Sean O'Casey: The Man Behind the Plays* (New York: St. Martin's Press, 1964), p. 145.

27. *Ibid.*, p. 146.

28. *Ibid.*, p. 147.

29. Burns Mantle, editor, "The Season in New York," *The Best Plays of 1934-35 and the Yearbook of the Drama in America* (New York: Dodd, Mead, 1935), p. 9.

30. Atkinson, "Two Broadway Promenaders," *Broadway*, p. 159.

31. Gish, April 1963.

32. Mantle, editor, "The Season in New York," *The Best Plays of 1934-35 and the Yearbook of the Drama in America*, p. 9.

33. Gish, April 1963.

34. Brooks Atkinson, "The Play: Fantasy: The Seasons in Hyde Park in Sean O'Casey's 'Within the Gates'," *The New York Times*, 23 October 1934, p. 23.

35. Gish, April 1963.

36. Eileen O'Casey, "I Leave the Stage," *Eileen*, edited, with an introduction by J. C. Trewin (New York: St. Martin's Press, 1976), p. 135.

37. Mantle, p. 395.

38. O'Casey, p. 135.

39. Mantle, p. 411.

40. "Dorothy Gish Sues to Divorce Rennie," *The New York Times*, 25 March 1935, p. 17.

41. Lillian Gish, with Ann Pinchot, *The Movies, Mr. Griffith, and Me* (Englewood Cliffs, New Jersey: Prentice-Hall, 1969), p. 323.

42. *The New York Times*, p. 17.

Chapter 25: The Road to Elsinore

1. O. Z. Whitehead, "Lillian," *Theatre Book*, vol. 1, no. 1, Spring 1978.

2. Lillian Gish, conversation with author, June 1961.

3. William K. Everson, conversation with author, September 1968.

4. Frances Tannehill, conversation with author, June 1997.

5. "Noted Movie Stars Back from Europe, *The New York Times*, 2 August 1933.

6. Helen Hayes, conversation with author, April 1972.

7. John Tsortakis, conversation with author, June 1990.

8. Richard Maney, "Lillian Gish — A Celluloid Saga of Tears and Poignant Pathos," *The New York Journal American*, 1937.

9. "Lillian Gish Ends Coast Visit," *The New York Times*, 9 September 1935, p. 24.

10. "Dorothy Gish Wins in Divorce Hearing," *The New York Times*, 27 September 1935, p. 24.

11. "Lillian Gish Ends Coast Visit," *The New York Times*, 9 September 1935, p. 24.

12. "Dorothy Gish Obtains Connecticut Divorce," *The New York Times*, 12 October 1935, p. 13.

13. Brooks Atkinson, "The Play: 'Mainly for Lovers,' a Comedy from England," *The New York Times*, 22 February 1936, p. 13.

14. Burns Mantle, editor, *The Best Plays of 1936-37 and the Yearbook of the Drama in America* (New York: Dodd, Mead, 1937), p. 431.

15. John L. Toohey, "The Old Maid," *A History of the Pulitzer Prize Plays* (New York: Citadel, 1967), p. 23.

16. Brooks Atkinson, "Welcome to the Players," *Broadway* (New York: Macmillan, 1970), p. 362–63.

17. Maurice Zolotow, "The Component Parts: Lynn Fontanne," *Stagestruck: The Romance of Alfred Lunt and Lynn Fontanne* (Greenwich: Fawcett, 1965), p. 23.

18. R. W. B. Lewis, "A Rooted Possessive Person," *Edith Wharton* (New York: Harper and Row, 1975), p. 458.

19. Lillian Gish, with Ann Pinchot, *The Movies, Mr. Griffith, and Me* (Englewood-Cliffs, New Jersey: Prentice-Hall, 1969), p. 333.

20. Linda Lee, conversation with author, June 1997.

21. Gish with Pinchot, p. 334.

22. Lee, June 1997.

23. Gish with Pinchot, p. 334.

24. Lillian Gish, with James E. Frasher, "Stageography: Lillian Gish," *Dorothy and Lillian Gish* (New York: Charles Scribner's Sons 1973), p. 308.

25. "D. W. Griffith Wed," *The New York Times,* 3 March 1936.

26. Tannehill, June 1997.

27. Daniel Blum, "1928," *A Pictorial History of the American Theatre: 1860–1970,* edited and enlarged by John Willis (New York: Crown, 1969), p. 238.

28. Blum "1920," *Ibid.,* p. 181.

29. Tad Mosel, with Gertrude Macy, "Degrees of Fame (1936–1937)," *Leading Lady: The World of Katherine Cornell* (Boston and Toronto: Little, Brown, 1978), p. 321.

30. Francois Truffaut, with the collaboration of Helen G. Scott, "The Secret Agent," *Hitchcock* (New York: Simon and Schuster, 1966), p. 72.

31. Toby Cole and Helen Krich Chinoy, "England and Ireland," *Actors on Acting: The Theories, Techniques, and Practices of the Great Actors of All Time Told in Their Own Words* (New York: Crown, 1949), p. 380.

32. "John Gielgud Arrives," *The New York Times,* 1 September 1936, p. 24.

33. "A Hamlet Out from England," *The New York Times,* 6 September 1936, IX, p. 1.

34. Gish, June 1961.

35. *Ibid.*

36. William Roehrick, conversation with author, March 1993.

37. Sir John Gielgud, in collaboration with John Miller and John Powell, "America," *Sir John Gielgud* (New York: Clarkson N. Potter, 1979), p. 215.

38. Sir John Gielgud, "New York," *Distinguished Company* (Garden City: Doubleday, 1973), p. 67.

39. Gish, June 1961.

40. Roehrick, March 1993.

41. "Gielgud Triumphs in Hamlet," *The New York Times,* 1 October 1936, p. 30.

42. Brooks Atkinson, "The Play: John Gielgud and Judith Anderson in a 'Hamlet' Staged by Guthrie McClintic," *The New York Times,* 9 October 1936, p. 30.

43. *Ibid.*

44. *Ibid.*

45. Roehrick, March 1993

46. Sir John Gielgud, letter to author, 17 May 1995.

Chapter 26: Changes and Adjustments

1. Ray Henderson, "Lillian Gish, Once of the Cinema, Says She Really Did Not Like It," *The New York Herald-Tribune,* 27 December 1936.

2. Lillian Gish, conversation with author, 1958.

3. John L. Toohey, "Both Your Houses," *A History of the Pulitzer Prize Plays* (New York: Citadel, 1967), p. 109.

4. Joseph Wood Krutch, "The Poetic Drama: Maxwell Anderson," *American Drama Since 1918: An Informal History* (New York: George Braziller, 1967), p. 301.

5. Alfred S. Shivers, Ph.D., "The Golden Years," *The Life of Maxwell Anderson* (New York: Stein and Day, 1955), p. 155.

6. Edmond O'Brien, conversation with author, July 1971.

7. Burns Mantle, editor, "The Season in New York," *The Best Plays of 1937-38 and the Yearbook of the Drama in America* (New York: Dodd, Mead, 1938), p. 6.

8. Lillian Gish, conversation with author, April 1967.

9. Martin Gottfried, "No Isotta Fraschini for Jones," *Jed Harris: The Curse of Genius* (Boston and Toronto: Little, Brown, 1984), p. 123.

10. Fred Hobson, "The Consolations of an Agnostic," *Mencken: A Life* (New York: Random House, 1995), p. 376.

11. Aileen Pringle, conversation with author, April 1989.

12. Anita Loos conversation with author, June 1972.

Chapter 27: Choices: Right and Wrong

1. Anita Loos, conversation with author, June 1972.

2. Lawrence Langner, "The New Regime," *The Magic Curtain: The Story of a Life in Two Fields, Theatre and Invention* (New York: E. P. Dutton, 1951), p. 337.

3. Sheila Graham, conversation with author, March 1960.

4. Allen Dwan, conversation with author, September 1975.

5. Burns Mantle, editor, "The Season in New York," *The Best Plays of 1938-39 and the Yearbook of the Drama in America* (New York: Dodd, Mead, 1939), p. 5.

6. Irving Settel, "The Twenties," *A Pictorial History of Radio* (New York: Grosset and Dunlap, 1967), p. 64.

7. *Ibid.*, p. 54.

8. Frank Buxton and Bill Owen, *The Big Broadcast: 1920–1950* (New York: Avon, 1966), p. 63.

9. Lillian Gish, conversation with author, May 1973.

10. Jerry Devine conversation with author, July 1970.

11. Brooks Atkinson, "The Play: On Their Golden Wedding Day in Dodie Smith's 'Dear Octopus'," *The New York Times,* 12 January 1939, p. 22.

12. Mantle, p. 5.

13. Lillian Gish, conversation with author, February 1968.

14. Burns Mantle, editor, "The Season in New York," *The Best Plays of 1939-40 and the Yearbook of the Drama in America* (New York: Dodd, Mead, 1940), p. 418.

15. Alan Brock, conversation with author, October 1980.

16. Gish, May 1973.

17. Alan Brock, October 1980.

18. Lillian Gish, with Ann Pinchot, *The Movies, Mr. Griffith, and Me* (Englewood Cliffs, New Jersey: Prentice-Hall, 1969), p. 343.

19. Ed Cray, "The Most Businesslike Manner," *General of the Army: Soldier and Statesman* (New York: W. W. Norton, 1990), p. 165.

20. Clifford Stonely, conversation with author, May 1965.

21. Myrna Loy, conversation with author, April 1969.

22. Charles A. Lindbergh, "A Letter to Americans," *The Barnes Review,* September 1996, p. 4.

23. Ed Koch, "A Museum for All of Us," *The New York Post,* 12 September 1997, p. 29.

24. Stephen Birmingham, "A Middle," *The Late John Marquand* (Philadelphia and New York: J. B. Lippincott, 1972), p. 126.

25. Robin Edmonds, "The Common Law Alliance, 1941," *The Big Three: Churchill, Roosevelt, and Stalin in Peace and War* (New York and London: W. W. Norton, 1991), p. 213.

26. Winthrop D. Johnson, Miriam Greenblatt, and John S. Bowes, "The Road to War," *The Americans: A History* (Evanston, Illinois: McDougal, Littel, 1991), p. 729.

27. Edward Wagenknecht and Anthony Slide, "Hearts of the World," *The Film of D. W. Griffith* (New York: Crown, 1975), p. 95.

28. O. Z. Whitehead, "Lillian," *Theatre Book,* vol. 1, no. 1, Spring 1978, p. 36.

29. *Ibid.*

30. *Ibid.*, p. 39

31. *Ibid.*, p. 43.

32. Gish with Pinchot, p. 345.

33. Whitehead, p. 46.

34. Sheila Graham, "The Garden of Allah: How it Began," *The Garden of Allah* (New York: Crown, 1970), p. 13.

35. Graham, March 1970.

36. Whitehead, p. 46.

37. Charles A. Lindbergh, "June 1941," *The Wartime Journals of Charles A. Lindbergh* (New York: Harcourt, Brace, Jovanovich, 1970), p. 504.

38. *Ibid.*

39. Lindbergh, "July 1941," *Ibid.*, p. 512.

40. John Mason Brown, "Prologue: Three Speeches, Three Worlds, Three Men," *The World of Robert E. Sherwood: Mirror to His Times* (New York: Harper and Row, 1965), p. 4.

41. John L. Toohey, "There Shall Be No Night," *A History of the Pulitzer Prize Plays* (New York: Citadel, 1967), p. 176.

42. Brown, pp. 4–5.

43. Joe Morella, Edward Z. Epstein, and John Griggs, "Confessions of a Nazi Spy," *The Films of World War II: A Pictorial Trea-sury of Hollywood's War Years,* with an Introduction by Judith Crist (Seacaucus, New Jersey: Citadel, 1967), p. 176.

44. Morella, Epstein, and Griggs, "Prewar Propaganda," *Ibid.*, p. 14.

45. Birmingham, p. 127.

46. Loos, June 1972.

47. "America Firsters, Denounced as Traitors, Were Patriots of the First Rank," *The Barnes Review*, p. 7.

48. Wagenknecht and Slide, p. 95.

Chapter 28: The Road Back

1. Edward Wagenknecht and Anthony Slide, "Hearts of the World," *The Films of D. W. Griffith* (New York: Crown, 1975), p. 95.

2. Anita Loos, conversation with author, June 1972.

3. Lillian Gish, with Ann Pinchot, *The Movies, Mr. Griffith, and Me* (Englewood-Cliffs, New Jersey: Prentice-Hall, 1969), p. 344.

4. Thomas F. Brady, "Hollywood News Highlights," *The New York Times,* 26 July 1942, VIII, p. 3.

5. *Ibid.*

6. *Ibid.*

7. *Ibid.*

8. *Ibid.*

9. O. Z. Whitehead, "Lillian," *Theatre Book,* vol. 1, no. 1, Spring 1978, p. 23–24.

10. *Ibid.*, p. 46.

11. Lillian Gish, with James E. Frasher, "Fourth Decade," *Dorothy and Lillian Gish* (New York: Charles Scribner's Sons 1973), p. 227.

12. Loos, June 1972.

13. Alan Brock, conversation with author, October 1980.

14. Jerome Lawrence, *Actor: The Life and Times of Paul Muni* (New York: G. P. Putnam and Sons, 1974), p. 265.

15. Brady, p. 3.

16. Lillian Gish, conversation with author, November 1958.

17. Bosley Crowther, "At the Rialto: 'Commandos Strike at Dawn'," *The New York Times,* 14 January 1943, p. 25.

18. Gish, November 1958.

19. Crowther, p. 25.

20. Gish with Frasher, "Stageography: Lillian Gish," *Dorothy and Lillian Gish,* p. 309.

21. *Ibid.*, p. 307.

22. John L. Toohey, "Look Homeward, Angel," *A History of the Pulitzer Prize Plays* (New York: Citadel, 1967), p. 296.

23. Burns Mantle, editor, *The Best Plays of 1942–43 and the Yearbook of the Drama in America* (New York: Dodd, Mead, 1943), p. 442.

24. Norman Nadel, "1939–1948," *A Pictorial History of the Theatre Guild,* with an introduction by Brooks Atkinson, and special material by Lawrence Langner and Armina Marshall (New York: Crown, 1969), p. 176.

25. Brooks Atkinson, "The Play in Review: 'Mr. Sycamore'," *The New York Times,* 14 November 1942, p. 18.

26. Mantle, p. 442.

27. Brock, October 1980.

28. Mantle, pp. 447–48.

29. Herman Shumlin, conversation with author, July 1965.

30. Gish with Frasher, "Fourth Decade," *Dorothy and Lillian Gish,* p. 226.

31. Joe Morella, Edward Z. Epstein, and John Griggs, "The Moon Is Down," *The Films of World War II: A Pictorial History of Hollywood's War Years,* with an introduction by Judith Crist (Secaucus, New Jersey: Citadel), p. 111.

32. Bosley Crowther, "The Screen: Plenty of Donald: 'Top Man'," *The New York Times,* 29 October 1943, p. 23.

33. Gish with Frasher, "Stageography: Dorothy Gish," *Dorothy and Lillian Gish,* p. 307.

Chapter 29: None but the Lonely Heart

1. Lillian Gish, with James E. Frasher, "Fourth Decade," *Dorothy and Lillian Gish* (New York: Charles Scribner's Sons 1973), p. 229.

2. Tennessee Williams, conversation with author, March 1980.

3. Charles Higham and Joel Greenberg, "Musicals," *Hollywood in the Forties* (New York: A. S. Barnes, 1968), p. 171.

4. Joan Bennett, conversation with author, March 1984.

5. Cornel Wilde, conversation with author, August 1968.

6. Margaret Truman, *Harry Truman* (New York: Pocket Books, 1974), p. 6.

7. Aileen Pringle, conversation with author, November 1969.

8. Mark Schorer, "Fall," *Sinclair Lewis: An American Life* (New York: McGraw-Hill, 1961), p. 660.

9. *Ibid.*, p. 661.

10. Anita Loos, conversation with author, May 1972.

11. Schorer, p. 660.

12. Lillian Gish, as told to David Brown, "Miss Gish's Challenge to Marriage," *The New York Journal American*, 12 October 1946.

13. Gish with Frasher, p. 235.

14. Alan Brock, conversation with author, October 1980.

15. Sheila Graham, "Of Cabbages and Kings," *The Garden of Allah* (New York: Crown, 1970), p. 201.

16. Brock, October 1980.

17. Bosley Crowther, "The Screen in Review: 'Miss Susie Slagle's'," *The New York Times*, 7 February 1946, p. 29.

18. *Ibid.*

19. Dr. Ralph Wolfe, conversation with author, November 1997.

20. Louis Calta, "Premiere Tonight of Mary Surratt," *The New York Times*, 8 February 1947, p. 11.

21. Gish with Frasher, p. 244.

22. Brock, October 1980.

23. O. Z. Whitehead, "Lillian," *Theatre Book*, vol. 1, no. 1, Spring 1978, p. 48.

24. *Ibid.*

25. *Ibid.*, p. 49.

26. Tony Thomas, "Life with Father," *The Films of the Forties* (Secaucus, New Jersey: Citadel, 1975), p. 204.

27. Rudy Behlmer, editor, with an introduction by S. N. Behrman, "David O. Selznick Productions, Inc.," *Memo from David O. Selznick* (New York: The Viking Press, 1972), p. 362.

28. Whitehead, p. 48.

29. Bosley Crowther, "Duel in the Sun," *The New York Times*, 8 May 1947, p. 30.

30. Lillian Gish, conversation with author, May 1961.

31. "Greta Garbo Back, Not So Elusive Now," *The New York Times*, 4 September 1946, p. 25.

32. Crowther, p. 30.

33. John Baxter, "The Stock Market of the Spirit: Northwest Passage to The Fountain," *King Vidor* (New York: The Monarch Press, 1976), p. 68.

34. Crowther, p. 30.

35. Thomas, "Duel in the Sun," *The Films of the Forties*, p. 194.

36. Colleen Moore, conversation with author, September 1967.

37. King Vidor, "Steel and Super Western," *A Tree Is a Tree* (New York: Harcourt, Brace, 1953), p. 207.

38. Whitehead, p. 55.

39. *Ibid.*, p. 56.

40. *Ibid.*

41. Gish with Frasher, p. 243.

42. Clive Fisher, "Fame," *Noel Coward* (New York: St. Martin's Press, 1992), p. 88.

43. Daniel Blum "1927," *A Pictorial History of the American Theatre: 1860–1970*, edited and enlarged by John Willis (New York: Crown, 1969), p. 232.

44. Blum, "1923," *Ibid.*, p. 201.

45. Blum, "1927," *Ibid.*, p. 231.

46. Lillian Gish, with Ann Pinchot, *The Movies, Mr. Griffith, and Me* (Englewood-Cliffs, New Jersey: Prentice-Hall, 1969), p. 351.

47. Gish with Frasher, p. 242.

48. Brooks Atkinson, "At the Theatre: 'Crime and Punishment'," *The New York Times*, 23 December 1947, p. 29.

49. John Chapman, editor, "The Season in New York," *The Burns Mantle Best Plays of 1947-48 and the Yearbook of the Drama in America* (New York: Dodd, Mead, 1948), p. 9.

50. Atkinson, p. 29.

51. Lester Polakov, conversation with author, May 1995.

52. Chapman, p. 369.

53. Brock, October 1980.

54. Richard Schickel, "No Casting Today," *D. W. Griffith: An American Life* (New York: Simon and Schuster, 1984), p. 604.

55. Lillian Gish with Pinchot, pp. 352–53.

56. Robert M. Henderson, "1910: California," *D. W. Griffith: The Years at Biograph* (New York: Farrar, Straus and Giroux, 1970), p. 110.

57. Donald Crisp, conversation with author, August 1968.

58. Gish with Frasher, "Stageography," *Dorothy and Lillian Gish,* p. 309.

59. Harry M. Geduld, "One Act Plays," *James Barrie* (New York: Twayne, 1971), pp. 87–88.

60. Gish with Pinchot, p. 361.

61. Cynthia Heimel, "Lillian Gish: Life with Mother," *The Soho Weekly News,* 28 September 1976.

62. Whitehead, p. 59.

63. Cynthia Heimel.

64. Whitehead, p. 59.

65. Gish with Pinchot, p. 361.

Chapter 30: Tubes in a Box

1. Brigid Berlin, "Lillian Gish," *Interview,* December 1978, p. 42.

2. *Ibid.*

3. O. Z. Whitehead, "Lillian," *Theatre Book,* vol. 1, no. 1, Spring 1978, p. 65.

4. Peter Carlsen, "Lillian Gish: 'Birth of a Nation's' Epochal Star in New York," *Architectural Digest,* April 1990, p. 238.

5. Lillian Gish, with James E. Frasher, "Fourth Decade," *Dorothy and Lillian Gish* (New York: Charles Scribner's Sons, 1973), p. 245.

6. Ezra Goodman, "The Little People," *The Fifty-Year Decline and Fall of Hollywood* (New York: Simon and Schuster, 1961), p. 314.

7. Rudy Behlmer, editor, with an introduction by S. N. Behrman "David O. Selznick Productions, Inc.," *Memo from David O. Selznick* (New York: The Viking Press, 1972), p. 362.

8. Lillian Gish, with Ann Pinchot, *The Movies, Mr. Griffith, and Me* (Englewood-Cliffs, New Jersey: Prentice-Hall, 1969), p. 361.

9. Richard Schickel, "At the Crazy Hotel," *D. W. Griffith: An American Life* (New York: Simon and Schuster, 1984), p. 548.

10. *Ibid.,* p. 549.

11. Daniel Blum, "1932," *A Pictorial History of the Theatre: 1860–1970,* enlarged and revised by John Willis (New York: Crown, 1969), p. 255.

12. Tony Slide, "Lillian Gish: Star of Screen, Stage, and TV," *Emmy,* January/February 1984, p. 28.

13. Lillian Gish, conversation with author, April 1963.

14. Charles Higham and Joel Greenberg, "Fantasy and Horror," *Hollywood in the Forties* (New York: A. S. Barnes, 1968), p. 57.

15. Bosley Crowther, "The Screen in Review: Selznick's 'Portrait of Jennie', with Cotten and Jennifer Jones Opens at Rivoli," *The New York Times,* 30 March 1949, p. 31.

16. *Ibid.*

17. William K. Everson, conversation with author, February 1971.

18. Raymond Sarlot and Fred E. Basten, "The Golden Years: East Meets West," *Life at the Marmont* (Santa Monica: Roundtable, 1987), p. 137.

19. Dr. Ralph Wolfe, conversation with author, October 1997.

20. Brooks Atkinson, "At This Theatre: 'The Man'," *The New York Times,* 20 January 1950, p. 28.

21. *Ibid.*

22. John Chapman, editor, "The Season in New York," *The Burns Mantle Best Plays of 1949-50 and the Yearbook of the Drama in America* (New York: Dodd, Mead, 1950), p. 9.

23. *Ibid.*

24. Alan Brock, conversation with author, October 1980.

25. Lillian Gish with James E. Frasher, "Stageography: Lillian Gish," *Dorothy and Lillian Gish* (New York: Charles Scribner's Sons 1973), p. 308.

26. Frances Tannehill, conversation with author, December 1997.

27. Blum, "1929," *A Pictorial History of the American Theatre: 1860–1970* enlarged and revised by John Willis, p. 243.

28. Tannehill, December 1997.

29. Clarence Derwent, "American Debut," *The Derwent Story: My First Fifty Years in the Theatre in England and America* (New York: Henry Shuman, 1953), p. 117.

30. Tannehill, December 1997.

31. *Ibid.*

32. Derwent, "Giraudoux and Shaw," *The Derwent Story: My First Fifty Years in the Theatre in England and America,* p. 265.

33. Norman Nadel, "1948–1958," *A Pictorial History of the Theatre Guild,* with an introduction by Brooks Atkinson, and special material by Lawrence Langner and Armina Marshall (New York: Crown, 1969), p. 224.

34. John Chapman, editor, "The Season in New York," *The Best Plays of 1950-51 and the Yearbook of the Drama in America* (New York: Dodd, Mead, 1951), p. 17.

35. Nadel, p. 255.

36. *Ibid.*

37. Brooks Atkinson, "At the Theatre: Lillian Gish in the Theatre Guild Production of 'The Curious Savage'," *The New York Times,* 25 October 1950, p. 41.

38. *Ibid.*

39. Chapman, p. 17.

40. Richard Williams, "The Gallant Gish Girls" *Life,* 20 August 1951, p. 115.

41. Bosley Crowther, "At the Cinema: 'The Whistle at Eaton Falls'," *The New York Times,* 11 October 1951, p. 49.

42. Gary Carey, "Unity and Disharmony," *Anita Loos: A Biography* (New York: Alfred A. Knopf, 1988), p. 249.

43. Norton Mockridge, "Forever Lillian," *World Telegram and Sun,* 11 September 1954.

44. "Lillian Gish in Role of Dog Health Aide," *The New York Times,* 1 February 1952, p. 44.

45. Gerald Clarke, *Capote: A Biography* (New York: Simon and Schuster, 1988), pp. 227–28.

46. Daniel Blum, editor, "The Grass Harp," *Theatre World: Season 1951–1952* (New York: Greenberg, 1952), p. 17.

47. Gish, with Pinchot, p. 383.

48. Lillian Gish conversation with author, December 1980.

49. Gish with Frasher, "Fifth Decade," *Lillian and Dorothy Gish,* p. 252.

50. Nadel, p. 236.

51. Gish with Pinchot, p. 362.

52. John Wolfson, conversation with author, November 1997.

53. Nadel, p. 236.

54. Brooks Atkinson, "Last Night at the Theatre: Lillian Gish Gives a Notable Performance in Foote's 'The Trip to Bountiful'," *The New York Times,* 4 November 1953, p. 30.

55. Louis Kronenberger, editor, "Plays Produced in New York," *The Best Plays of 1953-54 and the Yearbook of the Drama in America* (New York: Dodd, Mead, 1954), p. 315.

Chapter 31:
The "Comeback"

1. O.Z. Whitehead, "Lillian," *Theatre Book,* vol. 1, no. 1, Spring 1978, p. 39.

2. "Lillian Gish Gets Degree," *The New York Times,* 23 February 1954, p. 30.

3. Howard Thompson, "Seen on Miss Gish's Wide Screen," *The New York Times,* 2 May 1954, II, p. 5.

4. *Ibid.*

5. Elsa Lanchester, *Elsa Lanchester Herself* (New York: St. Martin's Press, 1983), p. 237.

6. Lillian Gish, with James E. Frasher, "Fifth Decade," *Dorothy and Lillian Gish* (New York: Charles Scribner's Sons, 1973), p. 255.

7. Lillian Gish, conversation with author, June 1961.

8. Charles Higham, *Charles Laughton: An Intimate Biography,* introduction by Elsa Lanchester (Garden City, New York: Doubleday, 1976), p. 187.

9. Lillian Gish, with Ann Pinchot, *The Movies, Mr. Griffith, and Me* (Englewood-Cliffs, New Jersey: Prentice-Hall, 1969), p. 364.

10. *Ibid.* p. 360.

11. Charles Higham, introduction by Elsa Lanchester, p. 196.

12. *Ibid.* p. 193.

13. William K. Everson, conversation with author, September 1970.

14. Lanchester, p. 239.

15. *Ibid.*

16. *Ibid*. p. 236.

17. Gish with Frasher, p. 255.

18. Higham, introduction by Elsa Lanchester, p. 188.

19. Marc Connelly, conversation with author, November 1978.

20. Julie Goldsmith Gilbert, "Treasure Years: 1938–1927," *Edna Ferber: A Biography of Edna Ferber and Her Circle* (Garden City, New York: Doubleday, 1978), p. 337.

21. Gish, June 1961.

22. *Ibid*.

23. Higham, introduction by Elsa Lanchester, p. 189.

24. *Ibid*., p. 197.

25. *Ibid*., p. 190.

26. Gish, June 1961.

27. Stephen Harvey, with a Foreword by Liza Minnelli, *Minnelli* (New York: The Museum of Modern Art, and Harper and Row, 1989), p. 216.

28. John Houseman, "1945," *Unfinished Business: Memoirs 1902–1988* (New York: Applause Theatre, 1989), p. 258.

29. Sam Kashner and Nancy Schoenberger, "Paradoxical Excitement," *A Talent for Genius: The Life and Times of Oscar Levant* (New York: Villard Books, 1994), p. 357.

30. *Ibid*.

31. Lawrence J. Quirk, "The Cobweb," *Lauren Bacall: Her Films and Career* (Secaucus: Citadel, 1986), p. 129.

32. Anita Loos, conversation with author, June 1972.

33. Donald Bogle, "A Hollywood Girlhood," *Dorothy Dandridge: A Biography* (New York: Amistead, 1997), p. 45.

34. "Post in Cabinet Asked for Arts," *The New York Times*, 27 March 1955, p. 65.

35. *Ibid*.

36. Bosley Crowther, "The Cobweb," *The New York Times*, 6 August 1955, p. 32.

37. Kashner and Schoenberger, p. 358.

38. Crowther, p. 32.

39. *Ibid*.

40. Quirk, p. 129.

41. Bosley Crowther, "The Night of the Hunter," *The New York Times*, 30 September 1955, p. 23.

42. *Ibid*.

43. Lanchester, p. 245.

44. *Ibid*., p. 239.

45. *Ibid*.

46. William K. Everson, conversation with author, November 1971.

47. Jack Gould, "TV: Lillian Gish Goes to Washington," *The New York Times*, 20 October 1955, p. 71.

48. *Ibid*.

49. Miriam Cooper, with Bonnie Herndon, *Dark Lady of the Silents: My Life in Early Hollywood* (Indianapolis and New York: Bobbs-Merrill, 1973), p. 57.

50. Lydia Lane, "Hollywood Beauty: Beauty Is What Makes Face Lovely, Says Lillian Gish," *The Brooklyn Eagle*, 12 December 1954, p. 20.

51. J.P. Stanley, "On TV This Week: Mr. Welch and Miss Gish," *The New York Times*, 5 February 1956, p. 11.

52. *Ibid*.

53. Gish with Frasher, p. 256.

54. John L. Toohey, "1938-1939: Abe Lincoln in Illinois," *A History of the Pulitzer Prize Plays* (New York: Citadel Press, 1967), p. 157.

55. Higham, introduction by Elsa Lanchester, p. 200.

56. Shanley, p. 11.

57. "Actor Portraying Booth Injured in Leap to Stage," *The New York Times*, 11 February 1956, p. 37.

58. Jack Gould, "TV: Lincoln's Last Day," *The New York Times*, 13 February 1956, p. 47.

59. Murray Ilson, "A U.S. Arts Board is Endorsed Here," *The New York Times*, 15 April 1956, p. 86.

60. Gish with Frasher, p. 256.

61. Gish with Pinchot, p. 365.

62. Alan Brock, conversation with author, October 1980.

63. *Ibid*.

64. Louis Kronenberger, editor, "The Season in New York," *The Best Plays of 1955-1956* (New York: Dodd, Mead, 1956), p. 3.

65. Whitehead, p. 67.

66. Brock, October 1980.

67. Gish with Pinchot, p. 364.

68. Whitehead, p. 67.
69. Brock, October 1980.
70. Whitehead, p. 71.
71. Neil Fitzgerald, conversation with author, March 1971.
72. Frank Carrington, conversation with author, October 1971.
73. Whitehead, p. 71.

Chapter 32: Just Her Name

1. Louis Calta, "Theatre Culled for 3 Centuries," *The New York Times*, 28 September 1956, p. 29.
2. "American Plays Given in Berlin," *The New York Times*, 21 September 1957, p. 23.
3. *Ibid.*
4. "Hall of Culture Opened in Berlin," *The New York Times*, 20 September 1957, p. 9.
5. *The New York Times*, 21 September 1957, p. 23.
6. Richard Griffith, "The Stella Life," *The Movie Stars* (Garden City, New York: Doubleday, 1970), p. 38.
7. Howard Teichmann, conversation with author, July 1963.
8. O. Z. Whitehead, "Lillian," *Theatre Book*, vol. 1, no. 1, Spring 1978, p. 73.
9. Daniel Blum, "1936," *A Pictorial History of the American Theatre: 1860–1970*, edited and enlarged by John Willis (New York: Crown, 1970), p. 275.
10. *Ibid.*, p. 326.
11. Lillian Gish, conversation with author, October 1958.
12. Brooks Atkinson, "Theatre: Eliot's 'The Family Reunion,'" *The New York Times*, 21 October 1958, p. 39.
13. Louis Untermeyer, "About T.S. Eliot and His Work," *The Cocktail Party* (New York: Decca Records, 1950) Record Album.
14. Atkinson, p. 39.
15. *Ibid.*
16. *Ibid.*
17. Gish, October 1958.
18. Bosley Crowther, "Orders to Kill," *The New York Times*, 18 November 1958, p. 41.
19. William K. Everson, conversation with author, October 1970.
20. Alexander Walker, "Riding for a Fall," *Audrey: Her Real Story* (New York: St. Martin's Press, 1994), p. 167.
21. Lillian Gish, with James E. Frasher, "The Beginning," *Dorothy and Lillian Gish* (New York: Charles Scribner's Sons, 1973), p. 9.
22. Ian Woodward, *Audrey Hepburn* (New York: St. Martin's Press, 1984), p. 179.
23. *Ibid.*, p. 141.
24. Albert Salmi, conversation with author, February 1969.
25. Alexander Walker, "All for Art: Lillian Gish," *Stardom: The Hollywood Phenomenon* (New York: Stein and Day, 1970), p. 80.
26. Charles Higham, *Audrey: The Life of Audrey Hepburn* (New York: Macmillan, 1984), p. 141.
27. Woodward, p. 179.
28. Barry Paris, "Huckleberry Friend," *Audrey Hepburn* (New York: G.P. Putnam's Sons, 1996), p. 162.
29. Higham, p. 141.
30. Lawrence Grobel, "Shooting in Mexico," *The Hustons* (New York: Charles Scribner's Sons, 1989), p. 457.
31. *Ibid.*
32. Warren G. Harris, "Motherhood at Last," *Audrey Hepburn* (New York: Simon and Schuster, 1994), p. 69.
33. Grobel, p. 463.
34. Salmi, February 1969.
35. Seymour Peck, "Then and Now: Lillian Gish," *The New York Times*, 17 April 1960, VI, p. 70.
36. Bosley Crowther, "The Unforgiven," *The New York Times*, 7 April 1960, p. 46.
37. Peck, pp. 70-72.
38. Stuart Oderman, "Lillian Gish: A Friend Remembered," *Journal of Popular Film and Television*, vol. 22, no. 2, Summer 1994, p. 53.
39. *Ibid.*
40. Colleen Dewhurst, conversation with author, February 1963.
41. Lou Jacobi, conversation with author, September 1997.
42. "Equity Vote Is Won by Regular Ticket," *The New York Times*, 26 April 1962. p. 24.
43. Gish with Frasher, "Stageography: Lillian Gish," *Dorothy and Lillian Gish*, p. 311.

44. Roy S. Waldau, "1931-1932," *Vintage Years of the Theatre Guild* (Cleveland and London: The Press of Case Western Reserve University, 1972), p. 136.

45. Henry Hewes, editor, "Plays Produced on Broadway," *The Best Plays of 1962-1963* (New York: Dodd, Mead, 1963), pp. 300–301.

46. Howard Taubman, "Lark by Shaw: 'Too True to Be Good' in a Pert Revival," *The New York Times,* 13 March 1963, p. 8.

47. *Ibid.*

48. Lillian Gish, conversation with author, April 1963.

49. Otto Preminger, "Life in the Sausage Factory," *Preminger* (Garden City, New York: Doubleday, 1977), p. 100.

50. Cleveland Amory, "Money, Manners and Morals," *Who Killed Society?* (New York: Pocket Books, 1962), p. 515.

51. Preminger, "The Cardinal Goes to Vienna," *Preminger*, p. 178.

52. *Ibid.*, pp. 179–180.

53. Alan Brock, conversation with author, October 1980.

54. Preminger, p. 180.

55. Brock, October 1980.

56. Bosley Crowther, "The Cardinal," *The New York Times,* 13 December 1963, p. 41.

57. Gish with Frasher, p. 311.

58. Whitehead, p. 83.

59. Anita Loos, conversation with author, May 1972.

60. Mary Hara, letter to author, May 4, 1992.

61. Mary Hara, conversation with author, June 1992.

62. Milan Stitt, conversation with author, May 1996.

63. Hara, June 1992.

64. Stitt, May 1996.

65. Howard Taubman, "'Coriolanus' and 'Romeo and Juliet' Open Stratford, Conn. Season," *The New York Times,* 21 June 1965, p. 36.

66. Stitt, May 1996.

67. *Ibid.*

68. *Ibid.*

Chapter 33: The "Singing" Empress

1. Irving Drummond, "Lillian Gish: Loveliest of Perennials," *The New York Herald Tribune,* 13 June 1965, p. 25.

2. Lillian Gish, conversation with author, November 1965.

3. George Abbott, conversation with author, November 1965.

4. Daniel Blum, "1944," *A Pictorial History of the American Theatre: 1860–1970,* edited and enlarged by John Willis (New York: Crown, 1970), p. 303.

5. *Ibid.*, p 343.

6. Guy Bolton, conversation with author, November 1965.

7. Abbott, November 1965.

8. Howard Taubman, "Theatre: 'Anya,' a Sentimental Musical," *The New York Times,* 30 November 1965, p. 48.

9. *Ibid.*

10. *Ibid.*

11. *Ibid.*

12. John Willis, editor, "Anya," *Theatre World: 1965-1966,* vol. 22 (New York: Crown) p. 37.

13. Willis, "Reviewing the New York Season," *Ibid.*, p. 6.

14. William K. Everson, conversation with author, February 1971.

15. Bosley Crowther, "Follow Me, Boys," *The New York Times,* 2 December 1966, p. 46.

16. *Ibid.*

17. Lillian Gish, with James E. Frasher, "Sixth Decade," *Dorothy and Lillian Gish* (New York: Charles Scribner's Sons, 1973), p. 274.

18. Howard Thompson, "Warning Shot," *The New York Times,* 8 June 1967, p. 52.

19. Richard Oliver, *Warning Shot* (Los Angeles: Liberty Records, 1966), Record Album.

20. Thompson, p. 52.

21. Lillian Gish, conversation with author, February 1968.

22. "Theatre's Loyal Star: Lillian Gish," *New York Times,* 11 June 1966, p. 21.

23. *Ibid.*

24. *Ibid.*

25. "Lillian Gish and Miss Wood Honored for Aid to Theatre," *The New York Times,* 4 May 1966, p. 53.
26. Lillian Gish, with Ann Pinchot, *The Movies, Mr. Griffith, and Me* (Englewood Cliffs, New Jersey: Prentice-Hall, 1969), p. 368.
27. *Ibid.*
28. Peter Glenville, conversation with author, June 1972.
29. Bosley Crowther, "The Comedians," *The New York Times,* 1 November 1967, p. 37.
30. William Goldman, "What Kind of Day Has It Been?" *The Season: A Candid Look at Broadway* (New York: Harcourt, Brace and World, 1969), p. 393.
31. *Ibid.,* p. 89.
32. *Ibid.,* p. 83.
33. Samuel Hirsch, "Hirsch on Theatre," *The Boston Herald Traveler,* 29 December 1967, p. 30.
34. Clive Barnes, "Theatre: I Never Sang for My Father," *The New York Times,* 26 January 1968, p. 30.
35. *Ibid.*
36. *Ibid.*
37. Goldman, "Crap Game," *The Season: A Candid Look at Broadway,* p. 257.
38. Lillian Gish, conversation with author, February 1968.
39. Lois Wilson, conversation with author, February 1968.
40. Gish with Pinchot, pp. 370–371.
41. Helen Hayes, conversation with author, November 1972.
42. *Ibid.*
43. *Ibid.*
44. Gish with Pinchot, p. 371.
45. Helen Hayes, with Katherine Hatch, *My Life in Three Acts* (New York and San Diego: Harcourt Brace Jovanovich, 1990), p. 242.
46. *Ibid.,* p. 246.
47. Gish with Pinchot, p. 371.
48. *Ibid.*

2. Howard Thompson, "Lillian Gish the Author Talks on D. W. Griffith," *The New York Times,* 18 April 1969, p. 32.
3. Lillian Gish, conversation with author, April 1969.
4. Thompson, p. 32.
5. Arthur Mayer, "Lillian," *The New York Times,* VII, 8 June 1969, p. 7.
6. William K. Everson, conversation with author, June 1969.
7. John Britton, conversation with author, June 1997.
8. "Lillian Gish Plans Double Exposure," *The New York Times,* 10 April 1969, p. 50.
9. Thompson, p. 32.
10. Everson, June 1969.
11. Aileen Pringle, conversation with author, April 1969.
12. Lillian Gish, with James E. Frasher, "Sixth Decade," *Dorothy and Lillian Gish* (New York: Charles Scribner's Sons, 1973), p. 288.
13. *Ibid.,* p. 278.
14. *Ibid.,* p. 279.
15. Henri Langlois, conversation with author, May 1973.
16. Gish with Frasher, p. 286.
17. *Ibid.,* p. 282.
18. "Lillian Gish: In Memoriam," *Journal of Popular Film and Television,* vol. 22, no. 2, Summer 1994, p. 51.
19. Gish with Frasher, p. 288.
20. *Ibid.*
21. *Ibid.*
22. Lillian Gish, conversation with author, May 1973.
23. *Ibid.*
24. Clive Barnes, "Stage: Mike Nichols' 'Uncle Vanya,'" *The New York Times,* 5 June 1973, p. 35.
25. Lillian Gish, conversation with author, June 1973.
26. Otis L. Guernsey, Jr., editor, "The Season in New York," *The Best Plays of 1973-1974* (New York: Dodd, Mead, 1974), p. 22.

Chapter 34: Full Circle

1. Mel Gussow, "That Lad Has Come Far from 'Lassie'," *The New York Times,* 2 December 1997, E3.

Chapter 35: Honors and Surprises

1. William K. Everson, conversation with author, March 1974.

2. A Musical Jubilee, Souvenir Program.

3. Sheridan Morley, "First (and Last) of the Moving Picture Pioneers: Lillian Gish at 75," *The London Times*, 19 September 1974.

4. Vincent Canby, "Modern Museum Is Celebrating Birth of Griffith with Film Show," *The New York Times,* 23 January 1975, p. 35.

5. William K. Everson, conversation with author, September 1974.

6. Lillian Gish, conversation with author, December 1975.

7. Clive Barnes, "'Musical Jubilee,' and Its Stars Glisten," *The New York Times*, 14 November 1975, p. 24.

8. Lillian Gish, conversation with author, November 1975.

9. Otis L. Guernsey, Jr., editor, "The Season in New York," *The Best Plays of 1975-1976* (New York and Toronto: Dodd, Mead, 1976), p. 15.

10. Alvin H. Marill, *Movies Made for Television: The Telefeature and the Mini-Series: 1964–1979* (New York: Arlington House, 1979), p. 236.

11. Ralph Haven Wolfe, "The Gish Film Theatre and Gallery: The Ohio Roots of Dorothy and Lillian Gish," *Journal of Popular Film and Television*, vol. 22, no. 2, Summer 1994, p. 58.

12. *Ibid.*

13. *Ibid.*

14. Ralph Haven Wolfe, conversation with author, October 1997.

15. Gerard Plecki, "Success and Experimentation," *Robert Altman* (Boston: Twayne, 1985), p. 103.

16. Peter Carlsen, "Lillian Gish: Birth of a Nation's Epochal Star in New York," *Architectural Digest*, April 1990, p. 239.

17. Plecki, p. 106.

18. Plecki, "Filmography," *Robert Altman*, p. 152.

19. Plecki, "Success and Experimentation," *Ibid.*, p. 106.

20. *Ibid.*

21. William K. Everson, conversation with author, September 1977.

22. Plecki, p. 106.

23. Viveca Lindfors, conversation with author, March 1980.

24. Plecki, p. 104.

25. *Ibid.*, p. 107.

26. *Ibid.*, p. 106.

27. *Ibid.*, p. 107.

28. Vincent Terrace, "The Complete Encyclopedia of Television," *Encyclopedia of Television: Series Pilots and Specials: 1974–1984* (New York: New York Zoetrope, 1985), p. 386.

29. Walter Kerr, "Supplementary Material," *The New York Times News Service and The Associated Press*, 23 September 1978, pp. 35–36.

30. William K. Everson, conversation with author, October 1978.

31. Plecki, p. 107.

32. Blake Green, "A Woman of Letters," *Newsday* 13 March 1997, II, B 3.

33. *Ibid.*

34. *Ibid.*

35. "Lillian Gish Lobbies for Old Newsreels," *The New York Times*, 20 June 1979, C 19.

36. Anne-Marie Schiro, "Modern Museum, 50, Has a 20s Party," *The New York Times*, 15 November 1979, C 8.

37. Anita Loos, conversation with author, November 1979.

38. Tom Buckley, "Broadway Pays Tribute to Ethel Barrymore," *The New York Times*, 12 December 1989, C 7.

39. Anita Loos, "Lillian Gish–A Tribute to a Trouper," *The New York Times*, 14 September 1980, II, p. 1.

40. Judith Cummings and Albin Krebs, "Notes of People: Gloria Swanson Tells of an Affair with Joseph Kennedy," *The New York Times,* 15 October 1980, B 2.

41. Cummings and Krebs, "Lillian Gish, 84 and Still at It," *Ibid.*

42. Albin Krebs and Robert McG. Thomas, Jr., "Lillian Gish: A Winner Before and a Winner Again," *The New York Times*, 8 April 1981, B 8.

Chapter 36: Taking Stock

1. Joan Juliet Buck, "Lillian Gish: Surprising Life of Hollywood's Demure Waif/Angel," *Vogue*, October 1981, p. 182.

2. *Ibid.*

3. Frederick Winship, "The Cameras Still Roll for the Queen of the Silents," *Sunday Morning Post*, 14 December 1986.

4. Buck, p. 187.

5. Winship.

6. Buck, p. 187.

7. Albin Krebs and David Bird, "Notes on People: The Untiring Lillian Gish," *The New York Times*, 8 July 1981, C 20.

8. *Ibid.*

9. Albin Krebs and Robert McG. Thomas, Jr., "Notes on People: A Night of Memories for Miss Gish," *The New York Times*, 9 November 1981, B 13.

10. Daniel Blum, "1908," *A Pictorial History of the American Theatre: 1860–1970*), enlarged and revised by John Willis (New York: Crown, 1969), p. 103.

11. Blum, "1913," *Ibid.*, p. 139.

12. Krebs and Thomas, *Ibid.*

13. Colleen Dewhurst, conversation with author, May 1983.

14. Irwin Molotsky, "Kennedy Center Honors 5 in the Arts," *The New York Times*, 16 August 1982, C 11.

15. Barbara Gamarekian, "5 in Arts Get Honors in Capitol," *The New York Times*, 6 December 1982, C 13.

16. *Ibid.*

17. *Ibid.*

18. *Ibid.*

19. Lillian Gish, conversation with author, March 1985.

20. Enid Nemy, "Lillian Gish, at 83, Transcends Style," *The New York Times*, 31 December 1982.

21. *Ibid.*

22. *Ibid.*

23. *Ibid.*

24. *Ibid.*

25. Leslie Bennetts, "For Oliver, a Night of Praise for 50 Years of Accomplishment," *The New York Times*, 26 April 1983, C 11.

26. Laurie Johnson and Suzanne Daley, "New York Day by Day: Floral Homage to a Fable," *The New York Times*, 2 June 1983, B 3.

27. Gish, March 1985.

28. John O'Connor, "TV: 'Hobson's Choice,' An Adaptation on CBS," *The New York Times*, 21 December 1983, C 27.

29. *Ibid.*

30. Gish, March 1985.

31. Aljean Harmetz, "Hollywood Honors Miss Gish," *The New York Times*, 1 March 1984, C 15.

32. *Ibid.*

33. John O'Connor, "Film Institute Salutes Lillian Gish," *The New York Times*, 17 April 1984, C 18.

34. *Ibid.*

35. *Ibid.*

36. *Ibid.*

37. Anna Kisselgoff, "The Dance: Met Opera Gala," *The New York Times*, 14 May, 1984, C 11.

38. William K. Everson, conversation with author, October 1984.

39. Peggy McCarthy, "Theatre Museum Planned in New Haven," *The New York Times*, 11 November 1985, XXXIII, p. 10.

40. Georgia Dullea, "Style: The Evening Hours," *The New York Times*, 12 March 1985, B 8.

41. *Ibid.*

42. Gish, March 1985.

43. Lawrence Van Gelder, "Recent Releases," *The New York Times*, 10 March 1985, II, p. 30.

44. Lillian Gish, with James E. Frasher, "Fifth Decade," *Dorothy and Lillian Gish* (New York: Charles Scribner's Sons, 1973), p. 256.

45. Leslie Bennetts, "50 Years for MoMA's Film Department," *The New York Times*, 12 May 1985, XXI, p. 1.

46. *Ibid.*

47. *Ibid.*

48. *Ibid.*

49. *Ibid.*

50. John O'Connor, "4 Part 'Huckleberry Finn' Begins," *The New York Times*, 10 February 1986, C 17.

51. *Ibid.*

52. Peter B. Flint, "A Doughty Lillian Gish Takes a Fresh Fling at Comedy," *The New York Times*, 11 May 1986, II, p. 1.

53. Thomas Clavin, "Alda Film Raises a Stir on East End," *The New York Times*, 12 May 1985, XXI, p. 1.

54. *Ibid.*, p. 4.

55. *Ibid.*

56. Flint, II, p. 1.
57. *Ibid.*
58. Clavin, XXI, p. 1.
59. *Ibid.*, p. 32.
60. Vincent Canby, "Screen: Alan Alda's 'Sweet Liberty,'" *The New York Times,* 14 May 1986, C 23.
61. Alan Alda, letter to author, 12 June 1996.

Chapter 37: The Last Reel

1. Cindy Adams, *New York Post,* 2 March 1993.
2. Peter B. Flint, "A Doughty Lillian Gish Takes a Fresh Fling at Comedy," *The New York Times,* 11 May 1986, II, p. 32.
3. Adams.
4. Aljean Harmetz, "Placating the Stars of 'Whales,'" *The New York Times,* 22 October 1987, II, p. 21.
5. Vincent Canby, "Film: Gish and Davis in 'Whales of August,'" *The New York Times,* 16 October 1987, C 3.
6. *Ibid.*
7. Harmetz, p. 21.
8. Whitney Stine, *"I'd Love to Kiss You…": Conversations with Bette Davis* (New York: Pocket Books, 1990), p. 254.
9. *Ibid.*
10. Harmetz, p. 21.
11. *Ibid.*
12. *Ibid.*
13. *Ibid.*
14. *Ibid.*
15. William K. Everson, conversation with author, September 1987.
16. Stine, p. 256.
17. *Ibid.*, p. 255.
18. *Ibid.*, p. 258.
19. *Ibid.*
20. Harmetz, p. 21.
21. James Spada, "The Lonely Lady," *More Than a Woman: An Intimate Biography of Bette Davis* (New York: Bantam, 1993), p. 616.
22. Stine, p. 256.
23. Harmetz, p. 21.
24. Stine, p. 258.
25. *Ibid.*, p. 243.
26. Spada, p. 617.
27. *Ibid.*, p. 619.

28. Canby, C 3.
29. *Ibid.*
30. *Ibid.*
31. Lillian Gish, as Told to Selma G. Lanes, "Mother," *An Actor's Life for Me!* illustrated by Patricia Henderson Lincoln (New York: Viking Kestrel, 1987), p. 37.
32. Lillian Gish, as Told to Selma G. Lanes, "A Christmas Like No Other," *Ibid.*, p. 32.
33. Lillian Gish, as Told to Selma G. Lanes, "The Gerry Men," *Ibid.*, p. 52.
34. Lillian Gish, as Told to Selma G. Lanes, "Summertime," *Ibid.*, p. 40.
35. Lillian Gish, as Told to Selma G. Lanes, "We Meet an Old Friend," *Ibid.*, pp. 62–63.
36. *Ibid.*, p. 64.
37. Lillian Gish, as Told to Selma G. Lanes, "Flying on Broadway, Landing in Hollywood," *Ibid.*, p. 73.
38. Ann W. Moore, "An Actor's Life for Me!" *School Library Journal,* vol. 34, October 1987, p. 144.
39. Zena Sutherland, "An Actor's Life for Me!" *Bull Cent Child Books,* vol. 41, November 1987, p. 48.
40. William K. Everson, conversation with author, December 1987.
41. Michael Buckley, "The D. W. Griffith Awards Ceremony," *Films in Review,* vol. XXXIX, no. 5, May 1988, p. 259.
42. Anita Loos, conversation with author, June 1972.
43. Buckley, p. 259.
44. Helen Hayes, conversation with author, February 1988.
45. John O'Connor, "Lillian Gish Looks Back on a Century," *The New York Times,* 11 July 1988, C 16.
46. *Ibid.*
47. "Letters to the Editor, "Sandy Shook Hands with Miss America," *The New York Times,* 12 September 1990, A 30.
48. Ralph Haven Wolfe, "The Gish Film Theatre and Gallery: The Ohio Roots of Dorothy and Lillian Gish," *Journal of Popular Film and Television,* vol. 22, no. 2, Summer 1994, pp. 58–59.
49. Lawrence J. Quirk, "Somebody's Fool," *Paul Newman* (Dallas: Taylor 1996), p. 321.

Bibliography

"Actor Portraying Booth Injured in Leap to Stage." *New York Times*, February 11, 1956, p. 37.

Adams, Cindy. *New York Post*. March 2, 1993.

Affron, Charles. *Star Acting: Gish, Garbo, Davis*. New York: E. P. Dutton, 1977.

Allen, Frederick Lewis. *Only Yesterday*. New York: Bantam Books, 1946.

"America Firsters Denounced as Traitors, Were Patriots of the First Rank." *The Barnes Review*, September 1966, p.7.

American Plays Given in Berlin." *New York Times*, September 21, 1957, p.23.

Amory, Cleveland. *Who Killed Society?* New York: Pocket Books, 1962.

Anderson, Robert G. *Faces, Forms, Films: The Artistry of Lon Chaney*. New York: Castle Books, 1971.

"As Lillian Gish Views Art." *New York Times*, VIII, July 1, 1928, p.4.

Atkinson, Brooks. "At the Theatre: 'Crime and Punishment'." *New York Times*, December 23, 1947, p.29.

_____. "At the Theatre: Lillian Gish in the Theatre Guild Production of 'The Curious Savage'." *New York Times*, October 25, 1950, p.41.

_____. "At This Theatre: 'The Man'." *New York Times*, January 20, 1950, p.28.

_____. *Broadway*. New York: Macmillan, 1970.

_____. "Last Night at the Theatre: Lillian Gish Gives a Notable Performance in Foote's 'The Trip to Bountiful'." *New York Times*, November 4, 1953, p.30.

_____. "The Play: Fantasy: The Seasons in Hyde Park in Sean O'Casey's 'Within the Gates'." *New York Times*, October 23, 1934, p.23.

_____. "The Play in Review: 'Mr. Sycamore'." *New York Times*, December 14, 1942, p.18.

_____. "The Play: John Gielgud and Judith Anderson in a 'Hamlet' Staged by Guthrie McClintic." *New York Times*, October 9, 1936, p.30.

_____. "The Play: Lillian Gish as 'La Dame aux Camelias,' at the Morosco." *New York Times*, November 2, 1932, p.23.

_____. "The Play: Lillian Gish in Phillip Barry's 'The Joyous Season'." *New York Times*, January 30, 1934, p.16.

_____. "The Play: 'Mainly for Lovers,' a Comedy from England." *New York Times*, February 22, 1936, p.13.

_____. "The Play: On Their Golden Wedding Day in Dodie Smith's 'Dear Octopus'." *New York Times*, January 12, 1939, p.22.

_____. "The Play: 'Uncle Vanya'." *New York Times*, April 16, 1930, p.19.

_____. "Theatre: Eliot's 'The Family Reunion'." *New York Times*, October 21, 1958, p.39.

"Backer of Duell was W. A. Harriman." *New York Times*, June 3, 1926, p.27.

Barnes, Clive. " 'Musical Jubilee,' and Its Stars Glisten." *New York Times*, November 14, 1975, p.24.

_____. "Stage: Mike Nichols' 'Uncle Vanya'." *New York Times*, June 5, 1973, p.35.

_____. "Theatre: I Never Sang for My Father." *New York Times*, January 26, 1968, p.30.

Baxter, John. *Hollywood in the Thirties*. London: Tantivy Press, and New York: A. S. Barnes, 1968.

_____. *King Vidor*. New York: Monarch Press, 1976.

Behlmer, Rudy, editor. With an Introduction by S. M. Behrman. *Memo from David O. Selznick*. New York: Viking, 1972.

Bennetts, Leslie. "For Olivier, a Night of Praise for 50 Years of Accomplishment." *New York Times*, April 26, 1983; C11.

Berg, A. Scott. *Goldwyn*. New York: Alfred A. Knopf, 1989.

Berlin, Brigid. *Interview*. December 1978, p.42.

Birmingham, Stephan. *The Late John Marquand*. Philadelphia and New York: J. B. Lippincott, 1972.

Bitzer, Billy. *Billy Bitzer: His Story*. New York: Farrar, Straus and Giroux, 1973.

Blesh, Rudi. *Keaton*. New York: Macmillan, 1966.

Blum, Daniel. *A Pictorial History of the American Theatre: 1860–1970*. Edited and Revised by John Willis. New York: Crown, 1969.

_____. *A Pictorial History of the Silent Screen*. New York: Grosset and Dunlap, 1953.

_____. Editor. *Theatre World: Season 1951–1952*. New York: Greenberg, 1952.

Bode, Carl, editor. *The New Mencken Letters*. New York: Dial, 1977.

Bogdanovitch, Peter. *Allan Dwan: The Last Pioneer*. New York: Praeger, 1971.

Bogle, Donald. *Dorothy Dandridge: A Biography*. New York: Armistead, 1997.

_____. *Toms, Coons, Mulattoes, Mammies and Bucks: An Interpretive History of Blacks in American Films*. New York: Viking Press, 1973.

Bowen, Ezra, Series editor. *This Fabulous Century: 1910–1920*. New York: Time-Life Books, 1969.

_____. Series editor. *This Fabulous Century: 1920–1930*. New York: Time-Life Books, 1969.

Bowser, Eileen. *The Transformation of Cinema: 1907–1915*. New York: Charles Scribner's Sons, 1990.

Brady, Thomas F. "Hollywood News Highlights." *New York Times*, July 26, 1942, VIII, p.3.

Broccoli, Matthew J. *Some Sort of Epic Grandeur: The Life of F. Scott Fitzgerald*. New York and London: Harcourt Brace Jovanovich, 1981.

Brooks, Louise. *Lulu in Hollywood*. Introduction by William Shawn. New York: Alfred A. Knopf, 1982.

Brown, Arnold G. *Lizzie Borden: The Legend, the Truth, the Final Chapter*. Nashville: Rutledge Hills Press, 1991.

Brown, Gene. *Movie Time: A Chronology of Hollywood from Its Beginnings to the Present*. New York: Macmillan, 1995.

Brown, John Mason. *The World of Robert E. Sherwood: Mirror to His Times*. New York: Harper and Row, 1965.

Brown, Karl, edited with an Introduction by Kevin Brownlow. *Adventures with D. W. Griffith*. New York: Farrar, Straus and Giroux, 1973.

Brown, Peter Harry, and Pamela Ann Brown. *The MGM Girls: Behind the Velvet Curtain*. New York: St. Martin's Press, 1983.

Brownlow, Kevin. "Lillian Gish." *Films and Filming*, November 1983.

_____. *The Parade's Gone By*. New York: Alfred A. Knopf, 1968.

_____, and John Kobal. *Hollywood: The Pioneers*. New York: Alfred A. Knopf, 1979.

Buck, Joan Juliet. "Lillian Gish: Surprising Life of Hollywood's Demure Waif/Angel." *Vogue*, October 1981, p.182.

Buckley, Michael. "The D. W. Griffith Awards Ceremony." *Films in Review*, vol. XXXIX, no.5, May 1988, p.259.

Buckley, Tom. "Broadway Pays Tribute to Ethel Barrymore." *New York Times*, December 12, 1989, C7.

Burke, Thomas. *Limehouse Nights*. New York: Grosset and Dunlap, 1917.

Butler, Ivan. *Silent Magic: Rediscovering the Silent Film Era*. With a Foreword by Kevin Brownlow. New York: Ungar, 1988.

Buxton, Frank, and Bill Owen. *The Big Broadcast: 1920–1950*. New York: Avon Books, 1972.

Calta, Louis. "Premier Tonight of Mary Surratt." *New York Times*, February 8, 1947, p. 11.

_____. "Theatre Culled for 3 Centuries." *New York Times*, September 28, 1956, p.29.

Canby, Vincent. "Film: Gish and Davis in 'Whales of August'." *New York Times,* October 16, 1987, C3.

_____. "Modern Museum Is Celebrating Birth of Griffith with Film Show." *New York Times,* January 23, 1975, p.35.

_____. "Screen: Alan Alda's 'Sweet Liberty'." *New York Times,* May 14, 1986, C23.

Carey, Gary. *All the Stars in Heaven: Louis B. Mayer's MGM.* New York: E. P. Dutton, 1981.

_____. *Anita Loos.* New York: Alfred A. Knopf, 1988.

Carlsen, Peter. "Lillian Gish: 'Birth of a Nation's' Epochal Star in New York." *Architectural Digest,* April 1990, p.238.

Carpenter, Frederic I. *Eugene O'Neill.* Boston: Twayne, 1979.

Castle, Charles. *Noel.* Garden City, New York: Doubleday, 1973.

Cerf, Bennett, and Van Cartmell. *S.R.O.* Garden City, New York: Doubleday, Doran, 1946.

"C. H. Duell to Wed Josephine Smith." *New York Times,* July 11, 1933, p.8.

Chaplin, Charles. *My Autobiography.* New York: Simon and Schuster, 1964.

Chapman, John, editor. *The Burns Mantle Best Plays of 1947-48.* New York: Dodd, Mead, 1948.

_____. *The Burns Mantle Best Plays of 1949-50.* New York: Dodd, Mead, 1950.

_____. *The Best Plays of 1950-51.* New York: Dodd, Mead, 1951.

Churchill, Allen. *The Theatrical 20s.* New York, St. Louis, and San Francisco: McGraw Hill, 1975.

Clarke, Gerald. *Capote: A Biography.* New York: Simon and Schuster, 1988.

Clavin, Thomas. "Alda Film Raises a Stir on East End." *New York Times,* May 12, 1985, XXI, p.1.

Cole, Toby, and Helen Krich Chinoy. *Actors on Acting.* New York: Crown, 1949.

Collins, Glenn. "Hundreds Gather to Mourn a Friend, Lillian Gish." *New York Times,* March 12, 1993, p.9.

Cooper, Miriam, with Bonnie Herndon. *Dark Lady of the Silents: My Life in Early Hollywood.* Indianapolis and New York: The Bobbs–Merrill, 1973.

"Court Holds Duell on Perjury Charge; Quashes Gish Suit." *New York Times,* April 3, 1925, p.1.

Cowajee, Saros. *Sean O'Casey: The Man Behind the Plays.* New York: St. Martin's Press, 1964.

Cray, Ed. *General of the Army: Soldier and Statesman.* New York: W. W. Norton, 1990.

Crowther, Bosley. "At the Rialto: 'Commandos Strike at Dawn'." *New York Times,* January 14, 1943, p.25.

_____. "At the Cinema: 'The Whistle at Eaton Falls'." *New York Times,* October 11, 1951, p.49.

_____. "The Cardinal." *New York Times,* December 13, 1963, p. 51

_____. "The Cobweb." *New York Times,* August 6, 1955, p.32.

_____. "Duel in the Sun." *New York Times,* May 8, 1947, p.20.

_____. "Follow Me, Boys!" *New York Times,* December 2, 1966, p.46.

_____. "The Night of the Hunter." *New York Times,* September 30, 1955, p.23.

_____. "Orders to Kill." *New York Times,* November 18, 1958, p.41.

_____. "Plenty of Donald: 'Top Man'." *New York Times,* October 29, 1943, p.23.

_____. "The Screen in Review: 'Miss Susie Slagle's'." *New York Times,* February 7, 1946, p.29.

_____. "The Screen in Review: Selznick's 'Portrait of Jennie,' with Cotton and Jennifer Jones Opens at Rivoli." *New York Times,* March 30, 1949, p.31.

_____. "The Unforgiven." *New York Times,* April 7, 1960, p.46.

Cummings, Judith, and Albin Krebs. "Notes of People: Gloria Swanson Tills of an Affair with Joseph Kennedy." *New York Times,* October 15, 1980, B2.

Derwent, Clarence. *The Derwent Story: My First Fifty Years in the Theatre in England and America.* New York: Henry Shuman, 1953.

"Dorothy Gish Obtains Connecticut Divorce." *New York Times,* October 12, 1935, p.13.

"Dorothy Gish Sues to Divorce Rennie." *New York Times,* March 25, 1935, p.17.

"Dorothy Gish Wins in Divorce Hearing." *New York Times,* September 27, 1935, p.24.

Douglas, Ann. *Terrible Honesty: Mongrel Manhattan in the 1920s.* New York: Farrar, Straus and Giroux, 1995.

Drutman, Irving. "Lillian Gish: Loveliest of Perennials." *The New York Herald-Tribune,* June 13, 1965, p.25.

Duberman, Martin Bauml. *Paul Robeson.* New York: Alfred A. Knopf, 1988.

"Duell Asks Trial on Perjury Charge." *New York Times,* March 30, 1926, p.12.

"Duell Case Goes to the Jury Today." *New York Times,* June 15, 1926, p.7.

"Duell Drops Gish Action." *New York Times,* June 17, 1927, p.23.

"Duell-Gish Troth Merely Unofficial." *New York Times,* March 31, 1925, p.23.

"Duell Is Tangled on Gish Dealings." *New York Times,* April 1, 1925, p.25.

"Duell Sues Mrs. Gish." *New York Times,* June 7, 1927, p.30.

"Duell Summons Rennie in Gish Row." *New York Times,* February 25, 1925, p.40.

"Duell Takes Stand to Deny Perjury." *New York Times,* June 10, 1926, p.27.

"Duell Trial Ends in a Disagreement." *New York Times,* June 25, 1926, p.25.

"Duell's Ex-Partner Aids Prosecution." *New York Times,* May 29, 1926, p.16.

Dullea, Georgia. "The Evening Hours." *New York Times,* March 15, 1985, p.8.

"D. W. Griffith Wed." *New York Times,* March 3, 1936.

Edmunds, Robin. *The Big Three: Churchill, Roosevelt and Stalin in Peace and War.* New York and London: W. W. Norton, 1991.

Edwards, Anne. *The DeMilles: An American Family.* New York: Harry N. Abrams, 1988.

"English to Win in Films." *New York Times,* March 28, 1926, p.26.

"Equity Vote Is Won by Regular Ticket." *New York Times,* April 26, 1962, p.24.

"Erred in Testimony in Duell-Gish Suit." *New York Times,* June 8, 1926, p.14.

Ethan, Morden. *Movie Star: A Look at the Women Who Made Hollywood.* New York: St. Martin's Press, 1983.

Everson, William K. *American Silent Film.* New York: Oxford University Press, 1978.

Eyman, Scott. *Mary Pickford: America's Sweetheart.* New York: Donald I. Fine, Inc., 1990.

_____. *The Speed of Sound: Hollywood and the Talkie Revolution.* New York: Simon and Schuster, 1997.

Farnsworth, Marjorie. *The Ziegfeld Follies: A History in Text and Pictures.* London: Peter Davies, 1956.

Farr, Finis. *O'Hara: A Biography.* Boston and Toronto: Little, Brown, 1973.

Fehr, Richard, and Frederick G. Vogel. *Lullabies of Hollywood: Movie Music and the Movie Musical.* Jefferson, North Carolina: McFarland, 1992.

Fisher, Clive. *Noel Coward.* New York: St. Martin's Press, 1992.

Flamini, Roland. *Thalberg: The Last Tycoon and the World of MGM.* New York: Crown, 1994.

Flint, Peter B. "A Doughty Lillian Gish Takes a Fresh Fling at Comedy." *New York Times,* May 12, 1985, XXI, p.1.

"A Florentine Story." *New York Times,* December 2, 1924, p.13.

Fraser, Antonia, editor. *The Lives of the Kings and Queens of England.* New York: Alfred A. Knopf, 1975.

Gamarekian, Barbara. "5 in Arts Get Honors in Capitol." *New York Times,* December 6, 1982, C13.

Gaver, Jack. "Recalls Griffith Film on TV Thursday 'Silents Please' Brings Back Fond Memory for Lillian Gish." *The New York Morning Telegraph,* June 20, 1961.

Geduld, Harry. *James Barrie.* New York; Twayne, 1971.

Gielgud, Sir John. *Distinguished Company.* Garden City: Doubleday, 1973.

_____. In collaboration with John Miller and John Powell. *Sir John Gielgud.* New York: Clarkson Potter, 1979.

"Gielgud Triumphs in 'Hamlet'." *New York Times,* October 1, 1936, p.30.

Gish, Dorothy. "My Sister Lillian: What One of the Best Comediennes of the Screen Thinks of the Art and Character of Her Noted Relative." *Theatre Magazine,* December 1927, p.31.

Gish, Lillian. "The Life–Giving Light." *Guideposts.* May 1982.

_____, as told to David Brown. "Miss Gish's Challenge to Marriage." *New York Journal American,* October 12, 1946.

_____, as told to Selma G. Lanes. *An Actor's Life for Me!* with illustrations by Patricia Henderson Lincoln. New York: Viking Kestrel, 1987.

_____, with Ann Pinchot. *The Movies, Mr. Griffith, and Me.* Englewood Cliffs: Prentice–Hall, Inc., 1969.

_____, with James E. Frasher. *Dorothy and Lillian Gish.* New York: Charles Scribner's Sons, 1979.

"Gish Betrothal Befuddles Duell." *New York Times,* April 2, 1925, p.19.

Golden, Eve. "Mae Marsh: The Natural." *Films of the Golden Age.* Winter 1966, p.32.

Goldman, William. *The Season: A Candid Look at Broadway.* New York: Harcourt, Brace and World, 1969.

Goldsmith, Julie. *Edna Ferber: A Biography of Edna Ferber and Her Circle.* Garden City: Doubleday, 1978.

"A Good Little Devil." *New York Times,* January 9, 1913, p.9.

Goodman, Ezra. *The Fifty-Year Decline and Fall of Hollywood.* New York: Simon and Schuster, 1961.

Gottfried, Martin. *Jed Harris: The Curse of Genius.* Boston and Toronto: Little, Brown, 1984.

Gould, Jack. "TV: Lillian Gish Goes to Washington." *New York Times,* October 23, 1955, p.71.

_____. "TV: Lincoln's Last Day." *New York Times,* February 13, 1956, p.47.

"Government Drops Suit Against Duell." *New York Times,* November 27, 1926, p.11.

Graham, Sheila. *The Garden of Allah.* New York: Crown, 1970.

Green, Abel, and Joe Laurie, Jr. *Show Biz: From Vaude to Video.* New York: Henry Holt, 1951.

Green, Blake. "A Woman of Letters." *Newsday,* March 13, 1997, B3.

"Greta Garbo Not So Elusive Now." *New York Times,* September 4, 1946, p.25.

Griffith, D. W. *The Man Who Invented Hollywood: The Autobiography of D. W. Griffith.* Edited by James Hart, with a foreword by Frank Capra. Louisville, Kentucky: Touchstone, 1972.

Griffith, Richard. *The Movie Stars.* Garden City: Doubleday, 1970.

_____, and Arthur Mayer. *The Movies.* New York: Simon and Schuster, 1957.

Grobel, Lawrence. *The Hustons.* New York: Charles Scribner's Sons, 1989.

Guernsey, Otis L., Jr., editor. *The Best Plays of 1973-1974.* New York: Dodd, Mead, 1974.

_____. *The Best Plays of 1975-76.* New York and Toronto: Dodd, Mead, 1976.

Gussow, Mel. "That Lad Has Come Far from 'Lassie'." *New York Times,* December 2, 1997, E3.

Hadleigh, Boze. *Hollywood Babble On: Stars and Gossip About Other Stars.* New York: Berkeley, 1994.

Hall, Mordaunt. "His Double Life." *New York Times,* December 16, 1933, p.12.

_____. "The Screen." *New York Times,* February 25, 1926, p.2.

_____. "The Screen: Annie Laurie." *New York Times,* May 12, 1927.

_____. "The Screen: One Romantic Night." *New York Times,* May 31, 1930. P.19.

_____. "The Screen: The Scarlet Letter." *New York Times,* August 10, 1926, p.19.

_____. "The Screen: Strange Interlude." *New York Times,* September 1, 1932, p.24.

_____. "The Screen: The Wind." *New York Times,* November 5, 1928, p.26.

"Hall of Culture Opened in Berlin." *New York Times,* September 20, 1957, p.9.

"A Hamlet Out from England." *New York Times,* September 6, 1936, IX, p.1.

Hanson, Patricia, executive editor and Alan Gevinson, assistant editor. *The American Film Institute Catalogue of Motion Pictures Produced in the United States: Feature Films, 1919–1920,* vol. F1. Berkeley: University of California Press, 1988.

Harmetz, Aljean. "Hollywood Honors Miss Gish." *New York Times,* March 1, 1984, C15.

Harvey, Stephen. With a Foreword by Liza Minelli. *Minelli.* New York: The Museum of Modern Art, and Harper and Row, 1989.

Hawthorne, Nathaniel. *The Scarlet Letter.* With a New Introduction by Willard Thorp. New York: Collier Books, 1962.

Hayes, Helen, with Katherine Hatch. *My Life in Three Acts.* New York and San Diego: Harcourt Brace Jovanovich, 1990.

Hefner, Richard. *A Documentary of the United States,* 4th ed. New York: New American Library, 1985.

Heimel, Cynthia. *The Soho Weekly News.* September 28, 1976.

Henderson, Ray. "Lillian Gish, Once of the

Cinema, Says She Really Did Not Like It." *New York Herald-Tribune,* December 27, 1936.

Henderson, Robert M. *D. W. Griffith: The Years at Biograph.* New York: Farrar, Straus, and Giroux, 1970.

Hergesheimer, Joseph. "Lillian Gish." *The American Mercury.* April 1924, p.397.

Hewes, Henry, editor. *The Best Plays of 1962–1963.* New York: Dodd, Mead, 1963.

Higham, Charles. *Charles Laughton: An Intimate Biography.* Introduction by Elsa Lanchester. Garden City, New York: Doubleday, 1976.

_____. *Ziegfeld.* Chicago: Henry Regnery, 1972.

_____, and Joel Greenberg. *Hollywood Musicals in the Forties.* New York: A. S. Barnes, 1968.

"Higher Court Backs Lillian Gish." *New York Times,* December 30, 1932, p.13.

Hirsch, Samuel. "Hirsch on Theatre." *Boston Herald Traveler,* September 29, 1967, p.30.

Hobson, Fred. *Mencken: A Life.* New York: Random House, 1995.

Houseman, John. *Unfinished Business: Memoirs: 1902–1988.* Applause Theatre Book, 1989.

Howe, Hubert. "The Film Wizard of Europe." *Photoplay,* December 1922.

Ilson, Murray. "A U.S. Arts Board Is Endorsed Here." *New York Times,* April 15, 1956, p.86.

"James Rennie Is Cleared." *New York Times,* March 12, 1925, p.6.

"John Gielgud Arrives." *New York Times,* September 1, 1936, p.24.

Johnson, Hugh. *The World Atlas of Wine: A Complete Guide to the Wines and Spirits of the World.* New York: Simon and Schuster, 1971.

Johnson, Joyce. *Minor Characters.* Boston: Houghton Mifflin, 1983.

Johnson, Laurie, and Suzanne Daley. "New York Day by Day: Floral Homage to a Fable." *New York Times,* June 2, 1983, B3.

Johnson, Thomas H., in consultation with Harvey Wish. *The Oxford Companion to American History.* New York: Oxford University Press, 1966.

Johnson, Winthrop D., Miriam Greenbatt and John S. Bowes. *The Americans: A History.* Evanston, Illinois: McDougal, Littel, 1991.

"Josephine Smith Becomes a Bride." *New York Times,* October 22, 1933, II, p.4.

"Judge Clears Room at the Gish Trial." *New York Times,* March 28, 1925, p.6.

"Judge Mack Unfair, Duell Declares." *New York Times,* June 11, 1926, p.8.

"Jury Is Locked Up at the Duell Trial." *New York Times,* June 16, 1926, p.7.

"Jury Picked to Try Duell For Perjury." *New York Times,* May 28, 1926, p.44.

Kael, Pauline. *Going Steady.* Boston and Toronto: Little, Brown, 1970.

Kashner, Sam, and Nancy Schoenberger. *A Talent for Genius: The Life and Times of Oscar Levant.* New York: Villard Books, 1994.

Katz, Ephraim. *The Film Encyclopedia.* New York: Perigee Books, 1982.

Kerr, Walter. "Supplementary Material." *New York Times News Service and the Associated Press,* September 23, 1978, pp.35–36.

Kisselgoff, Anna. "The Dance: Met Opera Gala." *New York Times,* May 14, 1984, C11.

Kobal, John. *People Will Talk.* New York: Aurum Press, 1986.

Koch, Ed. "A Museum for All of Us." *New York Post,* September 12, 1997, p.29.

Koszarski, Richard. *An Evenings Entertainment: The Age of the Silent Feature Picture: 1915–1928.* Berkeley, Los Angeles, and London: University of California Press, 1994.

Krebs, Albin. "Lillian Gish, 99, a Movie Star Since Movies Began Is Dead." *New York Times,* March 1, 1993, p.1.

_____, and Robert McG. Thomas, Jr. "Lillian Gish: A Winner Before and a Winner Again." *New York Times,* April 8, 1981, B8.

_____, and Robert McG. Thomas, Jr. "Notes on People: A Night of Memories for Miss Gish." *New York Times,* November 9, 1981, B13.

Kronenberger, Louis, editor. *The Best Plays of 1953-1954.* New York: Dodd, Mead, 1954.

_____. *The Best Plays of 1955-1956.* New York: Dodd, Mead, 1956.

Krutch, Joseph Wood. *American Drama Since 1918.* New York: George Braziller, 1967.

Kunitz, Stanley J., and Howard Haycraft, editors. *Twentieth Century Authors: A Biographical Dictionary of Modern Literature.* New York: H.W. Wilson, 1942.

Laffel, Jeff. "Sylvia Sidney." *Films in Review.* Vol. XLV, no. 9/10, September-October 1994, p.19.

Lahue, Kalton C. *Dreams for Sale: The Rise and Fall of the Triangle Film Corporation.* South Brunswick and New York: A.S. Barnes, 1971.

_____. *Ladies in Distress.* South Brunswick and New York: A.S. Barnes, 1971.

Lamparski, Richard. *Whatever Became of...?* second series. New York: Crown, 1968.

Lanchester, Elsa. *Elsa Lanchester Herself.* New York: St. Martin's Press, 1954.

Langner, Lawrence. *The Magic Curtain.* New York: E.P. Dutton, 1951.

Lawrence, Jerome. *Actor: The Life and Times of Paul Muni.* New York: G.P. Putnam and Sons, 1974.

Leab, Daniel J. *From Sambo to Superspade: The Black Experience in Motion Pictures.* Boston: Houghton Mifflin, 1976.

"Letters to the Editor, Sandy Shook Hands with Miss America." *New York Times,* September 12, 1990. A30.

Lewis, Phillip C. *Trouping.* New York: Harper and Row, 1978.

Lewis, R.W.B. *Edith Wharton.* New York: Harper and Row, 1975.

"Lillian Gish and Miss Wood Honored for Aid to Theatre." *New York Times,* May 4, 1966, p.53.

"Lillian Gish at Art Reception." *New York Times,* March 31, 1925, p.17.

"Lillian Gish Dies at 99 After a 75-Year Film Career." *The Star–Ledger,* March 12, 1993, p.5.

"Lillian Gish Ends East Coast Visit." *New York Times,* September 9, 1935, p.24.

"Lillian Gish Gets Degree." *New York Times,* February 23, 1954, p.30.

"Lillian Gish Here in 'Camille.'" *New York Times,* October 18, 1932, p.28.

"Lillian Gish: In Memoriam." *Journal of Popular Film and Television,* vol. 22, no. 2, Summer 1994, p.51.

"Lillian Gish in Role of Dog Health Aide." *New York Times,* February 1, 1952, p.44.

"Lillian Gish Joins with United Artists." *New York Times,* December 7, 1932, p.32.

"Lillian Gish Lobbies for Old Newsreels." *New York Times,* June 20, 1979, C19.

"Lillian Gish Opens Lawsuit in Person." *New York Times,* March 25, 1925, p.25.

"Lillian Gish Plans Double Exposure." *New York Times,* April 10, 1969, p.50.

"Lillian Gish the Author Talks on D. W. Griffith." *New York Times,* April 18, 1969, p.32.

"Lillian Gish Returns." *New York Times,* September 24, 1932, p.18.

"Lillian Gish Returns; Brings Mother, Ill." *New York Times,* June 5, 1926, p.7.

"Lillian Gish Signs." *New York Times,* April 25, 1925, p.16.

"Lillian Gish Sued by Film Producer." *New York Times,* January 31, 1925, p.15.

"Lillian Gish Wins Decision." *New York Times,* March 23, 1925, p.23.

Lindbergh, Charles A. "A Letter to Americans." *The Barnes Review,* September 1996, p.4.

_____. *The Wartime Journals of Charles A. Lindbergh.* New York: Harcourt Brace Jovanovich, 1970.

Lockwood, Charles. *Dream Palaces: Hollywood at Home.* New York: The Viking Press, 1981.

Loos, Anita. "Lillian Gish — A Tribute to a Trouper." *New York Times,* September 14, 1980, II, p.1.

"Mae Murray Wins in Court." *New York Times,* November 11, 1925, p.16.

"Mae Murray Wins $1,600." *New York Times,* November 17, 1925, p.11.

Mantle, Burns, editor. *The Best Plays of 1931-32.* New York: Dodd, Mead, 1932.

_____. *The Best Plays of 1932-33.* New York: Dodd, Mead, 1933.

_____. *The Best Plays of 1933-34.* New York: Dodd, Mead, 1933.

_____. *The Best Plays of 1934-35.* New York: Dodd, Mead, 1935.

_____. *The Best Plays of 1936-37.* New York: Dodd, Mead, 1937.

_____. *The Best Plays of 1937-38.* New York: Dodd, Mead, 1938.

_____. *The Best Plays of 1938-39.* New York: Dodd, Mead, 1939.

_____. *The Best Plays of 1939-40.* New York: Dodd, Mead, 1940.

_____. *The Best Plays of 1942-43.* New York: Dodd, Mead, 1943.

Marill, Alvin H. *Movies Made for Television: The TeleFeature and the Mini-Series: 1964–1979.* New York: Arlington House, 1980.

Mayer, Arthur. "Lillian." *New York Times,* June 8, 1969, VII, p.7.

Mayfield, Sara. *Exiles from Paradise: Zelda and F. Scott Fitzgerald.* New York: Dela Corte Press, 1971.

McCarthy, Peggy. "Theatre Museum Planned in New Haven." *New York Times,* November 11, 1985, XXXIII, p.10.

McConathy, Dale, and Diana Vreeland. *Hollywood Costumes.* New York: Harry N. Abrams, 1976.

McKinley, Albert E., Ph.D., Charles A. Coulomb, Ph.D., and Armand Gerson, Ph.D. *A School History of the Great War.* New York, Cincinnati, Chicago, Boston, and Atlanta: American Book Company, 1919.

"Mimics Max Steur Bullying Duell." *New York Times,* June 9, 1926, p.12.

"Miss Gish Appears Against Charles Duell." *New York Times,* May 8, 1925, p.22.

"Miss Gish to Take Stand in Duell Suit." *New York Times,* March 27, 1925, p.19.

Mizener, Arthur. *F. Scott Fitzgerald.* New York: Thames and Hudson, 1972.

Mockridge, Norton. "Forever Lillian." *World Telegram and Sun,* September 11, 1954.

Molotsky, Irwin. "Kennedy Center Honors 5 in the Arts." *New York Times,* August 16, 1982, C11.

Moore, Ann W. "An Actor's Life for Me!" *School Library Journal,* vol. 34, October 1987.

Morella, Joe, Edward Z. Epstein and John Griggs. *The Films of World War II: A Pictorial History of Hollywood's War Years.* With an Introduction by Judith Crist. Secaucus: Citadel, 1973.

Morley, Sheridan. "First (and Last) of the Moving Picture Pioneers: Lillian Gish at 75." *London Times,* September 19, 1974.

_____. "Interview with Lillian Gish." *Films and Filming,* January 1970, p.15.

_____. *A Talent to Amuse: A Biography of Noel Coward.* Garden City, N.Y.: Doubleday, 1969.

Mosel, Tad, with Gertrude Macy. *Leading Lady: The World of Katherine Cornell.* Boston and Toronto: Little, Brown, 1978.

Nadel, Norman. *A Pictorial History of the Theatre Guild.* With an Introduction by Brooks Atkinson, and special material by Lawrence Langner and Armina Marshall. New York: Crown, 1969.

Naremore, James. *Quarterly Review of Film Studies,* vol. 6, no. 1, Winter 1981, p.93.

"Nathan Denies Betrothal." *New York Times,* June 22, 1927, p.23.

Neade, Marion. *Buster Keaton: Cut to the Chase.* New York: HarperCollins, 1995.

Nemy, Enid. "Lillian Gish at 83 Transcends Style." *New York Times,* December 31, 1982, B6.

"New Strand Opens Biggest of Movies." *New York Times,* April 12, 1914, p.15.

"1920s: Economic Influences." *International Musician,* October 1996, p.24.

"Noted Movie Stars Back from Europe." *New York Times,* August 3, 1933, p.8.

O'Casey, Eileen. *Eileen.* Edited with an introduction by J.C. Trewin. New York: St. Martin's Press, 1966.

O'Connor, John. "Film Institute Salutes Lillian Gish." *New York Times,* April 17, 1984, C2.

_____. "4 Part Huckleberry Finn Begins." *New York Times,* February 10, 1986, C17.

_____. "Lillian Gish Looks Back on a Century." *New York Times,* July 11, 1988, C16.

_____. "TV: 'Hobson's Choice,' An Adaptation on CBS." *New York Times,* December 21, 1983, C27.

Oderman, Stuart. "Lillian Gish: A Friend Remembered." *Journal of Popular Film and Television,* vol. 22, no. 2, Summer 1994, p.53.

O'Leary, Liam. *The Silent Cinema.* London: Studio Vista Limited, 1965.

Oliver, Richard. *Warning Shot.* Los Angeles: Liberty Records, 1966. Record Album.

"Order in Lillian Gish Suit." *New York Times,* September 27, 1927, p.18.

Paine, Albert Bigelow. *Life and Lillian Gish.* New York: Macmillan, 1932.

Paris, Barry. *Audrey Hepburn.* New York: G.P. Putnam's Sons, 1996.

Peck, Seymour. "Then and Now: Lillian Gish." *New York Times,* April 7, 1960, VI, p.70.

Pickford, Mary. "The Lillian Gish I Know: A Star's Story of a Star." *Movie Weekly,* January 24, 1925, p.4.

"The Play: Nine Pine Street." *New York Times,* April 28, 1933, p.24.

Plecki, Gerard. *Robert Altman.* Boston: Twayne, 1985.

"Post in Cabinet Asked for Arts." *New York Times,* March 27, 1955, p.65.

Pratt, George C. *Spellbound in Darkness: A History of the Silent Film.* Greenwich: New York Graphic Society, 1973.

Preminger, Otto. *Preminger.* Garden City: Doubleday, 1977.

"Quarrel Enlivens Lillian Gish Suit." *New York Times,* February 14, 1925, p.68.

Quirk, Lawrence J. *Lauren Bacall: Her Films and Career.* Secaucus: Citadel, 1986.

_____. *Paul Newman.* Dallas: Taylor, 1996.

Ramsaye, Terry. *A Million and One Nights.* New York: Simon and Schuster, 1964.

Renoir, Jean. *My Life and My Films.* New York: Atheneum, 1974.

Robinson, David. *Hollywood in the Twenties.* New York: Paperback Library, 1968.

Rosen, Marjorie. *Popcorn Venus: Women, Movies and the American Dream.* New York: Coward, McCann and Geohegan, 1973.

Rosenberg, Bernard, and Harry Silverstein. *The Real Tinsel.* New York: Macmillan, 1970.

Rothe, Anna, editor. "Lillian Gish." *Current Biography.* New York: H.W. Wilson, 1944.

St. Johns, Adela Rogers. *Love, Laughter and Tears: My Hollywood Story.* New York: New American Library, 1978.

Sanborn, Pitts. *The Metropolitan Book of the Opera.* New York: Simon and Schuster, 1937.

"Sarlot, Raymond, and Fred E. Basten. *Life at the Marmont.* Santa Monica: Roundtable, 1987.

"Says Duell Kept Miss Gish's Profits." *New York Times,* June 2, 1926, p.7.

Schickel, Richard. *D. W. Griffith: An American Life.* New York: Simon and Schuster, 1984.

Schiro, Anne-Marie. "Modern Museum, 50 has a 20s Party." *New York Times,* November 15, 1979, C8.

Schorer, Mark. *Sinclair Lewis: An American Life.* New York: McGraw-Hill, 1961.

"The Screen: The Enemy." *New York Times,* December 28, 1977, p.26.

"The Screen: The White Sister." *New York Times,* September 6, 1923, p.17.

"Seeks to Drop Gish Suit." *New York Times,* June 16, 1927, p.25.

Settel, Irving. *A Pictorial History of Radio.* New York: Grosset and Dunlap, 1967.

Shaeffer, Louis. *O'Neill: Son and Artist.* Boston and Toronto: Little, Brown, 1973.

Shannon, William. *The American Irish: A Political and Social Background.* New York: Macmillan, 1966.

Shipman, David. *Cinema: The First Hundred Years.* London: Weidenfield and Norman, 1993.

Shivers, Alfred S. *The Life of Maxwell Anderson.* New York: Stein and Day, 1955.

Skinner, Cornelia Otis. *Madame Sarah.* Boston: Houghton Mifflin, 1967.

Slide, Anthony. *Early American Cinema.* New York: A.S. Barnes, 1970.

_____. *The Griffith Actresses.* New York: A.S. Barnes, 1973.

_____. "Lillian Gish: Star of Screen, Stage, and TV." *Emmy,* January/February 1984, p.28.

Spada, James. *More Than a Woman: An Intimate Biography of Bette Davis.* New York: Bantam, 1993.

Spears, Jack. *Hollywood: The Golden Era.* New York: Castle, 1971.

Stars of the Photoplay. Chicago: Photoplay, 1924.

Stewart, Gail. *Timelines.* New York: Crestwood House, 1989.

Stine, Whitney. "I'd Love to Kiss You..." *Conversations with Bette Davis.* New York: Pocket Books, 1990.

"Sues Lillian Gish for $5,000,000." *New York Times,* June 23, 1927, p.4.

Sutherland, Sydney. "Lillian Gish: The Incomparable." *Liberty.* August 27, 1927, p.54.

Sutherland, Zena. "An Actor's Life for Me!" *Bull Cent Child Books,* vol. 41, November 1987, p.48.

Swanberg, W.A. *Dreiser.* New York: Charles Scribner's Sons, 1965.

Taubman, Howard. "'Coriolanus' and 'Romeo and Juliet' Open Stratford, Conn. Season." *New York Times,* June 21, 1965, p.36.

_____. "Lark by Shaw: 'Too True to Be Good' in a Pert Revival." *New York Times,* March 13, 1963, p.8.

_____. "Theatre: 'Anya' A Sentimental Musical." *New York Times,* November 30, 1965, p.48.

Taylor, Deems, Marceline Peterson and Bryant Hale. *A Pictorial History of the Movies*, New York: Simon and Schuster, 1950.

Terrace, Vincent. *The Complete Encyclopedia of Television: Series, Pilots and Specials: 1974–1984*. New York: New York Zoetrope, 1985.

"Testifies Miss Gish Did Not Pay His Fee." *New York Times*, June 5, 1926, p.7.

"Theatre's Loyal Star: Lillian Gish." *New York Times*, June 11, 1996, p.21.

Thomas, Tony. *The Films of the Forties*. Secaucus: Citadel, 1975.

Thompson, Howard. "Seen on Miss Gish's Wide Screen." *New York Times,* May 2, 1954, II, p.5.

_____. "Warning Shot." *New York Times,* June 8, 1967, p.52.

"Three Liners in at Once Bring Jams on Piers." *New York Times*, August 21, 1929, p.18.

Toohey, John L. *A History of the Pulitzer Prize Plays*. New York: Citadel, 1967.

"Trials of an Actress." *New York Times*, July 3, 1927, VIII, p.3.

Truffaut, Francois, with the collaboration of Helen G. Scott. *Hitchcock*. New York: Simon and Schuster, 1966.

Truman, Margaret. *Harry Truman*. New York: Pocket Books, 1974.

Untermeyer, Louis. "About T.S. Eliot and His Work." *The Cocktail Party*. New York: Decca, 1950. Record Album.

Van Gelder, Lawrence. "Recent Releases." *New York Times*, March 10, 1985, II, p.30.

Van Ness, Chris. "Lillian Gish Remembers the Movies." *The Los Angeles Free Press*. November 2, 1973, p.6.

The Victor Book of the Opera. Camden: Victor Machine, 1913.

Vidor, King. *A Tree Is a Tree*. New York: Harcourt, Brace, 1953.

"W.A. Harriman Lent $6,000,000 for Films." *New York Times*, June 14, 1926, p.25.Wade, Wyn Craig. *The Fiery Cross: The Ku Klux Klan*. New York: Simon and Schuster, 1987.

Wagenknecht, Edward. *The Movies in an Age of Innocence*. Norman: University of Oklahoma Press, 1962.

_____ and Anthony Slide. *The Films of D. W. Griffith*. New York: Crown, 1975.

Waldan, Roy S. *Vintage Years of the Theatre Guild: 1928–1939*. Cleveland and London: The Press of Case and Western Reserve, 1972.

Walker, Alexander. *Audrey: Her Real Story*. New York: St. Martin's Press, 1994.

_____. *Stardom: The Hollywood Phenomenon*. New York: Stein and Day, 1970.

Watson, E. Bradlee, and Benfield Pressey, editors. *Contemporary Drama: European, English and Irish American Plays*. New York: Charles Scribner's Sons, 1961.

Watters, James. With photographs by Horst. *Return Engagement: Faces to Remember — Then and Now*. New York: Clarkson N. Potter, 1984.

"Weight Keeps Star Here." *New York Times*, July 26, 1927, p.44.

Wenden, D.J. *The Birth of the Movies*. London: MacDonald, 1975.

Whitehead, O.Z. "Lillian." *Theatre Book*, vol. 1, no. 1, Spring 1978, p.46.

"William McAdoo." *Newsweek*, February 10, 1941, p.17.

Williams, Richard. "The Gallant Gish Girls." *Life*, August 20, 1951, p.115.

Willis, John, editor. *Theatre World 1965–1966*. Vol. 22. New York: Crown, p.37.

Windeler, Robert. *Sweetheart*. New York and Washington: Praeger, 1973.

Wing, Ruth, editor. *The Blue Book of the Screen*. Hollywood: Pacific Gravure, 1923.

Winship, Frederick. "The Cameras Still Roll for a Queen of the Silents." *Sunday Morning Post*, December 14, 1986.

Woodward, Ian. *Audrey Hepburn*. New York: St. Martin's Press, 1984.

Writers Program of the Work Projects Administration. *The Ohio Guide*. New York: Oxford University Press, 1940.

Zierold, Norman. *The Moguls: The Power Princess of Hollywood's Golden Age*. New York: Avon, 1969.

Zolotow, Maurice. *Stagestruck: The Romance of Alfred Lunt and Lynn Fontanne*. Greenwich: Fawcett, 1965.

Index